W9-DEA-087

YEARBOOK RESEARCH & COMPILATION:

JASON R. PATER

ANTHOLOGY OF MAGAZINE VERSE

AND YEARBOOK OF AMERICAN POETRY

1986-1988 EDITION

Edited by

ALAN F. PATER

Introduction by
JAMES RAGAN

BEVERLY HILLS
MONITOR BOOK COMPANY

COPYRIGHT © 1988 BY MONITOR BOOK COMPANY

Printed in the United States of America

ISBN number: 0-917734-14-9

ISSN number: 0196-2221

Library of Congress catalogue card No. 80-645223

The Anthology of Magazine Verse & Yearbook of American Poetry is published annually by Monitor Book Company, P. O. Box 3668, Beverly Hills, CA 90212.

Preface

Much of the world's finest and most prolific poetry has first appeared in periodical literature: poetry monthlies and quarterlies, general literary magazines, college journals, etc.

Regrettably, most of those publications have limited circulations, and once an issue has been read—and the next one arrives—it is filed away and rarely opened again. But the wealth of excellent work contained in their pages—by both talented, promising new poets and well-known, established writers—should be kept alive, distributed more widely and be readily available. That is the *raison d'etre* of the *Anthology of Magazine Verse*.

After William Stanley Braithwaite ended his much respected annual surveys of magazine poetry in 1929, there was a lamentable gap in the important business of selecting and preserving in book form the verse of the day. That pause was temporarily filled with the re-emergence of the *Anthology of Magazine Verse* in the mid-1930's through the early 1940's by the editor of this current volume, but World War II then interrupted the continuation of the series.

Now, this new series of annual collections is aimed at re-establishing the purpose and spirit of the Braithwaite books on a continuing basis, and thereby providing a yearly barometer of the trends of poetry in the United States and Canada.

An effort has been made to include poems of various lengths, forms and styles, as well as a multiplicity of subjects and geographical originations. And the spread of magazine sources chosen reflects these criteria.

It should be noted that the sources included in any given volume of the Anthology constitute only a portion of the total number of periodicals regularly received by the editor and considered for suitable material. Since the quality of the individual poem is the main criterion for acceptance, the specific magazines represented in each edition of the Anthology will necessarily vary from year to year.

Magazine poetry best represents the era in which it is written—it is current, abundant, as varied in style and content as the numberless journals in which it is published. Its topics are today's issues and events, as well as the perennial ones. New poets, who, because of the current realities of the book world, find it difficult to have their work published in hardcover, fortunately have an outlet in the increasing volume of magazines that print new and original poetry. It is from their ranks that the future major poets will emerge.

Also part of this volume is the *Yearbook of American Poetry*—the first and only annual gathering of factual material in this burgeoning field. The *Yearbook's* directories, bibliographies and listings (to be updated with each succeeding edition) will provide a yearly record of information and reference material for the world of poetry—an area heretofore lacking a comprehensive information sourcebook of its own.

Together, the *Anthology of Magazine Verse and Yearbook of American Poetry* will, hopefully, be inspiring, stimulating, informative, and an accurate reflection of the state of the poetic form today.

Beverly Hills,   A.F.P.
California   April, 1980

Editor's Note

Individual 1986 and 1987 volumes of the Anthology were not published due to the illness of the Editor. Material from those two editions has now been included in this, the 1986-1988 volume.

Normal annual publication schedule has now been resumed.

Table of Contents

PART ONE

Anthology
of Magazine Verse

Introduction

POET AS PROPHET:
LANGUAGE AND THE DEMOCRACY OF VISION

by
James Ragan

Director of the Professional Writing Program,
and Instructor of Advanced Poetry,
Graduate School, University of Southern California

We are nearing the last decade of the Twentieth Century. Poetry has survived—and thrived—on the embattled experimentations of the *avant-garde* soon to become orthodoxy. The paradox and contradictions romantically spawned by imagination in the last century gave way to the co-existing absolutes wrought by reason in the next. What was traditional British to Eliot became "yawpish" American to Williams. What was once the Baudelairean "forest of symbols" soon became Stevens's "realm of resemblances." What from 1920 to 1955 pacified the New Critic formalism soon incited the heresies of the Confessional, Beat and Projectivist movements in the fifties and sixties. What forays into the anarchy of the mind first produced surrealism in the thirties soon became the providential source of subjective expressionism for the Deep Image poets of the seventies.

With the passing of each new decade, what remained constant was the cyclical nature of experimentation. Each new movement's re-creation of form and language produced its own version of that most flexible of concepts, "modernism," followed by a period of adjustment loosely codified as "post-modernism" (a term and principle ironically governed by its antecedent), all soon to become orthodoxies just the same. Always, the Apollonian and Dionysian forces are at play. What is ordered now will be freed later; what the mind seeks to objectify, the heart will with spontaneity subjectify; what the intellect fashions, emotion will tear asunder. From primitive forests to godly realms, from anarchy to benevolent tyranny, one fact is certain: relativity endures. As Pound said of his version of modernism's failure to create absolute change, "If I was in any sense the revolution, I have been followed by the counter-revolution." The only absolute that endures is to "make it new."

With the billennium soon upon us, there has never been more urgency than now to "make it new." Behind us, the legacies of the symbolist, traditional, and free verse strains of poetic achievement; before us the new challenge of saving language and form from their own narcissistic charms. As language falls victim to quick-paced trends of media communication currently dominating the universal psyche, responsibility for precision in words—written or spoken—currently in danger of being diminished, is in need of re-appraisal. The "You Know" generation of the eighties continues to populate the wordscape with mosaics of telegenically defined cliches. The multi-valence of metaphor has been replaced by minimalist no-speak, double-speak, and non-sequitur. And so it falls to the *anthology*, this most august of compendiums, to perform such re-appraisal. By providing a sense of "historicity" for the various and conflicting trends in poetics, the *anthology* re-affirms what for the poet must remain as the primary goals of his art: the exploration of truth and the innate urge to re-shape and re-discover language, his only tangible vehicle for the erudition of vision.

The *Anthology of Magazine Verse* for 1986-88, edited by Alan Pater, has proven once again that eclecticism is not lost on this generation of magazine editors devoted to representing in verse a multiplicity of visions. Indeed, the balance of wit and form offered in these pages is met with the counterbalance of colloquy and reform. What is not lacking in either is imagination. I recently began a *Los Angeles Times* book review with the assessment that one of the still sacred powers of poets in this period of intellectual recession is the ability to move and shape the minds of kings, who in turn move and shape the minds of society. While currently, it appears there are no kings (world leaders) with minds to be moved—or, perhaps, artists seem no longer inspired by that intention—it still remains for the poet, that beleaguered and irrepressible *shaman* of language, to persist in the pursuit of universal truth, no matter how irascible or anti-cathartic society remains in its response.

No one who reads the following pages will fail to be struck by the verve and compassion with which the poets have informed their verse in order to, in turn, move and shape the hearts and minds of a seemingly dispassionate culture. Indeed, even if one lingers on each poem for only moments, there will lie over these moments what Rilke called "the dimensions of gigantic intentions." Alan Pater is to be congratulated for his efforts in gleaning from so many traditions a modicum of poets, who in their best work continue to reflect the "dimensions of gigantic intentions" currently being published in America and abroad in the eighties.

One is delighted to see among the "older" generation of distinguished American contributors: Hayden Carruth, Jane Cooper, John Ciardi, Richard Eberhart, Thom Gunn, Daniel Hoffman, Maxine Kunin, Stanley Kunitz, Richmond Lattimore, Philip Levine, John Frederick Nims, May Sarton, Harvey Shapiro, Louis Simpson, William Stafford, John Unterecker, John Updike, Constance Urdang, Mona Van Duyn, Peter Viereck, and Robert Penn Warren. Each in his own way has weathered the shifts in the literary topography to remain steadfast in his own search for artistic identity in a decade in which the culture and the temper of the times are so distinctively in flux. Each continues to look forward beyond his own private domain to find some larger intention beyond the familiar.

Witness, for example, William Stafford's poem, "Looking for Gold," cited here in its entirety, which best illustrates the many "flavors" of experience, gained through man's symbiotic relationship with nature, as being most essential to man's quest for personal and universal identity:

LOOKING FOR GOLD

A flavor like wild honey begins
when you cross the river. On a sandbar
sunlight stretches out its limbs, or is it
a sycamore, so brazen, so clean and bold?
You forget about gold. You stare—and a flavor
is rising all the time from the trees.
Back from the river, over by a thick
forest, you feel the tide of wild honey
flooding your plans, flooding the hours
till they waver forward, looking back. They can't
return: that river divides more than
two sides of your life. The only way
is farther, breathing that country, becoming
wise in its flavor, a native of the sun.

Unlike Baudelaire and the Symbolists who saw man and nature eternally in struggle, nature for the contemporary poet can be at once seductive and benign. The "forest of symbols" here are realms of unseen truths often external and diversionary to the original goal, yet equally as revelatory. Time will not turn back on experience, says Stafford, "The only way is farther."

Stafford's poem is prophetic for the many poets of another generation, younger, yet equally as compelling, who have ventured "farther" in their crafts, "breathing that country, becoming/ wise in its flavor." Represented in this collection are Wendell Berry, Michael Blumenthal, Michael Dennis Browne, Raymond Carver, Turner Cassity, Rita Dove, Stephen Dunn, Sandra Gilbert, Michael S. Harper, William Heyen, Laurence Lieberman, William Matthews, Stanley Moss, Sharon Olds, Linda Pastan, David Ray, Gibbons Ruark, Gerald Stern, C.K. Williams, Miller Williams, and a host of others equally as gifted.

The poet in the latter half of this century, like Stafford, most suited to being called nature's prophet, is one who sees the past and future as the unifying factors of all art and one with whom nature shares the prophesy and the expedition. This is the sense of the best work in this collection. As in Richard Eberhart's "Sun-Make," where a "mirror of clouds" so exquisite as to exist beyond mortal description suddenly changes, as is the providence of nature, and what is past is now preserved in future, in words—the providence of art:

> This puff of clouds, mirrored so far away
> In a way that could not be imagined
> Made of thought beside the morning blue ocean;
>
> It was a system of light and distance so exquisite
> He thought it should remain perfectly wordless,
> Then the sky changed, he changed his mind, shaped this.

In the early 70's, as the Vietnam War was winding down, two books were published which were beacons of sorts of the twin strains of the personal and the mythic. While the influences of Bly, Ginsberg, Ashbery and Creeley in the sixties were still to carry on into the present, Galway Kinnell's *Book of Nightmares* (1971) and Ted Hughes's *Crow* (1970) were monuments of pure light to both deep imagists and rhetoricians; beyond this it was exciting to go. In Kinnell's straightforward, personalized expeditions of "wandering" and "wondering" through the long poem and in Hughes's detached voice of distortedly punctuated imagery, the use of enjambement, already mastered by a third bright light, W.S. Merwin, in his poem "The Way to the River," yet another evocation of "journey" from *The Moving Target* (1963), served in the hands of their masters to achieve brilliant heights in poetic diction. In truth, their essential collective accomplishment was to return the multivalence of metaphor back to the page after a long period of subjugation to the "literal" voice present in the Confessional, Projectivist, and Beat sensibilities.

By controlling the image through multiple levels of meaning, often aided by the powers of verbal unexpectedness and double-entendre, they freed the language even further than had their predecessors Whitman and Williams, Olson and Ginsberg. Like Bly, they also directed their attentions to the awesome and still powers of the earth and to a "consciousness in things" (an echoing of Martin Buber's I-thou), in part, perhaps, a response to the incineration of life and nature in a far southeast Asian country or to the violations of humanity across the cities of "Civil Rights" America. The powers of *surrealism* were in play "like dice in command of their own combinations," to borrow Merwin's line, and provided for an on-going process of new and exciting discoveries for the "self" and for the conscience of a besieged nation.

It is Wallace Stevens who reminds us that the great poems of heaven and hell have already been written; the great poem of the earth has yet to be written. With this in mind it was now the poet's intention to re-discover the earth. And with Kinnell, Merwin and Bly in America and Hughes in England leading the way, the new "young" generation, already obsessed with the exploitation of new forms, experimented with the multi-level approaches to exploring the conscious and subconscious levels of associative experience. What has resulted in the eighties are new attempts at individuality of vision and explorations of verbal and imagistic nuances, going beyond anything Dylan Thomas or T.S. Eliot might have wished. More in tune with Rilke or Neruda, theirs is a language of images, concrete and incitingly disparate. Existing in realms of "deep" subjectivity, the poems seek only to speak in their own language and with their own sensory responses. They fit the times. People respond to and speak more easily in images in a decade of image fitness and instant image replay. Maurya Simon's "The Sadness of Rivers" is one example of the consciousness-granting powers of what Bly calls "a sort of ground tone audible under the words of poems":

> The gratitude of stones is wide as the world.
> Their shadows are heirlooms the day hoards,
> along with the blessings of pebbles.

> Stones know the words under our tongues
> are their children: mutable, jagged, bold.

Whether experimenting with the molds of traditional form or protesting their boundaries, the poems of earth are still being tested. In perceiving the world with the "subtler life of the senses," William Carlos Williams may well have been the greatest influence on the "conscience of the eye" according to Donald Hall, and in his work poets found the impulse to explore the earth in images, grand and small, intricate and simple. But what Williams also taught us was that one of the primary concerns of the poet is to re-discover and reshape language, for, indeed, it is the word that has seemed to fail us in this "telegenically" inspired culture of the literal-minded, the narcissistic, and the over-abundant. And what of the "flavors" of experience?

It is William Meredith who in a 1985 *Paris Review* interview was asked, ". . . you average about six poems per year, why so few?" Meredith's response was, "why so many?" Meredith explains that he waits for a poem to be addressed not to "occupant" but to William Meredith. Astonishing experience doesn't happen very often. Meredith's response is crucial because his belief that poetry and experience should have an exact ratio offers important insight into the origins of the poet's creative impulse. "Daily experience is astonishing on a level at which you can write a poem," Meredith says, "but astonishing experience would be the experience which is not astonishment of reality but astonishment of insight."

And here is the key to appreciating so many of the fine poems in this collection—astonishment of insight. Indeed, we are reminded of Robert Frost who was fond of saying, "How many things have to happen to you before something occurs to you?" To Meredith, a poem starts with an insight "which gets a few words close to the ground and then the words begin to make specific the insight." Consider the few words "close to the ground" beginning Daniel Hoffman's "Stop the Deathwish! Stop it! Stop!":

> at least until the 21st century
> because the present is too good to lose
> a moment of—I would begrudge the time
> for sleep, but dreams are better than they used
> to be, since they enact the mystery
> that action hides and history derides.

. . . or Gerald Stern's "The Dancing," where the private mythos of his 1945 childhood in "beautiful filthy Pittsburgh, home/ of the evil Mellons," is set down in the images of ritualistic and celebratory dancing to Ravel's *Bolero*:

> . . . my mother red with laughter, my father cupping
> his left hand under his armpit, doing the dance
> of Old Ukraine, the sound of his skin half drum, . . .
> the three of us whirling and singing, the three of us
> screaming and falling, as if we were dying, . . .

Stern leaps now to the specific insight of a more universal mythos:

> . . . from the other dancing—in Poland and Germany—
> oh God of mercy, oh wild God.

This same theme of mythic awareness, reminiscent of Plath's invocation of the holocaustal vision in "Daddy," can be found in David Ray's elegiac "Bhopal," Michael Dennis Browne's "Mengele," and J.P. Horgan-Aguado's "Late at Night, The Cattle Take Over Matagalpa." Astonishing insight is not exclusive to historical or mythical orientations but is at the center of the deeply personal and transitory as well.

In "The Descent" one cannot fail to recognize the weight of anxiety grounding Linda Pastan's tribute to her ailing mother, whose "fear is using up the oxygen":

> . . . Now evening
> leaches the color from her face
> and in the leftover light
> it is hard to see where
> the descent will end,
> hard to believe
> it is death holding
> her elbow with such care,
> guiding her all the way down.

Or Sharon Olds's view in the poem "12 Years Old" of her sexually aware daughter diving into a swimming pool "rich with college boys" also sexually aware of . . .

> . . . her pale body
> plummeting through the air in silence and then
> entering the water with the charged thrust of her
> knife into the chicken when she is really hungry.

Likewise, the breadth and simplicity of insight colored by foreshadowing in Daniel Halpern's "Child Running":

> The playing child is one distraction, the warmth of the day
> another. The layout of the scene below demands attention—
> it is not a matter of description but of focus. The weather's
> holding. What's one ecstatic child running on the beach?

The difference between "description" and "focus" has always been the difference between experience and abstraction, the poem of "things" more than of "ideas," the "conscience of the eye" rather than the logic of the intellect, a point on which Eliot and W.C. Williams have always disagreed; and a balance between the two would have been most difficult to achieve had it not been for Wallace Stevens's principle of unifying "correspondences." Consider yet another balance most difficult to achieve between language and form in these informal times.

If, indeed, language must remain "freed" and not "tied" to the archaic and trite idioms revived by contemporary media, it is refreshing, then, to recall X. J. Kennedy's "Nude Descending a Staircase," a poem commemorating Marcel Duchamp's cubist painting, and renowned for its marriage of exquisite language and imagery to the function of form:

> Her lips imprint the swinging air
> That parts to let her parts go by.
>
> One-woman waterfall, she wears
> Her slow descent like a long cape
> And pausing, on the final stair
> Collects her motions into shape.

For in any art form—poetry, painting, music—there is involved a process of collecting all the parts, all the motions into a final shape. If it is true that the poetry of the older, more classic-minded generation seems to occupy itself with the power of ideas to awaken us to insight, then hearken here to the power of the word as image. The new generation appears to have given renewed emphasis to the unlimited powers of punctuation and syntax to accommodate the unlimited powers of metaphor. It is as if Rachel Hadas's invocation concluding "The End of Summer" were fashionably treasonous: "Not light but language shocks us out of sleep—".

In Michael Harper's "The Borning Room," feel the rich intonement of images leaping, one to another, and its final muted shock line resulting in insight reminiscent of the deep image tradition of Robert Bly and James Wright:

> I look over the large bed
> at the shape of my woman;
> there is no image
> for her, no place
> for the spring child.
> Her cornered shape dreams
> a green-robed daughter
> warmed in a bent room
> close to fireplace oven,
> warmed by an apple tree:
> the old tried to make it new,
> the new old; we will not die here.

"The old" who continue "to make it new" have not been lacking in youthful sensitivity nor in the younger generation's praise for the sensibilities that their art provides on both sober and humorous levels. Maxine Kunin's wit is exquisitely saturnine, not hokey, and directed toward memory, the real commuter of time in her poem "Surprises." When "after fifteen summers/ of failure" one hundred California peppers grow suddenly "like newly hatched sex organs" in her "Zone-three Garden," her conclusions?

> Doubtless this means I am approaching
> the victory of poetry over death
> where art wins, chaos retreats, and beauty,
>
> albeit trampled under barbarism,
> rises again, shiny with roses, no thorns.

Then follows the expansive vitality of Stanley Kunitz who philosophizes in "Passing Through" (on my 79th birthday), "Maybe I enjoy not-being as much/ as being who I am . . . The way I look/at it, I'm passing through a phase:". One voice, who for sixty years has been "passing through," enjoying "the victory of poetry over death," and who is without question the *savant* of the "fantastical" and "fact-tastical," is Robert Penn Warren. The disciplines of classic form, wit and allusion surviving in the mold of the New Critics are not without their titular model in this collection as one is asked again to consider the wonderment of achievement that Warren continues to bestow upon his verse. In these lines from his light and lyrical "Tulip-Tree in Bloom," we are treated with the ironic wit and extravagant turn of phrase we have come to associate with America's first Poet Laureate:

> She had married, he later heard. Oh, well, so had he!
> And children both. Contentment? Why not?
> Yes, a country was like a trap of propinquity,
> And memories blur like old mirrors, unsilvering spot by spot.

Even if one were to agree with William Carlos Williams's declaration that "unless the mind change,/ the old will go on/ repeating itself with recurring/ deadliness . . ." we cannot help but take pleasure in Warren's wisdom and discipline and in his indefatigability at eighty-three to persist in his craft as if he were looking forward still to writing his best poems.

But lest we become too impressed with the old line who continue to show us diversity and spontaneity, let me call upon the new who so capably make it "old." Consider Thomas Lux's villanelle "On Visiting Herbert Hoover's Birth and Burial Place" or Leo Luke Marcello's "Villanelle on the Suicide of a Young Belgian Teacher Soon to be Naturalized." In addition, the sonnet form, which through its brevity and concentration disallows too great a prodigality of words, is renewed by Mauro Mare in "Eternity" and by John Frederick Nims, who while "aging young," reforms anew his affinity for the idiomatic in "Closed for Restoration," a poem settled in the formal area of orthodoxy, yet decisively freed by the language of the colloquial:

> . . . Odds are, I'll never see
> That span again. If on Liguria's shore
> I lie, *Qui dorme in pace's* not for me,
> Stones with *le ossa* . . . or *tristi spoglie* . . . or
> Any such dismal lingo of the lost.
> Mine, *Chiuso per restauro*. With fingers crossed.

The first and final phrases seem oddly out of place yet appropriately witty in a sonnet form whose Petrarchan octave and sextet are strapped in place by a Shakespearean rhyme-scheme.

Such dancing in and out of disciplined rhythms and structures are indicative of the variations, subtle or profound, manifesting themselves in contemporary poetry and further evident in the off-rhymes of Peter Viereck's "Misty Mornings on the Cape," William Heyen's "While We Are Still Alive" and Pulitzer Prize-winner Rita Dove's "Flash Cards." Alongside, we still see the symmetry of *perfect* end-rhymes in John Ciardi's "A Trenta-Sei of the Pleasure We Take in the Early Death of Keats," while the perfect rhyme closures framing the self-conscious repartee between two poets in Mona Van Duyn's "Views" is for its echoing, contrapuntal effects—the closest mirror in measure and sound to a fugue that we have in this collection.

Contrast such closed forms and restraints to the open and liberating forms found in the prose poem of Hayden Carruth's "Dancing as Vestigia and other Considerations" or in the consistently muscular and colloquial tones of Philip Levine's "The Last Shift," Louis Simpson's "Publishing Days," or Stanley Kunitz's "The Round," with its reiterative epanaphora and the elemental imagery of a "bloated compost heap,/ steamy old stinkpile" reminiscent of Whitman. We have further trysts between the sonorities of the colloquial and those of the formal in Thom Gunn's "The Hug," Gibbons Ruark's "Postscript to an Elegy," and in the lyrical yet earthy imagery of Laurence Lieberman's "Banana Madonna" or the lyrical and lofty rhapsodic conclusion to May Sarton's "As Does New Hampshire":

> Only most daring love would care to mention
> So much, so simply, and so charge each word
> As does New Hampshire "mountain," "meadow," "bird."

There has evolved in this decade a kind of sublime narcissism—a preoccupation with art and with the poet's relationship to his art and to the other arts—that is pervasive and persuasive by its sheer inventiveness. While this in itself is not new, it is the proliferation of such poems that staggers, suggesting a preoccupation with the artist as an end unto himself and subjugating the poem to a participatory process. There are as many references within the poems to poets and authors living and dead (Bly, Cavafy, Cheever, Chekhov, Ciardi, Dickinson, Frisch, Hugo, Lanier, Kees, Reznikoff, Williams, Wright, Saroyan, Santayana, Wheelock, etc.) as there are to musicians and painters (Bach, Da Vinci, Monet, Hopper, Kazan, etc.). What is significant about this is the "self-consciousness" (not confessional) and "self-identification" under-girding these poems. The opening lines of Peter Cooley's "Van Gogh, Self-Portrait with Soft Felt Hat" echoes this familiar theme by suggesting a kind of subliminal involution that is crucial and necessary for the self-conscious artist:

> You who would die into some other,
> allow these colors of the sea and sky
> to take you in. Fins, wings. The elements are free.
> Released, you have only to immerse yourself.

The moment of sublimity is crystallized in the final image:

> . . . there is nowhere Vincent has not lost himself
> in strokes whirling the background up to his body's edge.

Cooley, by evoking Van Gogh, grants the positioning power of artistic equality to his own self-identity by addressing the creative process of the poet, who, like the painter, must lose himself in words whose elements owe their inspiration to the whirling background of imagination.

William Virgil Davis, a Yale Younger Poets winner, recalls such inspiration and self-identification in "Early One Morning My Son and I Take a Short Drive" as being that which one "almost might invent . . . on paper or in paint; so still we must/ imagine motion to believe in it." Another Yale Younger Poets winner, Bin Ramke, reflects on more of the poet's calling by evoking Rimbaud, still another master of "eternal motion," in the opening line of his touchingly humorous "The Attempt to Write the Last Poem of His Life." And Sandra Gilbert does more of the same by intoning Rilke in "After Thanksgiving":

> Lord, as Rilke says, the year bears down toward winter, past
> the purification of the trees, the darkened brook . . .
> . . . Now the mountains will settle into their old
> cold habits, now the white
> birch bones will rise
> like all those thoughts we've tried to repress:
> madness of the solstice, phosphorescent
> logic that rules the fifteen-hour night!

No anguished and long-suffering writer of poems will fail to recognize the significance of the last three lines as being reminiscent of Ted Hughes's "world-shouldering monstrous 'I'" whose "poet's imagination whirls with increasing wildness," or of Galway Kinnell's closing lines to "The Bear":

> wandering: wondering
> what, anyway,
> was that sticky infusion, that rank flavor of blood, that
> poetry, by which I lived?

What does this suggest? More and more poets seem to be focusing attention on artists as subjects or reference points in their poems at a time when poets are not receiving the audience attention they once enjoyed in the sixties when, for example, Ginsberg, Bly, Kinnell or the aging W.H. Auden and Robert Penn Warren commanded loyal followings. The realities of a diminishing audience, perhaps, also accounts for the preponderance of journals in which poets speak to poets—the only surviving witnesses, it seems, to their writing. In all, it portends a positive turn of events as it signals a new beginning, the "post-contemporary" grumblings of artistic self-evaluation and experimentation at a time when the "other," the reading public, has become a "listening" and "viewing" public. The sight and sounds of truth are not limited to the transcendental levels of the Emersonian "oversoul" but can be experienced with a "tape deck" on the "altar of a dashboard" in the confines of a car, as in Stephen Dunn's "Sacred." This echoes what has become the remains of experience or what survives in Richmond Lattimore's deftly ironic "The Idea of a Town": "This was America's/ unimaginative matrix of all our imagination and dreamstuff."

It should not be argued that poetry has fallen out of favor with the public, but that the public has fallen out of favor with poetry. Much of the poetry being published today appears not to be concerning itself with the universality of experience, insight, truth. Perhaps this has to do again with the "flavors of experience" and the lack of it present in the subject matter of a new young "telegenically" inspired generation of writers. It is no surprise, then, to find in this collection poems whose reference points are tributes to the memories of Presley, Keaton, Billie Holiday, and others allied with the overly familiar world of entertainment and media iconography. Here, of course, is a different kind of narcissism, one tied to subject as *cliche*. Into the nineties we go—with structures "deforming," language "deconstructing," and subject "trivializing," and instead of Dylan Thomas's creed, "Man be my metaphor," we now have "I be my metaphor." I am not speaking of the engaged and conversational self-conscious "I" speakers of Michael Blumenthal's "Lucky," Jonathan Holden's "The Scientist," or C.K. Williams's "Anger," but of the vast numbers of new writers leaving the writing programs "looking for gold," to cite Stafford's poem, without so much as a past to aid in adding "insight" to their future.

One final observation for the nineties. For years we have been influenced by the notion that to create imagistic poetry, one should follow the dictum, "no ideas but in things," as the very basis of poetic expression. Indeed, Williams was reacting to the over-classicism of verse and the New Critic orthodoxy whose adoration of the "iamb" and adherence to closed form and classic principles were to govern poetry for half a century. Consequently, since the fifties, Williams's notion of "objectivism" influenced an entire generation of poets practicing their craft in open forms reminiscent of Whitman. As Donald Hall points out, theirs was "a poem more of experiences than of ideas."

One begins to wonder at the proliferation of poets whose book publications by their numbers alone seem disproportionate to their ages and to their reasonable accessibility to world and personal experience. Poets at the relatively youthful age of 30 have five books (and chapbooks) published and are being pressured to publish more. Robert Bly once told my class at the University of Southern California that poets in the Creative Writing Programs across the nation should not be permitted to publish until they are forty. They had not enough of human suffering experience on which to draw in their writing. In China, a "man of wisdom" may not be heard from until he is at least in his sixties. I am not suggesting that such measures, as appealing as they seem, are reasonable solutions to the pressures of over-publishing currently in vogue in our utilitarian society. But I am suggesting that young new poets have taken Williams's credo to extremes. They seem to seek little balance between the heart and mind, the emotion and the intellect, and fail to value the power of "insight" which William Meredith sees as crucial to the very nature of the poem.

Perhaps the impulse to write about all "things" and "anything" with less than maturity of experience and with less emphasis on the cohesion of "ideas" has contributed to the glut of published poems in the many journals and magazines across America. Ordinarily, one would think that with so much activity going on in poetry today, America is at the healthiest stage it has seen in many years. Unfortunately, European, Asian and South American writers do not share this view. They have found American poetry in the last ten years to be obsessed with the "trivial" and lacking in "substance," exhibiting, if you'll forgive me, a "pimple on the neck" kind of urgency in its subject levels.

Open forms and open minds once seemed synonymous with American poetry in an open society in this half of the century. It seems now that "things" are all that American poets and minimalist prose writers write about in a time of self-interest and upward mobility, while "ideas" have ironically become the purview of the closed minds in the closed societies of Chile, Peru, Czechoslovakia, South Africa, the Soviet Union, and other countries similarly restricted in expression.

With this in mind, then, the irony is not lost on the editor's valued decision to publish here the translations of those poets who continue to speak to us beyond the restraints and borders of place, time, and experience. There are exquisite translations of such distinguished international poets as

Anna Akhmatova, Vicente Aleixandre, Gottfried Benn, Bertolt Brecht, Charles Baudelaire, Ernesto Cardenal, Rene Char, Eugenio De Andrade, Hans Enzensberger, Stefan George, Hsieh Ling-Yun, Harry Martinson, Antonio Machado, Osip Mandelstam, Czeslaw Milosz, Rainer Maria Rilke, Yannis Ritsos, Jaroslav Siefert, Gabriella Sobrino, and Boris Van. And these are so eloquently offered by such remarkable poet/translators as Robert Bly, William Jay Smith, Ed Ochester, Shirley Kaufman, Robert Hass, Julia Older, Felix Pollak, Pier Francesco Paolini, and Peter Viereck. In these translations thought and expressiveness are not closed, nor are the borders of form.

I have resisted the impulse to believe that Williams's attention to "no ideas but in things" has produced exactly that—no "ideas"—only "things," a cataloguing of images which for many has evolved as the principle aim of American poetry. I have also resisted the impulse to believe that the proliferation of writing programs and poetry quarterlies are the causes of so much ease and "politicking" with which writers find their works printed. But in answer to the first proposition, many poets in this decade seem to have re-discovered Wallace Stevens, who has at least offered us a beginning solution by proposing his symbolist marriage between "ideas" and "things" in his theory of "resemblances." And in answer to the second notion, writing programs and poetry journals have already proved their worth as the only supporters of the principles of art and creativity in a nation where the government's strong practice of anti-intellectualism and its on-going policy of depleting its already depleted arts funding has lately become even more bankrupt of generosity, spirit, and ideas.

With this in mind let me leave by the way I came—through the open window of vision, made clear to us by poets whose work remains timeless and universal. Consider the similarities in approach to merging past with future—a responsibility of the artist's birthright which the poet can never take for granted—from three recent Nobel Prize winners and one of our finest young American poets. Czech poet Jaroslav Seifert in "To be a Poet" expresses our deepest anxieties toward the failure of poetic inspiration on the one hand and the power of image as metaphor on the other through which poetry shapes our consciousness and future:

> In vain I snatched for ideas
> and frantically closed my eyes
> in order to hear the first magic line.
> But in the dark, instead of words,
> I saw a woman's smile and
> wind-blown hair.
>
> That's been my destiny.
> Behind it I've been staggering breathlessly
> all through my life.

One cannot fail to heed the "staggering" march of destiny in Czeslaw Milosz's poem "1913" which recounts the memory of that year's McCormick harvester "leaving" the past behind like "cut stubble" in his Polish fields while he experiences his first trip to Venice—only to awake:

> In a city where the traveler forgets who he is.
> In the waters of Lethe I saw the future.
> Is this my century?

Finally we hear from William Matthews, one of the strongest American voices of insight in the eighties, whose poem "Days Beyond Recall" recalls the true nature of the poet's experience with the timelessness of art:

> Learned Santayana described himself
> as "an ignorant man, almost a poet."
> By "poet" I hope he meant neither a career

nor a state of being (*cf.* angel; *cf.* wretch), but
a student of the future, and thus of the past.

Each seeks to merge the future with the past just as each attempts in turn to merge the poem with the reader. The 1987 Nobel Prize winner Joseph Brodsky says that the poet's vision is one of "exercising prophecy and perpetually redefining individuality through his loyalty to language."

Poetry is a conversation, Brodsky says, "and in the moment of this conversation a writer is equal to a reader, as well as the other way around, regardless of whether the writer is a great one or not. This equality is the equality of consciousness." In these pages please enjoy the true democracy of poetry's universal conversation.

Index of Poets (Dates in parentheses indicate year of birth, where available)

Index of Translators

*(Poems for this edition of The Anthology were
selected from magazines with cover dates of
January, 1986 through December, 1987, as well
as some from 1985.)*

POCKETS

Walking down the street she finds her hands
jammed into pockets, blue jeans tight
across the hips she likes to move to music—
barefoot, hair down, silver tape recorder

blaring loud. She's seventeen. Her mother
calls her Bluebell just to get a rise, goes off
to work the morning shift in almost white
shoes and cap and apron, while daughter

slouches over Cheerios, sips coffee, stares ahead
and thinks how much she hates the smell of books.
"Goodbye." And once again "Goodbye" as now she
turns a corner stained with leaf tattoos

from early rain, pretends she doesn't care
that she is pregnant from a skinny man
she slept with once, who'll never know, who
thinks of her as something he once tasted,

might again. She moves along, indifferent
to the aching bit of smoke from cigarette
she sucks. She's seventeen. All's possible. All isn't.
Today at school they'll see a stupid film.

Cedar Rock   KATHARYN MACHAN AAL

IN SUMMER DARK, WAITING FOR CHANGE

Some calm evenings
instead of statues or hide-and-seek
we'd trample down a circle
in the hayfield, dig a shallow pit
in the center, bring twigs from beneath trees
along the river, ball up newspapers
and light a fire. We'd take turns
laying flat page after page
across the flames. Sometimes an ash
would hover up, twirling or steady,
and we thought, if we waited long enough,
one might turn giant moth, wings
weakly flapping once before they beat
and beat away.

        But soon the dark came

and our parents, after calling
once too often, would stride out
to grip our wrists. Only sometimes
they'd stop—

        a hesitating step or two
inside the firelight, sit down—our mothers
hugged their knees—and watch
for flights our ashes never took.

The Southern Review   Wɪʟʟɪᴀᴍ Aᴀʀɴᴇs

HOMAGE

(to William Carlos Williams)

If you moved the eye of the poem
you could scan the whole yard:
oak trees, swept sand, altheas in bloom,
worn tools propped against a shed,
bright barrow in a cellophane of rain,
slow fowl in tow. What you see
depends on where you stand:
whether you see yourself a child
alone and glad, or not—mouth slack,
bare legs dangling form the lip
of red metal, chickens as stallions;
whether the chickens continue to peck
and cluck, shaking their white wings
free of rain and other strange
comings and goings, while you, a man
going blind, stoop to close your hands,
scarred and strong, around black handles,
to lift them toward a distant light;

or whether you, a woman at noon, turn
at the upstairs windowsill and see
through lace curtains brush strokes
of red and white, feel down your spine
the shiver rainwater makes, and cry out
with breath drawn deep as the ground,
"Oh Lord, the sensible world!"

The Georgia Review   LOUISE HARDEMAN ABBOT

ST. LOUIS BOTANICAL GARDENS

(The orchid exhibit)

In my glamorous pouch
baby kangaroos could nestle
but I'm built to hold water,
one ladleful per bird
Sip, friend, and travel.
Distracted by the jibbering plenty
of the jungle, *rest here,*
then carry the message in my cells.

Harlots' frillies in lavender plaid,
iridescent puce, and a boa
of plashing maroon down a stem
iced with glitter. What will fetch
the silent exclamation from a bee?
Come, friend, torch your heels
with my pollen. Carry me like a rumor
through the green waves of your jungle.

The world's most pampered flower—
we are velvet paunch, we are brassy blondes.
While outside, at 35° Fahrenheit,
squirrels wait in suspense
for the headlines of spring,
and in Australia wallabies
steal the crop of winter grapes;
we're cossetted and coaxed

by servile human hands, which keep
our silk purses steamy ripe. We dine
on the equivalent of larks' tongues
and chocolate. We are free
from that slum of hummingbird and drizzle.
Why bother with a mosquito's
languid toilet? Why bother
with the pooled vulgarity of the rain?

Poetry   DIANE ACKERMAN

A MASS FOR THE UNBORN NEW DEAD

There'll be a mass for the unborn new dead
In the basilica above the water,
Grey, green, blue, icy or aswirl with snow as it is
In Charlottetown, Prince Edward Island,
This Wednesday and many Wednesdays to come;
For the rich think they've no more use for us
And our cunning hands once we've built civilization
And want us off—gold watches clutched in lead.

Valerie will be there on my right hand, Michael on my left.
The Host will be on display the entire day.
Further action will be decided on
If not immediately, eventually.
The doctrine of limbo has been eliminated
As not much use in a situation like this.
Faith remains faith if only faith in life.
We will not substitute a faith in death
At the mass for the unborn newly dead.

The Antigonish Review   MILTON ACORN

OVER-KILL

In moments of love,

we experience hate

In moments of hate,

shards of passion

In moments of grief,

flamencos of laughter

In moments of hurt,

tangible healing

In moments of silence,

a vestigal scream

In moments of madness,

the ultimate truth

In moments of fear,

the spirit to conquer

In moments of courage,

an Achilles heel

In moments of shame,

Olympian pride

In moments of freedom,

a prison of choices

In moments of faith,

the fires of hell

At the moment of death,

Paradise Lost

Humanist in Canada   MONA ELAINE ADILMAN

SAVING FACE

*("Be humble and likeable to all people,
and specially to members of your
household.")*   *—TALMUD*

Should I be humble and
likeable to my own household
of one?

For what am I
if meek and mild
but a parody of traits
I've purposely labored to
shed in order to be honest
with myself—
What is self-directed humility
but self-indulgent pride?

And if indeed a divided house-
hold
can't stand,
in order to live with myself
and save face I'd have to
excommunicate that
teacher's pet:

Complacency is vain
and vanity disrespect—

So for one I say
an eye for an eye.
Charity begins at home.

   Jewish Currents   Carol Adler

BEATING UP BILLY MURPHY IN FIFTH GRADE

Who knows how it started?
We were the same age, but he was smaller
with wrists you could snap like green beans,
veins that showed blue runners through his skin.
His scalp was something dead beneath his crewcut
and I hated his pipsqueak voice,
his hanging around with us girls.

Then somehow he was face down on the pavement,
my fist banging his back.
When my girlfriends pulled me off,
he whined like a toy engine:
I had hurt his sunburn,
I would pay if he went to the doctor.

He was an orphan I thought I should be nice to.
His aunt was sending him to military school.

I was ashamed but still sickened
remembering his soft hands, his thin eyelashes,
the schoolgirl in him.

West Branch   KATHLEEN AGUERO

AN UNTITLED POEM

I finally wrote down the words
Which for so long I dared not say.
I have a dull headache,
And my body is strangely numb.

The sound of the horn has receded, then ceased,
But the heart's same old riddles remain.
The first light snow of autumn
Lies on the croquet lawn.

Let the last leaves rustle!
Let the last thoughts languish!
I didn't want to trouble
One who was used to having fun.

I've forgiven those dear lips
Their cruel joke . . .
Oh, tomorrow you'll come to visit us
Over the new-fallen snow.

They will light the drawing-room candles,
Their shimmering is more tender by day,
And from the greenhouse they will bring
Roses, a whole bouquet.

August, 1919, Tsarskoye Selo

Boulevard   ANNA AKHMATOVA
                                        —Translated from the Russian
                                        by Judith Hemschemeyer

WE DON'T KNOW HOW TO SAY GOODBYE

We don't know how to say goodbye—
we wander all over shoulder to shoulder.
It's already started to get dark;
you're thoughtful, and I keep quiet.

Let's go into the church, watch
a funeral, a christening, a wedding;
go out, not looking at one another . . .
Why aren't things like that for us?

Or, let's sit in the trampled snow
in the cemetery, let's breathe lightly,
and let you trace with a stick palaces
where we will always be together.

New Letters   ANNA AKHMATOVA
                        —*Translated from the Russian*
                                by Joan Aleshire

CROSSING

The brook works subliminally, running
past the house, through the dreams
of everyone who sleeps here—teaching
the language of change and continuing—
nameless, just mine here, but further up
Adams' Brook, and furthest Korzuns',
in the hillside where it springs. Farther down,
it's Smith's, and people I don't know
watch it flow into the Mill. Really,
it belongs to the rocks that make it pool
and color it clear brown, except where
sand makes it clearer. It belongs
to the cows, to cress, to wild mint
that scents my shoes. Later, in summer,
my mother will walk with me here.
We'll talk, as always now, of my father;
that loss will be with us, that break
in the rhythm of their days, when she cried
and shook his still body.

Will she think I don't miss him enough,
who feel him still here? Who have I loved
that I haven't watched leaving—drifts erasing
tracks that seemed so sharply etched in the snow?
Her fifty years in one place, with one man—
it seems wrong to be kept from knowing the world
shifts underfoot, that we live on change:
oxygen moving into blood, the brook here
moving past our slippery purchase. Balancing
unsteadily, encouraging each other,
somehow we cross.

The Virginia Quarterly Review   JOAN ALESHIRE

THE OLD MAN IS LIKE MOSES

Like Moses on top of the mountain.

Every man can be Moses
and bring forth the word and raise his arms

and feel the light sweep from his face
the old dust of the highways.

For over there is the sunset.
Look behind: the dawn.
Ahead: more shadows. Where lights pointed the way!
And he waves his arms and praises life
even as he dies alone.

Because like Moses, he dies.
Not with vain tablets and a stylus and lightning in high places,
but with his words broken on the ground, hair
aflame, ears burnt by their terrifying meaning,
the force still in his eyes, the fire in his lungs,
and in his mouth the truth.

To die is sunset enough.
A bit of shade on the line of the horizon.
A swarming of youth, hopes, voices . . .
And over there, the future, the earth: its limit.
What others will see.

Crosscurrents

VICENTE ALEIXANDRE
—Translated from the Spanish
by David Garrison

DREAM NEAR EXTINCTION

I'm sitting in the gravel road that leads
to my grandmother's, moving my bare feet
in a basin of dust soft as talc.

It's late afternoon. The wind is slow and laced
with the tar my grandmother is cooking, stirring
in a rusted barrel down by the house.

The tough grass clumped along the road
has dried stiff and sharp as razor blades.
A milk snake bellies through it blind.

My grandmother's stray dog, black as pitch,
watches me from the shade of the tool shed,
his breath pressing fast against his ribs.

The cattle are gone. The pond has gone
thick and shiny and dark in this sun.
I'm pressing my handprints into the dust.

I lie down on my side and trace letters into it.
My dress is the same thin yellow as the dust,
and the tar I'm breathing is all we have left.

The Iowa Review   DEBRA ALLBERRY

BARGE LIGHTS ON THE HUDSON

(For Dana and Mary Gioia)

Glass door to the balcony slid open,
We step from the party to a night so clear
Only diamonds could scratch it. Below us,
River barges look like floating dominoes,
And we seem to hear boatmen singing, but that may
Be simply chanties from another condominium
Along these cliffs. Hours, you say,
Should pass as slowly and as beautifully
As those lights on the Hudson. Leaning here
Against the railing, shoulders barely touching,
We play a child's game of connect-the-dots
To bring out of the dark a tiny tugboat
In which a phantom pilot, legs spread wide apart,
Wholeheartedly steers—his face
Rimose as the moon's. One by one,
Others join us, until all along
The balcony a line of men and women
Lean and whisper, staring down, and some
Say the river's asphalt, others that
U-galaxies drift there,
Or we are in a science-fiction movie
Watching starships in a planet exodus
Across the Coalsack. Soon, however,
The party flares up in the living room, those few
Who linger here grow silent, watching until all
Lights disappear toward Troy, and just the oars
Of Irving's ghost row out from Tarrytown.

Poetry   DICK ALLEN

THE POSTMASTER

A blue-haired woman in the house with trellises—
beautiful big red roses like crushed drinking cups
climbing up them toward the gingerbread—
would rise every evening from her widow's bed
to greet my father. The mail he brought her
wasn't much: a postcard from her niece, a flyer
from Montgomery Ward's; but he liked doing it,
he told me—it was something in his spirit,
that mysterious feeling that thrives on walking just
a step or two away from the beaten path
to do a favor. "Why not?" was always his answer
when someone questioned him about the other
people he befriended—like the Coshburns,
our town's richest family, its only blacks, so spurned
by our neighbors, so envied, that I never
remember anyone else out with us when we'd curve
croquet balls on their great green lawn. There were also
the Hiroharas, he back from the camps. We'd go

out bicycling and end up in their little garden
with the pool and small stone bridge and stunted pines
and pebble path, and boulders, flowers, and my father
would have some tea. He would stir
it awkwardly, his hands too big. He looked funny,
nibbling sweet rice cakes. Everyone knew he was crazy
for those people, people who felt wrong the way he did
at the end of the 1940s when the maples spread
over the oiled dirt roads, and red roses grew
higher and higher at the house of the blue-haired widow.

The Hudson Review DICK ALLEN

PLAYING THE GUITAR IN JANUARY

The fire loosens my fingers, the winter flows
out of my hands, and I open the case
and play. Tonight, for the tones
of this fire, I want to forsake all the music
I have ever learned, and feed them the lean wood
of a song found only
in its rising, in the smooth blaze of six strings.
Under the chords that my fingers assume
without my tending lies every song
in the world: known, forgotten, to be
known, or never to be
discovered. They are all here together

not even bothering to hide, for they know their numbers
surround them. And the chance
I will touch them tonight, even
for an unsuspecting sound, is less
than the chance I will ever stop
looking for their measure, unless

every song is the same house
and I have always walked in
through another door.

The guitar plays. Do I hear everything within it,
or nothing? Or is everything nothing but ashes
when it finally darkens from its own light?
My fingers ache heavily from holding
the strings, from making less of them
than they are; but only the dying

fire can stop me tonight. The wood will last
an hour, no more. Another gray blanket
waits over my bed on the floor above me,
and when the moon lightens the stairs
through the north window, the house will be clearer,
colder than I could tell.

Images GILBERT ALLEN

CULTURAL REVOLUTIONS

This one Doukhoborhouse left unburned.
A Hollywood film maker turned Canadian
had the inside redone in fine wood
and put in a stained glass window—flowers,
with the afternoon sun lighting them now.
My fellow guest, Marcus, a professor
of scientific method, outlines his trip
to Shanghai, where he let his brain be picked.
His mind is as orderly as a syllabus:
when research bosses asked him how to ask questions
about reality, he could tell them, 1,2,3.
My mind isn't orderly, so I drift into thinking
about the Doukhobors, "spirit wrestlers,"
who burned their houses as a protest
against the state, with cues from the Holy Ghost.
Tolstoy wrote letters that won them refuge here.
Marcus, an old Marxist-Leninist, made
his pilgrimage to China a few years late—
the true revolutionaries were in jail.
"One fellow I met may have been a true Marxist,
he asked the toughest questions." The Holy Ghost
of history spoke German first, then Russian,
then Chinese. Now it's silent. Nostalgia
is merely a bourgeois emotion; Marcus
knows that as he sits in a lavish house
mourning the class struggle. And I know
he's too constructive to burn anything down.
The dialectic that drives the world is a motor
torn loose from its moorings. Marcus and I
register the vibrations as ironies
as we chat under the stained glass bouquet.

Cross-Canada Writers' Quarterly   BERT ALMON

HOTEL PAINTINGS

Sitting in my rented room in San Francisco, staring at hotel paintings,
I wondered if, during my stay, I couldn't change them a little,
at least deepen the corrugated blue of this sea to a more rudimentary shade,
devoid of illusion, tone down the antic postcard green of the mountains
to a sheer austerity of space, preserving the dusty orange rooftops,
perhaps making them the main event in an otherwise marvelously restrained
composition of ochre and gray; and of course eliminate the plump white clouds
on the horizon. A modest ambition but I couldn't sleep. Why stop at that? I began
   to think
of all the other hotel rooms in the seedy old Glenwood and of all the paintings in them:
ruined still lives, awkward unshopworn apples, slightly obscene pears, shining blue
   vases
of tiger lilies and chrysanthemums no guests even bother to scorn; perhaps I could
   rescue them all

from this bleak rosy oblivion with appropriate alterations here and there,
bring them into a kind of eclectic glory; it might be the start
of a fabulous new career, moving from room to room, from hotel to hotel,
always a new roof over my head, free of charge, enough pocket money
for paints, avocados and bread, a serious reputation quietly growing
as a master restorer of hotel paintings. An intriguing scheme; but I got to thinking
if perhaps the most curious thing about hotel paintings
is not precisely that they occupy this peculiar place of unconcern
devoid of all distinctions, where there is neither doom nor deliverance
and where the most tawdry shade of rose in a background of reluctant green may turn out
   to be
the true color of beginning. Though it wasn't easy
to relinquish a grand career so rich in promise, revelation and change,
on the spur of the moment I gave it all up
with more relief than regret and, better still, time to explore
in my newfound freedom from strange ambitions the wonder of hotel paintings just as
   they are.

Grand Street   GROVER AMEN

THE CARVERS

We dig deep
carving into time
burrowing
to a cage of light

We are the pain
that secretly starts
with a glitter of stars
for the heart of the log

We shape what is seen
in shifts
not distinguishing
the breath from the fear—
the song from the knife

New Letters   ZORAN ANCEVSKI
          —Translated from the Macedonian
          by Zoran Ancevski, with James McKinley

WALKER EVANS: HOUSE AND GRAVEYARD, ROWLESBURG, WEST VIRGINIA, 1935

I can't look long at this picture, a Walker Evans photograph
of a West Virginia graveyard in the Great Depression,
interesting for the sharp light it throws
on poverty, intimate for me because it focuses
on my private and familial dead. This is where

my grandparents, my Uncle Adrian and my Aunt Margaret
I am named for are buried. Adrian died at seven, long
before I was born. Margaret died in childbirth in 1929.
The morning sun falls flat against the tombstones,
then spreads across Cannon Hill behind them. I see

how beautiful this is even though everyone was poor,
but in Rowlesburg, nothing's changed. Everything
is still the same, just greyer. Beside the graveyard
is Fike's house, with the rusty bucket, the tattered
trellis and the same rocker Evans liked. Miss Funk,

the school teacher, now retired, and her widowed sister
still live down the road out of the camera's range.
I remember how my Aunt Nita loved that mountain,
how my father told of swinging from the railroad
bridge down into the Cheat. Nita worked

for the Farm Security Administration too, as Evans did.
She checked people's houses for canned goods, to see
how many they had stored, and she walked the road
by here, every day. I can't look long at this picture.
It warps my history into politics, makes art

of my biography through someone else's eyes.
It's a good photograph, but Walker Evans
didn't know my family, nor the distance
his careful composition makes me feel now
from my silent people in their graves.

Northwest Review   MAGGIE ANDERSON

OLD FISH EYE

Cozy inside, I watch out in the cold
drinking their coffee over an open book
a former student and her friend. A look—
something about the way their glances hold—
tells me they're lovers and I'm growing old.
The glances that once held me till I shook
like any fish upon a baited hook
can't catch me now. I know the line is trolled.
Not that I'd say I've lost my appetite
so much as that I've wandered down the stream
to calmer pools where I don't have to fight
the current. I just watch the young ones bite,
content to rest among the weeds and dream
while on the line their bodies twist and gleam.

The Threepenny Review   JOHN ANSON

THE DEBT

My brother owes Con Edison $750
for knocking down a utility pole with his truck.
He totals cars, loses tools, burns furniture
with forgotten cigarettes, turns
everything to junk.
I remember when he was born:
I was 15 and ecstatic,
my mother 40 and exhausted.
I told my sister
it was wrong—our parents
making a baby like that one night
when they were out-of-their-minds drunk.
I said it made me sick them *doing it*.
but I wanted a brother. He was mild,
sad and wet—after school and weekends
I took him everywhere. I wheeled him to town
in a wagon, dressed him up
like a little clown on Halloween. Now
he reappears unemployed, dodging creditors,
a shabby young man down on his luck—
like a marker on a bet
against those lousy odds of our childhood—
a shadow calling me back.

Passages North   CATHY APPEL

HEADING NORTH

Day breaks
your heart: pack
the smell of tanning oil
beside your snorkels and
whip your bones to a raw
future, dragging along
the pain of sea birds,
white sails. Home again,
fighting your way through slush,
you are condemned to memories
of golden fish in coral reefs,
golden beaches blinding
your frosted eyeballs. Now
your slurred footsteps in wet sand
won't beat the walk light; nothing
the color of palm trees blossoms
on Tenth Street. Live, if you must,
with half-hour delays
in the morning rush, prophecies
of turmoil in the sky,
minutes painfully pieced out

for a thousand nothings;
but dream, in your bickering taxis,
of the slow wake of white hulls,
your purest vision turning in
upon itself, leaving
everything to chance except your life:
the sun on your pale back,
the lust of ocean along your skin,
a lifetime that's finally worth it
everytime you breathe.

Poetry PHILIP APPLEMAN

WHERE CHILDREN STILL WATCH

The rain beats the color from these cold hills,
Filling the crimson buds with their gold breaking.
The freshet becomes a turbulence; streams swell
With this first waking. Beneath the banks frogs thaw,
Snakes loosen, and roots curl upwards away from the crystalline cold.

If you came here in the time of the iris,
Or in the time of the tulip, or now in the time
Of the winter melting rain, you would come
To a place where childhood is still valid,
Where measurements, roads, stonewalls, the work of men's
Hands still has meaning, where children still watch
The raindrops sliding down the window.

And the walls that hold this small world still pull
down the green tendrilled sun from the cloud loud sky.

The rain stops: blue breaks white and barns dry.
We have all retreated here.
We have come here like broken kings whose short
Space of years has stolen every truth.
Come here to find the constancy beneath the messiness of being,
To find the security of mill ponds
Where trout lay their eggs on rotting waterwheels,

And those hands that built forgotten rooms,
And dreamed themselves asleep in a different world,
Lie content with taproots in their skulls,
And tomorrow's stars in our bare branches.

America STEPHEN APPLIN

SELF-PORTRAIT

Eyes, covered by thick glass, disguise the two,
four, a thousand parents who passed the blue
recessive gene by blue-hot touches in between
mending the plow or stirring the beans.

Mouth tries to perfect a closed design,
lips stretching since high school trying to hide
teeth that fought for space in a too-small chin
and practiced for hours natural grins.

Skin smooths over the face, guards a world
of feelings that pull and push to be heard:
of blood that rushes when the covers slip
when he takes off my glasses, presses open my lips.

Poetry   BARRI ARMITAGE

FILLING CANVAS

I have a vision of those ships, idle, near,
like many hands, just waiting to applaud.
The sand is sharp around them, ocean-bruised;
the sky is blue with battles to be fought.
Men wander in and out of tents, play cards,
and call it yesterday, wondering when
today will lay her neck across their blades.
The eyes of some men wander past me, fix
beyond a point on the horizon:
no farther than the walls of Troy, as close
as all endeavor. These men don't
long for sacrifice; they're merely stirred
by breathlessness to lusting after blood.

If I could paint, I'd paint the scene; it would
include the grace of waves before they cap,
after they roll away. It would reveal
the purity of color, virgin white,
the strength of steel that cannot quite be seen.
Beneath them all would lie the prompting face,
dark and light, two lips that kiss as if
selecting apples, or a hand. And slashed
across the top, forgiveness like a shroud
entangling all the thousand ships I'd die for.

There's something out there larger than myself—
the masts that pierce the stillness of the air
don't even touch it. Dogs sniff. Fires burn.
Time will tell: perhaps it's in an arm
that opens mornings, cleaving them like wind
splitting sheets or curtains dropping down
on Iphigenia's walk to that long altar;
I don't know. It isn't wind *I* wish for.
There's something out there, maybe love, but not
what I would paint if war did nothing more
than fill their—fill my—canvas with desire.

Shenandoah   ELIZABETH ARTHUR

WHERE HAVE YOU GONE
JACKIE ROBINSON

reds are devouring the world
while peaceniks in the west
give them aid & comfort
the nation lifts its weary arms
for one more shot of smack
smack smack smack

and here's to you jackie robinson
who played it tough but fair
and stood tall for america
till you grew fat & grey
hey hey hey
hey hey hey

through terrible summers you showed the way
when crazies yelled "nigger" from the stands
or whispered it in boardrooms
kicking sacks or kicking ass
you were the top
bop bop bop

heaven smiles on those who play
those who watch & pray
most of all those who work
tending the precious flames
we know their names
the ones who fight for right

but they are few
so many traumatized & hypnotized
please come back jackie robinson
son son son
son son son

Obsidian 11   ASA PASCHAL ASHANTI

BENDING TO HER BATH

she thinks of him:
how she will fill him with herself,
how he will rise to take her in.

Slowly, she extends a foot into the tub;
she does not want the pleasure all at once.

The warm is strong;
it rolls along the low slope of her calf.

And now she half-submits.
She sits and lets the water find its way.

She stays and stays,
then bows to lean her breasts
against the clear seam of the surface:
she dreams it is his mouth.

Gently she slides back
to rest her head aainst the procelain.
She feels the wet touch on her neck,
the water lick her lip.
How patient she is now,
how well-prepared.
Her body is a prayer she knows he'll answer.

Poet Lore   SUSAN ASTOR

POEM 15

The world is a cage
of universal dimensions.
No one will be left without his place.
For this one-time-only performance
we will all be huddled together—
white, black, yellow,
coward and hero,
worker and loafer,
East and West,
Catholic, Buddhist and atheist,
masturbator and fornicator,
confused and lucid,
ignorant and wise,
rich and poor,
all together,
contemporaries by chance,
almost like brothers,
ready to support ourselves for the last time.
When the curtain goes up,
without a doubt
it will be a one act play,
all too brief,
without any epilogue,
and thus nothing will be remembered.

Webster Review   ETELVINA ASTRADA
                                —Translated from the Spanish
                                      by Timothy J. Rogers

BIRDS ON A POND AT DUSK
TURNBULL WILDLIFE REFUGE, MAY 1984

At the Wildlife Refuge, waterbirds make
Mad chorus: yellowheaded blackbirds,
Those senile emphysematics, laugh

From reeds; coots bicker,
Thrashing the placid water.
Tree swallows burp like babies
While snapping up gnats and mosquitoes.
Canvasbacks skip love calls
Across the pond that mirrors wood and clouds,
Redwinged blackbirds make spastic
Song in the pines. I sweep my hat
Overhead to scatter mosquitoes.

A yellowheaded blackbird
Wheezes, swoops to a reed
With wings spread back, feathers
Fantailed, the cold reptilian
Claws wide open. Chickentailed
Baby grebes thrum like greasy
Evinrude trolling motors
Refusing to start. Canadian honkers
Sound beyond the wood. One
Ponderosa pine outtrunks
The rest, silhouetted at dusk
Like a Japanese silkscreen. The balls
Of my feet tingle, my heels ache;
Tucked in like a child
Under these dark clouds, I close
My eyes. The sweet smell of the pond
Spins me back to summer vacations.
A mosquito whines in my ear and, far
Away, sounds of the highway
Rush, a great horned owl moans.

The north wind rises, bruising
Needles; it rushes through the mossgrown
Ponderosa wood
Hundreds of miles inland
With the surge and fall of the tide.

Reflections dim on the water.
A ghostly heron looms
Overhead, veers toward the sunset
And glides to the horizon.

Night sets over me, leaving
Only the sounds
Of wings on the water.

The Hollins Critic   KEITH AUBREY

REMEMBERING WASHINGTON

Summer dusk in Washington; half-light,
Perfervid as a Shenandoah rose
In leafy shadow, laden with the musk

Of swarming summer evening reveries.
Glittering bridges bracelet the Potomac.
Early lights make stars about the skylines.
On the Virginia side, the Pentagon,
Crystal City, hard-edged, Arlington—
Taps pining the silent, buried, brave.
Westerly, Roslyn's rise; across Key Bridge,
Georgetown's parapets and steeple; then the sweep,
The patriotic postcard panorama
Of the capital city, city of my first love,
Resplendent as remembrance in the roselight.
The Monument's upraised finger lifts the eye,
Like the hushing gesture of an orator,
To evening's starry banner, lowered slowly
Over Columbia's rooftops, Federal buildings,
Vistas of bronze and marble architecture.
Behold the famous dome, lit up as if
Aglow with very freedom's shining dream;
And there, the pillared shrine where Lincoln sits
Keeping watch over the vast republic,
Remembering barefoot summers in Kentucky;
And there, by the Tidal Basin, the chaste temple,
Clustered by dogwood, cherry branch and pine,
Where Jefferson stands, restive, listening
To the rising hum of millions of free spirits
From Louisiana to the Northwest Passage,
And crickets sing of nights at Monticello.
Rose deepens into purple, then warm darkness,
Filling all the twinkling distances,
Distances I walked lost summer nights,
And walk and walk tonight in memory.

Kansas Quarterly   JOSEPH AWAD

AMATEUR THEOLOGY

Sometimes
the sky looks like the inside of a skull;
its clouds resemble the puffy white brains of a retarded God.
On such days I think the skyscrapers are acupuncture needles:
too weak a cure for too grave an illness.
Other times, its clouds look like white frilly silks
against the blue thigh of a vain God too silly to think of us.
Some days, clouds resemble the white mist a small boy-God blows over
his blue hands on a cold day:
the sun reminds me of a small fire barely enough to warm him
after a romp through the empty cosmos.
But there are those days, like today, when clouds look like
the discarded napkins of a vampire-God gorging himself on the day's dead.
The sunset is especially beautiful.

The Hollins Critic   JODY AZZOUNI

I AM DANCING WITH MY MENNONITE FATHER

We dance a carnival ride:
you try to make me feel
in your arms the thrust and turn
of the Ferris wheel, to give me
at last that ride I wanted long ago,
that you denied because you saw
my small body sway to gypsy rhythm,
my feet move in forbidden ways.

Under trellises we dance the leaves
I pinned on my friends' costumes
in third grade—*Welcome, Sweet
Springtime*—the garlands
I helped the teacher place
on their heads, backstage.

"It is all right," you say,
and I see how young you are,
how your damp hair curls.
But this is my fantasy. I should
tell you it is all right now.
I am no longer eight years old
in my modest dress watching you
in your black suit at the classroom
door tell the teacher I am not
allowed to dance.

You move back to see my silhouette
against the light. "It is all right,"
I say, wind moving the sheer, forbidden
gown—all right to look at the outlines
of my body, to tell me by your smile
that other men will find me beautiful.

We dance all gossamer things,
not even trying to keep our feet
on the ground. You whisper now,
as you never did, "You're lovely,
and strong," spin me down patio steps
to the path, let me go.

The American Scholar   ANNE-RUTH EDIGER BAEHR

STRAWBERRIES

My pail stands between us,
half-full, the berries dusted with sand
like fine sugar. I turn at Maureen's warning.
You crouch beside the pail, scrabble
among the berries, straighten
with both hands bulging. The pail

tips; berries cascade across the sand.
Strawberry juice spurts through your fingers;
runnels fill the creases around your wrists.
You don't know that this is meant
as work, meant to guarantee a winter's worth
of fruit. Careless of future lack,
you bite through sand, leaves,
deep into the berries' fleshy hearts,
fling them away half-eaten
as you reach for more.

Balanced between laughter and anger,
I look around my feet. Strawberries
everywhere, rosy and plump as little pillows
among the leaves. Enough,
the woman supervising says,
for animals, birds, and children, too.
Each one has a share.

I hug you, gather up the berries,
drop two handfuls in your pail. Maureen
moves across to help me pick.
I will take home enough berries
for one meal, maybe two.

Ten years from now, none of us will remember
how many berries we have picked today.
I will remember only you, sticky
from head to foot, staggering sleep-heavy
to the car. I will remember the morning sun,
the hot sand against our feet, the world
a bright, sweet garden full of fruit,
thickly scattered by a careless, generous hand.

Helicon Nine   REBECCA BAGGETT

UPON THE ANNIVERSARY OF HER SON'S DEATH

When her son died, Earleen canned peaches for three
months, stacking the polished jars
like sentinels on the countertops. These are
the measure of my days, she murmured.
Then came apple sauce, pumpkin pies, fruit cakes,
pickles, and on to the spring garden until
every calendar month of that first year lay
crumpled in the cardboard box she saved
for clippings. Births and deaths. Sometimes

now, close to sleep, she hears rocks click
in the garden wall, larvae stir under leaves
and fossils lay themselves out, uncoiling
like small fists. Above her roof, squirrels

turn twice in their nests, insects burrow
the easy bark. She struggles for sleep.

When she sleeps, she dreams. Tonight she sits
again, as before, dozing in a lawn chair
between the garden and the pool. Her son
is swimming, his frail arms tucked beside
his waist, pink feet whipping upward
to make a whale, the brown hair blown out
behind like seaweed breathing and his small
boxer shorts, one shot of coral, all
washed white in the flurry of that long suspension.

The South Carolina Review   JAN BAILEY-WOFFORD

GOING ON INSTINCTS

I belong here as much as anywhere—dusk, the river
bank I grew up on, slow wind among the trees.
Yesterday's storm hardly touched it. Down the road,
silo tops were ripped off, fencerows flattened,
a shoot of straw, they say, stuck in one elm's soft bark.

Here the few leaves that fell are lost already
in the soft mulch of the soil. As I go down
the bridge-slope toward the water, I do not move
a single shadow but my own, do not disturb the frogs
on either mud bank saying the one word they know, by now,

by heart. It is like memory, the land, like a lost self.
It is where I've come to find a past whose remnants
are everywhere—the humid air like an old loose skin,
familiar shades of green, the burrs, as I touch
the brush, like little ticks to be picked off again,

one by one. Even that sofa someone tossed from the back
of a pickup, years ago, is still here, still swollen
and heady as a week-dead cow. No man, no storm could
change this place enough that I wouldn't know it.
The river flows past me, past its banks, as it always has.

I stand at the edge of its black water, old
as memory, and watch a bat skittering above me
in the dusk light. He sees nothing, yet flits by
faultless and easy as a shadow in the low evening air,
neither of us minding which way he turns next, or for what.

Kansas Quarterly   DAVID BAKER

SNOWBOUND

Tragedies of clouds still stumble over us
stalled in cars and tractor trailers
along the highway blocked at a mountain pass;

but now a track team from a chartered bus
has shoved a van past a jack-knifed trailer,
and so, after long hours, a lane is cleared
for all the bickering parents and bratty kids,
for truckers zonked on speed and nattering on CBs,
for the long-hauler with straggly hair and no front teeth
who struck out in the snow to straighten things out
and who stomped back angry; for the snoozing salesmen,
for the old folks too shy to pee by the road,
for the teenagers yelling in hormonal fits,
for the wailing babies, for the diabetic
shooting his thigh behind a fogged windshield,
for the lovers feeling lucky at being trapped together
and just wishing it were night—
for all of us now inching forward in a glittering line
resuming our lives under a sweep of clearing sky.

Poet Lore   JOHN BALABAN

CITY PARK

The moon does not know
why an elephant
lives in this city park.
Why a red brick house was built,
straw provided,
water, a keeper.
Why offering her peanuts
the children cry, "Alice."

The moon does not know
why an elephant
lives in this city park.
But the moon provides.
In the locked park at night
it sluices Alice
with silver,
daubs moon designs on her ears.

Sing, Heavenly Muse!   JEAN BALDERSTON

HOUSE

("Whoever has no house now, will never have one")
                                           —Max Frisch

Of all building work, I like best
the bare structure before the roofs
go on—above it
blue sky, the metallic echo
of blows as they nail down
the boarding. Wood shavings, warm

sawdust, trucks bringing new planks
from the forest. A series of rooms
full of sky—uninterrupted
stories, space seeing sun
for the last time in decades. Morning
sealed before my eyes. My gaze
stills things—the many I know
that are gone. Drugstore with black and white
diamond tiles, black wire chairs with backs
twisted into hearts. Woolworth's
smooth wooden floor. Sanctums.
My home's a meager impression
of bare steps, a kitchen's waxen light
at the end of rain. A closet
with a fifth of whiskey—my parents'
wedding present—glowing intact.
Its darkening amber.

A failed shopping center pales as if to record
a slow cooling of the sun's rays.
What will remain of the flatness
that in time everything takes? Under the town's
thin blanket of lights. "It's inhuman,"
I'm told, "to expect a person to see beyond his own ruin."

Poetry   ANGELA BALL

THE MORNING AFTER

The morning after another
collective suicide, you go out
as always to get the morning paper;
as always, the freshly fallen snow
gleams white or the tidy sun
of a summer dawn rises; as always,
the milk bottles ring and
the croissants give off their scent; as always,
a little girl with a satchel
runs to school and trips and falls
and skins her knee, and there's much crying and in this crying
so much life.

TriQuarterly   STANISLAW BARANCZAK
—Translated from the Polish by Magnus J. Krynski
and Robert A. Maguire

THE SWALLOW WATCHER

(for Larry and Elliot)

Every house needs someone to watch the swallows,
someone willing

to half close the eyes, lean the head back
against a tall chair
in a garden, on a porch, in a courtyard.

It doesn't matter if a cheap paperback
falls wrinkled from the knees,
a wine glass dangles
empty from the hand.
What matters is the watching:
                                        following

the lifts and darts
of the small birds,
the racings and screechings over territory,
the jags and dips for insects,
the gliding on wind.

About the time
the neighbor's porch light comes on
and the sky
can't hold color any more,
the swallow watcher moves inside

to the glare of living room lights,
but he turns, leans
against the cool glass of the sliding door,
and stares out at the dark sifting down,
quiet as feathers, easy as wings.

The American Scholar   WENDY BARKER

LA PLATA, MISSOURI: TURKEY SEASON

In early morning light you see them rise
from the branches, give their feathers a shake,
and drop gently down to the ground, their cries

scraping through the woods to herald daybreak.
You must hold still, black as the trunks around
you: no movement at all, nor eyelid tick.

The absolute, in all the stalks, you've found
is just this: not stealth, savvy, camouflage,
but your mind's immersion in the will of dawn.

These birds you hunt know more than swale and ridge
or weather rising fierce in the sudden south.
On days when your luck runs along the ledge

in easy shot, you count the lives in both
light and dark, the sum total of your frames.
What you take away from these woods and off

the land is spirit you hold in trust. Names
of birds and beasts erupting like wild dill
upon your tongue say that you did not tame

one wild thing, nor cause the low sky to spill
its rose or blue. Your camera holds a way
to be, and you another through your will.

The Ohio Review   JIM BARNES

THE NIGHT TIDE

When we finally got to the beach house, the night tide turned.
The moon was setting beyond the marshes, Arcturus
Still bright above the hill, no wind, and the salt river
Moving back to the sea with a silent power
So deep that a yellow planet stood reflected,
Burning the same from the sky and its calm surface.
"Stay!" said the house, and the curtains touched our shoulders,
The broom fell at our feet, but we turned and ran
Beyond the oyster shells and the stunted oak trees
To where the reeds were bending in the shallows
And a few crabs scuttled sideways through the sand
Trailing paths of green fire that grew to tendrils,
Tendrils to leaves, then phosphorescent branches
Blossoming from our bodies as we swam
Sideways against the current. Then we stood
A moment on the farther shore and saw
The lamplight beckoning us from the little windows,
and once again we waded into darkness
And swam, half afraid, through the strong, sea-going water
Until we felt its slow release and rose
Reborn on earth. Then when we walked the beach
Our tracks still shone with green and instant fire,
And all that night we swam in a tide of stars,
And all that tide we bloomed in a tree of light.

Contemporary New England Poetry   KATE BARNES

DARK AND WHITE SONG OF
THEODORE ROETHKE

I call myself the dancing bear, and though
I'm big and blazing with a bleak desire
To lindy with a beauty—not some crow—
My truth, my skip through hell, is that gray fire
When Jakob Boehme saw a pewter plate:
A dish of sunlight serving up his fate.

That wretched cobbler of philosophy
Gave me abysses and auroras, too.
I swing between a mad felicity
And gobs of reverend gloom, the holy glue
That holds my squirming soul in one dark shade.
Each night I sew up holes, but I'm afraid.

Be close to me. I'm sick and shy and try
To dance my arrogance. A man's a bag
Of miracles—which cynics call a lie—
Yet if I can't turn ashes or a rag
Into a rose, I might as well lie down
In a Long Island swimming pool, and drown.

O love, when Dante found a name, your name,
I stole it for my bride. You stole me with
Your swaying bones, and we became the same
Slow rising butterfly. We are the myth
Repenting from a dream of solitude.
I dwell there, fat with you and sweetly lewd.

Be kind. I want to live. I try to live,
And herons whiten banks along the Nile,
Its sewers nourishing a fugitive
From calm. I wear a golden crocodile
Under my shirt. It brought me you and day
When all hope drained into mere boring clay.

Under my shirt I am like all of us,
A nakedness that craves eternity.
Sometimes I sing or groan; I make a fuss,
Am caged a while until I learn to be
Easy again with you. Lord, let that flame
Of horror bleach a bit, and I'll be tame.

Nimrod   WILLIS BARNSTONE

RESTORATION

I love to recover the quality
of things in decline.
To scour bricks, scale paint from stone,
to compel, with wire brush,
the flourish wrought by iron.
To refinish wood, solving for
forgotten grain.
To give, by weeding, our stone wall
back its dignity.
To left and right the borders of our lot,
to square the corners of our keep.

I have even dreamed: pushing a pushcart
I stop anywhere and start
doing what needs to be done.
The first building takes time:
replacing windows, curing the roof.
I know compromises must be made,
and make none, a floor at a time.

I work along an interstate
a century after Johnny Appleseed.

A modest people makes me chief.
(They, too, enjoy the hazy shine
of finished work by last light.)
Storm drains relieved, brick walks relaid,
a heritage of dust and wrappers
is renounced. The square square,
trim trim, the town for once
is like an artist's conception of the town.

Passages North   JOHN BARR

FLIGHT OF THE GEESE

(for Angela)

the ice on the river
is already breaking up
and the geese are thick
the porch swing stirs
and the dogs hold forth
at the mailman's step
the sky drifts apart
from the water's cold edge
and the cars don't see
the roar of your absence
and the hush of the neighbors
wash over me
come back
the turn of memory
fits the lock and the clock
and the candlelight
the late night breathes
while the stairs climb on
to the moon's clipped wings
the black cloud moves
past the lead glass panes
and the trestle speaks
the ice on the river
is already breaking up

The Cape Rock   CAROL BARRETT

ANTI-APARTHEID MARCH: KIRKSVILLE, MO

Saturday morning: we abandon our routine of donuts
and car repairs to gather on the college quad's wet grass
as the flat-faced brick of every building
deflects the sound of the marching band, practicing.
We are a college out in the grass, miles from a four-lane,
a train to Chicago. We struggle to care about more
than the rock on the road, arson downtown, the failure
of another farm.

We march through the gates of the quad, up High Street,
signs raised: "One Man, One Vote. Solidarity With
South Africa." We pass the Quik Trip, the Speed Lube.
Today we do not hurry. We reach the courthouse square.
Mennonites stare from their stalls at the Farmers' Market,
the bread and cheese they sell usually enough
to silence our hungers. Our first speaker begins.
Who are these words for? Mennonite children watch,
heads cocked, as if this were a signal to another galaxy.
Here we all are, staring into the distance,
a long way beyond this square of buildings in the grass.

Envy's Sting   MONICA BARRON

PLEADING TO A LESSER CHARGE

Above all, I regret what happened to the
cat. It was the blood I wanted to
drain out on the altar.
As for the rest of the damage, I was
drunk and bound to smash something.

Father Brown, I understand, has already
forgiven me. I thought,
even as I was piling the books for
burning, it wouldn't be enough. I have
found his god to be either
thick-skinned or sleeping.

Statues of Christ are known to bleed.
An uneducated man in Hoboken
shouts out in pure Latin while he sleeps
an obscure heretic thirteenth-century
philosophy. I was
stretched out in a pew. The morning's
first faint light coming through the
stained glass into the
smoke from the smoldering fire
made a multicolored gloom.

Where is this god who would once
blind a man for a few chance remarks?
Can't you see? Even the back of your hand
would be better than nothing.

St. Andrews Review   ROY E. BARROWS

VOICES

I spoke to God and Devil,
waiting for reply.

I whispered into both ears,
having seen two sides.

I told of men and women,
of youth and of age,

Of joy, love, goodness, beauty,
and their counterface.

Each question and emotion
met with silent dread.

One listened to the living
and one, to the dead.

Crosscurrents   ELIZABETH BARTLETT

LEFT BEHIND

Old towns die slowly.
Their tired blood runs thin
and sluggish with time.
Ragged grey feathers
of curled and peeling paint
crawl down the old frame houses
leaning in the wind.
Shreds of yellowed lace hang
like cataracts in the darkened windows.
Shutters flap and groan with age.
Vacant storefronts,
victims, done with business,
stare out at sagging curbs
and crumbling walks, streets empty
except for old shoes shuffling,
tired feet with nowhere to go,
but going there anyway.

Kansas Quarterly   NONA KILGORE BAUER

THE VIEW FROM AN AIRPLANE
AT NIGHT, OVER CALIFORNIA

This is a sight that Wordsworth never knew,
Whether looking down from mountain, bridge, or hill:
An endless field of lights, white, orange, and blue,
As small and bright as stars, and nearly still,
But moving slowly, many miles below,
In blackness, as stars crawl across the skies,
And ranked in rows that stars will never know,
Like beads strung on a thousand latticed ties.
Would even Wordsworth, seeing what I see,

Know that these lights are not well-ordered stars
That have been here a near-eternity,
But houses, streetlamps, factories, and cars?
Or has this slim craft made too high a leap
Above it all, and is the dark too deep?

Arizona Quarterly   BRUCE BAWER

MIDWESTERN POETICS

The unpromising meets the unexotic,
and we are home again, alone,
with this image of the possible:
these hills that anyone can climb,
the lowlands, reeds perched with red-wing
blackbirds, leading painlessly
to cemeteries and small towns
where voices are subdued and have no region.
A man paints enormous replicas
of Rembrandt's middle period on the sides
of barns. He is mad. He leaves.

Without elevations, hurricanes or
earthquakes, without geological alarms,
we learn to count the angles
in the sky and to admire four-barrel carburetors
in the muscle cars that combine with roadside
trees in the six-pack dark of Saturday.
It's not that something has to happen.
A man writes a letter to himself
and excludes the absolute: he is four seasons,
paths in third-growth woods, nature
that is endlessly familiar.

He is a silo: he stores, he feeds.
No horsemen raging down the mountains
flying banners, no vipers, just this and that
that could be anywhere but happen to be here.
The children grow up calm: they learn
about psychotic tantrums like tornados.
They plan. There is time, and more time
and more time after that to learn to love
the mild gifts—these apple trees, these
sparrows—in this marriage with a woman
who knows you, but will not kiss you back.

Poetry   CHARLES BAXTER

THINGS I CAN'T SEE

Blackbirds cry in the persimmon trees.
I can't see them

But I know that they are there.
They mock me with their screeches,
As the wind that
Shimmers through the leaves,
Peeling them like scales
From parched branches.

I can't see you,
Yet you breathe
Cool against my throat,
My flesh puckering
From the chill.
The blackbirds do not rest,
The echo of their voices
Sweeps through the limbs and back
To lodge again in their mouths.

A train rattles somewhere.
I close my eyes and see
The worn tracks quiver,
Shaken by the vibrating metal,
Now still as if the train
Had never touched them.

I strain to see the blackbirds,
But they have become leaves
Bending with the wind.
In my mind you are as real
As those blackbirds, those persimmon leaves,
Perhaps even more than when
Your shadow lies next to mine
On the soft earth.

Tar River Poetry   NANCY BEARDEN

IN RODIN

In Rodin, the damned
are cast in their bodies
& lamentations,
such comfort
as sorrow provides,
such inwardness—
this one
figure *Despair,* her whole
body straining
for release, each muscle;
& curled, almost
fetal, one foot
kicked outward & caught
in the hands, & her face
buried in her breast, as if
beginning to withdraw,

at last, into her dead
body: but she's
arrested in that perfect
form of her own
sorrow, set
carnal & unforgiven in the gate
of hell Rodin carved, body
after body, in
his cracked & tear-streaked bronze.

Southern Poetry Review   BRUCE BEASLEY

ABYSS

Pascal's abyss was with him everywhere.
Everything is an abyss. Anything
That is done, that happens, is thought; is put into words.
I can't begin to tell you how many times
The fear in the sound of the wind has made my skin creep.

The deep; the long white empty beach stretching on
Forever; the silence; the desire of falling.
God has written something on the face of the dark
In a hand absolutely sure of what it is doing.

I am afraid of sleep because I am afraid
Of a hole empty with horror. I can see nothing
Out of my windows but infinity.
My acrophobic spirit is falling in love—
To be nowhere, free of being, form, and name.

Raritan   CHARLES BAUDELAIRE
                                    —Translated from the French
                                    by David Ferry

POMEGRANATE

(for Christopher)

("because of the plenitude of its seeds,
  has a penchant for going wild.")

Son, how to tell you the eating
of pomegranate is the beginning
of all seasons, and just as the Jews
wandering through the wilderness remembered
with longing the pomegranates of Egypt,
you will never forget your first taste
of the heart's fruit: the way scarlet
flowers conceal the shape of a fist;
mysterious pink-turning-to-crimsom pulp;
the way your stained hands become memory

that shapes your life, your own
many-chambered heart that beats
even in its quiet moments of passion
more quickly than the clock;
how, like Persephone, you will
come to know each seed consumed
has roots in the underworld.

You will eat the small, translucent,
tear-shaped seeds more delicately
each year, remembering many who sought
the orchards of Solomon, only to find
themselves lost and alone
in a world where the heart
is an ornament.
My son, you are not alone:
you will weep and laugh
in the ancient garden where
men become boys and boys become men,
the land of the deep,
indellible, blood-red fruit
where both bitter and sweet stain
the lips and the heart
forever.

Passages North   THERESE BECKER

PERHAPS

Looking from the evening window
to see streetlights blooming above
the snow and last fingers of dusk
receding, I wish the scene were
neither dark, nor cold, nor empty.
Perhaps there should be a river
with barges and along the bank
an old man in blue cap smoking
a pipe, and a young girl riding
a red bike down a gravel path;
or perhaps there should be a field
of wheat, an undulating sea
of gold, and an Irish Setter
curled in a daub of light, and hawks
turning; or perhaps, just perhaps,
staring now into the darkness
I should see a coconut palm,
and a monkey high in the fronds,
and a woman in a flowered dress
sitting in the sand, her fine hair
stroked by an almost loving wind.
But if such were the scene, perhaps

nothing would be changed. The frail glass
would keep me from the old man's smoke
and his stories of river life,
from running madly with the dog
through the glad waves of waist-high wheat,
from sitting near enough to touch
the woman in the sun-drenched sand;
just as when I try to touch snow
to my lips I find it's only
absence I drink, uncertain if
the taste is more bitter than sweet.

The Southern Review   RICHARD BEHM

THE NATURE OF LITERATURE

(for Mary)

This windy afternoon the budded trees
rub a charcoal sky; the windows fill
with occasional light, watery rectangles
of yellow, now here, now gone, erased
by another drifting smudge of cloud.

We each work at our books, you
in the rocker with Byron, poet
of such empty afternoons, booming
out despair, me in the canvas chair,
idling among legends of Finnish wizards.

Night will come, crow, caller
of the darker dance, and you will dream
of Manfred on the heights, while I
sing horses into stones, and buds
by moonlight feather into leaves.

Yankee   RICHARD BEHM

FOR THE TEENAGERS WHO STONED THE ZOO BEAR

Could you listen, then, unmoved, to his sigh of resignation
as he lay down to die, sinless, to resist no more
beneath the dark hail of your stones?
Could you hear the deep resonant striking
of brick against broad back, great sides
that swelled and shrank in anguish, in confusion,
at the twilight sky raining down missiles where apples,
where candy and the warm spring rains had showered him?
Could you watch the deep, hopeless eyes
helpless to comprehend, to believe
he was not to perform yet this once more,
not to beg, even as you stoned him,

as you killed him slowly for your amusement,
brutally, in the hushed green park?
Could you live so, to find in this massive life
some soulless thing, some mere trifle
for your whim, your entertainment in its extinguishing—
you who were dead long before he died,
long before he lay his battered head on the cold,
the waiting, bloody concrete, a trickle of bright blood
from his dark, quivering nostril tracing the ebb
of his great spirit among the waste of rocks and bricks,
the shattered glass and flagstones,
the fragments of the paved and ordered world
made filthy by your civil touch?
You could, of course; for you could laugh, for whom no toll
might be too great, nor stone too heavy
for laughter, for mirth, for murder
in the soft spring sunset,
among the infected elms, the willows
weeping with shame, with shame.

The South Carolina Review   STEPHEN C. BEHRENDT

MOVING

Black is a verb
Moving through the shattered night
Breaking into day
With a fist dance
Against discrimination
Black is a verb
Moving through the European night
Holding onto Africa
With finger edges
Against racism
Black is a verb
Moving.

Black America Literature Forum   NOVEMBER BELFORD

ANOTHER SKY

There is no sponge to wash the sky
but even if you could lather it up
and douse it with buckets and buckets of ocean
and hang it in the sun to dry
it would still be missing a silent bird

there are no methods for touching the sky
but even if you stretched like a palm tree
and managed to rub against the sky in your delirium

and you finally found out what it felt like
it would still be missing the cotton cloud

there is no bridge crossing the sky
but even if you could reach the other side
by dint of memory and forecasts
and you proved it wasn't so difficult
you would still be missing the pine tree at dusk

because this sky is not your sky
however impetuous and audacious it may be
on the other hand when it comes to your own
you won't want to wash or touch or cross it
but the bird and cloud and pine tree will be there.

Poet Lore   MARIO BENEDETTI
—Translated from the Italian
by Richard Zenith

A HYMN FOR THE POST OFFICE

Inside this place of regulation
where paper and cardboard shuffle
dry as spirits waiting in line
to squeeze out of purgatory

and letters slip-slide into heaps
of yours truly and sincerely yours and even
a few loves among the circulars with
special offers exclusively yours,

now twinkles another sound—
a constant small music accompanying
sunlight pouring down Jacob's
ladders through shut panes.

Maybe it's a shower the tired young
postman is dreaming about at four o'clock,
or a spray of stars he remembers
from last night's porch with his girl,

or that carton of baby chicks mailed
to Maplevale—small yellow messages
singing about circles yet unbroken,
waiting in boxes to be delivered.

Calliope   ELINOR D. BENEDICT

FULL CIRCLE

The one remaining molar of a whore
who had died unclaimed,
bore a gold filling.

(The others, as if by secret agreement, had
dropped out.)
The undertaker's apprentice
knocked out the filling,
pawned it, and went dancing.
For as he said:
Only earth should return to earth.

New Letters   GOTTFRIED BENN
                                 —Translated from the German
                                 by Stuart Miller

THE POEM

is its own subject.

It is interested
only in itself.

No matter how
or where it begins,
it ends up talking
about itself

unshakable
in its conviction
that it is be-all and end-all,
center and cynosure,
the most fascinating
of all phenomena.

In this,
as in many ways,
it resembles us closely

and has much to teach us.

Tar River Poetry   BRUCE BENNETT

STATIONS

In the train's window I see my own reflection
and the passing towns: the highways running
across my cheekbones, billboards and houses
in my face, the occasional sky in my hair.
And the fine nature of my constraints becomes evident.

I took a picture of you once, sitting
in front of a low tree, and could not decide later
which was the more incidental—the green leaves
falling across your shoulders and into a patch

of soil, or you in your diminution,
without the intricacies of thought.

When I look back into the window, I see myself
fixed within a great movement. There is a rush
of wind outside which I know without feeling.
There are the homes interrupting the darkness
and the understood families within them.
I am sure that a thief is in one of the shops,
stealing something that he will not sell,
but regard with a pure and obsessive delight.

I think of you always in this gratuitous way,
as small as the jewel at the end of the crime,
and as enormous. I think of you limb for limb
as it were, in an isolation both grave and laughable.
And the abstraction astounds me, like the sight
of my face in the glass: a temporal etching,
a weird conclusion arising out of the blur,
like the naive sense of importance
with which we pursue our lives.

Four Quarters   KAREN BENNETT

IN THE SHADOW OF THE PINE

This ancient Scotch pine lived its faith;
Worshiping sun, air, water, earth,
It made of me a fundamentalist.

Now, ax in hand, matches in pocket,
I honor our forty years of friendship
By presiding at its crematory rites.

Unlike animals and birds, trees die
In public, their bodies racked with pain:
How far from fleshy green this brown skeleton.

With heavy heart and cleaving shoulder strokes
I lay my old friend low. As it goes down
It grabs my feet. I do not forsee my fall.

Luckily, I land on shoulders and neck,
And roll with the blow. Numb as a stick,
I lie still, waiting for my head to clear.

My first thought startles, then comforts me:
How much friendlier the earth has become
Than when I fell to it in childhood games.

America   PAUL BENNETT

TOKIWA AND HER CHILDREN

(A painted screen by Yokoyaman Kazan)
—Japan, 19th Century

You suppose we have been walking for days
among hills whose summer features I
probably know by heart, but in winter, all is blank.
Or that the snow must be as cold with sandals as without.
You suppose us pausing in a grim tale
of a woman lost, her children about to be eaten
if she cannot satisfy the white tiger's hunger,
and soon. I have taken the baby
inside my clothes. She mews herself asleep.
The boy whose hand I have steps into the air.
He looks wildly at the needles of the pine
as if they'd let an avalanche loose,
but those boughs, also with their hands full,
also won't let go. The oldest son
stands off from us three a little,
hunched so his clothes outgrow the body
he will have to fill with more than this
slender misery. The bamboo gate, lashed
like a shepherd's flute, stands
wreathed in spindrift snow across the ravine.
We have stopped near the edge. My cheek inclines
against the baby's fine-haired skull.
The boy's silk pants billow. The wind against my cheek
is breath upon a live, pink coal.

The Antioch Review   ROBERT BENSEN

HIDDEN IN THE DARK NIGHT

Hidden in the dark night
is the trembling of bright planets.
In the abyss of heaven
blind stars secrete themselves.

Like the voice in song,
flight is hidden in the air.
The sun disappears into cloud
like a ghost into dream.

Solitude lies hidden
in the solitude of sky.
And in the tenebrous forest
the paths of silence.

The Literary Review   JOSÉ BERGAMÍN
                    —Translated from the Spanish
                        by David Garrison

THE ECHO OF YOUR VOICE

The echo of your voice in my ears
seems to move away
and grow sadder, more afraid,
as it nears my heart.

As if, disguised by silence,
it were not the echo of a voice
but a living flame that touches my heart,
lights it, and burns it.

The Literary Review   JOSÉ BERGAMÍN
                              —Translated from the Spanish
                                        by David Garrison

TRANSMIGRATION

As kerosene climbs through a wick,
Or sap through oak by the slow
Fire of evaporation,
So moisture from the saltpan
Has scaled the flesh and feathers
Of this long-fallen crow,
And seeded it with crystals.
Alone with its blue shadow
As if on a shield of snow,
Half scavenger with a tough beak,
Now more than half a vessel
That might have served Versailles.
It challenges the sun
With a blistering salt eye,
Easy in the wisdom
That its fellows are nothing at all,
Serene in its lucky fall,
Its dazzling transmigration
From bird to the stabler kingdom
Of the gem and mineral.

Poetry   BRUCE BERGER

A CLASSICAL TEMPERMENT

As though in love for the first time, summer
extended its warmth and brought November
an unaccustomed lushness and ease. Then
this morning I am awakened at last

to a hard frost, and in the early light
I see crystals standing straight from the backs
of grass like coarse hairs on a young man's thigh.
All autumn I had dreaded this moment—

the winter's undeniable advance.
I had forgotten that nature possessed
such precise and formal beauty, but now
I'm grateful. This cold that came as I slept

has proven that I will always be drawn
to those like you who are distant and chill.

Nebo   DAVID BERGMAN

HASIDIC WEDDING

When I speak of the bride and groom
in their wooden chairs, hoisted up
over the heads of the celebrants, I speak
of crazy joy, though it's true
the women wear wigs, and the men,
too, cover their heads, as if righteousness
lies in what isn't
animal. It's true the men don't dance
with the women, just as it's true

the couple's faces are almost too brilliant
to bear, like white hot wax
from a candle. Still,
if I wanted to tell you the movement
of joy, it would be these
two, their arms held out
to each other, high up
over the wedding
in their chairs, not pale
and floaty as Chagall
would have painted them, but ferocious
hot, like what's inside
the earth. They have
to come down; even the sun does,
though the things of the earth
feel the burning
a long time after, even the night-
flowers, the moon-
flowers.

The Ohio Review   JUDITH BERKE

A DIFFERENCE

Machines pass on the road, so heavy
that the leaves of the young beech,
spreading in stillness, shake.

But on the river, slow waves
roll under quick waves,
causing the reflections of the trees
to ripple and to sway.

The Hudson Review   WENDELL BERRY

ATTILA THE HEN

Years after school has faded to a stack
of dust-fringed yearbooks on a closet shelf,
the dream returns to drag the truant back
by one delinquent ear. You find yourself

in class. You're either naked, or your name's
been called to give the answer. There she stands:
the teardrop glasses with the rhinestone frames,
a metal ruler flashing in her hands.

Artemis   ROBERT BESS

WINTER BROOK

Down where the thin whisper of brook undermines
the argument of the stone wall is
a small moment where the water pearls
into an ampersand of ice.
I go there often.
Like some county clerk's office where
recorded deeds signal
the rummages of life,
it tells me beads of rumors,
how the elm up the way slowly died,
how the trillium wait for
the quilting bee of spring,
how the old sclerotic spud of rock
at the bottom of that moment will outsee
my eyes forever.
Today
the sun barely glazes
this unleavened snow;
the air snarls the nose.
Down in this lower corner,
kneeling over this moment,
I hang my ear over this ampersand and hear
my own blood unknotting, breaching silence,
myself slightly echoed, slight echo that I am,
off the earth.
I listen farther, but no luck,
only the deft hardness of dying elm,
the waiting potency of trillium,

a rock whose eyes mine the coming earth
with the seeds of bone and hunger.
Down in the lower corner of my land
Delphi surfaces and caws.

Buffalo Spree   MICHAEL BETTENCOURT

THIS GARDEN

There is no excitement
in the dove's call.
We think we know
what he means, and that he would say it
whether or not we heard.
We think there is a garden

lined with poplars
and wrought-iron
benches, painted white,
where obedient children sit
studying shadows
among the pebbles along the walks.

In this garden
our mothers and fathers went out to gather
flowers and brought them home at evening.
Long afternoons, we learned
the patient twisting of sycamores
around secret, magical places . . .

                        Even now,
if I listen, if I look hard enough,
I can see where the cardinal
sings in the maple. So easily
the eye follows a blur of feathers,
translucent, throbbing, red.

But the mind
catches.

He pulses away across
fields still yellow. The sky
fades . . .

And this gray song under my window,
like an argument
so familiar nobody bothers
to listen. Or you
asleep beside me
in this garden grown
so quiet.

Ploughshares   ROBERT BIENVENU

THE TERMS OF ENDURANCE

The last bell has not yet left your ears
as your friends crowd in around you:
girls in reversible skirts—green plaid
to red—in powdered, white buck shoes.
And now the boys, ringing in
with their cleated wing-tips, autumn
sweaters still tight at the neck.

It is that time of endurance.

Together you watch an oval dish, boiling
with water. Beneath it, a bunson burner flame
flattens to an amber coin. Now observe,
the teacher tells you, dropping the body
of a pond frog to the jumping water.
In one motion it lands, senses, leaps,
its pale underside extending to an arrow,

a filament of light. The flame
is turned down, the dish replaced.
Within it, the reptilian body
languishes in luke-warm water—gradually
heated, heated, until the small
boil bubbles churn at the rim of the dish
and the frog turns its lifeless belly
to your face, to each face, presents
it slowly, like a sigh: *Here.*

And what does this tell us? the teacher
asks. You are stunned, unable
to speak, unable to comprehend yet
the terms of endurance. You think only
of that motion, the scorched belly
turning up like a sigh, and wonder
why the animal did not leap as before,
why it did not understand its own
tolerance, and why it would stay there,
in that water too long its element.
Heavy and troubled, you walk
back to your seat, past the blackboards
and the long mural of Civilization
and its Great Wars. On this cold autumn morning,
you cannot understand your own grief,
how it swells and recedes. Already
the instruments for Music
are arriving, bold and familiar;
the sleigh bells and castanets—and
for you the shining triangle, its one note
so perfect in your hand.

Carolina Quarterly   LINDA BIERDS

EVERLASTING PEACE

The garden. And here in the center of town
The smell of storm is in the air, moving
Westward, up the Elbe, towards Hamburg.
Apple blossoms glow whiter,
Then pink against the ink-black
Sky. Peace. Peace. Peaceful
Roll of thunder, moving this way. And I
Count the seconds before the flash, a child's toy
That once amused the gods. We creatures
Now have other little games going,
Like cherry-bombs, whoops! with a different flash,
A different thunder. The air stands still and
Smells of wind. The red clinker-bricks are still
Fragrant of the sun. And now
The blackbirds bicker at the cat, the
Mocking bird plays nightingale.
Sparrows whirr into the greenery. A miniature peace
Passes into evening, the world
Is in order. Here it comes, and
The first lazy drops drum on the edges of the
Roof. The black bird waggles one last
Fleshy bite from the new-mown
Lawn. And rain. Rain stirs the air.

The Malahat Review   WOLF BIERMANN
                                    —*Translated from the German*
                                    by Maurice Taylor

PHOTOS IN A PICTURE ALBUM

Master David Black,
In yarmulka, blue suit,
A carnation in his lapel,
Requests the honor of your presence
At his Bar Mitzva party.

People, frozen in a picture album,
Light candles, slice hallah.
Aunt Margaret dances on her little feet,
    Martha Wolfe smiles.
Uncle Hymie and Aunt Rachel already looking old,
Aunt Rosie like an Irish washerwoman.
Aunt Haya Leah, five years a widow,
    Zorach turning fat and gray.

Seventeen years have passed.
I look into a mirror,
    It lies to me.
I threw a shovelful of dirt into
    Aunt Margaret's grave.

Uncle Hymie and Aunt Rachel age no longer.
I held Aunt Rosie's hand in her last coma.
Martha Wolf is dead. Her husband has remarried.
Haya Leah and Zorach rest in little plots.

Each page of the album
Unveils a headstone.

A camera freezes time,
But time refuses to stay frozen.

Jewish Currents   HAROLD BLACK

OLD MAN, WALKING

He'll tell you it's never really a matter of will,
walking across counties he can recite by name
as if they were kin—*Alachua, Wakulla, Escambia*—
walking towards the cool patterns of mirages
on dust a mile away, following the stuttering
of poles growing small down a road that is here
only a hint at endlessness, the wind a breath
bright-edged with salt, a sea yearning towards
dryness, the sour drifting yellow of smoke
from stump fires.

Shimmering in the heat, cypress hammocks
spot the distance, and he says he can see
across this open pasture and down this road
great mountain-shadows held still
by lines of barbed wire, gaunt strings rusting
beside the road, something else to keep him walking.
In the tired openness of afternoon he settles
for a time under the one tree in this pasture,
listening to leaves rattle against the tree,

and he tells you there is power
in standing alone like this, branches scraping
a mosaic on the underbelly of the sky, swaying
in the promise of a sun too bright, too hot.
Then, led along by the heat moving
on dust a mile away, chased by the stillness,
he walks on, he says, because he has to keep moving,
because he never wants to know that where he is
is where he's going to die.

The Georgia Review   JOHN BLAIR

KITCHEN SURGERY

I don't remember what caused the bloodied nail—
a door slam, a hammer blow that missed, catching
the cuticle. I remember throwing wet snowballs

all the next day, my fingers going numb giving
the infection its chance: the purple fingertip
swelled to double size. So my father taped
my hand to the kitchen table, injected Novocain
in the vein at the base of the finger, touched it.
Can you feel that? I grabbed the table edge
and looked away at the row of black pan handles
hanging on the opposite wall, every muscle tight
but the hand. With the first cut a deep pain
flowed out over the numbness, only blood,
so he made a second. When he asked if it hurt,
I called loudly and slowly to the walls,
It's not too bad. My mother put her arms
around my shoulders, siphoning off some of the wild
static of pain. After the third cut he cried, relieved,
There it is! I stole a glance and saw yellow
oozing among the red. *But I thought there'd be more,*
he said, bandaged it, and gave me aspirin.
Maybe I didn't use enough Novocain. His eyes asked
for reassurance. Not knowing how much Novocain
a man would need, I said, *It'll be fine,*
and went upstairs where the real pain rushed in
like waves, with no father watching.

Poem   PETER A. BLAIR

A HOUSEWIFE'S OLD-FASHIONED FIRE

Not so much the faces, eyebrows askew, lipstick smeared as though
applied at dusk without a mirror, the expressions of animals you forgot
but once knew by name or the monotony of light
carved on furniture day after day, but the company you keep. A flame-colored
cockatoo sings of the meaning of life from its tall cage,
its songs blending the way light from a full, orange moon
paints the shadows of different trees. In every blade of fire
you hope for more. How one night, just fifteen, you turned your lips red
against the grass in summer moonlight. The barn
at the end of the meadow lit up the color of your lipstick
and in its next life you saw changing boundaries, constellations' light
reshaping your features, a kind of make-up, eyelids florid as roses
pressing against glass for release. In the fire is the face you saw
in the shop window yesterday, small as a piece of burnt paper in a landscape.

Black Warrior Review   LAURIE BLAUNER

SUMMER HOUSE

In the large house by the lake
we have installed our best loved
rituals—those we have no time or place
for otherwise—mornings on the porch

drinking coffee and eating fruit from plates
into which the sun spills itself,
the kitchen stool by the sink,
shelling peas into a blue colander, the house so quiet the plink of each
small green globe is heard as it falls.
On the side porch the faded seat pads
of an old wicker glider move to the music
of wind chimes. The air disturbs
our tea things and summer magazines.

Each day we follow the sun
to the lake's edge
or perhaps even out in the boat
to keep it with us longer. We row
carefully, pulling the silver thread
of wake behind us. All winter
we'll keep these images
at hand like prayer beads.
I'll be able to feel
the weight of your head in my lap
these summer afternoons. And sometimes
we'll need to talk,
reinventing the moment when it is both day
and night, as the lake holds the last fuchsia
of an August sunset,
while bats skim its shining face.

Passages North   KAREN BLOMAIN

WHAT'S WRONG

Even the light, exhausted
hours before it reaches the horizon, crawls up each morning
over the edge and collapses

flat out. Like a lung. It's February.
People are cold and unsympathetic. They want the sun
to set an example, bright, on time,

everybody doing the jobs they were hired to do.
This is the wrong time of year to talk reasons.
If a woman sleeps through

the alarm and the phone calls and the husband trying
to bring her to: to what? The world
is a sickness we succumb to daily, our own need

pulling us in. It takes courage
to listen to the details, what's the food like,
how does the routine work in this place,
where's the other way out.

The American Poetry Review   LAUREL BLOSSOM

LUCKY

Off to the market to buy a lottery ticket,
I consider the possibilities of luck: good luck,
bad luck, beginner's luck, hard luck, the luck
of the draw, and realize I am lucky, in fact,
to be here at all, along this benignly lit street
on a night in October, as luck would have it;
and I know that it's not just the luck of the Irish,
but any man's, to walk the streets of his town
beneath the shapely moon, and ponder
the dumb luck that brought him there, against
all odds, out of the vast lottery of minnow
and ovum, and that he has once again lucked out,
this very night, spent as it has been
without accident or incident, a small testimonial
to the quietudes that are still possible:
the only half-felt wish for some grand stroke
of luck that will change everything, that will
change, really, nothing at all, our lives being,
in some sense at least, beyond the vicissitudes
of luck and longing, the night being lovely,
the day finite. Many of those we know whose luck
has already run out, and we not yet among them,
thank the beneficence of Lady Luck:
our lucky stars just now flickering into flame
as the night lucks in.

The American Scholar   Michael Blumenthal

THE POND

History insults us. The slap
of ancestors, cataclysms
cindering the forebears, top
billing to chance or determinism,
man a gray cake of soap.

Who needs it? Heroic
wills in irresistible ascent,
villains mean and ultimately tragic
entice us. Things *meant*
to be—beautiful or catastrophic—

please like the cool surface
of a pond. There are swans there,
an oak proscenium blurs
the horizon, and everywhere
details rehearse their purpose.

Take those fat humming
bees to betoken fertility,

the breeze, of course, whispering
secret wounds, the morning glory
praising light and strangling—

it can go on forever.
Even in the cold strut
of dialectic we'll uncover
a cakewalk: sweet bonds that
we dream and will not sever.

Poetry   DON BOGEN

ON HEARING AN ALUMINUM DISC AGAIN
OF MY VOICE IN 1938

It used to be that my past was close by,
huggable and lovable as a best friend.
It was my past as a young man.
Now I have a mythmaker's past,
long, long.
This recording of my voice at eighteen
reduces forty-five tumultuous years
to an instant
and returns me to the redhead in the booth
at Wurlitzer's on 42nd Street
reciting his elegy to Hart Crane.
It's my voice alright,
but unstrained, unsuspecting, sweet,
listened to in those days
with fadeless enthusiasm and love
by that dear cluster
for whom I could do no wrong
and who, naturally, are all gone.
There is no other record of that day,
only the vivid myth I make
of a legendary boy
reading his poem on the very rim
of romance and catastrophe.

The Ohio Review   GEORGE BOGIN

A LANGUAGE

To speak a language till one's dying day
is of great consequence, you'll surely say.
For long years in that tongue I did no speaking,
although within my blood it went on shrieking.

And now I know: it's of great consequence
for long years not to speak a language once.

A tongue in which you're bidden to be dumb
is one that never will succumb.

Midstream   ROCHEL BOIMVOL
                                        —Translated from the Yiddish
                                             by Aaron Kramer

ENVOI

It is Easter in the suburb. Clematis
shrubs the eaves and trellises with pastel.
The evenings lengthen and before the rain
the Dublin mountains become visible.

My muse must be better than those of men
who make theirs in the image of their myth.
The work is half-finished and I have nothing
but the crudest measures to complete it with.

Under the street-lamps the dustbins brighten.
The winter-flowering jasmine casts a shadow
outside my window in my neighbor's garden.
These are the things that my Muse must know:

She must come to me. Let her come
to be among the donnee, the given;
I need her to remain with me until
the day is over and the song is proven.

Surely she comes, surely she comes to me—
no lizard skin, no paps, no podded womb
about her but a brightening and
the consequences of an April tomb.

What I have done I have done alone.
What I have seen is unverified.
I have the truth and I need the faith.
It is time I put my hand in her side:

If she will not bless the ordinary,
if she will not sanctify the common,
then here I am and here I stay and then am I
the most miserable of women.

Northwest Review   EVAN BOLAND

ESTUARY

Seagulls scare in a bluster of wings
and rise on the strain of their beating;
a sound much like the rush and catch
of our breathing in our moment of strain
and flight. I watch them stretch, and the sky opens.

Strange, here on this beach with you
and the sound of climbing flight, I remember
the noise of my uncle dying in a closed room,
breathing like the beating of trapped wings,
the pigeons he kept in a coop—scrape
of feather and bone against a wire cage.
Honed razor stillness sprung from walls
severed his final rattle of breath, and the sky
slammed shut. No wing could endure.

Herring gulls extend their black-tipped wings
against the sky, banking, skimming turns
through a smooth bowl of air.
I stroke your knuckles with my thumb
and your hand opens, cradles mine,
as we listen at the shore
to the calm rhythms of brackish waters—
land-held fetch of waves, the earth's rotation
deflecting incoming water to the right,
the nudge and tug of tides, the ride
of fresh water over salt.

We turn and plod up the beach,
clasped hip to hip.
We pause at the mouth of the river,
turn our faces to the sea breeze;
then we follow against the current
our passage back into the sun-torn,
unquenchable land.

The Literary Review   BERNARD BOMBA

METASTASIS

All day we sit in the bar watching
grey winter waves. A child is feeding
the gulls; a man walks out between
the hotel and the beach, his cane swaying
ahead of him like a dowsing rod.
And you tell story after story,
a Mississippi childhood built of words,
as colorful as Oz; it is as if
the chaos in your cells has set time
moving in reverse for you, unraveling
your life as it goes, till only
the oldest stories are still of a piece.

Midday, we stirred ourselves for a walk
and found the beach dappled
with flocks of birds flown in from the north,
all face to the wind, too tired
to be afraid. They rose up
decorously around our feet, hung

in the air, and settled down behind us
as we walked. Turning to look back,
we found them as unmoved
as if we'd been the wind.

Through the stories you tell, move
other stories that you do not tell,
of love that works its way through grief
and turns away too soon, days spent
with strangers on a winter beach.
The child has gone inside now.
Through the window we can see
the blind man out on the sand.
He waits, the wind in his face,
tapping a patient arc to guide him
back into the order of the walks.

The Southern Review   ADRIENNE BOND

FINAL GROOVE

I first danced there on the warm linoleum
of our kitchen in my father's arms.
Our hands clasped, feet scraping across the floor.
I felt so comfortable with this, my first dance—
as he led, and the music played on.
The needle scraped in the final groove.
I felt his grip release, our blood flow
from those fingers back through palms
toward centers as we stepped apart.

I danced easily through my early years
with this step—the basic box.
Much more easily than he had, for he
had high-stepped to Cotton-Eyed Joe in
Oklahoma, then swung his way in a waltz
across Texas, to find himself here in our
final dance—with the music too loud,
but still the same simple step—
the blood still
in those fingers that clasp mine.

Ploughshares   MORRIS BOND

MIDWEST

My heart is like Chicago's Union Station.
Once it was full of a thunder of arrivals, departures.
In the gusty ostentation of its spaces blinked
   tremulous Rebeccas, fresh as eggs from the farm;
and the pull of the trains boomed in its aortal vaults.
How the hicks hobnobbed, then shushed in the din, eyeing the moguls eye

those pigtails wobbling in the holes in straw hats!
It was big, big enough to contain the city.

Now it is filled with commuter regularities—
the lisping of papers, the oblong rumbles, the routine comings & goings.
In the club cars, under tables of bridge games, bobble the briefcases
  with their inbound sandwiches and their outbound stock quotes.
Cards coded with tiny symbols cover each other;
  the queen falls to the ace.
Back in the station the benches are glossy with waiting.
The place is written up in the guidebooks, a must for the ruddy tourists.
It is part of Chicago, this pump, this station, this heart.

Blue Unicorn   PAULA BONNELL

BROTHER

The subject had been a dream
you had about death, how you had sickened
and gone to sleep without thinking,
then found yourself walking under my window,
and I in a half-sleep would lean towards
you at your word.

The last of the dreams was yesterday:
you were in a car, satisfied
at last to let things be.

This time I knew, even in dream,
that 12 years ago the doctor saw something,
small as your thumbnail,
sure to kill by summer.

Artemis   BETTY BOOKER

UNDERSTANDING POETRY

Death be not proud . . . How proud we were, how tough,
You my arch-poet, I your paraphrase!
Our pyrotechnics set their wits ablaze:
Logic, trope, scheme, theme, structure, all that stuff.
I met them, matched them, made them call my bluff;
We thrashed it out, rehashed it forty ways;
Strutting that little scene, I played for praise
And won my share—oh yes, I had enough.

Death be not proud . . . When did the clapping stop?
Standing in that still house, remembering how
We sojourned there in joy, the joy that was,
I hear, Jack Donne, beneath your razzmatazz,
A quieter music. "If it be not now,
Yet it will come." Teach that, or shut up shop.

Poetry   MARIE BORROFF

BALLAD OF THE BACK

We who have become inured
by scale, watching South Africa
burn, Ethiopia dwindle, who flee into ciphers

of power, for whom even nakedness
has become an abstraction,
can learn from the life of the back.

It is the back that receives the rod,
that fetches and hauls.
It carries our life

like a house with many rooms.
In them stretch the corridors
where we chisel our days out of rock.

The back hides all that quivers.
It opens and closes like a door,
against others, against

ourselves. But it is also the back
which flows like silk beneath a lover's
hand, which shimmers like water,

like the open space in a forest.
It is a glade murmuring with voices.
It bears all the touch of the world.

Partisan Review   MARGUERITE BOUVARD

THE REST

You can take it with you,
you know;
in fact you must—
the silence between words,
those moments of pure,
thoughtless reverie when sharpening
a pencil or stirring soup;
the pause between breaths;
the stop between diastole and systole
for which there is no name;
the space between the notes
without which the notes would be
one long wail.

Overhead, in the tall darkness,
a plane seems to circle,
its engine stopping and starting,
then stopping for good
as the farmer looks up from his mystery
and listens to nothing

punctuated finally by a distant thud.
In the morning he will stand
between rows of corn
before the wreckage so out of place
and small in his broad field,
as cameras click and whir
and someone reaches out a microphone
and waits for him to comment
on what he understands but can't explain.

Southern Poetry Review   NEAL BOWERS

SEPTEMBER

From the other shore this morning,
a crane flew over here to stalk
the borders of this bed of reeds
beside my dock.
                          He walked
the shallows like the shadow
of a tall man lost in thought.
And once he hunkered down,
                                        held still,
then hammered at the water with his head.

What he swallowed, I couldn't see.
A sunfish maybe, or a baby bass.
I watched him for a while (or her,
I couldn't say), then turned to other cares:
the unmown grass, the leaking boat,
my dog's unkempt and matted fur.
Things fall apart all right.
And seasons change.
                          Already
the innocence of summer's drowned
in a flood of falling leaves.
                                        It seems
we're "well into the festival
of what is not eternal."

The crane took off for parts unknown.
I saw him rise and go,
admiring as he flew away—
the air of patience
he carried with him (or her,
I wouldn't know).
                          Cranes
take their time,
what time is theirs.
And so shall I, I say
to no one in particular,
no one being there.

I'll take
my time and husband it,
and harvest it with care;
my crop has not done well of late,
and I doubt I'll have much to spare.

Passages North   NICK BOZANIC

THE KING UNCROWNED

a statue
of elvis stands tall
on beale st.
an undue tribute
to a tone-deaf legend
with a nasal twang
singing sad refrains
of white washed
RHYTHM & BLUES
while delta bluesmen
pay their dues
in blood sweat tears & toil
enduring year after year
of trial
the constant denial
of entrance
even at the back door
of "mainstream american music"
elvis
        the king is dead (& gone)
& with him went rock & roll
& western aesthetics
now
america weeps the blues big time
over the cast iron memory
of a dead king
while the blues muse
lives on in the songs of
MUDDY B.B. BOBBY
BESSIE BILLIE & MA
swinging/singing/& saying
hell yea
the blues is alright
'cause the blues is real
& ROCK & ROLL IS A RIPOFF!
if you don't believe me
GO TO HELL! . . . & ask the king

Black America Literature Forum   CHARLIE R. BRAXTON

THE SHOPPER

I'm an old woman.
When Germany woke up,
welfare payments were cut. My children
give me something now and then. But I can
hardly afford anything now. So at first
I didn't go shopping so often, though I used to go every day.
But then I thought about it and went
every day again to the baker, to the vegetable store,
like an old customer.
I chose my food carefully,
took no more than I used to, but no less,
laid the rolls next to the bread and the leeks
next to the cabbage and only
after it was added up did I sigh,
rummage in my purse with my stiff fingers,
shake my head and confess that I couldn't
pay for those couple of things, and shaking my head
I left the shop watched by the customers.
I said to myself:
If all of us who have nothing
no longer appear where food is for sale
they might think we need nothing;
but if we come and can't buy,
they'll know how things are.

New Letters

BERTOLT BRECHT
—*Translated from the German*
by Ed Ochester

HORSES

I love your bays,
Your chestnut places.
I love the thunder of hooves
When all else slides away
Sidesaddle
And we are galloping, galloping
Into a warm red seething of blood.
I love your mane
Whipping at my eyes,
My shoulders,
As you ride me,
Urging me forward faster with your knees,
Until mare and stallion we race
Past knowing of each other
And plunge over backwards into earth.
As the flare leaves our nostrils
I nuzzle into you.

I love your bays
Your chestnut places.

Casper State Tribune Arts Section   MARY LOUISE BREITENBACH

JEALOUSY

The moon is full tonight, and shines between two clouds
Like an open robe. Its light grazes the river,
Which pulses through the darkness moaning and sighing.
The low sounds wake no one, but as you lie
Dreaming, unaware of this outer world, I stand
Outside, where stars blaze against the sky
Like candles in a cathedral on All Souls Day.
One, far away, burns for my dead mother.
And now another appears, suddenly puncturing
A black patch of empty space,
An old wound opening.

I've been exiled from your mind, sent
Downriver on a waterlogged raft;
My back's been turned to your yacht,
Anchored near a moonlit levee,
But above the rush of water flowing between us,
I hear strange footsteps walking the deck.
The waters of your dream are washing
Away my image, and floating farther
Downstream I think of this:

Those lonely, interminable nights
My mother waited up till dawn
Drinking and sobbing in the dark nonstop,
Invisible, except for the glow of a cigarette,
Which would flare with her breath and then go
Out, a star dissolving in the vast tide of gray
That even now is turning everything
Blank and forgotten as dreamless sleep.

The Cape Rock   MATTHEW BRENNAN

THE SCALE

The man doing life with no chance of parole,
Watching the walls grow visible in the first light,
Thinks how, all over the city, men wake up beside women;
Even the losers get lucky sometimes, but nobody
Gets lucky here, where they put you to make sure
You have no pleasure, and miss it constantly.
The guilt that had seemed almost nothing inside him
They had made solid, so that he could not look
Away from it to take some comfort from the sky
Without seeing bars also.

It could have been worse:
One hears that in certain countries, political prisoners
Are locked in boxes too short to lie down in,
Carried down to a cellar, and stacked like so many
Warehouse crates, in one dense tenement
Of tormented flesh soaked in its own excrement.

For someone, somewhere, this is actual; one of those boxes
Is where he is and has to continue being.
If he dreamed of a prison cell
With a bed and a toilet, he would weep bitterly
To wake in his box and find it all a dream.

This is the stone on the far pan of the scale;
Load what you will on the others; it scarcely trembles.

TriQuarterly   PAUL BRESLIN

WALKING THE CENTRAL VALLEY

through towns of secondary roads,
outside Weed, Cottonwood, Shingle-
town, Round Mountain, Paynes Creek—
past stick houses where the aged
stare out from porches on elbows

into the dry heat of a typical
summer day. Everything I own
in a bundle on my back. I have
an opportunity to feast

on images, to regard the trap
of appetites. I have nowhere
to be until August. Later,
witnessing sunset, a color lyric

mirage, I find an abandoned apple
orchard, a comfortable place to
apprentice myself, to read a book
before sleeping.

I have nowhere I have to be until
August.

Kansas Quarterly   PETER BRETT

YOUNG WILLY SERVICES
TWO MAJOR ACCOUNTS

My Dear Mississippi Kiddo:

I regret my unannounced arrival in Jackson
Before heading on for New Orleans,

But business takes precedence,
Dictates schedule, destination, comportment:
Best foot forward, articulate wit,
Now raw passion are de rigueur
If I'm to keep from risking my position
As mid-South rep
For Acme-Zenith Trouser of St. Louie, Mo.

Afraid of waking your husband,
I'm forced to leave this on your visor,
Escort that whore, Silence, to bed.
Dispossessed of your wet sex,
And missing your touch and tongue
To reassure me the remote geography
I stumble into is safe,
I'll grope for morning's door,
Borrow tomorrow on this unsecured note.

Ah, but then, I see this abstinence
As discretionary compliance, token sacrifice
When measured against potential gains.
How otherwise might we sustain
The feverish pitch of our alliance?
Besides, cake consumed without savoring
Only tastes sweet to the baker.
Anyway, let's not belabor slack time—
I'll be back in forty-eight hours!

—Mr. Willy

The Southern Review   Louis Daniel Brodsky

A RENEWAL OF FAITH

Tracking south in my fleet vehicle,
I whisper past the highway sign
Proclaiming Wilson and Lepanto,
Cruise between viaduct uprights
Approaching mile by minute Belle Memphis;
A specter, unnoticed as yet,
Hurling recklessly toward the River.

Whether seeking absolution
In Beulahland's baptismal stream
Or on Crusade to a Canaan south of Eden
Remains for me to ascertain.
Already my flesh has begun to quiver and itch
As if I were slipping in quicksand,
Naked, unable to scream for assistance.

Signs for Tyronza and Jericho remind me
I'm yet enslaved by Arkansas,
May not reach Mississippi by dusk.

But my apostate heart has faith
You'll be waiting in Oxford to jog with me
Through the humid gloom of Bailey's Woods,
Anoint my spirit with your buoyancy.

Ball State University Forum   LOUIS DANIEL BRODSKY

THE MAPS AT MIDNIGHT

"The right maps have no monsters."
Not so in the middle
of the night.
The right maps squirm
when you hold them.

Which way? you ask.
I shrug. A shrug
is not a map, but
an adequate gesture
in lieu of direction,

compass, or clock.
The right maps are just
loaded with monsters,
mirrors and desires.
Marco Polo knew this,
Magellan didn't.

The right maps make their
own monsters, fuel them
with the proper myths.
Which way? you ask.
I shrug. Ask them.

West Branch   DAVID BROOKS

CROWS

The crows stir up the darkness with their wings,
proceeding west; a stand of cedars mutes
their drifting cries, which last as if a hand
had gestured to design a word, then left

the meaning in the air. Black into black,
they disappear now. Even in the mind,
something about their form remains opaque;
I cannot penetrate to their idea,

remote behind that stern, deliberate rise,
the wholeness of their flight. The commonest
eludes us most. Among the folds of hills,
the corn will leap up, flaming in the wind,

as summer runs; when the crows come again
in waves above the quincunxes of green,
what will it matter then that alien wings
have just descended over me like death?

The Southern Review   CATHERINE SAVAGE BROSMAN

LOSING ARGUMENT

The branch is locked in a bank of snow,
the deer in their yards wait for the slow
turn of seasons, and I walk against
the wind that shreds itself on the fence.

Where am I going when I could be
home, a book propped on my knee
while others break the ice on the brook
or shoulder the snow their passage shook

from the weighted bough? I leave no tracks
on the hardened bank. I won't turn back
or even pause in my wintry trudge
to watch black water flow under the bridge.

But my surly will drags to mind
your silence, and the eyes you blind
to every gesture I shake before you
to bring you out of your stubborn euphoria.

Look how the stars have lost their hold,
look how the drifts on the roof have curled
close to the brittle window's pane.
Everything falls. I'm not to blame.

Four Quarters   T. ALAN BROUGHTON

SAWDUST CIRCLE

Magically in the meadow
I find a strange
sawdust circle.
The clamorous, glamorous
circus has gone.
Only the circle
within which
I play the clown
to an audience of cows
and the applause of crows
remains.

When beasts
trample it

and time and tempest
disperse the dust,
scattering the shavings,
who will know
what life
was sustained
within this ring
under the
BIG TOP?

Crosscurrents   VICTOR H. BROWN

MINOT TRAIN STATION

When we rode into Minot,
that silent town,
passed the blue station strung with cracked neon,
I saw your face glow like an orchid on glass,
dark eyes squeezed open from sleep,
felt your whole family
blow through my bones.
The train slowly smoked,
ground old gears to pull out on down tracks,
and the toy-tiny station with its single red wreath,
strings of green lights still coloring snow,
rose higher and higher until it could meld with a slate of stark sky.
I wanted to stay, slide over ice with roped baggage,
sit in that station, drinking steamed chocolate to warm my blood,
and, taking you with me,
burrow like mice into memories:
dawn-frosted streets;
shops where fruitcakes cost 10¢ a tin;
bright snowy plots
where all your kinfolk are buried.

The Centennial Review   TERRI LYNETTE BROWN-DAVIDSON

MENGELE

Don't tell me about the bones of Mengele;
the bones are alive and well.
Don't think to thrill me with tales
of the drowned bones uncovered;
the bones are alive and well
inside the sleeves of a suit this day
and carving out the figures of a fat check
or severing a ribbon with the ceremonial scissors
or holding the head of a child;
I tell you, the bones are alive and well.

Don't expect me to get excited
concerning the skull of Mengele;

the skull is alive and well,
the skull is asquirm with schemes this day,
and low words are leaving it at this moment
and other skulls are nodding at what they hear,
seated about the world table;
I tell you, the skull is alive and well.

Don't bother showing me pictures
of the remains of Mengele;
the remains are alive and well
and simmering in our rivers
or climbing into our houses out of the ground,
where they will not be confined
or sliding inside the rain out of the summer air;
oh yes, the remains are even there, I tell you,
are alive, are well, are everywhere.

The Iowa Review   MICHAEL DENNIS BROWNE

MY FATHER'S VISITS

You spot a loose nail on my porch and pound
it down so it won't snag me later when you
are gone. Hammer in hand, you prowl around
and around for something broken, something to do.
I think you think a father should only stay
to fix his daughter's house, then go away.

You jingle change in your pocket. Your coffee steams
the window where you stand and tell me how free
you feel since you retired. You spot one flame
of cardinal twitching. You explain how he
will survive this northern winter, burn back in May.
But, when I look, he fidgets. He flies away.

If you could stay just one more day I'd listen
to you describe the dawn, a racket of flak
as you flew over Italy, every mission.
Below you, unpicked olives gone gold, then black.
I'll never have time to get the details straight.
Your bomber staggers. I watch it fly away.

I watch it fly away with you inside,
breathing fast, a young blond bombardier.
Your buddy, the navigator, hugs your waist, hides
behind you. Your neck is wet with his fear.
Your plane leaves here at six o'clock today.
I'll stand at the gate until it flies away.

But I make you promise to come back in the spring.
Of course, you laugh, and slap your suitcase shut.
I'll never have time to ask you everything.
Sun on your skin in Corsica, the chestnut

shade where they let you nap after bombing those days.
What did you dream there? It's time to go, you say.

Prairie Schooner   DEBRA BRUCE

TANGLED LINES

The boat began to drift with the wind
which whipped down Deer Pond,
turned us against the anchors.

The loon which danced
all the way from the point
beside us dove and was gone.

White lines drifting
in long lazy S's
down into the hemlock water
tightened and ran
as trout after trout
took hooks fast
as we could rebait.

Anchor ropes twisted,
trout braiding our lines,
hats blown off down the pond,
my father and I leaned back and laughed

as he laughs today
from his stiff bed
where pale tubes drift
to intravenous racks
and the EKG monitor sketches
green peaks and depths
of his pulse and breath.

I was just there again, he says.
*Remember that day—the loons
and the wind?* And though his hand
is cool in mine, I laugh with him,
tangling our lines into memory.

Painted Bride Quarterly   JOSEPH BRUCHAC

CHALK

Today, after taking two ferries
Across Puget Sound and driving two hours up and down logging roads
Along the crumbling rim of the Pacific, I bet on the rain forest and won
Every tree in sight, every green flame
Of fern, every swollen mushroom and truffle, every wrinkled white
Log, and wet and spotted wildflower.

But what I really love was yesterday
When the chalk players, hunched over The Form, scratching
Figures on tout sheets and tablecloths, put it all on the #3 horse
In the ninth because (they thought) figures
Don't lie, while the woman drinking chartreuse
Margaritas at the window table, here for the one
Afternoon, picked the roan because (she said)
The green and blue silks were dazzling
In the swirling mist that paid $62.50
For the win. That surprise,
That woke me again last night,
Still smiling and willing
To bet on anything.

Tar River Poetry   THOMAS BRUSH

A FATHER CONSIDERS HIS INFANT SON

Always before your guileless eyes I stand condemned,
Guilty of the sordid crime of growing old.
Innocent was I when I was young,
But living tarnishes the soul.

Would that the world would leave your infant heart alone,
And maturity would never take its toll;
But living is the curse of being born,
And living tarnishes the soul.

Poem   PAUL BUCHANAN

THE LIFE WE SHARE

I can feel it,
as if this swimming were of my own
body, beyond maleness, able to sustain
the life it spawned.
My wife, six months pregnant, sleeps
lightly atop me, her yellow hair
covering my chest,
a ringlet on my right nipple,
belly to belly the way she likes
most after love. We need this
fusion of skin kept apart
too long. Her body,
once hard for the sleek fashions,
has softened in motherhood, developed
curves that mold to my flesh so perfectly
we are almost one,
closer than the coupling that made our child,
the fetus that moves to find more comfort
between us. Hardly breathing

I lie, not wanting to wake
the wife who could end this
feeling with a yawn,
with a slow roll to her side,
whose pregnancy has become,
for the moment, mine.

Ball State University Forum   MICHAEL J. BUGEJA

LOVE POEM TO A STRIPPER

50 years ago I watched the girls
shake it and strip
at *The Burbank* and *The Follies,*
and it was very sad
and very dramatic
as the light turned from green to
purple to pink
and the music was loud and
vibrant;
now I sit here tonight
smoking and drinking,
listening to classical
music,
but I still remember some of
their names: Darlene, Candy, Jeanette
and Rosalie.
Rosalie was the
best, she knew how,
and we twisted in our seats and
made sounds
as Rosalie brought magic
to the lonely
so long ago.

now Rosalie,
either so very old or
so quiet under the
earth,
this is the pimple-faced
kid
who lied about his
age
just to watch
you.

you were good, Rosalie,
in 1935,
good enough to remember
now
when the light is
yellow

and the nights are
slow.

Prism International   Charles Bukowski

FATHER

That is his chair,
his easy-chair.
There he sat.

The leather became brittle
under his body,
I never once laid my arm
around him.

Dark stains on the sides
where his hands rested at noon,
and the head above
lay in sleep.

Bent towards this side he
slipped.
Thus I found him.

Poet Lore   Hans Georg Bulla
*—Translated from the German
by David Henry Wilson*

BLIND MAN AT THE GROCERY

1
The blind man at the grocery
leans on his wife. Together
they trace the braille of melons.
They inhale their ammonia,
tap for soundness,
that efficient tongue.
2
His touch simple, pragmatic,
yet a caress. Her movements
are hiss.
3
True, she must translate distance,
but he in his dream of nasturtiums
translates oil
into air, moon into tar,
the wet sprawl of leaves blowing,
blowing, blown.

Artemis   Mary Bullington

"AGAINST THE NIGHT"

(for Father Raymond Roseliep)

From this uncertain vantage point of age
and pain, I think of how you lived for years
with your plain pine coffin in the spare room,
bought and paid for, at the ready.
Even from one as well prepared as I,
this brought a small reproach: was the poet-
priest perhaps a trifle morbid? "Not at all,"
you said. "Some damn fool might have gone in
for bronze. Besides, it makes a dandy file
for manuscripts and poems." And so it was,
and for my letters, thick with love,
and for Ivan, the wanderer, a bed
for curling tail to nose.

Three years ago this month, the rocket burst
inside your skull, and you fell headlong
into night or dazzle—who will know?
"Be in advance of all parting," Rilke wrote.
You took him at his word. At ease with dying
as with delight, you chose the plot,
dictated copy for the granite stone,
and bought the box, pulling the future
toward you, like a creature of the sea
suddenly in love with air, like a wild bird
blind with light.

The Georgia Review   JEAN BURDEN

THE WRITING TEACHER

I am forgetting the words,
he confided one evening.
We saw more often then
how his door was swung shut,
how the room began slowly
to slide into
unaccustomed hesitations,
a clutter of slurring
and broken phrase,
into an empty ruin finally
that each day filled
with the sunlight of what
we could remember
and the dark glimmering
of what he could not.

But now at last
he's found the word
he was looking for,

the clear sum
of untrammeled eloquence,
the shining wisdom beyond
sun and moon and stars.

Four Quarters   DANIEL BURKE, F.S.C.

FIRE IN THE ONION FIELD

(The soil in those fields is so rich it can catch fire.
Blazing black dirt isn't easily controlled. In 1964, there
was a fire in which a couple of thousand acres burned.)
                        —John McPhee

The mole never sees the sun
That warms his wiggling fur
Through earth so rich it burns
When a loose spark lands in a furrow.
The fire that summer scorched fields,
Roasted a million onions lying in dry cracks
Deep enough to hide a man.
The fire leaped gaps, rejoiced at the air,
Then dove into the earth and warmed onions
Until the green fingers at the cores began to steam.
Their strong perfume spread in smoke
To a mole's nose whose tip felt heat
As if a stray sun had exploded in the field
And lay there, puffing fire.
He burrowed to cool soil
And water that clings to onion roots in spring.
His throat, soft as an eyelid, swelled,
And he bit an onion, tore the crackling paper,
Longing for its water. But the onion burned him,
Made his blood tremble. Fire and water bubbled
In his eyes, and he clung to a hot root,
Dreaming of snow. His fur curled
And browned like elm leaves in September;
His paws fluttered, sent him swimming across the sun.

West Branch   DEBORAH BURNHAM

SARDINES

I am idling in Paris,
and none of my friends
can understand my craving
for tins of sardines.
"All the way to France,"
one of them says,
"and all you want to dine on
is sardines!" She sniffs,

in true French fashion,
and eats her French bread,
and drinks French wine.
I look into my sardine tin,
and I can see the history
of this famous city
written within its walls.
Henry Murger would have liked
sardines, even if he did
have to drink water with them.
Utrillo ought to have traded
his paintings for sardines.
Hemingway no doubt made
thick sardine sandwiches
rather than thin salmon
when entertaining Bob McAlmon.
Another of my friends
says that I don't even know
if they are French sardines.
I don't, it's true,
and only the nets they're in
when they're caught,
or the tins that enclose them,
and not the waters
in which they freely swim
identify their nationality.
But then, I've always thought
it might be the same for me.
And it seems ideal
to eat sardines in the Jardins,
especially du Luxembourg.
I tip the tin, and watch
the thin oil slide across
silvery scales, and I weigh up
everything I've seen.
Life is nicely balanced,
and I eat another sardine.

Hanging Loose   JIM BURNS

THE COMFORT OF A WOMAN

Last night I woke to the smell of furnace gas.
I dreamt you'd asked Charlotte to marry you
and told me after we'd tied
to a cyprus stump at Lake Conway,
after the bait-man had filled his plastic tubes
with crickets, then shook them down in our basket,
his hands shaking. You simply said, I love her.
You simply said, She's lovely, blonde, petite.
In reality, her hair's auburn, she's big-boned.

We cast out blue nylon. Three mallards
shook the gnats and mosquitoes loose from
mesquite leaves. When we oared away,
you told me why the females are drab
—because they nest and need
camouflage. When I returned to bed, my own
wife warm beside me, I tried to dream you good
fortune, whatever is good, a woman blonde
as a sunfish, small-boned as a sparrow.

Poetry   RALPH BURNS

THIS IS

Not anything like
Perfect, this is not
Old songs or rose gardens or
The Aurora Borealis. This is not
A crosshair zeroed to a ten-thousandth
Or Bumpo's bullets one on top of another
Nor the ultimate evolution of the triune brain
Or world brotherhood with feminist environmental protection or
Everybody deciding to let live and sticking to it.

This is more
Like two white not quite dead
Azalea petals on the bush in late
Overwarm January which, when the clean kill
Of the old squirrel sends him tumbling through,
Bounce, a little bloody, and bounce back.

The Apalachee Review   JANET BURROWAY

A STORY

We string our lives, like beads on a strand,
story by story. My mother, my grandmother
waiting at the door, looking across the fields
toward rising storms talked about the year
they lived on watermelon money, how they'd
hang wet sheets in the doors to cool themselves,
how it never helped. They'd tell about
the night the dogs, frantic at their chains,
barked until morning, and in the light
how they found circles of tracks around the house,
deep and deliberate—mountain lions
up from the river or down from along the bluffs,
drawn by the fresh meat they'd hung on the porch.
Riding home I always wanted to hear that story
again. And once, jerked from sleep saw,

I swear, a lion on the road. A story
I tell with some reserve, for there are always
those with their own version, who choose
not to see the flash of eyes beyond the headlights.

Cottonwood   LYNNE BUTLER

CHILDBIRTH

I cannot remember what it was like.
Here she sits in the lamplight,
mending her stockings. I must not be looking
at her for too long, else she scolds me,
slamming the door as she goes out.

I could tell you the fire roared
for two days. The rooster crowed so loud
I ordered the midwife to fetch the axe
under my bed. There was yellow brush
far up the mountain I watched
until night came. And blood.

I remember that. No thaw
will ever make me so afraid as I was
of that flood taking six sheets
to staunch, that still stains like a birthmark
the one I would not let them burn.

It was March. I remember her cries
like a pumphandle braying. I walked against
everyone's wishes outside to the spring
where the milkjars sat, chastened
to such irreproachable sweetness.
I knelt and drank gallons of sunlight.

Carolina Quarterly   KATHRYN STRIPLING BYER

BECAUSE IN THIS HOUR

Because my child sleeps
in this hour, because in this hour
his sleep is perfection, rivering
a faint light from his breathing across his cheeks,
too much like dawn itself, I can think about nothing
but the hourly resonant blue, nothing
but the glass of first milk set
by my window. What we know in this hour
will not hurt us: one rickety fishing boat
unbalances too close to shore
rocking a measurement of hourglass movements,
its yellow-slickered men bobbing
up and down like buoys,

and as though tiring an hour within an hour
for fish, a sky-mile within each minute of sleep
for my son, frantic grey gulls and heavy-headed
pelicans circle and dive, circle and dive
at odd and uneven angles from the black
appendage crane, waiting to pull
its full net aboard.

Mid-American Review   ELENA KARINA BYRNE

OPEN LETTER TO THE
POLISH GOVERNMENT, 1986:
ON THE SUBJECT OF PUTTING HIGHWAYS
THROUGH CEMETERIES

Please don't take the cemeteries.
We can't sleep when the dead fidget in air,
their frantic fingers hushing the wind.
We'll give bread, or pastures, even the trees
tucked into themselves like frightened children.
But please don't take the cemeteries.
For each stone there is a blossom, a tear,
an empty room where someone waits
long past the time the horseman
should have arrived.
Above each doorstep a darkening lintel.
What other pleasures have they
than rain in April, a sprig
of rosemary in an abandoned field?
They are the beginning of the dream,
where grief rises from the earth
and takes a human name—
If you take them away,
how will we know what to call ourselves?
Besides, they might fall in love
again. There might be families,
infants, a son with our eyes.
And if we should go to look for them,
some night when the moon is waning,
when our hair has turned white
as apple blossoms, our skin
paper-thin as birch,
how will you tell us from them,
how will you know not to tear
our bones from their sockets,
our tongues from our mouths?

Ploughshares   TERESA CADER

SPRING IN A FOREIGN COUNTRY

Over a clearing of stumps and
branches piled and tangled,
a hawk skims the wrinkle of air that
helmets the land, and you realize
that never before now have you
seen this place except as new,
as foreign as a book you struggled
to be able to read. You have never
known it as it is, familiar and
peopled; you can never love it.

The tobacco-yellow mulch
squelches under your shoes,
an ox unmoving
in a field so full of water
it reflects the gray
the hawk glides across as you
change the place by standing there,
the staple that will not dissolve,
the bullet that encysts and belongs,
foreign and intimate,
digested into place.

Amelia   MICHAEL CADNUM

NOTHING REALLY

I'm tired of that same average reflection
so ordinary in its aging.
I'm tired of shouting to be listened to,
of cupping my ear to hear.
I'm sick of waiting for people to die
and hanging around children.
I'm fed up with boots, safety pins,
passports, string quartets, kleenex,
and spewing wisecracks.
Dancing gives me the willies,
and I want to bolt except I have no plans.
I don't care about crabgrass, sprained ankles,
bad cheques or the Red Cross.
All of you everywhere bore me
and the only great jokes are my own old ones.
I keep raising the roof.It's all so much menacing hilarity.

The Antigonish Review   HEATHER CADSBY

YOU WRECK YOUR CAR

Maybe you'll live, maybe
some fluke will have

the emergency crew waiting
with their pants on. It could be
they weren't even sleeping, just
playing cards or eating fried chicken
at their station house, drinking
nothing but coffee, say, just two
or three blocks from your house.
It turns out they were ready,
eager, even, to make tracks
to your accident. They live for this.
Odds are you'll be light-headed,
too giddy maybe to notice much
about how their hands
dance, altogether, above your wounds,
how they pamper you to the cot, flatter you
against all that you deserve, to float
you to the hospital.
Your eyes will be failing, accepting
sleep, so you'll never know how,
even as you gesture toward death,
your angels are most alive.

The Chariton Review   SCOTT CAIRNS

IN THE MANNER OF M.C. ESCHER:
DAWN, BIRDS, CLOUDS

Glenda put the bird seed out last night
and Brian hung the feeder in the tree,
but I am first to see the cloud of birds.

I see it coming light against the black,
flocking at dawn against the greying sky;
one feathery cloud upon the still dark night,
and then day pearls. The darkling clouds begin
to break apart and fly across the sky,
still darker than the frigid silver air.

The grounded birds peck at their morning meal.

Then suddenly they rise, now darker than
the sky, exploding high above the house.
I watch. They soar black silhouettes, away,
becoming seeds before the wing—like clouds
of white and crimson flocking as the sky
hangs out the flying golden morning sun.

Blue Unicorn   RICHARD CALISCH

THE GREAT PYRAMID OF DES MOINES

I love your planes and spaces, I.M. Pei,
But why do you never drain the rain away?

Right in front of Roy Lichtenstein's *Great*
Pyramid your roof has made a little lake.
Why doesn't the American Institute of Arts and Letters
Care that in Boston your windows are falling on pedestrians?
In Sarasota, the college you raised
Is sinking back into the Everglades.
I hear the same thing wherever I go:
The man's a genius, but—*Look out below!*
Yet all your buildings win the big awards:
I guess this reconfirms that "Less is more."
Since you're making icons of our age,
Of course they run, crack, chip, peel, split, and fade.

Plains Poetry Journal   DAN CAMPION

IN A FIELD OF LANTERNS

The night sky is an eastern Nebraska county
in 1874. And almost the entire township, each man
and elder son, is out searching
every cottonwood clump and prairie
dip—and, O, how they must
love that child, patiently working
their way across the buffalo grass,
holding their lanterns high,
some of which begin to gutter because the kerosene
is running low; and every now and then
one of them stumbles and his light arcs
silently out. But they do not see,
in that swathe of groundfog, that white
shred of dress trailing from a hawthorne
snag, but keep steadily
walking, the bails of their lanterns
creaking, even now beginning to paraphrase the loss,
taking up where her light song left off.

Puerto Del Sol   KEVIN CANTWELL

THE PARROTS

My friend Michel is a commanding officer in Somoto,
            out by the border with Honduras,
and he told me about finding a shipment of female parrots
that were going to be smuggled to the United States
            so that there they'd learn to speak English.
There were 186 parrots, and 47 had already died in their cages.
And he took them back to the place from where they'd been taken;
and when the truck was getting close to a place called The Plains
near the mountains where those parrots came from
            (the mountains looked immense behind those plains),

the parrots began to get excited and beat their wings
   and press themselves against the walls of their cages.
And when the cages were opened
they all flew like arrows in the same direction to their mountains.
That's just what the Revolution did with us, I think:
it freed us from cages
   in which we were being carried off to speak English.
It brought us back to the Homeland from which we'd
  been uprooted.

Comrades in fatigues green as parrots
      gave the parrots their green mountains.
  But there were 47 that died.

The Agni Review
            ERNESTO CARDENAL
          —Translated from the Spanish
            by Jonathan Cohen

WORKING-CLASS CHILDREN: NEWARK, NEW JERSEY

I used to come here as a child,
the druid in me arranging
stones in little circles and
laying sticks at odd angles, thinking
there was some significance
in this, that it would stay
that way until I returned
in another life to continue
the conversation.

There was baseball then
as there is now on the
grass before me; there were
paper routes and braces
and, later, strange girls who
cared nothing for varsity letters.

How I came to live so far
away, so soon, so happily
is more than I care to remember.
The stones I placed here
have long since washed away.
What memories I have I could
have had in Iowa without returning
to this foul ditch, in this tiny park
on a polluted river.

But my daughter loves it.
She loves the noise of the trains,
the birds, the dirt, and the people.
She arranges stones in circles on
the grass and lays sticks at odd angles.

I close my eyes and rest with her,
knowing what she knows: that yes,
the magic is still here, despite
the murders, and the muggings, and the pollution.
It's in the gloves of small black Yankees
chasing balls off the diamond.
It is in the smoke-filled air breathed
by working-class children working at nothing.

The Cape Rock   MICHAEL A. CAREY

CAMOUFLAGE

So many piles of leaves are walking about these days,
disguised as humans, it must give pause.
Originally we meant only to fool ducks, dupe deer
into posing like St. Sebastian, but now it looks
like we are hiding from other heaps that mean harm,
that mean to steal us from our families and lovers
or steel us against the unhappy prospect of quaking
like so many aspens in the arms of winter.

Or is it simply that we mean to advertise a sincere
wish to become one with nature and quietly disappear,
toting our taped and silenced M-16's and Mini-14's
and other automatic acronyms of extreme prejudice?
There is big business in camouflage these days.
We can be anything we want to be at last!
A summer wood, an autumn wood, a big beige desert.
We can even be dead grass, we can be snow.
And let me not fail to mention our latest fashion,
Night. Night is very popular these days.

What we do not want to be is colorful; color is
suspect, a thing of the past, except for a week or
maybe two weeks in spring, during the spring offensives,
when even the desert forgets itself and laughs floridly.
Then it is safe to be a field of poppies.

But we must never forget the latest heat-seeking
technologies that have kept pace with our trade.
Telescopes so powerful they are capable of detecting,
at incredible distances in the coldest environments,
the small trembling heart of a mouse; o soldiers of
fortune and misfortune, they mean to find us out,
to discover in our iciest resolve a spot of warmth.

Poetry   HENRY CARLILE

WHAT PEOPLE MAKE

*(It's a little hard to explain to my friends at first what I
do. They don't really understand that people make kazoos.)*
        —John Battaglia in THE NEW YORK TIMES

They make wars, babies, sonnets, money, haste,
Fantastic visions, patent leather shoes,
Pledges to keep, paper towels to waste,
Long recipes for life and oyster stews,
Thick books contrived for everybody's taste,
Slim volumes only doting authors choose,
New glasses for the old when they're replaced,
And awkward pauses anyone can use.
For people stuck on sticking, they make paste;
For people stuck on answers, they make clues;
For people just plain stuck, or who are faced
With failure, they make big bottles of booze;
And for those seeking simply to amuse
Themselves a moment, people make kazoos.

Poetry   THOMAS CARPER

DANCING AS VESTIGIA AND
OTHER CONSIDERATIONS

Cindy won't dance for me, and God knows I know why, she is
Almost as screwed up as I am. But at least she knows how to
    dance, at least she learned.
I am always a sampan bobbing against the tide.
Sometimes when Cindy puts on one of her favorites, like the
    Beatles or the early Stones,
I catch her swaying and turning in the hall: but she stops when she sees me.
In ordinary circumstances the best I can hope for is when she dances with the
    vacuum cleaner, wearing her short shorts and the navy jersey, barefoot,
Swinging and turning around the room while I smoke my pipe
    and pretend I'm in a brown study.
The muscovy duck, according to Conrad Lorenz, perfectly exemplifies
The effects of domestication and denaturing: it flies, but it flies wobbly,
It walks with three steps for each sine wave of the head, like a ferryboat in a swell;
    it has lost its quack, which has been replaced by a whisper,
And so on. But how about you, Dr. Lorenz? Did you dance
    across the lawn with the otters and hazel trees?
Cindy and I dance in bed. This is our grace, almost perfectly
    expressive, our mating dance
That survives in the pure access of love against everything,
Against enforced sterility and all the dooms thereby implicated.
We dance every night in the semi-dark to the vestigial music of our blood.

The Southern Review   HAYDEN CARRUTH

I AM ASKING YOU TO COME BACK HOME

I am asking you to come back home
before you lose the chance of seein' me alive.
You already missed your daddy.
You missed your Uncle Howard.
You missed Luciel.
I kept them and I buried them.
You showed up for the funerals.
Funerals are the easy part.

You even missed that dog you left.
I dug him a hole and put him in it.
It was a Sunday morning, but dead animals
don't wait no better than dead people.

My mama used to say she could feel herself
runnin' short of the breath of life. So can I.
And I am blessed tired of buryin' things I love.
Somebody else can do that job to me.
You'll be back here then; you come for funerals.

I'd rather you come back now and got my stories.
I've got whole lives of stories that belong to you.
I could fill you up with stories,
stories I ain't told nobody yet,
stories with your name, your blood in them.
Ain't nobody gonna' hear them if you don't,
and you ain't gonna' hear them unless you get back home.

When I am dead, it will not matter
how hard you press your ear to the ground.

Southern Exposure   JO CARSON

GIVING VOICE

*(Behold, I show you a mystery; We shall
not all sleep, but we shall all be changed.)*
                    —I Corinthians 15:51

There is something about a trumpet blowing
at the end—the dead awakened, sitting up
in their coffins, reaching out through earth
become no more than a mist on their faces,
listening: but it would be more than music,
more than dark flowers opening toward morning.
Inside each thing I think there is a voice
kept to the last. You've heard that story:
the swan that sings only once, the stillness
before the storm. When something knows it is
about to break, it finds a way to speak.
What sound the world is saving, that it keeps
inside rocks and stones and trees, is half
of a long breath; imagining is the other.

In school, when I was a boy, the teacher said
if a tree fell in the forest, and no one heard,
then it made no sound. That man had no idea
that things speak when they are ready—not
to be heard, but because they are caught up.
First breath or last, dangling by one's heels
or one's neck, gasping in pain or in passion—
to give voice is to break silence, to summon
all that we have touched and seen and held
until the circuit of words and syllables
weaving about us like a wind, like the blast
of a trumpet—sounding out of nowhere, growing
stronger, coming closer—completes itself
and we are one with it, at last, and sing.

Images   JARED CARTER

CADILLACS AND POETRY

New snow onto old ice last night. Now,
errand-bound to town, preoccupied with the mudge
in his head, he applied his brakes too fast.
And found himself in a big car out of control,
moving broadside down the road in the immense
stillness of the winter morning. Headed
inexorably for the intersection.
The things that were passing through his mind?
The news film on TV of three alley cats
and a Rhesus monkey with electrodes implanted
in their skulls; the time he stopped to photograph
a buffalo near where the Little Big Horn
joined the Big Horn; his new graphite rod
with the Limited Lifetime Warranty;
the polyps the doctor'd found on his bowel;
the Bukowski line that flew
through his mind from time to time:
"We'd all like to pass by in a 1995 Cadillac."
His head was a hive of arcane activity.
Even during the time it took his car
to slide around on the highway and point him
back in the direction he'd come from.
The direction of home, and relative security.
The engine was dead. The immense stillness
descended once more. He took off his woolen cap
and wiped his forehead. But, after a moment's
consideration, started his car again, turned around
and continued on into town.
More carefully, yes. But thinking all the while
along the same lines as before. Old ice, new snow.
Cats. A monkey. Fishing. Wild buffalo.
The sheer poetry in musing on Cadillacs

that haven't been built yet. The chastening effect
of the doctor's fingers.

Ploughshares   RAYMOND CARVER

THIS MORNING

This morning was something. A little snow
lay on the ground. The sun floated in a clear
blue sky. The sea was blue, and blue-green,
as far as the eye could see.
Scarcely a ripple. Calm. I dressed and went
for a walk. Determined not to return
until I took in what Nature had to offer.
I passed close to some old, bent-over trees.
Crossed a field strewn with rocks
where snow had drifted. Kept going
until I reached the bluff.
Where I gazed at the sea, and the sky, and
the gulls wheeling over the white beach
far below. All lovely. All bathed in a pure
cold light. But, as usual, my thoughts
began to wander. I had to will
myself to see what I was seeing and
nothing else. I had to tell myself *this* is what
matters, not the other. (And I did see it,
for a minute or two!) For a minute or two
it crowded out the usual musings on
what was right, and what was wrong—duty,
tender memories, thoughts of death, how I should treat
with my former wife. All the things
I hoped would go away this morning.
The stuff I live with every day. What
I've trampled on in order to stay alive.
For a minute or two, though, I did forget
myself and everything else. I know I did.
For when I turned back I didn't
know where I was. Until some birds rose up
from the gnarled trees. And flew
in the direction I needed to be going.

Ploughshares   RAYMOND CARVER

SIMPLE

A break in the clouds. The blue
outline of the mountains.
Dark yellow of the fields.
Black river. What am I doing here,
lonely and filled with remorse?

I go on casually eating from the bowl
of raspberries. If I were dead,
I remind myself, I wouldn't
be eating them. It's not so simple.
It is that simple.

The Ohio Review   RAYMOND CARVER

PROPOSAL

*(for a new public building to be built
on the site of the burned-down city hall)*

It should be a barn built of weathered boards
to give shelter to whatever wild things
might deign to live among us. Raccoons,
owls, snakes, bats, anything
having from four to a hundred legs;
those that fly in the sun or live
in burrows—or in deep dung;
at home in decay that is damp and warm,
and spontaneous, like us.
And whatever rots, and moves in a rotten house:

fungi—toads and stagnant water,
apartments in dead trees.
Every allurement to coax the wild into town,
such as a wooden statue of St. Francis,
with holes in his head, and arms, and robe,
to harbor birds and wildlife.

Here snakes shall be exalted, and ants
have their cities; sparrows revered as eagles.
Rats? There are worse things than rats.
It would be worse if one day
we should have to compare ourselves
with ourselves—and so go mad.

San Jose Studies   ROBERT CASE

THE AUTOSCOPIC EXPERIENCE

The soul at death looks on the corpse it leaves
And after that dies or is put on hold.
It is a process easy to reduce
To painted birds on stucco walls, or breath
This side a mirror. As abstraction, view
And viewer one to one and poised to part,
Autoscopy is more the mask of gold:
The mummy's backward eye. Or is the gold
More narrowly—need, cost, implied exchange.
Must the eye cover for the heart gone out?

Emotion is investment capital
Like any other; it will be withdrawn.
Free, idle, high potential hovers, soon
To pick its site: another flesh astute
In ways to estimate another flesh,
And by and by a disembodied drive
Eternally in search of search; until,
Outworn by scrutiny, the body counters,
And the soul, the poor hardworking soul,
Having paid through the nose, must leave by it.

Poetry   TURNER CASSITY

BEYOND THE PICTURE WINDOW

Somewhere unknown the skunks are mating
with abandon cleaner
than our own. They are the act
and part to higher unity;
and I, one night, having placed a bowl of milk
on the gravel outside the picture window,
soon heard a different kind of lapping.
Switching on the outdoor light, I saw
a grateful sort of skunk,
its golden eyes opaque, its tail
a dainty fern curling whitely inward
toward its head—a fan, a canopy,
a plume of dandelions gone to seed—
yet more—more lovely, breezy and august. Turning sidelong,
the skunk proceeded with stately
unhurried waddle
toward the rosebush that grips
the wooden siding of our
home and discreetly,
modestly,
disappeared.

The Fiddlehead   NATHAN CERVO

SOMETHING REASSURING

about finding clean underwear and socks
in my dresser drawer sufficient
for seven days ahead.

When I get the feeling
we're all wandering
through Yellowstone under a full moon—
here a bubble   there a simmer and boil up,
straight ahead   geyser of steam and flung mud

and yes   heightened sense of danger—
I make for my dresser drawer,
steady where it stands   has stood   will stand
and count them out . . . seven sets of underwear and socks,
seven obviously expected days.

The Cape Rock   JANET CARNCROSS CHANDLER

COURSE OF CLAY

Notice, shrill bearer from morning to morning,
The long frenzied blackberries coiling their sprouts,
The earth closing in on us with its absent gaze,
A cricket's even song to lull our pain,
And a god showing up just to swell the thirst
Of those whose words are addressed to living waters.

Therefore rejoice, my dear, in the following fate:
This death doesn't close the memory of love.

New Letters   RENÉ CHAR
                                    —*Translated from the French*
                                          by Charles Guenther

NEARING SECOND LIFE

You are nearing second life
when you finally know which to look forward to,
—Monday or Friday.
When all the old accolades and trophies
start to look like prep-school artifacts,
charming, worthy of their pewter.
You know it because the pains that slice your back
into four aching quadrants
will no longer go away,
but take their place at your table
like background music.
Against this you will play the fine rare tune
that can only come with second life,
—not second birth—
for to be born again is to be naked still;
This is more the habitus of Socrates,
a hairy-chested timed exposure to the world
which is both confronted, and yet taken in
like hemlock, like the one remaining draught.

The Fiddlehead   RON CHARACH

SILENCE IN A CHILEAN PRISON

Far away from here you turn dark
And crouch alone like a light ray
Bent in the water.

The shadows of the iron bars across your
Head
And through your eyes drag over the
Bottom of stones.

Dreams pulled in under your throat
No longer speak.

The guards, dropping out of their chairs,
Strike at everything,
Hitting your lighted cigarette, your hands,
Your bones
Because you believe too much.

Life is like coral rubble, petrified,
And your eyes underneath, chisel-sharp,
Pierce the black night.

You must kill them with your silence.

America   JAMES CHICHETTO

A FIRE IN EARLY SPRING

The pieces I bring in are from a storm
that tore branches off a maple.
It was summer
and before the storm I saw
a snake draped on a limb.
His smooth body rested with the bough,
followed the curve, rode the slight motion
made by a breeze.
Later, the tree thrashed in the rain.
In the quiet afterward
I looked again and found only the limb
making its slow crawl in air.

As it warms,
the stove ticks with the tiny
contortions of steel.
Such a dance there is in things,
the shuck and draw of atoms
that do not die or disappear
but move,
perhaps, to a bone in the rib cage of another,
or to a green stick writhing in the flames,
gesturing for me to come inside.

Yankee   MICHAEL CHITWOOD

GUERRILLA TACTICS

Once they start paving,
it's all over:
first you lose the potholes,
then they erase the ecstacy of ditches.
Sandy fields yield asphalt and bloom
straight white lines,
diagrams for packing and living.

You wake up one morning and realize
the baseball field has been swallowed by Woolco
and second base is in Housewares.
You miss the smell of clean dirt
and the glue of mud on your fingers
and wonder if your grandfather
could harness a giant plow
and turn it under again
to rot
so everything could grow back.

Late on a warm drizzled night
when the streetlights stage musicals
in the damp air,
you climb on a black bicycle
and speed off out of the spotlight
down a dark street
with soft new black pavement
and plunge downhill
fast beyond confusion.

When the new neighbors see you
sitting bolt upright,
arms folded, eyes closed,
being sucked by invisible magnets
toward the unfinished road,
they lock their doors
and close the curtains.
They wonder if the town is safe.

The Pottersfield Portfolio   LESLEY CHOYCE

LEARNING THE LANGUAGE

Like an axolotl,
my newborn son eyes me
through the incubator's transparent wall,
mouths his message: *feed me, feed me.*

* * *

At seven months, he wakes at 2 A.M.
not to feed, to reminisce:
sorting the day's sensations,

practicing his vowels.
They roll over his tongue
gaining momentum toward morning.

* * *

Almost a year and still
he has no word for me.
He's moved past the rich round *O*s
into the long thin sounds of *e* and *i,*
has added the *da-da* that gets
the laughs at my expense.

Mama, ma-ma, I intone,
blowing up birthday balloons.
I let the red one go, fat heart,
and he careens after it, laughing.
Bye-bye, he says. *Bye-bye.*

Yankee   MARTHA CHRISTINA

VANISHING TRACES

In the mountains,
wild things
live a life we no longer remember,
walking in ever-tightening circles
as their world closed around them;
and we who can't tell the track
of a bobcat from the track
of a coyote, can't tell a hawk
from a sparrow,
intrude sometimes to look
at the unself-consciousness we have lost,
at the vanishing traces of a world left behind;
and we cry out for wisdom
while the unblinking eye of the cougar
watches aloofly from cover
as we tramp by, all noise and smell
and careless, empty destruction.

Crosscurrents   RENNY CHRISTOPHER

APRIL LIMES

New shoots emblazon the truncated limes
we said wouldn't grow. Hardly a month ago
their dull trunks under patina of rime
confounded hope. They offended in a row,
amputees in crabbed plots . . . Now, at home
with the whip and tang of April in the air,
these limbs, like broken bones or unfinished poems,

inspire and embarrass us to care
for what's easier still to denigrate: ourselves,
colt-legged; self-inflicting obloquies,
aspirations moldering on the shelf . . .
These trees are tough: tough enough to freeze
like Catholic girls in knee-socks in the snow,
then, sun-struck, to forget their prayers and grow.

Kansas Quarterly   BILL CHRISTOPHERSEN

A WEDDING GIFT

For forty years I've seen
that white house, the elms behind
green with the leaves of May
undimmed by season or time.
Lilacs as fresh as in
the spring of nineteen-forty one
before we turned to face
the sun. The angle of the
shadow's fall hasn't
changed in all those forty years,
nor does the lilac's bloom
fade, to fall as brown-stained tears.
The afternoon sun still
lights the clapboards white and shows
The yellow glaze I'd not
seen, the purples hidden in
the shadows of the grass.

Between my chair and the picture
on the wall, Miss Bradley
comes again, her paint box and
her easel strapped behind
her old velocipede with
its wormgear drive. She sets
the easel up just off the
corner of Frye Street and
Main, gives her baggy black
knickers a shake, lays out
her colors with a pallet knife.
From the open window
of my dormitory room
I watch again that odd old
lady put a stop to time,
to change, to fading bloom.

The Fiddlehead   ROBERT M. CHUTE

A TRENTA-SEI OF THE PLEASURE WE TAKE IN
THE EARLY DEATH OF KEATS

It is old school custom to pretend to be sad
when we think about the early death of Keats.
The species-truth of the matter is we are glad.
Psilanthropic among exegetes,I am so moved that when
    the plate comes by
I almost think to pay the God—but why?

When we think about the early death of Keats,
we are glad to be spared the bother of dying ourselves.
His poems are a candy store of bitter-sweets.
We munch whole flights of angels from his shelves
drooling a sticky glut, almost enough
to sicken us. But what delicious stuff!

The species-truth of the matter is we are glad
to have a death to munch on. Truth to tell,
we are also glad to pretend it makes us sad.
When it comes to dying, Keats did it so well
we thrill to the performance. Safely here,
this side of the fallen curtain, we stand and cheer.

Psilanthropic among exegetes,
as once in a miles-high turret spitting flame,
I watched boys flower through orange winding sheets
and shammed a mourning because it put a name
to a death I might have taken—which in a way
made me immortal for another day.

I was so moved that when the plate came by
I had my dollar in hand to give to death
but changed to a penny—enough for the old guy,
and almost enough saved to sweeten my breath
with a toast I will pledge to the Ape of the Divine
in thanks for every death that spares me mine.

I almost thought of paying the God—but why?
Had the boy lived, he might have grown as dull
as Tennyson. Far better, I say, to die
and leave us a formed feeling. O beautiful,
pale, dying poet, fading as soft as rhyme,
the saddest music keeps the sweetest time.

Poetry　　　　　　　　　　　　　　　　　　　　　JOHN CIARDI

SECOND HONEYMOON

Now the island is developed.
Beyond the wall of the ancient fortress
a housing project tames the hill,
a shopping mall crowds the edges
of Old Town.

But where we stay is quiet—
only the wash of surf
along the dark rim of reef
and the smell of tamarind trees
like buttered popcorn—
In the evening wind palm fronds clash.

At the church near Pirate's Cove
the priest's words like tired flies
drone against the stucco
and the natives, eyes lifted to the cross,
still clutch pink rosaries.
We believed then.

We remember scouting for private beaches
where we lay naked to the sun.
You tell me I was thinner then
but less afraid. Although
you swear we are not strangers,

It is hard to remember you.
Under plastic fans
the grey air churns;
our smiles protect us
from each other.

We watch lizards quiver through the brush.
They blend into leaves.
They become the leaves.
In the night I hear a mongoose scream
and dream that I have let you die.
I wake to rain.

Southern Poetry Review   PHILIP CIOFFARI

THE NEWS

I'm pulled back into life
by precious babble from the crib,
my daughter's voice
evolving into art
an archangel's height
above the highest beast's,
her matins.
I bring her in my arms
down from heights of dream
to our new day.
This union nothing can rive,
I think, our lives
a double-helixed wish
toward what's good.

I place her in the high-chair,
turn on the radio
and go to the cupboard for her bowl,
unbreakable plastic
decorated with cartoon creatures
in chase and flight,
caught in what passes these days
for eternity.
The morning's a song
I've heard many times before.
Suddenly into the shuttered room
a voice skewed by urgency brings word
of "the third-worst massacre
by a single assailant
in the history of the United States,"
bloody prints smeared on walls
of an Oklahoma post office.
Though the unspeakable seems distant
here in Ohio,
nearly everything's changed.
Only the child singing
for breakfast remains untroubled.
For a while longer her perfect ignorance
will keep her from the news.

The Southern Review   DAVID CITINO

CARD GAME AT THE ITALIAN CLUB

Surely it is more than pastime,
the backroom booths removed from the afternoon,
the stained fingertips stacking change,
the hands scarred from machine-shop years
waiting idle and damp for the cards'
plastic slap, the liquid coughs
welling up from the chest, then settling again.
From the bar, music drifts in, and
wing-tips tap on the oiled wooden floor.
But nothing stirs them or hurries
their pleasure; even the high idle
of homebound traffic, stalled and
steaming at the Route Five light,
can't crack Montovani's lush wall.
Day after day, deliberate and cautious,
they bid on the smallest stakes,
wanting only to break even.

Tar River Poetry   ROBERT CLAPS

ELEGY NEAR THE BITTERROOT RANGE

The trees lining the street leaf out,
And the one I thought was dead
Turns, finally, the darkest green of all—

Like the lake's color the last time fishing
In Montana, first blue, then green
As a thunderstorm rolled toward us

From the Bitterroots. Water never stays
Colorless, the way I never remember a feeling
Purely, mixing today and a day

Three years ago. We caught nothing, and I think
I disappointed him, wearing a bathing suit
Under clothes I never took off.

Like all of us, he was dying
Then, too, though first he went swimming,
Slipping into the lake only to bob there,

Beckoning. Now I keep seeing the face
I came to love, a face briefly present
Like the moon last night, a white disc

Scudding behind the clouds. Ashes
Over water, waves crumpled on a shore,
He has taken the body's longing

With him, how first it wanted food and sleep,
Then the warmth of someone else's arms—
For the longest time, someone else's arms.

NER/BLQ
(New England Review & Bread Loaf Quarterly)   PATRICIA CLARK

KELLY CHERRY READS AT HERKIMER

From city hosts by bus she came to Herkimer
To read to us five students: three in jeans and two
In ties and jackets. Her flowered stockings marked her
Like scabs upon her legs. The city was the red
Around her eyes; the South was on her tongue. Her poems
She kept clipped together in an old overhead
Transparency box. Then she read to us of love,
And Russia, and of love in Russia, and of her
Russian love, and of a frozen mammoth. Above
Us, in the lounge, idlers shot pool; in distant rooms
The hectored faculty attended meetings of
Great weight. But we were there to smell the scattered blooms
Blown from her lips, to cup our ears on tiled floors,
To catch the rhythmic drip of blood from open sores.

Blue Unicorn   PETER CLARKE

ENTERING

Snowed all last night, eight inches by morning.
After freeing the car from its defining igloo,
I went to cheer up the bent young pines
depressed with heavy weather in the back wood.

With each large shovelful removed, branches
sprang from the depths to their usual heights
spraying snowy seed on my reddening face
and in my open winded wordless mouth.

In the warm ache of this breath of fire
I stripped off my coat and sweaty shirt,
felt the cold stiff branches against my skin
and, touched by these deep green woods, there went in.

Blueline   ARTHUR CLEMENTS

THE YEAR YOU DIED

Snow patches on the brown fields,
white lambs, three days
into the world, nuzzling ewes stolid
in March sunlight, and your hair, Father,
whitening against the car window
as you drove me further up
the juts and muddy twists
of Bear Creek Road, jolting
past wooden shacks, wood
smoke rising

that day you carried me up
to "cat lady" Addie in her
rusted trailer with the hundred cats,
and you and I stood there, mountain-mute,
arms brushing, flannel against flannel,
in the feline sea, until you pointed
to the black kitten behind the black stove,
and when we both agreed "That one, with the owl eyes,"
you scooped it up and pressed
the dark animal into my willing arms.

Poetry   SUSAN CLEMENTS

DO NOT TELL ME THE CHILD IS DEAD IN ME

Having been here in this world
a total of 22,260 days, as of
this morning (on the 23rd day of April
in 1984, according to calendar time),

I know better than I did ten thousand days ago
how false the measuring of time is.

Do not tell me the child is dead in me!
The weight of those days behind me now
melts into each night's dream,
where I still stare into the sun
looking for the explosion
out of which will blossom
the dawn of the first day of a new calendar.

Kansas Quarterly   JOEL CLIMENHAGA

HOLLY

(for Tanya at eleven)

Did I ever tell you holly
doesn't grow in that too hot
place where I was born, and
that at your age a grown-up kiss
was forced on me behind my grandmother's house
by a fourteen-year-old boy I caught
stealing her grapefruit?
"Still green," he laughed, and threw them at me.
For that waste I took the blame.
Both these facts you'd find hard to believe:
that Christmas can happen without snow or
bright lights, and that a boy would want
to kiss your mother. I'd like you
to be innocent of such a kiss
for a few more years, Tanya, to have more days
like the crisp, cool morning when you picked
armfuls of wild holly at your Grandmother's
Georgia farm under an iced sky, nothing
to distract you but the rustling of dry leaves
as you made your way deep into the woods.
Holly fills every container in my house;
I want to keep it green for you: you want
it dried, to make wreaths and decorations.
Its turning brown doesn't bother you,
you don't worry about the berries, red
as your cheeks that morning you gathered
the branches, that are now falling; and
as we crush them with our winter boots, they
stain the floor like blood.

Passages North   JUDITH ORTIZ COFER

THE GREAT BLUE HERON

Above the lake swift mayflies wing
And dot the air in dancing bands.
Shoreward, the Great Blue Heron stands,
Coiled hunger in a silent spring,

Moveless, timeless, welded to wish;
And like him now my poet's mind
Outwaits its hope—as starved to find
A metaphor as he a fish.

The Antigonish Review   FRED COGSWELL

FACULTY OFFICES, CIRCA 1985

The young scholars inhabit these offices
but they're seriously ill, you'd think,
in view of the machines required
with big cords and consoles and screens,
lengths of paper chugging out into the light—

intensive care units, these offices,
with their high tech sounds and no smoking;
high tech but curiously primitive,
like Model T's or sewing machines or Linotypes,
some more like a rusty Morse code—

but the young scholars who jog and lift weights
are running the machines almost invisibly,
old books at the tips of their fingers,
old books sneaking a cigarette
and wanting, one whispered, to be left alone—

wanting to be old and difficult as always,
wanting no outside consultants
or CAT scan or extraordinary means;
old books wanting some iodine for a cut finger,
old books wanting the old bedside manner.

Poetry   JAMES COLE

AUTISTIC BOY

The earth is meant to harm him.
There can be no preparation for fear or pain;
no promises. His hand, curious to burn,
draws to the stove's fire.

With two fingers he taps the table and sings,
knowing nothing of denial.
He is dedicated to the sounds of the house.
Then there are noises locked in his skull only.

I strain to hear syllables
while he mimics the radio—his words
caught behind an endless smile.
He stoops to look into my voice,
young hands unsteady on my shoulders.

In the living room his brother plays violin,
mother paints, father walks to the window
and back again. Their firstborn leaves no trace
of crayon landscapes or cut-out hearts.
Again he goes to the cellar door,
turning the doorknob over and over
with no intent to open or close.

Poetry   KEVIN COLE

NAMING THE TREES

The forest dips its feet here,
rings the swamp with sumac,
beech, and butternut.
There are so many leaves,
we cannot find the sky.
Not yet.
Not before Fall.

But they are as mortal
as we, these trees,
whose flowering arms
wrap earth and water
with such urgency,
and that is why
I have brought you
to this place.

Why I call out names of trees—
hickory, maple, sweet gum.
So I will know them in winter,
find them though they change,
fall, lie buried.

It is, after all, the mortality
in you I love. It is why I lean
toward you, heavy with blossom.
Why over and over
I call out your name.

Yankee   JANE COLEMAN

WAKING IN GEORGIA

First light turns our sheets the color of skim milk
as we lie together, waking.

A woodpecker breaks the fabric of an oak
and day begins, a mosaic of lawnmowers and airplanes.

Thinking of our lives—rages of our parents—
we breathe a difficult element:
the shell-thin air, curved around the world.
    Blood bruises our veins.

Our dresser gives back its simple wood,
surfacing from the dark.
Dogwood rolls and boils in a generous breeze
our open window captures.

I turn to you
and feel my breathing tighten.
    Your face—
a pattern meshed in my brain,
                durable as skin.

Amelia   MARY ANN COLEMAN

INVITATION TO A GUNFIGHTER

You rode into town on a mighty tall horse, Durango
and now it's time for that last showdown

and the townspeople who sired you
have all turned against you
in their arrogance ignorance & fear
and the object of your love
is as fickle as the wind

and you're punch drunk as a skunk in a trunk
looting & shooting for pleasure—tearing up
their peace of mind

and they're all too scared to take you on—the gutless lot of 'em

and you're too bitter and fed up with the bad hand
fate has dealt you in the form of black skin
and deadly aim

it's time to get out of town, Durango
time to get the first thing smoking
go on and get on
to whatever is waiting in that wild, wild way out yonder

time to take that long slow technicolor ride

before they ambush you in the saddle
and leave you face up in the sun

                           WANDA COLEMAN

THE DIVER

On television, my sister emerges
three meters above the water
like something carved from light,

where she balances on the springboard,
and like a graceful sleepwalker extends
her arms as counterweights. A doll

of perfect will, she rules her fear
of heights by tracing little circles
with cupped hands and then drops her arms

to start the swift wing beats of a creature
who has taught herself not to fly but to land,
more intricate than flight for the twists

and knots and folded arms that make her appear
wounded in mid-air, beyond recovery, though
recovery comes quickly once she clasps

her hands, entwines her thumbs to make a sieve
through which the water passes and allows
her head to enter, then shoulders and hips.

And this is how I always see her, half-in,
half-out of water, her body perpendicular,
toes matched as if there is no place for

error in the world and all her body's
perfection was meant to disappear beneath
the splash—a light she carves and shatters.

Poetry   MICHAEL COLLIER

AT DAY'S END

At day's end, when the sun
paints the familiar roundness of the barrels
red—a tender, flamingo red—
one by one the old men from the poorhouse
in their uniforms of ashen doves
come for a drink at the door
of the wine shop under our window.
Every day for the old men at this time,
it's this—the passing of their Equator,
the moment when the baptism of wine
is the consecration of their patience.
Ashen doves, a little bit under a spell,
a little ruffled, they turn back then
to their silent gutters overhead
together with the sun that goes down—
the incredible sun of '38,

a florid flower that draws as in a net
real youth and unreal age.

New Letters   LUIGI COMPAGNONE
                                —Translated from the Italian
                                        by Bruce Cutler

AZALEAS AND THE CIRCUS

When I was ten, azaleas were things you
weren't supposed to ruin while playing
in the yard, and God knows I hit a few
as I kept from being "it" that spring.

Then, the circus was something not to
miss, in the pink dawn its train bringing
Max, the fire eater, and Wanda, the tattoo
lady, both in the caboose waving.

Men in white stars spun with girls who
twirled almost like cotton candy; swinging
far up in the high dark tent, slowly, through
the roll of the drums and the cymbals crashing

again, still. They will return this spring, new in
pink and white, a fragile bloom, clinging
above the sawdust. I will not pursue
their ruin; I prefer the safe azaleas, flowering.

The South Carolina Review   CARL CONOVER

EPITAPH

He loved all breathing things—mostly the small
Defenseless ones: a flower, a mouse, a bird
Could spear his heart; a storm of pity stirred
The sky-blue of his soul: he knew them all
So well, even their sorrows were his own;
The mateless bird's brief heartbreak scarred his heart:
Out of the reeking world he walked, apart,
Till time reached up and drew him gently down
Into the earth. The root, the worm, the flower
Are closer to him now than when he went
Picking his way through fields, indifferent
To snarling nations and their songs of power:
The weeds spring from his flesh and grave worms go
Carousing through his blood—but he would wish it so.

Arizona Quarterly   R. L. COOK

THEY PASS BY IN THE DARK, DRY AIR

In sleep I see fish.
Mostly, it's the fish I have hooked and dropped
thumping to the bottom of my aluminum boat.
The sand sticks to their sides
like bread crumbs,
and they flop, making near-death
swimming notions against my rubber boots.
It seems so wrong,
now that I caress a brittle fin in sleep
and watch bluegills float through the dry air,
beautiful as butterflies.
Now that I have put my cheek to them in sleep,
I feel sorry and afraid
that the waking up will end
and I'll ride out through that dry air
on the back of a pickerel,
a pale yellow perch leading the way
to the rest of them.

Southern Poetry Review   ROBERT P. COOKE

VAN GOGH, 'SELF-PORTRAIT WITH SOFT FELT HAT'

You who would die into some other,
allow these colors of the sea and sky
to take you in. Fins, wings. The elements are free.
Released, you have only to immerse yourself.
Blue cradles you, now you are born aloft, afloat,
passing into the dreamscape of this face
approaching calm. Cobalt, azure, sapphire:
there is nowhere Vincent has not lost himself
in strokes whirling the background up to his body's edge
and now across it: jacket, tie, hat,
and red beard blued, the cheeks, the brow, the eyes
blue bluing blue. In this gaze you may rest and enter.
These eyes have taken down the stars, walked corridors along the deep
searching for you. Turquoise, lapis. Sleep. Sleep.

The Virginia Quarterly Review   PETER COOLEY

CHILDHOOD IN JACKSONVILLE, FLORIDA

What is happening to me now that loved faces
are beginning to float free of their names
like a tide of balloons, while a dark street
wide enough only for carriages, in a familiar city,
loses itself
to become South America?

Oh I am the last member of the nineteenth century!
And my excitement about sex, which was not of today,
is diffusing itself in generosity of mind.

For my mind is relaxing its grip, and a fume
of antique telephones, keys, fountain pens, torn roadmaps,
old stories of the way Nan Powell died
(*poor girl!*) rises in the air
detached but accurate—
almost as accurate
as if I'd invented them.

Welcome then, poverty!
flights of strings above the orange trees!

The Iowa Review   JANE COOPER

THE WAITING ROOM

Under the lamp, you notice
a stopped-up hourglass
weighing down old magazines.
It has a lump in its throat.
You wonder if the doctor
wants you to believe
that time is a patient here, too,
its flow caught and held
on top of a plastic table
where the latest news
quit happening six months ago.
You feel the urge to operate.
You wish you could open
the transparent neck
and release something, the way
your life begins again, suddenly,
when they call your name.

Tar River Poetry   M. TRUMAN COOPER

EARLY MEMORY

My father and I would shower together;
according to my mother, it was the only bribe
I would accept for washing myself
after a day of five-year-old wildness.
We would gurgle fountains of hot water
while I dabbed soap on as few places
as would satisfy his vigilance.

Afterwards, I would watch puppy-eyed
while he soaped himself,

raising his shoulders so I could see
the tufts of fur beneath his arms,
and wonder how I could get hair
to grow under mine, watching, too,
his penis jiggle like a plastic toy
you punch only to have it bounce back,
water clouding my eyes,
running happily into my mouth,

Until one time his swinging arms
struck a bottle of after-shave lotion
perched on the shower's ledge,
sent it springing at him
like a small vicious animal
tearing a chunk of flesh from his arm,
mixing blood with water
along the tiled floor like a shallow cascade
over rusty stones, while I watched,

My legs heavy as mountains, my mouth
sealed shut. Sooner than my eyes' blinking,
he was out of the shower, had a towel
wrapped around the arm,
ordered me not to move lest broken glass
bite at my toes with their ruthless teeth—
water pounding me like my small fist
against my chest on the Day of Atonement,
commanding me to admit
to every sin ever committed.

The Hollins Critic   ROBERT COOPERMAN

EASTER SUNDAY, 1984

Christmas my father could tolerate,
a day harmless with gifts, feasting and football.
But Easter made him edgy; he would curse
everytime fine weather was predicted
for that Sunday. It wasn't
the miracle of resurrection
that he begrudged "The Catholics,"
as he lumped all Christians,
but the Good Friday pogroms he remembered
his parents telling him of,
when Poland was their special hell,
and America—Easter bonnets,
eggs and chocolate rabbits—
merely a dream of a heaven unobtainable
to the killers of Christ.

Through March and April he forgot
we lived in Brooklyn

with its synagogues and indifference,
and that Poland was just hearsay to him,
a horror story told by parents
that was sadly true; he forgot, too,
that here Christians greeted Easter
with sunrise services, baseball games
and parades, egg hunts for children
who might bark their shins
but not blame the Jews for their bruises.

Still, something of my father
survives in me: I, too, feel myself
growing angry before Easter,
nightmared by Cossacks pulling women
into the dirt of *shtetl* roads,
each drunkard hoisting an arm or leg
while her neighbors were forced to watch,
their breaths frozen in sunshine,
the eye of God complacent
upon Easter dinners, firecrackers
and the Statue of Liberty.

Poem   ROBERT COOPERMAN

SACRED COWS

I go out to try the cattle.
I could blow out the sun
of their liveliest calf

and their eyes would not change.
A god could leap
shorn of its blasted brain

and they would sit there still yawning,
chewing the air,
eyes blank as the sky

when a man's head explodes,
or does not explode,
or the world does or does not really end.

Stone Country   STEVEN R. COPE

ENDANGERED SPECIMEN

That snake you spared last fall is back.
("Look!" you said, spying the hatchling,
"a baby copperhead." With a nudge
from the toe of your boot, it was gone.)
Half grown, it watches me from the woodpile,
head raised above its bright mosaic coils.

As I walk the path in sandals,
rainwashed roots twist from the ground
and stop me cold, till wood is wood
and I can breathe again. You,
my naturalist son, would smile
at my layman's fantasy.

Yesterday I found snagged on a cedar branch
a loop of tissue skin that bore its print.
How many ghostly membranes will have peeled
from its cool elliptical eyes before
it is thick as the handle of the ax
I keep at the back door?

America   HELEN M. COPELAND

ELEGY FOR JOHN, MY STUDENT DEAD OF AIDS

In my office, where you sat years ago and talked
Of Donne, of how you loved
His persona, the bravado he could muster
To cover love's uncertainties,
Books still line the shelves, centuries
Of writers who've tried to make a kind of sense
Of life and death and, failing that,
Found words to stand at least
Against the griefs we can't resolve.

Now you're dead. And what I've got to say
Comes now from that silence
When our talk last fouled up. I allowed you less,
As always, than you wanted to say.
We talked beside the Charles, a lunch hour reunion
Of sorts after years of your postcards
(New York, San Francisco, Greece),
Failed attempts to find a place to live.
The warm weather had come on

In a rush. You talked of being the first born,
Dark-haired, Italian son. How you rarely visited
The family you so clearly loved.
I shifted to books, to sunlight falling
Through sycamores and the idle play of underlying
Shadows. When we parted,
All that was really left was the feeling
You deserved better. And yet I was relieved
Our hour was up, that we had kept your confusion

To yourself. We shook hands, you drove off to Boston.
Now you're dead, and I wonder
If your nobleness of living with no one
To turn to ended in dishonor,
Your family ashamed. Or if your death had

About it a frail dignity,
Each darkening bruise precise as a writer's word,
Saying, at last, who you were—exactly
And to anyone who would listen.

Poetry   ROBERT CORDING

THE BLOOMING OF SENTIMENTALITY

I hear it coming from the start,
the claptrap all shamelessly marshalled:
the hordes of muted violins
swelling and subsiding, the voice
wrenching to a wail I know
makes a cheapshot bid for my heart.

I keep it all at a distance,
looking askance at the hangdog eyes
or the child's squeal and her sparkling smile—
these images that must not count
because they are designed to count,
to demand the shiver of my skin
for the whimper of a half-pound pup.

Time after time I fend it off,
the chorus of grandmothers, roses, and tears.
It seems to fall from the sky,
to sprout from the ground by night—
rootless, and puffed with hope.
I focus instead on integrity:
wholeness and balance of mood,
visions that come from those depths
where freshness and honesty breed,
where clans of thin motives and still-thinner words
lack the power and desire to go.

But on one dark, soulful day
those violins rise up again,
so many that I picture a wave,
the sweeping bows like grain
rippling to the far horizon.
And through that deafening swell,
my lovers and family march uphill
to a flowered ridge glued on a crystal sky,
where the Enemies cannot reach them.
This *could* be the place, I suddenly think,
and I run to reach that distant height,
my arms outstretched and raised
in that gesture of exaltation
I have always seen but never known.
And then, I am beside myself as well,
cheering me on as I run.

I reach the sun-drenched edge and I know
I have cut off the dullness of reason
to set loose a burgeoning dream
that could give all my other dreams range.

Poetry   STEPHEN COREY

INTO THE WOODS

Vanishing for days, my father
would return unshaven,
the odor of evergreens and woodsmoke
on his clothes, his eyes
a pair of chickadees
darting from mother's face
to the faces of his children
as he spoke of lakes and rivers
where he had been and we might someday go,
disappearing like him
with a fly rod and a knap sack.

The face we remembered
and the whiskered face emerging
from the forest were never quite the same;
and we were never sure if he would bring
stringers of trout or just a kiss
for mother and a grin for us.
It never mattered. Leaving us,
he'd fall soundlessly from our lives
like a tree in the center of the woods.

And though we pictured him
crouched beside his fire
by the shore of some lake or pond
with a name as long as your arm,
we couldn't imagine the man
who days later would stroll into the yard,
freshened and whole again,
bringing us fish and kisses.

Blueline   PAUL CORRIGAN

TAKING LIBERTIES

My father would drive us
to the Sandy Shores
one Sunday a month.
In those days, even
ten-dollar motels
had a baggy clown
on the diving board, waving

his arms on the way down.
Pratfalls were good business.

We never checked in.
My mother spread her towel
over the last vacant chaise lounge.
I rubbed her back
with the white cream
from a wheezing bottle.
In the pool she touched
my Treasure Island float
with her cigarette
and told me if a clown
can surface so could I.
And my father and I sat
with our feet in the deep end
while he told me how
to treat women. If we saw
a couple enter a rented room
in their bathing suits,
my father told me the girl
was getting it.
Poor thing, he said,
and his eyes never left
the patternless drapes.

Free burgers were grilled
on a spit by the sea wall.
My father, with no room key
to prove his claim to food,
looked at my mother's shoulders
and picked up the bottle
of cream. I would watch them
from the shallow steps,
my eyes out of water,
and pretend
I'd never been
above the sea.

Kansas Quarterly   VINCE CORVAIA

A COUNTRY THAT I HAVE NOT KNOWN

This is a country that I have not known.
Mountains retreat and give the valley air,
Become hills only, shreds of blue. Fishbone
Bleached on blue rock takes me to my own bare

Rigging, swims me in my spirit upward
Past the smokehouse, past the sagging weir.
A trapper seems to know the place. The beard,
The tooth, the grease of him say this, the sneer.

He snaps a trap to show me how it works.
But I am well upstream by now, beyond
Whatever he can do. A grizzly jerks
A head to take the sun, takes air beyond
The river, off hind legs reared the hills.

Prism International   TONY COSIER

MEMORY

Ten years ago this morning, father died.
Light rain was falling: he went out to wipe
His Chevy down in a chill December drizzle.
When from the front door mother looked for him,
He'd stretched out by the far side of the car
Face upward with his arms crossed on his chest
Like a granite-carved Osiris or the Christ
Of the Last Judgment on the high Celtic cross
In the ancient churchyard at Monasterboice:
His body cold as stone and just as dead
In that instant—he lay in his plaid jacket
With hat still on—from cardiac arrest.

"Happy the corpse the rain falls on," flashed
Through mother's mind, remembering a phrase
From childhood and the days in Dunderrow
Up at the farm the Finns tilled on the hill
Above the Cotters' plowland in Shippool
Where Kitty first saw Jim across the fields
And loved his gold-flecked eyes and light red hair.

The Hudson Review   JAMES FINN COTTER

LACE

Each morning my Aunt Margaret walked through fields
Down into the winding streets of old Kinsale,
With the steeple of Saint Mulrose and tall masts
Glittering like bright needles in the harbor
Beyond the town hall and the market square
To work in Fahey's Lace Shop on Clare Lane.

She was so silver-quick, so sleight-of-hand,
They called her magic Margaret: she could knot
A baby's bonnet into a web of stars,
Doilies into snowflakes and scarves into frost
Delicately drawn and looped on windowpanes.
Designs appeared to leap out at her touch.

Now, her fingers quietly clasped in her lap,
At ninety-two still fastening the light;

Her hands become the lacework they created
From the crystal patterns of her needlepoint.

America   JAMES FINN COTTER

YOUNG HORMONES MADRIGAL

Then you were a boy and could
raise excitement in your pants
equally with bad or good
literature or circumstance.

Reading "Blondie," Joyce, or Farrell,
kissing Blondie, Joyce, or Snooks,
friction made you come a barrel—
fictions, girls, and comic books.

Was the world a dream, or real?
Who could really give a hoot,
dreaming of a real feel
of silky this or naked that?

Secret lusts inhabited
every lady on the street:
they were all at home in bed
admiring your prodigious feat,

even though they didn't know it.
Cousins, aunts, your mother's friends—
none were proof against your habit;
you knew both of all their ends.

Life was coming; coming, life;
death was Not Getting Any.
Even Holy Writ was rife
with tales of promised milky honey;

classes in biology,
civics, history, and Latin
were all crypto-anatomy,
the one idea to raise and fatten.

Cars were custom-made for just
one activity on earth:
for transportation, take the bus,
Ford's invention was a berth.

Nothing live was safe or sacred
if it forked or had a rictus:
habeas balloon, or snake,
mandrake root, gazelle or *corpus*.

Then you were a boy and could
conceive of nothing greater than

to have a limb of polished wood
and a friendly, tireless, helping hand.

The Iowa Review   JAMES CRENNER

SKATING AFTER SCHOOL

In the space between school & supper,
light flat as a china plate,
sky and ice a single seam
stitched by the black trees,
we raced over the railroad tracks
down the embankment
to the frozen pond,
mufflers trailing,
snow embroidering our flannel jeans.
Then out, onto the ice, blades dividing
the surface into geometry,
ice writing from an old language,
the calligraphy of snow . . .
And then, as the baggage of school disappeared,
became ephemeral as smoke from the bonfire
where we charred hot dogs, made dark cocoa
that burned our tongues,
we went back out onto the ice again,
feeling the slap and chock of the hockey puck,
the body contact muffled in layers of wool,
the ache of air inside our lungs . . .
And as the dark came down like a coffee cup,
we saw the yellow lights come on
up over the tracks.
But we kept on playing, icing the puck,
shooting straight for the goal,
legs aching beyond endurance . . .
Home, where the yellow lights are growing,
fills with the smell of macaroni & cheese
and muffins, but we stay out, still checking & hitting
wood against wood, our steel blades marking the ice
until it's a black board in need of erasing . . .
And, when we knew we could not stand it
any longer out in the cold,
we clambered up the banks,
always falling on the cinders,
woodsmoke and winter clinging to our clothes,
climbing, climbing, toward the steady yellow lights of home.

West Branch   BARBARA CROOKER

THE SIMPLE ACTS

(after reading Primo Levi)

The night before the train
left for Auschwitz,
some got drunk, wept and swore at God.
Others removed their shoes, lit
Yahrzeit candles, prayed. The mothers
washed their children, put them to bed.
Then in tepid water they washed
the children's clothes,
hung them on barbed wire
around the camp at Fossoli.

How this image holds me,
how it speaks of the simple
ordinary acts that make us human.

As the children sleep,
are sleeping still,
cotton underwear and thin socks
worn thinner at the heels
flutter in the bitter wind
small and white as hope.

Event   LORNA CROZIER

THERE ARE POEMS

There are poems in the typewriter,
but they won't come out.
I know they're in there.
I hear them whispering at night,
calling me downstairs
into sudden silence—
a cruel joke.

There are poems in my hands,
but the fingers are broken,
gone numb at the tip.
The hands gesture in mounting panic—
a mute misery.
If I could bend the fingers
I would beat fists on glass.

There are poems in the street.
The autumn trees are full of them
blazing cold fire out of reach.
There are poems in old men's eyes,
in babies' fingers; poems in the wind,
in street parades—in night screams
and morning silence.

There's a poem in the soft mustache
my brother dips in his beer
across the table,
making jokes to cheer me up.
I've heard his routine.
I offer him mine—
these words on crumpled paper
calling themselves alive.

Event   MARY ELLEN CSAMER

SONG OF RADIATION

If anything is magic, I am magic, I am everywhere.
Hide me in glass, bury me in salt, freeze me in ice, burn me in sun,
    I shall not leave you.
Wherever you go, I follow, inevitable, invisible, always inescapably there.

Drown me in ocean, I seep and seek you out:
Find you in the plants that feed the fishes,
Find you in the fish that feed bigger fishes,
I concentrate myself and find you there.
Cover me with earth, I wait until you dig me up:
Find you through the rabbits in their trenches,
Find you when you dig up contaminated shovels
(Left oh so carefully unguarded),
Cling to every follicle of hair on you.

Do not run from me, I am in your mother's milk,
Fast as the wind I run, I am in the air you breathe, I am coming,
Eat me, drink me, breathe me,
Forget me, turn your back on me,
Scratch at me, vomit me up, I am in you,
In your lungs and in your blood and in the marrow of your bones,
In your testicles and ovaries I celebrate myself.

And do not run from me in death, I shall never let you go;
I am in your children and in your children's children,
In testes, semen, milk; I live with them for half a million years.
Silently
I sign my name
on the genes of your forever.

The Pottersfield Portfolio   PETER CUMMING

RIVER TRIP

Riding down the shallow rocky Sheepscot
the trick is to stay centered
on the rubber raft.
You have to watch out for crazy currents

that will hang you up
on hairy boulders.

Falling off is not the problem—
it's the getting back on,
with the rear end of the raft
swinging away
like a
slippery fish.

You try to keep your eye out
for the clear chance and
you make frantic last minute choices
to go right—
or left—
only to nose into the bank.

But the hemlocks and cardinal flowers
don't get you where you're going,
nor the easy minnows
in the shallow pools;
so you push off again
for midstream.

Where are the others?
Your neck aches
from looking ahead
and the pace is too fast
when you aren't snarled up
in river weed.

But here, now,
as you near the mouth
leading to the sea,
the way calms down and widens out.
You can put your face on your arms
and float.

Ploughshares   DELLA CYRUS

EVERYTHING ELSE YOU CAN GET YOU TAKE

It's that kind of day.
Hay and panic grass
combed into rolling windrows.
Minstrel-faced sheep. A few
head of cross-bred Charlies.

No place we ever imagined
we'd be. No sea's edge
where a low wave sputters,
ignites like a fuse, and races
hissing along the shore.
No thin, viral mist fizzing

the windshield, gorges rising
grey as China in the rain.

Only this long roll of
space where day-lillies
leap any breaks in the fences,
flooding down ditches, orange
against the many colors of green,
—only the jingle and ring of
morning crickets in the dew.

Don't ask how long we've
been here, or why we stayed.
You fall in love with
a climate. Everything else
you can get you take.

The Iowa Review   ROBERT DANA

JOY RIDE

(for my brother Mike in Detroit)

Laid off, he drove to Texas
with his wife, two kids, a tent.
Came back burned, a mortgage
waiting to kick his ass.
Uncle Les got him a job driving trucks
north to Saginaw for a chain
of nonunion restaurants,
6:30 to 6:30, no overtime pay,
no pension. He watches his kids
on his day off while his wife works.

Today, after calling in sick,
he talks of quitting. Tunes up his car
in the street, an old Ford held together
with duct tape and mirrors,
then takes off on this first fine
April day down I-75 past the sign
announcing the number of new cars built, past
the brewery, the stadium, then south
into flatness to Monroe, home of La-Z-Boy
chairs, and down across the Ohio line
to drink in the first bar he can find
until he feels a fuzziness in his head
he can almost mistake for possibility.

You know the rest: he sobered up,
he drove home.

Michigan Quarterly Review   JIM DANIELS

GRANVILLE, NEW YORK: THE MUSEUM OF NATURAL HISTORY

In summer, when the sun
slants through
and smears the cages
of these sleeping beasts,
the smell of heated fur
nearly explodes,
for even the air
is stuffed in the land
of taxidermy gone amok.
In this peaceable kingdom
the rabbit disdains
the bobcat's teeth,
and hundreds of birds
stare straight ahead.

A barn that droops
like a half-dead horse
is backdrop for a farm
emerging from the wall
in shocks of real hay,
a branch, and a pond
of stiff, blue sheet.
Here the weasel
and woodchuck come to drink,
observed by an owl
and a three-hundred-pound
black bear—a bear
of infinite appetite
for boredom,
waiting to eat you alive.

Blueline   CHARLES DARLING

THE TIME BEFORE

Life was simple then;
The colors of green grass,
Blue sky, yellow sun.
Morning smelled of soap and
Toast. Houses drawn with
Crayons on squares of creamy
Paper had smoke twisting
From the chimneys,
A tree each side, winsome paths
Curling to the door.
The sun wore spokes and always
Smiled. All things small
Had lives of their own:
Bug, bird, snake or fish;

You could create an afternoon
From two caterpillars,
A bit of moss, some acorns,
Twigs and flower petals.
Rocks were friends to hide among,
Climb, throw into waiting pools
Where their wet thuds made
Quiet circles reaching out to touch
Your shoe. Trees were an
Adventure, ice cream an outing.
Christmas was so large it
Reached backward brushing November.
The best clothes had pockets.
Time was longer, and, when you
Stood at the start of a day,
The hours stretched wide and bright
Curling from your door.

The Piedmont Literary Review   ANNE L. DAVIDSON

EARLY ONE MORNING MY SON AND I TAKE A SHORT DRIVE

We climb into the car. The air is cold and clear,
the kind of morning one almost might invent, try
to get right, on paper or in paint; so still we must
imagine motion to believe in it. His eyes graze my face,
asking before the words pass between us; and then
the smiles, and quickly he comes to me, climbing over
the back seat to sit upon my lap. He drives the length
of one whole block in the clear air, sunlight alive,
warming the morning lawns and leaves, the spilt light
splintering into our eyes through shatterproof glass.

Ball State University Forum   WILLIAM VIRGIL DAVIS

A CLEAR DAY AND NO CLOUDS

The small white houses are proud
against the light blue sky. The trees
are bright green rows bordering the fields.
Beyond the end of the narrow road
the sea tongues the land. We stand
here, days like this, on the high cliffs,
as if at the only window in the world.

Arizona Quarterly   WILLIAM VIRGIL DAVIS

PULL CORD

By the time I get to the hospital
the strings that held my father to me
have been broken;
there are only puppet strings left—
lifting a shoulder when he breathes,
knotting in spasms so his hand
jerks and fumbles as I hold it.
Soon even these . . .
but they don't break quickly.
They loosen and,
towards midnight, his arms quiet,
the shoulder lifts less and less,
stops lifting,
and the long strings into my mind
pull as they break
so that all the memories
light up as he goes.

Quarry   DIANE DAWBER

UNEXPECTEDLY, THE CLEAR SKY

(in memory of Chuang Tzu)

Getting off work and walking home
. . . it's 10:00 a.m.
    and the weight of being awake all night
    is with me.
The harbour is an empty arc in cool blue light.
Though I look closely I can see no ships
and, turning to the north,
    I think of my lover.

This morning I feel
the opposite directions that our days take—
    she going off to her office
    as I return.
With perseverance we have an hour in the evening
and she so round, and pregnant, and tired.

In the Chinese market I wonder at the colour
of flowers, at the colour of the sun
    in fresh-washed bakeshop windows.
While my slow brain watches,
the entire catalogue of common sounds is swept up
into the pulsing whiteness of invisible stars;
    every uncounted sphere precise
    within the spreading whorls of the galaxy.

I move through an absolute world.
On the sidewalk outside my building

a man with perfect make-up
turns and smiles.

The Antigonish Review   JAMES DEAHL

I'M SATISFIED

I'm satisfied, I owe life nothing,
and life owes me just
a penny's worth of candy.
We're even, so now

the body can relax: day
after day it plowed, planted,
reaped as well, and even
squandered somewhat, oh poor,

poor animal,
its testicles now pensioned off.
One of these days I'm going to stretch out
under a fig tree, the one I noted,
exasperated and alone, years ago:
we are kith, we are kin.

Northwest Review   EUGENIO DE ANDRADE
                       —Translated from the Portuguese
                              by Alexis Levitin

THE SOCIAL CONTRACT REWRITTEN

They know another dog
has been here. They can
tell by the cursive yellow
writing in the snowbank,

a word or phrase ending
in an absurdly-stylized letter Y.
It looks like one of the
signatures on the U.S. Constitution,

so highbrow and eloquent,
an educated man's mark. Still,
we all three stop to stare,
like tourists, me, bundled eskimo-style

in my coat, and them
in their furs. While I
see fit just to look
with that outsider's detached,

appreciative gawk, they go a step
further, adding their own—less

elegant but perfectly legible—
scribblings to the near-empty

cold white inviting parchment—
making history with their
sincere, steaming urine in the
brisk flush of early December sun.

Passages North   LARRY O. DEAN

CRICKETS

You are the voice of the earthstuff,
the singing that melds the summers.
Sometimes I try not
to hear you.
Sometimes I strain to hear you over the ice,
and you are a warm breath,
the light of the hearth.

In fall you rustle amongst the dropped corn,
sing like a slow pulse.
The pale green chorus overlays the ground
of your voice.

They chirr and clack
at the front of the night.
Sometimes they forget
and sing when a light is thrown on them.

In the morning I see them clinging
to the buildings, and they are like
green still tears sitting on the brass
lip of the city.

Their voices snap in the fields
or shake in the trees,
elaborations of the fundamental
seven notes
about which the whole cycle
twists,
seven notes through the night, seven notes
through the storm's hail green sky,
seven notes,
earthstuff.

They always get through.
Your stubwing song
flies over the dreams
and gets the music to the
heart.

Kansas Quarterly   PAUL DECELLES

SHIMMY

Suddenly, one afternoon, while he stands
With his mouth in the shape of W—O—W,
His wife flounces from the shower,
Pirouettes, g-r-i-n-d-s a hip,
Skip-struts, bobble and bouncy,
Disco Aphrodite, slicks
Into the bedroom on a wave
Of towel and a pink and peachy
Hello-Sailor sidelong flick and flash of naked.
Teasing a leg, steamy, creamy,
She quivers, shivers, delivers
One last belly hump jelly roll
Fresh flesh jiggle—giggles—
and is gone.

Wascana Review   MARK DeFOE

PUBLIC DEFENDER

Silhouetted by flourescent light,
I watch from my office window
As early morning grays
First shadow, then define
Crows currenting, climbing
On funnels of warm air.

Often as a boy I woke
To the raucous cries of crows mocking
Our straw dummy staked among the cornstalks.
I never liked crows or their bible-cover black suits
Or how they avoid the hunt and chase,
Prefer carrion—corrupt and unclean—
And, with authority, beak their fare.

Still I dislike them.
But, with trial only three hours away,
Preferences are luxuries I cannot keep:
I circle back to my desk,
Eye the lifeless case sprawled across it,
Take my pencil, and peck.

America   FRED DEGNAN

THE CONDOLENCE

When he lay dying in the hospital
It was as if he couldn't bear my touch,
But he was like that sometimes, afraid of love,
Especially when he needed it too much.

I thought I'd sit by him and read, or pray,
Bring up old times that we could smile at now;
Then later, if he wanted, hold his hand
To make it easier for him to go,

Though he still struggled to get out of it,
And stiffened the little that was left of him
Against my comforting, as if he sensed
A darker lullaby than I could hum,

And kept the sliding bed-table between us,
More stubborn as the pain and fear increased.
"Let go, let go," I whispered, desperate
To draw the curtain and get on with grief.

When he grew weak enough I held him close.
We kissed. Then he went mercifully fast.
But that was how it always was with us,
Me needing him, him giving in at last.

TriQuarterly   TIMOTHY DEKIN

NEIGHBOURHOODS

The men in this neighbourhood
are cunningly intimate
across their wooden fences,
stringing morning glories tall
between the boards,
pulling roots beneath
each other's feet,
leaning on shaky conversations.

This is the way a man will pray,
sly in the presence of God.
Small talk, the weather this,
the wife and children that,
a voice of flowerbeds
withering for rain.
How are you? . . . I am a fence,
the weight of blossoms.

Some men pray with shovels, trowels,
others speak in waterfalls.
A scent of marigolds,
a wisp of rainbow on the breath.
Men will dig for bulbs, for rocks,
or train their plants to walk on string.
God, another neighbour now,
a fence of cunning clouds.

Watch right here: two men
are leaning on this very print
as if they were about to fall,

the words so small, a shovel slipped.
They are saying things about
the weather, how the flowers
grow both up and down, how
summer strains to somehow disappear.

Blossoms overhear each hint of sound,
both earth and wood extremely clear . . .
our bones are leaning on a simple word,
that's life, tangled in each other's flesh;
what's this, our conversations rise on
flower breath, spilling fence to fence,
the intimacy of neighbourhoods,
the small print in a prayer.

Cross-Canada Writers' Quarterly   BARRY DEMPSTER

THE SPANIEL

Piles of leaves at the curb again
And I think of Mitsi, how she loved to flail among them
And burrow in, dooming herself, it turned out,
To a shorter life in the world of cars
Than the life allotted spaniels in general,
However nervous and clumsy the breed may be.

Shrewd of nature to put its money
On the species only, not a penny on the particular.
The odds are good that the blue whale will endure
Unchanged, or changing imperceptibly,
While generations of particular pods
Beached on the bay shore in gales
Are doomed as surely as Mitsi was,
Mitsi who's gone with the sagging front porch
Of the brown and blue house on Granger Street,
The butterfly wallpaper in the front hall,
The bathtub with the fish decals,
The boy I was then, the young man
Who thought he was leaving them all behind.

All lost in the rockslide
While the species holds its place,
Tempting me to believe my deepest nature
The same as the nature of man,
To dismiss the differences,
To ignore the dock hidden among the leaves
Where a boat painted with my colors
Tugs at its chain.
Barely sunrise. No one on the water as I row out.
The brindled spaniel in the bow sleeps quietly,
Not wondering with me if the tide we're riding
Is the one I should have chosen,

Or why that cluster of gulls at sundown
Veered off after slowly circling.

Poetry   CARL DENNIS

ON COMMONWEALTH AVENUE
AND BRATTLE STREET

(For William Saroyan)

Last year the magnolias flared
like candelabra bursting into flame,
quivering as if they had never bloomed
before, astonishing sight everywhere.

And if a soft rain fell, it came
like angel breath, like gauze dispel-
ling the sweet excess of light.
This year the color is the same

and never was I more aware of fall-
ing petals. But only to compare
with those when we, a levitated pair,
walked above them all.

Contemporary New England Poetry   DIANA DER HOVANESSIAN

AUTUMN BURNINGS

My mother used to smell
my clothes to see if I'd been
near a fire. Back then, when
fall's leaves were burned
on streets, I'd stand close to watch
the season's leavings smoldering,
the deep orange core glowing.
I like to close my eyes,
knowing there was wisdom
in that burning, some gorgeous finality
I could feel, standing there. I hugged
that smoke blowing through my clothes,
a new wind biting my cheeks;
stood solitary watch, the beautiful
consummations all along the street.

Southern Humanities Review   PETER DESY

DOUBLE BIND

Life seems to set us tasks
adhering to some law

of the double bind,
like spinning gold from straw
while proclaiming it forbidden
to use a crucible
or spindle;

like Diaghilev
telling Nijinsky:
"Astonish me,"
while viewing him
with sardonic eyes
that denied they still
could be astonished.

"Astonish me," says life,
and when we complain
that the tools are hard to find,
adds, "I make the rules.
The advantage
must be mine."

The American Scholar   E. B. DE VITO

TO KATIE AT EIGHTY

The world's a small, small place,
   So very small
That once in one embrace
   I held it all.

Your lips on mine close pressed,
   I held in trust
All that the past possessed
   That is not dust.

Given your hand and heart,
   I held in fee
Of Space and Time and Art
   Their instancy.

Your eyes caress me now.
   O Skies, contract!
And Time, slow down and bow
   Before one fact:

The world's a small, small place,
   So very small
That now in one dear face
   I hold it all.

The American Scholar   PETER HUGH DEVRIES

BOONIES

The telephone linemen
came way out
in our woods
to hitch us back up
with the outside,
and the dog barked
ungratefully.

The storm last night
disconnected us
from vets, docs and public
defenders, deprived us
of gossip
and real stories.

Now that the linemen
have gone
and we're again
part of the world,
the telephone's quiet,
waiting to bring us out
of ourselves,
but we have nothing
to tell.

And the dog's asleep
on the floor,
nose half in half out
the door, ears
flopping down
all around her head,
not even dream dark
or dream cats
to bark at.

Now that we're connected,
give us a call,
tell us there's a war on
or a two-car crash
    out on 202,
any stupidity
to stir the air
or the dust.

Yankee   ROBERT DEYOUNG

MATTINA

Am feelin'
good, so good,
the room fills with me,

am filling it and the street
and part of the tree in the
northwest yard, and the love who
walks through it, meeting me at
the door, and me offering coffee
to her, just like in those
far-away days of child-
hood when you used to greet
something by tipping the little
hat of your soul, just in such miniature ways, the squirrels, the
sparrows, the little bits of
leaves and their tiny heroisms in
a fistful of wind; just like that
those things in one explosion, only
five explosions in the middle of
my room like the hub of a star; no,
like the hub of a man; no, like
the centre of my friends; no, like
the spokes of that generator, the heart,
going out to the world—that kind of
love, that's the tag-feelin' that
good. Morning in three hours. I want to
be ready for it, another blaze of blue
sheaves decking whole bunches of molecules; downright
amazing, now I hang such a mood on the
tail end of Venus up there and go risking
my neck on the planet, what the hell, the
day rushing at me like a car with full
headlights on. Some new lively people in the
front seat. Welcome. The door, this heart,
this baywindow, this flank of my
life for the taking.

Cross-Canada Writers' Quarterly   PIER GIORGIO DI CICCO

READER AND ADVISER

This Four of Clubs means that Christine will
come to you on nights of moon haze,
of rain on the thin streets mirroring the dark,
on nights of dogs signalling each other.
She will fill you with echoes and reflections,
memories of love throb and moss damp,
feelings of wave crest and sun touch.

The King of Diamonds indicates
that you'll awake some morning to discover
everyone you know speaking a different language.
Most of the buildings you're familiar with
will not be there and the sun
wil have drifted off to become much smaller

because you have analyzed Christine away,
reasoned her out of existence,
reached the conclusion that she's not possible.

The Queen of Diamonds says that even after
months have pulled the moon through its orbit
she'll appear to you sometimes, whispering,
"Must we know everything . . . must we analyze?"
Thinking only of her has made your friends seem
almost like strangers, often makes you say
preposterous things at the wrong time.

But this Nine of Hearts suggests that Christine
will return some night when flakes of moon
lie on the ground
and on the roofs of the fat houses,
and you'll finally realize that this time
the hand you touch, the voice you hear
is really hers.

The Spoon River Quarterly   JOHN DICKSON

SHAKESPEARE'S KINGS

You English kings, you're so much like we are;
You kill and die with shades of guilt between,
Yet majesty assumes our bones are there
To seize our flesh: we're in a chilly scene
About to stab; we plan to stop the breath
Of those who stand between a throne and us.
How full of royal blood is any death,
But in these halls the dynasties of loss
Were formed for useful doom. Royal guides,
Your juices spuming out more bubbled words,
You fall to night that's rising on all sides,
But leave us free beyond the warrior herds
Who mill about. Oh, troubled English kings,
You die all time yet live as each word stings.

Arizona Quarterly   ANDREW DILLON

MARC CHAGALL

He invented animals and flowers;
faces upside-down, painted airborne
droshkies, icons, red roosters, fiddlers—

green hands: on canvases drew images.
His studio for better or for worse:
sketchpads and pottery on the table.

A lamp and brushes, photographs of
Bella and his parents, an easel. Oils.
His hands explored the moods
    of lovers and clowns,

flying donkeys, nostalgia for Paris,
the wooden houses of Vitebsk,
    his youth. He said
what is the end of life but a bouquet?

Yankee   MARGARET TOARELLO DIORIO

THE APRICOT TREES

After the toothy limbs pruned in February
lay tangled on the ground, so that their snares
might claw or snap shut where you walked, one branch
arced up and bit your thigh, inside, and you
slapped the spot where blood seeped and trailed,
a red snailtrack pointing toward your belly.

After years of marriage and two years tending
four trees, our share of remnants left from orchards
that once shaded all these neighborhoods,
the cycle led us to imagine one
uncontested season of preserves and jams
glowing in the cupboard, in the half-dark.

One bough I hadn't braced in time soon snapped.
Late nights, to reach our door we had to lean,
silent and drunk, around that torn point,
then stoop beneath sagging arcades of fruit,
green, orange, gold succulence of summer
tedium when things ripen too fast and fall.

When friends stumbled away with knobby sacks,
they surely thought it no strange thing that we
would leave this place, each other, and the story
of the orchards, that we would give away
perfection's spoils to anyone who asked.
We had enough. Earlier, before the fruit

took form and force in bud, I sliced one branch
to follow the track laid in the cool moist flesh
by borers I couldn't find. For miles around
they've left their signs: a stone-glass bubble sealed
to trunk or branch, gemfire flared inside
false, perfectly imagined apricots.

TriQuarterly   W.S. DIPIERO

FISH PIER

Thousands of codfish
Glitter in open
Cases. They look
So still on beds
Of ice, I tiptoe
Around them. Gutted,
Dead instruments,
They will not trill
The high or low
Seas again. They lie
Quiet as knives.
They, too, were feared
By their lessers,
Squid and mussels.
Still, these losses
move me little.
Tomorrow they'll be
Wrapped in the news
Of today's paper.
Events surface
At this very moment.
At every moment
Bad things happen.
Death leaves a corpse
And violence often
A reliable witness.
But good deeds and blessings
Are mostly manifestations,
Too abstract for me.
The fish had faith
In open water.

Ploughshares   STUART DISCHELL

MITRE BOXES

In the garage, and under cellar stairs,
My father's tools are waiting. (His hands,

Twisted now, will never use them more
Than what they have already.) Bought.

Or thefted, piled together every way,
They serve a plenitude of purposes—but

Not to anybody now that they lie there
Uselessly; nor will they in time to come

For me, unknowing as I am of what
Those jaws were meant to grip, or why.

The tools I need to use, I own.
These tease me with the skills they say

I need and do not have, and he had.
Cast metal, pounds and pounds

Of it, awaits in chests, on shelves.
It tells me *Learn us quickly: quickly*

We are yours. I'd say *I do not want*
You, turn me loose—except a friend

Has taught me, gifting me his father's
Mitre Box, the thing to do with these

A father's leavings: not to place
Saw in the groove for sake of cut

And angle merely; but fit the hand
Where hand had been and, fitting, use

—If not in doing, then at least
In stepping into tracks made in a snow.

The Fiddlehead   JOHN DITSKY

GATHERING HAY

(Vermont, 1982)

Under a sky munificently blue,
We pack the last of the windrowed hay
Into bundles, fork and heave them skyward
Onto the pick-up and its unsteady pile.
Two acres in five hours. Seven loads.
By some, a half-day's work, though I'd
Dispute it. Back at the barn, we pitch
The hay up to the loft where already
A mountain of it has risen
Through our doings. Or rather, yours.
This is an art I have not mastered,
Has taken me twice the time to do
The half you've done, though I ache well
By any measure, enough to wonder
By what faith or will did the first
To settle here endure—Andersons, MacKensies,
Browns—who with scythe and pitchfork only
Heralded the winter in, survived, begat,
And made a life out of the stubborn land
They're buried in. It is a thought
I can't hold on to, a whispering here
And not quite here, before it passes.
For want of something better, I say,
"This last load killed my back,"
Thankful I lasted long enough to have

The ache I do, the sweet complaint.
But later, as we sit on your porch
Facing townward, the house behind us,
The stubbly field behind that, thick
Enough for your horse to graze on,
You say quietly, "It feels good
To have my hay in for the winter."
Just that, though your eyes betray
What you keep to yourself and hidden.
It's the old story of time and weather,
How too much water can cure a thirst
Beyond its wants, how some this summer
Have lost their first crop to the rain,
How some will lose the second, the cut hay
Rotting and fungal in the sodden fields;
How some may lose both, the farm, themselves.
You've timed this harvest right. Had luck.
Enough to go on for another season.
Enough, at least, to make you say,
Though ruin will in time undo us,
"It feels good." It is enough
To sit beside you
And hear you say it.

The Iowa Review   GREGORY DJANIKIAN

MY ISLAND

("No man is an island, intire of it selfe.")
                              —John Donne

Last night in Zurich,
Naked, in the arms of a friend,
I spoke of loneliness.

We are all islands, she said.
I'd rather be an island than an islander.
I'd rather be England than English.
Touché, I thought. John Donne is wrong.

Which island should I be?
Tristan da Cunha,
This dot on a map surrounded by blue?
No, thank you. Not that much solitude.
I'll pick the Finnish archipelago.
One of a thousand islands,
Small, granite, covered with soil,
Bearing moss, fir trees, mushrooms,
And berries ripe for the tongue.

Remember the taste:
Fresh pike, chanterelle mushrooms,
Yellow, picked minutes before?

Remember the rush from the sauna:
Naked pink radiance
Across giant granite boulders
Into icy Baltic waters?

To be a Finnish island, yes—
Smallish, softly covered with moss,
Silvery soft moss for my beard,
Fertile for delicacies, for lingonberries;
Solid, dependable underneath.
A neighboring island close by,
And waiting for the next boat to arrive.

The Midwest Quarterly   CARL DJERASSI

THE MILL IN WINTER

Below them, the valley cradles
the mill's dark body which lay
for a decade like a stunned animal,
but now awakes, almost innocent again
in the morning light. A pale disk of sun
pinks the crusted snow the men walk on,
the first thin columns of smoke brush the sky,
and the odors of coke and pickling acid
drift toward them. They taste metal on their tongues
and yearn toward the mill's black heart.
To enter, to shut out the bright cold air
is to enter a woman's body, beautiful
as ashes of roses, a russet jewel,
a hot breath grazing their arms and necks.

Black Warrior Review   PATRICIA DOBLER

BONEYARD

These people in the future won't be like us.
Oh no, they'll be kinder and their foreheads
will bulge past their noses with wisdom. They'll
have our pictures, of course, although they won't
be snapshots as we know them but little
holographs, three-dimensional photos,
so when one takes one from his pocket it will look
like a miniature twentieth-century person
is standing smack in the center of his palm.
There they are, they'll say kindly, the old
murderers, old child beaters, and they'll laugh
affectionately as one might laugh at a foolish eccentric
who knocks his head against a wall or takes a hammer
and again and again slam-bangs his own foot.

Then they'll put us in their pockets
and stroll off hand in hand. There won't
be many of them, of course. They'll just
be coming back, like trees come back
after a fire: first the green shoots,
like a green rug over the burned place,
then a few isolated saplings rising above
the charred logs, until the whole mountain
is covered with a new family of trees—
box elder and cedar, maple and jack pine—
and only in dark corners will there be traces
of the rich and wonderfully verdant forest
which existed a few brief heartbeats before—
black stumps, blackened foundations,
flat stones with people's names cut into them.

Ploughshares   STEPHEN DOBYNS

HABITS OF GRIEF

Back at his dad's is a lake
like this one, hornets buzzing
near the edge, one rowboat
clicking against the dock. My husband
tucks his hands into his pockets. His shoulders slump
under the dusk. His guilt is unwavering,
even as his grief wells and subsides.
Heat lightning makes no promises.

He bows to the water,
glances toward his fishing rod and tackle,
draws back. In an hour, he could catch
a bucket of perch. He hasn't taken the boat out
since his brother jumped from the Huron Bridge,

fourth suicide in this odd family,
each one the one we failed to suspect.
The answer is to leave
what reminds him of childhood, the lakes
he swam across, never winning.
He still has not learned to keep
his head down, face in the water.

He turns toward me, and I prepare
my hands to meet his face.
The stubble will be thick,
his collar damp, the lake quiet
behind him wherever I look.
This will never happen
to us, I practice saying, afraid
he doesn't believe it, either.

Ascent   LYNN DOMINA

SEA-LAVENDER

The low November sun's a porthole
through which an open furnace grins.
In the slanted light the surf
at Good Harbor curdles to foam.
A billion round and tumbled stones,
perfect granite turtle eggs,
break the panting of the suds
to rags of fleecy underwear.

I want to harvest this undulant
sea-glow the way Turner could,
but I haven't his way with cream
and vermillion, his capacity
to liquefy with a glance.

Glazed by the yellow light, my wife
wanders along the surf-pool
behind the beach, scouring for dried
sea-lavender. Finding none,
she plucks handfuls of mare's-tail,
decorative but unscented,
like art when it's least redundant.

Brassy as the grasping of the surf,
its equally eager letting-go,
I picture myself with this glare
all over me, gory as seaweed.
A figure left over from Homer,
perhaps: the hero who didn't go
to Troy, who pined in his armor
while children raved on the beach
and he gazed toward Asia Minor:

his thoughts, like sea-lavender,
mysterious, scented, out of reach
of the ordinary—thriving
in the speechless rhyme of the surf.

The Literary Review   WILLIAM DORESKI

MASKS

(For Joseph Campbell)

I collect masks—wood, metal, ivory—
Tricked out with feathers, shells, or monkey hair,
Worn by Japanese actors in *Noh* plays,
By dancers in Tibet to become demons,
By shamans in Siberia turned to bears,
By Luba witch doctors to ward off plagues.

I do not collect skulls. When an old sailor
Offered to sell one cheap that he had bought
From a New Guinea tribe in 1912,
I eyed and handled it but would not buy.
To own something that once held speech and thought
Would be, I feared, going too near the bone—

Though I believe it would have blended well
With those false faces hanging on the wall
Which men put on to meet their buried selves,
Talk with their gods, persuade their guardian ghosts
(The totem beasts painted and carved on poles)
To guide the living with death's riper lore.

The skull, too, is a mask: it never looks
Anything like the face that grows on bone.
Only the face seems real, the skull disguise.
Yet every mask is worn over the face
And easily slipped off. But the firm skull
Remains unchanged beneath the changing skin.

This ivory death on which we live survives

The Hudson Review   ALFRED DORN

BACON LETTUCE BANKRUPTCY

the time we have left together
this bunch of men and I
these brawly burly hearts
beating irregularly
worry tense with job insecurity
plus or minus by-pass surgery
and high blood pressure
these railroad men
with no experience at new job searches
having never even made out an application
when they started here as kids 30 years ago
these working class giants
watching retirement dreams dissolve
like solvent eating into grease
the time we have left together is spent
tasting the sale of this hundred year old railroad
talking about it at every coffee lunch or toilet break
work/layoff/bankruptcy
work/layoff/bankruptcy
like a stale sandwich from the vendor truck
we're sick to death of it

The Lake Street Review   SUE DORO

THE DIFFERENCE BETWEEN DUST AND SNOW

"One melts; the other remains.
Each snowflake is unique;
dust, though monotonous,
is entropy's goal.

"One, like a reptile,
assumes outside conditions;
the other, like a mammal,
perishes if it's too warm.

"Snow is man's nature,
ultimately nothing;
dust is Nature's god,
all, ultimately dry."

Though most cling to dead religions
fixed on these appearances,
who am I to set them straight?
Neither dust nor snow.

Webster Review   THOMAS DORSETT

FLASH CARDS

In math I was the whiz kid, keeper
of oranges and apples. *What you don't understand,
master,* my father said; the faster
I answered, the faster they came.

I could see one bud on the teacher's geranium,
one clear bee sputtering at the wet pane.
The tulip trees always dragged after heavy rain,
so I tucked my head as my boots slapped home.

My father put up his feet after work
and relaxed with a highball and *The Life of Lincoln.*
After supper, we drilled and I climbed the dark

before sleep, before a thin voice hissed
numbers as I spun on wheel. I had to guess.
Ten, I kept saying, *I'm only ten.*

Boston Review   RITA DOVE

THE OTHER WOMAN

The other woman lives where dangers
Dare and sings a song too sweet to float
Upon the kitchen air; she lurks beyond
The corner of the eye, and yet it seems
You see her everywhere, a shape that suits

As perfect as your shadow does, from
Head to foot. The other woman never wears
A watch while she makes love but knows
The time when everything is nicely done.
What's often difficult to understand
Is that every woman is
The other woman to every other man.

International Poetry Review   W. S. DOXEY

103 MOUNTAIN AVENUE

When I left the house that afternoon,
walking uphill and north to the crossroads
where every direction was as one,
it was still mid-summer. I was twelve.
It was frog-gigging and minnow-netting.
It was Mom Bates in a tight black bathing suit.
It was Dad Bates in a tight tan skin.
It was the Duke, the Dodgers and Ebbetts Field.
It was the future in the future tense.
The road was cracked like a dry creek bed,
there were shadows, sunshine and leaves.
And up ahead there was the swimming hole;
there was the shallow, there was the depth.
And set back ten feet from the road
and one brief bend below the swimming hole,
there was the big boulder I was sitting on,
there was the throne I was sitting on,
the sun's fierce fire annointing me,
annointing everything I could see. And then
I heard the darkness coming down the mountain,
I heard the snap of twigs and leaves.
And then it was the great buck appeared,
riding the crests of his hysteric leaps,
his eyes small suns exploding distances
to red realities, the rich conversions done.
As quickly, he was gone: across the road,
across Buttermilk Brook, across the trail,
the slope and over. Gone, a dream undreamed.
Gone, the intrigue of a normal sort of day.
When I came once again to the house,
it was mid-October, colored leaves and cold.
It was a zenith crossed, now empty, now dark.
It was a tenement rising deep from center field.
It was a buck's head on the yellow wall,
the eyes dead moons, dull, frozen and gray.

Blueline   GEORGE DREW

SHOOTING POOL AT SLEDDER'S INN

It's true
that my father ran the table:
three games in a row on the break,
then took the cue ball, and, walking away,
tossed it from one hand to the other,
watched the white arc blur in the dark mirror
behind the bar for a long time.
                                        I remember
how I found him there,
my mother waiting outside in the car,
and how he lifted me into the smoky air
to meet him face to face,
saying nothing,
and those men he had beaten all night at pool
turned suddenly back to their beers,
as people do
when it's past getting even.

They, too, knew the single high beam
shining through the window
was the same light searchers use to locate the missing
who do not come home after work from the bars
and who, in winter, simply vanish
out the back door,
the snowfield drifting under the stars.

Which is why I was there,
to protect him in my sleepiness
from any sudden urge to disappear
or, in anger, to turn slowly and throw,
with all his strength,
the perfect, white roundness of the cue ball
through the silent jukebox.

What I really know is that he smiled
to restore something dying in himself,
the way I do now,
slapping down two quarters to challenge for the table,
a friendly game
until it's clear which one of us must lose.

Tar River Poetry   JACK DRISCOLL

ELEGY

Every year, in fall, the land bears
Its harvest like a penance.
The corn rises, the melons swell,
And the absent dead recede like the sea.

In the garden, the black waves taste
Of salt and blood, and the curled furrows
Lap the melons with the same spare
Indifference as once they ground to dust

A hero's bones or a neighbor's cat.
Now in the turned earth is your flesh
With new sweat mixed, and in the field's rough grit
Is your last silence grown close to speech.

Here bean stalks braid the season's yield,
And there is sweetness in the split seed's breath.

Sou'wester   PATRICK DUDDY

SUPPLICATION

Dear God, let me die in my sleep, my poor soul
(in which I still believe, against all evidence)
seeping slowly out through the ends of my hairs
into the warm room. Or let it divide in two and slip
out through the nostrils with my last breath.

For I fear death. I am afraid of heights, and know it
is always a fall from a high place—what has nested
all those years in the head as *consciousness* lets go
and falls clear (by way of the heart, which it quashes,
a hand smothering a candle) to the soles of the feet
and keeps going, punching a hole in the earth.

For entry. Please, God, may I avoid the public
clutch at the heart as the sidewalk comes up, startled
recognition staring from the faces of pedestrians
into whose day I have offended this mortality.
Nor do I desire like some to die behind the wheel
with a rush-hour pulse, taking a passenger and several
home-bound commuters along with me. Yes. In my sleep.

With only those who populate my dreams taking notice—
quiet beasts with half-human faces, cow-eyed,
easily scared and starting off in every direction
at the slightest provocation, banging the surface
of the earth with their hooves. Let my death be so
quiet even these so easily panicked do not startle,
but graze placidly the gray fields of forgetfulness.

The Hollins Critic   JOSEPH DUEMER

WILDWOOD AT DAWN

Sunfish napped in the back bay,
Their blue sides brushing stones.

We crossed, and seemed to cross again,
A small white bridge covering
A stream, like a woman's hand
Laid down in the tall grass.
Waves roared in from the east,
The herring gull cried fire to heaven.
Dawn was a pink line on the sea,
Salmon-colored, slender, a fish.

America   LAWRENCE DUGAN

BLUE SPRUCE

It's straighter, denser than other
Silvered blues I've seen, more spruce.
Whatever points the trunk so straight
To zenith is more than pull of sun
And moon. Something drives it from below,
Aiming for polestar. The same force
Packs cool limbs to densest cone—
Mildest haven, toughest fort. It says
To deer, who devastate the yew,
Don't touch, these needles are sabers
To the tongue, blue ice to draw your blood.
It says to wren and rabbit,
Come in, perch here, crawl under.

Where the farmer dumped his ashes,
Next to where the barn door swung
And closed, the tree, abristle, thrives,
A frosty phoenix slowly rising,
There to reassure, to say to us
What can be done with ash,
With refuse from a ruined barn,
As if the one who kept his tally
On cellar door of woodchucks gunned
Is still there feeding roots,
Still helping something grow.

Blueline   GRAHAM DUNCAN

TO GUARD YOUR SLEEP

At night, sometimes,
When your sleep is deepest,
Your little dead dogs
Come back, leaping
About the house
Like fawns.
Sometimes, mornings,

When you awake,
You find their toys
Scattered about the room.

You can hear them lapping water
From the empty bowl,
Or crunching biscuits
That you never left there.
They prance through your brain
Like ponies.
Finally they settle down
Beside your bed
To guard your sleep.
O, may they stay for your waking,
Not in separate heavens.

Sou'wester   LORA DUNETZ

SACRED

After the teacher asked if anyone had
    a sacred place,
and the students fidgeted and shrunk

in their chairs, the most silent of them all
    said it was his car,
being in it alone, his tape deck playing

things he'd chosen, and everyone knew the truth
    had been spoken
and began speaking about their rooms,

their hiding places; but the car kept coming
    up, the car in motion,
music filling it, and sometimes one other person

who understood the bright altar of the dashboard
    and how far away
a car could take them from the need

to speak, or to answer, the key—
    in having the key—
and putting it in, and going.

NER/BLQ
(New England Review and Bread Loaf Quarterly)   STEPHEN DUNN

AUBADE

(After Philip Dacey)

To rise before the children rise,
before life as it gets lived
has begun, is to rise into the silence

of another time, is to think your children
safe in the half dark dawn,
the fog protective, the short morning
of childhood prolonged.

To start a fire before the children rise,
to open the blinds, break the eggs,
is to act-by-act
shed the night, the adult night
your children sense
and have slept through once again.

And when it's fully gone,
when all that's risen has moved
into niche or arc, after the wind
comes up, after the traffic starts,
you watch the children (stretching
toward what they must
and must not have) rise without alarm.

Painted Bride Quarterly　　　　　　STEPHEN DUNN

THE DONATION

The ten-car Interstate collision
has shucked me from the body.
My little heat ascends toward space,
and now, under the surgery theater
lights, they are lifting out my usable
parts to be reinstalled, to keep
some stranger going awhile.
Goodbye, old heart, old greased purple
fist. Keep slugging, just one more
inevitable rejection.
So long, kidneys, old beans.
Where you're going you'll find plenty
of work, plenty of dirty blood.
Look sharp now, eyes. I kept you dry
and open all those years, don't go
and cloud up on me now.
Honor our old bargain
with the sun. Remember the good pay
that came to us daily in gold and all
we had to do was wait—oh we waited
at high speed for that meeting.

Ploughshares　　　　　　EDISON DUPREE

SUMMER CARPENTER

At daybreak
I am beating nails

into plywood roof decking.
My hammer talks across the water
saying, "Good Morning! I am fine,
and alive and hammering this house
tightly together."
The saw below bites into new wood
and the resin smell of pine rises.
I stop to frown at my measuring tape
and call down the next cut.
I look out over the lake and smile,
knowing that there is something inside a man
that loves to put things together,
and knowing today that there is a joy
for me to fit and nail and glue.

Confrontation   WILLIAM DURBIN

ANGELUS

It's the metallic hour
when birds lose perfect pitch.
On a porch, three stories up,
against a copper window
facing the El,
a woman in a satin slip,
and the geraniums she waters,
turn to gold.

Beneath the street the blue clapper
of a switch swings in the tunnel.
Blocks away, a crescendo overtakes
its echo, and the reverberation
is passed between strangers.
Shadows quiver like sheet metal.
High heels pace off down a platform
like one hand on a piano.

There's a note struck every evening—
every evening held longer—
a clang only because it's surrounded by silence,
chimes of small change
from the newsstand, trousers
full of keys and dimes
flopped on a chair beside the bed,
the tink of bracelets
as her arm sweeps back her hair.

Poetry   STUART DYBEK

WAKE FOREST NURSING HOME: INTERVIEW
CLOYD, BORN 1893

As a carpenter, that's how I lost my eye.
A nail sprung up and jabbed right in.
That ws in . . . 1920 . . . I was twenty-seven.
I'd been home from the Great War nearly two years.
Here I'd been all through Aingland and France,
Been shot at and gassed, even got bayonetted
In my left leg by a Gerry. I kilt him, though.
I still gotta slight limp, but I got my life.
I come home to Louise as the war ended.
My uncle built barns and tobacco houses.
He learned me the carpentry trade and,
With the work regular, me and Louise lived right well.
I'd wake nights, for months after, though, from dreamin'
Of the tussle with the Gerry. Sometimes I'd see
His wife and kids standin' over me,
A knife in her hands, reachin' out to stab me,
Me pulling my bayonet outta his chest.
The little girl'd be screamin' and the wife
Rushed in on me, I'd feel that steel sink deep.
That's when I'd wake up screamin' myself.
After I lost my eye, the dreams stopped.
That mighta been the Lord's way of evening
The score. I took one o' his children in anger,
And he took one o' my eyes. I figure I paid.
I figure I'm right with the Lord.

The Sun   WAYNE EASON

SUN-MAKE

The sun, arising to a flawless day,
Shines on the right side of the vessels
Since the slight wind is from the north

And finds a strange single puff of clouds,
Bright white, at the far horizon to the south,
The only clouds in the perfect early day,

Making an astonishing effect not seen before.
For there across the water and on it
In perfect silence, stillness, long pause,

Is a gigantic mirror of clouds down on
The ocean, as if impossible to be there,
Immaculately great, statuesque and static.

In all the years he had seen this vast scene
This new phenomenon was astonishing, unique,
A mysterious new shape in the universe.

This puff of clouds, mirrored so far away
In a way that could not be imagined
Made for thought beside the morning blue ocean;

It was a system of light and distance so exquisite
He thought it should remain perfectly wordless,
Then the sky changed, he changed his mind, shaped this.

NER/BLQ
(New England Review and Bread Loaf Quarterly)   RICHARD EBERHART

HORNETS BY THE SILL

There is something about a hornet
That wants to get out. Though inside,
A marvel and danger to the guests,
Hornets do not fly wildly around the room

But persist in looking through the glass
As if it were not there, constrained
By they know not what, consternated,
Contending judgmentally for freedom.

I am free to watch their lack of progress.
It is Autumn. Soon it will be dead cold.
Winter will have defeated the hornets.
They want to get out of this perturbative room.

They do not know why they are acting in vain,
Desperate articulation, buzzing as if in pain.

Michigan Quarterly Review   RICHARD EBERHART

WHY THE SHAKERS DIDN'T WRITE POETRY

("All Beauty that has not a foundation in use,
soon grows distasteful and needs constant
replacement with something new.")
             —unidentified Shaker saying

I want to write a poem that ends:
I am wonderful. Love me.
A poem in which no one is raped, no one
dies in a Nazi oven, a poem that tries
to love everybody, knowing
it can't. It would be like you.
No plot, no big ending, and women
can walk out on it if they hear themselves
being turned to dust. I don't blame you
if you want to walk out. Want to?

Good. Let's go. Where we wish,
there we turn.

The world, for the Shakers, meant the nonbelievers.
The world for you means knowing
that somewhere a five-year-old boy is kept
on a locked ward where he bashes himself
off one wall and then another because
that's his way of loving himself. Pain
the only mother who would come back for him.
You would be another. Adopt him into the world,
let him be useful and something new; tell him,
Repeat after me: I am wonderful. Love me.

The Georgia Review   GARY EDDY

MARSH WALK

Flute trills, the yellowthroat dives
to the thick of the marsh.
Cattail fronds wave and feather in a throng.

I walk to clear my head,
receive the sacrament of morning,
put off what is owed me,
take long strides to forgetting.

With each month's delay
expectation dies in my throat, a song
caught in wind.

It is long between times.
Your voice no longer stirs the same chord.

I will believe only in these things
I touch and will be
touched only by these:

Dry crackle of rush.
Long wild wheat that hides
the bittern's nest; where bird
becomes grass, both are lost to sense.

Above me static plucks the line
like the feet of starlings.
The quiver of your voice tells me no more
than I need to know.

Blueline   SUSAN EDWARDS

ON THE OLYMPIC PENINSULA

(for Ruth McFarland)

Everything comes in pairs today . . .
a thin horizontal cloud
repeated in the white strip of surf . . .

a fisherman at one end of the beach,
another ahead at the rocky point . . .

and two of us, old college roommates
forty years later,
walking down the stretch of sand
with deep backdrop of driftwood,

making the footprints that will
show up in a photograph
as two long ellipses
coming parallel off the left side,
vanishing on the right toward
an invisible point of entry
from a strand landlocked in memory.

Crosscurrents   VIRGINIA EGERMEIER

AWAITING THE HARVEST

Out on the plains, for every
majestic silo rising out of the flat
fertile land, lifting its beautiful bounty
of wheat, corn, soybeans and rye
skyward like an offering to the sun,
the rain, the moon and stars,
another silo descends
into the black earth bearing
its harvest of fire.

Driving the prairie in high summer,
wind in my hair, the open highway
stretching ahead like a ripe field
awaiting the reaper, I have seen them.

Night after night, I see them:
armed, poised,
waiting.

Stone Country   W. D. EHRHART

THE NOBEL PRIZE

Today,
in accepting this prize,
I do so
not in my own name
but in the name of all those
who believed in me.
It is they
who truly deserve
this recognition.

Freedom of thought
is an ancient struggle
which only the heart can win.
Do you remember Pedro,
old teacher,
those rambles
which kept you
from playing cards with the mayor?
and that beadle
who always had
something inspirational to say?
And those miners
who accepted me,
a man who lives on the surface,
a stranger, uninvolved with
their subterranean lives?
They were the ones who,
in spite of myself,
prevented me
from burying my work!
For them,
this happiness.
For everyone,
this hope.

International Poetry Review   JOSE ELGARRESTA
—Translated from the Spanish
by Sara Heikoff Woehrlen

ASHES IN THE ADIRONDACK MOUNTAINS

Mist rises up the sides
of the mountain like breath
in cold weather.

The landscape arranges itself,
pictures in an album
that turn brown in my hands.

Picking up some earth, I watch
it make furrows on my fingers,
under my nails.

I shiver as I open the box
I carried here
to scatter my brother's remains
to the mountains, the wind.

My task completed, I become the last
of the family and
leave as the last truce of mist
disappears.

Crosscurrents   SUE SANIEL ELKIND

THE TIME IS RIGHT

When the things I'd
    rather not think about
        begin to outnumber those
I'd waste a little
    time on if I weren't so
        consumed by thinking
about what thoughts
    to avoid completely
the categories
    blur like droplets of
        water shifting
the patterns of dust
    on the window
        so that
nothing seems worth
    the effort except not
        thinking about anything

The time is right
    this afternoon's rain
        has thinned to a fine
mist
    the dripping
        from the eaves is slower
birdsongs are vibrating
    and I finally
        feel myself settle
into that deep silent
    thought I've been having
        for as long as I've lived

Passages North   DAVID ELLIOTT

MOOT POINT

Bringing you a handful of raspberries clinging
red to their bushes in the morning mist,
I've asked myself if they were worth the bringing.

It's someone else's thicket with a catbird singing
incomparably, from which I couldn't resist
bringing you a handful of raspberries. Clinging

to the rest, I dropped two spheres belonging
to you on the kitchen floor. Both were promptly lost.
I've asked myself if they were worth the bringing

since searching on the red inlaid I went banging
down upon them suddenly, injuring my wrist.
Bringing you a handful of raspberries clinging

to their bush resulted in a ticket and harangueing
on our way to the Clinic, for a red light missed.
I've asked myself if they were worth the bringing,

though I wanted to share the day's early ringing
out of sweet song and bounty. But why do I *persist,*
after bringing you a handful of raspberries stinging
us, in asking myself if they were worth the bringing?

The Piedmont Literary Review   ELAINE V. EMANS

SCENES FROM AN EXERCISE

The lake was much as he remembered it
from last week: yellow-headed blackbirds
blossomed on rushes, kricking,
and yellow-stamened water lilies preened.
Mallards paddled to his left,
and straight ahead the shore
was at peace with the sky.

A dragonfly ferried on his arm
while a loon, watching him, submerged,
leaving no ripples, only to reappear
farther away, laughing . . .

He was unaware of time—
and his wife called him twice
for dinner before he opened his eyes
in the next room, stepped off
his deluxe rower with its adjustable
hydraulic tension, its smooth flow,
and out of his dream.

America   ELAINE V. EMANS

THE TECHNOLOGY OF INSPIRATION

I am tired of the tundra of the mind,
where a few shabby thoughts hunker
around a shabby fire. All day from my window
I watch girls and boys hanging out
in the dark arcades of adolescent desire.

Tonight, everything is strict with cold,
the houses closed, the ice botched by skaters.
I am tired of saying things about the world,
and yet, sometimes, these streets are so
slick and bold they remind me of the wet

zinc bar at the Café Marseilles, and suddenly the sea
is green and lust is everywhere in a red cravate,

leaning on his walking stick and whispering,
I am a city, you are my pilgrim,
meet me this evening, Love, Pierre.

And so I have to get up and walk downstairs
just to make sure the city's still secure
in its leafless and wintery slime;
and it still is and yet somewhere on that
limitless, starlit sea-coast of my past,

Pierre's red tie burns like a small fire.
And all at once my heart stumbles like a
drunken sailor, and I, an ordinary woman,
am adrift in the *bel aujourd'hui* of Pittsburgh.

NER/BLQ
(The New England Review and Bread Loaf Quarterly)   LYNN EMANUEL

COME ON, TONIGHT LET'S HAVE FUN

Set the table,
My nymphet, my snare,
My twinge of remorse.
Let's lay upon the table
The tender shoot of your dalliance,
The ripe fruit of my torment,
The lavish tray of your spell,
My temptation's bitter voice,
The new wine of your passion,
The blood-red pomegranate of my desire.
Let's have some fun.

Webster Review   GEVORG EMIN
                          —Translated from the Armenian
                          by Martin Robbins

THE DARK ROOM

I don't need any vitamin A,
I don't need a lighter by Cartier,
I need no role, I need no gain,
I didn't order any champagne.

Do finally understand that I won't.
So don't.
Leave me alone.
Switch off the light.
Close the door and be gone.

I want no candles, I want no ice.
I have no need of your advice.

Take your roses under your arm,
I can do fine without your charm.

Do finally understand that I won't.
So don't.
Leave me alone.
Switch off the light.
Close the door and be gone.

Ah!   The dark room
is dark as blood.
At last!
That's better.
That's good.

New Letters   HANS MAGNUS ENZENSBERGER
—Translated from the German
by Felix Pollak and Reinhold Grimm

CYGNUS MUSICUS

Note the scale of tones that flies from a brass bugle
    and, trusting that Nature creates nothing in vain,
compare the horn's shape to the windpipe of a swan,
    that snaky tube of bony rings. You see
the bird's instrument is altogether equal
    to playing the music praised in antiquity:
those plaintive strains, a cello-like requiem
    murmuring through the reeds its prophetic sigh,
as death waves the swan toward asylum where
    no one may hear him sing, no other bird
break up the sacrament of his dying hymn.

Also in the windless glow of a sea-beach
    they sing before sunrise, says Oppian.
Pythagoras was so moved he began to teach
    that the poet's soul in death becomes a swan
so his divine harmony will not be lost.
    One night before Plato came to Socrates
the sage dreamed a swan hid in his breast;
    and hours from execution the swan sounded
to him like a joyous prophecy of the Good
    waiting for us there in the next kingdom,
and not some hyperbole of bestial dread.

Now it seems the swan's melodic gift is fading
    or one must be dead to hear it. I have stood
long hours by lakes and estuarine rivers
    and recall only a stridulous braying, though none
of my subjects was ever summoned by death,
    the singing master. I will go on straining
my ears in the twilight between hope and dread.
    I shall catch that mythic descant of the swan,

out of my senses at last to hear the singing,
    like a father who hears the voice of his lost son,
that supreme fantasia, the soul's returning.

The American Scholar   DANIEL MARK EPSTEIN

AND SO TO BED

To dinner we had Paul and Sam, my bosses,
and their young blonded wives (acquired lately,
at no small charge of alimony, losses
of stocks and children, both lamented greatly).
The trout was awful—thawed a bit and breaded.
Sam said he knew where corporately we're headed
(to hell, he thinks). Paul never says too much.
He drank almost two bottles of my best
French white bordeaux; I thought he looked a touch
green towards the end. His wife was tightly dressed,
skirt slit to the thigh (which, nudging against mine,
made me uncomfortable, what with the wine).
Michelle wore her blue denim suit, of course.
She looks less like a preppie than a horse
after a couple joints. I think she keeps
me back, of which Paul's drinking is a sign.
Then, much as always, after all departed,
she starts to strip. And here the poor tears started
(her fists curl up and shudder when she weeps).
I might have been gentler in what I said.
A final cigarette. And so to bed.

Ball State University Forum   RICHARD EPSTEIN

FIR TREE

The fir tree that couldn't stand up straight
is stretched out on the ground now.
I was tired of seeing it so dependent
upon a foot of clothesline to keep it upright,
the rope circling its skinny trunk
and tied to the iron railing of the porch.
I nursed it for five years.
It took just two minutes
to hack it down with a dull Boy Scout hatchet,
the children shouting "Timber!"
No longer on midwinter mornings
will I have to take the broom
and knock the heavy snow off its branches.
The weather will do it in for good, I thought,
wondering if I would really give a hoot.
What a humpback it was, what a drunken sailor.

I kept hoping that one more year
would make it strong enough
to grow the way it should grow.
But my patience ran out at last.
I found the hatchet behind the woodpile
and did the job as quickly as possible,
feeling sad and relieved at the same time.
"That was fun, Daddy," said my little son.
"Let's chop down another one."

Zone 3   DAVE ETTER

ISAAC

I sit in the light of my father's house.
All that's over, what went between us.
To be sacrificed, even the thought of it,
is insane, but we can live with anything—
change friends, desires, change what we covet
in our father's house, and live with anything.

In guilt there is no middle ground, in guilt
the mind revolves upon deception. Waste.

We went together to the sea and at the sea
watched sailboats tack a cold expanse.
The fact of life, he said, is that we change
each other, change, and never are the same.
Regard the shift and tend the sea
that each idea and man must cross alone.

Poetry   GEORGE EVANS

NE'ERDAY

(New Year's Day in Glasgow, Scotland)
"The houses are Glasgow, not the people—these
Are simply the food the houses live and grow on
Endlessley . . ."
                                        —Hugh McDiarmid

Urged on by the morning wind, legs suddenly
spastic, a small man with staring face
stumbles over the street and carefully climbs
the gutter. The Glasgow keelie welcomes the year
as he welcomes every week: swaddled in whisky.
The tenements yawn and traffic trickles onto
the street, past the shuttered pubs, the silent
bingo hall.
         Poetry hides in Glasgow:
behind the grey, graffitied walls, beneath

the black tarmacadam hills, under
the stares of incurious faces.
        Only a mile
from this window, soft green fields surround
dark pine woods. A river crashes over
falls, spills below a mossy bridge, and curves
to brown stillness. A castle's crumbling walls
look down from an overgrown sandstone escarpment;
the day that Scotland lost her Queen of Scots
is chiselled in granite. Beyond the river, over
the trees, the city stretches in sunlight toward
curving, snowcapped hills.
        And this, too, is Glasgow:
poetry down side streets, behind iron bars.

The Texas Review   JIM EWING

DEATH

(after an Egyptian poem of the Twelfth Dynasty)

Death, you are in my eyes today
as when a shattered man becomes whole,
as when, after a long illness, a man walks abroad

Death, you are in my eyes today
like the scent of myrrh drifting, clouding,
as when one crouches under the jib and the wind swells his sails

Death, you are in my eyes today,
like the odor of waterlilies, heavy and sweet,
as when one sprawls on the sliding banks of drunkenness

Death, you are in my eyes today,
as when one longs to see his house again
after a man has wasted years, decades, in captivity

Death, you are in my eyes today,
like the sudden unveiling of heaven,
as when one reaches a goal, great heights he never knew

Death, you are in my eyes today
like a well-beaten road,
as when one returns from the wars, home, home at last

Grand Street   ROBERT FAGLES

THE STRUCTURES OF EVERYDAY LIFE

In the shop's nave, where the wind bangs sheets
of tin against iron beams, barn sparrows
quarrel like old lovers. At five o'clock,
the lathes wind down from their long flight.
Black coils of steel loom from collecting bins.

In the washroom, photographs of wives and lovers
look down on the backs of men pale as shells.
Brown wrists and black hands lather and shine
in the light of one dim lamp, and blue shirts
hang like the stilled hands of a deaf-mute.

When the foreman sees his raw face in the mirror,
he turns away, shy as a young girl, sick of iron
and rust, the dead sun of the day's end. After
washing, his wet hair gleams in the open door
and he begins his dream of women in cool rooms.

Gusts seep through tin, making the thin music
the men live by. Drill pipe they scar knuckles on
clangs restless as planets on the rack outside.
The six-ton hoist drags its death chain. The sky
is a gray drum, a dull hunger only the plains know.

Like children at prayer, the men kneel to lace
their shoes, touching the worn heels of a life.
When they leave, the faces on their locker doors
turn back to darkness. Each man shoulders the sun,
carries it through the fields, the lighted streets.

The Hudson Review   B. H. FAIRCHILD

PORTRAIT OF MY FATHER AS A YOUNG MAN

(after Rilke)

The unbroken horse, all head, eyes like tunnels,
and you stand there laughing in chaps and bandana,
dangling a lariat with that light grace
only your hands held. Years later, at a lathe
among motes and shafts of light, those hands
flickered like fish, chrome handles spinning,
bit gleaming, biting in just deep enough
to hiss and make smoke wisps rise, while
your heavy body settled back in its deep
dream of success. You must have thought
of this: the skinny boy, all bones, standing
by the still unbroken stallion. Break life,
this picture said, marry, make sons and money.

The son who grew to see the lathes shut down
now holds the photograph in clumsy hands, searching
for the boy who broke horses for a dollar,
clowned in ten-gallon hats, laughed at failure.

Southern Poetry Review   B. H. FAIRCHILD

THE CHURCH ROAD LILAC BUSH

The best place to pick lilacs is on Church Road,
Across from the broken silo, the gray pile of the collapsed barn.
It used to be the Church's place. A colonnade of sugar maples
Still shades the drive, but the foundations have melted into green:
The ground ivy yearly softens the squared stone corners.
Lilacs roof and wall the empty space, their old branches gnarling
Into baroque twists, a thousand flowers foaming atop
The beautiful formlessness of leaves.
Of the corn once planted on the place,
Of acres marching single-mindedly into the sun,
Not a stalk remains. The soil gave out, or the sons left.
Their lilacs were always famous, though.
They couldn't say why: they'd toss a dishpan of water at the roots,
When they remembered, and hack off armloads for the parlor vases.
Nights, when they awoke, and lay listening to a flight of rain,
They almost understood the place,
When the scent of the drenched flowers seeped
Into their bedrooms, expanding slowly
Into the purple, the unexpected and gorgeous.

Blueline   SHERRY FAIRCHOK

THE PROTECTION OF DUST

(I have never allowed anyone to clean my studio, not
because I feared the disturbance of my work but because I have
always counted on the protection of the dust.)
                                                    —Picasso

Part of this year's dust is the spider
who came indoors last autumn
to spin her web. From her belly
she pulled a whole geography,
hollow forms of trapezoids and triangles
glued into the square join of two walls,
her world touching mine
at only four points.
It swung in cross-room drafts
like a suspension bridge,
and she clung to it like an engineer
trusting specifications above all else.
She starved
because the cold October air
had closed my windows to the beetles,
gnats and sow bugs that in summer
wander in. Her web broke
under the weight of dust,
her shriveled body fell. And then
the slow process of becoming dust,
flaking down from line to point.

Now the spring breeze stirs her fragments.
The broom whisks against the slick pine board
and the dust flies up
incorruptible.

The American Scholar   LAURA FARGAS

IN A CONFEDERATE CEMETERY

Dull, withered sorrow taunts my memory;
In autumn, under leaf-fall, echoes rage,
A lone wind moans a wandering monody
Which cannot soothe but seems a dirge of age
And mortal change. All death and dust now, name
On name, deep-lost beneath indifferent years;
Their valiant strength, and all their purple flame,
Ash of the ages now, far worlds and tears
Away. But here, and in my kindred heart,
Feeling in silence while the dark comes on,
Some residue of their old dream, their art
Of life, burns low and mourns a time long gone:
And mourns the death of memory, also,
The passing of time's wind on which we blow.

Voices International   WINIFRED HAMRICK FARRAR

CHAPEL

Rays of stained glass cross the floor to me.
The rope holds me back. Candles
in ancient holders tangle light.

Red and white roses renew guidebook wars.
Under the ornate gable of history
my mind shifts facts of a time gone by
to make room for more facts.

Rays of stained glass cross the floor to me,
and their momentum moves me from surface views
to the underlying sense of blessed quietness
where doubt is without existence and all
that matters is the sole, unspeakable event.

Plain and uncluttered, my heart at its steady
work of working out a perfect beat
sustains the high note of an ultimate motif.

The Christian Century   IDA FASEL

COUSIN NETTIE

All my life long
Cousin Nettie has come around
chewing people's ears off.
Truth is, she never stops to spit.
She's no chatterbox, she's a wind-up
Victrola that don't understand quit,
stone deaf when you try to work
one word in edgewise.

Plump and pretty, local Miss Italy
back there in the thirties,
she managed to get herself three good
husbands, who that clacking tongue sent
straight to purgatory. And glad
to go, I bet.

She's old, we're all old now.
Rigormortis has taken dead aim on
this family. Still and all, every day she
drags herself across the yard, comes on
over for coffee & complications, Frank says.
Last Tuesday, leaning in our
back doorway, she confides how
now, mornings, in the bathroom,
her only hope is
to cross her legs, and pray.

This is the first thing ever I've
asked her to repeat.

The Hiram Poetry Review   THOMAS FEENY

GROW! GROW! GROW!

*(News item: Researcher claims that taller children
perform better on intelligence tests.)*

The birth of computers created this craze
That glazes the eye with a glut of what seem
To be ream after ream of a high erudition,
While innate intuition suggests we debate
The dicta that state such enormous effusions
Of unsound conclusions.

The computer's astuter than many a tester,
Yet it gives the requester these odd correlations
And cryptic equations that fluently spout,
Beyond shadow of doubt, that if A exceeds B,
Then Y equals Z.

Thus here's a researcher, scholastic go-getter,
Finds higher is better, and taller is smarter.

The man's just a martyr to mountains of data
That urge him to state a new inference shaper.
And publish a paper.

The only decision we feel we can make
Is to know what's at stake because of this finding.
I keep on reminding myself to invest
(Play it close to the vest!) in some group that's in touch
With the selling of human growth hormone and such.

The Hollins Critic   ROBERT N. FEINSTEIN

MOWING

The neighbors are mowing their lawns today,
three of them—one to the back, another
to the left, and one across the street.

It is a modest neighborhood; some houses,
like mine, are peeling, others
have the neatness of retirement.

Democracy is in the grass: every yard
manicured to perfection every week.
Let it go too long and the neighbors

lean on the fence to remark, as to a mother
whose boy needs a haircut, Time for a trim,
isn't it? Getting a little shaggy here.

So there is always this rough music—duet,
quartet, trio as now—of power mowers growling,
an orchestra of our need to keep in control.

Painted Bride Quarterly   MARY FELL

AFTER SPOTSYLVANIA COURT HOUSE

I read the brown sentences of my great-grandfather,
As if—not even as if, but actually—
Looking into a brown photograph as old
As his writing is. In his sentences
Two innocent naked young men, Methodists,
Bathe in the morning in the Rapahannock River,
At Fredericksburg, Virginia, eighteen sixty-four.
Brother Pierson and I went out and bathed in the Rapahannock.
Returned to take our breakfast on coffee and bread.
I can see the young men bathing in those sentences,
And taking their breakfast, in the letter home.
We sat down on the clean grass, in the Garden;
Around us strawberries, cherries, gooseberries, currants
Were ripening, though not yet ready for use . . .

An unluxurious incense, intense, dry, pure,
Rises from this letter and from his life.
The morning air seemed to take up the song of our praise.
It is a wonderful honor to be here and to do good.
The river is flowing past the hospital,
Nearly as wide as the Delaware at Trenton,
And like it, shallow. I can see the young men walking
Through the early streets, on the way to the hospital,
With paper and jellies and clothing, all laden down.
The morning vapor is rising from the river.
There were about 200, some of them so young.
We wrote letters for them, bound up wounds, prepared
Delicacies. We prayed, and sang "A Charge to Keep."
The incense has the odor of old paper.

Contemporary New England Poetry   DAVID FERRY

MOVING FIRST

We pay the park fee,
drive into the late summer woods,
the trail coiling wide to narrow
around the hills.
We climb cement steps
to a wide-windowed castle.
Heat hovers over the table
where we eat our picnic lunch.
We marvel at the elk herd
running shy and free.
Later, I look for a restroom, am told
"Down that hill—the little castle."
The path long, winding,
no voices, no movement
among the damp leaves.
I hesitate, push oak-heavy door.
In the dim light, porcelain gleams.
I move one more step—
wrapped around the toilet
like a ribbon
a copperhead tilts his jaw,
             waits for each footfall
                      —the slant of light—
We lock eyes

I move first

Helicon Nine   CRYSTAL M. FIELD

STATION MUSIC

I wanted to crawl into it, become the bird of that music,
and float like white feathers in the dark subway station.
I wanted to plant myself like a sincere kiss from red lips
on the forehead of that strange woman who listened, in a long
black coat, in wet boots. I wanted the week to come to a calm end,
harming no one, like a road that ends in soft, orange leaves.
I wanted to be a calloused finger easing a few slow notes from that
seductive sax, or pulling a few taut strings. I wanted to miss the next train
and keep on listening, the music climbing the poles of the station,
infecting my feet, circling like a bee above a hammock—it was summer,
make no mistake, it was slow and summer, it was syrup bubbling,
thick grass blowing, it was all this in their lips and fingers,
it was the weaving of the sax and strings, like a hand in fur,
like a fur coat bristling, like a woman in black fur sitting down
to a white table, licking a spoon loaded with raspberries,
like a red fox alert in a field of snow, like a field that goes on a while,
in its own rhythm, a field that resolves beyond the barn, like hay
stacked neatly, like good hay aging, like farm boys growing strong,
a low whistle late in the afternoon, the feeding done, the hunger
rising in their bellies, their tough hands washed under warm water—
it was their day, they made their mark, and now this music,
far from them, this train to take us home, the long way in it.

Poetry   ELLIOT FIGMAN

GARAGE ORGANIST

While the Volkswagen weathers the seasons,
the church organ is parked inside.
He calls it his great whore and is not afraid
to spend his time and money on her.
Each time I visit, a change: pipes
stored in attic, others taken
down again (more range), wires revein
the floor, jigsaws of wood lie
with sawdust over fading grease spots.
For the third time this year, he breaks her
down, rebuilds, extends the garage, plays
fugues from Bach that ring in her pipes.
Once, long after his fingers stopped,
he swore he could hear her breathe, pumped
up, waiting to play cathedrals.

Visions   FRANK FINALE

T IS FOR *TAILOR*

You step up to his mirror
and you are transformed

into the world's most elegant customer.
  He screws up his hand behind your back
  and pounds of ungainly excess paunch
drop from you, as though they were your tucked-up hems
  let down. Deliciously he runs his palms

    along your body, smoothing
      down your rump, pumping
up your chest until it bulges through the seams
  in your old self's shirt. Slyly he slips
  you down to the naked truth. He lays
out brand new skin for you to try on, a nice
  set of muscles, a much better face.

    You must admit that you look splendid
      in it, and take it.
He sews you up in it, deftly trimming away
  the ugliness, tucking in snips of flesh
  to make it fit. Only intimate friends
will ever see the stiches that crisscross your sides,
  the delicate suntan-colored threads.

The Hiram Poetry Review   ROGER FINCH

LIZ MOVES US AGAIN

Another cold front storm soaks
the basement, leaving the stains
you can't erase before some
new stranger examines the floor.
Our departure sign has stood
two months in the yard; the house
groans, self-conscious, tilts
its good side toward the street;
near the shade corner the paint
peels where the water enters.

Nothing is different, we know,
than the last time we sold.
Four years, and out; four years, and out:
we might be a first family
watching returns, though this summer
you're saying the next rooms
are the end, that we're building
because you plan to die there.

So many flaws in these used houses.
You spend hours cleaning, and
I watch your face in the morning
when I'm leaving you in sleep;
and it seems to me you're right
this time to be pushing dust,

whispers of possessions fading from
the windows where they've spent the night.

And though this house may not forgive us,
its doors will still lock, its lights
will still throw themselves into the dark
where our blood will settle while you stare back
and tell me those constellations are ours.

Poets On   GARY FINCKE

THE DREAM OF HORSES

How familiar they are in the light of our dreams,
these huge fluent horses, dray and nameless.
Their eyes follow ours,
their skins ripple with flies and independence
unless we speak to them gently in recognition, as we would
the child of a friend dead

a long time. Once they were born
our equals, our legs and flesh
in the fields and roads, hitched to our hauls
by bit and sweat and necessity. Now
they are art—speed, stud, steeplechase—
or separate—statuary on show, luxuries of the rich—
or children's pets, or broken into glue, or eaten—
tintypes faded into history,
superfluous,
abandoned.

And yet they stand still, waiting,
ears swiveling to our voices, and we
stroke each knob of spine like braille,
trying to remember.
Their souls are their backs,
souls of our responsibility and design,
ghost-ribs of a ship where we rode and rocked.
And now the moon shaves light into silver
and they are great hulls, broken and spectral,
rising from the mind's black water
like the chipped eyes of wild creatures
gathered, for now, in a safe place.

Blueline   JEANNE FINLEY

SOUTH OF THE BORDER

(El Salvador, 1982)

Our game plan called for "even-
handed" diplomacy, but the password

was *hands-on*: we were going in
as healers, and salvation

was the ticket. As Americans,
we had a stake in the country.
The fact that we had only the vaguest
notion concerning our continental
neighbors created in us no sense

of urgency. We had a heritage:
Columbus had discovered the Indians
on his first try. When the political
climate took a swing, we would be

ready. And we were beginning
to like the sound of the word *junta*
—thoroughly masculine. We could handle
a whole nation of dirt farmers,
sorcerers, ancestor worshippers,

bossa nova dancers. We understood
enough about *guerrillas* to dictate
a book. We were going in deep, calling
the signals.

New Letters   CHARLES FISHMAN

THE DURATION

Ten minutes out of Harrisburg Depot
heading southeast on US-PA 83,
I spotted them.

The Greyhound rumbled across the Steelton Bridge
and there to the left out the dusty window
they stood in the distance.
I could see only two of the massive concrete cylinders
until we rounded the bend,
and there were all three.

Three Mile Island
jutting above the maple trees
sat under a cloudy, smoky sky.
Just downwind of the plant,
patches of farmland along the Susquehanna River
were spattered with lilacs and cows grazing the meadows.

Off Exit 13 in Newberrytown
trucks lined up at Reese's Diesel Fuel Stop
and the Robin Hood Restaurant.
A boy knelt painting an American flag
across the entire roof of Rutter Brothers Dairy.

Nestled in the Susquehanna beside Highway 83,
TMI stands waiting.

America   PEG FLAHIVE

CONCERTO NO. 2 IN A FLAT MAJOR

(John Field—1782 Ireland; 1837 Moscow)

In the poor doldrums of the day
The shuffling sails hung empty until John Field
Blew music toward them, and suddenly
They glided upon the ides of night,
And where he cast his anchors down, the moon
Could still look at the sun,
And I at once fell into the arms
Of my old love. There we thrived
In listening and delight.
As the first theme in exquisite isolation
Loosed from its violin, we implored,
Quickly come, and not too soon the second
Slid with delicate outcry on its mate,
And both, it seemed, stretched out
Their necks with water-weeds hung,
While on your right hand, mariner,
Burned the North Sea.

If this be not major music, live with it
a little while, live with it in the arms
Of your old love. The ache of gladness can draw tears
And make great memories of minor things
Such as the melodious tide let fall
And the rippling shore revealed.

In death be aware of us, sad Irishman,
    Once, having need of joy,
    We both made much of you, John Field.

The Paris Review   HILDEGARDE FLANNER

CHILD BURIAL

I was ashamed to think of anything
while the others remained blank with formality
and sorrow, but the casket looked small
as a lunch pail left behind at a picnic ground.
A breeze lifted my hair, a swirling
I enjoyed when riding carousel horses.
Our circle was immovable and closed,
a severe crescent stiff as snowfence.
To show respect, I chose the frozen posture
I learned at school when lining up

for vaccinations. I shivered as the family
stared, measuring my size and seeking features,
for somehow I resembled what was lost
and my presence suggested a queer rivalry.
It was difficult to keep still
as the day walked on, the shellacked box mirrored
swooping birds, the whole world spinning on it.
It must have been the hour when I daydreamed
in class because I could not follow
the relentless algebra of stones, dull rows
like chalkboards repeating a hard lesson.
I preferred the hot house lillies
which smelled like Karo and candle-drippings.
Then I tracked a distant cloud, a grey funnel
of rain which dangled like a stocking miles away,
but I did not look again at death or see
what it saw about me.
The priest closed his book upon a snowy tassel,
white as the glare of that moody winter, white
as silk bunting I'd seen at the mortuary.
It was not the same color as those ponies,
polished for summer and tethered
nose to tail like all the days ahead.

Poetry   MARIA FLOOK

HALLEY'S COMET

I envied the muscled arms of the older boys
who controlled the deafening buzz and spin
of the gas-powered model planes that whirled

each Saturday above a Bronx Park field—
up and down, restrained by two thin wires
predictably through orbits around those boys'

firm grips and concentrating stares. Weak-limbed
and amazed, I doubted I'd ever wake
like them to a universe where I stood like the sun.

Afternoons, corralled in the children's section
of the Mosholu Branch, I thumbed picture-
book astronomies and took in every page

as fact: Jupiter's miscounted moons, Saturn's unique
artglass rings, domed bases by the nineties
in cool Venusian valleys. And yet I kept faith

with one: that ominous Bayeux rocket stitched
above King Harold's crown, that certain
wonder, whose sky-length tresses in a photo from 1910

I never forgot. Even crouching like a hamster
once a week in Saint Brendan's School,
assured by nuns that desks could protect

against imploding glass, that a coat
furring me from head to toe could shield
my skin from radiation, that prayers mouthed

in stifling air would save me
for this world as surely as my miraculous
medal would save me for the next—even then I

never doubted the covenant we had.
Such scarred dreams have brought me
to this starred night, here where pines

and birches ring a meadow's open eye.
Tonight I know the world is straining
in darkness, puzzling at this predicted light.

I hold it in the glasses' circle, a wanderer
among the ancient gods and heroes—a fizzling squib,
slowly abrading in the black, like a meager promise

vengefully kept. When I lower my arms
and turn to walk back by flashlight, I am amazed
at how easy it was to let it go.

The Nation   RICHARD FOERSTER

THERE'S SOMETHING LEFT
OUT IN THE RAIN

When I sleep in strange houses, and it rains,
I rise up from my bed and stare,
bewildered, out the dark twilled windows.
There's something left out in the rain,
I say, but I can't remember what it is.
I can't remember, but something in my memory
rusts or shines or sinks into the earth,
lost now, but still of great importance.
A baseball glove, a shoe, a book or a tool,
a gift, once upon a time, owned
and forgotten. But more than this,
some ancestral awe of water. Floods.
Lost land. Precarious shelter. The rain
spins off the leaves of trees, the bark,
corners of strangers' homes and barns.
Or slides down the rails and steps
of fire escapes, dark as spears.
The axe? The fence posts? What?
What is it that worries me, half-recalled
from another life? Something long ago familiar
about the grasses drenched in risen drops,
the sparrows stretching dry their wings,
insects emerging from between cleaned stones—
the ancient rains that made them.

I don't know what it is at the eroding edge of mind
that sticks there like a summer-swollen door;
but the rain stops, and, while I sleep,
the wet world evaporates in slow inaudible sighs.

Yankee   ALICE B. FOGEL

I LIKE, AT RANDOM . . .

I like, at random, to wander among walls
Of ancient times and, as darkness thickens
Beneath a laurel tree by a rough fountain,
To remember, with heavy eyelids, sieges and battles.

In the morning I like, with iron tongs
And lightweight nails, to seek the tight-fitting piece
Where gears engage, or the cushion ambushing
The axle, and take off smoothly down the asphalt.

And climb mountain passes, follow shady valleys,
Furiously conquer fords. O new-born world!
I also like a linden tree's soft shadow,

The ancient museums, the faded madonnas,
And today's extreme painting! A naive sudden impulse.
The new inflames me and I'm in love with the old.

Seneca Review   J. V. FOIX
                                 —Translated from the Catalan
                                      by David H. Rosenthal

STILL LIFE WITH DIFFIDENCE

That still life painting on my friend's wall
looks like a decoration. It isn't art.
How often I've seen it, fading to neutral
like the draperies, an upholstery of the mind.
And yet the brush painted it with care,
a care, even a love for the thing itself,
believing that neatness and attention to detail count
like clean kitchens, sanitary bathrooms,
well ironed clothes, and supper ready
for you when you want it.

Anonymous fruit
peacefully overflowing the stiff bowl,
you've never demanded very much from the viewer.
You and that green, or was it brown, bottle
didn't push back the aesthetic boundaries
or reach new heights in artistry.
You've not been searing, riveting, gripping,

compelling, commanding, or domineering.
You compliment the furnishings.
You are patient with children.
I think you are art after all.

Event   ERIC FOLSOM

THERE ARE NO BELLS IN THIS HOUSE

There are no bells in this house.
Only the big bell of night—
We hear the moon ring.
You will know no bells here,
Only the bell-shaped blossoms
Of the snowdrop, though their shape
Is one of prayer, not song.
There are no bells in this house,
Or at least not the bell
You strained to hear. There are
No bells here, though your words
Strike like notes and your hand
Moves across the page like a bell
Swinging. There are no bells, I
Tell you, though the snowdrops' praying
Broke a big bell, shattering
The irretrievable note of winter.
There are no bells in this house,
But all the bells are beating—
The moon gong pounding roundness
Into roundness, the night shaking,
And the snowdrops' deafness
Sounding whiteness hooded onto
Whiteness—now all the bells
Are battering and the snowdrops'
Deafness is poured into the moon's
Roundness. But there are no bells here.
Only the moon drunk on its own whiteness.
Only the snowdrops drowsy in snow.
Just the sentence wagging loose, off.

Poet Lore   JAY BRADFORD FOWLER, JR.

ARS MORIENDI

The self-destructive may be
onto something, but too soon.
One day only is a good
day to die, and must be
awaited like revelation,
or the cessation of a

headache. Suffering is
part of the diagram, a
side-effect of birth,
the creator of nervous
systems and gods. Those
who escape its tutelage
float in a void of idiot
comforts and uncertainties,
as dead to the world as
the poet lost too long in
poetry. One must feel
along the edge of existence
to know its true outlines,
or to welcome the unexpected
transports beyond when they
one day, surely, must come.

Southern Humanities Review   RUSSELL T. FOWLER

PENELOPE GARDENING

Soon I'll be finished weaving ivy,
and the new vines
will be patterned and sufficient.
Arc will balance angle.
Green will bare
only in suggestion
the comely white
of painted steel.
Sunlight will wax the leaves
rainfall has cleansed.
My trellis will not need me
and I'll be freed
to obligation.
Soon—
unless tonight
another storm unties my bracings
and batters my poor branches
out of balance.
Unless tonight
another shoot
grows willful out of pattern.
Unless tonight
I dream
a whole new possibility
of order.

Poetry   SUSAN FOX

RACCOONS

They run single file from the henhouse
Where a beam of light weakens and dissolves
Into dark; the five hunchbacked forms eject
Like prowlers from a house within a dream.
The impeccable creekside manners,
The mask and tail, the carcasses pitiful
On morning pavement, all the paraphernalia
Of our affections now are lost,
Sheared from mind as we discover
How raccoons have come to dine on chicken.
The family, treed, at last illumined
In a perfect blend with
Slippery elm, presents us with an obstacle:
What to do. Hang a charm? Recite a spell?
Drill them with a .22?
The dog yelps from his chain,
Eager to dispose of these, our pioneers,
Returned to abduct our laying hens,
To hear the echo of our curses—
Or perhaps just to ease their young blood's
Hunger. No time to be soft or mystical,
I say. And yet, this midsummer night of
Starry solitude appears as distant
From a killing
As Parisian opera from a frontier brawl.
Creature populations
Have hit their yearly peak. Funny,
How this moment that I grasp fits snugly
To the midway mark of man's allotted time,
How it coincides with the cycle of a year
Beginning its slide toward winter
And the second half of life, and how
It reminds me of our child whose birth
Is nearly due. Yes, we shall leave erosion
To the cars that strike with light,
To disease and natural accident,
To the company of hunters—our closest
Neighbor scored three dozen coon last season
With assistance from his hound. Raccoons,
That we lure from woods with the strut
Of banty hens and chicks, beware
Of the dog huffing at your tree and
Barking at your moves till dawn.

Buffalo Spree   WALT FRANKLIN

THE LAUGHTER OF BOYS

The laughter of boys lights up after school
on the black asphalt parking lot

near my apartment picture window.
It is the cackle of a bonfire, but a fire
that crackles over a stack of green logs,
a sound that comes from so far in
I can't remember when it left.
And when I watch the boys
flick lit matches at each other
and dodge the bites of the yellow-blue flames
that hiss out on the ground like innocence,
I think of my life as burning toward an end.
But it is their laughter vibrating the glass
which I want to take back inside me.
It is the restlessness of being young.
If I could laugh in the company of myself
and not feel that other person inside me
holding his breath, saying *Be careful,*
don't embarrass yourself, then I might turn away
from the fatherly whistle that splits up the boys
like sparks and not watch them cup matchlight
under their chins, each a ghostly mask
bobbing home, dimming out as boys do.

The Iowa Review   JAMES FRAZEE

CHIAROSCURO

In the summer haze
the stick people
of the neo-primitives
are shadows of us all.

Sartre spent his life
as a whittler, rocking
on the front porch
of his perception.
Consciousness is intentional,
he wrote, and a sliver
of light sailed to
the floor beside his feet.

Now the chair continues
to sway, but no one
is there, and his shadow
is in retreat.

Crosscurrents   PAUL FREIDINGER

MURDER OF A POEM

Like wave energy
Strong as seaweed

Like far off music
Held in a shell

I tortured it
On jagged reefs

Pounded it to death
With stones

I buried the wild sweet thing
in the crossroads

Scattered six white roses
Over the grave

Because I like conclusions.

Crosscurrents   DOROTHY FRIEDMAN

STREET SIGNS

Today I come to the corner of Summit
and Westminster too late. The white roses,
having chased each other up and over the
limestone wall, lie shredded in the grass.
A caterpillar hunkers down in his cocoon
and across the scene, cottonwood fluff
drifts down like movie credits.

Yesterday, on the corner of Summit
and Westminster, I came too early.
The streets were being washed,
trees lined the fences, and a chipmunk,
with a face like a jasper stone, waited
at the mouth of his hole.

But once, I remember, on a corner
much like Summit and Westminster—
girls jumping rope, boys in the street
playing stickball, and suddenly, the thwack
of the rubber ball, the high hovering loop
of the fly: the children, arms slack, eyes up,
caught in the hung instant—the single
loop stitch flung gleaming before them, that
knitting back into itself creates the design—
and I, woven even as I stood, into the pattern
they would tell their children of.

Puerto Del Sol   ALICE FRIMAN

THE WHISPERING GEESE

Because we know it's only a matter of time
before the whispering geese reach the end of the river,

their webs inextricable from the vast
platform of blazing ice, wings raised
in a suggestion of escape,
we imagine the sounds they make make sense,
could we listen in the right way.
If we stopped and thought *death* with no hope
to gather into one whole or fragmented message,
the secret sense of several hundred
geese plummeting to the hard rock
bottom of the falls, each in its own spotlight
of ice, the crashing tonnage
of water would drown their noise.
So though we don't know what it means,
we listen as if to prayers to the
epitaph of the geese, shh, shh.

Kansas Quarterly   CAROL FROST

THE SINGER OF MANOA STREET

Reading Isaac Singer, I spring back
into my Jewish body. I take notes
on my left palm in a strange script,
although I recognize the word "onions"
and also "strategic demons." From somewhere
a gust of wind passes through me;
it smells like exalted soup. Shall I sew
a yellow Star of David onto each of my
aloha shirts?
                    Clearly, I must stop
reading Singer. One short work of his
seems enough to bring God's absence
into my room. Soon, while I am alone,
someone will look into my mirror who isn't me.
I remember my father, my mother,
my wife, all well-rested in the soil
of our American republic. These memories
are scarcely ideas.
                    It is too late
to put the book down. I'll go on
in my short pants, the nice fat boy still,
walking the streets of Honolulu,
observing how little remains
of my past. Each year there is less,
each year a fresh body of knowledge
moves through my blood and says,
"I'm home now. Just let me sleep."

Of course Singer is not to blame,
his job is telling stories. If I feel
more Jewish, it is personal, not too serious:

what I feel these days is like
last night's half moon. But I still won't sign
the Covenant, which chose me so eugenically—
"You're a Jew, kid. Don't chase after shiksas."
I'll think more about Jehovah, Who knows everything,
and also about how sly and careless nature is.

The Chariton Review   GENE FRUMKIN

THE WOMEN WHO CLEAN FISH

The women who clean fish are all named Rose
or Grace. They wake up close to the water,
damp and dreamy beneath white sheets,
thinking of white beaches.

It is always humid where they work.
Under plastic aprons, their breasts
foam and bubble. They wear old clothes
because the smell will never go.

On the floor, chlorine.
On the window, dry streams left by gulls.
When tourists come to watch them
working over belts of cod and hake,
they don't look up.

They stand above the gutter. When the belt starts,
they pack the bodies in, ten per box,
their tails crisscrossed as if in sacrament.
The dead fish fall compliantly.

It is the iridescent scales that stick,
clinging to cheek and wrist,
lighting up hours later in a dark room.

The packers say they feel orange spawn
between their fingers, the smell of themselves
more like salt than peach.

Contemporary New England Poets   ERICA FUNKHOUSER

PAIRS

An antique lady in a long black dress
sits on the sunlit porch selling her socks,
telling little boys to make a fist,
knowing somehow if the heel just meets the
toe the pair will fit . . .
A shy old man living alone
two doors down from grandmother's house,
breathes out air through his tufted nostrils,

says as I share his steps one glowworm night
that the Chinese army is a horde so vast if all
its soldiers two by two started to pass
me by that very minute I'd be dead and
gone when the last ones came.

Shadowy lady, spellbinding sir,
this dreaming manchild clings to you,
heals your solitudes,
weds your subtle magicalities:
those endless soldiers reappear,
after all these years they're marching still,
marching, marching in their stocking feet.

America   JOSEPH GALLAGHER

THE APPLE TREES

They look twisted
because
they draw fruit from under earth
into the air,
and this overthrowing
of gravity needs
the shotputter's backward
crouch, every bulge
concentrating on
the pure form of the sphere,
even those knots around the eyes
that have to meet the grimace of January
face to face, that have to endure
the leaves letting go one by
one as their body-sails learn
the updrafts. So what if,
in the journey from root hair to branch,
the fruit passes through
knees and elbows and comes out
gnarled, unbalanced, nodal,
moon-dragged all one way? Don't those
tears in the heart of each apple
resolve to try it again,
over and over?

The Georgia Review   BRENDAN GALVIN

COMING INTO HIS SHOP FROM A BRIGHT AFTERNOON

Like a local flurry or stars too small to use that spilled, iron
filings stain the dirt floor silver.

       In the center of the floor,

the forge, in the center of the forge, the rose the bellows angers.

He lights a cigarette on rose colored steel, then hammers the
steel over the anvil's snout.
                              Red sprays of sparks splash from
each strike.
               One gummy fly-specked window begins to allow a
sprawl of wrenches, brushes, punches, chisels, taps, gouges . . .

Coalsmell.
        Sweat.
               The distant blue his eyes are.
                                        There is a lathe
and milling machine, both homemade from scraps.
                                        He chooses a
lighter hammer.
               Now I can read the names on varnish cans and see
how the walls are layered under sawblades, snowshoes, an airplane
propeller, a loom.
                On the other side of the door at my back, the
light I came in from grows white like a blizzard or hot steel.

Hammer blows ring across the meadow too much like bells.
                                              He is
shaping a piece of earth.
               He is hammering it into what he wants.

He thrusts it back into the fire when it loses its blush.

The Iowa Review   JAMES GALVIN

SPRING, SATURDAY SUBURBIA

        The frenzied coupling of dogs, tireless wasps
        Chewing out the flat gray stuff of nests,
        Squirrels running like cats on fire
        Through oak and pine.

        It is that time and I have been watching it come.

        Next door, the neighbor is mowing his lawn
        As the one behind plays hero, slashing his boxwood
        Into flat and square defenses.
        Again, the mockingbirds drag sticks and string
        To hang their home inside my chimney top.
        The lucky male swings over one hind leg
        And the dogs cling and watch, end to end, primeval.

        The laugh of a child, then two, or more,
        Comes lightly on a wind that smells of dogwood
        Until the smoke of charcoal claims the air.
        Stubborn wasps hum and dodge my hand.
        And then the dogs drop apart, fall flat,
        Tongue-tired and empty on the ground.

For it is that time, again,
and I have been watching it come.

Kansas Quarterly   STEPHEN GARDNER

RAIN TO ROSES

From clean tight hospital
whiteness
my Irish Catholic mother-in-law
held my cold Protestant hands
and asked if I'd brought
my squash racquet.
She drifted in and out
of her self, and then
there was no sign of breathing.
The long arm of the clock
snapped forward; she lurched
awake and smiled, "It's not over
till the fat lady sings!"

My blue Air Force jacket
and Larry's dark glasses
disappeared the day we buried her:
Mom took just what she needed
for the flight to heaven.
She's up there smiling
in her macho outfit,
humming through the clouds
bringing rain to roses.
Thunder is God guffawing
at her jokes.

Orphic Lute   DAVID GARRISON

BREAKFAST SYMPHONY

Faster and faster the rhythmic groaning
of bedsprings
and a counterpoint of birdlike cries
tell me the upstairs neighbors
are making up last night's quarrel.
While coffee grounds spurt
into the glass dome of the percolator,
I whistle Beethoven's "Ode to Joy"
and, spoon in hand, conduct
an orchestra of thousands.

Midwest Poetry Magazine   DAVID GARRISON

SUMMER HASTE

On the map just an inch
from Boston, Martha's
Vineyard lay hidden in
dense fog. No planes today.

The bus wound around
like kite string
kinking at cottages
and mail stops till

lights dimmed inside
and most slept or left
us altogether. Now, Dot
and I stood in Woods Hole

watching red tail lights
fade into darkness.
The one bulb kiosk showed
a bench and our luggage.

Then the slow and even
tones of fog's brawny
horn had us
surrounded.

Tar River Poetry   TOM GAY

SAFE PLACES

Corners, for example. Corners
Of kitchens, in particular.
Or closets, behind the line
Of overcoats and jackets
Wrapped in cleaner's plastic.
In bed, quilt up to the neck.
Better even—under. Wherever
Doors are locked, double-locked,
Bolted. Windows barred. Drapes
Drawn. Walls covered with cork.
All the mirrors shrouded
With starched white sheets.

The Literary Review   PAUL GENEGA

PINS AND WHEELS: A METAPHYSICAL

Do stones in the crystal chambers of their souls
Move without meaning in their molecules?
Do even the smallest, the insignificant least—
Like dust on the tusk of the most revolting beast—

Detect in the flesh of the invisible
A sense of purpose?
                          If souls have knees that kneel,
And stones have brains that calculate the cost
Of energy, then even the busy flea—
Vastly underrated by the cat—
Plays a part in a delicate balancing act:
The pins and wheels that keep the world afloat.

Now when I feel the pitch and tilt of an ark
That I have been riding too lightly in the dark,
I praise the water flowing under my feet.

Studia Mystica   DAVID GEORGE

BEAUTY

Sometimes unexpectedly, unbidden,
Beauty comes. Not a downpouring of doves,
Not a Venus, sheathed in an ivory shell,
Not even the lenses of Stonehenge in its season—
Stones aligned to catch the sun as it moves
Mystically, majestically, through holes
And crevices.
                          Not even these spectaculars—
The light against the dark, the white ecstatic,
Stars falling and setting the sky on fire—
Take possession, or let the moment take
The horse high over the hedge with an unseen rider.

It comes when least expected, when the dark
Opens a crack to let light filter in—
A word, a look, a sudden realization.

Plains Poetry Journal   DAVID GEORGE

LOVE LYRIC

If I do not touch your flesh tonight,
     It will leave my spirit tattered
     Like a tendon stretched too tight.
Love's emblems? Might as well be funeral flowers
For all the pain I've had from being yours.
     Judge: is so much torment due me?
     Quench my fever, cure me, cool me—
     Wavering here, locked out and shattered.

New Letters   STEFAN GEORGE
                                        —*Translated from the German*
                                        by Peter Viereck

WOMEN AT FORTY

Women at forty wear their skin
like phases of the moon, like
crescents of pleasure bent to catch
all angles of light: the slippery
solstice, the fragile truce of noon.

Fresh from sleep, they are assured
that yesterday's paleness was but a sag
of light, an inconsequent fading.
They wear their fullness conscious
of its snagged regrets, the lines
that web around the blooming.

Women at forty afford the dark side.
As the womb grows tighter,
they learn the shift in the lover's eye,
his taste for firmer flesh,
the secrets he is still avoiding:
again and again, they've kissed the skull
beneath the lover's grin, know
as surely as they know his thrust,
that what is full will soon be waning.

When sadness comes, women at forty
go without fear to a shuttered room,
bless themselves, bed down believing
that each effacement is but a rest,
a teasing dark before they ride again,
pushing the clouds from their right-of-way,
pulling the sea behind them.

The Georgia Review   SONIA GERNES

EXISTENTIAL

Morning, & I'm taking notes.
The squirrels are at it
again. Someone has wound
them up, they go round &
round the tree trunk, playing
hide & seek, then sit on
their haunches like rapt
petitioners. There are dogs
in this neighborhood that
visit the same hydrants every
day of their lives; it is one
of their purposes, they dote
on it. The birds keep talking.

If you watch long enough, it's
just such activity that

causes the nausea to rise
like sap, as in Sartre's novel.
All that existence thrusting
itself forward, the fabric
falling apart, as when, at a
concert, suddenly, without
warning, the scene dissolves
into madness: 50 penguins saw-
ing away at boxes of old wood &
catgut, the applause like
water, the death of cellophane.

There are no answers, only
the same questions written in
lemon juice & held up, upside
down, to the mirror. Only the
names pasted like labels.
This is the hardest.
The spaces between words are
infinite; being itself
slips through them. And now,
late as usual, my neighbor
runs for her bus. It will
carry her to the city—
one small face among millions.

Kansas Quarterly   ROBERT GHIRADELLA

HOMESTEAD PARK

It's 1956. My father
Is wearing his suede jacket
And short-brimmed hat.
We are going for a walk.
The joints of the willow
Are budding, the sumac
Already have that smell
Like old paint in a can.
Because I am only ten,
I notice that his shoes
Are just the same as ones
He wears to work,
Only scuffed-up and older.
He is telling me about
My mother sitting in the sun.
Her teeth are like the flesh
Of lobsters! The sky is blue.
I think about the office
Where he works, humming
With its great white
Refrigerators, freezers

Filled with plastic food.
Because I am only ten,
The world is as it should be.
My father's jacket is brown
As his shoes, the skin
Inside the sycamores is green.
When my father tells me
The names of the trees
And the meanings of the names
He uses, he is like the face
Of the rock wall jutting
From the woods above us.
In my dreams the shadow
Of the valley runs down here
Along the edge of the creek.
But today, bright Saturday,
With my father beside me,
The sky spreads its branches.
The woods go back as far
As our house. Everyone
I know is still alive.

The Hiram Poetry Review   ROBERT GIBB

THE GARDENER

So thick a summer man as one
of snow, he stands stock-still
in the garden

and startles me, as I pass
on the dusty street, with
his odd murmuring. I see

bare feet, drooping belly,
torn pants, for an instant
stare into dull eyes,

then quickly look away,
too late to erase the shock
of that moist mouth,

as if I'd touched
an alien life that might
reach out and know me

against my will. But his hands
placed the strings where morning glories
scale like reckless lovers,

his breath inspires the trumpets
of the yellow squash, the strawberries'
red-toothed mesh.

And isn't it towards him
the sunflower's great insect eye
turns, over the chicken-wire fence,
for counsel, for radiance?

Contemporary New England Poetry   CELIA GILBERT

AFTER THANKSGIVING

Lord, as Rilke says, the year bears down toward winter, past
the purification of the trees, the darkened brook.
Only 4:45, and the sky's sheer black
clasps two clear planets and a skinny moon
as we drive quietly home from the airport,
the last kid gone.

The time of preparation's over, the time of
harvesting the seed, the husk, the kernel, saving
what can be saved—weaves of sun like
rags of old flannel, provident peach stones,
pies, pickles, berry wines to
hold the sweetness for a few more months.

Now the mountains will settle into their old
cold habits, now the white
birch bones will rise
like all those thoughts we've tried to repress:
madness of the solstice, phosphorescent
logic that rules the fifteen-hour night!

Our children, gorged, encouraged, have taken off
in tiny shuddering planes. Plump with stuffing,
we too hurry away, holding hands, holding on.
Soon it'll be January, soon snow will
shuffle down, cold feathers, swathing us in
inches of white silence—

and the ways of the ice
will be narrow, delicate.

Poetry   SANDRA M. GILBERT

SOMETIMES WE THROW THINGS
IN THE CAR, FAST

and take off, hurt, mad, kissing it all good-bye.
Most of us, maybe, have done that. I knew a woman once
threw an ice bucket, ten sweatshirts, and her high school
annual in the car, ripped out of the driveway spitting
gravel and didn't pull over until she heard a lone
killdeer cry on a farmer's fence post. I loved that woman.
I loved her crooked toes and her sweet seven-grain

bread fresh from the oven, and I loved the good fit
the front of my knees made with the backs of hers.
And much more. But she took off. I know why

she grabbed the sweatshirts, winter or summer
that's almost all she wears, and the ice bucket
(a gift from her maiden Aunt Jelly) she used for
cattails, her favorite quote flowers. But why that ugly
purple annual I'll never know—remembering high school
made her wince and shudder, and the annual's pompous
name, *Veritas*, she hated. The truth is, I don't know
if a killdeer stopped her or not. I only know
she likes their lonesome song, so every time
I hear one I imagine she had to stop. Maybe afraid
she also picked up the annual, read some gems

her classmates had penned in blues and greens
beside their pictures—as she did for me
one New Year's Eve when we polished off a bottle of cognac
in front of the fire, remembering things—remember the swell
times in Mr. Six's World Lit, and stay as sweet as you are,
and good luck next year with your fabulous modeling career!
The modeling line gave her the giggles—made her say Wow,
that was close. Then she read something that made her say Oh.
and shake her head. Little Timmy Noonan, she said, touching
his small jerky script. I saw it. You are perfect, he wrote,

and appeared to wish he could disappear through his collar.
Maybe she didn't read the annual. Maybe she just looked
at some black cattle standing at ease in the pasture,
their moony eyes slowly turning to face her. No,
that's awful. The crooked silo full of holes and all
those swallows perched around the rim like wicked spitcurls
are no good either. Little Timmy Noonan never
knew her, she said. No one did. She left. And jerky
words, moony cattle, silos, or listening hard
to birds calling up their own worlds
beside the road—none of that will bring her back.

The Georgia Review   GARY GILDNER

LOS ANGELES AFTER THE RAIN

Back home again on one of those bright mornings
when the city wakes to find itself anew.
The smog gone, the thundering storm
blown out to sea, birds
frantic in their joyous cacophony, and the mountains,
so long invisible in haze,
newly risen with the sun.

It is a morning snatched from Paradise,
a vision of the desert brought to flower—

of Eve standing in her nakedness,
immortal Adam drunk with all
the gaudy colors of the world,
and each taste and touch, each
astounding pleasure still waiting to be named.

The city stirs and stretches
like a young man waking after love.
Sunlight stroking the skin and the
promiscuous wind whispering
"Seize the moment. Surrender to the air's
irrefutable embrace. Trust me that today
even seduction may lead to love."

Too many voices overhead. Too many scents
commingle in the stark perfume
of green winter freshened by the rain.
This is no morning for decisions.
A day to ditch responsibility, look up
old friends and dream
of quiet love, impossible resolutions.

The Hudson Review   DANA GIOIA

FOR JOE WEAVER IN MINNEAPOLIS

I've heard that in the office
where we worked most of our friends
have quit, left for other jobs,
other towns. New people now
are sitting at the same desks, the faces
different, the company the same.
Hard to imagine these strangers
picking up the lives we left—
and no one noticing.

There is no one to go back to now—
only the still white lakes
circled by birch trees, the silent
riverways, the ashen
winter sky. The somber, prosperous
suburbs of Minnesota
set like a checkerboard of leafless avenues
and overheated homes. The snow
already settled on your grave.

So why return? Why search through
the present—when I already have
what I would look for? The memories
of August, of our walks beside
the bright lakes and river pathways,
unconcerned with winter, and of you

standing with your back turned toward me
facing the empty sky, looking up
into the infinite, inhuman blue.

Boulevard   DANA GIOIA

FLYING OVER CLOUDS

No earthly image—only clouds,
affluent clouds, seen from high above,
still bright at the approach of evening.

Soft valleys hidden in a snowdrift,
waterfalls of ice and air,
not whiteness but a dream of whiteness,
an innocence one may have felt
on earth—but only for a moment,

waking unexpectedly at dawn
one winter morning after a storm
to find the shabby blacktopped streets
immaculate in sunlight, glossed
by deep smooth banks of snow, before
the earliest car or footfall.
                              So strange,
this world the ancients never saw,
and yet their words now come to mind:
nimbus, cirrus, cumuli,
magic names to summon all
the scattered elements of air.

O paradise beyond the glass,
beyond our touch, cast and recast,
shifting in wind. Delicate world
of air too thin to breathe, of cold
beyond endurance.
                              And nothingness
that mirrors our desire—not of death
but of your fluent oblivion,
of insubstantial dusk and dawn,
your whiteness burning in the sun.

The plane flies westward, gaining time.
The dark recedes—and up ahead
the sky is cloudless, clear, and bright.

The Paris Review   DANA GIOIA

THE END OF A SEASON

I wanted to tell you how I walked tonight
down the hillside to the lake

after the storm had blown away
and say how everything suddenly seemed so clear
against the sparkling, rain-soaked streets
cold and bright as starlight.

I wanted to wake you up, despite the hour,
and drag you out into the dark
crisp air to feel the end of winter,
the cold we cursed so long
slipping away—and suddenly so precious
now that it was leaving.

But there is no one to come back to now—
only the night, its wind and rain, the chill
magnificence of its borrowed light,
the touch of this impossible season.

The Hudson Review   DANA GIOIA

DANCING LESSONS

Still brooding on the beat,
the needle scratching through each afternoon,
I remember how I sideswiped
the waltz and the hipsprung rhumbas, circling
like a crab with a clubfoot;
and how the hulking girls I pushed around
reeked of roses and sour milk.

Even now I can feel the way my ankles
sank in those slow shoes
when Miss Fahrenheit—too tall, too tan,
too beautiful to be
anyone's mother—first posed against me
and forced my stammering feet
into the blocked maze of a foxtrot.

By whose law was I pressed
to those ballroom drills, those lessons
in civilized desire, as if
my soles grinding through the grit
must pivot to a point serene
as the look on a dustmaid's face that moment when
the count grunts down behind her?

But outside those heavy hours holding up the dead,
I learned at last
what steps I had to take, moved by menace
and the moans of low women,
as all day the radio shook loose my dreams
and gave my body back to me
in a swagger of snares and dirty saxophones.

Poetry   ELTON GLASER

NIGHTWATCH

After we have talked over the voyages of our day,
prows pushing the waves of our separate worlds,

and after we have lowered the jib and main,
talking of the children, how their small boats

float or flounder in the night, then, if the hour
is not too late, there may be time to talk of things

that pass by like a storm in the currents of the sea
or cling like the gulls that follow our ship for days;

a question, perhaps, pointing toward some uncharted
corner on the compass of our lives, or a thought

that needs trimming, the tensions of conversation.
Sometimes, in the lantern's light, you'll read aloud

a line from a book, a lyrical chord like the waves
that keep us humble before the sea.

Then, again, the press of things, the preparations:
You for early rising when, coffee cup in hand,

you'll watch the sun break through that line
of trees to the east, and I to my papers until

the morning lark or dove lets me know it is time
myself to sleep, lie next to you in the bed,

bring the chill night air under the sheets.
You call out from sleep to check the doors,

the stove, the children—reminders that even
in this part of the night we are still near

sea winds we can't ignore lest some fear,
lurking like a large fish beneath the surface,

waits to swamp us in surprise. Then back,
with reassurances, to the room where

our breathing, slow and steady, rises
like waves in quiet communion before dawn.

Poem   MICHAEL S. GLASER

FOG

Driving the interstate in night fog, I know
only the white line on the right, and I cleave
to it like one of the faithful clinging
to a rattler and talking him into lordly
peace. I glance in the rearview mirror
hoping to see fog parting behind me, leaving

a patch of road visible to assure me
my course is true. I see only light,
nebulous as moonlight behind cloud cover,
and then two lights bearing down
and veering left as the truck
lurches, rumbles past me, rocking me
in a backwash of thunderheads. I scan right,
weaving in search of the shoulder, the slice
of paint pulling me down curves
no map knows, blind and trusting
at a reckless rate of fifty. The road
leans right and I hug the line, sailing
into the gray fog, and then catch
sight off the white V on my left spreading
away from me as I lurch and dip
onto an exit ramp I didn't want to take.

Poets On   MALCOLM GLASS

RED TIDE, A BEACH OF SALVAGE

A search plane splits the even light above the dune-vines—
blackened ones and the ones that bloom—
and toward the gulf, radios are crackling, trash blowing,
the rowed bodies primped and oiled regardless,
stylized eyes, the great waves' red blindness
wholly self-absorbed, bringing in the soaked wood
and sunfish, sloughing them off like scales. All night
it had risen through the half-dreamed sea,
thrashing at the ear's root that would be sleep,
blooming in the phosphorescent rows of breakers,
exploding the ripped cups and tow-sacks,
flailing them empty because there is no filling.

Half-bloated, barefoot, someone staggers off
into the blazed red cells, gull-shit,
scraps of the fat hand's waste the tide-lash saved,
and twists a cigarette cool, as if to plant it.
A few bathers are watching from the rows of closed eyes,
are nodding off, bellies shining,
the static dimming in a hundred separate sleeps.
Into the blackness of their eyelids, imaginary swimmers

in their future bodies are floating out
golden, wholly radiant on the surface of a steaming sea,
their pale, oiled arms burning steadily,
buoying them up through their sleep, even the hot breeze
rich at the salt heart's core, safe as vice,
as the day's heat comes down through their darkness.

Poetry   GREG GLAZNER

GIFT

Suppose I could finally look
at your leaving
as a strange favor.
The way MacLeish might have
when Hemingway left him
out on a sand bar off Key West,
letting him sweat it out
for five hours,
the tide rising to his neck,
a quick lesson in direction,
all points inland from there.

Say that I, unlike MacLeish,
could call it
an act of love, an unlocking
in key-broken waters.
And that I could even overlook
the fact that you never
came back to pick me up.

We wait and wait for our lives
and, when we finally notice
they've arrived,
we are up to our necks
in their going.

Say it's a gift, then,
to know what it is to be left
to my own craft, no boat
but the rowing, the hard
rowing back toward the unbroken
word of the shore.

Poets On   KATHI GLEASON

TO A WOMAN IN AN ELEVATOR

Have you ever seen
a Clark's Nutcracker, a bird
of the Cascades, drop within inches
of your outstretched arm before flapping off
to a pine branch? Even with the elbowroom
of divorce, I hesitate. If our hands
brushed, would it take long

before we hit the mattress,
this slow-motion striptease
that passes for love
in the weightless morality
of passion? Hesitancy is
a kind of sainthood. As in

other rooms, the rose-
petaled wallpaper in its cheapened
bloom, someone scraping off
make-up and flushing the toilet,
I've waited. Hesitancy is
a kind of friction, the wrong-way rub
of time.
        Oh yes,
I've waited too long for a door to slide open,
for someone to enter and welcome me
with the insides of her arms.

In an odd way
it is a marriage: falling
silently like this to the bottom
in a small room with a stranger.

Michigan Quarterly Review   JOHN E. GLOWNEY

A QUESTION OF AESTHETICS

He never wrote a letter without
the words "despair" or "terror"
as in, "Even as a child I knew
despair," or, "How to turn
this terror into art." How romantic
it seemed then, like living
a Russian novel. His final note
read, "Tell her our relationship
was fully satisfying in every way."

No one ever says how thrilling
pain is, how it takes you like
a lover, how your body cringes
before surrender. At first
you cry no, no, then swoon
into its burly arms. You should see
your open mouth, your breath coming
in harsh gasps. Trust pain to find
the choicest part, the marrow,
and suck out resolve, leaving you
limp. But oh, how you'll sleep.

The only burden heavier than pain
is boredom, want of danger. When I
teach *Anna Karenina* to young girls,
I say, "Every woman should experience
one disastrous love affair and survive."
How like a woman Anna was, to hesitate
because she could not bear to throw
her red purse away. How like a man
he was to put a bullet some place deadly.

As a woman who's survived, I see boredom
now as comfort, devotion as something
precious, and death in any form,
a slap across the face.

The American Scholar   BARBARA GOLDBERG

INSULT FROM A GYNECOLOGIST

Legs pulled, split into a Sunday wishbone,
I slide forward at the nurse's request
closer to the end, wondering
if anyone ever slipped
too far, over the edge
in the spirit of cooperation.
Trained in origami
or Maypole, she weaves a sheet
in and out my curves and corners,
until I am a table draped in white damask
ready to receive guests. Here
there are no candles. A penlight
will do. Long-awaited visitor

enters the room, his hands washed clean
as silverware and other narrow instruments.
He lowers himself to a chrome stool.
Like a union man bellying up to the bar,
he wheels in closer, finally arrives
at the banquet. I peek through
the open traingle my legs form
to catch him in the act of yawning.

The Chattahoochee Review   JUDY GOLDMAN

SARAH, EMILY

there must be no wrinkles,
things must be kept neat.
Sarah smoothes the sheets over
and over herself. her body
in the bed barely shows.
it is how she has always lived,
learning to sink
into the background.
the others were the ones
who made decisions.

she calls her daughter
by the name of her oldest sister,
long dead now, asks about

horses, have they been fed.
Emily says, *yes*,
Yes, it's all right,
when it's not.
Sarah is dying.
her fingers pick at
something in the air.
Emily reaches up,
closes her mother's hands
inside hers, like a locket.
it's all right, she says again,
all the machinery of language
gearing down to those words
of love, of departure.

Prism International   LEONA GOM

FIELDS IN WINTER

On a clear day, early,
You can see the pattern laid out,
But not as a man sees it.
You see white muslin, white thread.

Field after field, crazy-quilt
With all its corners meeting
Miraculously: you can see
The pattern laid out under snow,

But not as a man sees it.
He will think bales and bushels,
But you will think colors:
Corn-green, timothy, green ryegrass,

And how many years it took
To piece it together, seam it
Tight across the hillside
With its stichery of stone.

Contemporary New England Poetry   J. B. GOODENOUGH

INHERITORS

What is in the house,
Beloveds, I shall destroy:
Burn my balls of string;
Smash my blue crockery
On the kitchen's stone floor;

I shall slit the bedding,
My dears; empty
Curtains out windows;

Overturn drawers
Into fireplaces.

The house itself, my darlings,
And the barn, and the two sheds—
I shall set fire to them
One of these days,
When I am ready.

Then there shall be only
Ashes and burnt grass
And my own bad-tempered ghost
For my heirs
To quarrel over.

The Spoon River Quarterly   J. B. GOODENOUGH

CLIMBING MT. ISRAEL

The woods road, lined with sugar maples,
dwindles to a track. I pick
my way across a brook,
all purpose and joyless
proceeding. Who will miss me
if I don't return?
Great rocks lie where water
spilled them, a nightmare
of what's possible. Fieldstone
walls draw lines across
the land, rigorous as fear.
The accident is more real
than the perfect day.
I want to pause, to quit,
but there on the path above
sunlight promises a view.
Others can do, can do, can do.
Then there's a flower, dropped
on the trail, pink, like a voice
from nowhere, pines that screen
the sky. I remember a tree
still up and leaning, eaten
by woodpeckers, the high note
played by creaking trunk,
the applause of leaves. Legs
do my work, become steady.
Age, death, suspicioning,
away! Knees take the shocks
on the down hill. Thighs,
carry me up. Step over
tree roots, brake

against gravity. Go marching
while the arms and shoulders sway.

Contemporary New England Poetry   MIRIAM GOODMAN

CHOICE

So many crutches:
Adjectives, nouns, verbs,
Adverbs, interjections,
Waiting for me to lean on.

I choose
The dictionary of the heart.

Crosscurrents   RYAH TUMARKIN GOODMAN

FOUND

I fell in love today with a freckled-faced
    perfect love, namely my big brother.
He mends my broken dolly and buys me vanilla
    ice cream and takes me to the movies.

Today I really fell in love. My Mom.
    Hard to believe she has been here all along.
She is loving and always understands me.
    I can tell her everything and she listens.

I fell in love today with the only man I'll
    trust, my father, who used to be the
enemy. He calls me his little adorable girl.
    Helps me in all things and is strong.

Today I fell in real love, romantic love.
    My first boyfriend, who looks like a movie star.
When he carries my books and holds my hand,
    I think my heart will surely burst from joy.

I fell in love today. I mean powerful, all consuming.
    This is what all those books told about love.
I also spent all of today in bed with my lover.
    Passion is truly what makes the world go round.

Today I grew up and fell in love with my intended.
    How could I ever have thought of love before?
We spoke our vows together. This will be forever.
    We trust, adore, worship and love each other.

I fell in love today. Completely, head over
    heels in love with a black-haired angel.
Our first born son. A magical gift of love.
    There is no other love like this in the world.

Today I have not had time to even think of the concept
    called love. Too busy cooking, cleaning, caring,
driving, planning, worrying, teaching to even dream
    about love. This is after all a practical world.

I fell in love today. For the last and final time.
    My spouse left, saying he was in love with another.
My children flew away saying they had to seek
    their own true loves. My friends are loving new lovers.
I fell in love today. I fell in love forever with MYSELF.

The Hollins Critic   LENORE J. GORDON-FERKIN

THE DISCIPLINE

This driver, wearing his visor cap, his thick gloves,
steps down from the bus, into the blowing fog;
tries to attach the trolley head into the wire up above.

In the beginning, a contact; there is a crackle, a whir,
flashes of blue fire, then the head, like a live thing,
breaks loose, sways back and forth, back and forth,
like a goose beak, or recalcitrant snake.

Four, five times, the failure repeats itself,
but the driver is infinitely patient.
The power is up there, waiting,
he knows eventually the head will lock in the spot.
It is destined.

Event   ELIZABETH GOURLAY

ROUGH AIR

A mile into the sky our plane is
practically nothing. This turbulence
of air—also nothing, like the loose cells
that float within the eye.
Connecticut rolls and pitches below—
Einstein was right, mistrusting his own feet,
and so was Bishop Berkeley, for a plane
glinting unseen among leaden clouds,
droning toward the Atlantic unheard,
is no plane at all, a trick of wind
or blood fevering in the ears.

I'd say to the earth, *look up;* I'd say
to myself, *look down*—but this ride
across nothing rouses the nothingness
in my belly, as the country below
turns to propellor-whipped gray froth.

I'd say we have no fear worth mentioning—
we are a mile above and far below
the parallel lines of time. Instead, I grip
your hand and conjure our bed,
its landscape of tossed sheets, weather
of our mornings there with light diffusing
through venetian blinds—parallel lines that meet.

Ploughshares   DAVID GRAHAM

W.C.W. IN THE SOUTH

There I am, high atop the rockers,
Chiffarobes and convict-striped pallets
Piled atop the chugging Reo truck just like the Joads,
For god's sake, only my daddy is hopping jobs
Again and I read through my thick spectacles a sign,
Jesus Saves, as my mother screams, "Any fool
Would have insured it! Goddlemighty, Worth,
Are you ever going to learn?" And I read a sign,
Where Will You Spend Eternity,
As my mother sobs, "How do you think I feel,
Trailing off every Sundy while you suck
That stinking pipe?" and I nod, because I
Am a little sunbeam for God, and I read a sign,
Speed On Brother Hell Ain't Half Full,
As a Studebaker as old as our Reo
Lurches out in front of us from a caliche farm road
And my daddy swears softly, veers left, recovers, chugs on,
As my mother screams and sobs and screams
And the rain begins to bucket down upon us
Like a tall cow letting her fadookie fly
All over flat rocks, and I see a flock
Of drenched chickens in the pouring rain, and I see
Preoccupied farmers on outraged mules
Lolloping through the fields beside us as we chug, chug, chug
Onward to the answer to all these questions.

The Malahat Review   PATRICK WORTH GRAY

RAIN

I sit behind sheer curtains watching it rain.
Houseplants with dark, red leaves line my sill.
A wet cow snorts steam in the field.
I am very old,
And my eyes are tired from watching so much rain.
I half hear the call of evening in the black hearts of trees.
In the darkening kitchen the pears on my pantry are slowly
    turning blue.

Southern Humanities Review   JAN GRAY

ARS POETICA: LESSONS IN BREAD BAKING

Daughter, the shape you seek lies hidden in
the dough. Women before you have sought
the smooth form, the light rising. The secret
begins with your ingredients—soft wheat
nurtured by summer rains, ripened in autumn's
slow sun, or hard winter wheat pushed through
soil grown cold; yeast bubbling in the bowl where warm
water caresses it; honey or sugar,

something sweet to bind the flour and
encourage yeast to grow. Others you choose—
butter, eggs, milk, raw grain. But go carefully.
Too many mingle until the loaf is
neither rye nor pumpernickel nor
plain wholesome whole wheat. Bread cannot be hurried.
Allow time for each new element to
sink within the mix, to spread its cells

among others until there is no longer
flour, yeast, liquid, but merely dough. Your reward
is in shaping the loaf. Now there is substance
for your touch, sticky strands you flour and
mold into a long loaf or twist into
intricate braids, their secret execution
grown easy for your practiced fingers.
For baking, you need only patience to

allow the heat its work; that and
a good nose so you take up the loaf just
when the aroma fills your kitchen.
The finished bread you tie in a bag
and carry to neighbors. Back home, you search
cupboards of your mind for fresh
ingredients to bake into new loaves,
gifts you hunger to give the world.

Confrontation   CONNIE J. GREEN

THE FLYING DUTCHMAN

Look closer if his feet seem
to touch earth. A filament
barbed into his wide skull,
singing like an aeolian harp
in the wind, leads to his ship
there in the clouds, or perhaps
that cloud itself lifts his heels
clear.
        I confess mine are brown,
calloused, rough. A boy, I used

to push pins through the thickness,
but his are soft as eyelids, blue
veined like breasts inviting kisses.

St. Andrews Review   WILLIAM H. GREEN

STANDING IN THE DOORWAY

monday morning and the world is overwrought
from saying goodbye to sunday. 'goodbye,
sunday, goodbye': as if it no longer knows
how to say anything else; and there's still
the whole rest of the week to say goodbye to,
easier of course, sunday's like that lover
you just want to lie around with forever,
while the rest of the week's a seedy bill
collector: pay the cash, slam the door, good-
bye! ah, what a way to live when either way
it all ends up with that same goddamned word: goodbye.
such a paucity of vocabulary! such a crime
against 'the supple mathematics of language'
not to be able to turn things around, right,
not to be able to set the week in reverse,
not to be able to speak all things backwards,
which is, perhaps, what only a poem can do,
which is maybe the only thing a poem is for:
allowing all those weeks to reopen their doors.

The Ohio Review   ALVIN GREENBERG

BOOK OF HOURS

Mercati's "Virgo" from the *Book of Hours*
is an angel standing in a blue sky,
a museum poster tacked above our bed.
Her wings, waist and arms
connect a system of yellow stars.

If Mercati could have seen
the sky under our half-pulled shade,
he might never have believed in angels.
When reddened by the city
the sky is a wall

only the strongest stars puncture:
the ram, the bull, and the twins
fall out of circulation
like a bowl full of pennies on the dresser,
while our hearts

send up lone signals
to the dead space in our room.

Under the poster we lie in tandem,
or one of us awake
kisses the other sleeping.

The newsboy biking from house to house
tosses *The Post* against the dark steps
and wakes every bird inside a magnolia,
black eyes shining
like holes inside a hole.

Yankee   JEFFREY GREENE

OUR FATHER WHO ART ON THIRD

*("After all, he said to himself, it is probably
only insomnia. Many must have it.")*
        —"A Clean, Well-Lighted Place"

I stopped praying years ago, learned how
to think instead of love, or the icy mountains before
death, green fields beyond. Now I need
a quiet god, not to make the heart rattle,
a golf ball in a cup. Baseball fits best,
almost as if designed in sleep: the pickoff, brush
back, squeeze, suicide squeeze, stealing. It's no
heaven—it's here: slick skin and stitches of the ball
in hand reminding me of Ebba St. Claire, Atlanta
Cracker catcher built like crossed tree, showing us
how to throw, the ball an egg in the knotted
roots of his fingers. If he never made it, how
can we? Yet I wear before sleep the welts
and wrinkles of a glove, dream hand, grip the bone
handle of a Louisville Slugger, slap clay
from my spikes and go toward the dark as to
home, playing for the bunt, the sacrifice.

Poetry   WILLIAM GREENWAY

PART OF ME WANTING EVERYTHING TO LIVE

This New England kind of love reminds me
of the potted chrysanthemum my husband
gave me. I cared for it faithfully,
turning the pot a quarter turn each day
as it sat by the window until the blosoms
hung with broken necks on the dry stems.
Cut off the dead parts and watched
green leaves begin, new buds open.
Thinking the chrysanthemum would not die
unless I forced it to. The new flowers

were smaller and smaller, resembling
little eyes awake and alone in the dark.
I was offended by the lessening,
by the cheap renewal. By a going on
that gradually left the important behind.
But now it's different. I want the large
and near, and endings more final. If it must
be winter, let it be absolutely winter.

The Paris Review   LINDA GREGG

YOU TRY

every now and then
the mexican girl i met
on the beach north of san diego
comes into my dreams

she holds her face
in her hands and sobs
nothing comforts her

the sun is setting
as pretty as a postcard
but that does not help

porpoises are leaping
one after another
in the golden water
but that does not help

i offer her a hat
full of perfect shells
but that does not help

this is frustrating

she is just the kind of girl
you hope would visit your dreams
every now and then

but i have yet to find anything
that will make her smile

you try

America   DANIEL GREGO

THE COMING DAY

Up as usual in the dark.
An invisible woman starts to patch the day together
On a snow-quilt in front of my window.
A solid geometry of housefronts

Stiffens to attention; fledged pelts of hemlock
And spruce darken; dollops of snow grow to gleaming
On yew bushes and the rhododendron. The shadow
Of the paper-boy passes, his sack dangling
Like the seed-bag of some dawn-striding
Nineteenth-century farmer whose head swells with
Revolution. Moonwhite the garden lightens
And the moon, a peeled clove of garlic, pales.
The day quickens cold on my face when I open the door
To let the cat out and see the small explosion
Of snow in the child's raised hand who stands
Across the street with his brother, waiting
For the school bus. Every particle a seed
Of light. A bluejay bristles on the fence; his
Harsh anarchic screech rattles morning. Like old
Hand-tinted photographs, the world is taking shape
Out there: beige, olive-drab, bleached rust
On a sepia ground of air, the houses fatten. The trees
Grow shaggy dark, smoke-green, ricepaper white
With a faint flesh tinge of pink, and every second
Something changes colour, texture, shape, and words
Can't stop them. What are those old iron leaders
Thinking, I wonder, who lie awake at the walled-in
Heart of things in the big world, grizzled infants
Of history who strain to catch that dim murmur
Behind the centuries of wax in their ears. Do they
Imagine their own heartbeats? Does light go
Only to show them the whites of their eyes?
In Derrylin the mourners, more and more of them,
Creep between burnt-out schoolbuses and the dripping
February hedges, their coffins cocked and
At the ready. There is no going back. This minute
The undercover gardens on Wing Road grow cold
And bright. My nightshade cat scratches to come in
From the chill. The day opens before me its blank page.

Poetry   EAMON GRENNAN

LOTTERY

(for Naomi Shihab Nye)

Because she seemed interested,
and her dark felt hat was tilted back
like a confident wager,
I was trying to get across
to this Central American
woman how our North American system
of gambling works, mostly
the state-wide type: Pick-The-Right-Numbers-
And-Be-A-Millionaire-For-Life.
It's just blind chance, I was telling her.
I said it's the luck of the draw.

Oh, she said, in a kind of Spanish
that picked through empty pockets, like when
some soldiers come suddenly at night
through a village, with the soft pad
of animals, as though night
grew red eyes weaving from the jungle
where reality has become
altered, overruled,
and the first person who hears them
wakens, cries out slightly,
stirs their attention
so that they turn to that hut first
and throw open the shaky door—
but are the welcome soldiers
her whole village waited for, and knows;
so this person sighs,
offers the one with the worst uniform
a drink, a cigarette, some talk, whispers
Good Luck, hums her child back to sleep.

Yeah, I said, it's just like that.

Passages North   MICHAEL GREGORY

DAISY BUCHANAN, 1983

The estate a mile away and long since sold,
The garden ploughed and the house now level ground,
She supposes just the bay remains the same
And knows that even it has changed; boats, like cars, exist
As smaller crafts of pleasure now, and in the mist
That hides Connecticut, tankers oil the Sound.
In the dayroom, as the other patients play some game—
Coarser women, whose breasts (she notes) droop low—
She glances to her lap and finds she holds
The careless, weekly hand of her daughter in her hand,
Whose face is the earnest annoying white of the moon.
The window admits a shaft of sunlight and
She's warm (though she would never let them know);
She half-remembers certain green and linen afternoons.

She remembers well one green and linen afternoon—
It must have been last summer—when
They let her stay in bed till twelve, and then
Left her in the sun on the home's front lawn; soon
She felt supremely comfortable, iced-tea in one hand,
Watching the traffic light on Western Street
Turn like a leaf from green to yellow, red to green again.
The breeze felt pleasant and the drink was sweet.
But that was years ago. Or days, whatever.
When Pammy wheels her to her room the sun, spun gold,
Gleams east into her eyes; an orchid on the bedstand

Bends like a butler to greet her, with his single purple vein.
She thinks, I am an orchid. No, a craft of pleasure.
The estate was years ago. It's long since sold.

The Iowa Review   DAVID GROFF

THE CREEK

"Crik," they call it here,
changing the vowel, dropping the *ee*,
the high-pitched sound as sharp to the ear
as a kingfisher's screech
racing his shadow over the creek
on a hot June day.

From the bridge I watch my son
knee-deep in the Illinois silt
hunting for crawdads.
He really loves
this muddy water, each cloudy step,
the crayfish like crabs.

Just in his teens,
his new voice cracks as he calls
to his friend upstream,
the two of them laughing, cussing,
not knowing I'm here, words
I've never heard him use before.

Looking down at the water
swirl by the pilings, I remember
those fights with my father,
how startled he seemed
the first time I swore,
wondering suddenly who I was.

And now, in spite of myself,
when I yell at my son,
I want to know just who I am:
my father's voice
by some ventriloquist's trick
come back on its own.

I turn toward the house,
my son out of sight upstream,
only his voice flowing down
riding the current like a reflection,
his laughter over the water fading away,
some dirty joke I wish he'd tell me.

Farmer's Market   BRUCE GUERNSEY

THE BARN

Ankle deep in the sweet smell, I watched
from beneath the loft's ledge—a sanctuary
of mystery to me where sun filtered through
cracks in the tin roof. I knew Uncle climbed
up the ladder, three or four rough pine slats
nailed to cedar posts, and then disappeared
momentarily.

The sun hung in the crevices of his face as he
reappeared standing above me. His ragged frame
seemed to move within the soft overalls—
without even disturbing the material—
as he pulled the heavy bales to the edge and
slung them over by the twine. The mules stood
silent to the muffled thud as it landed.

In spring, when I asked to come up, I was told
snakes might be in the hay and in summer the
hornets would sting. This winter day I was just told
no. Instead, I leaned over the trough polished smooth
by the mules' necks to spread out a bale left over
from yesterday. It came off in neat squares the size
of sofa cushions.

The dented pail hung on a nail within my reach—
opening the hinged lid, a musty dust rose out of the
oat bin that filled my eyes and nose. I ran bare fingers
through the heap and remembered: it had been a good year.
Uncle had said not to walk directly behind them—
"Swing out far enough so a leg can't get you if one
was to swing out—they have to see you out the corner
of their eye."

These are good things to know, I've decided—eyes know,
but the truth is in the telling.

The Texas Review   JO GULLEDGE

FROM THE M.P.'S OFFICE

The letter
is from my Member of Parliament,
its address so personal.
"Dear Friend," it begins,
"I hope you have enjoyed your summer."

Actually, Mr. Whatever-your-xeroxed-signature says,
I'm not your friend;
I did not vote for you;
I did not enjoy my summer.
You see, I am not one of your percentages
which fell since last September;

I do not hold one of the 19,000 jobs
you claim to have created;
I have not exported anything in the first half of 1985; and
I am not a manufacturing shipment up by 12.7%.
I would gladly accept your invitation
and view the showhome you opened—
I want a healthier, more quiet, better insulated home—
except I can't afford to buy
and I have no car to take me there.
While you admired the "innovative products" at the P.N.E.,
I dreamt of boots for the children,
a babysitter for one night.
I could pawn your three-piece suits
into enough tuition for four years.
Yet you include me in all your accomplishments,
your ceremonial "we."
No, I have not enjoyed my summer,
I have not been to Expo
or Canada Place
to shake the hands of dignitaries,
to record my smile
on photographs labelled,
"Myself and The Prime Minister"
"Myself and The Minister of—"
"Myself and The Minister of—"

"Dear Friend," you say, "we can be proud.
I look forward to your continued support."

Event   GENNI GUNN

THE HUG

It was your birthday, we had drunk and dined
    Half of the night with our old friend
        Who'd showed us in the end
    To a bed I reached in one drunk stride.
        Already I lay snug,
And drowsy with the wine dozed on one side.

I dozed, I slept. My sleep broke on a hug,
        Suddenly, from behind,
In which the full lengths of our bodies pressed:
        Your instep to my heel,
    My shoulder-blades against your chest.
    It was not sex, but I could feel
    The whole strength of your body set,
        Or braced, to mine,
        And locking me to you
    As if we were still twenty-two
    When our grand passion had not yet
        Become familial.

My quick sleep had deleted all
Of intervening time and place.
I only knew
The stay of your secure firm dry embrace.

The Yale Review   THOM GUNN

ON THE DEEPEST SOUNDS

There is a pipe in big organs,
the thirty-two foot basso, the contrabassoon,

huge vibrating pillar of air, late autumn
when water rises in the wells,

the subterranean network of waters and wells,
and it is more a sorrow than a sound.

At this lower limit where the music ends,
something different wants to begin.

Body more than sound, body and darkness,
and late autumn, when the wells are rising;

but since it is lower than earth,
lower than music, lower than lament

—it does not want to begin, it does not begin,
and therefore it does not exist.

Now it is closer, now it is distinct!
Now it will soon be audible, far and wide.

Southern Humanities Review   LARS GUSTAFSON
—Translated from the Swedish
by Christopher Middleton and the author

THE END OF SUMMER

Sweet smell of phlox drifting across the lawn—
an early warning of the end of summer.
August is fading fast, and by September
the little purple flowers will all be gone.

Season, project, and vacation done.
One more year in everybody's life.
Add a notch to the old hunting knife
Time keeps testing with a horny thumb.

Over all these months hung an unspoken
aura of urgency. In late July
galactic pulsings filled the midnight sky
like silent screaming, so that, strangely woken,

we looked at one another in the dark,
then at the milky magical debris
arcing across, dwarfing our meek mortality.
There were two ways to live: get on with work,

redeem the time, ignore the imminence
of cataclysm; or else take it slow,
be as tranquil as the neighbor's cow
we love to tickle through the barbed-wire fence
(she paces through her days in massive innocence,
or, seeing green pastures, we imagine so).

In fact, not being cows, we have no choice.
Summer or winter, country, city, we
are prisoners from the start and automatically
hedged in, harangued by the one clamorous voice.

Not light but language shocks us out of sleep—
ideas of doom transformed to meteors
we translate back to portents of the wars
looming above the nervous watch we keep.

The Agni Review   RACHEL HADAS

MORNING GLORY

Sitting in the bath reading Bly
prose poems, it's early morning.
We're conspirators,
saboteurs, secret
foreign agents or something
to be awake at this hour,
my dreamy legs,
the steaming tea,
and you probably halfway
home by now.

Painted Bride Quarterly   JERRY HAGINS

THE DEATH OF A SMALL ANIMAL

In my child's room
a small animal sickens.
I feed it egg yolk
with an eye dropper every hour.
It eats, then burrows
into bedding of cotton balls.

I remember the first time
death insisted
on something small.
I refused to give it up,

until one day it disappeared.
My parents knew enough
of death to rid
themselves of small reminders.

In my child's room
a small animal lingers
among softness and swallows
yellow liquid.
I stay still
contemplating
its final container.

Prairie Schooner   SUSAN HAHN

A RED BLOSSOM

The country that is my country
is in the hands of armed men,
its soil a crushed red blossom.

Upon the country that is mine
sentries have descended. Loud
is the sound of their tramping
through the darkness of night.

Alight with processions and
bright with death is the country
that is mine, my own country.

Rent with lightning and thunder
is the heart of the sky that is
my own sky, my sky. The air reeks
with the smell of gunpowder.

Alight with processions and
flush with death is the country
that is mine, my own country.

New Letters   DAVID HAIDER
—Translated from the Bengali
by Lila Ray

RABIES

That gyroscope of buzzards, its secret axis
Fixed in the bearing of a cold flat disc of sun,
Is turning faster now, narrowing down
to the final point deep in the cypress bottom.

At first I hoped they'd found a rabid coon,
Or a possum, polecat, wild cat, rabbit, fox—
Whatever it was the hound got hold of late

Last night when he raised that sort of yelping howl
That always sounds more surely killed than killing.

But then, to ease a coiling in my mind,
I went down the winter rye to check the herd
And found her gone, Black Dilsey, 14-B,
Whose trembling calf leapt from the April green
And charged me like a loco bull, braying,
Wild-eyed mad at the tilting whirl of sky.

I walked the whole fence line to find the place
She'd broken through, for I hate to follow buzzards,
Who can only show where the carcass dropped and not
What desperate path she took when she left the herd
And plunged headlong through the hot barbed wire, down
To the creek to squirm on her back that one last time
In the water she craved but feared to drink, if rabies

Was the cause . . . But when I found her there,
Her bone-pierced knees trussed up in helixed vines,
Her ribs an open culvert to the stream that spouted
Like a fountain at her mouth, I left her to the birds;
Her washed and sand-packed brain is not a thing
For some county vet to slice and mount and stain—
That pinpoints only one of a thousand reasons
Life goes out with sudden rage and calm.

The Texas Review   MICHAEL CABOT HALEY

ALOFT THE HANG GLIDER MEDITATES

Chinstrap and helmet of white buckled
Against the wind rising from the cliff's
Old antagonism with the sea,

I become my own shadow one thousand
Feet below, a bat-black thing
Running on mist into the shore's spume.

Falling, forever falling through
The up-drafts of this winter wind's
Mindless, circumstantial weave,

I see the blue, indifferent smile
Of all horizons and the sun caught
On the comorant's pursuing wing.

Centered so in the endless centerings
Of these hostile dispensations
I trust the guile of my altimeter,

The reconciliation of a goggle's lens,
My wing's pterodactyl memory, a strut's
Weld: these things and fabric hold me

As I sink through the wind's unseen
Definitions towards the pardon of stones.
Yet, always at dusk, the sun goes down

And the wind dies on this undefended shore:
Being only of the sun, of cliff, of the wind,
I go down also to the dark compromise of sand.

Interim   JAMES B. HALL

SCATOLOGY

The first day in that new house
my mother warned us she'd heard a rat
had once appeared in our house's only toilet.
Check before you sit, she said.
This is known as toilet training.
This is known as teaching your children
not to dally in the only bathroom.

Her rat swam up from the sewers, she supposed.
At six, who's heard of sewers?
So much to digest, so many revelations.
You mean, running under our street
is what I flush, and swimming rats?
And what our neighbors flush, she maintained.
But where does it all lead?
The ocean, she supposed, where else?
Then eels and shrimp, I said,
and baby sharks could surface in the commode.
And it should make you think again
about swimming at the beach, she supposed.

The first day in the first house I ever owned,
a frog bobbed up amid my loved one's leavings.
She screamed for me to come and see.
Santa Claus down the air shaft, I supposed.
It was my chore to dip him out.
How could I flush a fellow amphibian,
exile him down there with the rats.

So now we know they come from the sky as well.
Rats, bats, toads, eels, who knows what else?
The lesson is to check before you sit and listen
before you flush. Be ready for the first
experimental nip, the feathery flick of tail.
And relax. Relax.
It's not like it happens every day.

Kansas Quarterly   JIM HALL

CHILD RUNNING

The little girl runs too quickly in the summer afternoon.
It is late afternoon and she runs along the beach,
    her parents nowhere in sight, no relatives, only
    the waves of the bay repeating alongside her

as she runs the hysterical, off-balance run of children
overly excited, anticipating, dramatic, out of control.
    It might be the small red boat at the end of the bay,
    or the heron following back the tide after herring,

or the group of children playing farther down the beach
with a ball. Something calls to her. As far as
    I'm concerned, there are too many boats alight in the bay,
    too many flying insects. I'm thinking of Marianne Moore's monkeys,

who winked too much, as I stand at night on this lawn looking at the lights
across the water, of her elephants with fog-colored skin
    during the overcast mornings here, of the day's events,
    the tidal movement on the beach, the weather and menus for tomorrow.

Every day there is one less day no matter what you believe,
or in whom. This, of course, discounting the afterlife.
    If you think too much about what there is
    you begin to lose what you have.

This is foreshadowing and it preoccupies me. In my hand
a piece of burnt toast, a grown woman asleep where I left her,
    her body curled around the shape I no longer inhabit.
    On loan, the makeup of what is visible at this hour.

The playing child is one distraction, the warmth of the day
another. The layout of the scene below demands attention—
    it is not a matter of description but of focus. The weather's
    holding. What's one ecstatic child running on the beach?

The North American Review   Daniel Halpern

WHEN FIRED FROM CROCKER BANK

    No
        way for the rose to
            bloom forever
          always
    the petals must fall followed
                by the leaves &
              the stem turns brown &
          brittle as
    the ground freezes &
             the snow swirls over
        everything
         &
    working Crocker Bank is

hardly sweet blooming anyway so
when the axe falls
there's no blood lost &
no petals to spread over the
weeping earth
only
a final check &
brief goodbye &
a little time to
taste the hills & bay again
away
from this financial
mortuary

The Fiddlehead   FRITZ HAMILTON

PORNO POEM: LETTER FROM AN EDITOR

We apologize for the delay.
It's just that time of month.
We're overflowing. Submissions
keep pouring in like blood.
We'll make no promises, though
those lines of yours show pain.
It's not the kind we want. Try
again. Your images are bloated.
Your verse is much too cramped.
Let it out, let it spill all out.

Forgive our crudity. It's just our
way: we're as horny as a toad or as
refined as a sip of Coors. If you'd
like, we'll send you a subscription.
No guarantee we'll do anything but
squander your funds on beer and tacos.
Sorry you're not Jong, Bukowski or
Blazek. But don't let that deter you.
Submit some racy verse and we'll do
headstands or expose ourselves for you.

Remember that while God created "J,"
he proved his true poetic worth by
giving us grants, SASE, and multiple
orgasms. But back to poetry. When
this is past: multiply & be fruitful.

Gryphon   KARLA M. HAMMOND

THE OWL

Twenty below again,
cat's water dish frozen in the pantry

and the woodpile low. Time
to bring down the big, dead elm,
to call up Duke and his brother Willie,
who has a cable and a come-a-long,
enough practice with big trees
to keep this one out of the river.

The trunk was so big even the blade on Willie's
old pioneer left the center,
a bent chain link couldn't be coaxed through the winch,
and a hung up limb that dropped when we
drove wedges hit Duke and Willie
and left Willie leaning his weight off the leg
he thought might be broken, shaking his fist
at the big tree he said he couldn't wait
to sink his saw teeth back into.

We winched her again, but the chain broke.
And you can't just leave an almost cut tree
for any stray kid to walk under when the wind comes up,
so we dropped her in the river,
the ice thick enough to hold,
about two feet deep there
and all of it ice after weeks so cold
you had to keep moving to survive.

And this, I swear, was worth it all:
a small white owl I'd never seen or heard
fluttering out of his hole as the tree fell,
having wanted to make sure, I suppose,
before braving the cold, perched on a nearby branch
and looked down.
What words are there for this?
As if the very spirit of the tree
had not fallen, but flown.
And Willie, even with his bad leg,
wondered if there weren't some way to catch it;
and Duke said, "no, it's a waste to time—"
all of us looking at the bird and the bird
looking back—"we'll have to let it go."

Blueline   CRAIG HANCOCK

RIVER AS METAPHOR

Post this: the title has slid
between the cracks. Only the tail
of the "y" is showing.

What's below rings bells
on our toes. Long ago history quadrilled
here. This river was rain (which is where
we came in), a lying down column, muscling

bends, currying stones.
Now when the wind whistles in with a question,
the aspen responds at once.

I begin to learn my life.
If the bird flies, I cry Feather,
point me toward Omega unwinding.
Water carries many mimes: fog, cloud, steam,
ocean, ice-sleet-snow, creek, and is part
of Total, as I am part of my Self. Try to place
your finger on where I begin, or end.

I marry the river,
instruct my body to listen
how deep my banks will hold at floodtide.

Stone Country   NIXEON CIVILLE HANDY

ISLAND, PERHAPS

In days like these it rains after days of unease
before the rains would fall; the earth so dry,
that water falls away, runs off the back of the world
into basins and low country, country unlike this.
You wonder where the mountain got its name, and why
I persist in thinking of an island.
There's no surf here, no salt water taffy
to pull us from our daily pains into a sleep that lulls
us into dreams. Like a remembered dream, the rain
falls, falling and racing in streams
along parched ground. It is barely summer, and you
stay far removed, in these mountains that I cling to,
while the world rains and I write this letter;
and you, perhaps, must push the thought of me
until it dislodges, spins, falls away to root
in someone else. You think of longing and my heart
must ache. I think of you and think that you must find it easy
not to remember me when the rain begins again.
That I cannot have the mountain and the ocean
is nothing in the scheme of things; that this rain
must be falling is nothing; that drought ends,
nothing; that I am remembering you
the way the earth finally remembers it has the power of rain
is like a catch in the throat; in time,
it will be nothing, too.

Artemis   CATHRYN HANKLA

REFLECTIONS ON WITTGENSTEIN

The sense of the world must lie outside the world.
In the world everything is as it is,

and everything happens as it does happen:
in it no value exists.
The sense of the world must lie outside the world.

In the world everything is as it is
and happens just so, and who would have guessed
the sense of the world must lie outside the world?
The sense of the world, outside the world, makes no sense
to the world, where everything is as it is.

Everything happens. Just so. And who would have guessed
that death, for example, is not an event in life
in the world, where everything is as it is—
in the wide windy world, where no value exists
and where there is no one who would have guessed?

Death is not an event in life.
It lies, senseless, just outside this world
of springs and falls, which are only what they are.
We do not even live to experience death.
We spring to fall and long to spring again.

Eternal life is for those who live in the present.
And so, however far apart the two of us lie,
in Wittgenstein's cracked mirror, we lie together.
It makes no sense, but I love you—you and this
dying world where no value exists.

Kansas Quarterly   TOM HANSEN

EYEWASH

All winter the grounded white swan
sprouts poppies
near her front door, the gray
cascading fountain emptied, its
shallow basin filling now
with snow. How many times
we snicker when passing her house
there on the corner,
the plastic daisies hanging
bright as summer from their woven
baskets, the sunflower rotating
out of season in a north wind.
She keeps to herself,
this recluse we come to know
by her alien love in a harsh
temperate clime,
the miniature white picket fence
near the sidewalk clearly defining
the borders of her world,
impeccable white mounds of
chrysanthemums kept in check

all year long. Yet,
after we bend ourselves
into the cold, after driving past
her corner through howling drifts,
our eye again pulls to the
pink, the orange, the flamingo;
in all this isolation,
thinking:
what we see
has nothing at all to do
with what is there.

The Small Pond Magazine   TWYLA HANSEN

DEATH OF TREES

The dry woods and dry crows send forth
a chorus of notes to weave a fable of trees:

The oak burns for love, hot enough to melt,
tight as still pieces of ivory.

The starlings come bearing black roses
and black rosaries for prayer in a wooden mausoleum.

The pine curbs its tongue, fearing the voice
of God, knowing that there is no hope.

The birches, loveliest of things in the landscape,
fear the sound of ax ringing on wood.

The small skulls of yews are embalmed
in phosphorus. No one loved them anyway.

The walnut tree we thought was immortal keeps
turning and turning under the weight of sparrows.

The heart will not start!
Now, for all its turning, it is very still.

The Wooster Review   CHARLES HANSON

SURVIVORS

Our feet sink in wildgrass.
We find the ancient oak,
alive nine centuries.

Its twenty-four foot girth
set into earth like a boulder.
Each branch thick as a tree trunk—
its bark a stone wall.

Survivor of almost a thousand winters:
sapling in the youth of William the Conquerer,

it has blossomed through the minds
of Da Vinci, Galileo, Newton.

Through launching of the Mayflower
to first rocket to the moon,
it has resisted plague, storm, drought,
repaired its wounds.

It stands in a field
plowed by an old farmer
who moves his tractor slowly
around its roots,
his face furrowed as the deep ridges of earth
he leaves behind.

Southern Poetry Review   HELEN B. HARARY

5:30 A.M.

I wake now as my father did
but not to an alarm or because
I have to ready myself
to work all day with machines.
How his hands knew the precise place
to slice the metal! I wake
only because the pigeons are squawking,
and last night's movie, of a man
dying before he should have,
still presses me into thinking
about time, this time, to have
to arrange these words, to solve
the hard calculations that teem inside
the head for years,
as the tree nods, the sun lifts,
and a father's back is seen again
walking out the door to work.

The Journal   CATHERINE HARDY

EARLY APRIL SNOW

The heavy snow covers
the elderberry outside
our window. My father,
under thick hospital blankets,
nods as the nurse who brings
his morphine tells him
the weatherman predicts
six more inches before morning.

When he falls finally
to sleep, I crouch on the window sill

and watch a plow trying to clear a path
as my father's rhythm of breaths
weaves through the silence.

I believe the doctors are right.
There is nothing we can do.

The Journal   CATHERINE HARDY

A WINNING HAND

(for Richard Hugo)

In this university town of winners, the wind is a blur through the dandelions and
nurtured grass on the lawn outside my office, and you are here, but have gone on, to
the buffalo-skinned dream that has fallen in the cracks between the small towns that
make a necklace from Medicine Lake to Missoula. Indians still dry jerky in the risky
wind, test the water for visions of buffalo who were more than just meat sustenance.
Aren't our bodies mostly wind? And are cursed, like the rest of us, with being able
to smell but not see the world we are crazy for. You knew that place, traveled it until
it drove you crazy, too, to think like one of the beautiful native misfits. In Albu-
querque, in either seventy-eight-or-nine, you stunned my students from Indian School
into returning to the ghost towns their memories had become, in that auditorium
built in a town spit into existence by dry lipped conquistadors who wanted only
gold and Indian wives. Someone must have prophesied what they feared. Nez
couldn't take it, turned wads of clay into glossy bowls, but they still weren't enough
to hold her words. She abandoned us in that auditorium for the corner bar of the
lost poets. After your last poem, your heart tearing us apart, we all left to find her
and had to chase ourselves out of that place. There was only the magnetism of
ghosts driving us back, into the winning hand.

I don't think I looked back, or believed you had ever gone. When I hit the Montana
border last spring during the last hard storm, the wind nearly knocked me over. And
it wasn't poetry I heard, but something like the moan and laughter of a player with
the best hand, a touch of luck.

This time it's all or nothing, and there won't be any more losers in this field of tens
and one-eyed jacks.

The Bloomsbury Review   JOY HARJO

NIGHT CRAWLER

To be an earthworm
is to be male and female
to breed and to bear
to lay eggs in a cuff
of clitellum and slide
it over the head
the open ends closing
to form cocoon—
an unloading of young.

To be an earthworm
is to be blind and mute
to mouth through decay
to surface in rain
and to breathe through
thin rings of skin
avoiding light and
seeking damp—a life
of shrinking and stretching.

Southern Poetry Review　　KATRINIA A. HARKLERODE

SOLITARY: EL PASO COUNTY JAIL

The best light leaks in the smoked glass at the right.
Light like this, you'd never guess this the fourth floor.
You crouch there in the dark of your cement den
Staring out through the barred light seeing things

The way one of those leopards at the zoo
That doesn't want to come out sees things. Only
You'd like to come out. You tear a paper match
In half lengthwise—doubles your cache. Quick strike

And its sulphur bulb blooms as a brief yellow-petaled
Light, its pollen igniting the cigarette
You handrolled. You jet the first grey-curled breath
Of it out into the hallway, flick the first ash

Into one of the styrofoam coffeecups or
8-oz. milkcartons that doubles as an ashtray.
Keys clatter. A metallic screech which starts,
Then lapses into a low groan, sets off a long

Slow rolling echo, as the cell-block door,
Which looks more like a metal-studded wall,
Swings wide like a bank vault or submarine hatch.
The guard, a partial eclipse against the backdrop

Of fluorescent light, stands clasping a giant key—
The size of one of those ruby red plastic keys
You gnawed on when you were 2 or 3—announces
"Dinner." It's served on styrofoam plates, was once warm.

You lean back, then reach out to pluck off chips
Of the paint that thick-crusts the bars: each layer,
A different color. Your scratchings finally
Bring the door's metal bones to light.

America　　　　　　　　　　WILLIAM HARMLESS, S. J.

SPROUT IN THIS

Even the giant, retarded oaks
begin to sprout in this
sleek after-birth of winter.
It is spring again in the north.
I've waited months
to see the men from the retiree home
worry about their hats.
Hello Sir, your green sweater
is in bloom again.
Hello Mam, isn't walking grand?
And how the little cars
park vividly against each other.
The neighbors are outside today
hugging their dolls and cats.
Mrs. Davis dons her kimono
and walks for beer.
The Mitchells finally decide
on blue for the living room.
How the metallic sun
ruins our dulled perception.
Green flashes here, a strip
of yellow flutters there.
March opens its mouth, mid-month,
and birds fly
out of the arms of strangers.

Carolina Quarterly   JOHN HARN

THE BORNING ROOM

I stand in moonlight
in our borning room,
now a room of closets
changed by the owners.
Once only the old
and newborn slept
on this first floor,
this boarded door
closed now to the hearth
of our wood burning.

I look over the large bed
at the shape of my woman;
there is no image
for her, no place
for the spring child.
Her cornered shape dreams
a green-robed daughter
warmed in a bent room

close to fireplace oven,
warmed by an apple tree:
the old tried to make it new,
the new old; we will not die here.

Contemporary New England Poetry   MICHAEL S. HARPER

WATCHING MARCEL MARCEAU

Mime is the art of interstices,
of what we call the empty spaces
between objects; the spatial gestalt
of true art that defines by implication;
like the essential space of a Zen garden.

The brush-strokes of his wordless world
are painted gestures that pluck from
human imagination the shape of all
things dreamed or possible to dream,
which, like divinity itself, conjure up a world.

Crosscurrents   JOSEPH HARRIS

IN THE ATTIC

The thick air smelled of dust and wood.
Shiny, blue-black wasps, dangling their legs,
bounced off the facets of the roof
with quick, electrical buzzes.
I used to stay up there for hours, sitting
on the rough floor, jagged with splinters,

paging through stacks of Life magazine.
Or I'd stare through the Gothic window,
past spider webs, dead wasps,
and the ragged nests the starlings
had stuffed into the bargeboard, to feel
what it's like to be in the treetops.

This time I was up there for a reason.
Years ago, in the top drawer of a dresser
my mother had painted Pennsylvania Dutch,
I'd found a bundle of envelopes
stained amber by the attic's heat,
like the mattresses piled on the old brass bed.

I'd been afraid to read them. Now,
I untied the dull blue ribbon.
It stayed crimped and folded from the bow.
The yellow pages crackled as I opened them.
They were written by my father, full of
ambition, jealousy, infatuation.

It was a side of him I'd never seen.
I had written letters like these
when I was fourteen, letters I'd burn
to see now. I read each one, one for every
day that summer. There was one from my mother:
blue ink on white paper, no envelope.

She described a view I knew by heart:
the lake framed by hemlocks, the mountain
reflected in the evening, its rock face
staring blankly. She said it made her think
of God. She said, yes, she would be his wife
if he was sure he understood what that meant.

The Hudson Review   JEFFREY HARRISON

THE WAR ARTIST

My brush did not even touch his death.
When I wake it is with the smell
in my nostrils. When this is over
I will never paint in oils again.
Every colour is full
with a kind of dying I have seen
and nothing I have done penetrates the surface
of these forms: twisted metal, a hand
and bone in a sleeve on the ground,
the curve of a ship on its side,
and fallen bodies rocked like infants in the tide.
This is no place to ask questions. I look around.
The subject repeats itself without end,
a heap where there was a life, a skull for a face,
I capture things after they have been.
Colour is my weapon against the call
of madness; my eye is a shell, my brush a gun.
I am in my way a soldier
paid to turn this farmland into hell,
do what I'm told and save my breath.
This is no place to ask questions.

Grain   RICHARD HARRISON

GEESE

The first thing is the sound:
not quite an animal sound.
It's May. The rotting dock
sways with my weight.
If you go under the water
it's too dark.
If you swim at night

you can't see what's below you.
What I've been taught
is to bring fear to life
instead of naming it.

The geese fly in, so low
they're having trouble in the air.
Perhaps they weigh too much.
Perhaps they're tired of flight.
It's too far south for them
to nest. My neighbor's kid
once chased them in his boat.
I remember him lifting the oar to strike.
They skidded. Their wings flapped.
They ran on water.

Something to do with fear and not with geese.
Something to do with being here
alone. Something to do
with what I choose.

The light is almost gone. This time
of night it gets so still
you hear what happens on the other shore
as if it were beside you. A dog barks.
A door slams.
I can make something of this fear.

The Cape Rock   JUDITH HARWAY

PICKING BERRIES

Look, children, I don't know any of these bushes
personally. You will read about them in books
later, and getting to know them in the books
is safer anyway. Still, they are of three classes
and all give fruit or berries of sorts: Sweet, Sour,
Bitter. The colours vary from red and green to
purple and blue or black. Some are nice to touch;
others seem to have a grudge against us, are prickly.
Yet another kind, sensitive to rough hands and misuse
would rather be out of reach: call it Poisoned,
or Poisonous. Even the bees buzz over it and pass
to the next; it defends what sweetness it may have
viciously. Mothers will advise you about it;
it's so beautiful it will appear to call out for you,
and then look the other way with your begging hands,
watering eyes and wanting mouth.

The Toronto South Asian Review   ALAMGIR HASHMI

IDENTITIES: AN ARGUMENT

Mice nibble the faces of cans
until one morning we open our cupboards
to find we cannot tell garbanzos
from beets. We have lost those names
the way we lose our children
who gnaw at themselves until we can
no longer read the labels we gave them.

Outside, seas turn thin, pelicans become
scooping beaks, weathers shift. And
just when we think we know
the parts of flowers, we discover
pistils in tongues pollinated
not by wind, but by the sweet dim
air behind a curtain. Nothing,
we learn, so night
as a blind man's parlour in the day.

Things change. Husbands fade, and friends,
and we are left with breasts that fall
over our ribs, with white hair between
our legs. We are looking all the same,
we products of busy mice. Say to yourself:
Old woman. Old woman.
Never mind if you were Alice or April or Viola.

New York Quarterly   LOLA HASKINS

SHADOW

The shower lasted maybe a minute. Even
before the sun broke through smoky clouds
my sister and I rushed out, screen door
banging, onto the dirt road to trample tiny
raindrop craters with feet calloused in the
long summer. The damp dust worked between
our toes as we skipped and pattered down to
the wooden bridge. There we stopped short;
a huge blacksnake lay sunning on the splintered
planks. My heart flipped and then settled back
uneasily into place. Blackie was harmless,
we were always told. But the day's joy was
spoiled. We sloshed soberly in the cool water
of the creek, feeling the dust grains lodged
between our toes while curious minnows, nibbling,
tickled our feet. When at length we dragged
through the settled dust back to the house,
we almost forgot to announce the rainbow.

The Great Lakes Review   LOUIS HASLEY

DRIVING INTO A STORM

Last night we burned feed sacks
emptied over the long cold. Falling
snow melted on our cheeks, clicked
on the sacks piled behind us.
You stood in your long blue coat,
a red bandana around the gray hat,
watched for sparks in the grass,
in the haystacks. Flaming sheets
of paper rose, swirled in the black smoke,
flew off southeast like crows.

Today my big hands grip
the steering wheel, knuckles scarred.
The plain gold ring is already scratched,
framed by two new calluses.
I'm racing down this road
into the snow. I sing, drink
coffee, think of the job,
ignore the clouds dropping low,
lower.

You've given me so many gifts
and now one more: yourself
in your blue coat, flames
at your feet, standing against
the dark
rolling clouds.

Passages North   LINDA M. HASSELSTROM

TWO DOZEN LINES FOR RICH

I sit here, rich, drinking coffee
At East Park Restaurant. My car
Needs a muffler and you ask why
I love poetry though you say you hate
The stuff. Last night we got to hear
A concert in the hall where my dad, who died
Last fall, often used to go, and thought
Of him a lot as we watched all the old
Guys hanging out at intermission.
(People at a concert seem nicely unemployed.)
You never knew my dad, of course, who was born
About as many years before you as Freud

Preceded me in birth. (And in the order
That we enter, Rich, barring accident,
We exit.) So I left that concert certain
I'd write to you today and tell you how
My dad loved his long life though hated

Poetry just like you. But I don't believe
It matters, since I know his life ended
Like a poem and yours, despite your letter, begins
To notice poems. The guys in the next booth
Are telling stories about piling up planes
At the Portage County Airport. My muffler's
Probably done. Thanks for writing, Rich.

Tar River Poetry   DONALD M. HASSLER

1983, SAN ANTONIO

At the end, it got very cold.
Pipes froze & splintered in tall glass buildings
& very old trees died.

Texas learned that ice sculpture is interesting
but not permanent. I got bitter early,
before it was fashionable, before everyone else

decided to act cheerful.
I was cynical all year long, listening
to hollow doors slam & cats fighting meaninglessly

in the middle of the night, listening
to my neighbor bang sadly on his drums because his wife
had left him, thinking only briefly

about the loss of love, examining tiny pale flowers,
thick among the dark leaves of the ivy,
glad it was not my own.

I learned that you can't say everything, that
what you do say means little, but means something,
though to whom I'm not sure. My father told me

that there are details that are not important, like
the fact that the typewriter is dirty, or that I write now
on a sunny day, surrounded by dead ferns,

or that my wife listens to me secretly from the next room
while I think that I can hear the soft stilled rush
of her breathing . . . I don't know that it's important,

but I never listened to his advice.

New Letters   JAMES HATHAWAY

AMERICANA

"The heart is unforgiving.
It strains to remember its hurts, rubs its hands
over the grit of bitterness again and again
until even that garden shrivels."

This voice rumbles meaninglessly through my head,
dry as the evening thunder. Here
in the supermarket, people wander, blank faced
after work, listlessly probing the shelves,
fingers searching, lost in the dark cavities
between the dry goods. I am trying to remember
something, where I am maybe, or what this reminds
me of, perhaps a dog somehow penned in a back yard,
whimpering, doing something. I don't think
it matters, at least not now.
In among the vegetables, everything looks the same,
has no taste, no color, no texture,
but plenty of fiber, which is important. I can't
imagine the country it grows in, perhaps none,
for the land around here, I think,
is all barren. In among the cereals I hear myself
chuckling. What a relief! At this moment
matter and antimatter are threatening to become one,
and humor is crucial. When the doors open,
this rugged bag is full, tightly packed with contents.
Outside, a child is singing to a pay phone.
I marvel that even here in the wilderness
the parking lot is a deafening storm of cars.
This is a distant memory of something—
the live beat of the air on a wet morning,
the warning sound a cardinal used to make
before a rain.

The Cape Rock   JAMES HATHAWAY

POOL IS A GODLESS SPORT

(For Ed)

I like the articulate crack
the cue ball makes
on impact, how it drops
what it's after and backspins back;
the chalk skids
on its bald surface, blue
and hard as water
or your eye, keen straight
down the line of the poolstick,
how the clogged air of lies
and smoke clears as you circle
the table, the next shot
plump on the rail, a duck.
You're on a roll, playing
collisions of intent and dumb luck.
We don't talk as I gather
a new game in the rack;
no one's put down quarters.

We could shoot hours here.
The bartender yawns and goes on,
pinball bangs free game.
We play off the angles, combinations,
the felt before each break
fresh as promise,
and let the rolling geometry
plot our next move.

Southern Poetry Review   JAMES HAUG

MOURNING THE DYING AMERICAN FEMALE NAMES

In the Altha diner on the Florida panhandle,
a stocky white-haired woman
with plastic nameplate "Mildred"
gently turns my burger, and I fall into grief.
I remember the long, hot drives to North Carolina
to visit Aunt Alma, who put up quarts of peaches,
and my grandmother Gladys with her pieced quilts.
Many names are almost gone: Gertrude, Myrtle,
Agnes, Bernice, Hortense, Edna, Doris, and Hilda.
They were wide women, cotton-clothed, early-rising.
You had to move your mouth to say their names,
and they meant strength, spear, battle, and victory.
When did women stop being Saxons and Goths?
What frog Fate turned them into Alison, Melissa,
Valerie, Natalie, Adrienne, and Lucinda,
diminished them to Wendy, Cindy, Susy, and Vicky?
I look at these young women
and hope they are headed for the Presidency,
but I fear America has other plans in mind,
that they be no longer at war
but subdued instead in amorphous corporate work,
somebody's assistant, something in a bank,
single parent with word-processing skills.
They must have been made French
so they could be cheap foreign labor.
Well, all I can say is,
Good luck to you,
Kimberley, Darlene, Cheryl, Heather, and Amy.
Good luck, April, Melanie, Becky, and Kelly.
I hope it goes well for you.
But for a moment let us mourn.
Now is the time to say goodbye
to Florence, Muriel, Ethel, and Thelma.
Goodbye, Minnie, Ada, Bertha, and Edith.

The Southern Review   HUNT HAWKINS

SOMETHING SAID

Nobody's out but a winter crow
and me, of course, inspector of snow.
I almost headed back, but no:

Till something occur or be made known,
I'll keep my back to the valley town
Where tomorrow's already written down.

Beyond the pasture smooth as a sheet
And the grey-green spruces capped with white,
Something is being said, but what?

Something about the way a rise
Articulates with trees and skies,
Which if we knew would make us wise.

Contemporary New England Poetry   JAMES HAYFORD

SIGHTING

I plan to stare at the horizon all day,
to relax my neck, let go my old griefs.
But the sloshing surf drags down my eyes,
provokes a squall of gulls, undermines
the castles of loudmouth boys. Sand and sunscreen
crawl in my sweaty suit. And lovers promenade,
rubbed over every tanned inch with coconut oil or Panama Jack,
the huge sea behind them soupstock of their own desire.

I try again. My eyes, lifted into the glare,
sting from last night's Piña Coladas, salt swim.
The planet rim I have in mind smudges in a Gulf haze.
I squint for distance: the farthest waves draw my eyes,
running off the world curve in a shudder. I see
whale bodies roll over, impossible in scale that far off.
Then the earth leans away to India or China,
becomes a map, and I have lost my place again.

There is no line, I cannot fix it.
No rubicon where ions, having enough of sea
or filling enough with sun, leap for and become sky.
These rowdy sand engineers must draw it when they go home
to school: beach and ocean a double stripe—
yellow, green crayola on construction paper.
Sky, a layer of stiff blue wax, rubbed hard
across the very top of the page.

Down the strand, three brown pelicans pop into flight,
straight off threatened species' lists, homilies for Mother's Day.
Sure enough, there are the unselfish gabble throats,
the martyred breasts, swollen feet from Audubon prints.
They wingbeat low in a tight unison, all dull feather

and hollow bone creaking above sunbathers in bright lycra,
trace the water's hissing edge—with unpredicted grace—
and finally out of sight.

Northwest Review   AVA LEAVELL HAYMON

MISSING CHILDREN

Now there is all this milk
Souring in the kitchen
Windows, and so many
Small flames circling unfed
In the fish-bowls. Everywhere
The houses look tired,
Heavy now that the children
Are gone. Some say
They simply wandered off,
Arm-in-arm, into their dark
Scribblings of trees,
And left nothing,
Not even a bright trail
Of breadcrumbs behind.
While others still hear them,
Singing, along the backroads
At night, their tiny
High-pitched voices
Vibrating in the fencewire.

Southern Poetry Review   ROBERT HEDIN

CORPUS CHRISTI SUNDAY, FLORENCE

The wild sun hurls itself into the square
crying, summer, summer;
and the church, that grand
delirium in pink and green,
sprawls in the window of the pastry store.
Hot noon-time here
shouts challenges against the grave
Franciscan dusk, villages where
streets smell of bread and wine;
say an Adonis jewelled with candied fruit and violets,
an ice-cream Orpheus in a thousand flavours.

Take it and eat—
all this, the Cathedral of Flowers presides
over Prato biscuits, chocolate cake
with cream inside, maraschino cherries,

crushed cones in the street, the melting
heat on nuts and nougat, all this.

Take it or leave it.

Descant (Canada)   MAGGIE HELWIG

THE METHOD

Stanislavsky, Vakhtangov, Pudovkin.
Slapped awake by your passion for movies,
for acting, and bundled into your sleigh
—straw, stars, the horse's breath a cloud of steam—
I careered through the streets of your dream.
After love, we listened to all eight sides
of *Boris Godunov.* What courage it must take,
I said, to pour out your heart on stage.

You frowned, beetling your handsome brow;
you were in Strindberg's *A Dream Play* now,
learning your role, a coal heaver in hell,
by studying the Bronx Zoo gorilla's
slow-motion rage. After that, you had to quit.
There was a baby coming, a living to get.

The Hudson Review   JUDITH HEMSCHEMEYER

RAILS

Rails lead out of town,
iron bands that held my father forty years.
When I was young and walking here,
rails could take me to the four corners of the earth,
even McAdam.
That was when I was young,
and rails had an end.
That was when it was summer,
and the days dragged on for hours.

These are the ties that bind.
You don't stop walking these rails
till you get off;
red ants will eat you alive
like they ate my father as he stood
one place,
paid by the ton,
moving fishmeal and tin.

I am on rails at dusk,
at dawn.
I walk alone then;
there's a bear in the woods, they say.

They're right.
I've seen his footprints in the sand,
heard shadows crashing through underbrush.
But while I am on rails
he has to come out
to face me,
or I will see him on rails
ahead.

The Fiddlehead   MARK HENDERSON

LEGACY

You divided your house evenly into 13 parts
for niece and nephew;
those adopted and natural,
the loving, the angry, the passive;
for those with children
and those only old enough to understand
that the end points of meridians
disappear into the poles and do not return.

Aloud, they read the will
under the storm windows of the living room.
To myself you returned letters—
brought by a cousin this winter,
lined paper with drawings of sharks
and boats and you and me on the wave's crest.
Letters on stationery, flyers, butcher paper
from Europe, Asia, the Blue Ridge, Smithsonian,
the Ile de la Cite—
and from the near edge of dangerous earth
you now understand.

I have searched for lost poems in the talus
of my paper and trunks. You had tied them in ribbon,
fantasy birthed, sent,
forgotten and lost in a child's year
spent away from you, colored by the silt of the Seine.

Now I have untied them,
pieces you have returned to join with me again,
gifts from the wiry skin of your hands.

When the house is sold and the silver paid out,
dust will remain on bluffs
overlooking your massive river,
your rich joining of arteries.
And the gods of Mosenthein Island swirl
the glacier of Minnesota lakes into
your Missouri heartland,

your legacy, the sand bars
and the currents of the Mississippi.

The Cape Rock   MARK HENKE

WANTING WINTER

So far I had only seen
one instance of the turning

of the leaves, one branch
like a bloodied hand
reaching over the road.

And I had only wakened once
in the just-rising sun to a frost,

the field behind our house
and the backs of our brown sheep
white and luminous. But these

beginnings in an otherwise
green world were enough

to stir in me my longing
for the leaves to fall;
and for the branches,

bearing nothing, to let rest
upon them snow and birds,

and hold these out to us—
the silence and the singing, each
making more of the other, and of us,

who walk out into it,
breath freezing, seed in hand.

The Georgia Review   CAROL HENRIKSON

WHILE WE ARE STILL ALIVE

(*"Why don't we find each other, and go home,
while we are still alive?"*)
                        —James Wright

I ease my seat back to try to doze,
and do, almost. A stewardess
brushes by in her cloud perfume.
How long before I'm home?

Terminal . . . I stand in a circle
for my suitcase. Paranoid eyes
jump from one suspect to another.
When was I ever home?

Businessmen in black wingtips
click along corridors to waiting cars.
At least my line is busy:
someone must be home.

Something went wrong somewhere
in our lives, or we would not be here.
I try the phone again. This time,
the right number, no one home.

I sit down, untie my shoes,
close my eyes to think something through,
but what's the use when a numb brain
droops from its stem?

I lift my suitcase to my lap,
drum it with my fingers, hum,
stand too fast, dizzy, a dream
cut through by the clear ache for home.

Automatic doors buzz,
but open only half way.
I bang into plate glass panes,
step back again.

Inside, outside the door,
I stand invisible in this form.
Why don't we find each other,
and go home?

Southern Humanities Review WILLIAM HEYEN

FINAL VIGIL

How dark the veins of your temples;
Heavy, heavy your hands.
Deaf to my voice, already
In sealed-off lands?

Under the light that flickers,
You are so mournful and old,
And your lips are talons
Clenched in a cruel mold.

Silence is coming tomorrow
And possibly underway,
The last rustle of garlands,
The first air of decay.

Later the nights will follow
Emptier year by year:

Here where your head lay and gently
Ever your breathing was near.

New Letters   GEORG HEYM
                        —*Translated from the German*
                                    by Peter Viereck

YOUR NAME SO NEARLY

Your name so nearly like
my own reminds me,
set at the head of a procession
of stark obituaric phrases,
that I am not immortal either.
For one moment I imagined
the press had beaten me
to the tape, left me lagging
a poor second; but then descried
the tell-tale letter that erects
our flimsy barrier, each from each
divided by one death-bell vowel
only. Well, we'll check it out
a time later when it's ripe
for comparisons and the exchange
of anecdote. Who hasn't heard
the cry from the laggard child
suddenly aware of comrades
moving on without him:
Wait, wait—I'm coming!

The Fiddlehead   JOHN V. HICKS

RELATIVITY

Our lives will not flash before our eyes.
Light travels the curved walls of time
like a train whistle that lowers
in pitch while diminishing.
But when the train doesn't swerve
at the turn, or a girl, sleepy, looking for
the bathroom door, falls between cars—the light
does not intensify. There is no inward curve, no
illumination.
              Her parents hope she didn't see,
didn't feel the bare rail, the clutch
of wheels. Still, they wish
they'd kissed her again, pressed every bone
of her body to their hearts,
like a fern making a fossil in stone.

They store her suitcase
in an upstairs room, an atom, intact.
Below, the clock sounds like the clack of ties.
For those on board there is no
relativity: the shriek
of the whistle does not fade.

The Michigan Quarterly Review   JANE HILBERRY

THE EYE OF A NEEDLE

A necklace of lakes
adorns wealthy west Minneapolis.

Nordeast, where the Slavs live,
had a lake, too. Dusty
Park Board maps show it drying up
early in this century.
Dredgings hauled across town
and dumped paid off, creating
a future railroad yard.

Downtown, today's brokers sit inside tall mirrors
like the Pillsbury Center,
where computers thresh
and photocopies feel as warm
as fresh bread. At noon,
grey and blue suits fill
the skyway system that runs above

the uncarpeted sidewalks
outdoors. There a whiskey billboard
shows a team of men
scaling an unobstructed peak
not to be found in this city.

Envy's Sting   DANIEL HILL

MOONLIGHT ON THE RAILS

Night, and the dashlights
angle towards the moon.
Speedometers howl
at their reflections.
Like a storefront, the sky
turns liquid green.

A car speeds east from Edmonton,
eventually crossing the North Sask. River.
The driver points at 60 in the sky
and the needle creeping up there—
the infinite gauge.

The passengers lean and squint;
they want to see their faces in the clouds
visible by moons
and the reflections I spoke of before.

The moon is light on the railroad tracks
and it will not quit
these parallel miles and hours.
I remember a boyhood,
a riding in cars in summer
and the curves of endless telephone wires
ending at the poles.

These moonlights.
Ticking.
The border must have passed.

Prism International   GERALD HILL

FENCE-BUILDING

Dividing the field into halves, we build,
fencing the air first, before we start
with posts. At the point clearest of trees
we dig the hole for the end-post by hand
(remembering the woman who had been caught
in a mechanical digger, wound up
like a ribbon, her hand catching
at the air, her husband standing by
helplessly watching).
We work it in one post at a time,
taking turns lining up and driving;
it is like target practice divided, the way
one crouches, to signal, behind a driven post,
and waits for the target post to disappear
into line and the other smacks it in.

It is a fence already, before the fence
is up. Although the horses refuse
to recognize the perfect, bright line
of posts, we walk back to our gate,
already a gate now, with its boundaries up,
and we walk on one side or the other;
we stay where the fence will keep us,
knowing now where it is going up.

Mid-America Review   SARAH HILL

THIS POEM WILL NOT HARM YOU

It contains only gentle words.
There are no death squads

waiting to claim you between
the syllables. The sounds of
explosions and death are faint
and belong to someone else's
nightmare. You can travel
safely here. It is quiet; rest
between the despair and loss.
Flowers grow carefully in this
poem. Their scents linger
through the rhythm of the
words. Turn each page lightly.
Surrender only as your tongue
imagines its taste. This poem
conquers nothing. Attacks
nothing. It shrinks from
aggression. From arguments.
Jagged voices. Turn the page
lightly. Streets in this poem
are filled with music. Even the
dead are light; floating
without the unfamiliar failure
of the grave. Turn the page
lightly. When you finish this
poem, sleep; think only of gods
and what you would like to ask
them. This poem holds no claim
on you, but release it gently.
Others have been tortured for
such thoughts. This poem doesn't care
about the color of your skin or what
personal atrocities you have witnessed.
Leave it quietly. It belongs to
you now. There is one final image.
Read it aloud.
One letter at a time.

The Antigonish Review   ROBERT HILLES

SUPPLY-SIDE THEOLOGY

Does God think riches trickle down and that
the plutocrat, with glut and gorge of gift,
soon shares his capital and spends his thrift
on indolent poor and fribbling bureaucrat,
that milk and wheat flour filter from our fat,
fat land to thin Third World, that shirts down-shift
from mannequins to men, that doctors lift
the curse of pestilence before too late?
Who in the world but God would pour down grace?
As barn-born baby, battered man, he cast
his lot with the down and out, not counting cost,

abdicated his throne for the human race—
so prodigal a father that he'd waste
the highest and best on the least, the last, the lost.

America   BERNHARD HILLILA

CEMETERY BY THE SEA

(Ha'iku, Hawaii)

There is a treacherous curve on Route 36
Where the gears grind
                                    in your rented metallic body
And the dead are nothing more
                                              than a hairpin turn
And a heartbeat away.

                              Above you,
A helmet of fire crowns
                                    the volcano's ashen head
While the rainbow-colored sails
                                              of wind-surfers
Gleam in the white-capped Pacific below.

One day we stopped the car
                                    and stumbled
Through a sunshower at dusk:
                                              13 wooden crosses
Misted with yellow light,
                                    rain borrowed from the ocean,

And a sense of the dead
                                    troubling the air
In suits of yellow flame,
                                    blowing through the bananas
And the split-leafed palms
                                    in spirals of yellow dust.

I believe we had come to lie down
                                              in the topsoil,
To remember something essential again,
                                                        something we'd lost—
The wild hair of the grass
                                    growing in circles and waves.

The eternal, low-pitched voice of the water,

The ancient swimming motions of the dead
                                                        touching our faces
As we breathed from the wet air,
                                              and quietly felt
Our bodies floating out to join them.

Grand Street   EDWARD HIRSCH

IMAGES

This photograph, that poem, these paintings—
When they emerge for showing, they seem complete.
The scene is set, all the characters drawn,
Their poses captured; this hand upraised; that motion
Frozen into a permanent gesture whose reason
Can be endlessly considered; the wanting
In those eyes that I imagine I can meet
In the darkness of pages, the false dawn
Of closed books. These pictures say what can be said
In the rectangular absence of voices,
But, by my hand, it is not enough.
I am always looking at the edges of these things,
Where any artist from a wealth of choices
Draws his line, edits, cutting out
The heart of the image while the whole world wings
By in silence, barely out of sight.

The Cape Rock   DAVID HIRZEL

WALKING THE HARBOR

Mr. G's jewelry sells forever
in a city made of seashells
and hair spray and rubbers.

Sand swirls forever into knotholes
on wooden porch swings and into
tiny pits in the asphalt streets.

On the strand, a few telescopes;
a quarter lets you see
forever on the waves.

Southern Humanities Review   HARVEY HIX

AN OPEN LETTER TO MOTHER NATURE

I wish clouds would learn
how to control their bladders.
I have given up on gulls,
those flying, inconsiderate,
incontinent wretches. And pigeons
are genetically beyond the pale.
The sun has superb manners and control.
Ditto the moon and stars.
But clouds are another, soggy matter.
If they are not yet toilet-trained,
don't issue them a pilot's license.
If they do not take their duties

seriously, then the obvious solution
is to keep them close to the ground
in the form of fog. But when they
matriculate to the laudatory level
of cloud first class, can't they
have the decency to take care of that
before they sail over my house?
It is most embarrassing to have a guest
in the garden be spattered, run to
cover under the porch, and ask me,
"What was that?" If I told the truth,
they would never call again. And,
quite frankly, I'm tired of using
the euphemism, "rain." It isn't "rain."
It's cloud urine, and I want it to stop!

Crosscurrents   ROBERT D. HOEFT

ALBA

This morning I turn thirty-three. I sit,
up before dawn, out on the porch and hear
the birds begin, listen for that dull roar
presaging sunrise, as though each day it

had to tear free of ocean. Or was this
one note its mantra, audible just now,
before the day's din drowned it out? And how
each day, as I was growing up, across

the Hudson I'd hear a train. When its song
dopplered away, if I rose fast and snuck
out in pajamas, I might hear the hushed
roar of sun, see its first light strike along

our tv aerial, each shimmering
inch bearing light to earth. I wanted to
grasp the rig's base and let the light pulse through
me to ground, to feel the crackling

force, the transformation. I wiped, instead,
dew from my slippers and tip-toed to bed.

Poem   ALLEN HOEY

PARTS OF A WHOLE

In the blazing fall of twenty years
I did not care about the shades of red
a dogwood turns through, trimming itself
for winter, any more than now I burn,
twelve years passed, to bum the open road

or change the world in a flash. War and rumor
of war persist. One steamy stretch of palms
exchanged for another; the same red leaves.

My son's voice, bright in dusk, asks this year
why the leaves turn color. I tell him cold
kills off the green, its dying lets the red
show through, the red since spring that's been there.
He squints down the still green lawn to the cold
glow of leaves, then turns inside to bed.

Southern Humanities Review   ALLEN HOEY

STOP THE DEATHWISH!
STOP IT! STOP!

—at least until the 21st century,
because the present is too good to lose
a moment of—I would begrudge the time
for sleep, but dreams are better than they used
to be, since they enact the mystery
that action hides and history derides.
The past drains from the present like the juice
of succulent clams left in the noonday sun.
I spent the better part of my long youth
prenticed to arts for which there'll be small use
in whatever work the future needs have done:
I can file a needle to a point
so fine it plays three sides before it burrs,
or split a hundredweight of ice to fit
the cold chest with a week's worth in two blows;
is there many a man around who knows
by rote the dismantled stations of the El,
or that the Precinct House in Central Park
was once a cote from which the lambing ewes
and spindly lambs and crookhorned rams set out
to crop the green? In one-flag semaphore
I can transmit, or signal in Morse code
by heliograph such urgent messages
as scouts and sappers a boyhood ago
squinted through binoculars to read.
I still can cobble *rime royale* by hand
—and may, though now, about as few use rhyme
as wigwag or sun's mirrored beam to spell
their definitions of the ways that Time
endows the present it consumes, or tell
how only in this moment's flame we dwell
save when Memory, with her hands outspread,
brings back the past, like Lazarus, from the dead.

The Southern Review   DANIEL HOFFMAN

THE SCIENTIST

Other fathers might cuss out a lawnmower
that wouldn't catch. Or kick the car.
Mine would simply stop. A physicist, he'd stop
and think awhile, his breath wheezing
through his nose—hiss and hiss, mechanical
until, abruptly, a solution clicked.
Then, step by step, arranging parts
in the sequence they'd come loose,
he'd direct at our lawnmower a logic
even that sullen machine couldn't refute.
Then, just as systematically, refit
each wrench upon its peg-board silhouette,
re-index every drill-bit, every nail—
this small, half-German intellectual
who, although he'd own no gun himself,
let me wear twin Lone Ranger cap pistols
on each hip. You couldn't tell
just what he thought of you. Had he hated
us, he wouldn't have shown it. When,
in that reasoning, mildly troubled tone
of his that meant he might
be disappointed in his son, he once explained,
In war, people hurt with tools,
I shuddered. You couldn't imagine what
he might invent. He was a patient man.

Crosscurrents   JONATHAN HOLDEN

A WORD ABOUT THE ARTIST

People used to call him "Papa Jeff."
He carved lifesized ducks from white pine,
thrumming current and light through each
incised and painted feather. Collectors
from everywhere would come and lean over him,
watching the wood curl against his blade, learning
about scapulars, coverts, primaries, and flight.

The pintail drake on the mantel is a favorite.
Look, his counterpart just landed out there
where high water stood last week. His mate
is laying eggs for the second year in the yard.
They know this is safe habitat even in fall.
Papa Jeff's art has never been wet.

His little private joke—
if anyone ever used his work as decoys
they would drive away their quarry.
All his birds' necks were sculpted
in the alert and warning position.

There was no warning for Papa Jeff that day,
shot by a hunter as he sketched black scoters.

America   GLENNA HOLLOWAY

OLD RUSSIA

I remember the pain and swollen bloat,
the years my body was not my own,
but I did not define my being
or number the reasons propelling my fate
as I delivered each of ten children
into the harsh cold
and pounded the wash on rough stones
before picking potatoes and milking the goat.
Perhaps my mind was not as big
as my feet and broad shoulders then,
when I knew I had to lift yoke, chop wood,
nourish the growth of a burden
in a part of Russia that has vanished.
Purpose was a plough and a pickel barrel,
as I sifted flour, nursed a child,
waited for *challah* to rise.
We wept, stitching a quilt
so long and wide
we thought it would never end
and nobody find our tears
buried inside the beet-red earth,
the orange-blue sky and gold leaves . . .
with the dreams of youth
lost in its seams.

Crosscurrents   ROCHELLE LYNN HOLT

COMMUTER'S LOG

Eighty miles of fog and moonlight,
headlights and jazz, the radio fading
each mile from Omaha. Enough times
down the route, and one discovers
the last secrets the land offers:
copse of maple along the river bottom,
gravestones loose in the collapsing
lip of a bluff, town lights marking
the platte of Nebraska City
pinched between two hills.

Late enough, and one can nearly
decipher the script of highway cracks
brought forth by recent rain,

subtext weathered into highway signs.
I reach out through the headlights,
concentration centered on that faint code
singing through the wheel:
                              radio waves,
vibration, lights off fog, mirrors,
the wind south-southwest. I am alone
and tired, with nothing between me
and this night racing in from everywhere.

Poetry   ART HOMER

SIDEWALK PEOPLE

(North Adams)

In this town turned into city,
turned into warm May evening
where the sun remains persistent,
the people on Main and Ashland
pass through the hour's heat
as others of their kind do
in other cities, in other elsewheres.
They are the sidewalk people:
old women in winter coats and kerchiefs
who play cards on beautify-the-area tables,
and old men in bald pants and panama hats
who keep bench company with newspapers—
those who live out of shopping bags,
those who window-shop away their emptiness.
They are the sidewalk people:
the loners and the drunks,
the strollers and the lovers,
the hang-on-the-corner crowd
and the stand-arounds and the lean-upons
who use sidewalk space and building fronts
to locate themselves in time passing.
They are beautiful—all, internal edibles
in their fantasies and dreams, alive
before dark settles in and they disappear.
They are the sidewalk people.

West Hills Review   MICHAEL HOOD

ONE DEGREE ABOVE ZERO

You have reached the point where you know
the resolution will not come soon,
that all night the temperature will drop,
reaching its lowest point in the hour
before dawn, that a lantern taken outside

on a night like this years ago shattered
halfway to the barn, that this is the start
of a winter when the river will stay frozen
clear to the bottom, like winters years ago
when some people got lost for good. And you
do what they must have done then:
you get ready for the winter, lay in a stock
of paper the way your immigrant grandparents
hoarded wheat for the winter, wheat to braid
and feed slowly to the fire with the caution
of a people who knew how long things had to last,
who knew spring would always come later than they
thought, or were told to expect, the whispered word
in their prayer, yours, *survival, survivor,*
in a world icing over, the snow drifting against the
door, and the life inside shutting down;
knowing the winter will be long, all resolutions
uncertain, that all night the temperature will
hover one degree above zero, and the sleeper
will wake to check the fire, then draw the blankets
closer, waiting out the silence, waiting out the cold.

Kansas Quarterly   JANE HOOGESTRAAT

WAKING IN AN UPSTAIRS ROOM NEAR ELM TREES

Waking this morning I saw
the room as from far off,
and the leaves printing the screen
were the leaves of a time before childhood,
my mother asleep, my father
rising for work as I lay
barely known in her body. Or were they
the leaves of my life before this one,
where I lived in the dust, or could feel,
through the skin of a fish, the flicker
of leaves over water? Or were they,
as I had believed, merely
the leaves of this morning, the room
unremembered in sleep, and my body
so empty it almost forgot me?
Then I woke to the morning the leaves
made me, in time for my child
waking, and even in time
to see at my window the first
sun on the sill, and could feel
how somewhere a brightness was filling
another world, waking without me:
its leaves, however unlike
the leaves I was watching, were waiting,
and the birds, as I wanted to name them,

were already there in the trees
woven of air, in the earliest
light, in the sounds of a place
I could come to believe on a morning
beginning without me.

Southern Poetry Review   PATRICIA HOOPER

LATE AT NIGHT, THE CATTLE TAKE OVER MATAGALPA

(Nicaragua)

Late at night,

when the soldiers and insurgents go to the hills
to kill each other for another's cause;
when the people of Matagalpa are snuggled away
beneath sheets and each other,
shutting out the sounds of distant gunshots,

the cattle take over the streets of Matagalpa.

Silently they steal into the streets,
empty but for the soldiers in the shadows
left behind to patrol the town.
No government curfew to stop them,
no lowing to give them away, busy with their civic duty;
they chew on the rotting refuse strewn along the streets.
Nothing wasted, they eat even the wax paper and plastic wraps
that once surrounded a Tootsie Roll or a side of beef
dropped carelessly by schoolchildren as they stepped over cow dung.

Early at dawn,

after the sun returns, after the killing,
after the soldiers and the insurgents return from the hills
to line up together in hopes of getting a piece of rare, rationed cheese;
as anxious mothers line up at the house of the dead
to identify missing relatives *(¡Dios mio! ¡Ni mi niño, ni mi esposo!);*
as the cattle also return from the streets,

the people take over the streets of Matagalpa.

And there is evening and there is morning.
And there is no Seventh Day.

America   J. P. HORGAN-AGUADO

FOR A NEPHEW—AND GRADE 11 DROPOUT

Like so many, he's "bright but—!"
The word is usually "lazy."
A smile comes hard with adults
Around. Barefoot, he's tall enough
To need a tail for balance.

His great disease? A need
For the Difficult to dance
Like a burlesque striptease floozie,
For the Boring to organize
As a ringmaster might a circus.

Then—and *only* then—perhaps,
He'd open his eyes with a yawn
Like a wakened forest
In Disney's cinema land,
Scratch his belly, feel himself,

And then—but *only* then—
Consider amazing the world
And us, stirring to life
Like a dead crater,
Out of the easy chair.

Anything of 3-ring interest here?
Mainly him to us,
His rumbly charm, sleepy or wakeful,
Whatever makes him seem—
Not *only* then but now—

A small child to tussle,
Ruffle the hair of,
Ever a nourisher of worry—
This excruciated long-legged sufferer
Of family love.

The Fiddlehead   LEWIS HORNE

MAN, COFFEE, MORNING

A thousand amnesias of childhood
Make one man.
He sits in the morning sipping coffee,
Looking out at Jerusalem glowing on a hill,
And doesn't know where he is.
He feels that if he played
The right band on the right record
He could find his way all the way back to America.

But only for a moment.
A moment. He turns instead
To the Hebrew paper on the table, whose shapes
Twine him insolubly to the future.

Midstream   PETER DAVID HORNIK

NAMING THINGS

Solid things have hard names,
like rock;
quiet things soft names,
like valley.
What if there were a person with no name?
What if she could choose her name—be tree
one day, be star or owl the next?
Today, I'd be the quiet
inside the lily of the valley,
gentle bell that moves but never rings.
Or the hush in a bird's throat
before he opens it to sing.

Kansas Quarterly   BARBARA HORTON

AFTERNOON WAS FADING

as I flipped wall switches, lit lamps
to slow the twilight, hold off the night.
Sudden as knife-edge, the lights failed.

I padded to the basement in stocking feet,
groped through hanging laundry, a soggy
shroud trailing over my head
while I fumbled in the dark, found
by feeling a knot of cables and the switch
box—drew back, spine cold, sucked air.

From somewhere—nowhere—
you bumped my arm, my hand
made some crackling, blue-flash connection

and the lights came on. I saw
the lights come on . . .
wakened to the dark alone.

The Hiram Poetry Review   WILLIAM HOSKIN

READING ROBERT HAYDEN ON A QUIET MORNING

Speech is an almost music we make
that only happens in the very now.
It rides the air between us,
travels down the body hairs
and plays its rhythms on the skin.
It can enter the open door of the ear
Like a kiss or a fist.

But what I am now holding in my head
is a record of speech that can be played

over and over on the circuits of my mind:
words of the living or the dead
offering their published witness,
muted echoes of bodyless voices
ringing silently in my brain.

As I read this pagebound speech,
this ship that ferries poetry,
this elegant daughter of song,
I heard what I have never heard,
see what I have never seen,
and through my eyes alone
feel many feelings not my own.

I would be lessened without these words,
prosthetic symbols stitched to my ignorance
with the strong gut of human knowing.
My imagination and the text extend
the sealapped shores of what is real.
Word by word, this manmade island
that all my searching years have led me to,
grows.
Soon I will be near enough to wave to you.
When you are near enough to hear me,
I want to read aloud to you.
Have you heard the work of Robert Hayden?

Painted Bride Quarterly   EUGENE HOWARD

BECAUSE YOU ASKED FOR A BEDTIME STORY

The time will come when nothing of any worth
Will be remembered by the connoisseurs
Of video games, computers, frozen foods,
The whole warehouse going up in flames
Or merely dissolving into molecules
Of Western Culture, particles of value,
The atoms spinning freely into the void,

The center sliding, moment by moment, sideways
Or into a darkness unrelieved by neon,
A formlessness we've dreamt of, after all,
Though never seen, except in inferior films
Or in those moments of our childhoods
When something shook the house, and no one came
To caress our brows or hasten us into sleep.

Poetry   BEN HOWARD

NIGHT FLIGHT LETTER TO WELDON KEES

I'm writing you after all these years
because people keep saying there is this
kinship of sensibility. Flying over Kansas
now, at a dizzy cloudless elevation, I can't see it.
But you with your cigarette and mustache
and your swept-back Nathanael West darkness so deeply
in love with the cynical tide of things, I can see
them ok in this book which I admit isn't mine.
I'm your age now is another reason
I'm contacting you. Word is you jumped
at 41; and here I am
clinging to every shred of time, by God, and wondering,
Weldon, how to live,
how to stay for one more kiss
in the arms of such mystery of heart
I can't manage it either. So
I was a PI and a tough
character
arguably ("Don't try me," was, anyway, always my advice).
So I loved without any particular restraint or shame.
I love you, too; does that make us similar? Did you
really jump, throw it all
into "them shark infested waves" like a prom queen
who's gotten old? Come on,
tell me I'm wrong (all of us
must be) as Ptolemy was wrong: that is
because the world is not logical,
is it? Think
how many have died like the solitary
tapping pattern buried in Mexico City for days
while the crews dug and wept.
Was it you, Weldon, lost in the hours of earth,
plummeting into the night smile
like a bird? Well, I think
you're a shit for going off like that, on purpose,
leaving us lonely for your profile, for someone
like you, but older
and hopeful. Not as dead.

Northwest Review   CHRISTOPHER HOWELL

SCALING THE HEIGHT OF STONE GATE MOUNTAIN

Walking-stick in hand, in the morning I set out for
                              the steep cliff,
And at evening stop to pass the night on the mountain.
Opposite my high cottage rise distant peaks,
Along which runs a winding stream.
Tall trees are my only courtyard wall,

Piled-up stones the steps and base of my cottage.
Towering rocks here and there obscure the path,
Which finally vanishes into a forest of thick bamboo.
People going up forget the way they've just taken;
People coming down puzzle over the old trail.
Evening waters rush gurgling over the rocks;
Night apes fill the air with their cries.
Is it all so unreasonable—this being lost in contemplation?
I would never half-heartedly keep the Way.
While my eyes enjoy the fleeting buds of spring,
My heart is as upright as an autumn pine.
I live in the usual way—awaiting the end—
In accord with nature and at peace with what will be.
I only regret that no one shares these feelings
And mounts this misty stairway through the clouds.

New Letters   HSIEH LING-YUN
                                            —*Translated from the Chinese*
                                  by Bruce M. Wilson and Zhang Ting-chen

LOVE LETTER FROM THE GRAVE: SIDNEY LANIER, 1881

I'm out of this. But you're still scoured by
each grief, each savagery the lockstep heart
is subject to. There is a balm
in Gilead, but you must carry on,
burning, acquiring the need for Gilead,

the legendary balm that soothes the soul.
Forgive my teasing. Although the body has
no elegance, it has the facts.
I can dissuade it for a little while
but it will win the argument. And soon.

Ten days at most. This letter is unfair.
Before you read it you'll have stood, a widow,
above the northeast corner of my face.
You may have wept. Or, maybe, for the boys,
you were dry-eyed, much braver than the day

required of you. What makes me speculate
about these damn unknowables? You said *goodbye,*
thinking that graveside word would end
our love, our commerce. Now I'm here with this—

a letter from the grave, confused enough
to be the whole man coming back to claim
the thin authority of a revenant.
I know it isn't fair, or kind. I know
it has a false poignancy no matter what

I say. Or fail to say. I know all this.
But I will tell you something stupid, Mary.

We dead don't get around much anymore.
We have no self-control. We are concerned with nothing
but ourselves. The Bible says there is a time

to refrain from embracing. We're almost there.
Forgive me, Love—though it may scrub
your red grief raw, I can't resist the chance
to come back just this once—this final time—
and kiss you when you least expect a kiss.

The Southern Review   ANDREW HUDGINS

DREAMS OF RELIEF: WHEN THE MIND AND SOUL GO THEIR OWN WAY

Dreams are void of morals,
values, proprieties and *ex post facto* laws.
Or so it seems.
I've yet to be arrested for
deeds done in the technicolor darkness
of my slumber. What freedom, dreaming.
But memory evades a multitude of
nightly adventures, scenarios of fantasy
in a nonsensical world where East and West
become North and South and faces
from the past pop up without calling first,
and much is lost to the dawn.
That's the way dreams are. Here, then gone,
forgotten with the years, with age, with
wrinkles multiplying around the eyes;
but that's life—waking life. In slumber,
years don't take their toll, rules are
abandoned, values evaporate like open wine,
and what takes place someplace somewhere between the mind
and soul, if remembered, sometimes provides
the waking flesh with the sense it's been
revived, renewed—on vacation in some tropical
panorama—or even been to bed with some old
flame from another era. How sensual these dreams
seem, so much more vivid than fantasy. The mind
and soul rebel, revolt—do what they want.
Perhaps the waking body will recall—perhaps not.

Kansas Quarterly   ROBERT L. HUFFSTUTTER

STANDING MORTALITY

A bad thunderstorm
Spooked my neighbor's
Horse last night.
This morning, my neighbor

Found her in his swimming pool.
She looked surprised to be there.
Her tail floated behind her
Like a bed of kelp. When
I asked him how he was going
To get her out,
He walked into the pool,
Put blinders and a bridle on her,
Then led her up the steps
Of the shallow end.
She bunched the muscles
In her back and flicked her tail.
I wondered at the fear
That drove her into the pool.
I wondered at my neighbor's
Easy acceptance
Of her fear and her calm
As he led her back
To her stall in the barn.
I wondered that I thought
She looked like a prisoner
Going to execution,
With the hope and serene
Trust of the faithful.

Passages North   PETER HUGGINS

CASE HISTORY

When she was twenty-three, she screamed
In Lord & Taylors.
They put her away
To teach her
You don't scream in fancy
Fifth Avenue stores
No matter how desperate you feel.

When she was thirty-six,
She took her blanket to Sixth Avenue
To send up smoke signals.
They put her away
To teach her
You don't send warnings
On busy Sixth Avenue
No matter what dangers you foresee.

When she was thirty-nine, she danced
On a pink Cadillac.
They put her away
To teach her
You don't profane

The gross national product
No matter how ecstatic you get.

Now she is forty-five.
She can greet any cop on the street.
She can look any shrink in the eye.
She's put her feelings away
To teach them
Home-tutoring is better
Than compulsory education.

The Hollins Critic   SOPHIE HUGHES

PENNSYLVANIA: SMALL SCALE STRIP MINING

Behind the local cemetery, crowded trees
jut limbs clashing for new position.
The trucks have come only this far.
It is nearly winter.

Crouched on the silent dawn hill,
a power shovel snorts furiously, becoming
a purposeful creature, scraping the earth like a starved hand.
These fields will be mud:

In spring, new life will not gather here,
squeezed out in the tracks of machinery lying still.
Rain and sun will struggle with this ground.
It is neither evil nor good.

Raw as any vegetable, the coal
is hauled away to fuel survival's necessary fire.
What is enough? Years ago, there were woods in this place,
deepened by the uncertainty of our childhood.

Whenever we came here, the dark
grew more remote to us than winter's darkness.
Here, we felt as much as children could feel of death.
We were in the time of creation,

sparked by every sound that moved
in the heavy tangle of vines and leaves
and drew us farther into it,
knowing our lives were seen, the earth stirring.

America   MARK HURDELSH

AMERICAN BEAUTY

While kerosene gushed out the spigot
into a gerry can by the back door,
Mother pulled jeans from a rusted line,
then hurried to stir potato soup.

Kerosene ran out for an hour,
soaking the foundation of our home
deep into dry soil,
down to the roots of our rose bush . . .

Climber, with its glorious red that bloomed
all summer at the corner of the house,
survived Ohio blizzards and tornadoes,
the only bright color around the grey farmhouse . . .

Farmhouse that stole my mother's youth
with its eternal clothes lines
and endless sucking oil stoves,
demanding as nine empty bellies . . .

Took her youth as surely as kerosene
strangled our rose bush.
"Don't anyone light a match!" she shrieked,
when she remembered.

I wonder if secretly she wished
it would ignite, flare red, bright
and brief as the roses.

The No-Street Poets   KATHLEEN IDDINGS

HILL

There is a hill.
On the hill is a house.
It lights up at night.
Wind passes from field to field.

There is an old couple
in the house.
Their only son has sunk into the south China Sea
in military uniform.

In the fall the old woman
closes the window of the house on the hill.
A withered leaf flutters
on her husband's mortuary tablet.

In the spring in the house on the hill
nobody is left.
Only the moon shines.
The highway runs below.

Now a hill disappears.
Drive-in snack bars go up.
Kids drink Oronamin C.
Wind passes from field to field.

New Letters   ITSUKO ISHIKAWA
                    —*Translated from the Japanese*
                    by Keiko Matsui Gibson

HOME OF THE RAZORBACKS

Homesick again, watching these buds break,
the high breeze spinning one-arm maple wings
like wishes. I feel the Boston Mountains roll
against me with their old soft green breasts.

I take it slow, from Alma, Arkansas, straight up
Highway 71, then bank left into the first curve
and its long pale overlook. I downshift shrewd
as a hillbilly, gauging what I can and can't do.

God relaxes his grip and I am free, climbing
with the expert trailer-trucks, easing from gear
to gear. Off the edge, miles of sweet green haze
are laced with dogwood, but I am holding the road
up Mount Gaylor to the last plateau where half-

hearted tourists shops announce in peeling paint,
"Highest Point in the Ozarks." Arkansas people like
the folds and crevices, so I am flying down the north
side, holding on, slowing into Mountainburg, West Fork.
Then in the dream I am on the edge of Fayetteville,

looking down into its mountainous Razorback heart
the way I want to know myself. It sprawls plush and deep,
jagged with civilization and haphazard streets.
This place is so clear and real it is almost death.
All my life, I have kept leaving it to stay alive.

The DeKalb Literary Arts Journal   FLEDA BROWN JACKSON

THE MURDER CITY BLUES

i dreamed i lived
in a city
where alleys were for cars—
not ravaged bodies—

where homicide detectives
had cobwebs swirling
around their professional lives.

and the muffled
pop pop pop i heard?

children breaking wind.

firecrackers.

empty popcorn bags
meeting hands.

a city where everyone died
of natural causes—

and no one listened
when i sang
the murder city blues.

Black America Literature Forum   REUBEN M. JACKSON

WORLDS APART

I can't help but believe the killdeer,
so deftly has it led me,
dragging its own wings away from a poorly
hidden nest before clenching back into flight,
and I can't help but believe in a love
that would make itself so vulnerable for its young.

It is hard to understand, but
only by leaving do we know what we love.

Before I left, you told the story
of the fledgling cuckoo who hatches in a sparrow's
nest, who spills out the native fledglings,
and is adopted by the vulnerable parents.
One night, in a city far from home,
I watched in amazement as two young men
who seemed more fierce than the cuckoo,
stooped to kiss some bag lady on the forehead
and pass her a dollar, a lady who had nested on a corner
with her dozen sacks and a cart.

Never have I felt so guilty
for what little love I could show.
That night, alone on a bus, I thought
you were the starlight nesting in the trees
that held every moment that had happened in your life.

In the pine woods along the coast north of here
starlight never touches the ground.
Somewhere in there the cuckoo will begin to sing.
I don't think there was ever a time we weren't
approaching each other through those woods.
I don't think there is a moment we have
that is not taking place somewhere else,
or a love that doesn't lead us, sometimes
deftly, further from ourselves.

Ploughshares   RICHARD JACKSON

OF ALL THINGS

The old man's face
rearranges itself
with each look, each thought,

blurring to match the color of the lake.
On the pier,
he baits the hook with a fresh minnow
& imagines the thick side of a walleye,
the dark eyes of a salmon.
He casts,
a long arching toss,
when suddenly a seagull dives
& catches the fish in mid-air.
From a distance, from the beach here,
it looks absurd:
a man reeling in a flying gull,
swerving back & down like a crazed kite.
The bird struggles, screaming
as the man yanks the pole,
reels, yanks, swears into the sky.
Finally, he pulls hard & the bird veers down,
smacking on the pier.
The old man nudges it with the pole.
Nothing happens.
In the red light of early morning,
he kneels closer & touches the gull.
Of all things in the world,
this is what he never dreamed
would happen.

Mid-America Review   DAVID JAMES

A PATTERN IN PIECES

I can tell you how to hold cold mornings
that are still as my hall mirror.
Take them gracefully
against your bare clavicle
because time is all that is left—
bone to skin to cold.
How very fortunate all we'll ever know
of prophecy is that it goes back to land.

Suppose we admit that going back
is directional, more real than the dark imaginings
of future.
When I look into my dog's eyes
revising the world,
I see our quiet walks up
through lawns of color.

I have always wanted to believe in a history
of self, in the gentle layering of family
on this uneasy, honorable earth.
Now I'm not sure
and I'm not sure it matters.

Today in the same old disguises
I blessed the dailiness of vision
and drove among the musky azaleas with my husband,
searching for the exact shade of blue-red
we thought we once saw.

I remember watching the light rise
like summer in the crocus bud and
ease into the hands of air
as though someone had touched me.
Perhaps the ghost of someone I love was there.
Steady rains half-lovingly rattle the rose petals.
In a climate of softness her full, pink roses
carpet the ground and I stand mindfully still.

Domestic Crude   JOYCE JAMES

TO MY AUNT DYING IN AUTUMN

You are a fallen leaf turning
to paper, the leaf one finds
after winter, a lacework of veins.
I lift you carefully to turn you
on the sheepskin, but even then
the parchment over your hipbone
cracks and opens. Your lips
move without a sound.

Here in the north, snow is already
falling with sudden wind gusts
lifting it back to the steely sky.
At the darkening window I see
the reflected bulk of my middle-aged
body, branches whipping into
its thickness. I remember
how I waited for breasts and hips
to round the thin rope of girl
I was, for that first drop of blood
on the tissue, a tiny bell trembling
inside of me. This summer
I heard it again in an English meadow
at Hadrian's Wall where we walked.
A flock of sheep, lambs with a ting,
ting, by a wall that keeps nothing out
or in, under a sky that whitens everything
except the sound of something
small and silver, ringing.

Poet Lore   JEAN JANZEN

MY GRANDFATHER'S SAYINGS

A hundred years from now what will it matter?
Everything goes wrong—so what else is new?
I'm looking forward to lying down and dying.

When you buy a used car you're buying
another person's problems. Just like marriage.
A hundred years from now will it matter

if grandchildren visit your bones? Used cars
break down. You can run on empty only so long.
I'm looking forward to lying down. Dying

is easy, it's living that's hard. The sun
goes up, the sun goes down. I won't understand
if I live to be a hundred. Nothing's the matter

with me—it's the world that's haywire.
If you can't sing, don't join the choir.
I'm looking forward to lying down and dying:

that's the only answer. I don't know the question.
Spit straight up and you'll learn all you need to know
a hundred years from now. Nothing matters.
Looking forward is lying. I'm down. I'm dying.

Southern Poetry Review   DAVID JAUSS

THE DEAD OF WINTER

These nights when the car is shoved
into the snowbank, old snow
heaped like slag and as hard,
when the sinister highway glitters,
our house slanted into the dark,
far away from the sun,
I've almost lost the desire
to be borne in the fiery chariot
to that fair and happy land
or even southern Iowa
for a month or so,

                          almost . . .

I've insulated the pipes,
banked the house with snow,
put plastic over the windows.
It's a matter of maintaining heat,
to simplify is the key,
to shed the useless leaves.
I always believed that constant
turning away might produce
a state of nonuniform motion by which
the universe would declare its intention.

In the dead of winter night
I listen. A timber cracks.
The house moves slightly.
It is only the polar ice
come into the yard again.
I put on my boots and coat,
look for the pick and the propane torch.

Ascent   LOUIS JENKINS

SALT OF THE EARTH

Self-indulgence can be dangerous. Imagine
being lured into an ice-cream parlor
and shot dead. Or straying
down the cookie aisle at the supermarket—
right into the steel-toothed jaws
of a bear-trap. Fortunately,
we humans know better.
                        But
the beast at the edge of the glade does not.
Proud white-tail buck—nine pointer, at least—
he paws the brown earth nervously, head up,
sniffing. Can smell the salt—but not
our bodies, sweat-stale even in the cold,
not the dusky gun-metal nor the faint acrid spoor
of overhanging death. We have taken care
to be downwind. Nor can he see us, blind
as he is, obscured behind our wall of fallen tree.
Tentative, he advances.

"Nice shot," says Stephen, later,
knotting the rope that binds the carcass to our hood.
Nodding, I acknowledge: indeed it was,
heart-shot at thirty yards. He stops
to wipe his forehead with a sleeve. "Heavy
sonofabitch, though." I nod again, silent.
"What's the matter," he asks. "No stomach for it?"
"No," I tell him, remembering
how the brown tongue had slid freely
over the bitter cube for a full minute,
while I steadied my aim.

Southern Poetry Review   ROBIN DAVID JENKINS

LEAVES

The summer leaves
of maples and sassafras
dance, sing and talk
with changing tunes,

for they live in the winds;
winds always change,
and with them
the tilt of the leaves.

I wish I knew the roots
that talk and rub backs
with the moles and worms;
they always know well

their friends,
and like a sunken stone,
never blow away
in the yellow wind.

Bitterroot   WALT JOHLER

AUTUMN MOOD

I knew what mattered was not
my wife and son working with me
to clear our leaf-cluttered lawn.
What mattered was the sunlight
that blurred the trees silver-bright,
and the leaves that sang their way
through the air, touched the ground
and hushed.
        —Until my son
asked me to let him go
with the friends who happened by,
and my wife surrendered to
the phone's persistent ring
and ran back in the house
and the prongs of my rusty rake
rattled in an air grown chill,
as I pulled still more dead leaves
into isolated piles.

Webster Review   ROBERT K. JOHNSON

RAIN

Rain, big drops, and few.
Drops that crater the dust.
Huge drops and far apart.
More
A footfall
Than a shower.
And in one house and another
The bedridden, hearing steps,
Sit bolt upright

In the sun that never left,
Fearing a thief
But singing out, anyway,

That you, uncle?
Mother, that you?

Yankee   THOMAS JOHNSON

CATULLUS 46

Spring light through starting leaves delights us,
blossoming trees in Harvard Yard and the fragrant
mud on Cambridge Common shake us out
of student lethargy and our winter stupor.
Time now to plan a tour of the famous sites
of New England, leaf through travel brochures
instead of textbooks, turn in our student visas,
see new friends in New York and Martha's Vineyard,
then head home—back pack, American Airlines:
various routes to summer north of the border.

The Antigonish Review   GORDON JOHNSTON

WHAT THEY DO

My father-in-law loves
to fish.
My mother-in-law loves
to read.

What they do is this:
they drive to one of his favorite
trout streams.
He slips into a pair of patched
waders. She
slips into a good book.

He listens to the water.
The sound
it makes as it wraps around
his waders and spins
out of sight. She
quietly swims
toward the shores of Russian
literature. Dreaming
of breakfast in a hotel
where no one
speaks English.

They go about their business,
floating in opposite

directions, yet always, somehow
meeting in the middle.
Soaking wet and
smiling.

Passages North   MICHAEL JONES

DISTANCE

(for J.)

I have never been a good judge
of distance. The time it takes
to travel and the measures, miles
or meters, are animals
Adam never named.
They croak their unsettling
chorus, their metered demands,
and I deny them the way passion
denies history, the way a wren
builds its nest against the wind,
in the same way I deny
your absence and the distance
I can never measure that sets
us apart. I would not be a martyr
at a distance, a new Adam
ready to call and control;
I would be willing to wander,
to say distance has its rule
and we have come under it.
In saying this, I see you are not
so distant, that what separates us
is not so large, as we imagine
where we could go and claim
that distance as our destination.

Plainsong   PAUL JONES

REASONS FOR CLIMBING

To become small.
To get to the top and sit
as though praying or waiting.
To dwell in the country of air.
To stare down
into the valley,
while part of you keeps climbing.

Also, to come back down.
After the sun has set,
in the dark.

To get lost on the path,
cutting yourself on the briars
and the branches,
carrying it all back
down with you, against its wishes,
falling back into your life.

Artemis   RICHARD JONES

JUST AN ORDINARY MONDAY

i was kissing kris kristofferson
when robert redford showed up early
for our midday tête-a-tête
just as the phone rang
with baryshnikov
he'd seen me dance again
and could we please just jeté?
but leonard cohen loved my lyrics
and keith jarrett wants to duet
and placido cries out 'diva' when i sing
then there's halston waiting pouting
till i try the spring designs
i'll wear for johnny, merv,
and maybe even phil
there's the doorbell once again
it's mike wallace and the crew
they're here to film me
with my fellow mense peers

just an ordinary monday

dawn is creeping through the blinds
to find the children
already dancing on my day

Waves   SUZANA JURSZA

WHAT TURNS BUT DOESN'T MOVE

What turns, but never moves is
white as cream. What shines but has
no fire, is the moon. What rises, never sets
is thought of you. And in the mountain
which is the head, in the cave
which is the mouth, and on the lakes
which are the eyes, I have lost
all sight of you. What gets smaller
the more I add to it, is a hole.
What goes through me, before it comes
to me, will be a riddle. I can see,

but I can't feel it, bitter smoke.
I can feel, but never touch it,
absent memory. It goes round and round
the house, but never enters. It's heard
moving through the rooms, absent voice.
It goes round and round the house,
leaves a white glove at my window
cold morning, early winter, shining frost.

Mississippi Review   RODGER KAMENETZ

THE GARDEN WALL

(Assolas House, County Cork)

Here the stones, in accents of moss,
clung flowers and vines, speak of chance
in change—of falling down to build up—
of remains, removals, the residual seed:
the necessity of walls in a garden.
By the waterside rhododendrons grow.

Still, the stream seems not to move, and
the water is smooth as it washes the dam
and runs among the stones downstream.
In wind, blossoms, bits of grass float
backwards, against a deeper current,
as if in memory of a source.

The garden wall refuses memory, has no
knowledge of beginnings, knows only the
present hour—keeping in, keeping out—
in ruin, in completeness, while the stream
beside moves like time, unnoticed and
still, in reflecting surfaces of sky.

Sewanee Review   PAUL KANE

ELECTIVE SURGERY

Growing up is elective surgery,
the doctor behind the mask
is me. I scrape the old face
from its bone and spoon it onto
a sterile tray. I could have kept
my father's chin, my mother's nose,
her eyes (those doleful beggars),
but I wanted the knife; the smell of blood
unfroze me and I sensed my womb
as it churned in its hollow place,
wrapped in thick bone.
Each month I howl for my life.

I carry myself to the forest,
the red-brown blood drying down
my thighs where it hardens like
bark. Here, in the shadows
of the wood, I carve a new face.

Event   JANET KAPLAN

DUST

We find it, a motionless rage, beneath the bed.
It grows without seeming to grow, its rasping heat knitting new goods

Even as we stare . . . scouring pads for the angels
Who polish forks in our dreams.

I think of an aunt who never loved anything openly, her remarkable
Sense of industry, her reverberating house, where one could almost hear

The emerald necklace of electricity rattling around on its clasped strand,
The minerals of Hell itching under the kitchen floor.

Which ancient civilization is in this batch?
Something we can never know.

Failed brother of snow, it rises weightlessly now under my lamp—
A brown vagabond made of landfill from the prairies of memory.

The New Yorker   VICKIE KARP

RIDING BIKE WITH NO HANDS

I have always wanted to.
Like I longed to match Mother's
perfect alto those Sundays
she sang into my ear,
hoping her pitch would stay there.

Harder than staying in tune,
it's been years since I tried to ride
no-hands, but under this pure sky
I sing *Christ the Lord is Risen Today,*
surprised I still know the words.

And my hands drop from the bars
in that quickening
I felt long ago when Daddy let go
and I coasted off in the lawn,

exquisitely balanced, absolved
from all attachment to earth.

West Branch   JULIA SPICHER KASDORF

HOW TO TURN INVISIBLE

Each night bored by the same celestial blankness:
the moon rolled into a little pill, the wind
a dollop less transparent: each night
a pint of vodka. And siestas,
Siestas. I cannot expostulate
with dawn when she arrives naked
under a blue slip. I know that clouds feel nothing,
sliced by the thinnest sliver of moon,
that the moon feels nothing, that from the moon's perspective
every coyote is redundant.
The only substance I can swallow like air
is air.

Southern Poetry Review   ANDREW KAUFMAN

CROCHETING AT THE ARTS FESTIVAL

When I broke my hand I could not spell:
Letters lie in little push-pulls of the pen.
Things that I don't know my hands know well.
My hands in darkness know to crochet when
a painter flashes slides upon a screen,
talks of influence and artists' tools.
My hands, the artists and the tools, unseen,
paint with their hook a tapestry of wools.

I listen while my hands entwine the words
of poets chopping out the voice of trees.
My hands clot views of pastured hills. Like curds,
a sweater clabbers, sets as tight as cheese.
My hands are dogs who guide a sightless shepherd's
flock, and in the dark my blind hand sees.

Kansas Quarterly   FRANCES W. KAYE

TO CHILDREN

I see you grow lovely, full of the earth,
and you open your small hands to me like petals.
I'm ashamed to show my face.
I can give you nothing.
I'm neither the sun, your mother
holding you to my breasts, letting you drink my milk,
nor the earth, holding the tray
of day and night in my hand, serving you
scores of beautiful and fine days.
I'm just an ordinary man,
but I think of

giving you myself.
Grow on my body,
Let my heart be scooped empty
by your powerful roots and stems.

The American Poetry Review   MANG KE
                    —Translated by Willis and Tony Barnstone

DRESSES

The attic a cemetery
of dresses. Smocked cottons,
fading the way bruises do. Imperishable crimpolene
of adolescence, gawky-coloured tents
for the twelve-course meals I made of slights
and snubs and inchworm desolations. The slip
for my wedding dress, itself entombed in plastic
at my mother's house; her dress,
worn by me, my cousin, waiting now
for its next occupant. Nightgowns (floral-
embossed cellophane) for my trouseau—
never worn.
Maternity smocks like empty birdcages
the doors banged open.

Silk and crepe; cotton and wool:
thieves of my nakedness. My skin a dress
whose seams keep splitting
so blood shows through.

Sometimes I steal whole afternoons upstairs
holding the dresses against me
as if we were dancing, or embracing
after some great grief. At times,
when I try them on and the cloth
nicks or gapes I can almost feel
who I am.

Cross-Canada Writers' Quarterly   JANICE KULYK KEEFER

DUCKS

For one thing, they're
not as big as swans. A
duck probably wouldn't
have made much of an
impression on Leda.
She might even have
laughed. But on their
high, cold flights,
their pain must be

considerable. On tv,
a fat duck used to bring
money down for Groucho.
That one and the one
that fluttered toward
my gun on a Louisiana
lake seemed as absent
as they were fat.
On late Novembers,
dozens of wiggling
Groucho brows have
found their way out
of dreams, moving
a sad silly song in
and out of the wind,
across a brittle sky.

Corona   GREG KEELER

HEARTH

What I want on days like this
is the cream
out of the milk of air,
the pale juice of October sun
gathered in one drop
on the tongue. I want
my body's grace and energy to move into
my mind. To sink

quiet as a stone and arrive
at the door of the "heart's
sitting room." I want to find what Rilke
found: the lamp lit, the fire banked, himself
or God—someone very very old—at home.

The Cape Rock   LUANN KEENER

GOING BACK TO THE CITY

The sun
has finished the small buildings, and the light
recedes, heading toward the bridges.
It has been years. Coming back
today was not the memory
of what you'd left here or taken to the next place,
but as if the streets you, too, passed
were someone else's life entered
by mistake you'd say, tired from walking.
A woman sweeps off the steps,

the familiar spirit of the neighborhood,
but doesn't look up. The clouds
are colored paper. What's puzzling
is how the buildings are part of the sunset
sinking down one wall, then the next.
Suddenly everything is changed: one skyscraper
electric blue, silver, rising above shoppers
and the man selling magazines. It glows
like a river seen from distant hills.

In the town where you were young, fireflies
rose from the grass like sparks.
Some nights your parents
would forget about you altogether,
and you and your three brothers would follow
the lights long after bedtime
as they moved off, higher
around the house and into the treetops.

You might have been leaving with them.
First the driveway, then the bushes
by the mailbox lost to sight,
the house and its lights fading
in the warm, dark air,
and that reflection in the building,
the city you no longer need, close by.
Oh, that is to come
back to you now: the world
inside you rising, tall buildings,
this sharp blue light and, beyond, the sky.

Black Warrior Review   DAVID KELLER

DUSTING OFF THE SORROW

All right, haul out the old blue shirt and shake off its
wrinkles, blow the dust off the lunch bucket, the bones
of the father and his sad rosary, trudge down another road
with what's left of hope in your left hand, the one that
can play no piano.

It's true that a man stands on his country the way he stands
on his gallows; it's true we are born on the birthdays of
our heroes and that we die, a few shriveled pieces of meat
on the saucer edge of the dawns that bring in the Days of
Assassination, holidays no one dresses up for.

And me, what am I doing boring everyone again, forgetting to
put the meals and the jokes in my songs? When will I learn
that the eye wants its reds only in roses, the nose wants to
smell what is cooked, the ear to listen to sounds filtered
through nostalgia like doves one remembers?

At a slight distance from here, perhaps only twenty years,
ice is waiting to form forever over the roofs of our houses,
snow is crouched like a cougar in ambush, and a melancholy
singer repeats the words of his people: when there is no more
bread, stones will do.

And I dust off the old sorrow again because of that and for
you, and I turn in the night as alone as each of us the way
we are when we run a single hand lightly up and down over the
edges of those sills that guard windows looking out and windows
looking in.

Tendril   DAVE KELLY

LAKE SEMINOLE

A heron turns head first, then wings
Toward fish eyes tilted to the sun.
On untucked legs, the bird
Waits for the waters to still, then
Sticks its head into the world
Refracted by natural light
But known by fish and bird alike,

While I sit in my rented boat,
Waiting with slight tension
On my untested line to nod
Its signal assent at my attempt
To pull a fish from this shallow place
Where even birds come down from the sky
To bite unbended reality.

But today I only catch myself
Casting about in my cautious way
For fish slipped under levelling waves.
And waking my still boat,
I glimpse a tail
By which I measure the whole.

For such is this or any place known
To me who sees through reflected light
Both realities in circling birds and
fish diving at the limits of sight.

The Antigonish Review   ROBERT A. KELLY

THE FRIDAY NIGHT LIFE

And when you came home from work not having gone out
with the girls to worship Friday night at the bar
and I was upstairs in bed listening to music
and you said how cute I looked in my jeans

and brown checked shirt
and I urged you to sit next to me
and I kissed you for the first time in months
and you didn't turn away right away
and your legs were open in their slacks
and I smiled
and kissed you again sweetly tenderly like
the immature person I am
and there was no hate in you
and I felt the miracle of the realness
and the humor in us
and kissed you on the neck where your curls
are bleached by marriage like mine
and still the same because I've always loved
your scented body
and on the lips and cheeks again then innocently gently
you got up disengaging
and said amazingly flirtatiously now be patient
you can't just barge in
and went glowing downstairs to make Sabbath
for the family
and I thought it was happening
and I was in my place
and everything was in its place.

Midstream   MILTON KESSLER

ON THE EDGE OF IT

It is early now, not even six,
And sleep is something that happens
To somebody else, to people we don't know.
The street starts to fill with traffic.
Each car and truck strikes like a match, flaring
Across an asphalt matchbox, burning away
Into silence. I am watching. The arc-lamp
Street light is orange. Twenty miles off
In another town you lie, unsleeping, eyeing
A digital clock. The blue numbers
Knock the minutes off with the glazed
Indifference of a gas meter.
You count the worries of your life—
The job, the kid, the rent-control board,
The empty, other half of the bed
I still think of as ours.
You sit on the edge in darkness.
If either of us were a smoker,
Now would be the time for it. We hold
Nothing in our fists but our fingers.
You're switching on your light now.
I, mine. We're switching on lights

In two countries. From a spy-plane
Or a hot-air balloon, someone
Could take us both in, could fit us
Into the same frame one more time.
From above, the earth seems to be burning,
Not in flames but in embers. Morning
Birds are screaming. The land between us
Stretches out, glowing, a bed of coals.

Calliope   ROD KESSLER

EAGLE HARBOR

Here's a picture of my father
in the morning north woods light.
My parents have just built on
a tiny, screened-in porch;
my father sits on the new steps,
elbows on knees, tired.

Around him, leaning against the house,
are all the well-worn tools
for moving the earth: the spade and fork;
the wheelbarrow, in use
as usual, half-full of dirt;
a length of pipe for prying
the rocks up out of their settings like gems.
And the house itself,
the white trim crisp against the siding;
the speckled, egg-shaped stones
from the lake, collecting in piles.
We come such distances

to be here, we sons; to see our fathers
leaning a little, life-sized.
For once, everything is at rest;
we'll remember it this way.

West Branch   CARL KIKUCHI

WHERE NO RAINBOW HAD HUNG FOR YEARS

No grapes grew on his land for years.
Only the dry hot wrath of indifference
    scorched by cynicism
Endured on the hard, cracked earth.

Years passed, and every hour he stretched
    his arms to heaven.
Sometimes false rains showered an hour
And then retreated on cumulous clouds,
Leaving hurt and caution growing with wet wrath.

But early one morning, on the edge of spring,
He stretched his arms in prayer for rain, and
This time the fingers knew that a monsoon
Had come to heal the land
Where no grapes grew,
Where no manna fell,
Where no rainbow had hung for years.

Obsidian   JAMES C. KILGORE

A NOTE CORRECTING THE
HOUR FOR DINNER

(after a theme by Christopher Boffey)

Afternoon. The sluggish hours ring
one, two, three, four, delaying evening.
That I may see you later makes me hate
the busy spangled light on cars and lake.
Innumerable windshields throw it back.
Innumerable fleecy sailboats tack.
Each sunlit fact makes you seem far away:
each couple over tea in that café;
each happy skateboard rider; each blond head;
each pigeon eating from a sack of bread.
Each index of the world's sufficiency
makes me stop dead: do you still care for me?
Or am I like a raindrop on a stone
that has the same expression when I'm gone?
Or like a drop of water in the sea,
won't you close up, without me, seamlessly?
Come when you read this note. You are the wave
whom drowning I have sought that you might save.
Stay me with ribbons of your smile and look.
Eat dainties from my hand. Sit while I cook.

The Southern Review   MARY KINZIE

AMAZED BY CHEKHOV

Whenever I see a production
of *Wild Honey,* say, or *The Seagull,*
I want to run up on stage
and drink vodka with the characters I admire
and knock the villains down
and have all the women throw themselves at my feet.
I forget that the people up there
are just actors who would probably freeze
or hurry off as the curtain came down
and that I would be hustled away by understudies,
eager nobodies destined for nothing better

than television commercials, if they're lucky,
but trying now to impress the stars
by the force with which they hurl me into the alley,
where I bruise and cut myself and tear my clothes.
As for my wife, well!
There would be a study in anger for you!
"You've embarrassed me for the last time,"
she'd say, and that would be the end of,
not a perfect marriage, but a good one nonetheless.
On the other hand, maybe the players would say,
"Marvellous! Wonderful! You're here at last,
old man! Have a drink!"
                              And that would be my life:
I'd spend the rest of my days acting my heart out
and getting these huge rounds of applause.
I would have to say the same thing over and over again,
but at least it would be brilliant.
And even though something terrible would happen to me
sooner or later, that's simply the price
that would have to be paid by a character
as well-loved as mine. Then *quoi faire?*
as one of Chekhov's impoverished Francophiles would say.
How's this: to get up some evening
when the jokes and the non sequiturs
are flying around like crazy
and make my way to the end of the aisle
as if to go for an ice cream or the bathroom
and get a running start
and fly up the steps
with a big stupid grin on my face
and just disappear into the light.

The Chattahoochee Review   DAVID KIRBY

COWS IN SNOW

From a distance they looked like Oreos
scattered over the snowy pastures.

But that was from a distance.
Up close they looked like cows, Holsteins,

enormous and stupid
and occasionally mooing in their sleep.

Or turning their long faces—all nose—
they look at you with their sad childlike eyes,

they lift their tails—
their great flanks shudder—and let fall

small brown aromatic apples of dung
steaming onto the frozen ground. Once

I watched men loading them, one after
the other, into trucks to be taken to slaughter.

Their eyes, their snow-flecked lashes,
glittered in the dark spaces

between the slats, hundreds
of eyes. And you wouldn't believe how hard it is

to wake them up. That's why the men carried
two-by-fours, to smack them across their foreheads

with, repeatedly, till slowly, sluggishly, they began
to walk toward the ramp behind the van.

I sat straddling the fence—
Oreos, Oreos—but that was from a distance.

Ploughshares   JAMES KIRK

JANUARY THAW

All day snow has spoken, sliding
from the roof with the prim satin *shush*

of my grandmothers' slips. The insistent
drip of icicles has been the only clock.

We know it can't last. The radio
is already smug with a cold front from Canada,

huge frozen tongues that will reach us
tomorrow. We are wedded to cold,

who drive its length each day, safe
and solitary. Even in summer we search it out,

digging deep into earth where winter
keeps its secrets. No wonder we are afraid.

The body betrays itself, seeking the warmth
of a second body, hiding under covers

as though darkness could save us
from the image of our need. My love,

I don't know how long we will last—I pace
the floor, overwound, and useless

without you. I'm tired. Defeated by ice,
by the long stretch of night that lies

before me. This is all I have to offer,
and even to me it seems slight.

Seneca Review   JUDITH KITCHEN

MENGELE

We were discussing nazis on the backyard lawn,
and drinking brandy in the late afternoon.
Two chickadees were mating in the grass until
the cat bolted after them, and then
they shimmered up into the trees and finished there.
Those trees, in the first muscle of summer,
lay down a colonnade of restful yellow light
which made a grace of dust and shadow.
I drifted away.
The thrum of our more moral tongues
became the dim cicadas. Just so peaceful was
the sea that swallowed him who forty years
before had murmured, "There, there, darling,"
to a little girl as he injected her
with poison; cooed to her while she writhed
and vomited and died; then ordered
her body destroyed with all the others.
All the others. He drowned; an old man;
maybe on one of those crowning days
when sometimes it seems right to slip
into the underwaves and float among the weeds
and settle on a breath of sand
in an ecstasy of rageless suffocation—
drifting away, drifting away.
And so our talk moved on to other things;
moved on and ended, and the far clouds moved on.
And in the quiet I at last could hear
the husky thermals shouldering a hawk
whose shadow froze the racing heart of prey
where the grass played loom to spiders.

Southern Poetry Review   ANDREW KLAVAN

DECEMBER POEM

How beautiful the dark, loose, ripe, glossy daylight comes
Without surprise. As if "to startle" meant to dart
Inward, grab what's to be had there, return full and
Ready. For what, the last month? Cold water, hard ground, half-bright air?
The short days stay like the others: like they've come from
The country house, back to where artificial light
Happens without success, fulfillment. Take the streets,
For example, indiscreetly bright. Crowded, too.
It seems as if more should be seen in this last act
Of every first year. But perhaps white rooftops hide
The audience, disguise it even to itself:
Gray light, an engraving we wish we could erase.

The Literary Review   EDWARD KLEINSCHMIDT

THE MINUET

The florid counterpoint of Johann Sebastian Bach
Drops note by note in the October night;
An imaginary couple of grave demeanor
Is dancing a slow and stately minuet
To a lovely ancient tune.

O you who hear nothing now,
O you deaf henceforth to all cries,
What has become of you, lovers of long ago?
Ashes and fragments of bone . . .
No one knows now the sound of your voices,
No one knows the form
Of your well-loved faces;
All of you is forever destroyed,
And only the charming heart of the old musician
Beats still to the gentle sound
Of the harpsichord.

Webster Review

KRISTAN KLINGSOR
*—Translated from the French
by Dorothy Aspinwall*

STUFFED RABBIT

It's last call when a man you've met
asks if you'd like a black russian.
All night, he's talked sports and half-
listened to you. Still—he has
a lean body and luxurious beard and you
like lean bodies and luxurious beards.
So you nod and take little sips
of vodka and kahlua.

Sandwiched in a cab, you begin to feel
dizzy and think you may have
a change of heart, but the man is already
rubbing your thigh, whispering for you
to just relax. You wish you were somewhere else—
your first trip to New York: the toy store
when you headed straight for the rabbit—
its bright eyes, the satin ribbon holding
the bell: how, stroking its fur,
you couldn't bring yourself to quite let go.

On the way back, you clutched the rabbit
in your pocket, wanting to cry,
dying to tell. Now, as if you'd lost
any say in the matter, you bite your lip,
and feel someone else's fingers
dig into the fur, tighten on the bell.

Ploughshares

LINDSAY KNOWLTON

SON'S VISIT

You enter the meadow catching
at seedheads, crows bloom over the wood.
A cicada cuts off its song
as you pass, but my ear follows
its rise over your head, a fine wire
grounded in my flesh, holding taut
the impossible canopy of my love.

As if cold, I draw my arms close
and lean against the door jamb,
its weathered grain paled to ash,
knots to milky scars.
I have become accustomed
to silence, the tap of flies
on the window, to remembering.

Crows settle back in the oak,
you stop by the raspberry canes
and pull berries with both hands;
behind you the meadow breaks out
like a city of spires.

Blueline   ANN B. KNOX

STAND-BY

Everything here
is on stand-by,
waiting:
the open door,
faded flowers,
your empty glass,
the silent phone.
My heart.

Midstream   CHARLES KORMOS

JÓZEK'S FEDORA

That morning they sent us
to sort out headgear
in that hut, you know,
near the crematoria.
All sizes, shapes, colors.
Caps, hats, bonnets,
hoods, berets, biggins.
Piles and piles of them.

Near one edge I spotted
my brown fedora

bought in Kraków
four years before
on Grodska Street.
I stared, thinking:
is it possible?
Am I still alive?
It stared back at me
as if in disbelief
that I was still alive.

I said to Mietek:
pinch me, pinch me.
I need to know
if I am still alive.

Midstream   YALA KORWIN

ON THE WAY

Mother and father are beginning to die inside me.
Thirty years after their deaths in the storm
they withdraw quietly from my rooms,
from my moments of grace.

I'm sure about it. Voices and words have stopped,
they're free now. They no longer visit
my house, but not because they are angry.
A living man must be on his own.

Somewhere father is getting up early,
walking around in his sandals, pretending
as usual he doesn't see how mother cries
as she knits a warm sweater for her son,
camped on the way in the night.

Poet Lore   ABBA KOVNER
                          —Translated from the Hebrew
                          by Shirley Kaufman, with Dan Laor

OLD WOMAN IN NURSING HOME

My world has narrowed
to the space around this bed,
without familiar odours,
worn furniture and creaking stairs;
orientation becomes difficult.

From far away my children send cards
that offer love in rhyming couplets,
their glossy coloured pictures
litter my dressing table
like prize ribbons offered at livestock shows.

I sit in hallways with strangers,
isolated by separate pasts
into a silence
I'm too tired to break.

Sometimes my tongue scatters past shame
through fragmented speech
to be chuckled over by nurses
until even my sins
are reduced to trivia.

The Antigonish Review   HOLLY KRITSCH

EXPLANATIONS

Take a sunflower in your hand and ask
why it grows—how long it lasts,
or from your window look at a child
riding his big wheel down the pavement,
or a mother hanging white socks
in the back yard summer.
How do you explain a kiss,
the daydreamer gazing out his window,
or that stranger in your looking glass?

The firefly winks in the August evening;
the cricket trebles his own goodnight.
Nearby, a leaf on the sycamore is turning;
on the lawn the rose of Sharon fades.
The hours fall in the hourglass,
and in the dark the whippoorwill echoes
the sound that pauses in your breath.
It will not last . . . will not last . . .
will not last . . . last . . . last . . .

America   PETER KROK

WISH BONE

She is thirty-one and thinking
of calcium supplements.

As if there is not enough
wrong with life,
she dreams of bones breaking,
splitting off into an army of skeletons:

The sorcerer's apprentice
casting careless spells
and spilling precious marrow
in buckets around her ankles.

The midnight fear clings
in mother-of-pearl beads
on her forehead,
curls her fingers and toes
into swollen shells.

On a shelf in the closet
are bottles filled with miracles,
one to keep the pincushion in her
chest still soft and beating,
another to iron out the seams
in her skin,
and a jar of tablets
to strengthen her cuticles.

Now there's a space
reserved for the pills
that will help keep
her back straight,
her arms and legs reaching
through years that fall
like clothing at her feet.

The Cape Rock   MINDY H. KRONENBERG

SURPRISES

This morning's red sun licks dew from the hundred
California peppers that never set fruit in
my Zone-Three garden. After fifteen summers

of failure, why this year do I suffer
the glut of inordinate success? They hang
in clustered pairs like newly hatched sex organs.

Doubtless this means I am approaching
the victory of poetry over death
where art wins, chaos retreats, and beauty,

albeit trampled under barbarism,
rises again, shiny with roses, no thorns.
No earwigs, cutworms, leaf miners, either.

Mother's roses climbed the same old latticework
trellis until it shattered under their weight,
and she mourned the dirtied blossoms more, I thought,

than if they'd been her children. She pulled on
goatskin gloves to deal with her arrangements
in chamberpots, pitchers, and a silver urn.

I watched, orphan at the bakeshop window.
It took all morning. *Never mix species
or colors,* she lectured. *It cheapens them.*

At the end of her long life she could reel off
the names of all the cart horses that had
trundled through her childhood, and now that I

look backward longer than forward, nothing
too small to remember, nothing too slight
to stand in awe of, her every washday

Monday-baked stuffed peppers come back to me
full of the leftovers she called surprises.

Michigan Quarterly Review   MAXINE KUNIN

PASSING THROUGH

(on my 79th birthday)

Nobody in the widow's household
ever celebrated anniversaries.
In the secrecy of my room
I would not admit I cared
that my friends were given parties.
Before I left town for school,
my birthday went up in smoke
in a fire at City Hall that gutted
the Department of Vital Statistics.
If it weren't for a census report
of a five-year-old White Male
sharing my mother's address
at the Green Street tenement in Worcester,
I'd have no documentary proof
that I exit. You are the first,
my dear, to bully me
into these festive occasions.

Sometimes, you say, I wear
an abstracted look that drives you
up the wall, as though it signified
distress or disaffection.
Don't take it so to heart.
Maybe I enjoy not-being as much
as being who I am. Maybe
it's time for me to practice
growing old. The way I look
at it, I'm passing through a phase:
gradually I'm changing to a word.
Whatever you choose to claim
of me is always yours;
nothing is truly mine
except my name. I only
borrowed this dust.

The American Poetry Review   STANLEY KUNITZ

THE ROUND

Light splashed this morning
on the shell-pink anemones
swaying on their tall stems;
down blue-spiked veronica,
light flowed in rivulets
over the humps of the honeybees;
this morning I saw light kiss
the silk of the roses
in their second flowering,
my late bloomers
flushed with their brandy.
A curious gladness shook me.

So I have shut the doors of my house,
so I have trudged downstairs to my cell,
so I am sitting in semi-dark
hunched over my desk
with nothing for a view
to tempt me
but a bloated compost heap,
steamy old stinkpile,
under my window;
and I pick my notebook up
and I start to read aloud
the still-wet words I scribbled
on the blotted page:
"Light splashed . . ."

I can scarcely wait till tomorrow
when a new life begins for me,
as it does each day,
as it does each day.

The American Poetry Review　　　STANLEY KUNITZ

TROPISM

(for Steven)

As the land pieces together,
I see the fields of New England
marked in clover and clusters
of early meadow rue.

I think of you in a warmer climate,
where bougainvillea drape jalousy windows
in wineshade flowers, where wild orchids,
domesticated in coconut husks, line your porch.

I have few names for these
New England flowers, single-file rows,

an abrasive array of purples
and peeking eyelet whites.

Here the muted light lasts longer,
gives me hours alone.
Like the stem of whorled leaves,
each line on my palm
stretches toward a more lighted place
I call home.

Crosscurrents   LAURIE KUNTZ

LOVE POEM AFTER TAKEOFF
OR
IN THE SAME PLANE WITH YOU

Look at the shadow on the earth, the tiny shadow that
flies with us

So the greatest of our fears remains
behind us below

Never is the probability less that one of us
will die much earlier than the other

New Letters   REINER KUNZE
—Translated from the German
by Lori Fisher

THE MOUNTAINS

I do not go to the mountains anymore.
Now that my brother is dead, I cannot go there
without weeping.
Certain trees remind me of him,
and the way the road winds, twists,
is so much like him, his difficulty.
Sometimes I say to myself
that all this sorrow will wear itself out,
that we were not meant to live forever in pain.
And then I remember those high places he loved,
the chill night air so unforgiving.

The Chariton Review   GREG KUZMA

THE GREEN MESSENGER

He comes
over earth feathered
with new green,
springy under his feet.

Now lavender stars
and bells caroling whiteness
wake in his path.
He comes,
and the mute strings
that have lain in the sleep
of trees all winter
are suddenly pitched
and plucked
to a green aubade.
Small leaves uncurl their throats.
Wet wings unfold,
and he comes.
The sun throws down
its gold unstintingly
on the hare's nest
and the shawl of the spider.
He comes,
and deep in a black cave
the she-bear nudges her cub.
The cold stone of the year
is rolled away—
and he comes.

Yankee   JOAN LaBOMBARD

LOOKING BACK

Each morning I assemble myself out of
images from my dreams, the way I will after
death when things I hardly noticed stay with
me like old photographs of times no one can
recall—someone told us to smile, touched our
lips with red, sharpened the wheat, filled in
my grandmother's hair, my grandfather's cheeks,
until it hardly mattered that we were together.
But in one dream last night my true grandparents
beckoned from the twilit pantry and I followed,
youth clinging to me like pollen. Everything
seemed familiar, both to the child moving forward
and to myself looking back, remembering.

Calliope   NANCY LAGOMARSINO

DO IT IN DETROIT

The nurses come in and wheel out
the teenager in the bed next to me.
They'll induce labor with pitocyn
so she'll give birth to her dead baby.
Ultrasound showed it had starved to death.

"Honey, ain't no way a baby's gonna
keep me from getting into my clothes.
If your figure goes, the delicious
ones won't even look at you, much
less ask you to get intimate."

They say babies in Detroit die
as fast as those in Central America.
There, they've got bullets
and bottled formula to deal with.
Here, you must contend with
criminal forms of vanity.

Michigan Quarterly Review   CHRISTINE LAHEY-DOLEGA

BLUE JAY

A sound like a rusty pump beneath our window
Woke us at dawn. Drawing the curtains back,
We saw—through the milky light, above the doghouse—
A blue jay lecturing a neighbor's cat
So fiercely that, at first, it seemed to wonder
When birds forgot the diplomacy of flight
And met, instead, each charge with a wild swoop,
Metallic cry, and angry thrust of beak.

Later, we found the reason. Near the fence,
Among the flowerless stalks of daffodils,
A weak piping of feathers. Too late now to go back
To nest again among the sheltering leaves.
And so, harrying the dog, routing the cat,
And taking sole possession of the yard,
The mother swooped all morning.

                              I found her there
Still fluttering round my head, still scattering
The troops of blackbirds, head cocked toward my car
As if it were some lurid animal,
When I returned from work. Still keeping faith.
As if what I had found by afternoon,
Silent and still and hidden in tall grass,
Might rise again above the fallen world;
As if the dead were not past mothering.

The American Scholar   PAUL LAKE

SEVEN HORSES FEEDING IN THE SUN

(for Patrick)

Yes, they were graceful.
They were many times graceful.

The pasture was quiet as a parlor—
They seemed to be grazing in lamplight,
Moving as if they were memories.

I didn't think of them again until October,
When I turned on a lamp one afternoon.
On the window, a bead of rain
    slid like a shuddering muscle—
Beyond it, slow obeisance of branches,
    adagio of bending—
The long strong hair of a daughter
    shaken out of a cap.
That was the way they moved.

In one certain light
They may breathe forever
In a place where the sun is raining
    shivers of summer,
And we say to each other always, "Look . . ."

The Ohio Review   MARGARET LALLY

NATURE, HOW SUPREMELY ORDERLY

In a desicated grove down at
the old homestead, fluttering
on glittering skeins of travel,
a caucus of magpies unravels
raucous parabolas from tree to tree,
chattering, jittering, jeering
an eagle poised southeasterly.

Bothered, that bailiff of birds
kicks twigs, polishes his golden beak,
bends his wings against the noise,
poses himself for flight in case
he sights some slight motion below.

In this avian geometry, the prey
of the eagle becomes carrion for the
magpies. When he hunts, they feed.
How rational, how clear the design.

It's like butterflies drinking tears
from the eye of the great sea tortoise.
To quench their thirst they must
first force the turtle to laugh
or cry. It doesn't matter which.

Blueline   MARGARET LAMB

A WEEK-END HAS TWICE AS MANY HOURS

A week-end has twice as many hours as a
week-day.
You will do something with your life on the weekend.
You will be able to stretch your arms in the morning. Be able to spread
your arms out
and dance like a dreamer. You will sing and be ready
to
sing in the shower.

You stretch. You spread your arms out. You make use
of the fact
that human gestures are available, even when you are
alone.
You stretch. You spread your arms out . . . like one who
is about to practice a whole new way of crying . . . or
really something quite different.

Frank

MARIANNE LARSEN
—Translated from the Danish
by George Johnston

THE IDEA OF A TOWN

There had to be a water-tower in a grove on the highest
point, and at the flattest the railroad yards and the stations;
at least one street a hundred feet wide running

through the entire town, to the ghost edges laid out
in blocks with nothing there but the sidewalks and hydrants.
The schools, unravished still by the moderns; the little

playground with its swings. The modest cluster
of stores and offices desperately down town. The movie house.
A handful of little apartment buildings. Beyond them, acre

on acre, on the straight streets (Race, Main, Front, Poplar),
the houses of the people, two story, with tiny
lawns, and swings on the porches. Remember? This was America's

unimaginative matrix of all our imagination and dreamstuff.

The Hudson Review

RICHMOND LATTIMORE

VETERANS HOSPITAL

In the lounge the TV turns to fuzz;
The green foam slippers move like clouds.
Puzzles are stacked on a corner table
Where the pieces drift slowly apart.
One man methodically attempts the putting

Together. If he finishes, it should look
Like the landscape pictured on the cover

Of the box: a sagging sky, a lazy green
Pond, some birches, a house, distant and
Tiny and cold. The man waits
For the moment of recognition—some
Color, some shape—until all is locked
Into place. The smoke of cigarettes
Caves in around the patients in wheelchairs.

There is never enough light in this room;
It turns sour in the drapes. One patient
Who is undergoing radiation for cancer of the throat
Has two blue crosses marked on his neck.
The man working the puzzle has a piece
That should be the sky if only it would fit.

Passages North   PATRICK LAWLER

FINAL RECKONING: AFTER THEOGNIS

Me? I feel safest in cemeteries.
Horizontal humans lie peacefully;
no anger or mischief in them, no hate
and deceit. Even if darkness comes
when I find myself standing near a slab
time and fierce squalls have tilted towards me
so that I think of the moles underfoot
tearing the flesh clean of the skeletons,
I have no fear or sadness. Why should I?
The dead are surely more fortunate
to be done at last with life's ills and chills,
with the lies needed for mere survival
and the mean compromises each must take
before he can call some small space his own.
Bah! The comedy's not worth a frog's fart;
only priests and rabbis think otherwise,
metaphysicians and crazed bolsheviks.
For myself, I love the tranquil boneyards
both for the evergreen moral they teach
and for the asylum they give against
the violent longings that agitate
the caged animals of Chicago
and Madrid, of Moscow, Belfast and London.
Tombs, I say, are reassuring when men
are swine, smiling wolves with capped teeth,
the cities reeking of scribbling whores
and those who need no bribes to pimp for them.
To these, O Zeus, send plagues! Destroy them all!
Don't leave behind a single specimen

and rid earth of locusts, snakes, and weevils;
let the new seedlings come up tall and green.
Preserve all poets mad and marvellous,
guard them from the fury of envious dust.

The Antigonish Review   IRVING LAYTON

THE MASSACRE

A man walks into McDonald's
dressed to kill in a black T-shirt
and camouflage pants and rat-a-tat
rat-a-tat rubs out twenty living souls
just like that, not one of them he knows. They say
he'd had a fight with his wife, Mary, but that's no reason
to shoot bullets into a one-month bambino
peacefully asleep in his crib or at two boys
alighting from their bikes, their mouths watering
for the big hamburgers sizzling in their minds.
Notching anyone his eye sights, even as far off
as the freeway, he also drills eleven hombres
holed up in the immaculate washroom
and then goes on to pick off the other diners
who've come to the restaurant for their last supper.
He picks them off like clay pigeons, but like they say,
'Who knows when the slug's got your initials on it?'
And now his name will be entered in the Book
of Records gee whizz and wow and all that
for the biggest one-man slaughter in America
because nothing is certain these days
except the human heart whose portals humiliation
and self-distaste have clogged with hate.
Death too's a sure thing, whose or when and where
only the good Lord knows and that's *his* big secret, eh;
but I reckon he means to keep it that way
for a long while yet or what do you think, Mister?

Descant (Canada)   IRVING LAYTON

PAPPA

Chair in half-sunlight, claiming
an unrepentant after-dinner nap on Yom Kippur,
he sits in his frame of smudged-charcoal beard,
Wedged fast asleep in the garden,
his tough farmer/book-collector's hand
half-possessing the *New York Times*.

A boy of twelve, and he scrambles
over the red barn roof

to feed his squabbling pigeons;
Swims in the ochre stream on a hot day,
Plays hookey, and hides from Torah study
in the afternoon—
A promising boy who wouldn't learn.

Wrinkles now crisscross the tanned forehead, wander
to busy eyebrows hedging his doubts
and aspirations;
Pappa shelters under the brim of his chosen
*baalegola** cap as he dreams
in his lost *shtetl.*

*Russian for "teamster"

Jewish Currents   MIRIAM LEADER

ROSIE'S BANQUET

(For Rose Lefcowitz, 1907-1984)

No kitchen more pungent
than Rosie's green hospital tent,
the nurses with floury aprons,
braids of garlic in their hair.
Through her filagree of tubes and masks
Rosie kneaded and strained, arranged
her last, most lavish, feast.

Sherry to baste the roast,
mandarin orange for the wild rice!
Her finest china
slipped from its quilted sheathe,
she laid each plate just so
on the rubbery sheet.
Mince the ginger, rinse the shallots!
Slowly, the cake must rise slowly,
each layer delicate as a moon,
o doctor, keep the oven warm,
poke your needles gently in my fragile crust.

Closing in, death dressed in his best
summer guest attire and closing
relentlessly in,
Rosie kept arranging all week
under the gauze and glazed hospital eyes
the meal we would no more eat
than Brueghel's wedding feast
or that other, more solemn,
last supper.

Webster Review   BARBARA F. LEFCOWITZ

TOMATO

You must have taken two or three bites
by the time I arrived, and what was left
looked softly and overwhelmingly like
the pink and red of tongue and cleft.
The vivid rows of pips like seed-
or milk-teeth in an open gum,
the sacs of luke-warm spit between
the unaugmented lining and
the cheeks' partitioning,
and the root of the fibrous tonsil
with its vocalizing flare
all bitten back, re-shaped again,
or smashed, irregular.
One more bite and the lot would go,
flushed redly down your long white throat
with the sudden suck and swallow
that only love keeps light.
As we sit in the car and talk of love,
a mark dries gently on your dress,
the latest in the traces of
our stabs at happiness.

The Antigonish Review   JOHN LEVETT

UNFINISHED BUSINESS

Sir, starting next month
Please accept my resignation
And, if necessary, find a replacement for me.
I leave a lot of uncompleted work,
Whether from laziness or practical difficulties.
I should have said something to someone,
But no longer know what or to whom: I have forgotten.
I should have given something away, too,
A word of wisdom, a gift, a kiss;
I've put it off from one day to the next. Forgive me,
I'll take care of it in the short time that's left.
I have, I fear, neglected important clients.
I should have visited
Far-away cities, islands, deserted lands;
You'll have to cross them off the program
Or entrust them to my successor's care.
I should have planted trees and haven't done it,
Built myself a house,
Perhaps not beautiful but conforming to a plan.
Above all, dear sir, I had in mind
A marvelous book that would
Have revealed innumerable secrets,
Alleviated pain and fear,

Dissolved doubts, bestowed on many people
The boon of tears and laughter.
You'll find the outline in my drawer,
In back, with the unfinished business.
I haven't had time to see it through. Too bad.
It would have been a fundamental work.

(April 19, 1981)

Ploughshares   PRIMO LEVI
—Translated from the Italian
by Ruth Feldman

SPRING THAW

The ground will break now, and metal
can be held directly in the hand.
Seems everyone's rebuilding.
Not just repair, like sealing leaks
or slapping on fresh shingles
to replace those blown away.

Ted is extending his kitchen—
three new sides already sketched
in standing wood. They'll have space
for stores now, honey and syrup,
grains sealed safe in Mason jars.

At the Morgans on the rim of town,
they're wrecking the garden wall.
Hired men with mallets meaning business
splatter chunks and clouds of gypsum
whiting like fertilizer
the stumps of last year's growth.
By July, the beans and cauliflower
will stretch a mile.

At the mill above the falls,
someone full of will and muscle
has dragged out the machinery
and gutted the inside clean
as a weasel leaves an eggshell.
He'll build his rooms where he wants them,
add a stove, and move straight in.

I've lived forty years in the same grey house.
Dad liked restful colors.
We painted over in what came before.
It was cheaper, too.

Preacher tells me we're new every day.
Like this water running over rocks,
we form the selfsame pattern,

a ruff of white here, a dark patch there,
but every minute brings a new cupful.

I sit on the riverbank choosing tools.
The sieve is lighter than the dipper.

Blueline   TONI MERGENTIME LEVI

OUT OF CHAOS

No wonder some prefer a narrow hall,
A single room where doubts die
Until possibility, that odd flower,
Returns its face.

The doors close and open every day.

The doors close and open every day,
And every day we hurtle toward the city.

Today I saw the usual human disaster:
Head in her chest, legs pocked with pink wounds,
fingers wrapped tight around a white handbag.

Then the subway doors opened and children
Piled in: the whole car filled with their high
Broken music.

At the next stop they all poured out;
The car was vacant, solemn, the air
Settled and clear—but she was still there.

Outside, a lilac bush blows to the wind,

And everywhere one looks,
A pre-Socratic flux
Streams down avenues
Of taxicabs and radios,
Mortality's parade crowned with neon and chrome—

As if we were beasts evolving toward a sentence
That breaks and disperses before we arrive
At the city we promised to build.

Partisan Review   PHILLIS LEVIN

THE PHARMACIST

In front of me, a cash register tolls.
I am shopkeeper and custodian
of a garden of crushed, dyed and rounded
herbs and exudates
of which my ignorance is enormous.
As more bottles crowd the shelves,

faith replaces ignorance.
Soon I am magician-priest
performing miracle healings.
The base metal of the register vanishes
through my alchemy and this is no longer a shop.
Each of the tablets carries my blessing.
They create small uprisings and realign organs.
They confer with micro-organisms
for a new homeland.
My incantations label the bottles.
So much passes through me
I must close once a week to recover.
The lids on the apothecary jars lift
with the power of dried rhizomes and roots,
and any potion in my hands
contains everything I believe in.

Crosscurrents   NORM LEVINE

THE LAST SHIFT

I had been on my way to work as usual
when the traffic stalled a quarter mile
from the railroad crossing on Grand Blvd.
Then I saw the moon rise above
the packing sheds of the old Packard plant.
The moon at 7:30 in the morning.
And the radio went on playing
the same violins and voices I didn't
listen to each morning. Back in the alley
the guys in greasy dark wool jackets
were keeping warm by a little fire
made from fence posts and garage doors
and tossing their empty wine bottles
into the street where they shattered
on the frosted roofs of cars and scattered
like chunks of ice. A police car dozed
across the street, its motor running.
I could see the two of them eating
sugar doughnuts as delicately as two
elderly women and drinking their coffee
from little Styrofoam cups. Soon the kids
would descend from these lightless houses,
gloved and scarved, on their way to school
with tin boxes of sandwiches and cookies.
They would slide on the ice and steal
each others' foolish hats and laugh
while they still could, their breath
pushing out into the morning air
in little trumpets of steam. I wondered
if anyone would step from the faceless

two-storied house beside me, all of its
rooms torn into view, its connections
and tubing gone, the furniture gone,
the floors ripped up for firewood.
Up ahead I could hear that the train
had stopped, the bells went on ringing
for a minute, the blinking arms of light
went from red to nothing. Around me
the engines began to die, and then
my own went. It was strangely quiet,
another town or maybe another world.
I could feel a deep cold slowly climbing
my legs, which wouldn't move, my eyes
began to itch and blink on a darkness
I had never seen before. I knew
these tiny glazed pictures—a car hood,
my own speedometer, the steering wheel,
the windshield fogging over—were the last
I'd ever see. These places where I had lived
all the days of my life were giving up
their hold on me, and not a moment too soon.

Michigan Quarterly Review   PHILIP LEVINE

AMERICAN COUNTRY

In the folk-art museum
the visitors are like wheat
looking at pictures of wheat.

A new crop springs up every few minutes,
craning for a peek
at tolework or fraktur,

only to be mown down
by a glimpse of quilts
or decoys far across the room.

Should a patchwork cow
devour them, or a painting
of a field return them to

the holy, golden city
of their dreams,
they would still pass.

Like the weather vane
in its glass case,
patinaed from a hundred years

of giving directions,
they no longer need to know
which way the wind is blowing.

The Georgia Review   ROBERT J. LEVY

NGAN DO IN GROSSE POINTE

Father arranged her
    stay with us
through Immigration.
    Yet, in a blue
month, she's shown
    no gratitude
for this country-
    club atmosphere.

Her face still wears
    the war in
Cambodia.
    Fire dreams of sons,
an ancient daughter,
    waken her, shaking,
afraid to break
    the imperial air.

A ravaged peasant,
    she looks Chinese,
speaks a bit of French,
    an old woman
at thirty-seven.
    Ebony eyes,
gossamer hair,
    her mouth, her sorrow.

Evenings, when the china
    & the children
have been cared for,
    she stares at the TV.
numbed to the guns,
    yet lit with a soft
expectancy, unaccustomed
    to continual laughter.
In time, she will own
    a house & house
cats & fashionable
    shoes & a face
the color of apricots &
    the view of the suburbs
that has no place
    for fire dreaming.

Buffalo Spree   J. PATRICK LEWIS

THE BANANA MADONNA

En route to Roseau
Valley Church, we pass defunct
sugar mills, a few

kept up as *ruins*—followed by lush crops
of banana trees and coconut palms, both casting much shade
and cooling our passage through St. Lucia's
rolling pastures. (Banana images, profuse in local Church
Art, glut our talk) . . .
Never have I seen so many unpicked bananas at once—
this plantation the richest,
so near to harvest: the thousands of green firm tubes wrapped
in bundles, thousands
of green hands upon hands upon hands—
fingers woven together, wound
about the stalks and vines . . . It's the great *Siesta*
of banana trees! The proliferant orchards
doze, Pater and Mater Familias Banana sleeping the long repose
of blessed hands crossed in their laps, crossed
over ample bellies,
green fingers interlocked. *Sleep. The sleep*
of bananas

toward harvest, while the sun's slow yellow light seeps,
dilutes the vine-tough green of rinds. I dream
the slow quiet goldening of the crops . . .
We leave behind the last plantation, bear right
down an elegant short cobblestone side road: "Here, stop!"

The American Poetry Review   LAURENCE LIEBERMAN

THE PAINTING FOR MY MOTHER

I make you buy the painting of the swans
as if it will make you live as long as it takes
all of them to enter the gold/green reeds.
They come out of the nowhere of marshland and float
under the vast sky. The tumor is smaller
on the x-rays this month; the doctors seem
pleased. I fly to Florida for your birthday,
your face as white as mine, your mind wandering.
Both daughters give you talismans
disguised as gifts: one a Chinese bell on blue string,
one a porcelain necklace with painted birds—
long-legged birds for longevity—their wings
open across a white sky, flying in place.

The Southern Review   MARTHA RONK LIFSON

THE EARTH FROM THIS DISTANCE

At twenty-five thousand feet life is the distance.
Here there are no seasons for the blind: the only road
Maps to the cities are the cracked blue veins

In ice that splinter off toward each horizon: the only life
In the lights of the oil rigs of Prudhoe Bay
Five hours behind us. At night we fly through the aurora:
Green ghost arms weave themselves around the ship.
A sense of rightness pulls us down to a pool of
Phosphorescent shadow; the pilots' gyros betray us
Straight, level. Here the magnetic compass turns
Aside. The sun rises by falling south.
We believe only what we must: dead reckoning.
We fly by the stars: follow what each instrument
Tells us: imagine the precise suggestion
That the world flies out of an artificial horizon.

North Dakota Quarterly   PETER HEARNS LIOTTA

THEY ARE DREAMING A LOT IN WARSAW
THESE DAYS, MARCH, 1982

among the police checking documents, they are
dreaming upsidedown the way people do in those
Chagall paintings, everyone's body elongated
and draped over the roofs.

the body stretches out so it can touch the ground
and the chimney smoke at the same time; a large face
can suddenly peer into a fourth floor window,
and feet can grow very large and bumpy so that
a shoe sometimes can reach from the front door
into the courtyard across the street.

the elongated body shows how we can stretch
ourselves when we dream, becoming longer like fibers
or taffy. it shows how we can melt and turn
almost to liquid. how flexible the human being is!
how we can pull possibilities out of ourselves!

and these long, floating bodies with large heads
and cheeks that touch in the sky near the clouds,
above the tv aerials and police helicopters,
look down fascinated at the small, metal tanks
that have parked at strategic intersections
with turrets turning slowing, near eye level.

The Massachusetts Review   LOU LIPSITZ

WHERE THE WIND STREAMS

south of Nassau,
letting me feel that winter
is a season,
is where I am—

chilled enough to remember Christmas
north, to hope for warmth,
searching for the same song,
sung again, lived again
in a future time hidden behind
the twisting trunks of mango trees—

I do expect to catch a glimpse
of angels in their spiraling of love—

Above the far-away rhythm,
muted boom, breakers on reef,
there surely will sing again
an infant cry cast along the shore,
coming to rest under phosphorescent
tree branches—

from the blanched wooden porch
where I stand, I do hear
rustle of wing and bush,
wind sounds bearing a love stream
suddenly sensible to time,
where redemption will last
longer than any flow and ebb
and a salt spray scent is
a sign across midnight

America   DAVID LOCHER

LOOKING FOR DAD

Your six kids search
for you all over Yakima.
We don't find you in the corner
bar, the lights low, your spirits
high, sipping one last brandy.
We don't find you sitting
on a bench, shoulders stooped,
waiting for the last bus home.

We find you miles from town,
lost, gazing at spring apple trees
in mid-February, in the west-
setting hills, blossoming
apple country, at home.

Now you are wearing your favorites:
red carnations, white spider mums.
In this air so thin and brittle
our voices will not break through
or ride the Ahtanum Ridge wind:
we six are carrying you
dressed in your flannel box,

so light we say you are not there,
you were heavier than that.

Ploughshares   KAREN LOCKE

NEW YORK

They say the City doesn't
sleep, but I know better.
I saw it sleeping, underground
on the trains, above
on sidewalks, in doorways. Only
the lucky ones have cardboard warmth.
They say the City doesn't
close, but I saw doors
always locked, wire barriers
around cement parks.
Everything; they say the City
has everything. I saw
it holding out its hands for more.

Crosscurrents   CHERYL A. LOESCH

WALKING

When I was green,
Green as the light beneath these leaves,
I used to say:
Today I will be sad.
Too bad for anyone who disbelieves
That I am sad today.
Green as the light beneath these leaves,
How sad I am . . .
I used to say.

No longer green,
Cool as the light between the rain,
I want to say:
Sadness has come to stay.
It is my middle name . . . but I refrain,
And going on my way,
Cool as the light between the rain,
I say: "Good-day . . .
Good-day . . ."

The Paris Review   CHRISTOPHER LOGUE

SORROW TREES

If there are fever trees, and they tell me there are,
I know where I've been walking. No one's named this
similar species, but sorrow trees exist. Look
how rain brings out the red, how wet the blackness
shines. Long patterns on these trunks
irregular and gnarled. Bark never peels
as eucalyptus does. My fingers move around the knobs,
trace the grooves they're caught in, as I am
caught: I heard of a man so lonely
all he had to hug was trees. Every day
I live like a botanist, examining these roots,
naming the dark veins of the leaves.

Yankee   JEANNE LOHMANN

FROM *LETTERS IN THE DARK*

I lay awake writing letters to you
In the dark—so I got up, felt alone,
And put on the light. I need someone.
There's a kind of intimacy that's closer than the bone
And can sometimes get into letters, more than anywhere.
It's communion with the dead, or more like prayer.
The dead are somehow refined, or are being refined.
When they answer back, it's in disembodied voices
From which all static and chatter stored in the cells
Have been magnetized off, buried, or even burned.
In the purgatory of the small hours the person
God might have first imagined stirs on the rock,
Pushes the vulture from his liver and begins to turn
His anguish into intimate words, or at least
Disembodied expressions of love disguised
As chatter and sent to a disembodied love.

The Hudson Review   HERBERT LOMAS

OLD FOLKS VISIT

Life clings to them; it is past
the time when they would hold it dear.
The tall elms along the street
shake down their darkening leaves.
School recess & children along the street. Noon.
Sun-serpents wind through the closed blinds. Those
cards left on the dresser, in case . . .
Medicare (red, white & blue-edged),
Medicaid for when the caseworker comes, later,
to renew the homemaker's term . . . *Asking,*

How are you feeling? . . . I feel, O
I feel. Did you ever see that painting,
the one of the artist's mother sitting
in the chair, yes, in a room, but that
is where it ends, where it goes wrong;
at such an age, one should sit on the roof,
one should observe the sky, and weather.
One should say, I am where you cannot come.

Kansas Quarterly   FRANK LONERGAN

AFTER THE FLOOD

When the water went down
we could see the top
of Maud Hatcher's house
minus the green shutter
that came off which she used
to float down main street
singing "Jesus Saves"
till the rescue boat picked her up
in front of Harvin's Drug Store.
83 and not a scratch.

A week later we found
Mose Green's restored Packard
at the bottom of Pine Hill
sitting in slime up to the fenders,
the windows caved in and
the thousand dollar paint job
scratched to hell.

Down at the A&P
John Thomas stood in water
up to his ankles passing out
the last of the canned goods
to the bay rum boys
who live under the bridge.
He thinks the insurance company
will give him a break.

Today the children are down
at the park playing in the rubble
of seesaws and swings.
The rain is gone; the sun's come out.
Maud's on the front porch fanning flies,
and out across the field
the mud is drying hard as stone.

Carolina Quarterly   BRENDA LONG

THE WAY TO THE MAGICAL ORDER

Run to the hill and pick
flowers and band them with sticks
Adorn the bundle with feathers
and speckled gold and blue eggs of birds

Go to the well and draw
water and fill a jar
Hold it up to see
the sun, clear sky, and trees

Enter the barn and pitch
hay and bed stalls
Milk goats and call
cats to drink from the white bucket

Climb to the loft and hang
your gifts from the highest beam
Let bat wings fan your face
Be blind like them. Dream

she nears you and all is won
She will whistle and air your lungs
with charms and music and words. Come
practice praising her name in tongue

The Texas Review   RICHARD LONG

THE SUMMER THAT NEVER ENDS

In the summer that never ends
We lie prone on the green hip of a hill,
Youth beating warm where skin touches
Skin, and the sun, through a shift
Of leaf-shadow, stabs at our lids
Till colored dots dance in the
Red darkness like crazed confetti.

The sweet breath of summer rises
Around us—wind of corn and clover,
Honeysuckle, watermelon, perfume of
Just-mown hay, of spaded earth. Across
The road in pollen-laden fields, amber
Clouds of bees undulate a wild harvest
Dance, a drone of unceasing joy.

In the summer that never ends,
The heat of August shimmers in layers
Of haze against a far ridge of dark pine,
And high above us a wide, lone V
Of hawk wings forever hangs,

Still as a brown brush stroke
On watercolor sky.

Stone Drum   VIRGINIA LONG

ADVICE TO A YOUNGER WOMAN

We used to say when we'd been
loved and left again,
"I think I'll move to a different town
and start all over as a virgin."

Who knew
how possible it was?

We misplaced the truth
and fixed our minds on
facts, as women do
who think they can defend
themselves. Thus our war
begins. We drag up the past
and aim it at our own hearts.
We try to set down the future
like a map.
Safe, but hungry,
we take refuge inside walls.

My young friend, you flash your eyes
like mirrors signaling distress.

Start over.

Imagine yourself courageous
at the gate of a different town,
prepared to live in that one place always
alone, without weapons, at peace.

You will become
that pure being about whom
the whole universe
revolves.

Helicon Nine   BARBARA LOOTS

THE WATCHERS

How many nights we've hung around
This Mobil Station at the edge of town,

Propped on Coke flats against the wall,
Breathing odors of grease and diesel,

As cars fly by in gales of wind,
Fanning the sedge beside the pavement.

Each passing car leaves us behind,
And in our mouths we taste the brine

Of the sea webbed in our blood.
Insects whirl in cosmic clouds

Around the yellow gaspump suns.
We float in the night's vacuum,

Telling stories of women scorned,
Of fistfights, and of husbands horned,

And sip whiskey from Coke bottles
To cheat the eyes of righteous people.

The L & N freight thunders north,
Lumbers along the valley floor,

Its headlight sweeping to and fro
As though looking for something lost.

Out in the darkness, mammoth hills
Rot with spear points in their ribs.

Caverns have leached their limestone bones,
And in the dark, dank depths of one,

An underground river rises.
Black water holds fish with no eyes.

The smell of cotton poison drifts
Up from the river bottom fields.

A whippoorwill whistles matins
In haunted woods behind the station,

And windows of late show watchers
Glow like distant spots of foxfire.

A patient, unbridled Pegasus
Soars each night on the sign above us.

The Texas Review   RICK LOTT

AN ICE AGE GHOST STORY

The shadow of the glacier still shapes
the Kaw River this evening.
Dismembered animals swim onto sand bars,
brilliant china-white bones
turned porous and umber.
They sprawl, scattered like driftwood.

Wild horses and boars,
giant beaver, bison, mastodons

washed from some lost graveyard
traveled from Lecompton to Lawrence,
Eudora to Bonner Springs.
On the voyage
they gave themselves piece by piece
to the mineral kingdom
and became tinny-sounding, bone-shaped rocks.

Tonight I will lie next to my husband,
fit my shoulder just under his,
my arms next to the sturdy box of his ribcage.
I will tilt my pelvis out of the way.
Hot wind will spread up the river valley
and stir grass outside our window.
Before drifting off we might remember
the lost spruce forest,
the lives of those enchanted beasts.

We will sleep in warm coats of flesh.

Kansas Quarterly   DENISE LOW

THE GRAND HOTEL "MAGIE DE LA LUNE"

The yellow, cratered road beside the lagoon
and vastly turquoise, tin-roofed huts
that set it off
from equally sallow beach.
Yellowed eyes glaring
through gap-toothed louvers
of murky cantines.
The pink hotel drive;
the lustrous dada
of seagrapes under the seawall,
studded with billions
of vermilion orangina cans,
party-colored condoms, rum bottles . . .

Like a benevolent giant,
dusk lifts the whole scene,
examines it briefly in kinder lights,
then flicks it tiredly away.
As the tour agents did long ago.

What is left now
is you and I, alone and fantastical
under blue-pomaded dreams of palms,
slow-dancing out of time and vogue
by the diamond, illimitable sea.

The Beloit Poetry Journal   FREDERICK LOWE

SOUND EFFECTS

Growing up by the railroad tracks
you are not aware of the whoosh
unless the train moans with grief
over its own passing.
                    Move
to a townhouse the highway runs past,
and once the novelty wears off
who hears the bluster of trucks
shouldering cars off the road?

Shelter your late years
among trees that filter
the hoarse wind scourging
the bleak seashore; the surf
growls at the door
of your ears, yet cradles
your sleep.
                    But wander
in the vast desert or climb
to the peak of a mountain,
the silence attunes your ear
to a footfall on the back side
of the moon, to the off-beat pulse
of solar wind, even the crackle
of fire in the hearth
of a remote supernova. Once
you deaden the world's noise,
its ubiquitous voice rings in your head.

Southern Poetry Review   ROBERT LOWENSTEIN

TO MY FATHER

Now you rest, at last, in peace—are calm.
I know you're dead, no longer do I fear
that you might die, no longer do I dread
your dreary, weary groan
which used to enlarge the bedroom:
your breath pleading for help
from my own breast's breath,
your howling eyes, entreating me.

I'm tired, you know. Now I fear not
to go to sleep,
to bend my head upon your bed,
and mix my fitful sleep
with your large un-human calmness.
And no more I feel the anguish
of being of no use to you like a foe:

I know you're dead, peacefully so,
and the silence here is back.

The Literary Review   LUCIANO LUISI
                        —*Translated from the Italian*
                        by Pier Francesco Paolini

NIGHTFISHING

In the last light waning
over the low, weed-thickened lake,
bats hurl themselves
through the still air
with the recklessness
of blind hunger,
mosquitoes whine
feverish for blood,
and my black jitterbug
walks on the water
indigestible as God.

Each shift of weight
makes us toss and pitch,
the uneven thrust of oars
propels us erratically from side to side
of our compass point;
the night air begins to chill,
and cold stars float in the water
as we lift our arms
and cast our lines into darkness.

Cottonwood   DAVID LUNDE

NOAH

It wasn't the closeness that bothered him,
the smell of women, the sweating flanks of horses;
not the boredom, after they had read all the books;
not the panic when he heard sloshing sounds
and thought of termites eating the walls,
building bridges in the hull.

It wasn't the food that bothered him:
lentils and garlic, onions in everything—
no fish, no eggplant, no salads,
no fruit in the bowl, no color on the plate.
He promised himself a vineyard when this was over.

What bothered him was the noise:
always, punctuating everything they said,

beating a dark rhythm for their singing,
pounding, hammering, day after day,
night after night, even in his dreams,
rain on the roof,
the wrath of God.

Yankee   JEAN LUNN

ON VISITING HERBERT HOOVER'S BIRTH
AND BURIAL PLACE

On the prairie's edge they buried the president,
and you can eat your lunch near his clean, shiny tomb.
Still, too many people can't pay their rent.

The grasslands beyond once covered with tents.
He was born here: for free you can see his house,
                                                  its tiny rooms.
On the prairie's edge they buried the president.

When he was boss, times were tough: what you spent
was what you earned and not a dime in banks accrued.
So many people still can't pay their rent.

Why, what is it, which way, how, can we prevent
our oblivion—some eat white bread, some get the screw.
On the prairie's edge they buried the president.

If I'm wrong about this I repent, I repent—
but don't too many dream of meat in their stew?
And so many people can't pay their rent.

This greed in our grain, why won't it relent?
The hunger, the longing—would it, if it were up to me or you?
On the prairie's edge they buried the president.
Still—so many people can't pay their rent.

Ploughshares   THOMAS LUX

SONG OF A 118-YEAR-OLD MAN

I been a quiet man most of my life.
My chess mate J. B could tell you
I haven't whistled or sung a song
since T. Roosevelt sat there in old D.C.

Silence like that dries a man up
& loses the song that wears his name.
Oh, he can walk & talk OK
but he lives in a desert without no shade.

But one no-sleep night, way late, I heard
a woman sing. I sat straight up
in bed & the feeling grew
that I wasn't no part of time.

Next day I told old J. B. that for a bit
I couldn't play chess. I was going all out
for singing lessons. "You can't even whistle
& how you keep your teeth in while you sing?"

To say the truth, my voice sounds like a rasp
breaking ice. But I'm steady & loud
& my inside desert's flooded
with good green things now.

I sang & sang till my teacher told me
to try out for the town musical.
I got the part of the old man
with three songs & the finale.

At first, in rehersal, they kept asking
if I was OK or wanted to sit down.
But before long they took me for a man
who knew where the high notes hid.

Makeup time, they said I didn't look old enough,
made me wear a white beard I thought a hash, but
it didn't hurt my songs. I stroked it & tried
my best to look old. They liked my willingness.

Opening night, J. B. kept watching my teeth.
Back stage, after, he said I sang better than
I played chess. He worried my beard would fall off
& people wouldn't believe I was 118.

It takes more than spins of this old earth to know
the difference between getting up & waking up.
Been on my feet more than a century—
only a couple of years back did I give up the beard.

Poem   ANNETTE LYNCH

A FABLE

Sir George Hooper thought, We each invent
a sometime-self, through an act of will;
usually it's a nickel wish we string
around our necks, reassured by weight
if not by gold:
        For example—Cage,
who'd been the gardener for many years,
envisioning the flowers into life,
and this despite a peaceful blind white eye.
Days he spent his time among the flowers

and nights among the clay pots in the shed.
He called the flowers children, or his lovers,
those times he thought to speak to us at all.

One night, after digging and tending,
after polishing his tools, he took
a hoe and rake and shears and hose, baling
wire and stakes—and fashioned a sort of man.
With his half-sight and furrowed hands groping

across the figure he had made, Cage found
the wood smooth, the metal cool—and the next
day we found only Cage's polished tools.

The roses haven't died, so far, the phlox
and daisies and salvia still bloom bright
on their stems; only what is different
is Cage, in his absence, in whatever
different garden he believes he tends.

The Literary Review   W. B. LYON

STONE FENCE POST

It's hard to hate the bulldozer,
though you almost do
because of what it's done, or been hired to do.
The old sheds, the one creeping up the hillside, the apple trees,
the big black walnut with a building built around it
because it was easier to do than to bring the thing down—
old Otto's crazy array and sloping backyard,
all brought down to this, grassless,
a dirt grade with a leaching field in it.
A new beginning, like an old man's, elsewhere.
A new beginning, then,
for someone with less shambling purposes,
the way the one shed simply went up the hillside
because it had to, eventually.
Then needing a new roof, with a new pitch to it,
one thing following another.
And all but endlessly,
because old Otto's quarter century's going under.
The bright pine frame of a new addition going up
juts off the house, white,
its hemlocks, its hundred-year-old maple
with a stone fence post jammed in its base,
the way the grey ice wagon seemed jammed where it sat,
and everything else.
Old Otto took what he could.
Books, antiques, buggy wheels,
all the hand-forged iron, horses' harnesses,
tradesmen's tools of sometimes uncertain trades,

stained glass, the strange paraphernalia of other eras,
picture frames, things loved once, or never loved.
And Otto went.
Otto and his wife went back where they came from,
unlike so much that's come so far.
Unlike anything ever really does,
especially us.

The American Poetry Review   RICK LYON

LOS OJOS (THE EYES)

When his beloved died he thought of growing old
In the closed house, alone with his memories
And the mirror where she used to look
At herself on a bright day. Like the gold
In the chest of a miser, he thought he would
Capture all of yesterday in that clear
Looking glass and the time, for him,
Would not pass at all, but would stand still.

After the first anniversary had passed,
He asked himself what they were like,
Her eyes. Brown, black? Were they
Blue—or gray? Good God! Is it
That I don't remember?

Walking along the street one spring day
In the silence of his heavy sorrow,
Aching heart, he saw some eyes
Shining in the shaded emptiness
Of a window. Lowering his own,
He smiled, continuing his way.
Like those! Like those.

Bitterroot   ANTONIO MACHADO
                                    —*Translated from the Spanish*
                                    by Lilly McCue

LETTER TO MONET

It wasn't until leaving
the Portrait Gallery & standing
in the clatter of tourists, pigeons
& doubledeck buses in Trafalgar
Square that I took to walking
down to the Thames, to lose dark
thoughts among the web
of quick turning alleys, bookstalls
& pubs.

> There, motorboats tossed
among the sunset's glitter
rocking in the waves; the spires
of Big Ben & Parliament stood breaking
through the fog; & over to the east
one young painter nestled
the river's edge, tracing the skyline
& shimmering landscape.
> Perhaps
it was vanity,
but as fog wrapped around, riverbirds
cooed & steel buoys rocked
& sounded on the water,
I snuggled close to the steel railing
overlooking the Thames &
hoped beyond hope—
as I wrapped a thick scarf against
wind coming on—the painter might
place, with a small black smear
just above the railing, or shimmer
of light just where the stone quay
reached down to the brown
& erratic waves, my soul here forever,
one crooked niche in an intimate landscape.

Poetry   MARK MADIGAN

STILL LIFE

> Think of me as the river
angling southwest
from center foreground
to the present,
>
> as the barefoot ditch
bisecting the pasture,
as the oxford creek
crossing the campus,
as the high-top river
sliding past
industrious years,
as the canvas stream
trickling under
naked, leaning trees,
>
> and be the moon
and moonlight
raddling the clouds,
>
> be the ripple
and the stones
wrinkling the stream,

be the bass
and brook trout
reaping the minnows.

Poet Lore   ARTHUR MADSON

THE TRUTH ABOUT BEARS

The old bear knows a game much like quoits;
he spatters water rings over the fish.

Slim trout rise to rub noses with air.
The tracks they leave are round as moons.

But the old bear waits for the fish that is strong,
rash, obsessed with the meaning of bear.

When the strong fish springs from the lake,
his tail strikes the bear with the strength of ten fish . . .

The force of the fish hits the bear
like the brush of a wing or the flick of a twig.

The bear strikes the fish with the strength of one bear.
For a moment the bear holds the fish in his mouth.

Fish against fur is paler than berries before they burn blue.
In the eye of the fish is the truth about bears.

Yankee   ELAINE MAGARRELL

DAYS

These days.
They are long and don't end.
I pretend.
If the days had only robbed me,
I would have been in a rage.
But where's my anger now?
The days merely contain.
Come, wave to me, I coax my day,
the way one waves to a little child.
But it doesn't seem to go away.
The days are not even in the way.

Leaning against a tree,
I am one with the sky.
There may have been days
I followed for a while,
as they softened in the light,
those I found among the shadows of my life.

A day behind the door,
one keeping watch,
another a ghost
wandering in the garden.
And one probably anxious to return.

These days.
Sometimes
they just move my mind
a little.
Like cattle crossing a road,
they pause without knowing and stare beyond them,
then walk on.

The Hudson Review   JAYANTA MAHAPATRA

FRESH PRUNE PIE

A poem about prunes—without remembering
Aunt Irene, living in her orchard,
twenty acres of dusty gray-green trees?

Powdery purple fruit in fall,
dropping upon smooth curried earth?
. . . a prune is never picked.

Irene made prune pies. Her recipe,
if there was one, was never written.
Crisp crust, halved prunes, unpeeled,
pools of butter where the pits had been,
a dash of salt to temper sweetness, her pies
warm from the woodstove, cream poured on
in driblets before eating: these were her poems.

Irene knew no poetry, but she knew prunes
fresh, plum-purple from her trees;
she knew plants and flowers and buttered things
and how to make prune pies for children.

Plump as a prune, Irene never grew old,
lives unwrinkled in memory.

America   JEANNETTE MAINO

HAWKS' WINGS

The sudden flash and turn
Of the speckled wings of hawks
As they dive through night air

Across roads of bleached white rock
Into roadside ditches,
Their eyes a topaz gleam,
Reminds me of those private acts
Performed inside the mind,
Those sudden turns of the will—
Momentous, but never seen—
And how the unimaginable
Is understood in an instant,
Like some beautiful creature
Set immediately before us;
Or some resplendent lake
Set cold and high in the pines,
Its fathomless blue depth
A quarry already mined,
The elaborate pattern
Of our lives a tale
Already told.

Arizona Quarterly   MARK MAIRE

DARK PREFACE

The blind—
They're barely noticed
Unless, as today, I see one
Nearly hit by a car; he freezes, then moves again,
A kind of sleep stumble, following some secret
Footage in the skull. His cane whispers
Through leaves on the walk—whispers
I follow at a distance, almost afraid
Of the eyepits, the face tilted back,
As if searching
For something gone from the sky.
He shuffles past deafening rock and the blankness
Of frat house windows.
On a dark street, I watch him disappear
Into a darkened house
And wait for the light,

Yellow as forsythia,
That borders my father's back porch
Where my deaf cousin and his signing friends
Are waiting for beer.
I pause at the door.
Delight creases their cheeks.
Words fill the eyes. The hands
Ballet; fingers fold and open, circle,
Figure the air and make it mean
Something funny this time. They laugh

A laughter so pure, you're listening
To nothing but light.

The American Scholar   PETER MAKUCK

CORONARY

(In Memoriam)

Time was trickling out; from it
a shadow shaped itself and love
took on an unknown brilliance
beside the stretcher, half-caught
in the hospital's clotted color.
It was Christmas Eve, a night blued and mysterious.
They graphed the rhythm of your heart,
the stubborn cry of existence.

And so we sang the Hallelujah with you
in the emergency room, *asepsis* stretched out among the psalms.
Time passed and war broke out between the man and his body.
So the odor of broom in early morning
seized hold of my hair
and I saw your heart, still loving,
and your arteries bearing rivers in them,
until a dust cloud blasted my eyes
and a sharp sound nailed my throat shut.
I had seen your heart, father!
No longer could an embrace give back to you the force of life.
Nor could salt, laughter, the sun, or the odor of broom.
I can only go back over your pupils rimmed with tenderness
and ask why, why does love make us old?

Seneca Review   ROSA ELENA MALDONADO
—Translated from the Spanish
by Claudette Columbus and David Weiss

MY MOTHER'S HOMELAND

My mother always said
your homeland is any place,
preferably the place where you die.
That's why she bought the most arid land,
the saddest landscape,
the driest grass,
and beside the wretched tree
began to build her homeland.
She built it by fits and starts
          (one day this wall, another day the roof;
from time to time, holes to let air squeeze in).

My house, she would say, is my homeland,
and I would see her close her eyes
like a young girl full of dreams
while she chose, once again, groping,
the place where she would die.

NER/BLQ
(New England Review and Bread Loaf Quarterly)   BELKIS CUZA MALÉ
—Translated from the Spanish
by Pamela Carmell

MY FATHER AT NINETY-TWO, SPLITTING THE DAYS

It's five minutes to twelve and the sun
glares in our faces—quite a phenomenon,
he says, to see the windows full of light
and everyone going about—at midnight!
The clock plays second fiddle to his brain.
An hour's nap, and he begins the day again,
washes, changes his shirt, and expects
his breakfast on the table. He respects
my worn explaining as a kind of busy
work, shrugs with courtesy. He is dizzy
with the earth's rotation spinning away
twenty-four to the dozen, each brief new day
a clone to the last. Like a match burning
meridians, he strikes his shadow's turn.

Seneca Review   CHARLOTTE MANDEL

FOR ME

For me, winter feels like
a belated gift.
I love her first
uncertain sweep.

Like the beginning of terrible events,
her fright is beautiful.
Even black crows are scared
before the whole woodless circle.

But the strongest is also most fragile—
the half-circle of temporal ice,
the blue of bulging rivulets
lulled sleepless . . .

New Letters   OSIP MANDELSTAM
—Translated from the Russian
by Michael Cole and Karen Kimball

EMILY DICKINSON IN HEAVEN

Gathering the leaves in autumn
one thinks of your leaves—
each gathered singly,

some to be sewn in solitary
prowess for your only book,
remaindered in a box,

a drawer, an upper room.
No one had to teach you
the New England seasons—

for 30 years spring pearled,
summer ached, and fall died
in your garden of delight.

Even the curious winter light
caught in a silent universe
(Western Massachusetts)

still burns *inside*
where things mean.
Each leaf, then,

columnar, ample as day,
inscribes your temple.
Here, stars gleam,

love's compass points,
mapping the unexplored,
the darkness of doubt.

In your heaven, constellations wheel,
pages turn. Kangaroo, Wren,
now your life opens: words.

The Journal   JOHN MANN

AN DIE MUSIK

Thank God for music! Drowner of the soul's
Loud chronic whining! O thank God for sound,
Exalter of spirit, power that unrolls
The folded trivial secrets that surround
And choke our perfect sense. O rush of notes
Lifting our love into divinity,
Hushing our hate and casting out the motes
From the world's eye! For once infinity
Is finite, being song. And all the moons
Are touchable and every living breath
Fused into certain meaning by these tunes
That shout so high the fallacy of death.

Give me a violin, a flute, a voice,
And I can make hell's embryo rejoice!

Helicon Nine   MARYA MANNES

THE BLIND COW

(La vaca cega)

Bumping her head on one trunk, then another,
mechanically going down the road to water,
the cow advances alone. She is blind.
A stone thrown with too good aim
by the farm-boy emptied one eye, and in the other
a web has formed: the cow is blind.
She comes to drink at the spring as she used to,
but not with the sure tread of other times
and not with her companions, no: she comes alone.
Her fellow cows, on ridges and in meadows,
in the silence of the fields and on the banks,
make their bells sound as they browse
green grass at random . . . She would fall.
Her snout hits against the smooth trough,
she edges backwards; but she returns,
lowers her head to the water and drinks in calm.
She drinks little, without much thirst, then raises
to the sky her enormous horned head
in a great tragic gesture; she blinks
over her dead pupils and returns,
orphaned of light under the burning sun,
wavering over unforgettable paths,
listlessly swinging her long tail.

Seneca Review   JOAN MARAGALL
                              —Translated from the Catalan
                                    by Nathaniel Smith

VILLANELLE ON THE SUICIDE OF A YOUNG BELGIAN TEACHER SOON TO BE NATURALIZED

("Truth is not merchandise.")
—Meister Eckhart

Children over 40 inches pay full fare,
but truth is neither relief nor merchandise.
What did you think you were buying, Jean-Pierre?

You buy relief with laughter or a gun, swear
those obscene Belgian curses, or theorize,
"Children over 40 inches pay full fare."

Your violence is unanswerable despair.
You have taken leave without paying goodbyes.
What did you think you were buying, Jean-Pierre?

A piano? passport? eternal youth? We bear
the judgment of those who do not realize
children over 40 inches pay full fare.

Mercy cannot be bought, and yet your unfair
silence buys our mercy, unmerited prize.
What did you think you were buying, Jean-Pierre?

You teach us more than French and music. You stare
behind your smiles, blood-soaked, and your laughter dies.
Children over 40 inches pay full fare.
What did you think you were buying, Jean-Pierre?

The Southern Review   LEO LUKE MARCELLO

ETERNITY

It well may be that I do love you well,
My pet. You turn me on, that *is* a fact.
You are leech-sweet during a kissing-spell
As though blood from my veins you would extract.
When you are close, I feel like being immortal
And can no longer stay within *one* skin—
While with my hand I knock at heaven's portal,
My feet in hell jump up and down like sin.
I don't know whether, now, it's me, alone,
Or the whole world, held in your arms and thighs.
Nobody is ever born, nobody dies.
Together we all came, and then were gone
In just a minute. Seeds, flowers and fruits
Gone with the wind.

The Literary Review   MAURO MARÈ
                                         —Translated from the Italian
                                         by Pier Francesco Paolini

GIRLS IN CROTONA PARK

As in a faded picture
girls have woven themselves
into the autumn dusk.
Their eyes are cool, the smile untamed and thin.
Their clothes are lavender, old-rose and apple-green.
Dew runs in their veins.
They're stocked with bright and hollow words.
Botticelli loved them in a dream.

Midstream   ANNA MARGOLIN
                                         —Translated from the Yiddish
                                         by Aaron Kramer

HER APPREHENSION

This morning, as I look out, I see
a doe feeding on the June grasses
in the back meadow. I call you
to join me, knowing
by the time you reach here,
she could disappear. Yet something
holds her until you come,
and we stand fixed in her apprehension.
It's not often, at this bright time
of day, a deer wanders out
of the woods. At dusk, the last
feathered light helps each emerge
and keep its distance.
Once, driving home late, I hit
a doe, crushing her rear legs.
She must have felt she was alone
or the fast light safe enough
to cross through. When I tried
to move closer, to kill her quickly,
she dragged herself across the road
and down into the darkness of a lake,
barking with all the bloody air
in her nose. She must have died
on her own, no matter how often
I dream up another night to drive home.
Today there is just air and field
between me and this new doe, and now
you near, still as meadow light, watching
her browse. The doe's guard bird is
the breeze, which brings us to her
faster than a headlight, so she can
prick up and bound away.

Tendril   GARY MARGOLIS

SKYSCRAPERS

Upon reflection,
these great structures grow
taller, or shrink smaller,
breathe, twist, prance,
fragment to atoms;
coalesce, to show
transient solidity,
image their beginnings, ends,
admit that their rigidity
is slave to circumstance.
Surprise, comfort, to know

they, too, are partners in
the universal dance.

Crosscurrents   ELIZABETH MARION

TUNING-UP

Strings seek
An accurate, authoritative A.
Unrelated notes and textures
Are flung into the air.
The instruments' potential
Becomes concrete and harshly audible.
Here is Beethoven's Fifth,
Or Schubert's Ninth,
Or what you will,
Scattered, like the shattered
Fragments of a broken vase;
But, unlike porcelain, capable
Of being miraculously,
Ecstatically reassembled
Into a cohesive and melodic whole.
And as the cold and bracing air of dawn
Is hailed by energetic devotees
As the best part of the day,
So this raucous, discordant display,
Vibrant with anticipation, ranks
As the best part of the concert.

The Antigonish Review   MARGARET MARSHALL

MARTY'S PACKETTE

The neighborhood's not the same.
The tax collector chained
the double doors of Marty's Packette.
Hands in their pockets, customers bunch up
at the glass to read the legal notice
and wave to Marty locked inside.
The tax man didn't know he sleeps in back.
Kids need candy, a video game.
Last stop before home, men
in pickup trucks need a six-pack,
like to shoot the breeze. Marty
also handles milk, bread, soft
drinks, processed cheese, ice cream
bars and batteries. Stuff to tide
you over. Sometimes in spring he sells
marigold plants. Pumpkins in October.
Once in a while he gets fresh rabbit meat.

Marty's in there now
consuming the perishables.

The Journal   SANDRA MARSHBURN

IF I WERE FIRE,
I WOULD TORCH THE WORLD

(Cecco Angiolieri: S' i' fosse foco, arderei 'l mondo)

If I were fire, I would torch the world;
If I were wind, I'd rage till it turned blue;
If I were water, I'd drown the world anew;
If I were God, to hell it would be hurled;
If I were Pope, then I would be enthralled
With cheating my Christians, the entire crew.
If I were Emperor—know what i would do?
I'd chop away till every head had rolled.

If I were Death, I'd go and visit father;
If I were Life, from father I would flee:
Not to take sides, I'd do the same to mother.
If I were Cecco—whom I happen to be,
I'd leave all worn-out wenches for another,
And take the young and lovely ones for me.

Boulevard   CHARLES MARTIN

"I COULD WALTZ ACROSS TEXAS WITH YOU"
(for T. R.)

Of course I'm excited
when you ask me to move
the desert in three-four time.
It may be jerky, brambles
sticking to our clothes,
but our feet toughen with each measure
sweeping us further and smoother;
nothing can stop this momentum,
not even the burn
from our grasping turns,
the dizzy air of sun, or our panic
for a polka that wants to run past rhythm.
Air lifts, assumes our voices,
lost in steps, in the beveling
of our words, syllables curve
skyward from our pivoting bodies.
The slope of our phrases gives
shoulders to the moon;
and there we balance
the moon with our thoughts,

luminous, gliding horizontally, not knowing
when the prairie will end.

Southern Poetry Review   MARY E. MARTIN

PAIN

(for Armando Valladares)

We all expected to see you lame.
Some *wanted* to see you lame.
When you walked toward us,
we imagined you crawling. It was
like waiting for a train that suddenly
turns into a wolf: it howls
as it runs into the station, its eyes
blind you like headlights, you step
into its mouth as if it were a car, you
think of tunnels and the next stop
as you're being devoured: you expected
a train and can't imagine anything else.
We waited with a wheelchair for a man who
could've used a new pair of shoes.
We asked the obvious questions:
if half a life of torture really
softens the bones until the body falls
like a ruined shack, if rebuilding
the shack is worth the trouble. And when
someone mentioned pain, the word rising
from its metaphors, you tried to laugh.

Your mouth opened like a small wound.

The Iowa Review   DIONISIO D. MARTINEZ

THE FINAL YEAR

It was the year when the abandoned cottage in the woods
    was sold for fire-wood.
The woodcutters came with their truck
and tore it down in three hours and a quarter,
and even took with them the well-frame.
It was not very large when they detached it from the well.
They did not even bother to smash it up,
but put it up on the bed of the truck just as it was.
And there it sat, a little gray chest covered with moss.

When all was quiet again,
the weasel came out of the old fireplace.
She called to a cuckoo from the forest,
and the two of them held a devotional hour.
The cuckoo sang a cuckoo hymn.

By then everything was over.
Nothing after that was as it was before.
But still the summer sauntered forth,
loosening its grasses and garlands.

New Letters   HARRY MARTINSON
                    —*Translated from the Swedish
                    by William Jay Smith and Leif Sjöberg*

MORNING LIGHTS

(for Marge Piercy, 2-17-84)

The early morning traffic
Weaves its way into the waking world,
Past churches and restaurants still asleep,
Past pedestrians carrying upon their backs
And minds the weight of being,
Bearing to their work the cold comfort
Of breakfast, with the ease of moving
For the moment toward destinations
They know that they can meet.

And in the clear east, the sun rising;
And in the west, a magnificent moon
Descending; while here the rhythms
Of morning are formed and monitored
by stoplights and pulsing turn-signals
Punctuating the paling dark,
Responding neither to moon nor sun,
Nor to cooing dove, or owl, or lark.

Southern Poetry Review   JULIAN MASON

THE OTTER

(at the Ak-Sar-Ben Aquarium)

I am startled at the fervor that must
have been his life, to seem, even in
death, stuffed, so vital.
His fur is a dusky brown, the hairs
thick, coarse, and silently radiant—
silver along the throat.
He must have been black and sleek in
the river water—faster than fish,
swimming down carp and trout, despite
the dartings, twistings, rococo
circlings.
More often, he was so crafty, so swift
a fisher, he would strike them
broadside, before they could shift

a fin.
Ears and nose valved against water,
he corkscrewed, then cannoned through
the current, long tail ruddering
behind.
Backwards, forwards, he swam both ways
with equal ease, equal grace.
And he moved better on land than skunks
or badgers—ran better than raccoons.
More playful than a cat, he was eager
to body-surf down rapids, or, leaping,
folding forelegs in, to sled down a
snowbank and out in a slide
onto the ice.
But now, here he stands: poised on a
log, webs showing between his wide-
fanned toes, thick tail curving to a
point,
whiskers bristling like straws
from his face.
Brown taxidermist's eyes stare fiercely,
forever, at the opposite wall.
He has just emerged from the river.
He is scanning the trees for the sound
he just heard, when the bullet rips
through his belly, and he rolls into
the mud, body slinky as a snake's,
his ears still hearing that gunshot—
but permanently deaf to the words and
noises of the tourists.

Envy's Sting   KENNETH C. MASON

UNSUSPECTING MORNING

The morning, green and unsuspecting,
Dawdled around our weedy barn,
And there stood father—
Stern as a hatchet—
He was about to kill a chicken.

He had been chasing it
This way, and that;
The chicken squawked and dodged,
Stumbling with terror.

Father caught it,
Twisted its neck,
Held it beneath the blade
While crickets chirped,
And blood ran down the stump.

And suddenly, I remembered
A cold, spring morning
Back in the city,
In our Georgian dining-room,
Where I, shiny with life
And my fresh curls,
Waited for father,
Saw him stride in
With courtroom-eyes,
March to our big bay window
Where his incubator stood.

Bewitched as if he gazed
Upon the magic of all time,
He smiled:

The shells, his precious chicken-shells,
Were cracked, crumbled, abandoned,
And out in front there was the quivery choir—
The wet heads lifted—
The feathers gold
As little bastard daffodils.

The Spoon River Quarterly   MARCIA LEE MASTERS

HUNTING

This was a week of turtles on the road,
six-inch battered hard shells stranded in the sun
as they struggled to the far side foliage.
The word *tortuga* pattered on my brain.
I toted three myself and rescued one
from dogs—I thought.

It came out of the woods in the jaws of the mutt
who uses my yard for short cut.
I talked her out of the tortoise.
At least she dropped it, moved away
as I moved to the mail box.

When I came back, she'd disemboweled it,
four thin pups feeding, neatly and in order.

Knowing I was near, she raised her head,
hiding the guts with her jaw,
her eyes beseeching.
Like the eyes of a woman once
who begged our trash in Nicaragua.
"Quiero basura, Señorita, quiero basurita."

This was no sporting prey.

America   EVELYN MATTERN

DAYS BEYOND RECALL

Learned Santayana described himself
as "an ignorant man, almost a poet."
By "poet" I hope he meant neither a career

nor a state of being (*cf.* angel; *cf.* wretch), but
a student of the future, and thus of the past.
The older our poet grows, the more past he has

to love and powder and dandle, nostalgia
being a dotage, and so he can use up
his dwindling future like a cake of soap,

or he can turn to that future expectantly,
the way a Jesuit might search his mirror for a skull,
and from the mists of waking and shaving

a skull will burn like Birnam Forest.
Or he can seethe along the fuse of his ignorance—
almost a poet, almost a future, almost dead.

NER/BLQ
(New England Review and Bread Loaf Quarterly)   WILLIAM MATTHEWS

SCHOOLBOYS WITH DOG, WINTER

It's dark when they scuff off to school.
It's good to trample the thin panes of casual
ice along the tracks where twice a week

an anachronistic freight lugs grain
and radiator hoses to a larger town.
It's good to cloud the paling mirror

of the dawn sky with your mouthwashed breath,
and to thrash and stamp against the way
you've been overdressed and pudged

into your down jacket like pastel
sausage, and to be cruel to the cringing
dog and then to thump it and hug it and croon

to it nicknames. The exhausting mysteries
of the self grow gray on the far horizon, but
the frosted windows of the schoolhouse gleam.

Ploughshares   WILLIAM MATTHEWS

FOR MY STUDENTS

(Peace goes into the making of a poet
as flour goes into the making of bread.)
—Pablo Neruda

If I have taught you anything,
may it be this: I said

have flour and water
always at hand—
bake bread.

Of your eyes, mouth, breasts,
womb—let this be said:
"She had a gift
for the world. She could
bake bread."

Whatever poems you write (or
live), remember that I said
everywhere men long for food
and freedom.
Bake bread.

In the end, it was the thing
Christ gave. He said:
"Take. Eat." Could you do better,
O beautiful women?
Bake bread.

The Antigonish Review   SISTER MAURA

A PORTRAIT OF MY FATHER

At the kitchen counter
He carves a peach into
Small pieces, then brings them,
One by one, to his mouth
And chews slowly, then waits
To see if it stays down.
If not, he leans over
The sink, then wipes his lips
And tries another piece.
He's telling his body
That he's still in control,
That nothing can take this
Simple function away
From him, the cool sweetness
Of fruit from his shrinking
Tongue. Tomorrow he will
Attempt a pear, apple,
Or plums, and, like now, lose
Most of it, but still carve
And eat until he tires
Of standing. Embarrassed, he turns
His head to cough. He asks
Me the same questions as
This morning nodding at
My replies. Good peaches,

He says when he turns in,
Leaving all lights burning.

Northwest Review   KERRY PAUL MAY

MOURNER

How poetic of our country neighbors
to have called their dog Mourner.
As to why he howled from four o'clock in
the afternoon until a half-past seven Louisville
factory-sundown, nobody had the faintest clue.
Over the fence, we saw him squatting on
hind legs, a black and white rather dowdy,
big, comic Doberman pinscher. Some felt he was
dangerous for being so sad. Against the
car garage, he was a one-dog *I Pagliacci*;
the red sky like proscenium lights about to
fade. His grieving belligerence brought
emotions to my childhood that, without
him, I might not have otherwise had.

The American Scholar   JANE MAYHALL

SPRING PLANTING

(This is the season when our friends may
and will die daily)
—Robert Lowell, "Soft Wood"

Last year's sunflower stalks blacken
at dusk, their huge exploded suns
droop like the heads of mourners,
frozen in sombre procession.

I carry my seedlings from the car—
snap peas, radishes, an experimental
pole bean . . .
                My little green homunculi,
my hostages to a future season, you've
hardened in April's tonic breeze.

We say you'll bear in so many weeks,
that we'll be here to share the fruit—
it's easy to imagine the future wrong.

The four-year mimosa tree stands pale
and spring-naked, a body's length taller
than last year, and seems to belong.

Years back, at Temple Israel Sunday School
on Saturdays, we donated flattened one-dollar bills
for planting trees in new-born Israel.

Survivors would "make the desert bloom"—
Reform American kids helped prevent erosion.
I imagined dark enormous pines,
my father's sweet name
a plaque on one I'd never find . . .

My friend, your last days among us,
you were such a frail leaf tossing
in pain's hurricane, until morphine
finally took you to sleep with my other
lost ones in a distant forest . . .
                                    I place
the flats on the ground by a rusty trowel.
Soon, when the mimosa blossoms again,
its delicate pink blooms will sway
in the cape's harsh wind, and drop—

oriental creature, its feathery flowers
are evanescent as the colorless smoke
your last cigarette blew across by room.

Poetry   GAIL MAZUR

AWAKENING TO FOG

Fog covers the whole city,
and awakening to its mist,
we put off rising, as if
more sleep might burn it off.
On the river are foghorns
and the cracks of ice floes breaking.
In part built of last winter's snow,
they yield now to spring warmth.

We, too, yield to the heat,
pressed prematurely out
like hothouse blossoms.
Above, a thin rainbow
circles the shrouded sun,
parodying that clear ring
within which our sights move.

Except for no salt spray,
it might be an Alaskan coast,
or the Antarctic.
We think of our own needs for travel,
how long we've been at home,
satisfied in our tight circles.

Our dreams go drifting back
like floes into the fog,
emerging unaccountably

in long beds of iris—yellow
and blue and hazy in the sun.

The Hudson Review   JEROME MAZZARO

NOSE POEM

Funny, the way I've started noticing scent,
as if my nose is seeking its primal role now
when it's hardly appropriate. I catch myself
remarking upon subtleties of odour
no one else discerns, waxing eloquent
on smells I have no words for.

It wouldn't be so bad if I could sniff discreetly,
but with these narrow nostrils I must inhale
in deeps gusts, flinging weighty air
to the very depths of my being, saturating
greedy sensors with the data they crave.
Hosts look at me askance, guarding the kitchen door;
grocery clerks stare, unashamed, at me
lifting their wares to my face in indecision;
even the cats look at me warily
when I bury my face in their fur
breathing their secret language.

Event   RHONA MCADAM

EVERYDAY PLACES

This is the house that Jack built—
before the paint can peel, the shutters will crumble,
before the chimney collapses, the eaves will sag,
the walls will fall to the scraggly ground;

and this is the kitchen where Jack kneels
with white knuckles beside his wife,
arranging the pots to catch the rain,
picking up pieces of shattered glass;

and this is the wife who swipes the floor,
her twisted flesh lumped on her back,
her back bent and her arms extended,
who opens the door for the cat who growls;

and this is the son who claws the daughter,
who strokes the cat and threatens the wife,
who cracks the window and scatters the glass
to stick out his head to look at the cow;

and this is the cow jumping over the moon,
looking down to laugh at the couple below

who face each other over the puddles,
who move to the door to gaze at the sky,
and catch the cow at the height of her climb,
who are watching, watching, longing to follow.

The Georgia Review   ELIZABETH MCBRIDE

2 A.M.

it's been so long since
I called someone at 2 a.m., we
didn't have kids & it would be 1 apt.
to another, black lines across the city
or across the towns, the fields & fences
between my city and yours. the lines
were greyhound buses streaking
across the night, our voices
flickering in our cold kitchens like those
old fourth-of-july pinwheels kids once had.
it's been so long, and it's
2 a.m. now, but I don't know
anyone to call, even in Cal. where
it's earlier and not beyond reason.
outside, the streetlight makes a long
elliptical patch of light on the
suburban pavement, a stray tom
howls in the hedge. no one has a light on,
no one. the old man who used to work
in his workshop all night sawing and
singing is dead now and the boy
across the street who studied has gone
to the seminary. I think of calling you
but that would be unthinkable; your wife
would answer a harsh, angry hello,
hello, who is this, and you would
worry: the parents? the kids?
the wailing cat is up against
the window now, wanting to
mate with my Persian.
the cat outside wants in.
the cat inside wants out.

The Creative Woman   JANET MCCANN

BEHIND THE STUCCO HOUSE

Beneath the ridge of acacia,
coyote talks and no one answers.
I have a .22 and a Kool.
I stretch my legs and smoke,

and the voice rises and falls
above the cacophony of pink
granite stones and brush.
This isn't allowed, to howl
in midday, the sun high over
the Osunas, over eucalyptus
and Mexican laborers.
Three chickenhawks loop,
their wings motionless, the air
hot and steady beneath them
where coyote raises a snout,
trusting the pack will return.
Tonight, they will scavenge
rabbits, mice, ground squirrels,
even the tangerines
ripening in my field. I'm not God,
there's no mercy in my heart
for his ragged ears and hide.
The gun is cocked and coyote
flattens like a housepet.
My palms are the Mojave,
my ears hear nothing but heat
rushing with blood.
Tomorrow the ridge will be silent
and my cat will stalk beetles
in the iceplant, and the only enemies
will be black ants tickling
my naked feet.

The Fiddlehead   SHARON MCCARTNEY

CITY LANDSCAPE: ORDER

Skyscrapers are rough and rugged nouns
    which form a patchwork quilt.
Public buildings are pronouns,
    plain and free of beauty.
Co-op condominiums are adverbs,
    with grace and appealing facades.
Apartment buildings are verbs,
    solid and strong-durability and homely charm.
Townhouses are adjectives,
    unique and soft, with singularity.
City parks are conjunctions,
    connecting city man with nature.
Museums are interjections
    linking past and present: creation of order.
—Factories are prepositions,
    free of opulence, practical units
        of city landscape.

Arizona Quarterly   EDWARD PATRICK MCCUE

SUNPORCH

A Wyeth painting, is it? It could be.
Clean parallelograms of light are laid
Across the mauve, grass-matted, concrete floor,
The rocking-chair, the yellow bench. The door
And range of windows looking out to sea
Are calm as plane trees casting luxuriant shade.

I think of various plane trees: one that stands
In a Platonic dialogue, one we saw
On Cos, the island of Hippocrates
(Planted by him, but guarding for centuries
A Muslim saint), and others in other lands;
And here, also: Zeus-like, deserving awe.

In less than awe of the porch furniture, I
Sit in a straight wood chair at peace with all.
The sea, the morning light, the sunlit room
Float me above the boring cries of doom
From yesterday's newspaper. I bless the sky
And the broad earth, and let silence to Silence call.

America   HAROLD McCURDY

WIND AND HARDSCRABBLE

It's wind, not rain, dry cattle need.
Vanes of windmills spinning all day
    turn lead pipes into water.
Wind makes metal couplings sough
like lullabies. As long as there is wind,
    calm steers keep grazing, believing

there is always water. On still days
        steers are nervous,
    lashing their tails at horseflies
always out of reach. They stomp
flat hooves and tremble, bleeding,
    and thrust their dehorned heads

between barbed wires. When it blows,
        steers don't need heaven.
    Wind is mystery enough.
They rasp dry tongues across salt blocks,
    eyes closed, and wind brings
    odors of grainfields miles away.

Even in drought they feast,
the curled grass crisp as winter stubble.
    Parched, they wade still pastures
        shimmering in heat waves

and muzzle deep in stock tanks
filled and overflowing.

The Atlantic Monthly   WALTER MCDONALD

THE MIDDLE YEARS

Now it begins, the soft insinuation
of ferns through spark light. The final
campfire flame is gone, unless we breathe
on embers. Shadows of piñons flare up

and fall away like ghosts. You whisper,
Will these coals live? Nothing
that breathes risks even this much light,
to be seen by strangers so deep

in the forest. For hours we gave ourselves
to simple tasks, unfolding, the clang
of steel on steel stakes for the tent,
sticks to build one fire for water

that boils without getting hot. This high
in the mountains, air is scarce as friends.
Close on a common stone, we watch rose embers
wink like mountain lions. The last sparks

fling themselves away from this spinning
planet and burn up in the only air there is.
All those years to make a roof for children,
gone from us faster than sparks.

Now we are back to beginnings
deep in the mountains, one fire at a time.
Stars are our comfort, and ferns that sough
and hover over us all through the night.

We lie in eiderdown and hold each other
a long time, silent. Later, I wake
and listen. The quick cry of a coyote
rises in the distance, the sound

of wings lifting, eagle or owl.
Nothing else for minutes, only your
steady breathing, asleep, believing
nothing's out there that shouldn't be.

The Journal   WALTER MCDONALD

MOON, RAZOR, EYE

the knife that does not draw blood draws heart
through blade instead of blade through heart

this knife is sharper and more polite
it is honed against the broken edge
of soon-only-forever, and the blade,
coated with its stickiness of loyalty
and love, can be used in public for deeper cuts

the knife that does not draw blood tears love
from its center, and draws caricatures
where you drown in your best features
this knife draws ugliness, draws cruelty
and you are the stick figure, full
of the pretty poisons, of friends and families
leaving behind trails visible only in the right light
like the silver threads of snails or sea snake tracks
like a thin cloud slicing the moon's single eye

and you wonder how you could have missed it all
how you could have missed a thing that moved so swiftly
inside its own deadly silence while you drank the false warmth
of evenings full of the scent of flowers or the old smells
of school books, umbrellas, rain slicks moist with what home
was like when life was simple and the only bloodless
scrapes were knees and dreams where you awoke falling
into line behind the leader, the father or mother, the trail
that led nowhere when you were still too young to care
later you learned the names of all the things that hurt
and if the knife shakes you loose of its tip
you will learn to wait for blood only you can see

The Georgia Review   COLLEEN J. MCELROY

WINDSURFERS

Everything is plausible this summer: I have no idea what I'm
doing, where I'm going, my mind is dimly lit and empty. You've
heard this before. We stayed awake for hours looking at each other
and smiling, then fell asleep. In the morning, our eyes opened at
the same moment like four cherry blossoms on one bough. Irony
is no longer a large part of my life, imagine that! Everything is
changing, everything is plausible, and I now see that wisdom
and knowledge can never co-exist. Oh madam, I embrace you
with all the spring breezes and starry nights of all my lives,
with all the darkness of this radiant moment, with what I hope
is the blindness of wisdom, more than instinct, less than intuition.

And since everything is plausible this summer, I suggest a quiet
part of the beach, the stony part, less crowded than the sandy,
and there is no one there. There are two kinds of people: those
who like the stony part and those who like the sandy. And there's
my friend Andy, he likes the Sandy. Andy Panda and Sandy Stone.
Please don't show this poem to anyone. Windsurfers, four of them,

come racing out from behind the distant rocky point, and one turns
abruptly and heads for shore, the others stopping to watch him go,
then turning and heading further out. I guess he just remembered
he had to make an urgent call. And so we eat cherries and spit the
pits among the stones. The water is cold, the sun hot, the breeze
cool, the sky blue, your breasts radiant with love's intelligence.
I enjoy my confusion as it is, and refuse to view it with irony.

Descant (Canada)   DAVID MCFADDEN

WALKING AROUND THE BLOCK WITH MY DAUGHTER

After she banged out the Bach minuets,
both of us thought we could use a walk.
No one, I told her, danced that rapidly then.
The women curtsied first and gentlemen
bowed like this, right hands floating like doves
in fall above those wheatfields to the west.

Snow, hard on the sidewalks, held my eyes
down to its cold sparkle. She had a surprise,
she said, in her desk at school, something she
made for me, but maybe I wouldn't like it.
Her voice quivered, waiting for me to say,
"Don't tell your secret. Save it for the day
I come home late from work and all these robins,
fat in the mountain ash, shrivel with cold."

Then she skated across the ice-hard snow,
flowing with intricate, random designs,
the sweet winter symphony in her veins
moving along her legs deep into her boots
like nothing Bach thought of in his minuets.
And overhead the hardy robins cheered
as "Yes," my daughter said, "I think you'll like it."

The Ohio Review   RON MCFARLAND

THE HUNTRESS

I buried my hunting bow
in the backyard;
the first big rain
exposed it like a spine.
There are many things buried
in that yard:
arrows broken in half,
cans of food,

their labels loosened
by dampness,
and a guitar packed with dirt,
mute.
I know exactly
where these things are
in case I ever need them—
they either lurch
toward the light
with each rain,
or stay lodged underground
like bullets lodged
beneath the skin,
travelling toward the heart.

West Coast Review   LYNN MCGEE

THE ASTRONOMER BESIDE HIS TELESCOPE
LOOKS WITH HIS EYES OUT HIS WINDOW

I think of myself as moving.
On the surface of a planet
I know im my mind I
Move breathtakingly and that
I rise and fall and rush
Across a universe with a star
Around which I move,
Though only in my mind.
For to my eyes it moves across
My window and I am still.
But I feel myself moving,
Looking out on rain-soaked
Shale of a classroom hall.
I move inside with emotion
Thinking this is what I feel,
Feeling in spite of thought
The orbit of my blood.
I see in things how my soul is,
I feel the beauty of things,
Red leaves on the oaken chest:
I move with visions—
A friend in a flannel shirt,
A woman in a cotton dress,
And all those who move around me,
Around whom I move,
With whom I rise or fall or rush
Through an emptiness I love
And fear and cannot comprehend.

Kansas Quarterly   REX MCGUINN

HARM'S WAY

I have a friend who lives desperately
as an answer to the world, as if the world
had asked him a question. He lives as though
he might be called to account for our suffering—
for his and everybody else's. He lives to be ready.

In this age, poets do not say forever,
nor do lovers. I refuse to count my losses.
My friend calls me foolish. Mornings, I watch
the valley fill with rain. I watch the puddles
where the deer drink, the fox and the dove.

Stay out of Harm's Way, an old woman once
told me, and I froze, wondering if Harm
was the man with the red hands and a raw face
who lived next door, who knocked the lid off
the garbage can, smashing glass in the morning.

Now I walk the steep hills and ridges
where the soil is thin, happy in the solace
of roots like the tendons of a human foot.
I am learning the patience of small animals:
staying out of sight, hiding in the shadows.

Tar River Poetry   DAVID McKAIN

PRIMER

Three years are long enough to learn
how to count, brush your teeth, get toilet trained.
Long enough to start thinking Mister Rogers is dumb.
Three years are long enough for magic marker to wear off
for a scoliosis brace to fix things
the smashed fingernail to grow back.
Long enough to outgrow Cinderella bedrooms
afternoon naps, seven pair of shoes.
Three years are long enough to lather peanutbutter
between thick slices of disappointment
a single parent walking
in autumn desperation long enough
to learn from children
to find horsies in marshmallow clouds
find the creamy center of a Twinkie.
Long enough to turn around and find
the man who regularly finds horsies
making peanutbutter sandwiches in your kitchen
with your children
like he wants to marry you.
Three years are long enough thank you
that when he's gone for three days

calls and says goodnight
to each of the children
you are left to sleep hungry
in the very center
of your marshmallow bed.

The Antigonish Review   LINDA BACK MCKAY

THE WORLD ON THE HILL

We had our own world there in that night.
We would lie on the quiet hill
needing the dark to hide our anxious faces
as we removed each other's clothing
and awkwardly felt for sex, embarrassed
to be so much out of control, to be so
controlled by the confusion of genitals,

so ashamed to be so adult while so young,
and proud to be so young, yet so adult.
But it was not pride
on our faces that we were trying to hide
with the darkness of that night.
We would lie for hours afterward, our hands
locked together, our eyes locked
onto a single silent thought only the stars
over that stilled hill could know.

Laurel Review   LOUIS MCKEE

NIGHT TRAIN

The clangor grips my memory. But then
To shut the crowding, chugging, wheezing out,
We closed the door and slept, cocooned within
Our room, impervious to dark or doubt
Until escape became a patterned way,
The risks and leavings strangers to defeat
Until the restless searching spawned by day
Led to encircled darkness and retreat.

Not now. Tonight, when jostling, whistling start,
No longer isolated from the throng,
I find a seat and listen as my heart
Locks with the churning wheels. Within its song
I hear your voice, and everything is one . . .
Night, clangor, end, beginning, rising sun.

Orphic Lute   CARMELITA MCKEEVER

IN A LARGE CAMBRIDGE BOOKSTORE, A.D. 1985

(after Cavafy)

1.

When I went into the House of Books
I didn't spend my time upstairs
where the usual trades and MMPs
are touted and sold like cereals
in their neat, alphabetical rows
and their Madison Avenue packaging
with the photos on back, the phony
praise—all so alike, all "Brilliant,"
"Dazzling," "Masterful" works of art,
or scholarship, or popular psychology.

No, I made straight for the stairs
that led down into that scurvy hole
of a basement, where disheveled racks
listed under the dust and two-bit
paperbacks from a decade or more ago:
the long-out-of-prints and secondhands,
the Perennial Classics and also-rans
with their lurid, misleading covers,
their crude, ephebic marginalia.

I didn't hold back. I let my fingers
wander along their smutted spines,
where so many others had roamed before.
I felt their papyric pages, dark
as Turkish tobacco, crumble at my touch.
I lolled and languished among the stacks,
feasting on their buried treasures
the way some daredevil of pleasure
would drain a bottle of heady wine.

Maybe you think it's a scandal that I,
a poet, have to scrimp on books this way.
But you're wrong. Because what kind of poet,
what kind of struggling artist would I be
if I bookshopped more conventionally?
I say: Better to read no books at all
than browse among the common shelves.

2.

But as I was climbing up those stairs
that groaned like a sinful bed, you
were just coming in the door
and, for a split second, our eyes met.
Then I hid myself behind an upright
while you hurried by, hiding
your face in a vintage *Books in Print*,
and blundered on down the stairs

to look for a book you wouldn't find
any more than I'd found mine.

And yet the book you wanted I had to loan,
and the one I wanted—I could tell
by your strained, myopic eyes—
you had for me. But caught by surprise,
we passed these bargains by.

Boston Review   MARTIN MCKINSEY

SPIN THE BOTTLE

The butt end of a Coke bottle spins to me,
   the mouth to a redhead, her green dress
spread over a black and silver leg brace.
Empty of words, my head a balloon, I follow her
limp from the room out into welcome darkness.
I can think only of how in the fifth grade
someone stole the placard of polio dimes
and now, two years later, shame and guilt harden
my tongue like the macadam road we walk on.
My first walk with a girl, the bottle has given me
one who could be my mother the easy way
she takes my hand to stall us, her hip
turning us to the rocky shoulder to sit,
all the while chattering in the great gaps
of my words. When she pulls us down to our sides
and her tongue burns mine, I answer—
forgetting the brace pinching my knee and all else
except one breast like a moth at a window—
until a car downwind whips out of an S curve,
its lights flooding us whiter than albinos,
the rocks we lie on snowed over.
                              As we scramble up,
blinded in that glare, I know at once
why my speech halts, why polio loves legs,
why, a year later, trying to take my turn
on a backseat with the neighborhood girl,
I will freeze up—silent, naked and soft.

Emry's Journal   KEN MCLAUREN

THE SUMMER KITCHEN

Her grandmother's garden at the end of the laneway, filled
with the skeletons of sunflowers. A day with warm sunlight
and dust by the window in her grandmother's house with
its yard of tall grass. The paths through the milkweed.
And paths through the flowers on the grey and blue

linoleum that lead to the bottom of the stairs. Whispers
coming from upstairs. They don't want her up there where
her grandmother is. But why not? She's big enough.

They say she can play in the kitchen. But keep away from
the stove and don't go near the cellar door. There's a
hole at the bottom of the cellar stairs, in the dark down
there. A real pit, big enough to swallow a little girl.
Yes, it could swallow her, and when her daddy went down
he took a flashlight and then she watched him solemnly,
listening to his steps on the stairs as they grew fainter,
afraid of losing him forever. But he was very careful.
And wasn't he changed when he came back up, slightly out
of breath from the climb, blinking in the kitchen's bright
light? Didn't he seem more of a father, and brighter, too,
as if the trip down to the pit had coated him with something
fine and luminous?

Event   ANNE McLEAN

THE DIGGING

(for Sarah)

It is that time of year,
the hedgerows hung with bittersweet,

potato time.
How early the cold has come this year I'd say
if we were speaking.
We're not. We turn our spading forks

against the earth. It's stiff,
the Reds and Idahos hard as stone
or soft as old tomatoes,
a total loss.

Once it was us against the beetles, blight,
whatever was not potato. How they flowered,
rows and rows
in white. Now look.

We give it one last try—and there,
far down in softer soil, a seam of them,
still perfect.
One after the other, some red, some Idaho;

we hold them up to the dying day,
kneel down to sift for more. Abruptly,
in the dark of earth, I come upon your hand,
you mine.

Yankee   RENNIE McQUILKIN

REMEMBERING MY FATHER'S TATTOOS

Sweetheart, the one for my mother
would have said in red and green, a heart
by the hand of a failed artist in Dallas or Newark.

One would have been for a woman in France,
someone he'd loved twice
before the Germans got to her on their way to Belleau
(the scent of her dark hair stunning him
in nightmares for forty years, the lingering
Etude in E she'd played on the crank-machine)—
Norma, the pale name under the faded bird
that could be a peacock
or a phoenix.

A third would have been for his mother,
least distinct of all, another heart,
misshapen, another woman left in the wake
of his frozen anger. In the heart, the word *Mommy*.

Passages North   PAUL MCRAY

BACH, WINTER

Bach must have known
how something flutters away
when you turn to face the face
you caught sideways in a mirror
in a hall at dusk,
and how the smell of apples
in a bowl can stop the heart
from beating, for an instant,
between sink and stove
in the dead of winter when stars
of ice have spread
across the windows and everything
is perfectly still—
until you catch the sound
of something lost and shy
beating its wings
against those darkening stars.
And then: music.

Ploughshares   JANE MEAD

WAITING FOR THE PALE EAGLE

The world is winking
at us all the time

Take for example
that red-winged blackbird
we have admired and
grown tired of admiring
poised on the curve
of cat-tail stems
in every watery ditch
from Idaho to Florida
epaulet crimson in the sun
One day on a drive to Wichita
I saw that thousandth
or ten thousandth blackbird

From below its crimson patch
a glint of yellow winked at me

Sunlight sang across the ditch water
I remembered the polished turning
of plowed ground near Dyersburg
The light-edged scales
of a moccasin sunning
on a cypress in the Combahee
The pale eagle rising
in the moon's face
Wind through the car
window laughed at me
See—it was always there
All you had to do
was look—and look—
and keep on looking

Kansas Quarterly   STEPHEN MEATS

A STATION ON THE COMMUTER LINE

I was waiting on the platform for the train into the city
    the morning I saw her,
a stranger to me, waiting on the far side for the express
    to the outer suburbs;
and when through the early rain we glanced at one another
    over the theater sign
like two people across a common border, it was mysterious,
    but a kind of solace,
and when the express arrived and swept the platform clear,
    I felt happy for her.
I have stood on the platform after the morning rush hour
    among those left behind
when I have had glimpses of those curiously agile worlds
    which cats must see
in mirrors, and in the waiting room of our small station
    more than one morning
I was reminded of an estuary where manatees lay sleeping

as the light came down.
Our small lives can be dazzling, like pennies on the rail
    after the train passes,
for something goes on sleeping here with a great patience
    and often a great calm,
as if across our quiet lawns a transfiguration has passed
    and made our possession
seem a dispossession, with light entering it by a new way.

O beautiful sunken animals, O consciousness in all places,
    I, too, have been waiting.
I have stood on the platform after the commuters departed
    when the station lay empty
and in the spectacular music our cells make I have heard
    only a great happiness
as the distance runners began coming in one after another
    toward their best times,
kicking out harder and at the line opening up their arms
    as though to embrace
what they had come to, a new self they are joyous to see.

The Ohio Review   JAY MEEK

WEEDS

She planted marigolds because they kept
the bugs away; their ridged bitter gold
glimmered like coins against the ivy and swept
brick of the walkways. She piled all the old
oak leaves from last fall around
the thick camelias with their waxy shine.
In rows of alternating spice—silvermound,
mugwort, tansy, basil, sage, parsley, thyme—
her garden spread outward from the center,
an orderly progression from bergamot
to spearmint, satisfactory and shared.
But at the farthest point from where you enter,
there, in the road's shadow, in the central spot,
she left some weeds untended where they flared—
stubborn, ragged, unassimilated, wild.

Southern Poetry Review   PETER MEINKE

SO MANY AMERICANS, DRIVING LATE
ON COUNTRY ROADS

*(The most likely time for a fatal automobile accident is
one a.m. Sunday morning. Often these accidents involve
a single car with one passenger.)*
                            —Newspaper article

It's always this place that calls you. You
turn a corner at the edge of town,

the wheel in your hands the outline of a shape
you no longer understand.

Like the dozens of drivers all over America
who parallel you tonight on other country roads,
you stare through a horizon of curved glass:
the asphalt deepens into a starless sky.
Your wallet is full; you believe you could accelerate
for years. You don't realize you're following a blinking line
of drivers, their names in smeared ink
of Monday-morning obituaries.
Their histories yellow in basements,
like your headlights fading beyond the gravel shoulder.

The speedometer turns over. The dashboard
flares. This place always calls
you, its voice softer
than your velour seats, calls you
to close your eyes
and meet it head on.

It's the simple end that is best.
Beyond that first sharp curve,
a single tree waits.
Never a witness. Perhaps
a lone dog whose ears straighten at the
impact. It limps the other direction,
deeper into woods, while twigs
tick like an overheated engine cooling.

Poetry   BILL MEISSNER

SURVIVAL

I stand on this stump
To knock on wood
For the good I once
Misunderstood.

Cut down, yes,
But rooted still—
What stumps compress
No axe can kill.

Midstream   SAMUEL MENASHE

CONDEMNED MAN DIES IN FLORIDA CHAIR

Shaving, I hear the familiar hitting of a fly
trapped between pane and screen, such a faint,

musical sound I barely realize
the panic and last energy of life required
in protesting death. Then winter sunlight
beams off the vacant lot beside my house,
yesterday healthy with snow, but now
patchy brown like a dog's vagrant hide.
Even the thermometer, tilting in rusty calipers,
blushes up toward fifty-five, though it's January,
whose warm days are merely the beast's
nursing his fresh-sliced foot before the kill. Whatever
dooms that fly and all its leaping
turns my thoughts away from detail and toward
winter's long swoop of gray, and how a man accepted
death today

like the grim evening news, pointing with each jolt
at the executioner paused in his room—
my childhood god of death and fear. Sometimes
I feel so merciless, cruel words surging
over hard-formed love, or caught within like slow,
electric strangle holds, until the doomed man, quoting
Jesus on the cross while crowds protest in a muddy field,
sounds too empty and easy. We choose
our place apart, shielded by glass or hellish masks,
or flung blindly between two barriers, stalked
by the fast encroaching paw of winter.

New Letters   MICHAEL MILBURN

THE FUTURE OF BEAUTY

I pause at the word *aesthetic* while the crowd
of clear twelve-year-old eyes assesses me.
They have not thought to ask
what *beauty* is, but the word *aesthetic*
is somehow beautiful to them—
the odd slide of vowels and the click
of the idea shutting off at the end of sound.
Their tongues prepare the *aesth*— but each
will wait for the next moment alone
to whisper the whole new word.
It is not animal, plant or plaint,
but idea, less manageable than *love*
or *hate*—more in the category of *grief*
or *anguish*, those refinements of *pain*
they are all anxious to know
in what they prefer to call The Future
since they have been told it belongs to them.

The Antioch Review   LESLIE ADRIENNE MILLER

WHITE OWL

Past carriages of bone,
Cobweb stars and sleeves
Of snakeskin, high in the rafters
Of the burnt-out barn
I found a scraggly white owl;

His flattened face
Pressed like a foxglove on a page;
His claws, his talons,
All peeling like the bark
Of aging silver maples.

And staring at his eyes,
so watchful, so alive,
So far beyond death's symbol,
I thought of you: old love,
Old vows, enduring still.

The Centennial Review   MICHAEL MILLER

IT'S IN THE BLOOD

When I was a kid
my father would get
what he called tipsy,
and even when my whiskers
had begun to show
he would lean down
unsteadily and kiss me
like some huge aunt
and chuckle when
he saw the flush
redden like a sunset
down my cheeks.

He never outgrew this—
not the getting tipsy
or the kissing; in private
or in public, it was a pain
I had to bear,
standing stiffly, lowering
my solemn eyes to accept
his parting kisses,
welcome kisses,
kisses any time
the wine flowed freely.

Now I observe
cool bargains struck
between fathers and sons:
the perfunctory grin,

the straight look in the eye,
the solid, sober handshake
when they say goodby.
Yet I lean down and kiss my son,
bestow both curse and blessing:
I've become my father's man,
the kissing
and the drinking kind.

Envy's Sting   PHILIP MILLER

PHOTOS OF FATHER

Five dozen photos but not one shows father
as he always was—boot drunk, ripping through each day,
or weeping over what seemed nothing, nothing:
lost spectacles or a broken glass, some small remark
he took to heart. Yet we could curse and threaten death,
and he would laugh like a doomed man, pour out a drink,
and light up a Camel before our firing squad of words,
then pick out his own to fire right back.
All these pictures show him as well trimmed
as a supreme court justice, sober as he looked
in his coffin, hands folded, posed for posterity,
beaming, letting the camera get its eye-full.
Best for us to remember him that way, I guess,
except for those shots I couldn't keep
from taking as I stood half my life
gawking, letting my wide eyes take him in.

The Cape Rock   PHILIP MILLER

1913

I betook myself to Italy right after the harvest.
The McCormick harvester in that year 1913
Moved across our fields for the first time
Leaving behind cut stubble unlike that left
By the sickle or the scythes of the reapers.
My factotum Yosel rode to his kin in Grodno
By the same train, but in third class.
I had my supper there in the refreshment room
At a long table under rubber plants.
I remembered the high bridge over the Nieman
As the train wound out of an Alpine pass
And woke up by water, in the bluish-grey
Radiance of the pearly lagoon
In a city where the traveler forgets who he is.
In the waters of Lethe I saw the future.
Is this my century? Another continent—

We sit together with a grandson of Yosel
Talking of our poet friends. Incarnated,
Young again, yet identical with my older self.
What strange costumes, how strange the street is—
And I myself unable to speak of what I know
Since no lesson for the living can be drawn from it.
I closed my eyes and felt the sun on my face,
Here, now, drinking coffee on Piazza San Marco.

The Threepenny Review   CZESLAW MILOSZ
—Translated from the Polish
by the author and Robert Hass

MEDITATION IN WINTER

Take one of the lesser stars,
the ones that flash in and out of vision
because they are so far away,
and think of what a cold and lonely place
it must be.
In this we see the poignance
of the specific, the one blasted and wrinkled
fruit in a sea of trees
sweeping over the long, low arc
of hills in Florida.
It doesn't matter how much universe
cascades over our heads
making the eyes want to relax
into the whole circumferate arch of a night
sky. The one reef still breaks
off the Galapagos. The ash of a volcano
that choked one man to death
is still as repeatable
as making love. And if, somewhere,
one creature opened its arms
in an impossible bliss of re-creation,
leaning outward toward all that signifies
Life, Yes, still that hope
would lie changed and unchanged, seen and unseen,
felt and not felt, like
the endless waves
of tree and sky and water and light
that keep the one thing
saved and broken.

The Ohio Review   SCOTT MINAR

WIFE OF MILLHAND

(Lowell, Massachusetts, circa 1875)

In the photograph she wears black,
hands folded in her lap, lips pressed together,

as if the photographer had told her not to smile.
His was a serious business,
the preservation of the family.
Her hair pulled behind her ears,
waist cinched into whalebone, a pose
she held only a few times in her life.

Afternoons at four when the whistle blew
she watched the men walk home by the canal,
as she stirred soup, having scraped the bones.
Sheets dried in loops above her head.

On the floor played the children,
who arrived one after the other,
beyond her control, her teeth clenched.
She knew she would lose at least one
or two or three of them
to typhoid or a kick from a horse.

Maybe she tried to guess
which ones would by luck outlive her
and allowed herself to hold them longer in her arms.
Maybe half of her already lay
with a little one
in the crib of his grave,
her heart gone hard as the stove
she fed the living from.

Contemporary New England Poetry   HELENA MINTON

A KNOWLEDGE OF WATER

I love the way the cows go down to the water
and wade in deep, till the nostrils rest
on the pond's copper film. In July,
when the oak shade bakes like a shut loft,
all the cattle walk off into coolness, feel
their heavy meat lift.
     So the body
they drink from consumes them, becomes
a eucharist busy with flies. This stink
of pond slime, piss, and rotting possum
swallows till their giant taw eyes
gaze across the surface, where the light
changes every move.
     And I believe
they can nearly take it in, like a drink,
the ripple, slope, fence, pines, sky,
and they walk from the pond onto earth
with a knowledge they will bear,

crossing dry pastures at dusk, single file,
their wet flesh heavier than before.

The Georgia Review   JUDSON MITCHAM

ISLAND HAMMOCK

Everything I love in motion
measures time.
Blue flags fold,
knot themselves slowly in green.
Fireweed flashes on a distant shore, then
dies away.

The tide rumbles,
rises within a granite cave,
a continual rhythm, dip and pull,
dip and pull of invisible oars.

My cradle of rope sways
beneath a finer weave of threads
shimmering, cast in a fitful breeze
across twigs and branches.
Wisps of silk glisten,
unravel, and floating down,
end in shadows.
No spider will be
mending these.

Everything I love in motion
marks my time.
No permanence,
no safety net is spread.
Loss lives here, in
the web of seasons.

Yankee   JUDITH W. MONROE

THE FASHIONABLE, SUCCESSFUL WRITERS

We are the fashionable, successful writers.
We have a string of awards and titles attached to our names . . .
Ho hum . . . ho hum.
See how famous and admired we are.
We have won all the prizes to be had.
Aren't we important and celebrated?
Our success is not ephemeral and transitory.
We are not some trained seal
—some popular T.V. Star or Athlete.
Our fame is not like theirs—ad hoc, diurnal, gone in an instant.
No, our talent is not some vulgar whim of the moment;

Our genius belongs to the ages.
See how admired and courted we are.
But don't try to intrude into our small inch of spotlight,
for we'll hack you down with machetes and machine guns
—with every weapon we possess . . . ho, hum; ho, hum.
We are the smart and well-recognized writers.
We are very successful, indeed.

Envy's Sting   ALBERT J. MONTESI

HOMECOMING WITHOUT YOU, LAUREN

This weekend last October
We stood for snapshots by
These black gates, leaves
Cartwheeling across the Yard,
A vague sense of yellow and
Crimson that seemed to brush over
The tedious details. What
I remember are clouds like terry
Cloth, these plain buildings
Disfigured by ivy, tremendous
Oaks and maples unimpressed
By wind, and your fingers,
Long and delicate like the clasp
On a brooch, how they abandoned
Holding back your fluttering
Hair for my waist. I concentrate
On that moment until I no longer
Hear the Square's traffic
Grumble, and people bumping
Past are like turns in my sleep.
I breathe in deeply again
And again, air filled with lies
About your presence, that same
Scent of wet leaves, my shoulders
Expecting your hands. For a moment,
I can believe what the woodcock
Believes as he reiterates
His speech, his startled glide
From grass to nest:
There are no years. Only seasons.

The Sun   DAVID MOOLTEN

IN GRATITUDE TO PISSARO FOR HIS
WOMAN AND CHILD AT THE WELL

It is real noon in the picture by Pissaro.
We did not know how gray we were, how tired,

until we looked, unspooled in the light nets
of the painter; the thatched greens
and wickets of the little orchard, the
patch of pink, trowelled earth behind it.
A watering can tips where it was dropped,
seems to dream in its improvised texture.
The woman leans in a forgetful space,
propped by substantial folds of apron,
her hand falling open in a fine, cool gesture.
Then uncurl.
Having come so far, with so much effort,
discover what really matters: that is,
moss, and Pissaro's red tiled roofs
absorbing their spatter of color over and over.
Here's moisture, pooled and blue,
the bricks of an old well.
Pissaro's trees collect the sun and hold.

The Literary Review   BARBARA MOORE

BURNING THE TOBACCO BED

Together in the March air, one on each side,
we walked the full length of the fire,
the mound of hickory, pine and fir,
and, with our rakes, separated the limbs,
then combed the pieces as they burned.
At dusk, a light wind stirred the bed,
lifting up flames in a spiral of light,
then spread between us millions of sparks,
father and son, face to face,
smiling through fire, brilliant to each other;
and for one moment, in mackinaw and faded hat,
holding a rake handle, you were God.

In my own bed just before sleep, I still hear
rakes touch, clear notes of steel
rising above ripples from the creek,
and I watch underneath me
the long rectangle of embers
sink slowly into the earth.

Passages North   FRANK D. MOORE

COPPERHEAD WALL

From the window she watches
the snakes among the rocks.
Some fool her into believing

they are leafless vines until
they stretch out on ledges
in the sun. One flat-headed rock
emerging from dirt she thinks
is a snake gone to stone.
If they make any sound at all,
it is like the hum of planes
high over the valley.

She welcomes the first freeze,
the wall silent with ice.
Now the snakes cover the ground
of her dreams. In the dreams
all childhood shrieks,
Mama, come with the hoe;
and the earth is the earth
until she steps on it,
and they writhe,
diamond-backed, coiled,
yellow, fuchsia,
long as jump ropes.

Kansas Quarterly   JANICE TOWNLEY MOORE

THE VISITORS

They like to come here. Pleasant sidestreets pave
    smoothly among the stones;
    a parking place at every grave;
a quiet suburb where the distant mower drones.

Instead of one they'd snarled at, he or she,
    or nagged with angry tears,
    the dirty, worn perplexity
they had endured at last in silence through the years,

there is a polished stone and the mown grass
    over the buried dark;
    there is the shadow that will pass;
there are the muffled cars that glide and softly park.

Let there be no tears; let the easy plough
    creature from creature sever.
    Death is no inconvenience now.
At last no need for talking, talk all stopped forever.

Wasn't this peace, this clippered prettiness,
    this silent presence here,
    this still and sterilized caress
what they had longed for always, always held most dear?

Contemporary New England Poetry   RICHARD MOORE

WHAT'S DONE

My father stepped from the waiting room
when I was born, and walked the long hall
to the nursery where the babies, crying, all
looked the same; he held his tears and called
all the nurses "dear," aware he feared how soon

he'd see my mother, wrapped in her nicest nightgown,
propped on pillows, still in pain. A boy
he'd hoped for, but as labor came, he had no joy—
she pushed, he paced, for hours, sorry
this child was made and bound them now.

As I grew, I never saw my parents kiss;
I thought this was how parents were
until I saw my friend's father
touch his wife, sure, familiar.
And when my mother died, my father wept, missing

her now she was gone; and I, his grown son,
couldn't then hold him. He's remarried now; his wife
reminds me of my mother, frail, her life
maintained by her intelligence; she kisses him and laughs
at his reticence. When I kiss him I sense

him drawing into himself, feeling what's done is done.

Passages North   DUNCAN MORAN

ORD

In boot camp at Ord everybody was dead serious
about the training
as our Korean war machine ground down
to the terminal idle that continued
to chew up kids.
There were a thousand tricks to be mastered
in those sixteen weeks, packed
denser than a Pound canto.

Gradually I learned that just two things
relative to the rank of
private
were essential to surviving the moment
and whatever might come after:
anonymity and the M1 rifle.
So I perfected myself in the firing
and cleaning of that edgy equalizer,
and slept whenever I could through the rest of it.

. . . And it turned out in the platoon
I had a clone—

same height, weight, eye color and the like—
named Morgan. Put fatigues on us
and our mothers couldn't tell us apart.
So naturally the cadre
was constantly mistaking us, too—

he'd yell, "Morgan, clean the shit cans!" or
"Morgan, police the wrappers—
I wanna' see asshole and elbows!"
And Morgan, the poor bastard, plodded
week after week through this plain case
of mistaken identity and never did catch on.

The last day,
when we were fully trained and terrified,
the cadre asked, "Well Morgan, how does it feel
to be a killing machine?"
I said it felt piss poor and that the name
was Moran. He stared at me
like he'd never seen me before,
which of course he hadn't.

The Threepenny Review   MOORE MORAN

AN ACT OF GOD

Houses hang from cliffs in northern California.
People expect to drop off into the Pacific
or whatever else lies beneath, and the
insurance companies, who love a good risk,
invest heavily in the short-term. They bank
on the epicenter's last known address.

But when the earthmovers took down a hill
for the new Ramada Inn on State 123,
they left a red brick house sitting uneasily
on top of a red clay bank, and when it slid
finally into the parking lot, it came
to rest on three new Toyotas

that were lined up at attention
for the dealer's midyear convention.

Northeast   RONALD MORAN

SIGODLIN

When old carpenters would talk of buildings
out of plumb or out of square, they always
said they were sigodlin, as though anti-
sigodlin meant upright and square, at proper
angles as a structure should be, true to

spirit level, plumbline, erect and sure
from the very center of the earth, firm
and joined solid, orthogonal and right,
no sloping or queasy joints, no slouching
rafters or sills. Those men made as they were:
the heavy joists and studs yoked perfectly,
and showing the dimensions themselves, each
mated pair of timbers to embody
and enact the crossing of space in its
real extensions, the vertical to be
the virtual pith of gravity, horizontal
aligned with the surface of the planet at
its local tangent. And what they fitted
and nailed or mortised into place, downright
and upstanding, straight up and down and flat
as water, established the coordinates
forever of their place in creation's
fabrics; in a word learned perhaps from
masons who heard it in masonic rites
drawn from ancient rosicrucians who
had the term from the Greek mysteries'
love of geometry's power to say,
while everything in the real may lean just
the slightest bit sigodlin or oblique,
the power whose center is everywhere.

The Atlantic Monthly   ROBERT MORGAN

JET TRAILS

Only on the clearest days in this
upstate climate do you notice
the contrails etched above. We must
be under some great air lane, for
by afternoon the whole heaven
is chalked and cobwebbed in all depths
and directions as a cowtrailed
pasture. The ropes of cloud once laid
on a still day have nothing to
do but settle for hours swelling
like yarn left out in dampness, twisted
out of shape by crosswind, sometimes
broken in sections but sinking
closer, thin as comet tails,
until they get so near and vague
you can't tell where their crystal stops
and a wisp of cirrus begins;
while surface currents erase their
last definition and late sun
gilds the whips of confetti and
tatters we're already breathing

like the cleaned air of history,
which is our only oxygen.

Carolina Quarterly   ROBERT MORGAN

THE MOTH

The giant moth we found between two windows,
trapped in a locked house, as we were walking,
stopped us a moment: how
it clung to the inner glass

impassively, moving its wings slightly
in torpor. It was like a mask in a case,
with two vast eyes that glowed
violet, rimmed with gold.

But ours was helpless love. So we went on
under the rain of maple seeds in the wind.
The heads of trees were exploding,
the attic windows swarmed

with many fragments of torn sky: shattered
peace and shattered forms driven across it.
Then, fired from ebony,
came random shots of the storm.

We cowered. But we ran with a strange joy.
Exhilaration, sudden death, in the air
and in our breasts were joined,
and the great moth we'd seen:

what had it been, a map that chance had drawn
of our world? It barely vibrated its wings
as if not to feel again
the narrowness of the space

where the wild, perfect pattern had an end.
In those wings, trembling, heavy, the moth bore,
hooded in dust and shadow,
every color, every form.

The Malahat Review   A. F. MORITZ

OLD, OLD LADY

The rooms in her small apartment
are now too large,
the distances to bed and table
too far, the place,
a spooky grand hotel
of frightening shadows.

Tottering, tiny,
she'd like to slip
into a cradle, tucked in
by momma, and be rocked
gently back, gently, gently
into a small warm darkness.

The Creative Woman   LILLIAN MORRISON

OBIT FOR SALLY E.

*(Investigating officers found that the pack of
dogs had escaped from a fenced-in area
surrounding a small house in the woods . . .)*
      —from an evening paper

"Only a small skull and a few long bones
Were found"—the evening paper said,
But there wasn't the slightest mention made
That Sally Eppingworth was dead.
Most of us had seen her—maybe once or twice—
Poking sticks at things along the road
Or pawing through some pile of trash
For anything to feed the pack of dogs
That she had gathered round her place
To ward off evil—make it safe.

And as I read the news my mind flipped back
To a story we once read in German class
About how Death can build a door.
I don't remember much—*Tod* and *Tür* come through—
But it seems there was a couple who
Boarded up their home with such great care
They thought that Death could never, ever enter there.

But Death was boarded in, not out,
Just as it was for poor old Sally
Who must have fallen with a stroke
In the safety of her yard—among her friends
Who couldn't watch her suffer there upon the ground
And saved her from the thing we all most fear:

Lying helpless, useless and so very much alone
In some God-forsaken place they call a nursing home.

The American Scholar   M. E. MORROW

ANTE BELLUM

Before the war, the sun rose over green fields and blue seas,
glass towers reflected its light by day and shone a bluish
    white at night

Before the war, trains ran on time and nearly empty,
driving was permitted anywhere at any hour and everyone drove;
airports became twenty-four-hour shopping malls

Before the war, citizens complained of the tax on their income and property,
the price of the groceries that filled their carts;
destinies hung on a half-cent rise or fall in the value of the dollar

Before the war, workers went on strike to protect their pension funds from inflation

Before the war, the market was bullish:
Litton industries created a thousand new jobs and paid no taxes

Before the war, alcohol's popularity reached an all-time high,
also yoga, jogging, drugs, cosmetics, registered charities, letters to the editor and
    food food food

Before the war, deterrent was a household word;
Knowing the closest to the blast die instantly without pain,
people crowded into cities and drove each other mad

Before the war, faith made a comeback,
flowers grew in spring, dew drops
clung to their petals, reflecting
in their tiny globes the sun and earth and all

Arc   COLIN MORTON

EXCHANGE OF GIFTS

You gave me Jerusalem marble,
gypsum from the Judean desert,
granite from the Sinai,
a collection of biblical rock.
I gave you a side of smoked salmon,
a tape of *The Magic Flute*
—my lox was full of history and silence,
your stones tasted of firstness
and lastness, Jewish cooking.

You took me where a small boy came up to me
and asked me to dance him on my shoulders.
So we danced around Genesis and the Songs
of Solomon. He clapped his hands to be riding
the biggest horse in Judea. I cantered lightly
around Deuteronomy, whirled around the Psalms,
Kings and Job. I leapt into the sweaty
life-loving, Book-loving air of happiness.

Breathless, I kissed the child and put him down,
but another child climbed up my back.
I danced this one around Proverbs and that one
around Exodus and Ecclesiastes,
till a child came up to me

who was a fat horse himself, and I had to halt.
What could I give you after that?
—When I left, a bottle of wine, half a bottle of oil,
some tomatoes and onions, my love.

Poetry   STANLEY MOSS

FIRST LOVE

An Oriental poppy
was fully opened in the morning:
a cup of flame-red petals,
the sun swimming through its veins.
I looked and saw one of our bees,
a new bee on its first day out of the hive,
with smooth shiny wings and a plush golden body.
It was rolling around madly
in the center of the poppy,
in the deep black pollen.
And though the pollen baskets on its legs
were full, bulging with the rich powder
of the flower's life, it couldn't leave
the source of so much opulence
or the sweet swift-flowing nectar.
I watched it roll around and around
like a shameless drunk,
having raided the storehouse of pleasure.
On its back with such abandon,
on luxury's red silken sheets,
it knew only joy there, that bee
who had never before seen a flower
or a garden.

Crosscurrents   ELAINE MOTT

LOCH NESS

I pride myself that I am past the time
Of faith in far-fetched Things, of putting stock
In tales of slithery beasties in the slime
Beneath the surface of this brooding loch.
I know that things we see sometimes appear
Because we want them to. The unicorns,
The fairy ring, the succubus, the queer
And Satan-spawned affretes, with tails and horns,
Are creatures we construct. They don't exist,
Except in minds of fools, and the unfit.
I know these things, for I'm a scientist.

But there are times, I privily admit
    Their presence, in despite of what I know.
    For if we quit believing, they might go.

Blue Unicorn   Cᴇᴄɪʟ J. Mᴜʟʟɪɴs

THE CASKET MAKER'S PROPOSAL

Ten years out of high school—long enough to know
That summer's nothing special after all—I was hauling
Boxes out of state, a major sale for a little man like me.

She asked to come along, needed a rolled-down window
And that sense of stillness you get when you're moving fast.
I said sure because I never took her out enough.

We drank beer until our speech fell free as loose change
Jangling on the sidewalk, and then, deaf from road noise,
Caskets on the flatbed fit to rock right through the cab,

I popped it. Just asked it like it was *What time is it?*
And blind with love's sudden puff, she kissed me going 70.
All I could think about was owls when you find one

Out of happenstance, and you'd believe the whole white moon
Was taking off not three yards from your face.
She was thinking: Finally, finally. He's not much,

But at least his work is steady as it comes. People die.
We passed a three-car pile up in the eastbound lane,
Big toys some giant kid tossed topsy-turvy.

Like anybody else, we gawked. It was the first time
I'd ever seen a dead man out of formal clothes,
Splayed over a guardrail, his head suspended in the weeds.

I thought: Death is real, but so is everything this woman
Sitting next to me will do or say to make it less so.
I turned on the radio to find the song we'd need to remember.

Tendril   Fʀᴇᴅ Mᴜʀᴀᴛᴏʀɪ

SEATTLE TO MINNEAPOLIS, 1946

    The Union Pacific
    was packed
    with homebound
    soldiers,
    my Grandma and me—
    collecting Army patches
    in a panatella box,
    gray tanks embroidered
    on red fields,

guns emblazoned
on blue skies.

The Lieutenant lay
on the other seat
coaxing me to nap,
to let wartime penicillin
the Wenatchee doctor
had given me with
mustard plasters
heal congested lungs.

He slept, tie undone.
In my lap
I sorted tanks
and thunderbolts,
heard Grandma
laugh with the soldiers
as the fast moving sun
shot through
afternoon train windows,
ricocheting off
buttons and bars.

Mid-American Review   KATHERINE MURPHY

FRIDAY NIGHTS 1964/ PAT O'BRIEN'S 1984

(for Mame Sims)

The bosomy pharmacist's helper, flask in purse,
beans and tomatoes spirited with a fifth
of Muscatel Red cooking low every Friday night
in the second story kitchenette next to ours
beside the railroad, is dead.
                              Not that I heard.
Just that I suddenly missed the way she
absentmindedly reached for the empty pint
for the third time, or the way the beans cooked down
raising a stink. The way now the piano's
pounding out "Peg O' My Heart" and the air
sours with vomit. The way one's mind wanders
reading a book, returning to find it's years later
and unfinished.
                   I was a girl those nights
she'd invite me over to jointly fight the silence.
Steam hanging on the ceiling above the beans
like scattered rosary beads, glazing the window
overlooking the abandoned depot, softening
the leaves of the red and white geranium.

I was tracing my new husband's name and mine
on the window when I saw her reflection, seemingly
old and foolish, dance with itself. Awkwardly,

unaccountably, I turned to dance with her
to an Irish patriotic song.
                                   The train thundered,
raining roaches from the cupboards,
collapsing the bed from the wall, skipping
the music in the grooves of her 33's.
She led me out into the hall where we had room
to waltz.
                    And that's how he found us,
coming home from work. He never said anything.
His axle-grease-nails just lifted the needle
from "My Wild Irish Rose," and we stopped dancing
as abruptly as we'd begun.

The Spoon River Quarterly   KAY MURPHY

THE PAINTERS

(for Sonya)

You were startled to find me in the basement
when you came down to do laundry.
I was hiding from the painters and the heat,
lying on the floor with my hands
behind my head, thinking of nothing.
I saw you look out a window at the gritty knees
and splattered shoes of the outside crew.
And we both could hear the inside men
upstairs moving their rollers up and down
against the walls.
You hesitated, then put down your dirty work
and joined me on that floor.
How pleased we were by this—the busy men
outside moving ladders, tying back bushes
and trees, and above us, the placing
of drop-cloths on the furniture—so much
going on around us and soon even our cut-offs
were too much to wear.
When the heat went down, we went upstairs
to the new walls of our old surroundings.
Our own love-sweat mixed with the smell
of the paint. It was a place we left
not long ago and had come back to,
but better than we remembered.
We didn't know then that our daughter
was conceived, how the mixing of liquids
inside you could produce such brightness.
And outside, the foreman waited for us
in his truck, taking care of invoices,
figuring out his next job, estimates
for the future.

Passages North   PETER E. MURPHY

NORTHERN EXPOSURES

(For Richard Hugo)

You hear the roadhouse before you see it.
Its four-beat country tunes
Amplified like surf through the woods.
Silencing bullfrog and red-tailed hawk.
Setting beards of moss dancing
On the dim, indeterminate trees
That border the two-lane blacktop.
Docked tonight, you reveal the badge
Of the farmer, that blanched expanse of skin
Where cap shades face, babyhood
Pallor above the sun-blackened jaw
Bulging uneasy with a concrete grin
And the inevitable need to weep.
Don't you think we live and breathe
In the meantime, in lockstep
With dawn, sunset, brawling dawn?
Even now, you await secrets worse
Than the few known ways a seized sky
Will come to survive your pity.
But on another far field, celebrated
For its arrivals and evictions, you learn
To be beautiful, never leading
A sensible life, playing ball in the early dark,
Fighting for a taste of the sweet spot
In this uncut land, this straight-edged air.
Whadya want to know that isn't yet a mystery
Somewhere, a confidential stumble, heat
Lightening, a first-rate backseat turndown?
So it is that later you track high above
Familiar tamarack and ash, beginning
The next inaccuracy alone, and again,
Remembering that everything east of you
Has already happened, on the same cold ground,
In a swarm of time, finally spiked home
To your surprise, nails flung to the air,
And us all thumbs to the hot hammer-licks
You hear from the roadhouse before you see it.

Poetry   G. E. MURRAY

SOLILOQUY BENEATH THE NIGHT

Often, when we were building
The doghouse & busy
Putting the fencing up
In the heavy dew-swept grass
In the dirt & the rockspattered loam
In the curse of a twisted nail

Bent against a cold November sun
I saw you & measured you & took you
For granted, for something
You were not
& felt ashamed

This morning I woke & left early
Your side, warm & rolled out
& went to the kitchen window
& pressed against it
& looked out into the dregs
Of a gray dawn—
There I seemed to see the doghouse
Uproot itself & disintegrate, & the fence
Bank up against the windy pines
& fall,
& lock with gnarling roots

All as if love, its labors
Had given way
To the rude December quiet
To the nothing
The stillness
The cold encroaching:
A few dead branches, the silent contumely
Of winter

The Fiddlehead   TIMOTHY MUSKAT

EXCHANGE

Red maple sparks burn away summer
as I try to remember the detail of green
lapsing like childhood inside me.
In the lull of long shadows,
hydrangeas erase super highways
and K-Mart has yet to be built.
I run through the shade of old houses
where kitchens are yellow,
the Mass is in Latin, and the name
of our only Black family is Brown.
The elms are still strong,
and I'm full of right answers
as I play under trees until dark.
The green slips away,
when far in the distance
the town clock strikes night
and a dry leaf crosses my palm
in a hand-to-hand trade
of this season for that.

The DeKalb Literary Arts Journal   JOAN ROHR MYERS

ELVIS PRESLEY

I want to get the screams in here—
the ones we danced to, shook to, laughed at,
hoping they'd never stop.
Screams we knew nothing about really
as we watched him jiggle and sneer,
his legs like electric rubber bands
which snapped so gorgeously in those zones
we were forbidden to claim. *Zones*
were for parking, and we understood that,

our bodies carefully sectioned into spots:
above the neck (was that why it was called
"necking"?) and *below*, like heaven and hell.
It's both, isn't it, and as we watched
that earthquake on the Magnavox,
our mouths knew something was happening
with unstoppered noises all the way through.
How many saints applauded in our tongues?
How many victorian souls?

Our parents stuck out their thick hands, too—
over their ears, over our eyes, all over
the press, their finger shaking NO in the air,
as we shook free of their world, the new
holy rollers, and they knew it.

The Journal   ROCHELLE NAMEROFF

VINEYARD CONJURING

One thing calls another thing to mind,
and by these tricks of conjured memory
I lose myself in what I try to find.

Ocean. Oak Bluffs. The end of June. A blind
piano player. Misty drinks. I see
how one thing calls another thing to mind.

Words clustering in moonlight off behind
The Island house under a light-laced tree,
I lose myself in what I try to find.

Among the campground cottages entwined
with gingerbread and salt-air fantasy,
each thing calls another thing to mind.

Lantana. Lobster pots. A drifting line
of poetry unwritten, not to be.
I lose myself in everything I find

until the porches fill with dark, resigned
to end this lazy, late-night reverie.

Nothing at last calls anything to mind.
What have I lost? What had I hoped to find?

Yankee   MILDRED J. NASH

PENOBSCOT PROFILE

At seventy, my great-grandmother
closed her ears to introductions,
needing no new people.

At eighty, she stopped buying furniture
or turning her old mattress.

No new clothes after ninety.
The rows in her closet stayed.
She approved their creases.

At one hundred years, she was finished
buying newspapers.
The old news went into her mind
and stayed there, caught.

Every glance into her eyes
was a page of weddings, obituaries,
and yesterday's steady weather—

blowing north-northwest,
pinning trees to earth.

Artemis   VALERY NASH

WAITING

It's just a short ride by Twin Otter,
Two hours south to nowhere: Schefferville, Quebec,
An accumulation of "more bars per

Capita . . ." where the railway ends. Flecked
In red dust from the strip mine, this
Is civilization, for us. All it lacks

Besides anything to do, is women, missed
Even more by those who don't head straight for
Letters waiting, Poste Restante, but off to get pissed

down at l'Orignal d'Or
Where they fly in strippers for a Saturday act.
This week, Miss Nude Florida 1974.

But I find other matters distract.
In fact, I'd rather be

Headed back toward the tundra,
the moss-choked lakes

crocheted into a landscape,
sponge-like from the air
and more so on the ground

Where sunset comes with its
own certain foreground
of blackflies,

Where the land hasn't yet recovered from
the ice age before last

And we find ourselves,
in the stillness,
waiting for the glacier.

Shenandoah   DAVID NEELIN

BECAUSE THE AIR

Because the air hides nothing,
and dogs squat unashamed,
and squirrels argue in public,
and birds bathe in full view
of the cat who openly means them harm,
and spiders spin their deadly lace,
and flies kiss dung not caring who watches,
and fireflies flash aimlessly without regret,
and grass doesn't care if it's stepped on,
and trees don't take it personally
when they're stripped of their leaves,
or long for happiness or innocence,

he thinks that somewhere inside him
a life as quick and unafraid as these
must be hidden, buried beneath a city
of padlocks and façades.
And he thinks if he could dig deep enough
through the layers of fragments,
the arrowheads and bronze coins, the chips
of pottery, lead cups, wooden clubs,
clay tablets, hieroglyphs and alphabets,
he would find at the source a heart,
his own, perfectly preserved and beating.
Brushing away the dirt and ruins of human
history, he would see it was the shape
of a leaf, a leaf that clung to a branch
with such inexplicable grace that he felt
moved to part his lips and utter *leaf*,
the sound of which made it fall.

California Quarterly   ERIC NELSON

MY BROTHERS TELLING THE STORY OF OUR FATHER

I don't even need the words
anymore to know what they're saying
across the kitchen table,
to hear them telling the story
that could go almost anywhere
on one more beer, that grows so big
as it goes along I think at first
it must be some other life
they are speaking of, not the one
that just walks in the mornings
out to the mailbox, then sits all day
in the same chair
smoking cigars, but the one
that keeps coming out right.

Listening from the back porch
tonight, I think how our real lives
must be ones
we would have lived;
and when our father jokes sometimes
about dying,
how we can't say love
outloud, but how they're saying it now
with this story
and how it holds us up.

Tar River Poetry   LESLIE NELSON

CONCERNING STARS, FLOWERS, LOVE, ETC.

Make it easier, they say, make it easier. Tell
me something I already know, about stars or flowers or,
or happiness. I am happy sometimes, though
not right now, specially. Things are not going
too good right now. But you should try
to cheer people up, they say. There is
a good side to life, though
not right now, specially. Though the stars
continue to shine in some places and the flowers
continue to bloom in some places
and people do not starve in some places
and people are not killed in some places
and there are no wars in some places
and there is no disease in some places
and there are no slaves in some places
and people are happy in some places
and in some places people love each other,

they say. Though I don't know where. They say,
I don't *want* to be sad. Help me not to know.

Event   JOHN NEWLOVE

HUNTERS

The skim ice, ribbed faintly as a leaf, floats
outward from the sand, smashed by the rubber boots
of my father and his father as they shove
the duckboat in the darkness into the pond
and climb into its intricate nest of reeds
and willows, my father in the bow, his father
sculling, the shotguns buried in the strange
island of debris, their camouflage.
Through mist patches guided by the touch
of darkness beyond darkness, visible
to their excited senses on the shore: trees,
Mt. Pleasant and Mt. Tom, glimpses
of stars through thinning cloud: they scull
silently toward the outlet and the river,
toward the dreaming ducks, like Indians,
Pequawkets with their throwing nets and arrows,
drifting into the night, dreaming of mallards,
redheads, canvasbacks, black ducks and teal,
deep in the center of a dream, in the still
bosom of the water, in the center of their lives.

Tar River Poetry   P. B. NEWMAN

WARSAW, 1944

I do not know the German word
for spring.
I walk unhelmeted by the tombs,
sleep houses do not answer me.
Only the Angel of Death
has a majesty by mortal lights.
The trees are tortured.
I was a wild palm.
My potato-sized wounds
will not give me a Sabbath meal.
Utmost sorrow.
Words are in the chimney's dust.
There are no walls for the dead.
I am older than cemeteries.
I wish to take a cablegram
to the nations.
History cannot call out my name.
My initials circle the world.

I imagined a future so easy.
Where are the ancient prayers
of my fathers?
Sister is gone.
My work is interrupted.
What is the Polish word for life.

Midstream   B. Z. NIDITCH

NEIGHBORS STRANGERS TO ONE ANOTHER

We know homely and intimate things about one another.
We know paint/no paint. We know angles. I know
that their barn is slumped away from the prevailing wind.
We both know the wide rivermarsh between us
and the ledgy tongue of spruce woods which divides it,
giving us each a false boundary.
They are—this is—the house on the other side
of the marsh.

They know, because the eye is drawn by a kind
of human gravity: when I went to bed,
my light, one star, dark.

I know, because I watched the smoke rise,
that they slept late this morning, that the kindling
was damp, that at last the fire caught.

Maybe we both keep bees. Maybe we both
favor red hollyhocks. Maybe we have nothing in common,
but we are important strangers to one another nonetheless.
I am—they are—the neighbors on the other side
of the marsh.

Blueline   NANCY L. NIELSEN

CLOSED FOR RESTORATION

Our gaudy years in Italy! In between
Those years and now, some thirty. I'm back today.
Eye, stride (and finger in guidebook) still as keen
—Only, rebuffed by barriers. *Ma perché?*
Brancacci Chapel? The Borromini dream,
Our shiver of pleasure? San Clemente's floor?
The monster's Golden House, weird walls agleam?
All? *Chiuso per restauro* against the door,

Giving us pause. Odds are, I'll never see
That span again. If on Liguria's shore
I lie, *Qui dorme in pace*'s not for me,
Stones with *le ossa* . . . or *tristi spoglie* . . . or

Any such dismal lingo of the lost.
Mine, *Chiuso per restauro*. With fingers crossed.

The Yale Review   JOHN FREDERICK NIMS

LUNCH IN CHARLESTON

While at a nearby table sat the late Fay Bainter
Or, at any rate, a startling replica
(With that famous *I suffer a lot—don't you?*
Look on her contenance), commiserating
Earnestly with a trio of other ladies
Under the palms and ceiling fans—my salad
Arrived, a rainbow manna on damask snow,
And so intrigued was I by the nearly erotic
Blending of cantaloupe and curried chicken
(Clearly recruited from one of Charleston's most
Aristocratic coops) and frosted grapes
And one quite regal strawberry, that I
Was tempted—please forgive the Faulknerian
Ramble—to reply to the late Fay Bainter:
No, hardly ever, and especially not now.

America   JOHN NIXON, JR.

PAPER PEOPLE

The only people who outlive their ages
Are paper people: Hamlet, Lear, the Moor's
Malignéd mate, still vital on the pages.
Ink is the darkest blood, but it endures.

Arizona Quarterly   JOHN NIXON, JR.

A COUPLE IN OLD AGE

Every evening my wife and I
sit in the kotatsu* face to face.
How can a woman
grow old so grotesquely?
How can I
match her so well?
Two such monsters
live together under the same roof.
Without the power of enchantment,
without the charm of enchantment,
two broken ornaments
sit deep in silence.

*A small stove with a coverlet fixed in a square box in or on the floor. People sit around it, putting their legs under the coverlet—a familiar sight in the winter in Japanese houses.

Webster Review   MASAO NONAGASE
                            —*Translated from the Japanese*
                                by Junko Yoshida

THE ABILITY

You never lose the ability to say your name using the thirteen
colours of language.
Once you've grown graceful, it's hard to be clumsy,
once you've grown old, it's impossible to ever be young enough
again. I know how to use my days when necessary.
A little salt and pepper on the omelette, a glance out the window.
Just about anything can be worked into this fine mosaic.
Pencil cases, hardballs, Babe Ruth's favourite saying,
the last thing John Donne ever wondered about.
This cloud plateau, where angels have gathered
for a six-inning game without gloves and without outs,
hangs in the air like an airplane pasted to the sky.

Descant (Canada)   KEN NORRIS

ANDRE DAWSON, AT THE HEIGHT OF HIS CAREER

The man is the consummate ballplayer;
he can hit, throw, run, flag down
the most wicked line drives to center field,
steal a base when it's necessary
or just desired, gun down runners
at the plate, and, batting, make the ball fly
as if it had wings.

It doesn't matter
that, this season,
his knees are shot
and he's been relegated to right field,
that he's struggling at the plate,
in the heat of July hitting .230,
making errors and slowing down.

Just look at him playing
between these lines:
Andre Dawson, at the height of his career.
Within this poem
he's at the top of his game
forever.

Descant (Canada)   KEN NORRIS

TRACKS

I.
In the spring I used to wander along the deserted railroad tracks the old telegraph
    lines ran beside,
the pale green wires strung from heavy glass insulators, crystal-blue to aquamarine,
    veined with imperfections,
each one as big as a fist or a heart, bending the sunlight in on itself.
Every few miles there'd be an abandoned house just off the tracks, paintless, warming
    in the sun,
and inside, shafts of light curtaining the walls.
I'd walk long distances inventing stories for those solitary houses—
bones rattled along the knotty joists; the old man who lived here, who could heal
    burns with secret words,
hung himself from a beam in the attic on a day just like this . . .

II.
The towns around there were scattered like debris from an explosion;
at night they glared against the bottoms of clouds in three directions, plotting the loop
    of the highway.
At home, I'd sit on the porch in bulblight, watching breezy shadows of insects curve
    across the floorboards and up the wall.
Once, a section of ash drifted into the light, though there was no fire for miles—I
    remember it settling to the floor.
Back then, my parents were always arguing, and their voices flared through the open
    kitchen window.
In a lull, I had to ask my mother twice what makes that chirping sound outside.

III.
Some days there would be a change: a pile of trash kicked around or a circle of ashes
    in a doorway.
I looked for things in those heaps, in dusky piles of broken glass, in ashes,
looked until the heat lifted, until the dark corners grew cavernous,
until, outside along the wires, tree frogs began calling down the rain.

The Ohio Review   GLENN NORTON

WITHOUT RAIN

That summer of long drought
we tiptoed on the ridges
afraid of the friction
if we kicked two stones together:
as if the mountain were already flame
and we were locked in the past,
as if the world without rain
could only be real
in a flash: at night,
in late August chill,
we huddled at the campfire
stamping on our sparks, cupping them
in our bare hands, staring out

at the coyote's eyes
consumed with reflected fire.

Crosscurrents   D. NURKSE

LEAVING TEXAS

Once you start wanting to get out of Texas,
it's all over.
The land can't love you anymore.
The cenizo bush hides its face
and the sky wears a robe.

"Texas is Texas and Marion is Marion," you said.
Out west the snow had just begun to fall,
the Guadalupe Mountains sank to their knees.

Ranchers in Marfa swear their horizon
can see things; it's been happening
since the Indians, lights flaring
like giant lamps.
One man said they chased him.
He went back to Houston.
He had nothing else to say.

Maybe that's why some folks live in Texas—
to feel like a tiny word on a huge paper,
not sure if the paper listens, or sees, or reads.
And why other people work hard to go away.

Painted Bride Quarterly   NAOMI SHIHAB NYE

FIRST FROST

The cat stretches on the window-sill
watching the yellow leaves drop
like shot down birds in the pale morning.
Last night was the first frost,
the one that brings down all the colors,
absorbs brown, gold, red,
even the green of the grass,
and leaves them silver.

I open the door and the cold presses around me.
Outside, the air is a frozen sheet, it spills
over into the water barrel, leaving a jagged circle
of glass. I lift the ice and hold it up
to the blue beyond the clouds.
My thumb warms it, it drops
and shatters without a sound on the cement.

In my hand, beads of bright water
slide from life line to heart line.

Blueline   JEFF OAKS

HOPPER'S *EARLY SUNDAY MORNING*

(for Joe DiTucci)

Just a row of store fronts
in the early morning light,
the sun just gilding the
apartment windows overhead,
their shades only half drawn,
as if indifferent to the light.
Or so it seems. But look:
See how the windows lean away
from the oncoming light;
see how the barber pole,
slightly tilted, inclines
with the lengthening shadows;
see how the door frames shift,
right to left, as if to shrink
from the sun's citric glare.

This is city light: diffused
by mists from the East River,
refracted by smog from Con Ed
smokestacks—a light so piercing
Hopper must have dipped his brush
in acid to catch the bleach sunlight
on tenement bricks; he must have
blended soot with pigments to get
the gloom of darkened store fronts;
then smudged in loneliness
in monotones of vertical
to suggest the nighthawk people
in upstairs apartments
waiting for the light.

I want to enter that painting.
I want to lift one leg into
the frame, climb in like a burglar,
and be one with the shadows.
To hear that early morning silence.
To feel the coming of the light.

Kansas Quarterly   WILLIAM P. O'BRIEN

POEM FOR DR. SPOCK

I, too, when I die do not wish
to encumber my friends with the burdens

of sorrow: I want a simple ceremony,
twenty minutes or so, a few poems,
a brief testimonial, a tear or two
against plain black velvet—and
as for the corpse, burn it, scatter
the ashes around my asparagus plants,
which need large infusions of lime,
or throw them in the eyes of my enemies
and let the mourners go off to a party,
a staid one where the waiters pour rivers
of *Dom Perignon* and nobody has to worry
about money for once; and later,
a wild one with live music, a reappearance
of the Bonzo Dog Band, if possible, and
recapitulations of every drug popular
for the last fifty years, laughter
and solidarity for days. Let them stay
as long as they wish and go off
satiated, prepared again for the world,
and let the mouse of grief
gnaw at their hearts forever.

Western Humanities Review   ED OCHESTER

CUTTING WOOD

1

After the war,
my father put away his leather flying helmet,
bought a farm and planted strawberries,
corn and potatoes, pushed his days
into the earth like seed.
Each October he walked hard fields
into the woods, dragged windfall branches
to the barn. He taught me to swing
the small axe where we cut and stacked
winter heat. Those weeks before he died
he carved a bird from a knot of wood,
hung it from the mirror with twine.
Each morning his eyes
caught its flight.

2

The chain saw shrieks all afternoon,
bites firebox lengths
from eight-foot logs I feed
along the sawhorse cradle.
Sweat runs down my breasts
and I imagine my hands slipping,

fingers dropping like sawdust.
My father's axe broke large branches
with a quick, sharp sound. When finished,
he buried the blade deep in the chopping stump
and I leaned on the handle,
watched his handsaw rush across
smaller wood. Once he gave me
a can of sawdust, and I fattened pincushions,
a stocking doll with brown embroidered eyes.

3

Two weeks
and ten cords stack the shed.
I count growth rings
on the last log—twenty years,
an hour of fire. I sweep
sawdust into plastic bags,
suddenly think, "pincushions,"
and fill a coffee can
with sawdust. I pick up
the hand axe, split October afternoons
from kindling logs. Somewhere
my father smiles
at the smooth arc of swing,
the clean snap of each cut.

Tar River Poetry   ANNE OHMAN-YOUNGS

STREET PEOPLE

*(I know I am dirty. I know I am ragged. I do beg
around the country-side, as I needs must. It is the
way of paupers and homeless men.)*
—Book XIX, The Odyssey. T.E. Shaw

We find a temporary sanctuary,
street people, vagrants, mentally ill,
untouchables in the public lavatory
at Port Authority and Kennedy International.
We ride the subways up, down, and back
and linger in warm lobbies of corporate centers.
To sleep lying down is to invite attack.
This is how we survive the long winters:
The body gets cold but works up a kind of fever.
We go to a building, recently condemned.
When it snows, sometimes, if we must, to a shelter—
and then it's onto the street again
where we own nothing and nothing owns us.
With some, it's habit, others, lousy luck.
We've been evacuated from our rooming houses.
A lot of the younger ones just got the sack

and quite a few of them even have degrees.
My friend Hermione here recites Shakespeare.
We sit near the grate and she quotes the tragedies.
You know—Hamlet, Macbeth, King Lear.

Confrontation   JULIA OLDER

12 YEARS OLD

When my girl and her friend walk away from me
at the swimming pool, I see her friend's
sweet stick legs, thin as
legs drawn by a child, and then I
see my daughter's curved hocks and
haunches, her hips that behind my back have
swelled until they taper delicious as
chicken legs, the liquid meat of the
thigh. Her joints gently grind and
suck and rock as she walks in rich
innocence toward the diving board, her
chest flat as a plank, the front of her
torso meek and raw as a kid's; but her
ass delicately flashes its signals:
Soon, now, the gold glow of the
warning lights. She mounts the ladder, her
skin twinkling wet as the basted
broiler half-way done to a turn; she
sways her frail way down the board
waving its wand in the air, the water
far below her rich with college boys; she
grins toward me, her head slick, and
takes the plunge, her pale body
plummeting through the air in silence and then
entering the water with the charged thrust of her
knife into the chicken when she is really hungry.

The Paris Review   SHARON OLDS

MY FATHER'S SHIRT

I used to joke about being my father; I
used to say I'll just give up and become my father,
but now there is no one else to be him—
a week after his death I open my suitcase
and pull out of it, slowly, as if
drawing a limp blue and white child out at birth,
his shirt his wife gave to me, and it
still smells of his house, that smell of
mold that I love because it smells of going to him,
opening his door and there from his chair he

rises slowly, such a big man in such
dark pants, with such a shiny face, such
dark eyes. The smell of mold is the
smell of the world under the rug and
beneath my father's skin now,
behind his eye. I put on the shirt and my
breasts look absolutely terrific in it and I
smell so wonderfully green with mold—let the
second half of my father's life begin,
let him find happiness as a woman.

The Atlantic Monthly   SHARON OLDS

TO THE MUSE

So what if your name is "Burning Bush"—
hair like fire, that bright,
that red. And fingers delicate
as birthday candles. So what
if you look a little eerie,
so pale and thin astride
that bony nag.
               Still you are
the luminous madonna—both lodestar
and throat-lump in one.
                    Without you,
my voice is poured into the void
and my words are lost, so hear me
as I cry across the dark to you.

Because you are sole owner
of the voodoo lute that raises ghosts,
I come with this request—
                    appear to me now,
translate this rub of skin on skin,
its music of risk,
into the cosmic note you alone can hum.

Ploughshares   GREGORY ORR

AIR

I stood in the pines on the cliff
above the sea. Each needle held
a drop of water, then the sunset.
A deer rustled in the brush,
and we both ran. When that winter
was over, I was two thousand miles away
between two cornfields in a car
on a moonless night. The silence

was beautiful and frightening.
Day comes to Columbus weakly,
diffused and mottled like the broken
vessels in a thigh. Where
does a man walk out into
the pure air of his own life?

The Journal   KEVIN ORTH

MEDIEVAL SYNAGOGUE, TOLEDO

Five hundred years after
they drove the Jews from Spain
signposts (both Spanish and in Hebrew script)
now guide the tourist to the synagogue.

No sense of guilt invests
the neat map in the case, the diagrams,
"Centres of Judaeo-Hispanic Culture":
red cotton linking names like Cordoba,
Seville, Segovia, while your mind
flies on to Amsterdam, Salonika,
and to Majdanek and to clouds of smoke.

What is it in this simple rectangle
that silences the noisy tourist crowd,
makes them tread softly, speak in whispers?

And I, who never cared about my origins,
am strangely moved by this calm dignity,
decipher clumsily
the fine gilt writing with my long-lapsed eye:
Melekh ha-olam
and
Adonai.

Crosscurrents   EWALD OSERS

AUNT ANNE

She had come home to the Midwest, but not to die.
She had an air that got her across streets
and brought her purse back before she missed it.
She wore a hat and white gloves to show
she came from New York.

In the end, she grew too vague to live alone.
She wrote too many checks for too much
and she never subtracted. She smoked in bed.

One day her brother handed her her purse
with the checkbook in it and put her on a plane.

He cried a little and waved to her back
as it disappeared.

She kept her hat on.
She smoked when they didn't stop her
and walked the aisles carrying her gloves.
The stewardess strapped her in for the landing,
then handed back her purse
and took her down the gangway.

In New York, someone kissed her.
She smiled and straightened her hat.
"Who are you?"
"I am your daughter Sandy."
Aunt Anne peered up at her, still smiling,
and asked, "By whom?"

West Branch   EMILY OTIS

THE WHITE RABBIT

You practice death
like this.
You wear your own ghost.
In the white snow,
you welcome your disguise.

You let the wind
blow through you
on its way to breaking twigs
for firewood.
You let the wind push
you as the snow leans
in fright against a house.

Winter wants to settle
your life in this cold.
A dispute it has
against your fur that fits,
against your heart's heat.

Already the earth
has given up its shape to
the falling snow.
You, too, should give up
the radomness of your paw
prints that makes
the hunter stop and wonder.

Already one bullet in his
gun belongs to your body.
Your dark eyes will learn
that when light

abandons them, the stew pot
had heard about you,
and luck was waiting for
your one loose foot.

Poetry   SUE OWEN

AT THE BEACH

The waves are erasing the footprints
Of those who are walking the beach.

The wind is carrying away the words
Two people are saying to each other.

But still they are walking the beach,
Their feet making new footprints.

Still the two are talking together
Finding new words.

New Letters   KEMAL OZER
—Translated from the Turkish
by O. Yalim, W. Fielder and Dionis Riggs

THE OPEN DOOR

The door to my den opens
As if someone has come
To see me; some stranger
With a score to settle
Which he has held against me
For years, though I was
Unaware of offending him.
Yet how can I be sure
The wind did not disturb the door,
Proving that the mind forms
Its own propositions.
Listen, I can hear the door
Open and close. This time
I believe he may be for real.

Crosscurrents   GARY PACERNICK

THE BOSTON SUITCOAT

The first day I held a gun
we found an old farm abandoned,
its single road wild and overgrown.
The windows long-gone
to target-practice;

the cellar-door torn open
where a bear winters.
Inside, a rusted stove
cold a hundred years;
on the door-hook,
a tangle of leather harness
and the Boston suitcoat.

Pockets puckered,
the lapels made lace by mice;
inside the inscription—
Nels Ingraham, Tailor, Boston.
Some long-dead gentleman-farmer
wore this coat to worship;
the blue pinstripe
gone grey,
a birds-nest inside the breast-pocket.

Worn back to town by me,
inheritance
and emblem
of shapeless adolescence—
late-night parties,
walks by the river at dawn—
and still a perfect fit.

The Antigonish Review   MICHAEL PACEY

SILENCE

Silent night. Here in the forest
I hear no noises, no, none at all.
    The worms are at work.
Birds of prey do their job (certainly).
    But I hear nothing.
Only the frightening silence. So strange,
so scarce has it become in this world
that no one remembers how it sounds,
    now no one wants
to be with himself for a minute.
    Tomorrow

once again we'll put off true life until tomorrow.
No hatred of living or sorrow at being alive:
    strangeness
at finding oneself here and now in such a silent time.
Silence in this forest, in this house
    in the middle of the forest.
Has the world ended?

Chelsea   JOSE EMILIO PACHECO
                              —*Translated from the Spanish*
                                by Linda Scheer

THUNDER

For the busy stocker, stacking
pop bottles like trophies,
for the hung-over mechanic
and the leather-handed farmer.
For them and for the stooped plumber
and the postman's angry daughters
I drive this car to win.
A slithering snake of sweat
crawls down each aching turn
of my body; for gripping
the wheel, I sit hunched
in this sweltering car, wearing
flame-resistant clothing. Power
I ride is engine—wheels
and frame—iron rails
they call a cage. My strapped arms
may be saved from bloody rags.
And if I bleed across the course,
red flags wave to cool my blood.
Only the true fans know
why I choose to race like fate
around this beaten track of mud,
driving not for silver dollars
rolled like wheels
nor for the trophy girl's champagne kiss.
But when the air burns
with methanol and speed
and fire barks from every header,
the thought of silence blows away
in dust and thunder—
and I'm alive forever.

The Southern Review   WILLIAM PAGE

THE ART OF REDUCTION

First he believes this meadow in all its abundance
is his, entirely, with thousands of green surprises.
Then he knows he can't live with such confusion. True,
the grass is not very high, it comes up to his knees, or
maybe only to his ankles. And yet it's a maze, deceptive.
There isn't a single path; there are endless paths.
He can go where he wants. He gets lost.

So he chooses reduction. Not a meadow, just a patch
of lawn. Not even that, just three blades of grass.
Not three, not even one (and this, he feels, is the crux
of the matter), not even a blade but rather a painting
of a blade. This is the essence.

Finally, after he hangs it on the wall, he understands.
This painted blade which includes the whole meadow,
removes the whole meadow as well.

New Letters   DAN PAGIS
                                    —Translated from the Hebrew
                                          by Shirley Kaufman

NO VISIBLE STARS

How can I begin to understand
and speak of the human
significance of the aberration
of starlight, tonight,
when there are no visible stars.
I think, instead, of the giraffes
standing in their tall closets
in the dark, and the hummingbird
with furiously beating wings
under the frosted skylight
above the unsleeping heads
of the giraffes, and the man
in uniform lighting
a cigarette, locking the doors.

The Iowa Review   GREG PAPE

THE MARINER

(for Richard Kenney)

This wide-plank skiff of a table
is rigged for travel,
with a sunny window at my back.
I sit alone here, spinning
an old globe beside my chair, its skin
of colors, planet of my own.
I list the places I would go:
the outer regions of my hands,
the tiny nerve-ends twitching in the night,
the peninsular foot, the nether bowels,
the mucous caverns of my inner ear.
I set my sails each morning after breakfast,
pulling sheets from a lefthand drawer,
taking a pen between my teeth.
The spirits seem to blow
four ways at once or, mostly, not at all.
Even Agamemnon had to slay a daughter
just for winds to carry him to Troy.
I, too, have slaughtered my kin
for motion, for a poem to waste.

Now I spread my charts,
correct my compass, and lay down a course
through the next few hours.
May the gods who brood upon these open waters
ease my way, direct the passage
of this fragile craft,
this sloop of self I angle into day.

Poetry   JAY PARINI

AS TIME GOES BY

I may have forgotten her name,
Yet the image of her dark eyes
And the warmth of her lips
Are implanted deeply in my heart.

Whenever the wind blows, or rain falls,
I recall the night she stood
Under the dim street light
That often casts its glow on my small windows.

Even if my love for her remains
Only a sweet memory,
I cherish my special affection
For her deep within.

Autumn leaves fall on the bench
Where we used to sit near the lagoon
On warm summer days, or in the park
On bright autumn afternoons.

The fallen leaves decay as time goes by
And become part of the soil.

Even if my love for her has become
But a chapter in my life's history,
Thickly covered by fallen leaves,

Even if I have already forgotten her name,
The warmth of her lips
and the touching gaze of her eyes
Still linger in my heart—in my cold heart.

The Antigonish Review   IN-WHAM PARK
                                    —Translated from the Korean
                                    by Hyun-jae Yee Sallee

THINGS OUT OF PLACE

1

For weeks at a time everything stays in place.
Plates stack themselves in cupboards discretely,

sturdily by kind:
salad, entree, bread and butter, dessert.
Cups hang from careful hooks.
Siverware lies dutifully in compartments
lined with brown felt.
Spoons consort only with spoons.
Knives have converse only with knives.
Sweaters fold their arms and stay put.
Blouses can think of nothing more delightful
than to line themselves up row after row
like children unnaturally still at a fire drill.
There's not a stray paperclip,
not a barrette on any floor.
Even the toothpaste obeys my will completely.
What I want is what comes out.

2

First a slight disorder.
A residue of dried toothpaste under the cap.
Then the dustmop drawing under its smooth route
items that have no business being there:
two pennies, a rubber-tipped bobby pin,
a couple of inches of perforated paper
torn from the edges of several stamps.
It has begun.
Soon chopsticks will mingle with knives and forks.
Teas will jumble their nations—
China indistinct from India.
Further into chaos, leaves of non-teas
(mint, hibiscus, rose)
will mingle with the real thing.
And anything can happen next.

Envy's Sting   CATHERINE N. PARKE

FROZEN LASAGNE

Heavy aluminum packets of pasta,
marked with masking tape
and a ghostly thin-penciled date.
We'll eat more
comfortably come Sunday:
there will be enough
time for storytelling.

Earlier, the kitchen swarmed with smell:
garlic like a flock of hornbills,
terrible and shrill. Sauce
bubbling in its fen, a bayleaf
potsherd pulled from the mire.
And the pasta!
Bandages worthy of

a line of Ptolemies.
Exotic, plain-style New World
lasagne spelled with an *e*—
that final letter rare and valued
as a saint's tooth under glass.

While back in the Old Country kings
are still dead, and lasagne
as we know it was never served.
Even more fanciful: Grandmother
is a Jew, but she keeps a little
something for the end of the world.

Can anything important be said
of food? We've eaten;
it should be enough.

Shenandoah   ALAN MICHAEL PARKER

GOING HOME

It has been the year of the butterfly,
All those butterflies in Marquez' novel,
Swarming around love, swarming around death,
Moving against their penchant for space.

And all those butterflies in the Blue Ridge,
Swooping like loose souls into the light,
Claiming those clearings cut for the traveler,
Burning the air, first yellow, then blue.

And now this one that flew in my face
Alarming those memories folded and calm,
Scattering those pieces of petrified years
Into flashes of yellow and angles of blue.

Poet Lore   MARTHA PARKER

HISTORY

When I was eleven,
my younger brother and I
would get ourselves up
at six o'clock on Saturday mornings
to walk through empty town
to play hockey at the rink.
We were taught
to make our own breakfast
and get away quietly ourselves.
One Saturday, when we got up,
our father was already sitting in the kitchen
with the radio on

listening to Churchill's funeral,
live from England.
There, in the dark morning,
he told us solemnly
that this was history.

The Antigonish Review   BRUCE PARSONS

A DRINK OF WATER

Was it a dream
or waking
in the dark
makes you sob

so piteously?
Whichever, come on,

we'll blunder through
the living room
to the big window

squared off at the moon. Shock
of light going into the familiar
bathroom greets us.

Here's a drink of water.

And another? Thirsty fish.
There swims an inkling

of a smile as your head goes down
on the pillow, buoyant

and deep.

Event   JOHN PASS

A WALK BEFORE BREAKFAST

Isn't this what life
could be: a walk
before breakfast, with the sea
opening its chapters
of water and light,
flexing its silken muscle,
pulsing back and forth—
a kind of accompaniment
to breath? Along its rough edges,
shells and small birds gather,
the rick-rack of life
in all its stages: feather
and fish bone, those sandcrabs

that we see only by their tiny
pinpricks of absence.
All summer we eat when the tug
of appetite tells us,
make love at odd moments,
the sand beneath us
as pliant as flesh.
If we refused to leave,
would our skins turn
the amber of beer glass?
Would we learn to walk always arched
into the wind, half naked
and vulnerable and tough
as seaweed, leaving behind
not footprints
but the discarded carapace
of our other life?

The Atlantic Monthly   LINDA PASTAN

THE DESCENT

My mother grows smaller
before my eyes, receding
into the past tense slowly.
It feels like an escalator down,
she whispers, half asleep.
I lean over the rail
and there are vistas,
whole histories spread out:
my own father in a landscape
where each blade of grass
cuts like an eyelash caught
in the eye, making a sharp edge
between what is known
and what is merely guessed.
Is it her childhood or mine
that glows with that light
only pain remembered
can throw? Fear is using
up the oxygen. I must
get used to the change
in the air, how thin it grows,
and how strange it is that beauty
can become the ache
in the bone that proves
you are alive. Now evening
leaches the color from her face,
and in the leftover light
it is hard to see where
the descent will end,

hard to believe
it is death holding
her elbow with such care,
guiding her all the way down.

TriQuarterly   LINDA PASTAN

THINKING ABOUT FRESH WATER

Such meditating starts in the esophagus, blown
Bone-dry by a wind that whipped across the Lakes,
Over the Alleghenies, and down on us valley-dwellers—
By mid-March gone a bit barmy waiting for spring,
Crocuses a kind of credo we enumerate.

A glass of fresh water. To desire is to have.
No mausoleums need rifling, no banks need robbing,
No incantations need mumbling. Plainly, water
Comes to us without mischief or risk, it flows.

A glass of fresh water. I think I see through it,
Although I see my eyes in it if I hesitate
Before drinking. I know, too, it protects itself
By coldness: I dare not gulp it down, must sip,
Extending its life. And it is never quite still,
I see, watching it from the corners of my eyes,
The same eyes I saw in it. We call water clear,
But more and more it becomes a little mystery
In a universe of relative mysteries.

The experience of fresh water. The upper lip,
The tongue, the mouth, each parched piece of the flesh
That longs for spring is quenched. Breath in the smoothed
Throat glisses in and out, speech unravels vowels
And clips consonants. How can poems be written
Without fresh water? The making mind discovers
New farmings, birds unimagined, echoing voices, in
Its own backyard. Does the water rise, rinsing tangles
From the tawny brain? We say we float in water,
But perhaps water floats us, upward into light,
And isn't light and lightness of light our need?

If sometimes I pour myself into a glass and rest
On the window-sill attending the doings of the street,
Reflecting some parts of a world—the maroon car,
The snow-flurry clouds, the khaki and blue walker
Cowering in that scorning wind—the water's secret
Name stays hidden (even the saint had to use adjectives:
Multo utile et himile et pretiosa et casta).

So I praise it, praise one of the good things, and drink, drink.

Blue Unicorn   KARL PATTEN

THERE MUST BE

There must be room in love for hate.
Allowing love to behave like a lung
allows hate in—and out. But the state

of nakedness this natural act requires—
have we the natural strength for it?
Or do we, after all our building, tire

of breathing because we are breathing so hard?
Having worked so long. Having built and rebuilt.
The four lungs in this house breathe with regard

to the continuance of our lives
and have the power to squall out the memory
of their earliest squallings, protests that survive

building and meaning. They can take love in
and breathe hate out and so manufacture
another part of the structure we determine

to live in. While there may not be room
enough for hate, there will be rooms constructed
from its labor. Presume that love has room

for all other emotions, and resume, resume.

Michigan Quarterly Review   MOLLY PEACOCK

MY COUCH IS HAUNTED

I'm sure
of it.
If you sit
anywhere else in
the room, it invites
you over.
When you comply,
it isn't happy
with mere sitting.
"Lie down," it sighs and
you are powerless.
Good intentions are not
enough, this thing feeds
on aching backs,
sore feet.
Expanding, its orange glow
enfolds your pains,
mesmerizes your mind,
encourages the day to drift
away.
Hypnotizing, it purrs,

"Close your eyes"—
and you will,
you will.

Calliope MELISSA PEO

FLAMES

(for Marissa on her second birthday)

Your cries eat through the folds
of night like fire. My body
bolts from the bed
like an old engine from the firehouse
down the icey street. Down
the hall I go whispering, "Buballa, what's wrong?"

What I find is you wailing, rubbing your eyes,
scorning the dark for its sting
and dance of night particles dripping
like spiders. As I take you on to my lap,
who can say what we make in the dark
rocking, you clinging to me
as I stroke your petal skin? Two swans
sailing under a bridge. The coconut
tree upholding its fruit. The philosopher
and her denial of denial. These designs do not
approach your midnight fragrance.
Slightly lilac.
Something of nutmeg.
The salt of your tears pressed
to my cheek like a cool honey that will never
wash away as your fingers roam blind over my face to shape
the boundary of what we are.

So now I've dowsed your nightmare out,
adoring the dark for bringing us this close.
Tiny candleabra rocking inside
this old engine riding
giddy toward dawn.

Northeast Journal JANE LUNIN PEREL

THE HERON

I walk the shore about to leave
the north country forever,
its sliding fogs, the wide dustless light
that kindles the green wave,
my small house under the wings
of a double spruce,
the yellow graves on the slope a cove away

where the families lie—
scent of blackberries sharp,
                    sharp
in August air.

I search for a stone like a starfield,
a stone of stones flecked with mica-dust of stars, .
glacier-etched with orbits, streaks, whorls.
I will carry it far from here.

A rain of gull cries falls
out of the sky like stones.
From far I see the great heron cranking home,
fog on its wings.
Leave . . . leave the stone, it cries.

This country ticks in my wrist.
I can let the stone go.
I let it fall from my fingers.
I let it fall from my fingers.
I let it go.

The Hudson Review   MARK PERLBERG

MAYBE

Maybe
if we tried again
we could be as happy
as two Inuit kids in
Disneyland on Xmas Day.

Or maybe
it'd be Spring again
& we'd go to the park
& you'd hurl handfuls of
cherry blossom petals in
the air to let the wind
swirl 'em over our head—
a blizzard of confetti.

And maybe
we could both forget
my inability to suppress
frivolous flirtation (so you say)
that I call friendly exuberance,
forget your galling paranoid
negative nihilism (as I see it)
that you call realism,
forget all this resentment,
all this searing cynicism—

and we could both feed
again on mutual respect.

But it's not bloody likely.

The Antigonish Review   KAREN PETERSEN

MONOLOGUE OF DEATH

In the final hours
Before any of the gray light filters through,
I awake and gasp for the thick air,
Feel my lungs, inflate like stubborn balloons
A thick moist air that one comes to know
From wandering the wet woods in the fall,
Or the same smell that expands the nostrils
In the summer swamps at night
When one inhales that something wet.
Something wet, sometimes dead, sometimes very much alive.
It is then that I lift the slimy rocks
In search of movement in the mud,
Fleeing the reflection seen in streams
Only to see my face carved as a totem at the top of a pole,
Feeling the weight of those below,
Watching birds fly straight away from my eyes.
It is the moment in which I speak the sacred language of children
And turn the bloody sacrifice into a game of innocents,
Only to find that the dreams no longer create a separate world.
I fear, too, that I have spoken another sacred language,
Turned forbidden stones, seen the wrong ancient rites.
I am compelled to this monologue.
I pronounce it, breathe it, live it; chant it:
Ashes, ashes, we all fall down.

Pembroke Magazine   DAVID A. PETREMAN

SECOND SIGHT

On the day after my death—
white dogwood, flowering cherry
flame in the sun—

The black-topped road runs down
to the curving mouth of the road—
and the oaks stand tall
in the lucid space of themselves.

In the park across the road
small dots of color move.
Like white gazelles, the tennis players glide
after the yellow ball.

The merry-go-round spins round
in a blur of reds and emeralds—
Cars in their metal freedoms
sweep the road.

The world I knew—but the world I knew transformed—
seen through other eyes.

The white sun shines.
Crevices in the walks
thrust up green shoots.
An ant runs down
into the cool, dark caverns
below,
and the windows of all the houses blaze with people.

This world—but this world known
through other eyes—
as it always should have been—
and was—
                    on the day after my death.

America   PAUL PETRIE

VALENTINE SHOW AT THE LINGERIE SHOP

You adore this day smack in the center
of the worst month of winter
given over to the heart. To roses,
chocolates, to these tokens
of affection. An outrageous redhead
and a blonde parade expensive intimates
before the husbands nudging one another,
crotches itching as they shift
in their seats and whisper. Classy,
this show. Sex dressed up nice.
Not undressing. You might consider
the very sleazy barker outside
Topless Bottomless on Bourbon Street.
He'd pull the door open and breathe
at you, passing by slowly getting
your eyeful: some stripper bumping her snatch
at the faces staring up from a tiny table
trashed with watered-down drinks,
cigarettes, dollar tips. *No cover,*
no minimum he'd rasp in your hot ear,
and you'd know he meant your life
was empty without the nasty times
ahead inside. The pasties and g-string
gone. Topless, bottomless, the wild night
down to nothing. But you know all that
is past, won't be back, so don't

drift off. It's February, and maybe this
next bit of red lace and black silk
on the leggy blonde's pale body
is it, the gift you came here
on this cold night looking for.

The Ohio Review   MICHAEL PETTIT

UNDER MID-AMERICAN STARS

That time again, we drive past the stadium
where thousands jam at dusk to see up close
what we will see while spread leisurely
on blankets like other families on the hill
below the carillon. Among fireworks
of children, we wait to be thrilled by sky-divers
poised at the open door of a plane that climbs
a wide spiral; unlike the swarm of bugs
above us. I light a Muriel Coronella, as much
for the sound as the protective smoke, the final
syllable flicking at the roof of my mouth.
In nervous numbers they shape their humming
elsewhere, propelled by tiny engines
that do not stall like the plane signaling
the dive, ribbons of red, white and blue
trailing a triple plunge like patriotic
suicides until they pop their silk pods
over a target of grass, one only moments
from losing air support and falling into
the crowd . . . but that's tomorrow's headlines.
Just now the first rocket whistles up
the sky, freezing the hillside like a flash
photo in a spidery burst of fiery, slow
descending segments. A good audience, we oooh
and aaah, rising to point out our favorites,
then lie back under a stoic moon with cold
drinks and popcorn still warm in Tupperware,
mid-American stars burning like an afterglow.

The Spoon River Quarterly   ROGER PFINGSTON

THE BALANCE

Most boys learn to balance
two-wheel bikes with Father

at their side, pushing, holding,
encouraging, until the moment

Father drops back, unexpectedly,
and Boy—riding on his own—

spins out across the world.
But I was away on business

the birthday we gave you
your bike. Five-year-old,

you rolled it into the wide
European courtyard, parked

by the front steps, climbed,
mounted, pushed off, pedalled

into the gravelled drive,
fell, dragged it back, straddled

the saddle, fell and fell
and fell and fell again.

And when I returned home, after
dark, you were waiting there:

"Look! Look at me!" You biked
proud, erect, perfectly.

My balanced son, the world
that took you in was devoid of me.

Chelsea   ROBERT PHILLIPS

THE HOUSE

Usually, when the sun comes up,
the stars are erased without warning.
Today, I walk to the old bridge.
The sun leaks over the horizon,
but night holds on
in the moisture of the air.

On the far side of the river
I walk among the trees,
most of their leaves already gone.
Quail flash from the thickets,
disappear as quickly as breath.

I look across the water,
see in the distance the house
my father and his father built,
stone and lumber tugged by horse
through the tall grass.
I let a leaf go into the river
to watch the water really move.

I look back to the house.
Inside, my mother drains the bacon;
my father grumbles and rubs
his stubbled face awake in the mirror.

The sun is up but indistinct.
Moisture gathers in droplets
on isolated stalks of weeds
and husk-colored grass.
The fog grows heavier and
the house fades into it.

A drizzle begins.
A crow calls, bursts into flight
from the top of a tree, dissolves,
and I start toward the bridge,
lose myself
walking on the deep, wet leaves.

Passages North   RANDY PHILLIS

LONG TRAIN RIDES

never begin that way. When you sit
in the car with destination firmly in mind
and the jaws unlock and wheels start grinding,
the subway is only climbing out of the tunnel
into a moderate light where you notice
black birds returning,
and you are not nervous even though
this arrowhead formation signals change.
The heat of last night's feelings
still sends chills flitting up your spine
and the smile, glowing.

But the train clenches, its doors open,
an older woman with pins in her hair
sighs as she sits next to you and again after
she has settled down. She worked hard
for that incessant chirping of paper bag
and the cheap panty hose snagging.
You tense up again, then relax, allowing
the mind to quiet down and wander slightly off
course, and you watch the grids of light
welcome you into Manhattan
as the current of change rotates through you.
Somewhere some connection has been made.

The Texas Review   MAUREEN PICARD

WHATEVER THE WEATHER

But what of those things we left
In closets: pants and shirts too small;
Notebooks filled with deliberate, looped
Script; tedious games we were proud

To admit we loved? As a child, I loved
Everything! On the back porch, housed
Beneath a table, I sang the same song
Over and over until my voice gave way.

Later, an ankle sprain kept me indoors,
While a plane buzzed so low the windows
Rattled in their frames. Life knew no end
Of tragedy—the brown shoe my brother lost

Running through a muddy April field.
I never realized summers were hot until
I reached puberty. For me, the air of late
September reeked of a cramped schoolroom

And filled me with dread. Like that
Injured pigeon we found on a cold, soaking
Night huddled in our doorway. The next day
Its cardboard box on the back porch,

With its slice of white bread like
A clean mattress, was empty. My mouth
Dropped in a wide *O*. It had never
Occurred to me it'd actually fly away.

Ploughshares   JOHN PIJEWSKI

IN THE SAUNA

I sweat like a Swede, the North pouring
out my pores like a busted faucet.
But no matter how much I eye the glass door,
the efficient wall clock or the chilled
awaiting water, my Jewish heart knows better.
I will sit here, glued to my hard seat
like a yeshiva *bocher*. Alone, I will sigh,
tracing my troubles back to the Second Temple.
In the sauna, I can remember my *zayde* and his ritual
shvitz: the wooden water bucket and stiff branches.
Among the sleek muscles and nautilus machinery
I give thanks for my purified, prune-skinned body—
amazed that it keeps my head from falling off,
that health is at once an accident and a psalm.

Midstream   SANFORD PINSKER

AMAZED

My brother's small son
Stands next to me,
Tells me there are teeth in the trees
Eating leaves from the branches.

Faster, the wind begins to move
Beyond the clouds, deeper into our autumn.
I stoop down to hold him,
Feel his small limbs wrap around me.

Through the kitchen window
I watch my mother chop onions,
Carrots for our stew.
She moves toward me,
Rubs the steam on the pane with her sleeve and
I see how the lines of her face
Grow deeper and she more careful of her fingers
And the knife.
She sees me and we smile for a moment.

The boy picks up a rock,
Looks at me, throws.
Rings of water in the pond run from the sinking stone,
Move toward him, then are lost in reeds.
He looks as though he dreams
And follows each ring until
The wind blows and it is gone.

We come to the table,
Bowls full and bread on our plates,
Steam rushes up from the cut loaf and dark stew.
In the silence of the moment before we eat,
Leaves move on branches and a sound
Like our voices rises into the wind.
I have come to the dying time of year
And am amazed how I welcome it.

Passages North   DEBORAH PLUMMER

RIVER HOME

Behind him
the sleek new wing:
its odourous rooms,
its corridors so noisy
with the wailing of
old women grown fearful
by mamma's abandonment.

He sits in the autumn
dusk by a smooth lawn
sloping to the water's edge.
A freighter passes,
guided on by channel lights.
Aboard, its crewmen write to
sweethearts in their sunny land.

Upriver looms the bridge
where forty years ago
he watched a young man
tumble from the sky.
He dreams of eagles; but
hears the voice of seagulls
quarreling in the distant wake—

And soon another,
calling gently from the porch.
He rises, turns into the dark.
Lit from beneath,
trim rows of shrubs
in beds of sparkling gravel
are his own markers home.

The Antigonish Review   DON POLSON

HOMAGE TO JOHANN SEBASTIAN

(Three Centuries Later)

In our synthetic days
you are reality.

You invent themes which stand
orderly, clean,
structured as bone
which underlies the transient flesh.

One measure certifies another
in patterned fugue.
Your elegant partitas
part the listening air.

Sound's architect,
you build cathedrals in the mind
where harpsichord and organ,
oboe, gamba, flute
praise passion's purity,
heal life's disorders,
promise us
eternity.

The Christian Century   CARYL PORTER

EVENING WALK

Moving under the green elms,
    dog jingling at my feet,
Passing houses with huge screen porches
    that hide behind flowering snowballs,
    white and pale pink . . .

Rounding the corner lot where
    the dandelions have gone to seed
    and the hollyhocks grow tall
    as the old shed roof;

I hear the summer siren of the katy-did
    humming overhead and the sun
    feels warmer at the sound.
Somewhere, forgotten chimes play endlessly . . .
    laughing in the wind,
    while I smile inside.

Buffalo Spree   JANICE K. POSTERA

UN-BUCKLING THE LINES

When you took my shirt off over my head,
the shirt lifted like a wing
ready to take on wind,
and I was shivering.
The night air climbed up
out of the yellow field around my house
to stroke my back and remind me
of all the promises I'd vowed to keep.
And when you found my belly, my breasts
with your lips, I knew I should have been
saying no, but nothing in me said no
as I raised your shirt and saw my mouth
going down the slide of your belly.
Lit by a pale-gold light, I rose to your breasts,
and eased my way back to your mouth.
The fallen clothes at our feet
were a useless argument against the fact
that we were climbing up onto my bed, naked.
I was no longer shivering from the cold;
it was the touch of your hands that made me
move like that, the sudden relief of your flesh
on mine. You began to paint my body
with your fingers, each touch another blossoming
of color, until the river broke a sudden
burst of color from the center and I knew then
that something in my life
had shifted,
and nothing would call it back
to what it was before.

The Massachusetts Review   CAROL POTTER

WINTER'S INSOMNIA

Winter is approaching, steadily,
    like a white army, and the trees

are all standing around talking
about it, their hair colored
just from thinking. The river gives
up its ghost to the cold,
and everyone I think of
wants to be remembered.

                             Sleepless,
our losses fall out of the air like snow.
I want one thought to wander
deep into a thicket,
its tracks disappearing as it goes.
But the cat in the refrigerator purrs,
its claws hover in the air.
Farmhouses float across the dark,
and on the other side of the mountains
a city casts a red glow.
As if from a great distance,
I hear snow beginning to fall.

Poetry   JOSEPH POWELL

PEPPERS

My father likes them hot
and grows every variety known
to burn the worst. Jalepenos
hang in clusters like green bananas
down the rows we are walking,
our arms full of bread bags.
Picking so many of them, finally,
that our fingers sting
and our eyes fill with water.
"The little yellow ones
with the purple tips are the hottest,"
he smiles, "bouquets."
Funny, I am thinking
how an arrangement of flowers
could burn like that, for the way
they land in your stomach.
"Hottest damned pepper
I ever got a hold of," he goes on
proudly, egging me on.
"Take as many as you want.
Take them all," as if their leaving
could be a credit, proof of his garden
and his skill.

The steaks sizzled on the plates
and we lined up enough peppers
for every bite. It was our usual
summer ritual to burn out the truth.

The same rule applied: whoever cries,
is out.

Ploughshares   SUSAN POWELL

BALLOON FLIGHT

The surprising joy of
Being robbed! After the first shocked
Sense of violation,
Of having been so crudely *known*,
And after the bored
Detective had listed our losses,
And we'd gone to the consulate,
And canceled our credit cards,

The sudden recognition, driving north from Barcelona
In our rented car—
Not stolen! A mercy!—
That three hours of looking at the divine
Melancholy of Christ
Crucified in polychrome, of a saint unzipped by the saw,
Of Mary grave with private knowledge,
Were worth more than a thief could imagine wanting.

And then, crossing the border
Without passport,
Waved on by the indifferent guard,
An elation as of ballast cast off,
As of floating upwards together, free,
Windborn, anonymous—
Nothing left to lose
But each other.

Commonweal   CHARLES W. PRATT

AT THE SPRING

A young girl stops at the spring,
her figure soft
against the green bank
thick with August secrets.
The dipper is cool
in her summer hands.
Raising it to her lips
she cannot know the secret source,
layers of limestone, agate,
slate the color of storm-stained sky—
what ancient fallen stars
trapped there finally burst—

how eons parted rock and earth
to quench her thirst.

Poem   PHYLLIS E. PRICE

DON'T I KNOW YOU?

Part of the puzzlement of being
sixty is that everyone I meet
reminds me of someone else I've met.

It's as though memory is an old,
round clay-jar that stores
the seeds for next year's fields.

Haven't our paths crossed before?
As children perhaps? On a play-
ground or in a classroom or . . .

It drives me crazy—this groping
to recall, to pinpoint. On the other
hand, it's comforting—there are no
total strangers. Each person is
a patchwork. Has pieces of other
people stitched here and there and
scraps of other seasons everywhere.

What is it about you? Voice, set
of eyes, expression, mannerism,
laugh, shape of your head, the way
you walk? Were we neighbors once?

It is as though grace is a prevailing
wind that twist-turns all the winter-
berry trees in one direction.

Surely, I know you? your face is so
familiar. Maybe we made small talk
on a train. Shared a meal. Maybe,
some festive night, we danced together.

Webster Review   KATHARINE PRIVETT

TRYING TO CATCH THE HORSE

He capers, buttocks to the slanting snow,
the first of the year.
Cow thistles, still prickly and green,
lean with the rush of flakes.

For three hours
I've tried to catch this horse,
stuffing the bridle down the back of my pants,

holding out apples, sugar lumps.
One sniff, and he clatters sideways
to the pasture's edge.

The barn and the house have disappeared
behind a wall of white.
The squall surrounds us.
I cradle a carrot in numb fingers,
trudge again. He veers out of sight.

But his whinnying pulls me to him.
He begins as a shadow in the blizzard, grows
until my hand can touch flank and muzzle.
And with a twist of muscle, he's gone.

I've clumped after lovers like this,
snow filling my boots, caking my socks.
They are easier to catch and lose
than this damned horse.

Poet Lore   ROSE PRUYNE

FRIENDS TALK ABOUT MOVING
TO THE EAST COAST

In a hot kitchen, canning beets
that look so much like the hearts of small animals,
I am alone with the midwest.
Air is heavy and pink with the scent of summer phlox,
quiet as an attic.

I am not a moth to be attracted
by satellite pictures of those bright cities,
volcanic orange, flaring up along the coastline.
But each friend who leaves stirs up thought;
grasshoppers clicking along the row of bent sunflowers.

Is there no value in perennials?
I am content, of a morning,
to drink my coffee out beneath a hackberry tree,
to keep still while a hummingbird works her needle
in and out of the rose of sharon. Then a friend
returns from the city, her life a charm bracelet
jangling gold experiences before me.

For a time the tree seems small
and hummingbirds move on the bush so slow.
A fisherman at night, his boat trusting
the still waters of a farm pond, catches the evening.
After stars intensify, he enters the dark light
of his own house, a different man.
Do you believe he needs designer clothes,
an entertainment center, that string of big fish
which threatens to take down all our sturdy boats?

Carefully, I place my beets along the window ledge,
watch sunshine settling purple in the bottom.
Nothing moves, except a vital color streaming.

Passages North   NANCY L. PULLEY

URBAN RENEWAL

Wherever I go in this town
I hear the wallop of jackhammers
and the patacake patacake
of workshoes on scaffolding.

The hardhats have no time
for winks and whistles,
only for blueprints of what
the business pages tell us

we most need—another
gourmet restaurant, a more
accommodating highrise
for the muggers to hang out in;

and on my own corner, a luxury
hotel the oil moguls will commandeer
to break the tension of their flights
from other cities to other cities.

Samisdat   CONSTANCE PULTZ

DEDICATION

To all who will not wake
Ever again in spring
As apple blossoms break
Like surf at dawn, I bring

This wreath of words. Although
The dead grow used, no doubt,
To silence, and wind will blow
Their restless dust about,

I have an empathy
For all with whom I share
A common destiny.
When jonquils scent the air

And once again the sleek
First robin is in song,
I think of that land, oblique,
Where winter is overlong.

The Lyric   JOHN ROBERT QUINN

MIDWEST WINDS

Corn-fed cattle, loins
tender from flatland grazing.
Alfalfa hay in rolls, bales, stacks.
Pig lots with wind in the wrong direction.
School bus, swirled by brown dust
down gravel roads, slicing cornfields.

Father with a fishing rod: "I'm going to go
drown a few worms at the mill dam."
Going fast in the porch swing
trying to touch
the wall without whacking it.
Window fans in the kitchen stir
fried chicken, yeast rolls, corn on the cob.

Ripples in the Wabash, "Hello, Goodbye, Hello, Goodbye . . ."
Sitting in lawn chairs under the hackberry tree
waiting for a good breeze,
eyes full of black loam.

Artemis   CAROL RA

BUGS

The patience of the creatures
weights the web and turns
a crumbled habitat into
a useful ruin.
Animals endure the distance
in the coping.
Some give voice to dessication
and some enjoy the underbark.
An ant's epiphany is crumb
from here to there, and
man's is beauty on a pin.
Cicadas sing a famous ode
while mantises, pragmatic,
gnaw the notes.
The spruce, like man,
is filled with silences and
universal rhythms.

A Poem in a Pamphlet   FREDERICK A. RABORG, JR.

RIVKA HAS A MAN'S HEAD

I'd love to marry a man
with a university diploma:
a doctor.

I'd love to live in Kiev
learn French, German,
maybe English;
read literature,
go to the theater,
study art.
I want to know
music—
sing play the violin,
wear stylish dresses,
have my hair like in Paris
piled high on my head
(my hair, not a *sheytl*).
I want to have evenings—
people visiting.
I want to be smart.
          In Tarastcha,
they say a girl who knows too much
has a man's head.
My husband has a broad brow;
he sits with the Talmud
dawn till midnight
wrestling with the texts,
the fine points—
a real scholar,
eyes weary,
pale,
he sits
among the *fayneh yidn*
at the Eastern Wall of the *shul*.
I run
the shop, five children, the house.
I've never been
     to Kiev

Helicon Nine   DORIS RADIN

BAD WEATHER

Not all days of the year are miracles;
some are fragments of glass after the rock,
some hang like rotting fruit about to fall
in a patch of nettles, some are chambers
thick with brown gases and fog; some, too,
beyond a canine snarl, are locations
of limbo where the unbaptized soul sits
on the shores of a warm river, staring
at transparent minnows and jelly fish.

Reaching the miracle of a good day
is a personal problem demanding

knowledge of exits, for God is always
busy paring fingernails or rubbing
rainbows to a fine lustre, which remind
us all that world's end won't come by drowning.

Prayers tend to choke in cumulous clouds;
so music helps, and reading, or getting
dirt under your fingernails or cycling—
anything that says your heart's still pumping;
but then you wish for that special action
which, irrevocable, alters the look
of time and startles you by the water—
like learning to say up yours to Caesar,
like whipping merchants out of the temple.

The Antigonish Review   KENNETH RADU

THIRD GRADE SISTER OF CHARITY

(for H. M.)

Sister Amadeus chalked the sky of a circle
and showed us how the soul is always white.
We looked at the slate. She showed us how

in this coal dark universe I counted badly,
one, two, three, seven, and gypped her
change for a Coke bottle. Always

in her white circles, I lost my soul.
She told us how each time
she blacked out the sky with the eraser head

I had sinned mortally, that an all black soul
is damned to emptiness. And I knew it.
So the next day at recess, playing tag,

I mimed my damnation. Eye balls dilated,
sins staring through the pupils, I scatted about
in circles, scared like the devil to be *it*.

Crosscurrents   JAMES RAGAN

THE ATTEMPT TO WRITE THE
LAST POEM OF HIS LIFE

Rimbaud did it, gave it up, like cigarettes,
and went on with the rest of his life.

I'll write a novel. I'll make a movie.
I'll sing in a rock-and-roll band.
I'll make end tables in my basement,
and late at night my wife will call down
that she is going to bed. I will follow

in an hour or so and watch her sleep,
me sitting on the edge of the bed
on the edge of sleep, still excluded
from her dreams as from my own.

I'll have heart attacks. I'll have gray hair.
I'll have a son in my dotage.
We'll blow bubbles in the bathtub,
glistening spheres rising.
We'll play with his boats, his sea serpent
washrag. Then I'll clean his secret parts.
While he fumbles with toothbrush and paste,
I'll dry his legs, his feet which turn
inward, reminder of the closeness
of the womb, of the wounds
     of Oedipus. Otherwise
     we shall be together
     perfectly fragile.

The Southern Review   BIN RAMKE

FOUR-HANDED: FOR MY DAUGHTERS

For once, your unresembling heads bend
together, rapt in this rapid play of string—
pluck, slack, shuttle over, and ply,
until your fingers seem to fly
beyond their dumb harnessing of wrist.
The music of shape after riddling shape,
cradle, God's-eye, cage-of-tigers, noose,
appears, dissolves upon your witching hands
until I look away, dizzy.

Children, did I teach you this,
that you should know to net and rig
the space between yourselves so skillfully?
No, some Eskimo or Pawnee crone
has dreamed you how a looped cord
contrives the snarly world anew
the oldest way.
What *have* I taught you, daughters,
your thumbkin of a father?
Have I taught you how to be each other's
nimble armature of love to wind,
or how to tell the false twining from the true?
Questions I must ask myself,
me, the great saver of string—
not you.

Seneca Review   JAROLD RAMSEY

THAT SPRING

That spring I loved
no one, so was empty
for letting others' sadness fill me.
The girl next door, pregnant,
betrayed, played Roy Orbison
all night—*Love hurts, scars, wounds, mars.*
My office-mate, deserted by his wife, flicked
her photograph to ashes—she curled into a lip,
a lash, a smudge
of memory. *Love's poor fools*, I thought,
and hugged their griefs
like flowers. I walked the neighborhood
brimming with what I called Desire's best,
true Spring, nothing
between my five senses
and sap, grass, leaves.
I could have been a leaf, pure chlorophyll
urging towards its palm-sized share—
—so organic. The chow whose bark had been cut
chased my dog with sounds like 83-year-old Tennyson
reading *In Memoriam* on Edison's wax cylinder—
—more music of hopeless love—couldn't he smell
she'd been spayed? I slept dreamless, my back
to the window. Love
was all behind me
and so far ahead
I could not make out a brightness, a frizz
of silver hair, syllables clogging a larynx like grackles
or someone crying, joy's shapes a year down the road
waving and waving. *Tell me again*, I would ask
the girl next door, my officemate, *how love mars.*
I couldn't get enough of their sadness
or of those iridescent blue-black birds
like bruises rising from lovers' skins,
borne aloft by such huge, thumping hearts.

Poetry Miscellany   PAULA RANKIN

JUDY

As a girl, she unzipped milkweed pods,
peeled silky hairs from the shafts,
touched the thick milk.

She sat naked in the creek: water
foamed through her fingers and knees.

This was before her breasts grew too fast
and drew sneers from the boys at recess,

before her father yelled
when she forgot to sit with knees shut

in a dress . . . and long before a man threw her
to the ground, saying he loved her.

Now, she goes to the quarries with a group of women.
They take a German shepherd and a rifle.

They unbutton themselves, their flesh set free
in the rock-washed water.

They loosen their laughs in the air—
laughs that climb
in backward waterfalls.

Passages North   J. R. RANSOM

JUST WEST OF NOW

My dad and all who've chopped the stalks
of corn to mix with hay remain
among those having still a higher
calling in this world: they've vowed
to stay out west for good. They view
this urge as one of sustenance
and livelihood—they'd sooner die

than think to leave. What *if* they live
with a firm resolve I'll always lack
about the place? I live convinced,
instead, that memory's the thing to keep
a place intact as is, *as was*,
or to arrange it as it never was
and never could be, which is what

I'd much prefer. In point of fact,
my father has been gone for years
and never touched a scythe. He moved
west from Detroit and took
up golf. My uncle was the one
who bought up plots of land in Idaho,
bailed Dad out, then stayed.

What's more, I've heard these days
of pestilential hoppers eating livestock
feed and shrubs. When all is said
and done about the place, even the Rockies
sometimes fall short, as they did
the time before the last time

I went home. The night before
I left again, the moon swayed

in a hammock and I lolled, thinking, "What if
they *do* live for some higher kind
of good here? Next time, for sure,
I'll stay and let the real thing take
the place of reminiscence." And the baling
machine rose and fell, settling all
the fresh-cut into familiar rows,
a universe of closeknit gravestones.

Michigan Quarterly Review   DIANE RAPTOSH

TREASURING THE SNAPSHOT

(In Memoriam, Samuel Cyrus David Ray, 1965-1984)

To go about the indifferent city
cradling a snapshot, precious
because it is all that is left,
is not a futility, but simply
a quest for him still, each time
we are broken. It is not
like those girls in *Cosi
Fan Tutte* who cup
the lavaliere portrait, coo
to it happy, though his girls
remember him, too, treasure
their copies that fade.
Image is all that we have,
shielded by palm, in a place
where we sat with him—empty
chair now. And at home, marks
on a wall, firm in lead pencil
—degrees on a tide gauge—
each level aspired to, etched
as in stone, first
at my thigh, then most years
leaving their marks. Top line
is my man-child. What
shall I do with this wall
where he stood patient and smiled,
tall while the ruler pressed
down his curls? No image
took hold, and thus,
like most walls,
it takes what we bring,
has nothing to say.

The Georgia Review   DAVID RAY

BHOPAL

(I've often wondered how it is at times
Good people do what are as bad as crimes.)
         —CLOUGH

Eyes open, glazed like isinglass, the fire
behind gone out, this child of Bhopal lies
in his shallow grave of cinders—no time
for weeping as when we lost our son Sam
and stood, hands joined, to wish him well in some
life beyond. In fact, he might have gone on
to Bhopal just in time to die again
at just three months. Not likely, but who knows?
One thing that's certain, though, is this: Third World
or one beyond, they're all our children now,
though borne by millions in brown arms and black,
and not much mourned by those who think their own
are wonders, others somehow less. And thus
I'll say good-bye to this son, too, and yours.

College English   DAVID RAY

FOR SAM: LOOKING BACK

Far down the lane
a fence leans,
and you lean on the fence.
A wood thickens dark
behind you.
The sleeves of your
plaid shirt are
elbow-rolled, as always,
and you look back this way.

You look back this way
with that smile that is
snowdrop-shy and wistful
despite your rugged stance.
In photos we've often
caught you laughing,
sunflower-bright:
you falling in deep snow,
fishing in loon-haunted lakes,
glistening from an after-sauna swim.
If this were a photo—
the fence leaning
and you leaning on the fence—
I would enlarge it
to bring you closer.

We would bring you closer
if this lengthening lane were not
a ribbon of sadness.
We would lean beside you,
say what will always
be unsaid although
we say it daily
to rocks,
to wind,
to pillows,
to altars where candles
keep the words burning on.

Poetry Review   JUDY RAY

WRITING IN VIRGINIA

In this concrete-floored study
The cricket's chirrup drills through
My head like a torturous
Needle. I locate the source
Behind a cobwebbed bookshelf
Which I inch out from the wall
Thinking to chase outside the
Shiny jumper. My movement
Brings silence. I can find no
Victim in dusty shadows.
I push the shelf back in place,
Pick up my pen, now hearing
Only wind brushing gold leaves.
Quiet enough for slow thoughts.
Too quiet. I imagine
The cricket's crooked legs crushed
By the shelf—such punishment
I did not intend, nor such
Assertion of an assumed
Hierarchy. After a
Quarter-hour of this remorse,
I hear a tiny chirp crack
Out. It gathers voice, speeds up.
Gladly my pen now follows
Its rhythms, the anapest,
The trochee. And when a host
Of quarreling birds, raucous
And cacophonous, blusters
Into chaotic chorus
Outside my window, I laugh,
And words fly free off the page.

Helicon Nine   JUDY RAY

NAMING THE SAUCE

Kamante, the chef who couldn't read,
memorized his recipes one by one,
naming each for the day
he made it first: the sauce
of the day the gray horse died,
the sauce of the day the tree fell.

What would I name this pot
I'm stirring now? The kitchen
is so quiet, a blank yellow sheet
of sun cast across the stove.
Something is missing—the juncoes,
those small gray shadows on the sill.
They have followed winter, wherever
it has gone. Maybe this is the sauce
of the day the juncoes flew away,
the sauce of the day the snow left.

My son bursts into the kitchen,
commandeering the patch of sun.
"Let's climb Pink Hill!"
I imagine the redolent slope of pine,
the first chirr of the blackbird
bearing us aloft, fringes of buds
surrounding the trees like a red breath.
As we approach the meadow pond,
the banks will be drenched with snowdrops,
the mating ganders lordly in the water.

I pull away from the stove, put down
my spoon. This is the sauce
of the day the sauce
was set aside to climb Pink Hill.

Family Circle   SUSAN REA

MISUNDERSTANDING

He had had just enough of education
and religion to mix him up. He would shun
all forms of nature, like birds or animals,
in the fear that he could not understand their falls,
their flights, their eating habits, their habitats. He felt
so incomplete he stayed inside a room and dealt
himself solitaire all day, drank icewater
and played short pieces on the Wurlitzer.
Nothing helped. He heard the owls, heard the dogs,
heard the willow branches against the croak of frogs;
he heard the music that came out of the wood ibis.
His problem was that he could not understand all this.

So he played the piano, sketchy sorts of tunes,
one-half of the Moonlight Sonata, revisions of Blue Moons,
the left hand part of Liszt's harder pieces of fire.
He played all night long his half-hearted desire.

The Midwest Quarterly   ALISON REED

DANIEL BOONE IN NEW YORK CITY
MARCH 1979

He came here yesterday, immortal from Kentucky,
A barbarous familiar, striding the pavements,
His body soon much wearier from the hard blocks

Than ever from the miles of frontier forest,
And everywhere he looked he saw betrayal—
At Rockefeller Center, Bergdorf's, the Plaza,

The zoo in Central Park, the smog and roar,
Doctors, museums, clergymen, and shops,
And a Nuke leaking badly over in Pennsylvania.

Then, suddenly, in the midst of all that death,
An over-the-shoulder glance revealed her presence,
Tall and blonde in a long black coat and boots,

Passing a window of many Chinese horses,
Vitality walking in the now lemon light of the city,
Something about her like the wilderness he loved.

He saw, he felt, he deeply knew, this girl,
His everlasting earth mid glass and steel,
all of that transfigured and blonder than the sun.

The South Carolina Review   ENNIS REES

WHO FEEDS AND SHELTERS US

Our last dog, a hand-me-down
afghan hound, was done in
by his pedigree, by ancestors
who hunted lions with the kings
of Egypt. He brought home
neighbors' chickens, rabbits
flattened by cars, and once
when he snuck into blind
Mrs. Henning's house,
an ermine cape she'd laid out
to wear at the Daughters
of the Eastern Star.
No punishment stopped him,
not even chicken guts

tied to his neck till they rotted.
At the Shelter, we lied and prayed
someone else could tame him.

All creatures come into the world
with stirrings that bubble up
in dreams. I remember
a castle on the craggy shores
of Denmark, shapes without faces
moving through the halls,
or a wilderness hut where
the only rule was live
as best you can.
I was born in Orchard Park,
New York, during the Great Depression,
woke each morning to the same
worn strawberries on the walls,
my mother's clatter in the kitchen
setting the rhythm of my days.

Who feeds and shelters us
seizes our souls, to still
the wildness twitching at our limbs
in sleep.

The Ohio Review   JENNIFER REGAN

DEMOLITION

Atop the roofless framework of a building,
a demolition man swings his sledgehammer
at the chipped remains of plasterboard
and bricks beneath his feet.
He toes a narrow ledge four stories high
and sidesteps only when huge hunks of wall
collapse beneath him, falling to the street.

We sidewalk supervisors wonder how
he does this, careful not to undermine
his sole support, the spot he's standing on.
If we have stumbled into potholes,
he measures gain on a descending scale
and levels everything—
buoyed by his dark ambition.

The Nation   JAMES REISS

ELIZABETH I ON THE DEATH OF EDWARD VI

My sweet consumptive king reigns from his bed,
His face as white and secret as a pearl,

The surface growing slowly in a curl
Of sand enclosed in a lost sea. Hopes fed
On stars and trumpets at his birth are shed
In ink and secret signings or a furl
Of crackling parchment while my prayers still swirl
Before his eyes, lost letters at his head,
Words spent. I know he will recall the fine
Red brick of Hatfield, chisms carried, long
Bright books, green leaves we read. While God's grace still
Endows his breath, he'll know. Despite the chill
Hands of Northumberland, the hungry throng
Of crowns and thrones, his last words will be mine.

Inlet   CAROL COFFEE REPOSA

CAR RADIO

An in-joke and the long days faltering
at the edge of fields just visible as we
drive on, the windows shuddering in twilight,
are parts of the songs. And we are travelling
faster all the time, no way to keep
up with them. Between ourselves and the night
coming on to uneasy towns like smoke,
the songs are a commitment we do not make
that gets made for us. Our own words reshaped
into the reliable, broken speech of the next
town and all those after it. As we
drive on, we see each one of them escape
us, certain that it will reappear in the context
of another song, the in-joke of the whole country.

Poetry   DONALD REVELL

DAMAGED ANGEL

I didn't want to be gruff,
but neither do I want to step
              in time
to every request. Perhaps
too many years
of living in a small room
with a small bed have clipped
my soul.
              The early years were
                   spacious:
I stood at the start of another
migration, eager to strip
                   trees
and erase shadows. Wings

flew high. But I could not fit
the trickle of blood that ran
along the chin.
         I am not suggesting
the two are irreconcilable, or that I should not
have stretched across this chasm, but a hobbled
        explorer
needs time—besides,
here in this room, I have no
crutch; a damaged angel
        long ago
left my side.

San Jose Studies　　　　　　　　　　WILLIAM J. REWAK

THE OFF SEASON

"Stay in shape, for Christ's sake,"
coach said on the last day of school.
"Get a job, haul cement, just don't
hang around the damn pool, all greasy,
and drooling after tits."
        We cleaned
out our lockers and lunged into summer.
Most of us did work: construction,
painting houses, mowing lawns. Eight
to four-thirty, home for dinner, out
to play ball until ten. That
was June, July, August.
        And most of us
did have girls who whined about everything
we did, chewed gum, and winked
at each other, went to every pick-up game,
walked tight beside us as we wandered
home, feeling each other between street lights,
passing slowly between buildings where we
lay our lips against each other, rubbed,
and hoped to hell that God or coach
would never know.
        In the fall, we
got our new books, ran five miles
after school, and worked harder
on our weak left hands. Coach
never said a word.

Elkhorn Review　　　　　　　　　　JACK RIDL

HALF LIVES

I watch a chameleon leap
from a fence and snap up a pair

of love bugs, joined, moving sideways
by my feet. They say the female
is most disordered by the male's
collision as he gashes in,
cranes her around, and drifts off like
a speck of soot from a wood blaze.
Yet who believes such old hearsay?
The air over the parking lot's
filled with them and their black shells mashed
into windshields. I set the chaise
back, and watch the purple sky boil
in the south over some green
woods. Now there isn't anyone
by the pool. The aluminum
umbrellas tilt their disks at clouds.
And the smell of rain, as I knew
it would, sends the small lizard back
to his bush. The book I am no
longer reading nevertheless
offers the sentence, "They were twins,"
to the perfect reader of such
puzzles. The first drops hit the page,
and I think of the half lives I
was party to. Tchaikovskian,
unwilling to allow the slant
of thought, the storm drives in full-blown.
I gather the book to my chest
and walk home by the bulb-lit pool.
In the rain, I do not know if
the dark still matters now, or what
I still hold against my heart.

The Southern Review   DAVID RIGSBEE

SERIOUS MOMENT

Whoever cries now anywhere in the world
cries in the world for no reason,
cries over me.

Whoever laughs now anywhere in the night
laughs in the night for no reason,
laughs at me.

Whoever walks now anywhere in the world
walks in the world for no reason,
walks toward me.

Whoever dies now anywhere in the world

> dies in the world for no reason,
> looks at me.

New Letters   RAINER MARIA RILKE
                                        —*Translated from the German*
                                                by Robert Bly

AUTUMN'S END

I've seen for some time
how everything changes.
Something stands up and does things
and kills and causes pain.

Day after day the garden
changes, is not the same.
What was yellow goes
to gold in a slow ruin:
that was a hard time for me.

Now I stand clear of leaves
and look through tree after tree.
Almost to the sea far off
I can see the earnest,
heavy, threatening heaven.

New Letters   RAINER MARIA RILKE
                                        —*Translated from the German*
                                                by Robert Bly

AUTUMN DAY

Now is the right time, Lord. Summer is over.
Let the autumn shadows drift upon the sundials,
And let the wind stray loose over the fields.

Summer was abundant. May the last fruits be full
Of its promise. Give them a last few summer days.
Bring everything into its completion, Lord,
The last sweetness final in the heavy wine.

Who has no house will never have one now;
Who is alone will spend his days alone,
Will wake to read some pages of a book,
Will write long letters; wander unpeacefully
In the late streets, while the leaves stray down.

Raritan   RAINER MARIA RILKE
                                        —*Translated from the German*
                                                by David Ferry

PEOPLE AT NIGHT

Nights are not made for crowds.
Night separates you from your neighbor
and so you don't seek him out.
And evenings, when you light your room
to look people in the face,
you must consider: whom.

People are terribly distorted by light
dripping from their faces,
and if you watch the unsteady world
piled up in confusion,
they gather together at night.
Yellow shine on their foreheads
drives away all thought.
Wine flickers in their glances,
the heavy gestures they use
to understand their talking
hang on their hands,
and with them they say: I and I,
but mean: Anyone.

Webster Review   RAINER MARIA RILKE
                        —*Translated from the German*
                                  by Paul Morris

SHORT REVIEW

Newspapers: titles, titles, deaths, births, wars, deaths, marriages—
the same ones we read about last year. The bag over there with the
    surgical instruments;
a long marble table; the other one, green: billiard table.
The good-looking boy with the tray listens behind the door.
Anatomy: didactic, tiring. The invariable. And anger all hollow.
Late at night a perforated moon comes up. The clouds run over the hills.
Old chimney sweeps sit on the public park benches,
quiet old men, with bronchitis, retired now. "A black hole," they say,
"the world is a black hole." They're quiet. They cough. They don't get angry.
Analysis of soot, dissolution, blackness reconstituted. Across the street,
behind the curtains, the light comes on. A little girl is playing the piano.

The Iowa Review   YANNIS RITSOS
                          —*Translated from the Greek*
                                  by Edmund Keeley

PASSAGE

Hold up the mirror, show me my face;
show me what I have become.
Ah, there are lines I can never erase.

I remember the years of ruffles and lace
that linger forever for some.
Hold up the mirror, show me my face.

I have been earning a sense of place.
I know where my heart comes from,
yet there are lines I will never erase.

Youth is the runner losing the race,
age tallies the aggregate sum.
Hold up the mirror, show me my face.

These are hard years to welcome with grace,
marking the beat of the drum.
Ah, there are lines I don't wish to erase.

I am content, there's no need to trace
what memory is eager to plumb.
Hold up the mirror, show me my face.
Ah, there are lines I would never erase.

The Creative Woman   JOAN RITTY

ILLINOIS: AT NIGHT, BLACK HAWK'S STATUE BROODS

(For Robt. D. Sutherland)

The forests I believed in,
Where pathways were open,
Come to this:
Duck decoys,
Picnic tables,
Oak furniture,
Faces in mirrors.

Where is my father,
Who thrived
On a trickle of water,
Could feast
On skunk or buzzard?

My mother, whose hands,
Weaving like sand in the wind,
Took in birds
To mend their broken wings?

The land is old and tired,
It sleeps in its own shadow.

I cannot kneel
To touch the soil.
The wind in my ears
Makes everywhere

And nowhere
My home.

Poetry   J. W. RIVERS

FRIENDS

There, under the Delacorte Clock
    In Central Park
It began again
    for me
Not outside the park
    where vendors' smoky fires
    scented the air with chestnut
    and pretzels the color of gold
    cost nearly as much
Not afterwards scanning the city
    from your wintry Olympus
    all watertanks and spires
    a Mondrian design

But there
    on the narrow stone path
    under the stopped clock
It started up again
With your hand's deliberate touch
Awakening mine

Wascana Review   HELEN MORRISSEY RIZZUTO

MAY ON THE WINTERED-OVER GROUND

Automatic as the amen of chard
gone rhubarb-red to seed, I again sit
and again feel for the easing of knots
I bound myself with without my knowing.
Amen to the small death strokes inside,
to their minority, to my more-than-
50-percent wanting to flourish
despite the strain easing more slowly now,

slow as whole days. On my knees in the garden,
I tear second-generation weeds from root
and willing earth. On the dark, unsure ground
where spirit grows its wheat, I kneel slowly
down. Stars do not come out inside the chest.
Work, love, song are the sound of the chemical
hoe and nighttime angel moving hill
to small spinach hill, preparing my yield.

The North American Review   RICHARD ROBBINS

NIGHT TUMBLES INTO TOWN BY RAIL

(Everything you want a train to do, it does.)
—overheard in a Chinese restaurant in Phoenix

We attend to small details first:
what to wear, who to call,
getting there on time.

Night tumbles into town, bruised
and swearing. I look at you,
the way you connect to me: arms and legs—
and slowly the words form on my lips:
Boxcars.

We settle smaller matters
by the exercise
of our own deliberation.
It is all scenery:
trestle bridges, depot houses.

More important matters,
such as the curve of our bodies
and the bodies of those we love:
a hazy shoreline seen from a train window
as we pass—who can tell where
water ends and sky begins?

The Ohio Review   KIM ROBERTS

BUILDING THE BARN DOOR

It is snowing and your brother,
back from a foreign war, has come
to help build the new sliding barn door.
Wrapped in green parkas, you two
first square the frame, 16 by 16, then nail
the cross brace. As you hammer the cheap spruce
boards, you think this time he's all right, the nails refusing
to fly from his hand, his mouth open with words, not screams.
Duck walking down the opposite side,
he says he's been off the Thorazine
for months, the clear snow shining from his eyes.
It's nearly zero and a wind down
from the hill, but he won't go in
until he bolts the 2 by 6, the galvanized
guide and runner, until the door rises
to cover the dark mouth of the barn.
He won't even look at the lights in the house,
the smoke rising from the chimney, until
the handle's on, the padlock, the rectangle
of rubber cut and tacked to keep the weather
out. Even as you say your feet are numb,

the wind's driving water from your eyes,
he stomps through the crusted snow, bends
to bevel the door's edge for the tightest fit.

The Virginia Quarterly Review   LEN ROBERTS

MISPRONUNCIATION

When my father called cows,
he'd stop the blue Ford wagon
by a pasture beyond a narrow ditch,
lean out the window and moo.
They'd look up, chew, swish their tails,
and some would wander over to stare
through the barbed wire. I wondered
what kind of cow they thought he was,
what he'd let slip from his mouth.
But maybe they had that same tolerance
the front seat had for the back.
Distracted from squabbling, we kids
begged, Daddy, do it again,
and he smiled and mooed,
and one of them mooed back,
obliging, we imagined,
as if theirs were not a separate tongue,
as if some sound were the truth
we all could retrieve at will.

The Ohio Review   GAYLE ROBY

WAITING ROOM IN MISSOURI

I watch false cool air
hold summer at bay,
wait for a tap, a probe,
a logical explanation to tell me
what my lack of pain cannot.
The insistent clarity of light
leads me to expect answers
pointed as the tips of leaves,
their hearts ripe with glare.

Rivers plumb our bodies,
keep a promise with the past.
Nine years the impulse
drowses deep in our cells,
a gargantuan parody of gestation.
We say, "No news is good news."
We say, "Listen to your heart
beat time with the wind,
the thunder in your blood."

Still, I wait,
afraid that when I know
it will be too late.
Faces here open like snowpox
the morning after an alpine shower.
When I dream heaven,
it's black and white.

Poetry   JUDITH ROOT

MEMORIAL CANDLE

Its flame is half way down now,
it has eaten three days of mourning;
          I am reminded
how you shivered in the sun
though covered by sweater, lap robe
whose knitted orange, red drummed
hot summer—like the boy upstairs
          playing rock-and-roll,
sure he'll never be cold with old age.

Father, this candle wax seems your body
melting in time's mouth, whispering
          that one day
cold and warmth will be irrelevant.

As I watch the fire's tongue lick up wax,
I recall how you spent most of the day
          with your eyes closed,
as though rehearsing your final sleep.

The rabbi said that hell lies in wandering
out of God's presence in hungry search,
          like this candle's fire,
sucking up wax as though eager for rest.

Inside the candle's high, round glass,
as I stare at its frozen landscape, I find
          my own winter,
watch its ground slowly dissolve.
There's no way to walk past grief
unless once more I try to journey
          on the road that leads
where there will be no more wandering.

Images   ROSE ROSBERG

WINTER, CHICAGO

Winter impounds the waves of Lake Michigan
          With one too-curious child caught in the frozen

Undertow. What I want to see cannot be seen
   From this window, like the clock that once ticked
At the end of my grandfather's telescope.
   The child and the clock are overgrown
By time and buildings. My grandfather is dead.
   He could tell time by the clock on the Wrigley Building,
Twenty-three blocks south in its white gown.
   In my childhood insomnia I could tell
Time by the binary lights of these buildings,
   Punched out like code for a nightmare machine.
For one hundred hours now, it has been sub-zero;
   Since Friday, thirty-six thousand cars have stalled.
Smoke unfurls from the North Side rooftops,
   Wool découpage atop the flat, photographed zones.
The trees below are lassoed with lights,
   Gold constellations blurring the straight avenues.
Snow sits on the shoulders of the statues
   Like the light of grace. A frozen horn ignites.
The barrio darkens, a cold oven.
   Only the snow burns a sweet, blue flame.
My life is a city on the head of a pin:
   Each block rehearses its epicenter,
The horns blare, the caryatids shiver.
   My grandmother and her sister soon will sleep
Through the city's frantic decibels.
   Though I guard the window like a sentinel,
Death cannot be seen with a telescope,
   Nor can the dead child be recovered.

Now sirens wail, a blue codicil.

Ploughshares　　　　　　　　　　　　　　　　　　　　Jennifer Rose

THE LIGHTHOUSE

I want to keep the Chatham Light, to live
among the big, bell-like and moving things
with purple beach-pea blossoms opening
and closing, day into night the beam
rising across the foam.

Summer stars and roman candles have drowned
themselves hissing down against the black
and gold-lit sea, washing with sailors' caps
at the last thin curve of the Cape, the Light
a pulse of safety when a child
awakens, feels car headlights rake
ceiling and bed, the emptiness of space—

and crosses to the window and looks out.
Then daybreak of the lighthouse swings,
goes steadily across the wall—

a blinking owl at the windowpane,
dragging the mirrored blackness out,
bringing a shining seaweed twig or flowering wave to shore.

I want to live like that, set on a knoll
behind a great and watchful eye
that sends its light out and takes nothing back.

Midstream   LIZ ROSENBERG

POETRY READING

Escape deferred, as when, in fits and starts,
The visiting poet, mumbling at the podium,
Says: "My final poem." an end to the tedium!
But adds: "In eleven parts."

Southern Poetry Review   FRANCIS COLEMAN ROSENBERGER

RELIQUES OF THE POETS

Spiteful, ungenerous, unkind,
So runs the record, time out of mind.
Biography teaches: In any age
The best of the poet is on the page.

Arizona Quarterly   FRANCIS COLEMAN ROSENBERGER

INSTRUCTIONS TO MY HUSBAND, SNIPPING MINT IN OUR TINY CITY BACKYARD

Step over the potted basil,
don't graze my red geranium
with your outsized shoe.
But look—you've caught
a begonia spray
in your pants cuff!

Begin again.
Travel to the fourth slate
near the fence, push back
the tangle of wired ivy
and ivied wires
draped there.
Be gentle.
Don't disconnect
the electric
or the hydrangea.

Duck the clothesline.
Move to the left two lilies,
follow your nose from there.
That's it—the first sprig
upright by a stone.
Use the cuticle clippers I gave you.

Work your way back to me now,
but slowly . . .

very slowly.

The Hollins Critic   ABBY ROSENTHAL

WITH TIGERS' TEETH

Try this. See how loosely
words of push walk out on you,
trippingly bitter, alluring
as they strut with unspeakable airs
to tempt with their easy numbers and
that satisfying smack of brevity:
No! Stop. Move. Go.
Some with four letters you know
and others that come in quick drag:
Get out. Lay off. Shut up. Shove off.
How they disdain, dressing down in
accessories of staccato décolleté:
the shrug, the simple smirk, the snort,
perhaps a gauntlet of crumpled-up laughter.
So fliply complete, such variety!
With what power to choose, so American!

Contrast, if you will, words of pull,
that tug of war with tigers' teeth:
I'm sorry. I didn't mean it.
Feel them chafe and pinch? That's your
throat contracting, retracting
as though the very sounds would
stuff your tongue back down:
Give me a chance to explain . . .
All toothy pathos and awkward ignominy,
lead-coated, sloppy with ellipsis:
No, stay. I was wrong, forgive me.
(Sometimes they aren't all that bad.)
Don't, now, here. Aw come here.
(They don't have to be grovelled . . .)
Give me your hand.

Give it here. Your hand.

Carolina Review   J. ALLYN ROSSER

POSTSCRIPT TO AN ELEGY

What I forgot to mention was the desultory
Unremarkable tremor of the phone ringing
Late in the day, to say you were stopping by,
The door slung open on your breezy arrival,
Muffled car horns jamming in the neighborhood,

Our talk of nothing particular, nothing of note,
The flare of laughter in a tilted wineglass.
Or we would be watching a tavern softball game
And you would come short-cutting by, your last hard mile.

Dissolving in chatter and beer on the sidelines.
How did that Yankee third baseman put it, tossing
His empty glove in the air, his old friend
Sheared off halfway home in an air crash? "I thought
I'd be talking to him for the rest of my life."

Talk as I may of quickness and charm, easy laughter,
The forms of love, the sudden glint off silverware
At midnight will get in my eyes again,
And when it goes the air will be redolent still

With garlic, a high note from Armstrong, little shards
That will not gather into anything,
Those nearly invisible flecks of marble
Stinging the bare soles of the curious
Long after the statue is polished and crated away.

Poetry   GIBBONS RUARK

HIGH IN THE CLEAR SKY

High in the clear sky the geese return.
Their cacaphonous voices reach me as whispers
and I can hear, almost, the steady sweep of wings.

They yaw to port, dipping slightly,
glide across the meadow through my study window,
open against such chance encounters,
cross toward the bookcase, turn again,
to drop into a pond hidden somewhere
in the forest of my pencil cup
where fatted buds peep from yellowed bark.

At that moment I know drugged winter has died,
that the ink has begun to flow.
Out across the lawn into the night
I send the gentle tap of rain,
watching new earth rise,

take deliberate shape on the dry,
rattling husk of a white season.

Blueline   PHILIP M. RUBENS

TOURISTS FROM FLORIDA REACH
NEW MEXICO

(for an elderly aunt)

That day in summer we got stuck atop
Mt. Capulin, we did not know about altitude's
Effect on carburetors, their need for oxygen.
But we learned. Later, in town, the wind
Blew cottonwood feathers; we thought it snow.
Sure enough, we saw the snow atop
The foremost Rocky range, fluted, silver
Spread raggedly, as with a butter knife.
Now your oxygen machine stands by
Your bed, and the tube winds like
The road to Capulin; once more we're short
Of breath, and far off, I think, you see the snow.

The American Scholar   LARRY RUBIN

CROSSING VICTORIA FERRY

(Vancouver)

For sixty minutes we are in the wind
Learning what it is to skim the straits
Like any gull, leaning for balance, tight
Against the axis of the air. Tilted,
We turn, prow drawn magnetically
Into the narrows between the islands, while people
Point to trees and rocks, as if a new
Dimension waited on the shore. Strangers
Speak, in this strange realm, where only
Water can be real. The gulls know
All the signs, and weave their silent laughter
As we toss our bread, bribing the gods with crumbs of earth.

The Southern Review   LARRY RUBIN

THE BALL

Jogging is not for me: too boring.
Running is dull, walking uninspiring.
So I have started taking a ball with me:
a pink, bouncy thing, a child's toy.
I throw it up and forward, run under it,
catch, throw again, bounce it, scoop,

bat, kick, anything to keep it in motion
and my body going after it, my mind
not on running or walking, but the ball.
It is not simply its symmetry,
which stabilizes its bounce, a
predictable, controllable bounce,
but its ascendency over gravity.
At the peak of its leap it seems
to kiss the fingertips, weightless,
balances there like a feather.
Oh, just another diversion to make me
forget the pain that comes from too
much of a thing that must be done.
I'm certain there's a metaphor in this,
the ball some symbol, the road and running
something more, but I won't press it.
It is enough that the ball bounces high
and away from me and keeps me gladly moving.

The Lake Street Review   PAUL RUFFIN

EDWARD HOPPER'S "NIGHTHAWKS"

This diner, like a prow of garish light,
cleaves the sea-green shadows.
Inside, the one waiter halts in the glare, gripped
by that lean man's gaze.
And the man's companion, with her long red hair,
stares at a matchbox, hovers

in a memory. The waiter gapes. He wonders
why the hook of these strangers' noses, their
hooded eyes, their bony shoulders
squared as if by the pull of wings
are enough to call up whole regions of cliffs,
and precarious darkness—why their silence

rasps, like the screeching of hawks.
It could be this woman's a singer in dives.
She's weary of swooping for low notes, sick
of bows and bleak come-ons.
And this man, perhaps, is a salesman, accustomed
to distance, practiced at sighting

slim chances from far away,
dull hungers stirring, where no one else would.
Each knows how the day thins to paper, how soon
that paper yellows and cracks.
They perch here, their long fingers barely meeting,
speaking through touch alone,

two creatures strayed from another realm.
In his white cap and jacket, the waiter

shivers. But he hasn't learned when to be wary.
He pays too little heed to that other,
who hunches forward, lifting his glass,
his beefy back turned

in the dark dead center of the scene.
Why is *his* face kept secret, and why
does he seem at ease in these too-bright quarters,
facing the blackened stores outside?
Does he own those buildings, their
half-drawn shades, their brick the color

of muddied blood? Vacant seats, like mute accomplices,
line his side of the counter. He's the kind
who draws a bead from in hiding,
who plies the usual trade of bringing
high things heavily down to earth. The kind
who deals in feathers, cheaply.

And across the street, a cash register sits
in the darkened window of a store.
As if, all night, the emptiness keeps shop.
As if each pays for his passage and his guise
on this glass ship, drifting, through bitter straits,
toward no end other than morning.

State of the Arts   LAWRENCE RUSS

LATE IN LIFE, SHARKY FALLS FOR THE MUSE

Be a pal, gimme a break, a kick in the nuts
for inspiration, a second of your own sweet time,
Babe. Gimme the straight poop—biff in the kisser.
Gimme the goods, the works, a poem that kills
like a slug in the ticker, the whoosher,
the thinker, a poem that goes like a house afire,
my house with me in it yelling for my life.

I need heart? Gimme a heart, gimme
three or four hearts that ooze at the cut,
the gash you give. Gimme the gash, Hon,
your shiv in my ribs, breath in my mouth,
the ghost of a chance. Before the goons
press the button and the fat lady sings,
or the guy in the bright nightgown comes
and hands me a blue minute with my name on it.

Artemis   DAVE RUSSO

LOUVER

Back home after weeks at the beach,
you long for that sound again

and lean into the August air
but hear only your familiars:
trains coupling and uncoupling in the far yards
or riding low out of town.
Even so, the night seems good.
The sidewalk cracks have found a new beauty
since you last saw them,
and the leaves leaning
toward autumn now seem thick
and bright and immortal.
The sea is still with you,
sighing and pumping its long regrets
so that far-off cars
whisper their tires like surf
and a quick breeze scents the street with brine.
Some louver in space and time
is ajar and you slip through.
You walk with one foot on wet sand—
water seeping in at each step—
and the other on cement
that shifts and takes your prints.
As you near home, these parallels
braid and cross and veer away,
then twine again.
Grass and seaweed mix
and trains set out to sea.

The Chariot Review   VERN RUTSALA

HOUDINI

It is not technique with lock
and strap that does it, not
shazaam or flibberty gibbit,
no collusion among hats and
rabbits, no trick tanks
or boxes, no wax impressions, no
secret heel compartments, no
unscrewable teeth, no saw the
width of a hair, no hidden
tank of air, no able assistant,
no distraction at the last minute:

it is the name—Houdini—whispered,
finally, after he has trained
his stiff hands to work lightly.
Houdini. It means "free instantly."

The Centennial Review   KAY RYAN

THE CONVEX

I think of ecstasy as water.
The full moon: habitual and dull.
I prefer the mountain to the valley:
above the timberline, silence
precedes the child, and the accidental
scrub seizes one with beauty.
I spend evenings in my wingchair
imagining the moment before my birth,
the rush of air before I descend
to need. My fears take flight
to a boy's balloon, to a file
where my name has not been written.
I want to break the circle of my life.
Plenitude, vial of torpor,
how I hate you.

Ploughshares   IRA SADOFF

FISH GALORE

I think of Bob Strong, my pleasant, corpulent godfather,
Driving me, a small boy, in his little car along the
    Gulf Coast,
The restless water off to the right, and always a cool
    salt breeze;
And that day over the water the pelicans diving and
    emerging, diving and emerging,
Each with a beakful of fish,
And Bob said, chuckling (what an affable man!),
"There're fish galore out there, Robert, fish galore."
I remember the pelicans well, going about their business,
Awkward but efficient, flapping heavily away, fish-laden.
Memorable birds, surely.
But the lodgment and fixing of memory came from the
    word "galore,"
Unfamiliar to me in speech, sonorous and surprising in
    its sound and its placement,
The exotic Gaelic adjective following its noun.
A gift of language. Galore. Fish galore.

Ball State University Forum   ROBERT SARGENT

AS DOES NEW HAMPSHIRE

Could poetry or love by the same lucky chance
Make summer air vibrate with such a brilliance?
A landscape which says little—

Grave green hills diminishing to blue
Against the foreground of a long blond meadow,
While from the near pine elegantly falls
The nut hatch's neat syllable—
A landscape which says little,
But says this simple phrase so well
That it takes on forever the dimension
(Space, sound, silence, light and shade)
Of which a summer's happiness is made.
Only most daring love would care to mention
So much, so simply, and so charge each word
As does New Hampshire "mountain," "meadow," "bird."

Contemporary New England Poetry   MAY SARTON

COPPER ON TIN

My *bàbeh* Mindel put her pennies
in the *pìshke*
when unruled shapes
threatened judgment.
A school test, summer trip,
job interview, even
a track meet would be met
by the sound of copper
dropping on tin.
Audible only to the heart
were the prayers, uneasy pleas
flowing inward from
those silent, telegraphic lips
in the New World's New York.
Once I teased her faith,
having finished eighteenth in a race.
"One place for each step of life,"
she said, "and you didn't even
break a leg."

bàbeh: grandmother
pìshke: a small box kept in the house for
  collecting money to give to charity

Crosscurrents   JOEL SAVISHINSKY

WOODEN FLOORS

We smooth off their rough edges,
Polish them, let them absorb,
From speakers of sophisticated
Sound systems, the deepest vibes
Of our best music, and though things
Appear smooth on the surface,

Ours is an uneasy occupation at best.

It's as though their own wisdom
About things sustains them, and
When they can, they slough off
Their polish, resort to roughness,
Irritate with their small signs
Of rebellion: nails thrown up
Slightly at the edges of rooms,
And, under the hammering of our
Feet across their planks, squeaks
And complaints of discord,
As if they're quietly but
Defiantly reminding that their
Music once ran rings around ours,
Virtuosos as they were of xylem/phloem.

Poem   RICHARD SCANLON

ART IN THE MORNING

White sky unbroken by birds, wet shells of grass,
porches beaten by grey paint, this is today's
still life. But you arrive, an insistent portrait,
your large body breaking the straight lines of the house
across the way. Outside the door you say my name.
I'm across the street with paint and canvas
and I watch you shake the door, raise your voice.
My brush glides quickly over the canvas,
suddenly calligraphic. The anger of your brows,
the S of your spine as you turn and leave:
These are now strokes and points in black.
I sign the painting and when I look up
the landscape is solid again, still life, unbroken.
I paint over the brush strokes you inspired,
I paint in primary red and blue and yellow,
the old porch and wide sky glisten on my canvas.

The Malahat Review   LIBBY SCHEIER

A FACE TRANSFIGURED BY LOVE

Perhaps in the basement of a public building,
along a fluorescent-lit corridor at night,
with soft straight light brown hair with red highlights,
you sit waiting for me, combing out your long hair,
one leg carelessly flung over the side of the chair,
lightly pushing yourself around the slick waxed floor.
It's raining outside. Soon the others will go home
with their dates for the night, and we will be alone.

In still another public undress rehearsal,
I enter a darkened theater like a ritual
of other worlds of new flesh to be conquered—
then, having worshipped there, having done everything
already from afar, I see you in soft light
forming temptations almost too cruel for life,
starting forth on another inches-long journey
into the darkest dream of my necessity.

Such dramatizing of this rapture is easy,
thinking of something else when what I am doing
is dangerous: how, collar up, stomach upset,
I am sliding through shadows, your silent escort
along dark sidewalks lit only by the faces
of the public buildings' windows in the rain,
reflecting back to me all my fear as I run
into the center of darkness from which I come.

The Ohio Review   DAVID SCHLOSS

BLUE THREAD

Passover morning, snow
stands sacramental on the air
of a formal tension.
The house is clean,
however soiled the ground.

Memory persists through diaspora,
of a high regard and a time
to grow free. Ceremony
demands me of itself.

How often must we exit
from this arid dark?

The season remembers
and reminds.

The Fiddlehead   AARON SCHNEIDER

SPRING AND THE BLACK HOLES

When green things grow, in glowing spring,
I attend to nature for a time, dreaming
That there is meaning, something, beyond
What I can tell, not merely the Heaven and Hell
Of whirling galaxies, not Byron's dreamless sleep,
Or merely to be part of the dust that swirls,
And someday to be sucked in, as by
A celestial vacuum cleaner, a black hole,
Into a what? another universe, still dust?

A what? The soul must be my vademecum
Or life and spring become intolerable.

But I am trapped, caught in the trap of life,
The spring of death. Yet it's not death
Which is the worst pain of my soul;
It's *rerum natura*, it's the black holes,
It's the not knowing, not being allowed
Which is allowed even in bright spring,
Even in prime spring when green things grow.

And suppose there is no dreamless sleep? Suppose
We wake somehow to feel again
And what we feel is endless pain,
Pain of time and space being born,
Birthpang of stars, the spaceless yet infinite
Pain of the black holes, where time, perhaps,
Runs backward, or, worse, does not run at all,
But leaves your shadow magnified stiff,
Frozen forever upon its lip,
While every molecule, still
Sentient, is smoked and rayed apart,
While still, while still, though somewhere else,
Green things grow, in glowing spring.

Isaac Asimov's Science Fiction Magazine   E. M. SCHORB

LIVING THE PRESENT LIFE

You have to have a very good memory
To live like this,
With ice crystals rising in the spine,
To sip the orphan's thin soup
While dreaming of goulash.

Above the landscape of your ancestors
Clouds come down like white promises,
And you swear you could abide
The domestic calluses
And love even a brief life
Hoeing parsnips, and grow wise
Watching the bees
Tick at the latticework.

You have to think back
A thousand years, when the Slavic tribes
Fell prey to men from the east
Raging on horseback, dragging
One of your relatives by the hair
Through blood and green grass.

You have to remember the smoothness
Of the heel on cobblestone,

The thick walls of the village,
The look of the crows even then
Dressed in the mystery of corn.

You have to examine in poor light
What has remained: two photographs
Of a house, and a letter
Scrawled in a language you do not
Understand, that welcome you,
Call to you, a distant arm raised,
The white sleeve billowing.

The Georgia Review   JOHN SCHOTT

IT IS NOT YET MORNING, BUT
MORNING RISES

It is not yet morning, but morning rises
In dreaming eyes, though strangely

Vast, and a morning like evening.
In dream I attend to the changing sky

And its rustling sound, its rasping
Dry and tindery sound like autumn leaves.

It is not the sound of autumn leaves,
But a change in the sky, some final stress

Of extremist weather, or of weather's end.
Then lines appear like veins of leaves

On the high, cold blue, and shards of it slip
To wheel in the air, careening the way

Bright leaves drift down. I watch the sky
Shift steadily down with emptying eyes,

Leaving blankness there, a whiteness not light—
The air, the blue, all dimension gone.

Then I wake in a room I have never seen,
In an unknown world, though my own.

Familiar birds sing familiar songs,
But differently now, from trees whose whispers

Arouse the doubts that pilgrims know
When they step at first onto newfound land.

The Hudson Review   ROBERT SCHULTZ

TRAPPER NELSON

Following the ducks, their rock heads
sharp and slant across the granite slope,

I remember this place—so suddenly
and in such detail (even the shadows,
the lines of my pack) that I stop:
knowing when I move it will disappear
as if we always live out of the corners
of our eyes and what passes for old
is what we almost avoid. I have never
been here before, of course; never held
still on this trail like a man before
a rattler; never told you so certainly
I've had such a place in mind—the cairns,
rock flowers, the grey slip of snow
against the west ridge of the morning.
And you scarcely matter in all this,
since you stood clear of the picture
then as now . . . What *then*?
It could be sunstroke, I've refused
to wear a hat, the air so open.
No: five days in, I've come dead
center. What can I have seen before
except the center? And now,
saying I am losing it again,
saying it couldn't last, I motion us
anxiously forward. The place is
already fading and we must be
getting on. Some yards ahead
I wonder how you at fifty-three
keep so close despite the climb
and whether, if I look back,
I'll catch you looking away
from me, your old and eldest son,
the one you'd set your eyes on,
the one you'd figured for, the one
who keeps coming back out of failed
nowhere to lead you through wilderness,
who has to know what it is you'll see
of him when you so suddenly remember.

The Texas Review   HILLEL SCHWARTZ

WINTER'S NIGHT

The snow . . .
all the street intoxicated with it.

A passing car's headlight
disturbs the intelligence of her eyes.
"In sleepless dreams, I know you,"
She tells me.

And like the snow blowing across the deserted street,
a smile spreads across her face
and her green eyes slowly lift.

I look into them
and see old Van Gogh
sitting in a lonely field
of twisted cypress trees
forever blue, mysterious and possessed.

Then, as the street light comes on,
her white slim hand
(whitened by eternal snows) reaches
into that deeper dark we walk together.

In the distance, the lonely tooting of a taxi horn.

Crosscurrents   GUY SCUTELLARO

INDIGO BUNTING

Not much of anything is blue: the roadside chicory,
Vipers Bugloss (a prickly flower mixed with pink),
our Eastern Bluebird flying the edge of extinction.
I watch an Indigo Bunting flash blue, then disappear
into a stand of gray-green willows by the swamp.
When it appears, a breath is exhaled on the air
like a swimmer emerging from a mountain lake.

I remember my mother's party dress embroidered
with a shock of blue butterflies: a chrysalis
from which I could emerge a finished woman
to flash blue across the landscape, then disappear
behind the leaves to sink unseen into the fork
of sleep, free to fly blue into my dreams.

I did not know she had cut her rope of shining
hair, plucked her heavy eyebrows to a pencil's line
to mimic other creatures of the world. As a child,
I liked best her plainness: her large well-shaped
hands as cool as leaves, their knuckles big
from chillblains. Yet I remember those butterflies
clustered around her as if she were a summer lilac,
its homely flowers covered with colored wings.

Seneca Review   SALLY BENNETT SEGALL

IS IT OK TO SAY HEART IN A POEM?

("we finally hid from English because it had too many corazons,")
—Sandra McPherson, "Conception"

When I say "heart"
I mean the literal place,
the organ between the lungs,
the stepchild of the sternum,
the acrobat of the vaulting ribcage,

the drummer that drives the whole body,
reverberating in the blue chorus of the wrist
or along the collarbone, I mean
the largest muscle, that red athlete racing the sun;
I mean the physical fruit of the aortal tree,
the junction of body and soul
where blood and air marry in a nuptial chamber
and molecules are exchanged like money
in the marketplace of the skin.
I mean the dead switchyard, sometimes resurrected
by thundering fists, blue bolts of current.
I mean highways where inner becomes outer,
where the world lights up
all the small campfires of the cell,
and the body's exhaustion feeds forests.
I mean a city where we inhale the public
and exhale ourselves
and, born, begin breathing. I mean
the life that is hidden
to the one who lives it, the foreign language
only tropical peoples speak freely.
I saw you standing in the snow.
My heart was a field.
I sat within it.

Carolina Quarterly   REBECCA SEIFERLE

TO BE A POET

Life taught me long ago
that music and poetry
are the most beautiful things on earth
that life can give us.
Except for love, of course.

In an old textbook,
published by the Imperial Printing House
in the year of Vrchlicky's death,
I looked up the section on poetics
and poetic ornament.

Then I placed a rose in a tumbler,
lit a candle
and started to write my first verses.

Flare up, then flame of words,
and soar,
even if my fingers get burned!

A startling metaphor is worth more
than a ring on one's finger.
But not even Puchmajer's Rhyming Dictionary
was any use to me.

In vain I snatched for ideas
and frantically closed my eyes
in order to hear that first magic line.
But in the dark, instead of words,
I saw a woman's smile and
wind-blown hair.

That's been my destiny.
Behind it I've been staggering breathlessly
all through my life.

Ploughshares　　　　　　　　　　　JAROSLAV SEIFERT
*—Translated from the Czech
by Ewald Osers*

TROUT

The sudden, almost forgotten
pulse of the line
announcing success:
a small splash,
the sharp tug of chance.

Landed, one must find
the anal spot,
insert the bright blade,
slit all the way
to the gaping jaw
clean and quick as light.

The tail will twitch
momentarily, disputing death.
The eyes will glaze
within minutes,
the colors fade
to something less than true.

Inside, the futile cluster
of red roe, the flesh
there tender,
necessary, sweet.

St. Andrew's Review　　　　JOHN T. SELAWSKY

CATCH

The fish nibbles the glass.
My son believes this is love
and traces a figure eight
for the obliging golden mouth
that follows each abstraction
like a student of fingers.

Later, outside, my son and I
play catch. The ball rises
like a bubble in the air: fly,
grounder, grounder, fly—
each toss a secret between us.
These are the random motions of love.

Yankee   CARL SELKIN

VACATIONING IN POMPEII

We have been vacationing too long in Pompeii.
When I speak, your eyes wander across the bay to Naples.
The wine is old, full of ashes.
It must be the smell of sulphur from the north
that makes us so irritable.
Inside the hotel a dry cough,
sandals scraping across the floor, loosening grout.
A dog in the doorway sniffs at the mountain
and drops like a stone over the sill.
My voice is extruded into silence.
It is too hot for anything to happen.

When the lava came,
everything was caught in an ordinary act,
a cat leaning forward to lick its toes,
sparrows perched in the lemon tree,
beggars sitting cross-legged at the gate.
What they found was only cold rock,
space trapped inside,
the shape of something disintegrated long before.

Crosscurrents   JOAN SEVICK

WAITRESS

To all the waitresses in white, blue, yellow, green
starched and stained uniforms, for Sue, Mary, Betty,
Joan, Thelma, Donna, and Ladonna, and for Ann,
may the largest, meanest, shaggy, honey-colored grizzly
of a brother guard you, protect you and bless you
from boors who talk of life, from bores who talk
of nothing, from mothers who talk of daughters, from daughters
who turn to drunks, from drunks who turn to lovers,
from preachers, pimps and poets. On that last night
when your legs turn to water and the water turns to stone,
may he rise and, opening his great hands, give you every tip
you never got, green and fresh and just-picked lettuce.

The Chariton Review   TOM SEXTON

HOLY CURTAIN

My mother loved the beauty
of words
that joined together
my father loved
the letters
that flowed from his hands

My mother's words
a thread of grace a thread
of benevolence
spread over them
sheaving them
into an inner
melody

My father's letters
symbols he loved
threads of silver
with threads of
gold
on Holy Curtains
of a synagogue

My father left to me
no silver no gold
only
the tip of a thread
and swarms
of letters

May my
poem
to him be
a little curtain
hanging
in glory

Midstream   AMNON SHAMOSH
              —*Translated from the Yiddish*
                      by Ada Aharoni

GRANDFATHER

I imagine I'll look much like him in my seventies:
gray and wiry as a stand of swamp maple with wood
grain in my face and knots in my hands.

Grandfather made me a toolbox containing saw,
hammer, level and angle the year I started school.
I could see Eagle Lake in his tales: hunting,
trapping, fishing, logging, poor farming, visiting

Indian camps in the deep woods, nearly half
of the children dead before twenty.
Wrangling army horses in Texas, cavalry marches
in Mexico, yellow fever, steam railroads and ships,
stories that taught my hands to turn to any job
of wood or metal, practical machines.

I thought I had lived in his time, but he
was not like me: harder, more restless. Grandpa
didn't like kids, politicians, officers, and told
the worst jokes I've ever heard. He liked me better
after I got married. If he ever read anything I wrote,
he never said. When grandmother died he drank too much,
then quit smoking at eighty-one and cut down on rum
at eighty-four. Took up with a widowed childhood
sweetheart he hadn't seen for fifty years and went
on a kind of pilgrimage: Maine, Texas and Mexico.

We'd play poker or cribbage for pennies. I'd win
and he'd figure two hours of fun was worth forty cents.
Nobody could talk him into living past ninety.
He bought a new suit for my sister's wedding
or his funeral, "whichever came first." But Grandpa
died as he'd promised, and six grandsons carried
the coffin in mud season. Mother and I cleared his room:
every gift he'd never used was labeled to return
to the giver—clothes, watches and money
divided down to the penny.

A New England show of affection, I guess,
all ship-shape with that last independent breath.
An older, colder loving and grieving:
the flight of wild swans.

Passages North   Richard Clark Shaner

THE GRIEF-STRICKEN HEART

Why is my heart so wrenched with grief
yet not one tear can flow?
And life is always dark for me
no matter where I go.

Why is the sun not here today
to warn me with its glare?
I have no garment, after all,
nor any shoes to wear.

And am I fatherless as well?
without a mother, too?
Where are you, brothers, sisters all—
are any left of you?

O why, despite my grief, have I
not one more tear to shed?—
Perhaps because the time has come
for *Kaddish* to be said.

Midstream   S. SHENKER
                            —*Translated from the Yiddish*
                            by Aaron Kramer

FOR CHARLES REZNIKOFF

I agree, Charles, to read and write
by daylight is a great pleasure. So
I sit by my window
this Saturday morning intent
on putting words to the page,
not as carefully as you placed them there—
I haven't the patience or the art—
but in my quick time, in my slapdash
fashion, to celebrate the morning light
and to say that to arrive at 62 years,
which I will do next Monday,
and still to take pleasure
in writing marks me as a lucky man.
And to have known you and your
great sweetness for so many years
of your life—and in memory still—
makes me doubly lucky.
                              There is
such good company at the common table.
We sit there, each with the work in his hands.

Poetry East   HARVEY SHAPIRO

EAST HAMPTON READING

John Hall Wheelock at eighty stood up, book closed,
and recited his poems. They were written in his head
and were in his head still, keeping the sea wind
and the long sunlit beach where he walked and composed
his lines of a gone world, borne now
by the sea wind, scattered on the sunlit beach.

Poetry East   HARVEY SHAPIRO

MEANWHILE

In the empire of labor-saving devices
that keep life at machine's length,

our future
depends on an endangered species
of love-intensive persons
willing to walk, not drive,
the second mile—
to use their naked hands to touch
the quick of things inside
their packages.

Let us keep silos
for silage and carry banners
to oppose our own entrenched
insanity and staunch the hedonistic hemorrhage
some joker branded
the economy.

Meanwhile,
in my elegantly designed yet still unfunded
environmental research project,
I continue to investigate the misty origins,
the delicate circadian rhythms,
Lady,
of my love for you.

The Atlantic Monthly   ROGER SHATTUCK

SPRING'S AWAKENING

Oddly assorted bedfellows, frost and thaw
ruckus under their scanty quilt of clay.
To them, spring comes as the final straw.
Their tortured nights are pictured plain as day
in sudden humps and craters that we find
in garden ground upheaved and undermined.

Tossing about, all elbows in the cramped
embrace to which their restless kind are fated,
their lust for loamy struggle never damped
in all the years since they were strangely mated;
neither has known the other's throes to yield
to careless calm. Their bed's a battlefield.

Curious: what they fight is what they share—
a sullen trance where serial nightmares reign.
Scouting the damage spades will soon repair,
shouldn't we feel less ready to complain?
Our cruelest dreams have yet to match the girth
of these, that wrench the surface of the earth.

Poetry   ROBERT B. SHAW

A DISTANT CRY

Walking the ravine edge,
He smoked and listened for the distant bird
Whose night cries he'd come to know,
Sensing at the same time the way
The lighted rooms cut his shadow from the house.
Even so, he could almost catch
The thick sweetness of the cream
She'd be touching to her face right now
And count with her the movements of the brush
Down her long, brown hair.
He remembered the periods of their love
When he'd done this stroking for her.
Now, heavy with another child,
She'd wait only for him to bathe the boys.
Then he and she would lie, pretending sleep,
With her roundness pressed against his back
Until, her breathing calm,
He'd go outside again for smoking,
And wondering whether the night bird
Shrieked loneliness or lament.

The American Scholar   LUCY SHAWGO

THE RELATIONSHIP TALK

God doesn't need us!
Do you understand that? Can
you comprehend vastness? Can
you possibly imagine our
primary color, stick figure bodies
making one iota of difference
in His life—which is all life
and no life at all at the
same time?

We can't bring Him food—
be serious, no Friday night
meatloaf or even fish like
the old Fridays. He doesn't
eat. That'd mean He depends
on something. God is no
dependent.

We can't give Him shelter—
not at the U.N. or the Astrodome
or even the whole state of
Wyoming. He doesn't need
shelter. What's He gonna do,
make it rain while He's sleeping?
I bet He doesn't even sleep.

The world rolls around day
after day and we're born,
then we're dead. If He needed
us we'd never die—not without
a phone call or a tree on fire
at least.

No, God doesn't need us
but He probably does love us.

That's the way I feel
about you,
Marietta.

Puerto Del Sol   M. E. SHAY

THE ANNUNCIATION

This is the honest grace of her body:
that she is afraid, and in this moment does not
hide her fear. That as the pink-robed angel
bends before her pure with the power of lightness,
she wants to turn away, she cannot look
into the angel's graven face. Because the child
meant to form in her will change her.
Because all she has known will dissolve,
pulling back from her like water.
For there is so little softness in me,
she thinks, and my hands are simply empty,
my hands that don't know how to fill.
I am no more than these shadows now
darkening the garden, no more
than these rigid, frightened hands.
She bows her head; her arms are crossed
against her brittle ribs. The lilies
should have closed by now, she thinks,
and still they have not closed.
Look how they breathe, such white hungers,
white mouths. And she, who must enter
the fear of her waiting, the door
of her waiting, no longer wants to see them
breathing, their smoothness like the angel's
steady face. She would lie down on the stone floor
and curl up there without thinking.
Until in the cave of her body
she might feel, without willing it, a tenderness
begin to form. Like the small, ghostly
clover of the meadow, the deer hidden
in the hills. A tenderness like mourning.
The source of love, she thinks, is mourning
That worldless loss by which we come to see
the opening of these lilies, this doorway

arching onto gardens, the child that will soon form
inside her body, this loss by which we come
to bend before the given, its arms that open
unexplained, and take us in.

The Iowa Review   LAURIE SHECK

PARIS BOULEVARD, 1839

Because of the film's long exposure,
this early image by Daguerre, a street-scene,
is uncluttered by walkers and carriages.
Only a man having his shoes shined is captured—
the first person ever to be photographed.

But what of the bootblack? you might ask.
He is the usual lumpen; literally, in fact,
a black mass at the dandy's foot.
There's nothing more to be said for him, being
one of the poor and religiously with us.

Nonetheless it's true: the man looks
remarkably locust-like. The swallowtail
cut of his coat forms the hard wings,
leaving us to imagine his harsh song,
his summer, unpleasant and devouring song.

But he is so small, ant-sized. The most
intricate details are the tiled roofs and
cobblestone street, whose bricks appear almost
as etching-lines seen after the acid
has cut the plate for, say, a new franc.

Release him and he'll invisibly
plague the boulevard humming with summer,
and all but strip the saplings lining the sidewalk.
It is the leaves' shadows that assure us
fashionable Paris is out in full, inaudible voice.

Michigan Quarterly Review   MARC J. SHEEHAN

WINE DAY

We have made every Tuesday the Wine Day,
which makes Wednesdays the day to recover,
and Mondays the day to anticipate.
On weekend mornings, we rummage through
bins of wine at the Bacchus deli, comparing notes,
holding jugs up to the light, thumping corks.

Inevitably, we begin to speak with French accents
learned from movies, my hat becomes a *chapeau,*

the everchanging wine clerks begin to treat us with
more respect. We begin to get a discount.
The basement fills with bottles of wine, the neighbors
stare as we unload cases and cases from the hatch of Le Car.
The only utensils we own are corkscrews.

When we are finally unintelligible, when the
cellar can hold no more wine, when the shock
absorbers of Le Car are no more than soggy corks,
only then do we open a bottle of *vin ordinaire*
and sit on the front steps of our humble chateau
with a baquette, and toast in solemn tones,
Liberte, Egalite, Amour.

Passages North   MARK SHELTON

ASTRONOMICAL

(Paxico, Kansas)

Shooting stars in Perseus,
luminous dust of creation,
come smoking out of the dark
and disappear as fast as we blink
back sleep. From August wheatfields
we watch bits of planets exploding,
some astronomical number
of grain ripening in the dark.

Dimmer but more constant,
a satellite glints across the galaxy.
What speed to witness—
this man-wished thing,
unbound from the earth's slow round,
sailing across the face of suns and moons.
What speed we ourselves move at—
846 miles per hour rounding the earth,
64,000 miles per hour around the sun,
and the galaxy turns on a center
north of Hercules, spiraling
43,000 miles per hour—as we drift
in and out of sleep in Kansas,
the grainfields ripening,
crickets pulsing, no wind.
The night, still.

The Southern Review   NEIL SHEPARD

EMPTY ROOMS

The best of what we owned, down to a handful
of days, already gone, given over

willingly to the last, replaceable: all glass,
not to tempt breakage in transit; brass lamp
and chairs: nothing sacred when you measure time
in one place as the young measure summer,
too suddenly at an end, ready to do it once again.

In our imaginary house on that corner lot
with its lattice that a glance can't balance,
the cherry desk once ours, all spindly legs like a foal,
would fill a sunny wall beside a window.
The floral oval rug that slid us
across the parquet floor another year would
underscore the largeness of the rooms.

We collect ourselves, lost treasures culled,
holding to this moment of found strength.
Once packed, we'll carry open space
unsettled weeks, the pattern so familiar. *I can
load what I own on my back as before I met her.*
Again, commitment to this way revives
the sounds of life shut up in empty rooms.

Blueline   STEVEN SHER

ANDERSON THE ICE MAN

Everytime she'd hear him
coming up the gravel road
my mother would say, *'Da
goy is du.'* His white truck,
the word ICE in letters
a frosted blue.

Like Barnacle Bill in the song we sang,
unshaven, coarse, beer-bellied,
he fought an unwinnable battle
with the brylcreamed forelock of hair
that kept falling in his face,
with the stained brown trousers
that would slip
past the frayed elastic
of his underpants
(my mother, glancing at me
would sigh as if to ask
what more can you expect)
as with monster tongs
he wrestled the giant cubes.

His children usually accompanied him.
The girl, blonde, smelt like lemon suckers,
the boy resembled an illustration
out of my birthday copy of *Huckleberry Finn.*
Shy, they huddled by the doorway

taking in the particulars of a cottage
inhabited by Jews.

Then, one winter, news reached us in the city:
Anderson and his truck had fallen
through the frozen lake: drowned, gone,
not to be recovered.
That summer the lake was
unseasonably cold. When I did swim
I imagined him somewhere down below me,
grizzly-faced, eyes bloodshot,
bilious,
his monster tongs poised
ready to snap.

Descant (Canada)   KENNETH SHERMAN

NUTCRACKER SWEET

(To Violet)

A most rare fruit was I,
so to speak: a tough nut to crack.

Bullies with bulky fists
tried hard, grabbed me,
pummeled me,
flung me to the floor,
stomped and swore.

Belles with delicate hands
picked me up, squeezed
me, shook me, looked
at me askance,
then tossed me back
into the party bowl.

Even one with probing fingers
who supposedly could
identify a nut
by its tough, woody covering,
declared me "nux vomica."

But only you
with a tender caress
cracked me open,
pried me from my shell,
and loved me to pieces.

Poem   MICHAEL SHIMER

THE WANDERING YEAR

Last August I looked out the window by your bed
and thought, for a moment, the silver maple

in the neighbors' yard was full
of tropical birds, green
and green-gold, breathing in unison.

In October, the maple stretched into the room
and traced thin gold branches
on the quilt. A brittle leaf moved
along the sill, and the seeds of the pomegranate
we split for breakfast

were garnets you dripped across my thighs
and strung onto the strands of light.
The sky, in January, was so smooth a child
could have skated on it. You walked
under that sky, a bag of birdseed in your arms,

snow glinting like age in your beard.
For the first time I saw that
the silver maple was truly silver,
its limbs bare, its bark
sleek with ice. Even if I stayed still a long time,

I knew that the planet would steadily circle
the sun, and the seasons catch up
with me, one way or another.
The ancient Egyptians counted 365 days, exactly;
over the centuries,

their year wandered, each month occurring
in a different season. But this is spring:
the ground thaws and loses
its pavé brilliance.
The tulips you arrange in a black bowl

on the table are no less stunning
than if they flared from the lunar seas.
Beside the forsythia, the gingko is pinching
off bits of March or April sun, salting
them away for fall.

Poetry   ALEDA SHIRLEY

GO IN GOOD HEALTH

Like all good women, I am in love with my doctor.
His coat flows like wisdom.
The mirror on his forehead
Shines like a miner's:

He digs for diamonds
In the dross of my flesh.
If I could see what he sees,
Feel what he touches,

(I'm not even sure where everything is!)
I would know a great secret.
I would know myself.
His hands sail the sea of my body.

My bones are water:
My brightness dazzles.
I am whole: he rests on an island,
Anchors my heart.

I am attached.
These men,
How much they know of us!
They fix names to organs and ailments

We didn't know we had,
Discover us in places
We can't even see.
We are investigated, invested with meaning.

We re-robe in the euphoria
Of knowledge.
The lover supplies an image,
He makes us real.

Come closer: let me kiss you:
Open your eyes.
I bloom like a dancer
Across the strict pupil

I open like the eye
Of a needle.

Southern Humanities Review   DIANN BLAKELY SHOAF

STALKING THE FLORIDA PANTHER

(Everglades National Park)

Camped near fresh tracks, we wait.
Such blackness—the leafy horizon
closed shut like a fan.

The fire burns in whispers.
All night it has eaten itself
like a trapped animal

down to glowing red bones.
We lie on separate hummocks
in this river of grass,

the water moving
as stealthily as I imagine
the cat—its plush paws

dimpling the black muck
as it hunts. What I know:
that desire spreads like light

without doctrine. By morning,
the sawgrass will shatter
the swamp to a million

glittering shards. Now,
moving for each other
in the darkness, our skin shines

like flares. I want to think
the cat is watching as our bodies
pull the wilderness in.

Poets & Writers Newsletter   ENID SHOMER

THE BULLPEN CATCHER CONSIDERS HIS CONDITION

With the big leagues out of my grasp, I lean against
the dugout wall and dip half a can of Skoal snuff.
The acrid smell of Texas City sinks onto the field
at dusk, oily, like the inside of a
plastic soda pop bottle. There's that to look
forward to, and mosquitoes biting like mad.

But I love this no-frills minor league,
the scraggy-faced teenaged girls who come
to watch us, their thin hands scraping
for popcorn in carton bottoms, solid bellies
rising toward ivory halters, boots tapping
every night to the same song by Jerry Jeff Walker.

Death is so far away tonight, like Thanksgiving
or my own childhood, and we're here slinging balls
as if having money piled in banks is something alien,
as if this is all the love we can give or take.

The Texas Review   PAUL SHUTTLEWORTH

FOR THE NEW YEAR

Our rabbi tells us not to live in the past
but on Yom Kippur to remember.
How can I remember
the grandmother I never knew?

For the New Year, Mother
teaches my children to braid challah.
Side by side we weave the loaves, watch

through the oven door
how they fuse like trees at night.

We thumb black and white
photos from Poland. Grandmother
stands beside ten children.
Behind them her flower garden,
stripped: chrysanthemums and asters clipped
by townspeople to honor their prince's birth.

Grandma, you lean against the fence
rereading letters your children sent
from Argentina, America, Israel,
begging you to flee. You watch the old
familiar road turn black with soldiers.

Midstream   JOAN SELIGER SIDNEY

THE SNOW FALLS

The snow falls with abandon, falls
every which way down. Each intricate flake
covers the scarred earth with its white coat.

How light a caress, this inch of snow:
It touches the tree, clings to the wires,
the dandruff of angels, a celestial worry

over all things. Now the mouse huddles
under leaves, the mole digs deeper,
the owl glides quietly, offering resolution.

The moon hangs above it, a cold query.
Sparrows circle from the chimney like ashes,
while the cat peers steadily from the skeletal

shadow of the fence. In the wave's swell
a shark turns suddenly
unappeasable, a whale swallows chiliads

of krill. So the world groans and dissolves
into itself. In this darkness the thing happens:
lives become other lives, are cast up

for the moon's clear inspection, pox-faced,
wearing a dark coat and hat. Sometimes he seems
about to comment. The surf erases another line.

All this hunger and movement, this striving.
The snow throws itself down in pity
from the order of heaven where things are clear

as the horizon retreating from a space shuttle
or the edge of Africa, a calm and simple line.
From there the snow comes, an infinite army

who throw themselves down, wings and all,
in utter abandon. Each tiny hosanna
patterns the air for a moment. Each small

forgiveness lights upon the earth, dissolves.

Midland Review   ROBERT SIEGEL

ZOMBIES

I don't even know the name
of this plant, so common
it must be second nature
to any nature poet
worth his pollen.
It has managed
a small white flower.
I keep it in the bathroom
on a rickety table
I scrounged from the dump,
where it gets next to
zero sunlight
and too much of the mornings'
squint and stumble.
The last stiff to live here
left it to me,
and I have mainly ignored it
as I've mainly ignored
the bums and drunks
that haunt like novice zombies
the streets of this town.
It has endured the winter
in a room without heat.
It has survived
on ashes and grime.
It has been toppled
and uprooted twice at least.
I don't know how it
goes on living
in that shallow plot,
turning its leaves
as if they were hands,
as if they could cling
to a smidgen of light.
Those zombies must be slumped now
in the alley back of Sunshine Mission,
stretching their arms
as though to pull themselves up.
This half-dead plant
must be growing, even now,

toward the room's one window
painted shut.

Shankpainter   JIM SIMMERMAN

PROBIE DAYS

Our lack of bibs and caps
symbolized our subservience
those first three months
when we learned to scrub
the stained and stinking
rubber sheets   scour and sterilize
the bedpans   stand when addressed
by seniors where everyone
was senior   and to take it
from any nurse
harassed enough herself
to need a victim

We learned well
the endurance we'd need
to face the next three years
and gave each other strength
more than sisters could
with laughter   off duty
sitting together in a curtained booth
uptown in the White Lunch
retelling our days   our pecadilloes
sipping our five-cent coffees
smoking forbidden cigarettes
down to the last shreds
held with medical care
forceped with bobby pins

Quarry   LOUISE SIMON

THE SADNESS OF RIVERS

The sadness of rivers is their aimlessness.
Though the edge of the world invites them,
they refuse to go beyond themselves.
Even the wolves of destiny can't persuade them
to forsake the lyric poem for the epic.

The contentment of trees is their protocol:
always bowing good-day, waving good-bye,
they make a ceremony out of greening.

They even put up with the coal-hearted crow,
with ruptured kites, and an armor of snow.

The bitterness of mountains is a solid fire,
fueled by air, by an envy of clouds.
With hearts of granite, mountains are unmoved
by the sight of swans reshaping the skies,
by the slow deaths of free-wheeling stars.

The joy of roses is a breaking of silence;
their fragrance a translation of light.
Their marvelous bodies spell out desire
in the coldest year of exile, when hunger
sings in the ice and despair licks itself.

The wisdom of oceans is a holy invention.
Though waves love to confess their passions
to unlistening shores, the ancient scrolls
of spindrift retain their pearly secrets,
the waters of oblivion seal their doors.

The gratitude of stones is wide as the world.
Their shadows are heirlooms the day hoards,
along with the blessings of pebbles.
Stones know the words under our tongues
are their children: mutable, jagged, bold.

Poetry   MAURYA SIMON

JANUARY 1, 5 PM

A dim star over the pine fades
and sputters, while behind
in the grey street, a tune is piped,
its halting notes not quite
a song you recognize, yet melodic
enough to lure your imagination.

What was it you once expected
to have by now: certainties,
facts about light dissipated
through miles of stratosphere,
the knowledge of infinite
kindness, clarity, absolution?

There continues this coming to terms,
so like decoding a stranger's
slack arrangement of phrase, or glimpses,
above the pine's crest, of starlight
which stalls, flares, teases
out of the incipient dark.

The Southern Review   MICHELLE BLAKE SIMONS

PUBLISHING DAYS

Sitting at a desk with my feet up
on the bottom drawer, reading manuscripts,

I have a vision of an author, in his underwear
at the typewriter. Through a window
come noises: boys playing ball, the diastole
of traffic. But he is oblivious,
typing away faster than I can read.

Now and then I leave my desk
and stroll about . . . look out the window
to the Hudson, where the ocean liners
tie up: the *Elizabeth,*
the *New Amsterdam,* the *Ile de France* . . .
and sit down again. The work is pleasant,
undemanding, and underpaid.

*

I go to literary gatherings
where editors rub elbows with authors
and agents. There are familiar faces:
Mailer, Styron, Baldwin, Bellow,
and many that have since disappeared.

The room is filled with smoke, a hubbub
of talk about paperback sales
and Hollywood contracts. The door keeps opening
with more and more crowding to get in,
like the cabin scene in *A Night at the Opera.*

*

Sometimes I take the train
to Old Greenwich, Connecticut,
where the head editor has his house.
There the party is continuing . . .
more novelists, more literary agents,
and some of J.B.'s more personable neighbors:
a corporation lawyer, say, or psychiatrist.

We play games like Twenty Questions . . .
a game, I recall, in which you choose
one of the people in the room
and they all guess, by asking questions,
which one it is. Questions such as,
"If this person were an automobile
what kind of automobile would it be?"
Frequently this leads to a discussion
of the person's character . . . sometimes flattering
and sometimes, definitely, not.

*

One weekend there is a hurricane
and flood warning. Cars come up Old Clubhouse Road
from the beach, honking their horns.

But J.B.'s house stands on higher ground
and, he assures us, we are in no danger.

With time, things that never happened
seem as real as things that did.
The house is floating out on the Sound
with lighted windows, and a voice
from inside it, faintly heard,
is asking, "If this person were a vegetable,
what kind of vegetable would it be?"

The Hudson Review   LOUIS SIMPSON

LEAVING IN THE DEAD OF WINTER

Ghosts push up through soil, pale mushrooms
and Indian Pipe clusters, the little saints.
Let the land moulder, October, November.
Oaks look finished but they will come back.

Some pretend to be dead and lie morbid
on the ground. Saplings rise from the rot.
At night, phosphorus glows
in the heart of the oldest stump.

It is natural to live with decay,
to notice the life of a tree and say we die
many times, mutable, all of us.
Still, one must learn how to act,

when to come, when to go.
Here is a scene. In wintertime,
a woman packs to go someplace.
Torn photographs fall to the floor. She sees

herself, and the one man she loved, young.
He looks dependable. Now she smashes a red
crystal bowl, and wants to cut everything.
Wait. This is not the end.

The woman drives away fast.
Or take it from this point of view—
leaving Cherry Mountain in the dead of winter
you look up and see a backbone sticking out,

huge curve of the ridgeline
shaped like a great whale beached and dying.
The ground has already stiffened.
No one can live this close to death.

Indiana Review   NANCY SIMPSON

DESERT LYNX

Bandit-cat,
you stood on a high plank
at sunset, spots over eyes and muzzle
to blend with grass, head high,
almost too slender for the weight of fangs.
Something in dying light turned you

from silhouette to a ripple
of fawn muscle a yard long
walking down a network of planks,
eyes never leaving mine. You made no sound,
and I read later how you were trained
by Egyptian princes to hunt pigeons,

outrun gazelles and bring them down
on desert sand in moonlight.
You would not jump
onto chairs, through fiery hoops, snarling
and pacing predictable lines.
You reach the ground and walk
straight at me. I almost hear

small paws that pound and leap, blur
of leg and turning flank, fangs
closing in bloodwarm shadow
a night like this. We stand
a foot apart, needing the fence between.

Soon I will be gone, and my smell.
Small light killer, I wish you free
to run, mate, and kill
again, pitiless as sun.

The Antigonish Review   MARTIN SINGLETON

DRIVING THROUGH KANSAS, EATING A PEAR

I squeeze the cold sweetness
of this breast-like fruit
between my tongue and teeth
and recall the two of us
stealing fruit one Sunday afternoon,
me coiling around the limb
like that first snake, tossing you,
solid on the earth below,
the small green pears.

The fields I cross now
are tossed with green,
their golden wheat an early summer
blessing, even though this year

it's half the size.
Combines work the fields
cutting paths (Moses
parting the Red Sea, I think
you would say), walls weaving upright
on both sides.

I think of you, also crossing Kansas today,
headed north through Nebraska in your own car,
each of us leaving our midwest lives
for a time.
The telephone poles string out
as far as I can see, crosses
that will bear our voices state to state.
I would ring you now, bound for Eustis,
ask you to consider how our lives return
to us in unexpected ways, how it is
not our hands which hold
what matters most.

Kansas Quarterly   ANITA SKEEN

THE LIBRARIAN DECIDES ON CRYONICS

Just his head, stuffed with children's books
and the thin yellow cards of the catalogue,
tissue ruffled and scored with red letters
of microfiche. Right and left halves,
aisles where the bad novels grow worse
and the good novels go unread.

And not that it was easy to make this decision;
when he met the cryologist at a party
it was doubt and mixed drinks, the cherry
of the lush present dangling on its thin stem
into their glasses. Just talk.

That's when the books reached into his life
with their thin jackets and took his loved ones,
one by one: a father, an aunt, the grandmother
whose jellies well-deserved their local reputation.
It became obvious, the fragility of life,
the slim volumes filled with their choices:
die or be frozen, freezedried.

He'll have a new body, though. It's expensive
to freeze a body, one so footnoted with cancer
and bad vision as his will be.
Hats off, then, to the librarian,
his head that is, strapped in a museum case
in a one-way glass building,
catalogued and paid up through 2200.

With all the time in the world to kill,
and the entire backlog of the humanities
to take his time on, thawing out and catching up.

Poetry   JUDITH SKILLMAN

SETTINGS

It is easy to grow used
to prairie, expecting
only crops and drive-in signs
from town edge to horizon.
It is easy to lose the fear
of violent June evenings,
sky turning to green whirlwind,
to settle like old houses
on the undermined land.

But some move away. They try
to find new settings, willing
to face lives of long winters
if it means lakes, to risk
hurricanes by being near shore.
It is sometimes all they need.

Others go as far as rain
country, where the flattened
dome of Mt. St. Helens looms
on clear days. Evergreens
and laurel become their borders.
A half mile uphill the road
ends. On the other side,
beyond a gate the color
of morning sun, a trail winds
for miles through the hills.

Crosscurrents   FLOYD SKLOOT

YOUR DAD ON A HARLEY

I'll probably never own a Harley
but in daydreams; between work and home,
sometimes I do.
And it's better now than when I owned a Triumph

back in high school—
the nine second quarter-mile was too important then—
"Let's see if I can bury the needle!"

.....95.....105.....125—"there she goes!"

But now, dreamriding my Harley,
I cruise over the Harbour Bridge on my way to town

and watch men in bright green dorys
hauling shad from the slippery water.
I glance now and then at my oil guage and tach
and feel the deep, slow rumble beneath me.
I stop at red lights and stop signs now.

Then, after two, maybe three
chrome-cruises around the square,
I twist back to you, your sister—
and your mother with our new child
revving slowly towards life

inside her.
I'll probably never own a Harley—
and probably never be content
with these ordinary reasons why.
In daydreams I watch me
finding newness in all that I see around me.
while riding a loud, lonesome

desire for myself—just to be seen.

The Fiddlehead   KURT SKOV-NIELSEN

THE GIRLS IN THEIR SUMMER DRESSES

(after a Short Story by Irwin Shaw)

He looks at her and gently caresses
her hand, says, "Darling, let's take a walk."
Outside, the girls in their summer dresses

parade down fifth avenue. It depresses
her to see him seeing them. She says, "Let's talk."
He looks at her, and with his lips caresses

her cheek. With a smile, he dismisses
her fears, mere foolishness. It's not his fault
the girls in their summer dresses

are attractive. He confesses
it's she he really loves. A woman walks
past. He looks at her, and with his eyes caresses.

"You want them," says his wife without expression.
"I can't help it," he says, "I love them all,
the girls in their summer dresses,

the girls in their offices, with their eyeglasses,
the actresses so young it breaks my heart."
He looks at her, and in his mind caresses
the memory of his wife in her summer dresses.

Kansas Quarterly   MARCIE SLEADD

SUNDAY DRIVE

Beyond the window, fields of milkweed pass.
The engine's hum and the spinning wheels beneath
Are like the drone of voices far off
In the front seat. He sees in the glass

The hover of the peaks and his own face
Skimming across the darkness. Shadows
Sliding off the slopes lift up the Queen Anne's lace
Buoyant as the stars above the meadows'

Rising mists. The face that speeds along beside
Meets his wide stare (eyes of a schoolteacher,
Eyes of a scientist?). The distant glide
Of all the stars is entrusted to his care

As he voyages out among them, connecting
Them like numbered dots in a puzzle book.
Those three stars make the belt of Orion,
And sequestered over there in a nook

Next to the moon the Seven Sisters shine.
He can almost hear them talk, their glimmering
Like whispers of what he will become
(Scientist like Dad; schoolteacher like Mom?).

The round world spinning spins beneath the tires
Until the fields borne along on rivers
Of white mist seem to float in a blur
Through the face looking in as if the fields were

Dreams dreamed till they came true. The road
Spinning faster catches up to the tires
That slow to a standstill beneath the turning stars.
His eyes slowly close on the eyes of the world.

Boston Review   TOM SLEIGH

JOY OF MAN'S DESIRING

(for Nancy)

Above the neighbor's power mower
and traffic passing in the street,
rise "Jesu's" intermittent strains
from my wife's upright piano—
still beautiful, in spite of halting
time and faulty fingering.
Did Johann ever dream
his immortality would
flourish in the fingertips
of unaccomplished amateurs?
Could he have imagined

the crazy drone of gasoline,
unlikely as this love song
to a carpenter from Galilee?

In this most unholy age, I
long to turn to God's own son
for strength and inspiration.
Instead, desire inclines to objects
slightly more profane;
to my darling's downy arms
sporting ten unruly thumbs—
the strains they still awaken
within these wanton bones.
In moments such as these,
we come to realize
it's essence that survives
the buffeting of circumstance;
that melody, like faith or love,
is all we ever seem to have.

Poem   GERRY SLOAN

IOWA

They prefer their Old Style
in abundance, spiked with tomato juice,
string cheese on the side.
It is a land of odd strengths.
Farmers lose their young faces
as they feed the soil, filling
barges that pull the Mississippi behind.
There's one Bible from God,
one *Register* from Des Moines,
and the truth hides in them both.
Corn grows beyond the sunset, parallel to nothing.
The fields give their ears,
and the stalks turn brown.

Poem   J. D. SMITH

REVENANT

A decade later I stray far back
to the cabin on Catalpa Pond to find
a fallen wall, spartan appletrees barren
and breaking, the pier collapsed. Where
are the chairs I fashioned
from the windblown elm, where
the slate roof of the shed
I wrote in, smoking my bulldog pipe,

hunched in a wool jumper, tossing
hickory onto the coals? The plumbing
froze years ago, while
something wild chewed the sheet
music to fugues. Shattered glass
of the one unwooden window recalls
a black widow's pattern, and coltsfoot
grows with panic gress through cracks
in the kitchen floor. I hear
the scrimmage of mice in the molding,
wind in the bat-heavy rafters. I believe
the patient ratsnake yet waits beneath
the boards. I believe the storm-oak's
resident hawk still peers through leaves.
I believe the earth fertile and a flock
of redbirds ready to sing if I can
again lean back and listen,
find in my blood the tone of this season,
find the ghost light I used to study
as it burned on the wilder shore.

Cold Mountain Review   R. T. SMITH

COMING BACK TO THE OLD EMPTINESS

So my grandfather rises
from the depths of The Depression
to flail my father (then a child
younger than my small son)
with an electric cord
in the basement of the house
on College Avenue,
the scars visible fifty years later
on my father's back and thighs,
and etched deeper in all of us—
my brother, sister and mother—
than that night's rage
meant to inflict.

My grandfather is dying tonight,
the madness of eighty years—
the drunken women he dragged home,
the gamblers and bootleggers for whom
his family gave up their beds,
the endless, unrememberable
moments of cruelty
told now with a sigh and the
closing of my father's eyes—
all of it crumbling,
like the demolition of an old hotel
collapsing room by room,

coming down absolutely
but in a motion all too slow.

I could see it otherwise,
from a distance and with dispassion,
but for the night my grandfather,
a Christian and reformed drunkard,
opened a drawer filled with knives,
guns, clubs, ice picks, razors—
a collection of murder weapons
purchased from a local magistrate—
and told me the story of each,
laughing at the moment of death,
then held a silver dagger lightly
to my throat, grains of sweat
beading in his palm.

Because we suffer impossible love,
my father grieves tonight for his father
just as I grieve for mine,
and my son, safe in his bed,
will learn of these cruelties
only in a poem, which itself must
someday crumble, its dust rising
in final dissolution.

The Arts Journal   STEPHEN E. SMITH

CHRISTMAS POEM

I cannot write a Christmas
poem for you,
not with all those slick verses
oozing through the mail,
the schmaltzy music whining
on the radio.

But what I can do
is tell you of a December
afternoon in 1957
when I sat in Miss Judy's
fourth grade class
listening to the radiators clank
and staring at my scarred desktop
and how Danny Chapman,
hunched in the seat beside me,
looked up suddenly and whispered,
"It's snowing!"

I looked up, too,
along with the rest of the class,
out the tall warped windows,

across the empty playground
to Idlewild Avenue,
and saw that it was true:
the first graywhite dust just drifting
the blue cedars.

If you are an old believer,
even on this bluest of December days,
I would give you that pale afternoon,
the chalkdust scuffle of shoes
on the worn floor,
those children's faces
eager as light.

Buffalo Spree   STEPHEN E. SMITH

LENS IMPLANT

Faint-sighted forty years,
I, the old misanthrope, totter
into the world of surgery.
A metal probe elicits
my cloudy cataract, chops it up.
Another sucks it out. Measured
earlier by a green-tipped
tube, my new eye, plexiglass,
is stiched in. Medicated,
I see Voyager, golden nebulas,
a circle moving around ruby lips.
I fear nothing, not even my past.
Within two hours, I go home.

Light pours about me.
It makes all things holy, creases
in familiar faces, ugly shoes.
Garden vines and flowers
trumpet hothouse colors.
Brightness pervades my winter's dark,
pierces into the future.

Blue Unicorn   VIRGINIA E. SMITH

LATE NIGHT

The chimney thrush, snug in soot,
weeps a soft note. I stir beside you.
A long season has begun in this cold place
where we have bedded down, tasted ice.
Stars appear, in dreams, and when I wake

I cannot mark the time, or you.
The old branches from an elm outside
creak through your sleep. You startle,
then settle into dark. It's weary here.
I wrap wings around my head.
The black night is strange
and you, a stranger.
Your eyes are windows to the light
and now they're closed.
My spirit sails off, feather-wise;
at this hour
the dreamer risks the dream.

Yankee   ROBIN SMITH-JOHNSON

DODGE ELEGY

A flatbed for your heap,
the stove-in doors, crazed wheels,
all your worked-over and overworked parts
showing through your sides like the joints of a butchered cow . . .
I watch you ride off,
old friend, old green metal mother
where I rode the waves of eight years,
born out of you again and again,
with each journey across the hills
a little more free, a little more sure where to go.

The times I thought we would die together,
on ice or in pelting darkness,
strafed by semis runaway along hissing curves—
even then you kept me light of foot,
steady as a lucky heart.
This last year you kept moving
in spite of yourself, your age, and the weather,
like an old lady climbing up to the P.O.
for the letter she does not really expect.

Where the maniac's wagon pushed you to the house,
my husband's car nosed into your side,
a small fish speared to a bigger fish,
deep furrows run with broken glass.
I would believe it's all we're made of
or all that our carelessness leaves behind
but for your courtesy light
working at last,
all night from your wrecked hulk
keeping watch over the lawn's trenches.

Yankee   SUSAN SNIVELY

IF I COULD KNOW

If only I could know
what you think when you see me;
what life-purpose there is
in a butterfly's flight;
who controls the matings
at midnight,
who remembers the stockstill plains
in Cumberland,
who's humming a refrain
in the halo of a lamppost
while the dilemmas wither;
who skirts the moon zones
entombed in a space
of perfect enclosure,
who waits for something different,
the certainty of impunity.
                            Amour, amour!
If only I could know . . .
Let's not complain.
I spend my days
and you
                            look around!
Apparently we've had our fill.
Nothing we stand to lose
if the Pharaoh's gold is lost.

And yet,
we are not happy.

The Literary Review   GABRIELLA SOBRINO
                            —Translated from the Italian
                            by Pier Francesco Paolini

MISS PETERSON

Miss Peterson often comes back to the office in the
late evening, not to work, but vaguely worried, as
if the typewriters might need to be covered over or
the potted plants on the windowsill might be thirsty.
The young girls lean their scarlet mouths over their
afternoon keyboards, making fun of her, but there's
so much about anxiety that they haven't yet learned,
can't possibly know until, like her, they've worked
thirty years in the same office, still underpaid and
always punctual; nowadays she is entrusted with the
keys to open in the morning, but the bosses stop
telling jokes when she enters the room.

Event   JANICE SODERLING

ATOMS

My four children, all conceived on the dank squish
Of coal mine floor, swarm to table and couch for the mass dinner.
The sullen antidisestablishmentarianism

That bore them up from the cool flicker of dim-lit coal
Still keeps Darla railing at strangers who stare sadly at our shack.
I showed a stranger once the mine's dark opening,

And heaved my blue bicycle in just to watch
Its clatter disappear and the surprised stranger stare more keenly.
That night Darla and I swirled pools

Of colloidal clay water with our feet,
And the hazy light caught both bikes' glint and the proper slush of mud
To take our bodies' joyful arch and imprint.

I felt the chromosonal deoxyribonucleic acid careening
From within my body to hers, a spout that settled to a warm suspension
Thriving and combining in the beginning of a child.

And standing up—Oh!—I felt the nuzzle
Of her skin on mine, teeming with the vanilla smell of mud and secretion.
Later, as the aching dusk seeped through the forest,

Darla pedaled our recovered bicycle across grass
So green that it was purple in the twilight. A gaggle of mushrooms
Mushroomed in my flashlight beam, and the cool air

Tendrilled into every alveolus in my lungs,
Filling my blood with dusk. And cresting the ragged hill
Lawning our house, we saw the usual havoc

Of our world strewn on the porch, and pressed
Our bodies together before passing again to an ordinary life
Spinning with extraordinary atoms.

Poetry Northwest   JAMES SOLHEIM

THE CROSSING

I am growing old,
yes, I am growing old.
Once I looked over wet, green fields:
the grass was tall,
it moved in the wind,
it hid swarms of life—
birds, mice, crickets and ants.
I walked through it and it parted,
shoulder-high, soft as my hair.
The river was a distant track, catching light.

Now I am at its banks.
I will put up my tent:
I will look at the stones,
ground and polished for a million years.
I will look at the stars;
their light has travelled for a million miles.
I will look over at the hills;
they are dry and brown
and their paths are strewn with bones.
What lives there but buzzards and wild dogs?—
They are as far as, once, the river was.

Yes, I will camp here:
then I will cross.

My eyes leap to cows' udders,
swollen before milking;
to mountains;
to young girls;

sometimes, at night,
my hand goes there,
dreaming.

The Fiddlehead   JILL NEWMAN SOLNICKI

MEMORIAL MAKER

Pieces at the end of a game,
The headstones on the lawn

Gleam in the early sun.
I do not see him at his

Dusty work. He is inside,
In the shadows just beyond

The door, but the sound
Of the airhammer, the steel

Chisel gripping the granite,
Tripping over it, chipping

The stone out, rips the morning
Open like a grave. Does he

Remember them all, I wonder,
While he cuts the names, cuts

The dates, cuts the farewell
Messages, those eternal

Identities finally with stone's
Finality telling them who

They were, who they are:
The Beloved Husbands of, the

Beloved Wives of, the Beloved
Fathers of, the Beloved Mothers

Of, the Beloved Sons of,
The Beloved Daughters of.

If anyone has the right to be
The town drunk it is surely

This cutter of sober stone.
Apprentice to journeyman to

Master-maker of memorials,
His life is covered with the dust

Of love. But dust washes,
Memories come clean. This is just

A job to him, and if every night
In the dark behind his door

He dreams the same dream, then
He dreams of the perfect stone,

Flawlessly straight and smooth,
The letters equally sized, spaced

And deep. He dreams this dream,
Or does not dream at all.

The Literary Review   J. R. SOLONCHE

REMINISCENCE OF AN AMATEUR

I might have played it otherwise
had I been master,
if not of fate or of the situation,
or some appropriate technique;
I might have had a draw from it,
a balancing of forces,
or at least made interesting mistakes,
deviating from the text,
had I been master of complications
or capable of solving
the problems I myself composed;
I might have played it otherwise
and not have played the game I did,
tempted by the sacrifice
for the glory of the gesture,
good tactics in the service of poor strategy;
in the last analysis, an ordinary game
as pretext for subsequent annotation—
had I been master of the moment,
had I been master of the theory of the opening,
knowing the intricacies of my trade

at least sufficiently
to have committed errors and not blunders.

The Antigonish Review   DAVID SOLWAY

ON STARLIGHT

Dead stars deceive us. Like figures
in a dream they are
undeniable
and bright; their light
seasons our eyes
as if they were alive.

Telstar's tricks are of another ilk.
She is neither unintelligible
nor dumb; she does not move
with the galaxy, but lies on the
lax sky
and speaks
in tongues both clear and intricate.

It is still our habit to look up in awe,
to sigh and point,
though few of us, these days,
could find our way by following the stars.

This new one, huge, near the horizon:
if it were not man-made! I fantasize
that I could follow it,
run under it like a free animal,
easy, easy, leaving the village, finding
the high land. I would hold my face up
to the sky. I would hold the star in my eye
all night, like a feast of light.

International Poetry Review   JANE SOMERVILLE

AWAY

More land slowly passed
than someone could ever know.

No one was admiring the red wildflowers
at the edges of the fields.
Farms seemed deserted.

Only birds looked from their wires,
chirped inhumanly, while I did not stop
moving past fields endless to every horizon.

Then one day, slowed down to 30,
I entered Liberal, Kansas;
Warrensburg, Missouri; McComb, Illinois.

I downshifted to join the flow
who cruised confident they belonged there.

I would've stopped at the Burger King
if I had known the countergirl.

I would've parked in front of the green house
and walked in the door: "Do you remember me?"

But I was already leaving Westminster, Maryland,
a last bench advertising insurance
where the bus stops. I was merging again

with soybean fields, distant red silos,
a few trees in clumps where only birds live,
passing freely and singly away.

The Bloomsbury Review   JOSEPH SOMOZA

CAMEOS

When the train moves off,
the night lies shadowed,
the tracks making their way
through tree after tree,
among hours marked
by light and dark.

Tonight I watch its headlight circle,
cool as a white finger,
through green embankments of spruce.
Bit by bit, it picks out and lights a world:
a hawk roosting its life away
on little more than air,
and the skull of last year's fox
nailed to a tree.

Sometimes it all comes clear,
the moon pouring vivid branches
through each window pane.
Why can't all the moments crack open
like those trees that become
so full of revelation
when the train wanders at midnight?

I see the train light pause and take
one snowy skull, saying this is it.
Then it moves on, saying the same,
over and over, the same.

Chowder Review   KATHERINE SONIAT

BRIEF SPARROW

(for Lauren Mesa)

Think how little depends on us—
not summer, breath, nor wings;
how all of it, once we leave, will continue:
mountains and trees, earth's passengers,
Chekhov, horses on a ridge,
granite as heavy as years of unfeeling.

Bede tells the story of one brief sparrow,
frightened, confused by smoke and noise,
who'd blundered out of the night through the eaves
where the men debated in the meadhall
some question of massive consequence.
I can't recall, can you, what they spoke of?

This "I" we treasure, this capital letter
with feet as flat as its Keaton hat;
this so-called "self" in dread of extinction
is, face it, nothing and everything,
whether we contemplate hard matters
or reach for more passions to tear into tatters.

The sparrow flew out by the opposite eave,
from dark back to dark. "Such is our life,"
a speaker said, bringing silence;
"a short while in the light." The talk
took on after that a strange gentleness . . .
more than the usual charity.

Poetry   BARRY SPACKS

EMILY DICKINSON ISN'T IN

We've traveled up to Amherst to see E.D. It's my last
day in New England and why not, among poets, pay my respects?
My companion is laconic. After all, these small New England
towns are old bones to her and with an arthritic hip, lifting
up stairs looms as anything but thrilling. We've called ahead
to make an appointment, since this house is occupied by faculty.
New Englanders have a certain practical cast. A waste not.
Surely they understand we mean today, not Tuesday only, as stated
in the guidebook. The house is attractive and understated,
like so much of her poetry; a two-story brick with white trim
set back from a trafficked street with small sign announcing
its historic importance. Nothing here is flamboyant or
assertive (where Twain in Hartford builds gabled gingerbread,
a gilded brick, pattern painted with indoor garden, billiard
room, porch hammock and bicycle). We sit on steps framed
in full summer leaf and green; trees, a garden, paths and
privacy. No one comes to guide us through. A pleasant

vacancy suffuses the humid air. No accent of grief slashes
the afternoon. Miss Dickinson simply isn't in.

Kansas Quarterly   LAUREL SPEER

FIRST LOVE IN TWO DIMENSIONS

Wandering through palmettos and scrub pine
In Sarasota, I find the magazine
Buried in the sand of the lot next door.
I exhume it. Careful not to tear
The pages stiff and crackling as dead leaves, I drink
In every picture, reverent as a monk
Poring over his parchment. It's Christmas
In July, and there at the center—unwrapped as
A present from a gift box—lies the woman.
The breath of a boy is small; since she has none,
She takes all of mine. A triptych of desire
Held by two staples where her underwear
Isn't, she dries out my mouth. At Holy Cross
Junior High, the priest warned my all-male class:
The fires of hell rise to consume forever
Any who think impure thoughts. I grow hotter
The more I stare, seeing her lips smile
Yes to things I don't know how to ask. I feel
My heart thudding so loud I'm sure that soon
I'll burst into flame. Burying her again,
I'm as cautious as a pirate—
Ten paces west of a Spanish bayonet.
Through summer, between swimming and fireworks,
I come back to let her strike the sparks
That will burn away my childhood. Though ash
May be all I'm left with from the rush
Of those days, beneath its layer the embers
Lie with her. I still feel them smolder.

Poetry   MICHAEL SPENCE

HONEY IN THE WALL

In the attic the bees swarm.
The great mass of their hive
hidden behind plaster
drips honey down the wall.
We smell it in the bedroom,
search for it in the kitchen,
put our ears to the wallpaper
and hear their low song.

We did not expect to taste sweet
in our own house,

did not anticipate the danger
of finding what we want
so close to the heart
of our lives.

Just knowing it's there
we begin to want more
than we'll ever be able to have:
the honey without the sting,
the song without the threat,
sleep without darkness.

We lose our taste for spring.
We curse
the unpredictability of dreams.

Blueline   SUSAN FANTI SPIVACK

WALKING TO THE MAILBOX

We found a turtle stunned by sunlight
dozing easy with half-shut eyes,
and as I bent down, my little Rosemary,
strapped to my back, stirred and
murmured. When I held its knobbed green
body up, her quick breath moistened
my ear, while the turtle, dazed
by eternity, made perfect unto itself
by so many million years, looked
back at my little one, all wisdom
and danger, trouble and delight
unfurled in the slots of its yellow eyes.

Hunched on the ground again it broke
from its trance, sinewy legs
reaching out, the green skull
of itself tottering slowly away,
made strong by wearing its
own death outward as I did
rising up with Rosemary.

The Virginia Quarterly Review   KIM R. STAFFORD

THE WAY TREES BEGAN

Before the trees came, when only grass
and stones lived in the world, one day
Wanderer heaped up a mound of mould
from dead stems and breathed on it.

You could look for miles then; sunlight
flooded the ground, and waves in the air

combined with billowing purples of grass
when you stared over open hills.

That mound stayed still in the sun, and at night
it quivered a little in the grass-rippled wind;
but Wanderer forgot and went on over miles
where shoulders of rock hunched from the ground.

You know what began, after warm and cold,
after trembles and sighs that gradually
awakened:—a tiny, furled-up leaf
spread out in the wind and waved like a hand.

Time was slow back then, a thick
slow golden syrup that flowed
over everything. It was good to the leaf
and to others that came, waved, and were gone.

Till now—trees everywhere. Wanderer
touches them in the spring, and they remember
how lonely it was. One little leaf at a time
comes out and begins all over again.

The Southern Review   WILLIAM STAFFORD

LOOKING FOR GOLD

A flavor like wild honey begins
when you cross the river. On a sandbar
sunlight stretches out its limbs, or is it
a sycamore, so brazen, so clean and bold?
You forget about gold. You stare—and a flavor
is rising all the time from the trees.
Back from the river, over by a thick
forest, you feel the tide of wild honey
flooding your plans, flooding the hours
till they waver forward, looking back. They can't
return: that river divides more than
two sides of your life. The only way
is farther, breathing that country, becoming
wise in its flavor, a native of the sun.

Yankee   WILLIAM STAFFORD

MY SISTER SWIMMING SIDE BY SIDE

Gently balancing on the wing
of an intelligent whirlwind,
in parallel desire,
my sister, swimming side by side.
—Charles Baudelaire

We swim out of darkness and into light,
the water a swarm of bees on our skin.

The world blurs a little around the edges,
but I feel you close beside me,
matching me stroke for stroke
the length of the pool.

Like two dolphins turning, we turn,
smooth and synchronized, unplanned radar,
and we keep going like this
length after length. I know you
are aware of this rhythm, too—
the rhythm nearly everything in swimming.

For nearly a mile we swim like this,
before something breaks my stroke—
a thought of my above-water life,
so different from this life where
there is no need for talk,
where everything is simplified and sleek.

Days later, we speak about what happened,
how we swam together, how even
if we planned it, we could not
do it again: our parallel desire
rising and surfacing like the water
that bound us long before this.

Pinchpenny   SUE STANDING

AUTUMN TWILIGHT

The day slips imperceptibly, drawing behind it
through the low window its low colors,
as though you willed it with your slender hands
you raised from my embrace.

The black star of your hair
rises for me, shining,
astride my heart,
while the dry ivy on the window thrums,
a fading black and distant drum
of our still-tangled seconds.

The day slips to gray, to black,
scattering leaves, drawing from the sky
the dull white ceiling of hollow clouds—
and a relief of mountains, facing us now,
flashes above, rising
and falling.

The Literary Review   NICHITA STANESCU
—Translated from the Romanian
by Thomas C. Carlson

A SHORT FICTION

1
War was raging
in the hills of paradise.
We were running short of money
but, all in all, thought ourselves fortunate
to have such keen memories
of ale and mango we had shared
near the sea.

2
Aldo was such a handsome liar—
in cashmere slacks, his rosewood guitar
leading us from one palace
to the next. I recited verse
to shepherds on the steppes
and thought often
of crossing the sea
in a skiff made
of Egyptian reeds.

3
From a balcony
near the great river
we heard the dark waters turn.
Boatmen came up from the riverbank
blowing their clarinets,
dancing a peculiar jig.
We removed our shoes,
threw our glasses at the moon
and went down to the street
with a mind to dance.

4
That was long ago;
and now we are old men
tending vegetables in the wind.
But occasionally
Aldo brings out his rosewood guitar.
We throw our glasses at the moon
and set out for the palace
prepared to dance.

Cottonwood   PATRICK STANHOPE

GRATITUDE

As if you could wake me completely
from my dreams, you'd come in the night,
dragging a shadow too big to fit through my door,
always bringing your voice.

You'd take me away
to the bathroom,
stand me by the toilet,
and pull my pajamas down
like candlewax melted around my ankles,
as if you could ever make me melt.
I was a bed-wetter,
and you were going to put an end to it.
But I could dream you gone, even then . . .
a little drunk on sleep,
slight trace of a smile floating on my face,
eyelids twitching, giving you the quality
of an old movie. I would make myself fall
off the edge of sleep, and fade away
from the cellulite heaps of you
plopped on the side of the tub,
demanding I pee
. . . *right now, god damn it!!* . . .
And each time I stand in the night
and pee against the wall of some gin-mill.
it's for you, Mother,
it's for you.

Poets On   JOHN L. STANIZZI

THE HUSBAND OF THE CIRCUS FAT LADY

Someone has to do the shopping
while she works the matinees—
otherwise he does odd jobs,
feeding the animals,
cleaning their cages and
the manager's mobile home.
The extra money helps.
She always has the center stage,
but he doesn't mind—
being thin as a rail
he blends into backgrounds.
Sometimes at night,
after he's washed her down,
she balances him on her knee
like a ventriloquist's doll
and tells him about the audience,
the teenage mocking,
the children's wide eyes
and the turned heads of ladies
who really wanted to look.

Ascent   LARRY STARZEC

BEATITUDES, WHILE SETTING OUT THE TRASH

The sparrow in our fig tree cocks his head
And tilts at, so to speak, his daily bread
(The sunset's stunningly suffused with gold).
A squirrel on the lawn rears and inspects
A berry in its paws and seems to hold
The pose of a Tyrannosaurus Rex.

The clothesline's plaids and stripes perform some snaps;
A page of blown newspaper smartly wraps
A fire hydrant in the day's events;
And there's engaging, if pedestrian, song
Ringing its changes from a chain-link fence
A boy with a backpack walks a stick along.

I park my rattling dolly on the curb
And set the trash among leaves gusts disturb.
Then, hands tucked in my sweatshirt's pocket-muff,
A mammal cousin of the kangaroo,
I watch my breath contrive a lucent puff
Out of lung-exhalated CO_2.

Small breath, small warmth, but what is that to me?
My steps retraced, the bird's still in his tree:
He grooms, by nuzzling, a raised underwing;
He shakes and sends a shiver through his breast,
As if, from where he perches, counseling:
That *Blessed are the meek,* for they are blest.

The Yale Review   TIMOTHY STEELE

LETTER FROM CALIFORNIA

(for Stephen Dunn)

My friend, farming was easier back east.
Each spring, a few thoughts
randomly pressed into the soil.
Each autumn, dependable as cabbages
& beets, a crop of neuroses
for the long cerebral winter.
There was always that time
when the muscles lay fallow & the brain
yielded harvest after harvest,
interrupted only occasionally by dreams
of softball games in January.

Here, it is always warm,
& difficult for things to grow.
But how could I have known?

My oscillations had that vague
westward direction. I prayed fervently
to the God of San Francisco.
Well, here I am; I've tried almost
everything & now sanity.
An unusual choice, but one
of the few a man has left
when he's backed against the Pacific
& has been running for so long
he knows, by now, his self
must be halfway across the Rockies,
moving toward another rendezvous.

Kansas Quarterly   DUANE STEFFEY

WALKING UP THE HILL

With a few quick strokes
a pine tree displays itself
in the right foreground.
Fishing boats like spiky water-insects
coast the sunlit bay,
their shiny gear dragging nets.
A pelican reconnoiters for fish
in a bare light the color of sun,
skipping stones on the ocean.

From houses above the road, flights
of laughter and conversation
stir me, drops of white wine
shaken from a glass. I yearn
to be on a summer porch
that overlooks the sea, fitting
links of talk into meshes
with people I don't know.

The pelican's angular form
plummets heavily
into the waves. A woman
leads a Dalmatian down the hill,
her eyes on the horizon, where sea
and sky are rubbed to a half-tone
by a thumb of fog.
At the top of the hill
I have it, almost all.

Even among friends, I am often silent.

Passages North   HANNAH STEIN

PAST TIME

(And then my heart with pleasure fills
And dances with the daffodils.)
—W. Wordsworth

Now that we're middle aged, we're reciting Wordsworth
on the front porch on a Sunday afternoon finally
savoring the words like the strawberries in the
collander between us, letting the words bypass our
minds and slip into our hearts so that even the most
innocent phrase catches at our feelings like a thorn
and makes us weep. It's odd when a friend or, even worse,
a stranger arrives and we're on the verge of tears
over a line that once bored us.

There is no explaining the impact of words. The kids
are half grown, some of our parents have died,
we have lived half our lives and, in that time, enough
has happened to strip daffodils down to their truth.
Perhaps we should hide poems from the children
until words take on the power of memory or hope,
until they darken like storm clouds or glitter like
the face of the sea under the moon. Then the poems
are spoken with the import of weather, of celebration
and defeat, then words swell like silk banners far
above the page, and simple conversation is as tender
as a hand stroking your hair.

Tendril   JUDITH STEINBERGH

THE DANCING

In all these rotten shops, in all this broken furniture
and wrinkled ties and baseball trophies and coffee pots,
I have never seen a post-war Philco
with the automatic eye
nor heard Ravel's *Bolero* the way I did
in 1945 in that tiny living room
on Beechwood Boulevard, nor danced as I did
then, my knives all flashing, my hair all streaming,
my mother red with laughter, my father cupping
his left hand under his armpit, doing the dance
of old Ukraine, the sound of his skin half drum,
half fart, the world at last a meadow,
the three of us whirling and singing, the three of us
screaming and falling, as if we were dying,
as if we could never stop—in 1945—
in Pittsburgh, beautiful filthy Pittsburgh, home
of the evil Mellons, 5,000 miles away

from the other dancing—in Poland and Germany—
oh God of mercy, oh wild God.

The Ohio Review   GERALD STERN

ROOMS

Some days when you're shopping
and you can't get past the furniture floor
where model rooms, built side-by-side
like an enormous doll house
leave you transfixed with their promises—
the all-white bedroom, say,
with its raised hearth and bite-sized logs,
light glowing through pleated shades
as it would on a day when nothing bad could possibly happen—
you imagine yourself waking among clouds of pillows,
walking barefoot across tiled floors
to lift the shade and look out on the hills of Tuscany
or the white cubes of a Greek village stepping to the sea.
You feel the pull of that room like a magnet
but you move on to the Art Deco setting,
shiny with lacquer and chrome, Cole Porter
in the background, two martinis on a silver tray
and you, in black with pearls.
It's what you are, it's what you wanted all along.
Then the show's over
and you're wandering among sale-priced coffee tables
when grief hits you like a terrible headline:
Lives Lost. Empty Rooms.
All the way down on the escalator
the dead sing you their sad songs.

New Letters   JOAN STERN

BALANCE OF POWER

It does me good
to watch cold come to light
in these hills
because I'm through
splitting a winter
of birch and maple
and, pipe lit, collar up,
feel the burning
heart in horizon,
stop long enough to recall
tomorrow you will be gone
ten years. Geese will wave
past the house, and old hornets,

drunk on sun, will stagger
from clothesline to porch rail.
The urge to fly has brought me
the happiness of knowing
I can't. Look down that road:
Wind relays the quiet
belief in life
lasting another day.

Yankee   BARRY STERNLIEB

KINSWOMAN

When a woman dies,
there is a sound
in the room
of the repetition of distances, all short—
like the small dripping of snow

or the final bee
rasping, resting on a branch
before it drops.

When a women dies,
the voices in the room know
nothing more to say,
so they fall,
like dust in the shaft
of sunlight that lies across
her whitened bed.

Cottonwood   TERI R. STETTNISCH

GOING OUT TO SATURN

If you go out there,
you will find no evidence
of lichen or living crystal
or toppled cities.

It's all ammonia rain
and crushed-head moons,
bone-killing cold
and noons that take your breath away.

In that splendor of rings and eons,
you will be one atom of dust
that says of itself, I am,
and nothing listens, and there is no damnation.

Within that empty ship whose orbit is forever,
you may, if you wish, write letters

or sermons, or make music,
as I make this.

The American Scholar   DOLORES STEWART

FLIGHT

The choking de Havilland
shakes its wings and dips
at three hundred feet
below the black ceiling,
touches down and taxies easily
toward the old end of the airport.
Seeing Kansas City again, Rose, is not so hard,
though the first time it was
freezing and beautiful—the night, the circumference
burning, illumined still brighter by the cold,
high air, and I was waking in your arms
on approach at 2 a.m. half my life ago.
                                        This time
I'm half in love with death, my wife
tells me, fly as though my life were over.
The children have her face, her stunned look,
press around me and wait among the debris
that's mine and not mine. I look out constantly
at the weather, she says, when I should be listening.

Rose, alive then, your hair streaming
against my eyes like power off a black wing tip,
two hundred-fifty knots, and a window open,
we lived on air. I know
you were only half in love with me, half
with the speed we kept clear to Kansas City.
Where the world stops overnight, they used to say.
Where some stop forever.
Above all the shitty corn, over the littered towns,
gliding in low tonight alone over the abortions,
the small deaths, the years of waste.
Coming into Kansas City on instruments,
Rose, what a pretty town when you break through.

Mississippi Review   FRANK STEWART

DEAR WEATHERMAN:

Will it rain
like the figurehead of a ship
or simply drizzle
low fires on the prairie?

Will the high pressure
push across my childhood
thirsty for salt or
remain steady like the ankles
of a horse?

Beneath this remarkably
clear summer sky,
we glimpse tomorrow's
red face, probing the dead
sculpted tree trunk
of yesterday.

I have seen your smile
in the soft dark of radar.
I have heard your whisper
in the silence after rain,
"One of everything, to go."

Dear Weatherman,
tell me where the percentages lie,
umbrella or coffin,
tell me which—
With only two hands,
my arms are long enough
to grasp only one.

Crosscurrents   JOHN STICKNEY

WHAT HAVE YOU HEARD LATELY?

What have you heard lately from Sulphur Trestle?
Nothing, huh? Nothing worth telling.
No news is bad news.
Nobody got killed? A tree never fell on nobody?
Not a soul smashed to jelly in a side-swiped flivver,
Or blowed up at a sawmill?
Dag-gone!

Hey! You say Buck Sampson got six months
For taming his high-stepping floozy,
Though she deserved every lick he hit her?
Now you're talking!
So Lily Jenkins went crazy and stripped in the courthouse square?
And you and your ex-wife are still going round and round?
And "Gone With the Wind" is back at the Bijou?
And that old doll who broke us both in
Is still switching her tail about town?

And how are you?
Doing no good?
Me either.

New Letters   JAMES STILL

CHRISTMAS AT BLUE SPRING

Christmas Eve we camped at Blue Spring,
Bug, Mark and Catie, Sarah and me;
ate sandwiches by the guttering sun,
put our tent up in a scrub oak wood,
lit the lantern and played slapjack
from our sleeping bags. It was odd quiet;
once raccoons squalled over crusts, and trains
shook our sleep twice during the night;
the hammer of their running earth drove
into our bones. Their horns, leaf-
filtered, still woke up Sarah, crying.

In the morning I made coffee, fried eggs and bacon,
and we all walked the white shell road
shivering in our slept-in clothes
down to water steaming from its spring
into the frozen air. No one else was there
to see, mangered in eelgrass,
a newborn manatee by its pale mother—
and all down the run, far as the river,
thousands of fish: carp, bream and bass,
stockstill in the silent flow
no more than a fin apart,
pointing the way.

Webster Review   MARIE STILLWELL

MEMOIRS

A spool of song
unwinding line by line
rolls underneath my door.
It's not a tune I know;
but once on a Paris street
a man in a blue beret
went whistling by,
and I remember.

Arizona Quarterly   MARY STIRLING

FOGGY NOTION

It is midnight and a slice of moon
Reflects off branches of the trees
We sat under. I walk in the dangerous rain and watch
Cars roll home toward hangovers
And vows that seem important
During the short hours between breakfast and betrayal.

There are many wrong solutions
To the crossword of our families and jobs. All the Downs
Are film stars and islands off the coast of Spain.
Everything Across is money in one of its masks.

We struggle on through marriages and reruns
Of the seasons and the rain. One can't even
Eat dry chicken and peas on a tray in safety. A gorilla
Or a topless girl is bound to turn up
With birthday greetings and
A kiss on the cheek from Aunt Harriett.

I wear expensive, ugly modern clothes and stab people
With jewelry. Music is the rope we grab
From the windows of skyscrapers, where we sleep alone
With memories of festivals and fields
And years when unsafe sex brought only babies.

The tears fall and the pages turn, revealing answers.
They backstroke toward us on the waves
Of sure forgotten things,
Then flip and disappear as the tide rolls out.

Poetry   ALISON STONE

A TRENTA-SEI FOR JOHN CIARDI
(1916-1986)

(Love should intend realities: goodbye.)
                    —John Ciardi

In the beginning was the word, as noted
(in the end, too, if truth be known)—
Mercy next, then Love, and, gravel-throated,
a distinctive Grace enduring as the stone.
From these were made a better man than most.
We say good-bye today, old crow, gruff ghost.

In the end, too, if truth be known,
was clean white paper waiting under a pen—
a gift of hand, eye, ear, and knucklebone
from Boston to Vermont and back again
to Jersey, Georgia, Key West—in every state
he came to talk and stayed to celebrate

Mercy next, then Love. And, gravel-throated,
the man became the word on which he fed
until he fed us all—and what he quoted
was from the major kingdom in his head
comprised not least of children's poems—crows,
pythons, sharks with teeth in rows.

A distinctive Grace enduring as the stone
or bronze or steel sculptors bring to life

he brought to his—and ours—though not alone,
for one enduring grace became his wife:
To her he'd bow and gratefully concede
that men have always married what they need.

From these were made a better man than most
who moved the word from mind to pen to writing
and made the books from wisdom and a host
of wars he never seemed to tire of fighting,
especially those he thought he'd surely win
(as well as some he reveled in like sin).

We say good-bye today, old crow, gruff ghost.
That's never worked before—and will not now.
No good comes of good-bye. Instead, a toast
(in whatever form the authorities will allow)
to you—to us—in minor fifths and thirds.
Along the way you found we'll find the words.

The American Scholar   JOHN STONE

THE DEAD PIGEON

Once in Venice, in St. Mark's, I stopped
to watch a child, a girl of two or three,
bending to study a pigeon that had dropped
dead as a duck in that pure certainty.

I think now of the other death in Venice—
of Aschenbach not rising from his chair,
of gondolas and their enduring menace,
and of the child, her wonderment and stare.

Death divides us all to shape and shadow—
pigeons, children, old men on the beach.
Those left must learn the language of the widow
to speak to those who move just out of reach.

Two have made it back, according to Word.
Neither one was Aschenbach—or the bird.

The American Scholar   JOHN STONE

NAMES

My grandmother's name was Nora Swan.
Old Aden Swan was her father. But who was her mother?
I don't know my great grandmother's name.
I don't know how many children she bore.
Like rings of a tree the years of woman's fertility.
Who were my great aunt Swans?
For every year a child; diptheria, dropsey, typhoid.

Who can bother naming all those women churning butter,
leaning on scrub boards, holding to iron bedposts
sweating in labor? My grandmother knew the names
of all the plants on the mountain. Those were the names
she spoke of to me. Sorrel, lamb's ear, spleenwort, heal-all;
never go hungry, she said, when you can gather a pot of greens.
She had a finely drawn head under a smooth cap of hair
pulled back to a bun. Her deep-set eyes were quick to notice
in love and anger. Who are the women who nurtured her for me?
Who handed her in swaddling flannel to my great grandmother's breast?
Who are the women who brought my great grandmother tea
and straightened her bed? As anemone in mid-summer, the air
cannot find them and grandmother's been at rest for forty years.
In me are all the names I can remember—pennyroyal, boneset,
bed straw, toad flax—from whom I did descend in perpetuity.

Contemporary New England Poetry   RUTH STONE

DESCENDANTS

Plumed seed-tops traced the passage
Of the rain as it veered in, then swerved away.
A Hereford grazing near the fence looked up,
White jaw grinding back and forth. A magpie
Squawked and shook its feathers, disappeared
Beyond the path now overgrown with brush.
We pushed dead lilac limbs aside and,
Kneeling, read the broken headstones—HOOFARD,
FROWEIN, JONES—farmers and their women, children,
Who just a century ago had stood
Where we were crouching, hats crumpled in their hands,
And prayed to something far beyond the rain-
Streaked meadow, their feet, like ours, scraping earth.

Buffalo Spree   ROBERT JOE STOUT

ROUTINES

It is the commonplace that keeps us sane,
the ritual smile, the key that turns the lock.
The skull holds to its flesh while these remain.

Like a child's prayer, the often sung refrain
that in the dark he clings to like a rock,
it is the commonplace that keeps us sane.

Wood smoke in fall, in spring sweet smells of rain
and northbound flights of geese flock on flock,
the skull holds to its flesh while these remain.

Even bitter breakfast cup and lonely train
and in the evening the long silent walk;
it is the commonplace that keeps us sane.

We hold to our remembered paths of pain,
chanting the daily rhythms of empty talk.
The skull holds to its flesh while these remain.

We count the days that bring us to a cane,
the minutes marching by on every clock.
It is the commonplace that keeps us sane.
The skull holds to its flesh while these remain.

The Hollins Critic   BRADLEY R. STRAHAN

I THINK OF VIRGIL'S FARMER

I think of Virgil's farmer; he counts his sheep,
pulls the burrs from their wool;
his dog, black as a mulberry, stands beside him,
tail wags, tongue hangs out. I watch him lug a rock
on the steep terrace, shove it into a wall;
prune back grapevines for new growth,
drive the plow share into the recalcitrant earth.

He comes home at sunset, washes under the plane tree
by the door, sits down to brown bread and cheese,
a comb of honey. This man doesn't care
whether words are felicitous—the pigeon his gossip,
the crow his depravity, the hawk his eloquence.

At Bergama where Mark Antony stole the library
and shipped it to Cleopatra, a farmer scythes hay
by the ruins of Hadrian's Gate; red and yellow
flowers in the grass fall beside the broken columns.

Books mold, paper crumbles, the stolen library
burns at Alexandria; poetry goes up in smoke,
science flakes in the ashes.
Who wastes a life on words should know better.
They fall from the bright air like Icarus and are gone.
Rocks remain. Burrs keep growing.

Mid-American Review   ANN STRUTHERS

SPEAKING FOR MY FATHER

I'm just not the type to walk smiling
through the door, calling "Daddy's home!"
It's true. I never hope my kids will run
to climb my legs, tumble me to the floor,
snatch the silver fallen from my pockets.

As I watched my father do, I just come home.
Kiss your mother. Brush sawdust from my crewcut,
eyebrows, ears. Then retreat to pick ripe beans,
pull beets, check berries. Or with smoker, straw hat
and net, tend the bees. Or creaking like the Tin Man,

a metal spray tank strapped across my back,
to the apples, pears, and peaches up the hill.
Yes. My stride's deliberate, my steps
too far apart for company. All true. And alone,
I forget the whine of saw, ringing bang of hammer.

I know I hardly talk during dinner, attending
only to my food and plate. But, like sandpaper,
the chatter of six children grates, circling
the table; at times I clench as if I'm swallowing
nails. You've seen my face as I push the meal aside.

No. I don't change my pace for you, touch your hair
and smile. But with bruises on my hands,
misshapen thumbs, I offer what I can: smooth-finished
wood, the reddest berries, silver pails of honey
filled with every word I want to say.

Buffalo Spree   DIANE SUDOL

PACHYDERMIST

(for Diane Fossey)

> throughout childhood to the present time,
> the unity of life and death has been expressed
> by the circumference described by my trunk . . .
> —Marianne Moore, "Melanchthon"

Not knowing how to be myself for myself,
I study the elephants in the Great Rift
Valley. Delicate nuzzlers, they crop
high branches to tuck in mouths as pointed
as geometry, as commodious as Jonah's bed.
I think how communal life grew among them
with their trunks. Dependent as humans on
mothers, grandmothers, aunts, the young
learn to collect leaves in tons, to extract
salt from stones by mastery of trunk, tusks
and foot as deliberate and nice as mine
of the needle I used to obey the rules
of my mother's world. We, too, wandered
from place to place, consuming whatever
was there, our huge needs insatiable,
pressing always for more and more.

My family's ancient history is as much
beside the point as the forty million years

described by an elephant's trunk, as I live
their life on this plain between old, long
extinct volcanoes. While I see their wide
ears and backs swaying across the veld,
I am comforted. They touch each other
with trunks that detect more easily than
words what feelings are. In a dream I, too,
am belly-big, fan-eared but stuck between
salt rocks in the night cave of Kitum.
Roaring and thrashing I see all I know
lighten beyond the cavern's mouth—mother,
grandmothers, aunts, huge shapes too far away
to touch, outlined by the rising sun—
beyond them, acacia trees, bushbucks running free.

Michigan Quarterly Review   JANET SULLIVAN

TREE MAN

(for Juan)

The morning traffic begins its slow shuffle
through the city
Don Manuel slips past our garden gate
on his way to the factory
He is happy. Our bright red tomatoes
are leaping into sun
We've been awake all night

I have come from another country
one you made for me
with words. It was dusk there
but the sky gathered its colours
for a final fling
and the birds were sucking
the last flecks of light from the shadows

I watched you
You leaned against a tree
and the tree leaned back
I cannot explain except that you changed skins
Your eyes grew green and vegetal
and the tree breathed in you
blooding your breath with leaves

When you hold me now
I taste earth in your mouth
scent the musk of forest on your body
am loved as a tree loves
with all its roots and branches

The Malahat Review   ROSEMARY SULLIVAN

HOURS

When hours bend towards morning,
you will track me down
heaving handsful of white gravel
against my window.

When my season bends toward morning,
the old year will appear thin,
an old sweater lying on a deserted beach,
salt hard, sea memory clinging.

When my whole life bends towards morning,
knuckling to the hard freeze,
snow will lend a false light
to suspend roof tops like wharves.

The trees will change into odd posts.
Then you, or the snow, like migrant birds,
will take flight, wings spreading
like a wish, battering the air.

Helicon Nine   HARRIET SUSSKIND

ENDING IT

The best collar frays
in time; if my mother
were here, she would cut
it off, turn it inside-
out, and sew it back on;
and what is over could
crouch unseen and forgotten,
a weightless riding.

If you were here, and not
at the far end of my useless
life, I would take love off
like a thin refusal, and show
you the ragged edges, the
threadbare excuses I make
for my absence; and, naked
from the waist up, I'd

try to be impartial: clearly
one of us must leave, but
how can I go outside like this?

Poetry Northwest   DAVID SWANGER

UNDERWOOD FIVE

Always ready for stirring fantasies,
you hold more secrets than a psychiatrist's couch.

What I put in I get out, discovering
in the process of stating. So mute, so receptive,
something like some men's perfect wife.
Always in neutral, yet ready to go.
"Underwood Five" you call yourself, as if
you were a pastoral conspiracy. Certainly
there's a dark side; your silence is
the world's silence, too much choice that
makes despair. What I can say to you you've
probably heard before—by now you can sort out
who plays for real. Such knowledge could make you
lonely. Are you lonely? What would you say
if you could speak with your own entire voice?
Would you ban me from your Republic
to get some rest? You who have been lied to
so often, would you lie in return? You,
used by so many, each with different rhythms
and techniques, how do you retain your sense
of service? Don't you want to rush out sometimes
and be pure unexpressed emotion, non-referential,
the moment plunged in, taken so in that none of it
so much as clings to you afterwards? How do I
free you? How do you free yourself? To ignore you
would be the death of both of us. At night,
lights out, your head still ringing with
another's words, do you wonder who you are?
And the more you take it the more you get it.
Such is the stoic's fate. But I am no stoic.
I am lonely. Speak to me.

Southern Poetry Review   BRIAN SWANN

A SENSE OF DIRECTION

It was moonless the night I drove my son
to the Fargo airport after my father's burial.
Coming back, I lost myself
not so much in the roads, which though they weave
together neatly as a tictactoe box have,
like the town, become less familiar
with each visit, which themselves have become
a return associated with the nursing home,
the graveyard among the wheat fields now
that the house is sold and only one aunt remains;
but in some inner sense I lost my bearings.
Those two male lives which bordered mine,
like railroad tracks constricting it at times,
now follow their own compass. I drive alone,
all direction lost to the dark
in which I cannot find my father's voice
although my son's holds my ear, a fading diesel call.

The wind comes in my window like
the breath of silence where my father spoke.
It is as if the opening of the earth for him
has left some door ajar and I,
in this vast room of fields, am shivering in its draft.

Poets On   KAREN SWENSON

FLYING

When her granddaughter, who is the pilot, shouts "Clear!"
through the cockpit's open window and the prop begins
like the earth to make circles we can't see
so we must go on faith the sun will rise again,
my mother says from the back seat of the C-182,
"You'll have to close that window.
I'm blowing to pieces."

                                                     And I know
she remembers the yellow biplane back in 1924,
a splashy flower among the small wild ones
on the county airport's weedy strip; how my father
handed her up as the wind rippled her skirt,
showed her the joystick, the pedals for turning
the rudder right and left, how she looked down
through the floorboards and saw the grass.
"The engine fell out," she says, to explain
why they didn't elope in that plane seen mostly now
in airshows, a woman strapped to the wingstruts
and spinning above her fate, while I try to imagine
the crankshaft twisted on the runway,
pistons and cylinders scattered in the dirt.
And all that happened afterwards
flies back because I was there at that destination
they came to slowly anyway—
her frightened face, his anger,
blows, my mother crumpled at the bottom of the stairs,
the engine of their marriage dead;
and then the single mother's life she followed
with its one faint star a pilot keeps
when the whole sky goes dark, a navigator's star,
                    as now her granddaughter
sets the plane's wheels down on the tarmac
and my mother says, "Why, I hardly felt us touch,"
although the three of us have for years.

Ploughshares   JOAN SWIFT

KAYAKING AT NIGHT ON TOMALES BAY

Kayak on the black water,
and feel a gold feather float in the air.

Pick up a red shard in the dirt,
and feel someone light a
candle and sing.

A man may die crashing into a redwood house,
or die as someone pries
open an oyster.
A kayaker may hit a rock, and
drown at the bottom of a waterfall.

Is the world of the dead
a world of memory? Or a world of ten dimensions?
Calculate the number of
configurations to a tangram?
Compute the digits of pi?

Kayak on the black water,
and feel the moonlight glisten the pines.
Drift, drift, and drifting:
the lights of cars on the road take a
thousand years to arrive.

Tyuonyl   ARTHUR SZE

PRAYER

The Deer-Crossing signs are riddled with bullets,
practiced on pre-season,
and now heads of deer
tilt from car roofs, distracted.
We are their only predators.
This is our season.

The stars fatten like pearls.
Not enough light to read your face by.
And useless to wish on, as restless
as we are, growing or shrinking.
All we can do
is lend our bodies to life.

Listen, in the tall bushes a bird crying out
in a voice so like a grieving woman's,
it wrenches the apples from the trees.
Dear mother-of-pearl, firmament
in which we graze, scatter your milk.
It's so hard to feed at God's body.

The Georgia Review   DEBORAH TALL

MEN AGAINST THE SKY

From my porch I see men walk against the sky
on wooden skeletons of new roofs.

Their hammers tell me
they're raising the horizon.

The sign foretold condominiums by September.
Here it is the fall, and naked cement blocks squat,
blunt tokens in a monstrous Monopoly game,
on the last empty lot facing the boardwalk.

There's no pretending this delay means stopping
higher buildings, more expense,
for when I face the south I see
they're boarding up the sea.

Mornings I can still face east and watch the sun
filter through the spruce. By close of day,
when pollution from the city dyes the evening rose,
there's no escape—they're boarding up the sunset.

Even at night the clicking tracks
tap tap tap a warning:
one day we'll wake and find
they've boarded up the sky.

San Fernando Poetry Journal   PATTI TANA

MIDDLE-AGED-MAN, SITTING

(for John Cheever)

I never felt bad much until I was forty,
and then guilt arrived one evening.
It was as old as you would expect,
with a bad cough, fumbling across the room
towards the edge of the chair and sitting
with its face in its trembling hands
the way my father always sat.

The next year it was envy,
streaking in a classic black Porche
through another long weekend, something
new-wave but classy on the Dolby—
lolling until three in tropical hot-tubs
full of Binaca and Pepsi-Lite,
with sexual acrobats in sequined Danskins
working high without a net.

At forty-three, I'd hate to think
that this is what it means
to grow even a little old.
Tonight, on the back stoop,
after dinner with a warm beer in
one hand and the hose in the other,
watering what's left of the honeysuckle
and watching the swallows swoop
and dive beyond my neighbor's roofs,

I imagine regret tomorrow,
a possible smile on its crooky face,
going through the trash in the alley
as it chooses what there is to choose
and keep, from what I have thought
I was only throwing away; but no—
I know now how it is taken,
piece by dreaded piece.

Passages North   BRUCE TAYLOR

BECAUSE I DIDN'T TAKE THE PICTURE

February 28, 1985, Fairmont, West Virginia.
The plain motel stands in front of you,
the rolling, snow-patched WVA farmlands,
a few distant cows and a picnic table behind.
A gallon of red jug wine colors the gray
scene. You stand and laugh with the others,
plastic cups toasting the frozen air.
Pete looks for all the world like Ferdinand
Marcos with a silly wool cap pushed on his head;
Jim looks like my father in fatter days;
Tom looks not quite like anyone except, perhaps,
a linebacker or someone's nearly forgotten cousin;
and you look as you'll always look to me,
like those pictures from your childhood, a sly
sidelong glance at whoever took the picture.
You tell me to take the picture;
I leave the camera in its box.
Now, in some bottomless future, no one
need wonder whose faces those were smudging
the implacable landscape; no one need guess
our ages when the shutter clicked or try to date
us by our clothes, invent lives for us they wish
they'd had. Now they'll know who and where
we were that day so long ago—and they'll know
it was I who wrote this, the real picture.

Puerto Del Sol   JAMES TAYLOR

FAMILY TONES

When my sisters and I once
Shrieked at the injustice
Of one wearing what another
Had ironed, when we still
Exploded about the empty
Communal shampoo bottle late
Saturday, when we snarled

About whose turn it was
To wash dishes and bellowed
Over a locked bathroom door
Moments before a date,
And we were enemies before
And after we were confidants,
Life was too loud for love.

Now, as we quietly untangle
The knots of sibling stress
And softly straighten those
Threads which bind us blood
To blood, as our whispers
Weave the past into pleasant
Patterns, as our soft-spoken
Understanding fuses ragged
Pieces of memory, as silent
Touch mends the repeating
Pain of present tears, we
Find life knitting with each
Gentle click of days, our
Lives in even, parallel rows.

The DeKalb Literary Arts Journal   SALLY TAYLOR

END OF THE WORLD

The day of the end of the world
will be clean and ordered
as the notebook of the best student.
The town drunk
will sleep in a ditch,
the express train will pass
without stopping in the station,
and the band of the Regiment
will try to play forever
the march that it played 20 years ago in the plaza.
Except that some children
will leave their tangled fears
in the telephone wires,
to return crying to their houses
without knowing what to say to their mothers,
and I will carve my initials
in the bark of a linden
thinking that it will serve for nothing.

The evangelicals will leave for the corners
to sing their hymns as usual.
The crazy old lady will parade with her parasol.
And I will say: "The world can't end

because the doves and pigeons
are still fighting for grain in the patio."

New Letters   JORGES TEILLIER
                                          *—Translated from the Spanish
                                                  by Mary Crow*

TROPICAL ARCHITECTURE

What seems to have been lacking
when I first admired the palm trees,
the Royal Palms,
was remembering how certain Egyptian columns
swell out like slender ladies
neatly wrapped down to the feet,
to a mathematical elegance of line
found, more often than not,
in natural things—
like those horizontally banded trees
rising grey-brown straight
toward parenthetical curves,
and a bright green Modigliani neck
above which unwieldy coiffures
click and interlace in the breeze.

The Hudson Review   PATRICIA TERRY

MILLY HAYES, FREE FROM THE SHACKS

In a shack too hot for summer, with the air going nowhere
    and the flies wanting to come in to settle down,
    I thought, maybe I would marry him.

In a shack he left me in with my words crumpled on the floor
    and my favorite *Lovingkindness* like a candy wrapper
    after the sweetness has gone, I thought, maybe
    we could work something out.

In a shack called home because he was in it, and I woke
    to the sun thinking it was him but all that glow
    now gone to a darkness he says will not be ending,
    I thought, wait a little and even the world turns back.

The world turns now in an apple tree with my hand
    up to a fruit like a sun.

The world turns the wind to sweep up the branches
    coming around me in a hug.

The world spins the day into the long sweetness of work,
    soft as grace on the hearts of those who have nothing
    at home to go home to.

In these slow, heavy moments I will not rush through,
I think: these full luminous apples. These leaves,
cool on my mouth like a respectful kiss.

Mississippi Review   ZONA TETI

THERE IS A SADNESS

I keep it locked inside a box,
inside a room, locked
inside of me. The walls are painted gray.
In this place, nothing else can exist.

For some, sadness is an elevator shaft
where they fall endlessly . . .

for others, a pile of promises,
broken and snapping in fire.

And many say it is the rancid breath
forced from lungs, past fangs,
turning to steam that condenses to form
a long rolling tear
reverberating
across the hills.

Sadness is a grave. We place whatever is dead
at the bottom, shovel and kick dirt
until we can stand in the daylight,
only to place flowers that decay
like discarded flesh,
then walk away, wishing we could turn back,
breathe life into it,
and maybe laugh again.

Croton Review   MARK THALMAN

LOW TIDE AT GABRIOLA

The water has pulled back
                beyond the reefs.
Starfish, seaweed, multi-sized crabs
and boulders swarming with barnacles
are left stranded
at the mercy of the noon-tide
                            sun.

The seaweed stinks—
the greens, oranges, reds paling
as colour-giving wetness
is sucked out into the
dead stillness of air.

Even the seals on the rocks
have dried out dead-brown
as we walk the tide's low
               edge,
and I wonder if crabs
     starfish
     seaweed
and barnacled boulders ache
for the incoming baptism,
or long to enclose the sea.

Event　　　　　　　　　　PHILIP THATCHER

MORE JAYS

During breakfast this morning I watched two jays
building a nest in a hickory fork.
Driven by the season, filled by the fire
greening up bluegrass, blazing soft rays
into jonquils, they sped about their work.
My empty grapefruit wheel will soon retire
to my compost heap, become rich earth.
By the time the jays warm black-speckled eggs,
the tree will have stirred awake, spread leaves.
I look at my children, quick-catch my breath:
they're changing so fast. No use begging
the gods for time—all's allotted. I leave
my table, this center of our nest,
caught up in spring's irresistible zest.

Kansas Quarterly　　　　　　JIM THOMAS

TRAIN

The sound *is* haunting,
lonesome,
even when it isn't
steam. We need the night
train's aching song,
still, to coax us from
the stillness
of sleep, to help us
recall the people
we left at lights-out,
and who left us.
We need this moving
and unseen train
to sound our isolation—
those who go,
and those left behind,

waving
in either direction.

CutBank   GARY THOMPSON

MOST BONES ARE BOWED A BIT

Try taking the straight lines
out of any landscape
and you'll probably find yourself
erasing telephone poles and wires,
houses, roads, antennas, fences,
streetlights, signs and bridges.
Most trees grow a little crooked,
rivers bend, shorelines squiggle,
hills are pocked, flatlands lumpy.
Birds don't fly straight,
smoke must be coaxed up a chimney,
flames, like clouds, are anarchists,
lightning flashes jaggedly,
and even the horizon is rounded
by bent sunbeams.

Crosscurrents   JOHN THOMPSON

THE LIGHT ON THE DOOR

Something about that old house we passed
In the last town. Orleans? Coventry?
The door with long glass oval.
The pale light, failing light, canted on the blind surface,
The glow from the bevel rainbowed,
Caved in on time, on history.

Nothing in nature so catches at the well of sadness
As this, nothing. Not evocative mist
Slow-wreathing through budded woodlands,
Not breeze-blown, rippling lake water as it laps ashore,
Not warm violets shaded,
Not airy honeysuckle lattice.

This pang can come anywhere. What is the reason? I think
Such light, lilac, slopes across lives almost ours
That we didn't have—a weight
As of a slumbering presence within the walls
Of old houses, an immanence
Brooding. What we longed for.

Almost as if we could open the burnished door,
Step inside a hallway, a rose-dark room with high ceiling,
And, looking out from the other side

Through wavery glass of a tall window, find life in a lost year,
Old sunlight, rung chimes. Shimmer
Of the possible. Out of reach. Ours.

The Hudson Review   PHYLLIS HOGE THOMPSON

SHAKY CHARLIE TALKS ABOUT HIS YOUTH

In North Dakota we plant early, and we
open the ditches before the river thaws.
The water you get must last.
We sow more seed each year than we'll need,
in case the spring's dry and the summer hot,
or the cattle will die next winter.

He said this at harvest time on the Marne,
in the earthquake evenings with no stars,
the farmland shaking like a slaughtered cow,
and in the machine gun mornings, the tin
cups, the coffee burning his numb lips.

And he said it again, alone in the muddy trench,
his hearing stunned, his limbs quaking.
He was saying it when they found him,
and he repeated it like a liturgy
to the sterile hospital walls.

Forty years later, he still talks about it
as his sister smiles and helps him drink
coffee. Her grandchildren laugh at his stories—
Shaky Charlie. Every month she drives him to Fargo
where he says it again and the doctor laughs.
They all remember the prairie of his youth.

Cottonwood   TERRY TIERNEY

I DO NOT REMEMBER THIS

Trees, this time of Spring, begin to grow
more and more noisy birds. The wind once
again learns how to play the chimes.
The birds learn again how to play the wind.

We, on the other hand, remember all of this
from before. Like last night at dusk,
birds skimming low over the lake.
The sun begins to lift itself higher and higher.

There is no sorrow for the slow death of Winter.
Daffodils and forsythia attend its funeral,
and we are comforted once again by
the color yellow, and red-winged blackbirds.

We know there is some strange energy
in the air, no matter where we are.
Every year we want it to become part of us,
to remove rocks forever from our eyes.

So pray, dear memory, we may forget the past.
And chant at dawn the odd words of our
waking dreams: I do not remember this,
I do not remember anything like this.

The Sun   WILLIAM TIMMERMAN

BRANDYWINE

The gold field spreads out from the river
like a dusty wing. The air is dry and hot.
It could be August—but it's March.
We are out walking, the whole family, single file,
along paths that were impassible
when we first came here late last July.
Then, the river banks were covered with vines,
thistles, briars—such a weight of green
we all stopped fighting anything but thorns and heat—
and humidity so high it was like living inside a mouth.
Today we all walk silently. It's as if we've reached a clearing
inside ourselves where there is exactly
what stretches out before us: to the right, a field gold
with dead grasses, to the left a wide, slow-moving river.
Around our feet, red winged beetles flutter up,
drift to rest on the bent grasses, the few new leaves.
We round a bend in the river and see two canoes
drifting sideways to the current. Nosing close
to the bank, they buffet each other. They are both
filled with men. There is loud talk, laughter, among them.
They are probably drunk. They are all young.
"What's happening?" they ask me. They assume
we are alone, my son and I. Even when you pass them,
five minutes later, I'm not sure they will connect us,
we seem so separate. This is accurate
as the day is accurate, and for a moment painless
as an unbaited hook scraping again and again
the river's quivering flank.

Southern Poetry Review   HEATHER TOSTESON

THE SINGER

It is May, and she is a long way from Ohio.
Light floods the restless room,
catching the faint sag of her chin.

Distracted, you take a drink and curse the crowded heat.
She stands there singing in this sweating light,
stammering the words to another country song.
There is no wind and her hair moves softly toward you.

She sings, she moves out of the light
and into the olive dark; shadows you had not seen before
come down over her eyes, and her pale fingers
tremble with the words.
When one hand plays against the shadow's billowing edge,
you see her fingers broken and ragged,
the knuckles dry and weathered like rope.

Singing like this, she forgets everything:
the audience, the desperate appeals of the drunks.
She leaves herself out.
And after she has finished and gone,
you walk for hours, dumb and glad.
These streets are safer, housed in amber light—
the small wind through the leaves, the words you cannot say.

The Chariton Review   ANN TOWNSEND

A PROPOSAL

    May's up on crowsfeet
    this morning, crisp
    as our bacon, the cracked corn
    I scattered on the walk
    a snack for the blackbirds
    between roadside meals.

    Crow, they say, is braggadocio.
    Worse, they call it deathhound,
    meathawk, a warning.
    I say call it the bell of this day:
    regal, preposterous,
    the perfect black act.

    A crow will eat its father
    neat to the feather,
    call for its cousins
    to join the last sweetmeal,
    a feast on filial meat
    to beak and holy bone.

    I say we could eat one another
    for breakfast.
    We could pick the flesh
    of our new dead
    in communion, calling it
    Brahma, the bloodwine.

Think of your mother's rib
on a spit, turning
like the slow wheel
of universe. Afterwards,
how clean the bone of love,
how she would fly back to you.

Poet Lore   JUDITH BALDWIN TOY

ON RECEIVING A GIFT OF A DIGITAL WATCH

There is no twelve to twelve
on the clock of my mind.
There is no now
of ticks and tocks,
of nights and days,
of winters and springs.
There is no now that joins my past
from twelve to twelve.
No now that passes into memory.
Now is now as dead is dead.
It is not wound up with life
Like lust with love,
or love with death.
Now is the watch of death
on the clock of my mind.

I mind your gift in honor of my birth.
On the face of it,
a sequence of numbers punctuated by two dots.
Two dots on: two dots off—
a momentary stare turned blank.
Without motion or sound,
without past or future,
the dots are there again,
simply there again and again and again,
like the genes of time replicating
now and now and now
on the digital of my mind.

Northeast Journal   PAUL TRAINOR

PRAYER FOR THE IRISH SETTER

Two red dogs come running
toward you from the street.
They shake their heads, their feet
tear at the windfall like hooves
as they see you and turn wide

in a curve across the lawn,
all joints and feathers,
jaws slack, tongues, leathers
blown back, their raised eyes
wild, flaring like horns.

Once they were hunters,
but those who thought they loved them
lost themselves in their beauty.
Now they are blood ruined
and trying to get away.

Behind them someone is calling.
You pray they ignore his voice
this time, refusing to stop
until they clear town, disappear
into raspberry, thistle

multiflora rose,
that they search there
among the blossoms and thorns
for what still remains
of their interrupted lives,

and that some morning,
in the limpness of your own sleep,
you will hear their delicate
footfalls outside, and worn
nails scratching below your window.

Zone 3   ROBERT TREMMEL

WHAT REMAINS

Whitened by frost and salt, narrow roads
stitch what remains of these farms to the landscape
in patterns as precise, from above, as maps.
Seen from down here, they inhabit us,

refuse the impartial view. Though we can't
define exactly the season's dry obsession
with stalk and branch, we see the gist
of alders advancing past lines of downed fence

and sense something in the way buildings
dispose themselves at dusk—barns leaning,
houses with windows boarded, shingles rotted,
hollow gestures against December's threat.

Bucket in hand, the only man we've seen
all day rounds the corner of a swaybacked shed,
stares hard as we drive past—
                              my dead grandfather

come back in his old red mackinaw
to finish the evening chores, remind me again
of something important I didn't do.

Canadian Literature   ERIC TRETHEWEY

WALKING BACK

I have no business here, a bearded stranger
circling the block, beginning to draw looks
from the man pruning his forsythia, the housewife
who calls the children in from jumprope. Dutch elm
disease has thinned the landscape, let afternoon
sunlight glare off grass and sidewalks. Everything
looks too new. Our house is green now, with patio
and lawn where tufts of rye grass used to stall
our mower till my father called it quits and took
to working weekends at the office. Even
our frontyard maple's forgotten my mark beneath
thirty-five new rings. Up the street,
Skrija's grocery store has lost its musty heart
of oak and penny candy. A neon sign
announces "Guns and Ammo" above barred
windows and a yellow metal door. Still,
there's the bump at Sixtieth and Grove—ready as ever
for the next no-hander showing off for his idea
of the girl who'd like his looks—and the blue jays
and the locusts and the tack of ripe asphalt.

Like those who stare, I wonder what I want,
whether I'm dangerous or simply need directions.
Today, hundreds, maybe thousands of us search
the old neighborhoods for clues: initials in a sidewalk,
a rusty nail pounded in a tree, a wish still floating
near the school, where a small ghost, waiting on the last
bell, rubs the shiny nickel in his pocket.

Poetry   WILLIAM TROWBRIDGE

THEY DO IT ALL ON PURPOSE

They do it on purpose, you see.
When they meet and gaze into each other's eyes and see something
they like when they speak seriously sometimes insincerely both
full of grandiose bravado and deep emotion and cheap motives and
veiled sad mysteries gnawing at them from the past when they
first touch and then again and an emotional explosion jolts them
and clear thinking heads for the door when they kiss when they
join flesh and find their time together precious and every day is

grander and brighter and they are joined in soul and become one—
All this they do on purpose.
When they begin to relax and get lazy and stop looking and begin
speaking less flippantly and more seriously though at times
insincerely and veiled sad mysteries begin raising their tortured
heads and solid ground becomes mud when they get scared and
lonely and see nobody but strangers even when they are holding
another's flesh against theirs and they sleep on a bed of gravel
and the nights are long and sleepless and days are spent in
stupors when dreams of other times and places other names and
faces begin and all they want is escape when they chop it in two
and wrench away and leave a bleeding stump where once if only for
a short while there was something good and they depart screaming
lies on their lips and embrace terror only to become another of
the other's sad veiled mysteries and they kiss a lot goodbye and
learn to walk like ghosts—
They do it all on purpose.
Get it?

Kansas Quarterly   ROBERT C. TRUSSELL

BLUE, ALL THE WAY TO CANADA

They say the Cheyenne were partial to Chryslers,
for the Chrysler is a well-travelling car
tolerant of abuse and virile in a fray;
and the Cheyenne were people of the far horizon,
always on the move, war-partying it up,
chasing the buffalo and the good times,
running north to see their cousin the Sioux,
and then south again when their welcome wore out.

Spring and fall, off they'd go, the whole nation
packed into upwards of five hundred Newports,
generally white four-door models gussied-up
with warpaint zig-zagged on the fenders,
and the back seats piled high with tepee skins,
lodge poles, firewood, squalling kids, pemmican—
all that Cheyenne caboodle rolling along
on big under-inflated whitewall tires.

Riding shotgun, skirts hiked up and dirty toes
propped on the dashboards, the women suckled babies
and fooled with the radios, while the braves
up-and-downshifted, jockeying for position,
each one of them as handsome as Elvis Presley
before he got all weird and fat and Vegas—
Chrysler after Chrysler sliding through the grass
under a sky that went blue all the way to Canada.

The Literary Review   JIM TUCKER

RITUAL

My sins gather on the correcting tape.
I press Tape Load Lever A to the right
(it always works—the diagram is magic),
turn Tape Spool B slightly clock-wise
(no reasons can be given)
and remove Take-up Spool (lift heavenward).
In my fingers the rejected letters spiral
frantic as a prayer wheel;
I toss them away. The collected errors are gone.
My hands are not even dirty.

Negative Capability   MEMYE CURTIS TUCKER

POPCORN MAN

The kettle tweet tweet cracked the night:
The popcorn man wheeled his barrow into view.
He had hot chestnuts, peanuts and candied
Red apples in the long front tray,
And in back, in the lighted glass house,
Warm popcorn lay in drifts against the panes.

The popcorn man came from where tales live.
He was stumpy, with sinewy summer arms
And a weathered face. Off season
He would be a woodchopper or seaman, any job
That had time in it for whittling,
For he had a carver's hands and eyes.
He wore baggy trousers that bundled
At his shoes, and a race-goer's cap.

The singing steam brought parents
And their children into the street.
The two-wheeled barrow stopped at the curb;
He let it down on its long back legs,
And opening the glass doors began scooping
Popcorn into thin white bags. He poured
Salt from a metal shaker and butter
From a chipped enamel kettle,
Staining the paper.

From summers before he knew us, and we
Him, not by name
But as a part of summer,
Coming and going through the cooling
Streets summer after summer.
And then one summer he stopped
And never came again.

America   JOHN TULLY

RACCOONS, THE MOST ARTICULATE

Even in dreams these masked hawkers of sound
pad in on slippered feet, gaze at the moon,
sniff their fastidious noses, and tilt their
sensitive silver-tipped ears to catch vibes,
too high-pitched or faint for most receivers.

On summer nights, when a bright moonwedge
mirrors itself in their green-gold eyes,
they are trilling and churring songs
that shiver the spine, screeching like owls,
or humming their kits to sleep in tremolos.

In August, they watch the corn patch from the woods,
pull down experimental stalks, testing for honey
or gold. Always they know when the ears are ready.
They drink the sweet milk by moonlight—
it dribbles down over their whiskers and tasseled chins.

They may be the last voyeurs,
able to see in all directions,
rolling round pebbles between their hands for joy.
Each night they sharpen claws for the prowl,
pausing only to test for scent and sound.

Southern Poetry Review   JEAN L. TUPPER

THE STRANGER

I was always a stranger.
Sometimes I thought myself in everyone's hands,
between light and shadow,
my voice among the voices.
A friendship like a bird's heart
would soak my hands.

And suddenly things turned their back on me,
leaving me in the center of a light
so pale, so cold . . .
Like bones.
Like fish just died.
I trembled. I looked
at the back of things—
napes, spines,
strange heels
the confused reverse of smiles,
the saddest and dustiest secret
that no one confesses to. I tried to
leave that light in which nothing
seemed—nor was—as before.

Why me?
My lips froze
with sadness.
What if I existed
without seeing myself exist!
Perhaps for so little . . .

When the light formed again
and my body revolved in everyone's hands
—between light and shadow,
my voice among the voices—
a distant memory would oppress me.
I am still a stranger.

The American Poetry Review   JULIA UCEDA
—Translated from the Spanish
by Noël M. Valis

MY MOTHER IS NOT WATCHING

from the door as I start my first
walk to school. I am not afraid,

though this crisp eyelet
dress feels like someone else's skin

and these houses—
tall faces turning

away. This morning
my mother gets to stay

where she chooses, raising
one shoulder, cradling the phone

so her hands are free to coat each
nail to a shield over each

pale finger. Smoke from her cigarette
curls across the table like the breath

of a visitor, the glamorous
woman she secretly loves.

In this dress I'm her dream
and no one's daughter.

School is a story whose ending
she tells me she doesn't know.

Now she opens the paper to follow
a war far away, while I march

into autumn, beneath the fences
and high windows which in time

I won't see—just
the blackboard worn thin

with words that vanish
each night. I will find my way

through their sounds, a song
unwinding, and one day

I will open a book and not
notice I'm reading.

Poetry   LESLIE ULLMAN

FIRST TRIP TO THE FUN HOUSE:
CRYSTAL BEACH

In the densest Fun House mirror
I widen like a toad to the edge of space
while, miraculous, upside down, pinhead to pinhead,
I float above myself, widening upside down to nowhere space.

Oh, you can do it with soupspoons:
upside-down in the bowl, right-side-up on the back.
I did it when I was eight.

But here in the Fun House, in public, it is terrible,
and I squirm, knowing your twelve-year-old eyes
see my ten-year-old distortions.
Then, even/Steven:
your skirt blown up above your shoulders,
arms flapping: modesty.

In the Fun House it is all One Way.
We line up for the spinning disc that no one can cling to
and the giant barrel that tumbles us, helpless,
to the two-story-high no-way-back oblivion slide:
oh, darkness: threads, cobwebs, screams.

Over my shoulder, I watch your mouth twist.
"Close your eyes," I say.
Your nails dig into my shoulders;
your legs lock my waist.
"Next time we'll be grown up, maybe," I think, letting go,
staring into the whirlpool dark coming toward us,
closing my eyes as the first threads of darkness change.

Then I hear your scream:
it is terrible,
an inverse mirror floating, terrible,
above my mouth's screaming.

The Southern Review   JOHN UNTERECKER

ODE TO ENTROPY

Some day—can it be believed?—
in the year 10^{70} or so,
single electrons and positrons will orbit
one another to form atoms bonded
across regions of space
greater than the present observable universe.
"Heat death" will prevail.
The stars long since will have burnt their hydrogen
and turned to iron.
Even the black holes will have decayed.
Entropy!
thou seal on extinction,
thou curse on Creation.
All change distributes energy,
spills what cannot be gathered again.
Each meal, each smile,
each footrace to the well by Jack and Jill
scatters treasure, lets fall
gold straws once woven from the resurgent dust.
The night sky blazes with Byzantine waste.
The bird's throbbing is expenditure,
and the tide's soughing,
and the tungsten filament illumining my hand.

A ramp has been built into probability
the universe cannot re-ascend.
For our small span,
the sun has fuel, the moon lifts the lulling sea,
the highway shudders with stolen hydrocarbons.
How measure these inequalities
so massive and luminous
in which one's self is secreted
like a jewel mislaid in mountains of garbage?
Or like that bright infant Prince William,
with his whorled nostrils and blank blue eyes,
to whom empire and all its estates are already assigned.
Does its final diffusion
deny a miracle?
Those future voids are scrims of the mind,
pedagogic as blackboards.

Did you know
that four fifths of the body's intake goes merely
to maintain our temperature of 98.6°?
Or that Karl Barth, addressing prisoners, said
the prayer for stronger faith is the one prayer
that has never been denied?
Death exists nowhere in nature, not
in the minds of birds or the consciousness of flowers,
not even in the numb brain of the wildebeest calf
gone under to the grinning crocodile, nowhere

in the mesh of woods or the tons of sea, only
in our forebodings, our formulae.
There is still enough energy in one overlooked star
to power all the heavens madmen have ever proposed.

Michigan Quarterly Review   JOHN UPDIKE

RETURNING TO THE PORT OF AUTHORITY: A PICARESQUE

(Some New Yorkers refer to the Port Authority
Building, where all buses enter and leave New
York, as the Port of Authority)

Where are they going, the crowds that pass in the street?
I had not thought life had undone so many,
So many men and women, seeking the port of authority,
Safe anchorage, harbor, asylum.
                                        Late at night
They are the voices on the radio, asking the hard questions;
Or they don't ask. The homeless, the hunted,
The haunted, the night-watchers
Who can't wait any longer for morning,
                                        where are they going?

Returning, revenant, I see Eighth Avenue is a poem,
Seventh and Broadway are epics, Fifth an extravaganza
From the winos and freaks at its feet in Washington Square
(Past once-white buildings, long-ago sidewalk cafes
Behind grimy privet, Fourteenth Street's brash interruption)
To the crossover at Twenty-third.
                                        At Thirty-fourth,
The mammoth parade of department stores begins,
And, on the pavement, a cacophony of hawkers
That stretches beyond the stone lions, the bravura
Of Forty-second, to a kind of apotheosis
At Fifty-ninth.
                        O prevalence of pinnacles!
O persistence of uniformed doormen sounding, in the rain,
Your peremptory whistles! On Madison and Third
I am assaulted by florists' windows
Bursting with tropical blooms, I'm magnetized
By the windows of jewelry shops, by vegetables
Displayed like jewels; I'm buffeted
By the turbulence of this stream
Of life, this lyric, this mystery,
This daily miracle-play.
                                        What impossible collaborations
Are being consummated in cloud-high offices!
How many sweaty love-acrobatics are being performed
Behind a thousand windows
In the tall imperturbable hotels!

and all day long
The restless crowds pass in the street,
Eddying and flowing like the tidal rivers,
And I am carried along, flotsam like the rest,
Riding the crest of the flood down to the sea.

Tendril   CONSTANCE URDANG

A CHILD TALKING IN ITS SLEEP

The child talking in its sleep, in nighttime,
knows words that no dictionary includes.
Our ear is helpless,
our knowledge—just a hindrance.

These are words—pebbles, words—earth-lumps,
and have lain untold for ages.
These are night-words, words—owls
that secret themselves in the room before the wind of dreams.

These are worlds that come from darkness.
Their form senseless to the thought.
Their sense is already gone
but they still hesitate to follow it.

New Letters   VLADA UROSEVIC
—Translated from the Macedonian
by Zoran Ančevski, with James McKinley

BOSTON

I would never dedicate a line to you,
I swore. I wouldn't think of you again.
I'd slipped on your wet cobblestones
more than once, I'd been deceived, and bitter.
And I hated your John Hancock Bldg.,
those precise green windows looking out
in cool astonishment. I'd never trust a Yankee
city again. That pounce over the heart,
the long tearing cry of the gulls. The crashing rain.
All of this distasteful to your quiet,
meticulous streets with their superb
self-possession, exclusive and serene.
Defining themselves through themselves, classy
non-referentiality. Maybe I should be blind, too.
But I can still feel the way that large, twisted key
fit into the dark and heavy door, the door I had
to sink all my weight against for it to open.

The Small Pond Magazine   NOËL M. VALIS

THERE ARE SOME WHO HAVE TRUMPETS

There are some who have trumpets
and flugel horns
and serpents.
There are some who have clarinets
and gigantic ophicleides.
There are some who have big drums.
Brrum   Brrum   Brrum
and ran   tan   tan.
But me, I only have a kazoo
and I kazoo
from evening until morning.
Me, I only have a kazoo
but it's all the same bag to me if I play it well.

Yes, but that's it: do I play it well?

New Letters   BORIS VAN
                              —*Translated from the French*
                                        by Julia Older

TRUE NORTH:
A CELEBRATION OF AMERICAN WOMANHOOD

And O, the hay of her hair, the smell,
The sweet American girl self—
The yeast of prairies rising to her cheeks,
The hops in her bones content. I have brushed her

With a beard and without,
I have sung the little birds in her throat asleep,
And dreamed in eastern European cities
Of heat, like peach fuzz, on her limbs. It isn't

That she has more charms than European
Ladies who never shave their legs,
Or bathe themselves no more than twice
A week in the summer. No, it's the American

Loaminess of her—the pure salt wit,
The waves in her eyes when your hand's on her knee,
And how she tosses through the night
To bring you home. O true, *True North!*

Pulpsmith   LLOYD VAN BRUNT

ANOTHER CHANCE

Today the pond froze over,
where the preacher last year,

born in Holland, skating
as spring came, drowned.

Later, I'll work over again
the poem I wrote last night,
tired and sad, but still
in control, like the skater

he once was, when judgment
stood up straight against faith
and had its way with him,
and always gave another chance.

Artemis   CHARLES VANDERSEE

AUSCHWITZ PHOTOGRAPHS

I.

By what coaxing, call, or shouted
order does he pose, this one old man,
still in wing collar and necktie,
his wrinkled overcoat on which
someone has pinned a dog-eared star
falling away to show a well-cut suit?
He does not seem to see the camera
blinking at his dignity. His eyes
reflect a culture walking naked
to the flames, marked in its passage
by the simpering smiles upon the faces
of the safe keepers of this place,
the stricken looks of those they guard
waiting their turn to be destroyed,
embarrassed by the spectacle
of civilization committing suicide
in a state of indecent exposure.

II.

There must have been noise in all this
company—trains arriving, trucks, feet
scuffing the dirt, commands, the clatter
of dishes, greetings, sobs, curses, prayers
or, faintly in the darkness late at night,
a whispered song to soothe a sleepless child—
something of the sort there had to be,
long since taken by the moaning winds,
vanished like smoke from the unspeakable
ashes, and not one breath of it can be
recalled. Is it time's mercy on us that
we cannot hear the sounds of those we see
impressed upon these pages? Would any cry
we could imagine coming from their mouths

be loud enough to drown the lack of it,
the utter silence of their fixed regard
pounding like heart's blood in our ears
when, wordless, we raise our eyes to eyes?

Jewish Currents   JOHN VAN DOREN

VIEWS

First Poet:

I fly all the time, and still I'm afraid to fly.
I need to keep both feet on the ground, the earth
within reach of my eyes. In airports I comfort myself
by assessing others—look at that handsome necktie,
the weave of that suit, the portfolio (people of worth
are going to be on this plane), the pearls on that shelf
of expensive bosom, the hairdresser's art! All this
tells my shuddering spirit that God wouldn't tip
my seatmates, all these important people, from sight.
Once the stewardess passed the word that Liz
would be joined in Rome by Richard Burton, who was up
in First Class. I have never felt so safe on a flight.

Second Poet:

I, too, fly all the time, and still I tremble.
I arrive too early and sit there sweating and cold.
I read at a book but can't make out what it means.
I look around at the others as they assemble
and make a collection of the dowdy old,
backpacking young, slouched in their dusty jeans,
men who have business suits of the wrong size on,
Frizzled Hair, Greasy Hair and Drooping Hem.
Humbly they live and humbly they will die—
this scroungiest bunch of people I've ever laid eyes on.
Surely God has no special fate in mind for *them,*
I tell myself, like a plane falling out of the sky.

Poetry   MONA VAN DUYN

MISTY MORNINGS ON THE CAPE

If the sun would only come,
The sky could leap free from the grass.
Hands that are lost without home
Grope for each other and pass.

Missing each other, they grope,
Hands that are lost without home.

That cloud on the grass would leap up
If only the sun would come.

Yankee   PETER VIERECK

STILL LIFE WITH OLD MAN

He arranges things so carefully now—
the morning bath and stroll,
afternoons to read and write
a few spare words for friends
he never sees—
the last bus ride downtown,
hours he hasn't slept with cracking walls,
and how he hates the fluttering
wings of pigeons in the park.

Most things are threadbare and precise,
what it comes down to after all—
not wisdom, not even the lack of it.
He finds it impossible to explain,
like the closing lines of a poem—
one more immaculate ending
to make us for a moment
think we see
more than we really should.

Ball State University Forum   MARK VINZ

SARA'S TERRACE

Thirty five minutes from Rome
I could name all her herbs in Italian:
basilica, rosmaria—like names of the
church ladies who would nurse her that winter;
the thick bronchitis would finally kill her
three hundred days from that day; she came out

from the four cool rooms,
watering can balanced on a tray,
steel braid coiled around her nape.
Blue-green tiles framed the trellis,
peach roses just touched her hair as she walked
the tiny walkway in the sun.

"So, still the same president in America?"
"So, your garden, you still scratch like a chicken?"
And she led me to a huge clay pot
spilling oregano stalks laden with the soft green buttons.
She knew the bus stop,
the corner drugstore, three neighbors & the church.

I was the last from America to see her
alive. I counted: seven children, eighty years,
three sugars in her espresso, two petals
stuck to her black silk stocking.

West Branch   JUDITH VOLLMER

KANSAS WEATHER

She lies, they say. Embroiders her stories,
and more. She is eighty-four.

Her hair is blue, because out of the blue
comes the blessed, bearing fruits

celestial. Without a little death
she would have nothing.

Her husband died at sixty-two.
His hands were blue

and gnarled as the bark of the cottonwood.
When she was young, when her blood

was high, crops often failed, and children died.
It was not lovely in those times.

It was blue. And duplicitous as ever. But when misfortune
undergoes a transformation

into something other than it is,
then comes the time to forgive

the tiny lapses of the natural world,
the unnatural frizz and curl

of the water parsnip, for instance.
She ponders the circumstance

of imperfection and invents, where necessary,
to save her soul. Her commentary

on the texts of things is always true.
Most clearly when the air is blue.

The Yale Review   SIDNEY WADE

INSPECTING THE GARDEN AFTER DARK

A few things I know: I know that you're my son.
This back yard is your home, and you are
crawling on fat knees over this mound
of black dirt, dragging your diaper the way the night
is dragging a wet moon into the sky.
You can say *mama* and *daddy*. But you whisper

mama to onions and *daddy* to the asters.
I've already lost you. Or maybe never had you,
safe in your crib with blankets by the night light.
The asters know your kiss. It's wet as a slug's.
What do you have to do with these morning glories,
unpacking leaves, hundreds of them escaping
with umbrellas, holding their homes in their own hearts?
See how the cabbage patiently folds one day
after another over his secret name?
If I could, I'd peel your days away like leaves
and finally find the name that's yours.
I think back, December, May, leaf by leaf
to last year at this time, when your heart
was a wish in God's mouth beating to get out.

Poetry   JEANNE MURRAY WALKER

THIS SIDE OF THE WINDOW

(for BGD)

You'd turn your snow-dotted cheek my way
and ask, "What is it? What's wrong?"
And I'd watch how they settle—night's idlers—

there on your lashes—big, lazy, sleeping
ones. Perhaps I'd smile. Perhaps I'd
drag you down into the snow to make ourselves

angels. Or perhaps we'd laugh the dogs silly,
break into a fresh dash, and run to its end
the song of falling snowflakes—all the way

back, you and I, to the kitchen window
standing lit in the dark—waiting. But I'd never
tell you how, only a moment before,

I felt sure each snowflake held in its palm
a quiet "Hello" from each of my dead ones,
drifting through that other snowy evening-

world each of us, alone, carries with silent
vigor for as long as we live. And if you asked,
I'd say, you and I, we'd run a strong, laughter-

bound snow-run home to the light.

The Journal   BRUCE WALLACE

THE FEAR

Our old dog's frightened of the wind.
When a front moves through, she senses

the pressure before the sky darkens
or the air stirs. Firecrackers wake her.
She cowers on back porch or crawls
under kitchen table, inconsolable.
At night she sleeps more and more
under the bed—and that's not enough
when the curtains billow and streetlight
floods the sill. Nothing assures her.
No touch comforts the quaking in her soul
at far-off fireworks or rolls of thunder,
or the hush of dawn rain. I wake
to her watchful silhouette.
I leave my hand on her back, but she
listens, stiff, and shudders a little
from time to time. So we get up,
at least, to wait for the morning paper
and for sunrise, or for whatever it is
in snow or rain she knows is there.

The American Scholar   ROBERT WALLACE

BARN SWALLOWS

All morning they've flittered,
erratic, to the pond,
pinching mud in their beaks, then straw,
to daub under the porch eaves.
The nest grows, cosy as a woven bonnet.

I wonder why they chose
to build right over my head,
while the whole barn they're named for
goes begging? They dive-bomb me once
with every small load,
the thin air turned palpable, dangerous.

With one thrust of my putty knife
I could undo the day's work
and send these mad hatters packing.
Instead, I move off to a safe distance
and watch them stitch the air,
looping the thread of their flight
against me, pulling it tight.

Sou'wester   RONALD WALLACE

BURNING

Sunset. The front yard catches fire;
sparks start from the blackened grass,

rise in the stammering air:
So many fireflies, or stars!

Dear, the old world is burning;
tomorrow the new world will flare.
We'll awake to the conflagration:
boneset, bee balm, love grass, blazingstar.

Sou'wester   RONALD WALLACE

THE DANCER'S ZOO

The dancers, their years and tons
and yards of flesh—so much
mortality in motion, so much
anxiety aquiver to the strokes
of rock and roll—shake it,
shake it for oh what a night, shake
an amazement, just one more time.
The floor does crack up
to keep from crying.

You love them, the dancers,
magnified cartoons of health,
the flutter of their greasy flab,
their bloated butts and breasts
ballooning over tiny painted feet.

You love them, the dancers,
like elephants, pimping hippotami,
mastodons trained to play
proletarian jazz or body-music
to disguise the prostitution of retreat.

At Dorothy's Medallion, the dancers
gyrate to the tunes of grotesque taste,
unempowered to purple sequin, glove,
or otherwise prince off their shame; so,
black to the core, they dwarf your lust,
seducing the lies for which you daily pray.

The Cape Rock   JERRY W. WARD, JR.

JIM HEARST: FARMER, POET, TEACHER

Growing up, he learned the order
of the seasons and the demands
of the crops. He learned that cows,
neglected, die, that fields untilled
grow weeds, that the heart untouched
grows rocky, that the spirit untended

shrivels down, and he learned hard
that a broken neck can take you off
your feet forever at nineteen.

First he grew corn, raised calves and pigs,
stretched tight, straight fences and gave us food.
Then he had to learn to plant honest words,
and harvest poems that give us the strong
rich taste and smell of both the black Iowa
earth and truth.

At a time when most men hunkered down
before their many years, he sprouted
like a great green plant,
for he had learned to stretch taller
than most men can on tiptoe,
to put plows in the heavens
and pull down stars into the fields.

Farmer's Market   ROBERT WARD

TULIP-TREE IN BLOOM

At the time when the tulip-tree, even then rare, bloomed
By the edge of the cloistered lane,
They met, and each mildly wondered if ever again
It might be assumed
That such accident would bring them face to face
In another such astutely designed, lovely, and lonely place.
Would they part with a nod of civility—
Or stand with a tentative smile until mutual timidity
Of youth made them pass on? Almost surely not,
For spring sun was reddening westward to gild earth's heaven.
But secretly he stubbed the turf with the toe of a boot,
And his tongue went dry, his brain drained. But how could he leave
Without some recognition of her own, and beauty's, worth.
At last in panic, he set heel firmly where boot-toe had scored earth.

He mumbled something. Was gone.
She, too, with no backward look, or word, was gone,
Her gaze idly wandering the gold-flecked hill
As idly as in some store she'd pass someone never known.
But unconsciously now—or half so—she kicked at a stone.

She had married, he later heard. Oh, well, so had he!
And children both. Contentment? Why not?
Yes, a county was like a trap of propinquity,
And memories blur like old mirrors, unsilvering spot by spot.

Twenty-five years later, or so, he said to his bigger son,
"Get out the Ford, I got business over to Tarleton."
They get down the road, gravel then, but in good condition;

Then spotting the county line, the old one's keen eyes
Began to scan road-brush for a gap that might come by surprise.

"Take yore next turn left, up that lane," he said. "And slow,
For it used to be rough, and a spring's just iron, you know."
"I'd help," the son said, "if you'd say where you're trying to go."

"Just an old man's craziness, to see if ever yet
Anything's the same," he said. Then: "Hey!—that tulip-tree's gone!"
"Tulip's rare," the son said, "and dollars pay axe-handle sweat."
"Yes, rare," said the old one, slow, "yet it seems they might leave that one."

"What next?" the son asked, but got no reply,
For the hard, blue old eyes were staring at vacancy.
Or was it at something that had taken the place of the sky?

At last: "On to Tarleton. I used to have friends thereabout,
And might just drop by to see how they're making out.
At Main Street, the light, just turn right and on to the end."
"But that—that's the graveyard!" "Shore is," the old one said,
"And that makes it easy to find a friend,
If it happens at last he's decided he's dead."

Son parked the car and snoozed in the shade,
While his father, weaving from stone to stone, made
His prowling way, just now and then kneeling to peer at
Some name or a date, this or that.
And at last found one where he crouched, and lingered. Then woke his son.

The Iowa Review   ROBERT PENN WARREN

A PRAYER TO FEET

Brothers, little lookalikes, planted
right there on the ground
like two solid citizens,
like fenceposts, little
founding fathers
with your roast beef, prehensile
piggies fat for market,
your empty stay-at-homes,
your littlest, highest-pitched piggies,
good old Charter Members,
literalists of the body
pledged to be the sole support
system, day laborers—
this is just to say
don't fail me now, don't
back up or down or out,
don't get cold, or settle
for less, just keep in line,
out of trouble, on the straight
and narrow, and walk us

out that door and down that road
with style and grace.
In the name of the torso, the arms,
the legs, and the head, amen.

Yankee   MARY ANN WATERS

MORPHO

In his *Journey to the Jade Sea,*
"one of the world's greatest walkers," John Hillaby,
tells the story of the ebony child
raped and strangled
near an acacia tree in the bush in Kenya.
The game-warden who found her was mesmerized
by two large, blue-green, rarely seen butterflies
trembling upon her glazed, staring eyes,
opening and closing their wings.
Those butterflies were attracted to moisture,
lapping with their spiked, black tongues
the shallow lagoons of primeval water.
Hillaby doesn't specify, but they were probably the *Morpho* butterfly,
each lulled in the mirror of her dissolving eye.
Beauty and beauty often go hand-in-hand—
"what an attractive couple," we say—
but some beauties are too terrible to bear.
I've only seen a dead woman once,
outside of the Ridgewood Funeral Parlor.
In Amsterdam I wandered into a bar
where a three-hundred-pound nude, quite dead woman
shaded the jungle of a back-room pool table.
The club was hers, and she'd left provisions in her will
for the local populace to swill
the remaining stock in a sort of wake.
She was doused with beer
—the felt was soaked a deeper green—
and there, between her enormous thighs,
one silver-blue, scratchless, polished and buffed
            billiard ball
was blazing!
            I was hypnotized.
I think that combination was beautiful,
or was near to what we think of as beauty.
Still, I couldn't look for long.
My duty was to accept another beer
and hoist it, in her dubious honor,
remembering, in another pocket of the world,
the mutilated gift with butterflies upon her.

The Georgia Review   MICHAEL WATERS

CARROUSEL

Raven to blackbird,
Redwing to oriole,
Oriole to house wren,
So the seasons go;
Dulled autumn warblers
Arrive before I know.

Catkin to columbine,
Bluet to chicory,
Chicory to aster
To hazel witchery.
Before the leaves are counted
Their fall is aging me.

Groundhog to cottontail,
Rabbit, chipmunk, fawn,
Whitetail to the harvest
December's rifles spawn;
The bloody roundup rattles me
As certainly as dawn.

These mix their sequence
And accelerate:
Crow, coltsfoot, clover,
Cattails, wood duck, corn;
Unceasing aging
Knells a warning horn.

And all of this is journey . . .
Safari . . . caravan . . .
Vacation, leave, sabbatical
Inevitably blend:
Calvary and Bethlehem:
Origin and End.

The Lyric   CHARLES A. WAUGAMAN

CALLING THE CATS

They have independent natures, it is widely said,
and I remember this every time I call the cats
and they won't come at night when I want to go to bed.
I go to the front door and call them by name—
I am too self conscious as a man to call "Kitty! Kitty!"
But they never come anyway—as though to prove a point.
I go to the back door, repeat the same process, listen
carefully to the sounds down close to the ground,
watch the top of the fence to see if I can catch
in the darkness a still darker leap of quietness.
Hearing none, seeing none, I pause, nevertheless,
and look out at the still darkness once again,

wondering whether they are within earshot but pay no
attention—meaningless shards of sound adrift in moonlight,
only the pine trees moving with a rhythmic pulse
and variety of vernal breath, as silver in the moon
as the voices within me. But no cat returns, no
answer to the bedtime call. They will only come
to the window sill sometimes in the hours between
our drifting off and our nocturnal habits. They appear
as part of the night, to come as scheduled Venus comes
to sit beside the moon and drift into your sleep.

Webster Review   ROBERT LEWIS WEEKS

TO THE DOG DYING

In her eyes there is a longing to not move.
She shivers in the warm room,
Old enough so the deaths overlap,
So the numbers of years begin to add up
Long past coincidence
Grows into something more tangible,
Like disease.

The light is short;
Into our path the trees' shadows fall
On our cruise around the block
Sniffing sex, pissing where we please
On the neighbor's lawns.
Seven times how many years she is
Is her dumb fate,
And she is not full of the human things
To keep her
When the scents fade.
Human things cannot keep her
Alive as we had imagined all these years.

Tendril   BRUCE WEIGL

DEAD MAN'S FLOAT

Meet me tonight on the far bank
of the *Neversink River.* At the stillest hour
between needling of cicada and scratch
of cricket there'll be a long stretch of time
until new light opens and the soft moan of doves
rejoins the steady whoosh of wind in the trees.

This river's just begging for it. Not one
soul has ever seen the bottom, despite
that clearest, most silver green of waters.
We can look straight down, and down so deep,

but not a thing slams our eye, or darkens it to ground.
So out of dusk's mild air, dive in: the diagonal swim
is endlessly cool. It seems we could make it through to
some opposite surface, where, as on the globe's other side
spun round in the teacher's hand, for someone else, submersion
is just beginning. Instead, such lovely suspense of the vertical
glide, and suspension of what can't be the next-to-last
stroke, since there is no last one. We'll put it to the test.
If this place proves true to its name, no lack of breath
will let us really fall. With no final floor for any
landing, this smoothest plunge can't ever fail.

Seneca Review   REBECCA WEINER

BARN CAT SUMMER

(for Mark Cox)

Sometimes I climb the silo
on a full moon night, tie myself
and a six pack to the top rung, smoke
and drink one after another and slowly
scrutinize the flickering details
until I can see the waterswollen
satellite in the amber bottle and lob it
high over the corn crib's
horizon of slats alive with raccoon shadows.
Under the cover of a temporary
stillness I never want to come out from,
that sickly sweetness when a wingspread
white owl drops out of the dark
and I know
I can say the thing that makes
every beer-bellied, chain-smoking
hump of self-pity as quietly
beautiful as a butterfly drying its wings,
then apologize to the bullfrogs
for the interruption, my skin
prickling with love for the humid night, love
for my heartsick vegetarian,
who built a funeral pyre for a peacock, then
smelled the flesh and ate
the thing down to its fragile
skeleton—love waiting for love's
apparition to appear in her nightshirt and say
come down before you break your neck, all
that endless arguing—and I can't
remember what sent me nowhere
you could see from a silo, foolish
one, her voice disintegrating
into beerglass fireworks over pissed-off
coons, frightened and careening

into brush, the sparking sunrise
end of my cigarette sailing after them as I
say don't come back but if you do
I've got two little twisttop darlings left,
one for the bad guy of your dreams, one
for you, if you can catch it.

Poetry   ROGER WEINGARTEN

CARL SANDBURG

In Sandburg, I
taste 5¢ popsicles,
hear the bone-rattle
of September cornhusks,
see lightning bugs
in a Ball jar.
He dashes out from
afar,
and lures me
back to childlost,
Midwest summers.

Blue Unicorn   CYNTHIA WELBOURN

THE BREAKFAST TABLE

He and she are old, and faintly
Addled, faintly: sharing the chairs together
At the breakfast table, after fifty years
Belonging to the chairs more than
To each other. No longer treasuring her,
He scorns those trivia she treasures, pays
Little heed to her gather of keepsakes
From life's past storms, or to what they portend
Of her future and less faint addle.
Why does she cherish like secrets a bent
Breakfast spoon, a cup that does not
Match his own, that funeral's albino
Flowers still rusting against the last photos
In an album, the lost cat's discarded
Whiskers laid neatly all one way
In a paper napkin, with the blacker ends
That thickened at the follicles? Nothing
Of his is hers, he knows, among all
The absurdities of her keepsaking, nothing
Except the chairs and the sitting together
Upon the chairs to share the breakfast

Table and its riddle of where one another's
Secrets have been keeping for fifty years.

The Texas Review   NANCY G. WESTERFIELD

ENGLISH ROSE GARDEN

(Oh! Blessed rage for order, pale Ramon,
The maker's rage to order the words of the sea . . .)
—Wallace Stevens

Strolling clean aisles, corners
that meet like squares on a chessboard,
I search for a scent in these obedient
flowers. Birds don't sing or stain
the wall of the fountain where
a lion's mouth roars water. Blooms
fall on soil that refuses weeds.
I look for slugs. No tender leaves
attract their trails of slime
across the dampness. Only brown edges
of sullen petals hint at possibilities.

In measured circles, women speak,
arms covered, to leaves floating
in cups painted with roses, petals
that never drop or die at the edges.
I understand now why men stood
on this path and yearned to hear
waves wash through mangrove roots
or the sound of camel bells.

The Cape Rock   DIANE WESTERGAARD

IN MEMORY OF QUINTUS HORATIUS FLACCUS

(Parcus deorum cultor et infrequens)

Out of a quiet sky the lightning exploded
into a pole not twenty steps away.

How quickly
the mind lights up, like a computer terminal.
Before the thunder had finished unrolling
back up the sky,
we knew it was not a terrorist
or gasmain exploding. Merely
static electricity, its sudden overload to the system.

We moved on to another parking space
and even later, coming out of the movie,
we walked wide of that particular pole—
a simple precaution

against what is not supposed to happen twice,
out of a sky that is not even angry.

We've come a long way from the blasted oak
and God, the Father, throwing
spears at us for no good reason.

We've not come all that far from adrenalin
charging the brain; the circuitry
smoking like the altar of the god
at Thebes. There's something. Something to live up to.

The Chariton Review   BRUCE WETTEROTH

THE WAY IN IS THE WAY OUT

I was older than the others
and walked into the laboratory
through the reek of decay and formaldehyde,
shutting the door behind me;

sunlight fell in rectangles
over rows of sheeted forms
and the bones of dangling skeletons
and the prosector
performing his last task
of dusting the tables;
there
in cylindrical jars
pig-faced foetuses goggled
and students nudging past
set a bare brain quivering;
was this
the soft coral where
Tennyson saw a blind life?
Eliot's multifoliate rose?

I joined the others beside the cadaver:
laid on its cloth-covered chest
scalpel, forcepts, needle and scissors;

and the first cut
was the putting together.

Event   PAT WHEATLEY

THE LETTERS

Every week since freshman year
I wrote my mother. It was my one
and only claim to the status of Good Daughter
and she worked it—boasted of it

to her friends whose children only wrote
when funds were low or a new grandchild
was born. I was glad to do it.
It eased my conscience for the fact
that I'd rather write than visit.
And it was nice to know that some-
one cared about the new porch steps,
the acceptance from a magazine that
no one ever heard of, the quarrel with
the neighbors, the good tenant
who went into the monastery, the
death of the favorite cat. If
she had kept those letters, I'd
have a diary of all my weeks, an
invaluable resource for
future biographers. Of course
she didn't. The attic would have
sagged with twenty years of boxes
full of letters. People just
don't save them anymore. And now
there's no one interested in those
new tires I got at discount rates,
the awful poetry reading, the cold
that seemed it would never end, the
good French wine. I sit and stare
at a sheet of paper in the typewriter.
It is not her I miss.
It is myself.

The American Scholar   GAIL WHITE

NET, LAKE, SIEVE

Here are these mirrors,
one broken, one framed in red,
and three in neat little boxes
that hinge open.
Look at yourselves for one minute.

While you look,
cells are sloughing off,
atoms are multiplying,
the light is changing.
No two instants are alike.

You with your sweet hair
clinging about your face;
you with your loving black eyes,
and you, who have dared
to reveal yourself to me,

look, look hard
into the brittle lake
of our fragile morning.
Only the eye of the mind
can record us whole.

Crosscurrents　　　　　RUTH WHITMAN

ON THE RETURN OF HALLEY'S COMET

Omen, apparition, long-awaited peacock's tail—
who will not ask you, as you flicker fifty moons wide,
of news from some other earth, afraid for this one?
Is there another world for us to embrace? More lives?
Or do we shuttle like you, back and forth,
from black to blackness, an unaccountable freak,
an orphan among stars? In our written history
we cannot keep the appointment with the Self—
the hour when the fist breaks, opposites crystallize—
while you double back out of the ox-blood arctic
of Jupiter's gravity, across the Babylonian tablets
and the lives of Confucius, Attila the Hun,
Seneca, Cortez and Twain—a matchflame lit
from ice hurtling through necessary violence.

Your eternity remains a predictable seduction
with each of us here plunked into ground,
a branch of star wormwood tangled up with the beyond.
Three million years ago we did not share the slumber
of the tapeworm's eyeless world. The last three
thousand were given to clashed swords, ghostly sparks
and ornaments and, perhaps, only the next three million
will tell if the earth will take cuttings watered
with sweat in years of drought, if our poor roots
will cut to the fat loam, draw blood from eternity,
make our moment mortal and understood, or whether,
like you, the crown of the skull will remain as wide
as the heavens above and as difficult to read . . .

Poetry　　　　　　　　　　　　　J. P. WHITE

WINTER

The moon so bright tonight
that three crows flying low cast
shadows like scythes
through the cornfield
they gleaned months back. The road

is dirt-familiar. Fences I know
post by post stretch out

their strange new selves
on the ground. The spruce creak
overhead, smoke-soft. Out here,

no one around,
I sing a little and heat
fills my throat. I love my boots,
slap of rubber on calf. I love how
the song never cracks, for once.

I want to walk on and on, keep
going as if no house
were waiting, no friend stood
by the kitchen window, heating
something in a small saucepan.

A car down on the main road turns,
headlights butt against the hill,
fall back. The crows pass down
a gully of air. Cold sloshes
in my boots, has me turning,
taking back every footprint I cut
black into the white frost.

Ploughshares   NANCY WHITE

WEBS

That time again
when spiders' spinnerets
secrete silky webs;
that time when orb weavers
reweave their spiral webs each night,
spinning

by touch
alone in darkness;
that time when shamrock spiders
eat the old web
strand by strand
each evening,

creating a new one before dawn;
that time when grass spiders
attach long signal strands
to their funnels,
and insects—touching their webs—
unknowingly give the signal

for their own demise;
that time again
when worlds within worlds,

    linked by a master design,
    appear in overnight miracles,
    and we dream

    that we could be thus reborn
    anew, each day a different
    working of strands;
    that in such webs
    we could catch fragments of youth,
    store it for use

    in some long winter night;
    that we could reweave the past
    into silken webs strong
    in autumn winds
    and be studiously attuned
    to the slightest tremor,

    the faintest tapping of the strand.

Inlet   JEAN WIGGINS

BILLIE'S ROSES

Just one song he hears me sing
and he says, "Lady, you are what they call
beautiful." One song and he starts in

with the roses. Don't he know
I don't like roses? But he is as smooth
as piano keys, rides me

up and down like an old tune:
a bunch of white to match my spotlight,
red for the fire that sparks and burns

in each melody. He brings it all . . .
bangles and bracelets and cool, pearly words
that wrap around my neck

tight as the tourniquet around my arm. He says
he wants me, says he'll take care of me. And me—
Well, I say I got things to do.

I can't help it. I don't like roses. The thorns prick,
too many needles. The smell of them goes from sweet
to sour too soon. And him, he'll be gone just as soon.

Tonight, maybe I'll sing a song about them roses,
drop the buds gentle to the mike and watch all the petals
burst through dark.

Passages North   NAN WIGINGTON

GOLD

Leonardo always trembled
when he began to paint,
for when he tilted, in his mind
                he saw the pregnant mothers
pushing their baby carriages uphill, hope revealed,
attack helicopters bobbing and dodging
                across a battlefield.
Fat cooks waved their ladles before an excellent meal.

Such are the dangers of genius, real or supposed,
of one who lives merrily through childhood,
then learns that by picking up a pen, a hammer,
he can create a world. One night the burglar
steals into a bank with his glistening tools,
to spend his life locked up, dreaming of gold.

Without telling Congress, Thomas Jefferson
buys Louisiana, and a colonial nation
races toward California.
And the novice writer, as he's been told,
begins his novel, "The moment I entered the room,
I knew I'd been there before."

The Ohio Review   Peter Wild

LEISURELY LUNCH

From leftovers, you improvise.
I hover around with chitchat, wrench
at jars, finagle some caresses,

uncork the *Est! Est! Est!,* devise
new ways for pirating your kisses,
unquenched by stalling pats and smiles.

Keeping all intact, you supervise
both my maneuvers and the meal, and soon,
pouring the wine, grazing my arms,

you serve it, our coy enterprise,
even the dressing I've concocted . . .
And soon, so soon, it's time for tea.

You sip it leisurely—your eyes
imply a secret recipe
that makes such noondays linger on.

Above the plates, two circling flies,
freeloaders, buzz in idleness,
just goofing off. We've half an hour left.

The Antigonish Review   Robert Wiljer

ANGER

I killed the bee for no reason except that it was there and you
    were watching, disapproving,
which made what I would do much worse—but I was angry
    with you anyway and so I put my foot on it,
leaned on it, tested how much I'd need to make that resilient,
    resistant cartridge give way
and *crack!* abruptly, shockingly, it did give way and you
    turned sharply and sharply now
I felt myself balanced in your eyes—why should I feel myself
    so balanced always in your eyes;
isn't just this half the reason for my rage, these tendencies of
    yours, susceptibilities of mine?—
and "Why?" your eyes said, "Why?" and even as mine sent
    back my answer, "None of your affair,"
I knew that I was being once again, twice now, weighed, and
    this time, anyway, found wanting.

Ploughshares

C. K. WILLIAMS

THE AGING ACTRESS SEES HERSELF
A STARLET ON THE LATE SHOW

For centuries only painters, poets and sculptors
had to live with what they did as children.
Those who trod the boards—I love that—
said their first stumbling lines into air.
Some do still, but most of us who are known
and loved for being people we are not
have reels and reels of old film unrolling
behind us nearly as far as we can remember.
We drag it everywhere. How would you like
your first time doing something to keep repeating
for everyone to look at all your life?

How would you like someone who used to be you
fifty years ago coming into this room?
How would you like it, never being able
to grow old all together, to have yourself
from different times of your life, running around?

How would you like never being able
to stop moving, always to be somewhere
walking, crying, kissing, slamming a door?
You can feel it, millions of images moving;
no matter how small or disguised, you get tired.
How would you like never being able
completely, really, to die? I love that.

Poetry

MILLER WILLIAMS

FOR LUCINDA, ROBERT, AND KARYN

I leave you these, good daughters and honest son,
to have or toss away
when all is said and done:

a name that rocks like a boat; some thoughts begun;
a fondness for instruments I didn't play.
I leave you these, fair daughters and far son:

a sense of the probable (the one
sure anchor for the brain); a place to stay
as long as it stands. When all is said and done

you'll share the glory I won, or might have won,
for things I said or things I meant to say.
I leave you these, tough daughters and rocky son:

a tick no springs or brain or batteries run;
the valley in the mattress where I lay.
When all is said and done,

I'll leave my unpaid debts to everyone,
a slow love and resentment's sweet decay.
I'll leave you to yourselves, my daughters, my son,
when what's to say and do has been said and done.

Yankee   MILLER WILLIAMS

SOMETHING NEW

My sweet land is not yet growing
with honeysuckle and shadow.
Along the creek slopes, moss clings
to winter, damp fibers ringing
the memory of wildflowers and sun.
All winter I have felt jonquils
bursting from my skin, cats crazy
for warm rolling grass,
the silver flames of spring colors along my creek.
I know if one more season comes,
a chance will rise for me
to brush these stray failings back,
to rush once more at love
as if it were seasonal,
the sound of wings, the color of light.

Poem   PHILIP LEE WILLIAMS

A PIECE OF TEXAS

It is true Texas—
land of hills, windmills and whipporwills,

where hound dogs chase jack rabbits across fields
of cotton and corn, and the possums and armadillos
scamper for cover.
The land spreads eastward to meet the dawn
and westward into crimson sunset and blue twilight.
It's a golden inheritance. Part of it belongs to me,
        and it's for sale, sale, sale!

The panorama of pretty pictures are masterpieces.
Ponds of clear, sparkling water mirror the faces
of coyotes, foxes and coons; golden autumn leaves
frame portraits of the deer and the songbirds.
Cattle, sheep and horses graze in green pastures
near a red barn, and roosters crow on fence posts.
Mockingbirds trill heart-touching songs at sunrise.
It's a piece of beautiful Texas—for sale,
        and going, going, going!

The pictures shift and change with the seasons.
In spring, bluejays and cardinals fly over
the blossoming wild plum; mother cottontails hover
with their babies in the bluebonnets and buttercups.
In summer, night winds strum tunes through tall trees
standing like silvered harps in moonlight.
The scenes soon shift to autumn reds and golds;
then shift again into winter landscapes
of crystal ice and softly falling snowflakes.
We are sacrificing a piece of Texas.
        It's going, going, GONE!

      *   *   *   *   *

It is SOLD—
a piece of Texas crowned with a billion stars,
putting on the greatest show Earth has ever seen!
It's GONE—a man's gloryland, a woman's dreamland,
a child's wonderland,
a piece of Texas signed away with five names
scribbled in black ink—
all these beautiful things
exchanged for a few pieces of fragile paper—
        and a piece of my broken heart.

Encore   MARJORIE BURNEY WILLIS

ALLHALLOWS EVE

Absorbing smoke
from Camel cigarettes,
my mother slouches
in a corner arm chair
farthest from the door.
As I enter the house armed

with books, the screen door,
snapping shut behind me,
she offers no welcome.
Dim light makes only
her outline visible,
shoulders rolled forward,
coffee mug refilled
with bourbon. I venture
a greeting. In the answering
silence, I watch her hunch
toward the ashtray.
Outside, October leaves
rustle across concrete;
brown pine needles drip onto
dusty flower beds; shadows stretch
arms against stucco walls.
I grope through darkness
to my room.

The Centennial Review   JILL WILSON

IMMORTALITY

A flat white light falls
from the window, drains color
from the distant landscape
which hangs like a photograph
framed by watery curtains.
When the bell rings again,
and an infant is wheeled in
curled on its plastic tray,
you recognize the small blue
features of silence. Your fingers
trace lips still closed
on their dark river, the soft
fists grasping nothing
but dusklight, the buried eyes
rowing toward the world. It seems
you have always known
the stranger in your arms:

You listen to the slow breathing
of a memory without origin
and imagine this is how happiness
arrives, like a shadow lengthening
from a previous existence,
a music spilling from your dreams
and carrying off these gloved
smiles, these heavy-scented flowers.
You wonder if the white seas
of eternity sing like the heart

rocking in your hands.
Across the room the darkening

mirror gives up its anxious faces,
closes its book of pale words,
and toward sleep you fall back once
again into the empire of the body,
as if it alone were capable of faith.
Through the window you glimpse
the anatomy of clouds, the stars
pulsing through the membranes
of the sky, as night, crying
softly, flows from the earth's
bleeding side.

The Hollins Critic   WILLIAM WINFIELD

PLACES

Today in tiny Roslindale where
my most recent concern was finding
a good parking space   A man
has come to speak to the Cambodian
children who go to Winter Hill
School just up the street
from St. Theresa's   I watch the

news clip on TV introduced by a
pretty anchorwoman with perfect
nails   "We are survivors" he tells
them   "My story is your story
The story of the Jews in the
Holocaust   The Armenian genocide
We are a part of a history we must

never forget"   I see a young boy
place his hand on the shoulder of
the girl in front of him   His
fingers tighten and when she turns
to comfort him the camera catches
a look in her eyes that is
punctuation to these words   His story

Her story too   There they are
Kids from Winter Hill School   With
pictures on the walls and pencils
in their desks   Come back to tell
that there are places where they
murder children   Places where
they wake to bombs   Places where
blood still slides like the sea

Cottonwood   SHARYN WOLF

NOW I WEAR

Now I wear a strong-seamed cloak
you have given me against the bleakness of your season.
And I pace and repace the autumn
garden where I caught your heart's faint odor—
in the blackened vine two figures disappear,
joined like the maple's twin seed.

You sit with your back to the entrance,
hermaphroditic in this limbo. You're an old woman
bent over a square of dark embroidery.
You're a boy hiding his nightmare.
You hesitate. You've become the echo in mid-flight.

Before I'm with you, I can feel
a clear hunger burnish walls to gold.
I trace a familiar path across your shoulders
and taste the lichen's melancholy,
its endless chain-of-being turned to dust. I remember
how even in the current of your sleep you braced yourself
against the gesture latent in your hands.

And I go to meet it, so it will not happen.
My legs signal and like a kite
I snap and unfurl,
held in the breath you took to tell me something.

Carolina Quarterly   DEBORAH WOODARD

NIGHT CAFES

Some come like awakenings,
Some as expectations realized.
Some are advertised
Miles before the highways
Bring us to them.

Neon, brick and glass,
They illuminate memory,
The uncertain black faces of fields.
Their duty is to measure, in light,
Long voids of continental night,
Force darkness to recede
However briefly, however falsely.

Or, night cafes are not so much places
As intangible things, states of dreams
One needs to feel, longs to know,
Some vague warmth,
Company during nocturnal wanderings.

Inside them,
Real ones with fluorescent glow,

Imagined ones ahead in asphalt mirage—
We are all beginning to look the same:
Edward Hopper retrospectives
With souls scratched by the soul of Münch.

Crosscurrents   CHRISTOPHER WOODS

A REPLY TO THE JOURNALIST WHO INFORMED THE RUSSIAN PEOPLE IN *IZVESTIA* THAT THERE WAS NO SANTA CLAUS

When the arsenal of obloquy is rehearsed,
It seems better not to exist
Than be named as a warmonger imperialist,
A bloodsucking stooge of a parasite.
Say what you will,
This unreal fatman was never a Trotskyite.

The fripperies of capitalism are held up
To the grim light of truth. The pup
Little Jimmy wanted, the wind-up duck,
Monopoly game, drum, dump truck
And doll are all the creatures of bucks.

So much for altruism and this myth
That ignored the state. There are no gifts—
Only duties, facts, schedules, jobs, shifts.
Everyone is equal—you earn your keep.
Roll over and get a good night's sleep;
No one is coming down the chimney
To frighten children and disguise the sordid
Inequities of gain. You are safer than safe.
No dream will ever let you escape.

Poetry   BARON WORMSER

CANTEEN

With rope and iron stakes, I pitch
the regulation tent, raise it
to a taut right angle of green canvas,
a tangent to the weedy square
of rocks and clay that served
as our backyard in Vinings, Georgia, in 1968.
With the collapsing spade, I scratch a hole
where my hip will lie in sleep,
comfortable, a flexing bone
protruding into earth. I lay down
the liner from your poncho,
camouflage mottled in green.
This makeshift floor weighs ounces,

smells like machine oil
under the mildew of the tent.
I gather fist-sized stones
for the circle of my fire,
sticks of pine, maple, beech,
handfuls of dry pine straw.
My canteen is full of apple juice
and I am ready to battle the mess-kit.
The tent flap folded back, I watch
the fire burn orange, then blue,
listen for crickets and tree frogs.
I think of you at Omaha Beach, my eyes
full of documentary footage,
"The World at War," "Victory at Sea."

Now what's left of bivouac
is this dulled steel canteen,
and I keep moving
to smaller apartments.
The box where I keep it
is in one home
or another.

Kansas Quarterly   THEODORE WOROZBYT, JR.

MY FATHER GIVES ME STILTS

Deep summer, the spots under the swings
already mud hard, he leans the stilts
against the barn for me to find. I swing out
from the cherry tree where I spend
that dreamy July, and he's watching
from the tractor when I grab the pine poles
wrong and fall over hard. I hear him laugh
that chesty laugh, slosh through
wet grass to show me how.
"Here, you grab them from the front,
you wrap your arms around like this!"
And off he goes, clomping down the road,
picking his big feet up off the gravel,
right through puddles, grinning back
where I stand in my skinned knees, clapping.
He yells, "Once I walked two miles
on these, just to see if I could!"

Then I learn, and I tower everywhere,
one whole summer better than the rest,
preferring my grand and awkward height
to the earth, "flittin' in the heavenlies
again," Mom says, her philosophy that
you have to come down sometime.

But two feet up I disagree, and Father smiles
from far off as I pole straight-faced
over black clods, cement blocks, everything.
To be like him whenever I choose, gaining
his stature on a whim! The mischief sticks,
and I almost never fall.

Passages North   JAN WORTH

THE SKULL OF A SNOWSHOE HARE

I found it in the woods, moss-mottled,
hung at the jaws by a filament
of leathery flesh. We have painted it
with chlorox, bleached it
in that chemical sun, boiled loose
the last tatters of tissue,
and made of it an heirloom,
a trophy, a thing that lasts, death's
little message to an eight-year-old boy.

What should it mean to us now
in its moon-white vigil on the desk?
Light from the hallway makes it loom
puff-ball brilliant, and I look.
For no good reason but longing
I am here in your room,
straightening the covers, moving a toy,
and lightly stroking your head—
those actions I have learned to live by.

If we relish the artifacts of death,
it's for a sign that life goes on
without us. On the mountain snows
we've seen the hare's limited hieroglyphics,
his signature again and again
where we've skied. And surely
he has paused at our long tracks there,
huddled still as moonlight, and tested
for our scents long vanished in the air.

We live and die in what we have left.
For all the moon glow of that bone
no bigger than your fist, there is more
light in the way I touch you
when you're sleeping: the little electric sparks
your woolen blankets make together,
the shape of your head clear
to my hand in the half-light,
and this page, white as my bones, and alive.

The Chariton Review   ROBERT WRIGLEY

TO MY WIFE

Beauty wears out—
It blows away like sails
Spread out to the wind.

The trousseau, smelling of sweet basil,
Sleeps in a walnut chest—
The sleep of virginity.

The downy mattress and the satin quilt have gone.
Dealers in second-hand wares have very, very deep sacks.
They never return what they buy.

Those happy moments
That blossomed when hope kissed them
Have turned into flowers dried on their branches.

Beauty will wear out, except
The beauty, like a ripe fruit, of the woman
With whom, for years, you have shared a pillow.

New Letters   OZCAN YALIM
—Translated from the Turkish
by O. Yalim, W. Fielder and Dionis Riggs

THE MIRROR'S OTHER SIDE

The mirror that I held
showed your past imperfect
and your present indicative.
Just ask Alice the dangers
of lingering in the looking glass:
you are suspended
in one-dimensional space.

If the image crumbles,
it must be due to
a flaw in the mirror.
Go, Narcissus, find another glass.
It is so much easier
than finding yourself
and loving someone else.

Crosscurrents   DENISE STAMP YANNONE

WINTER RAIN

I dream for awhile now in California,
Only it is raining differently
From what I have ever seen before—

The orchard, lake-like, as if swelled by snow—
And will not stop until it's flooded.

I dream the plum trees are alive,
But the return of the birds can't save them.
And the clouds are edging my mind in gray,
Though I am asleep, and my eyelids
Cannot push them away.

I dream I am walking through the rows,
Under a lattice of leaves and branches.
I feel the rain come down as if it were dying,
I hear the sounds that grow behind me,
And see footprints in the water for the first time.

I dream the weight of the trees on my chest,
And each breath grows less than the rain it's timed to.
I push the trees into the air with the strength
Of my hands. I see my feet sinking,
And the birds are circling, but will not land.

Poetry   SEVAG YARALIAN

THE UNIVERSITY BOWLING ALLEY AND LOUNGE

We, here at the institute,
have forsaken existence and essence
for the clean crash of ten pins
on a hardwood floor.

Classes are taught, dissertations written,
but only the names remain the same:
The Form and Theory of the Spare;
Eros and Thanatos (the frankly feminine
curve of the pin and the blackness of the ball).
Approaches to Deconstruction.

There are, of course, intellectual risks:
The ambiguity of a split.
The constant chance of a gutter ball,
the unimaginable zero score.
And always, always,
the potential for heartbreak
in the beautiful woman who brings
beer from the bar.

The Cape Rock   DON ZANCANCELLA

SEEING MY SON

Splitting wood on the snowy slope that drops
behind my house, I take a breather from

a knotty slab of hickory and look out
over the frozen lake. Goalie, I call,
the wind taking my voice and raising spindrifts.
Goalie! Again, louder. Dropping the maul
and starting down to get beyond the trees,
I suddenly see him, a dot on the disc of snow,
the blankness stretching from the bristling
side of the mountain—little lake,
but like the tundra now. Black-hooded Goalie,
little moonface, fat and padded, the dog
bounding before him like a loose basketball,
almost out of bounds—both so small,
I think they must disappear. Four years old,
so bleak, so brave, so far away
and in focus, absolutely silent, falling—
lying still just once, too long—up again,
circling back, the dog making larger circles
around him. All that space for running! It makes
the emptiness look fun. I should call him back,
but then? I have work to do before the storm.

    Later, beside the stove, the dog stretched out
at our feet, the house so full of noise and warmth
that an icy peace will seem to grow, elsewhere,
I will read to him and his little brother—
eyebrows, eyelids, close as a Holbein portrait—
"This Is the House That Jack Built," which they know
by heart. I don't see into that. I don't
see anything but snow. Goalie. Goalie.

Yankee   WILLIAM ZANDER

DAYLIGHT IN THE SWAMP

It is a long time since I smelled pine sawdust
Fresh and clean, a little resinous pitch
Still in the smell, when it is as fresh as it was
In the hurried, transient mills of my childhood,
Each gnawing its share of wartime profit.
It has been a long time since I heard the scream
Of the circular blade, scream shifting tones
As the sawyer brought the log
Against the blurring teeth.

I was a tallymarker, once, in a little mill.
Edgerman also, and splitterman,
And we sawed oak, as well as pine,
So I know, too, the smell of fresh-cut red oak
So green the sap sprayed when the metal bit,
and my shirt grew damp from the planks I piled away
From my side of the saw,

Before I left the mill for another war.
It is pine I think of now, the smell of pine.

That mill is gone, with others of its kind.
Our clearings overgrown, the sawyer dead.
The chuffing engine that drove the belt
That ran the mill
Is rusted junk, long since.
An axe scar on my leg still shows
From days in the woods when we cut the logs
To haul back to the mill.

We were a low milestone between
Paul Bunyan, Bangor Tigers and today,
When juniper and blackberry contend with new growth timber
Where our clearings were.

And yet, across the years, sometimes
A memory engages, like the old mill gears,
And I could swear I smell again
The aromatic death perfume
Of Yankee pine.

The Emrys Journal   JOHN P. ZANES

CHAMPAGNE ON THE M

(For Sara)

We climb the night's spiral
trail to the giant
concrete M
masoned to a steep face
above Missoula, climb one I-beam leg,
whitewashed and looming—the northern lights'
ladder of soft blues
runged in a Gemini rain—climb to celebrate
33 years of breathing, the miraculous
stamina of the heart and how
everything finally comes down
to this involuntary rumble
and punch of one fist-sized muscle.

Sara the veterinarian pulls a magnum
of "American Pink Beauty" from her pack
as if delivering a calf or lamb,
and I swear we can hear champagne
fizzling in a drizzle high above
the city's neon-streetlight-traffic buzz,
hum, and hiss. So fresh from cloud,
this rain tinctures
our sparkling wine to an elixir
we drink looking up

through long-stemmed crystal, a fairyland
goblet of stars. We huddle closer,
still catching wind, and learn
how hearts have hop-step
ways of keeping cadence
with one another. Our glasses clink
to miracle, to muscle—clink to love
above Missoula—sound so unique
the universe skips a millisecond,
listens,
then gallops with us into pure blue stride.

Poetry   PAUL ZARZYSKI

WHITE HEARTS

I would have to be an angel
to stop this diminishing—
November, dark prelude,
a gray and pressing sky.
I would have to be a leaf
still threaded to a tree.
But in this season,
I feel myself wizening
and know I will soon talk less,
move in smaller ways.

I'll eat winter
squash, orange and heavy,
in bites from a wooden spoon;
read Russian novels
beside a fire.
Forgetting my dream
of water rushing over fields,
I'll remember bulbs,
white hearts
rigid in winter ground,

and stories I've heard
of Eskimos gathered
under domes of snow.
How they sit hungry and speak,
while outside, Death,
the Snow Walker, moves
over frozen tundra
Until the Old Ones,
seeing their young grown bone thin,
give up their own bodies,
walk slowly out to meet Him.

The Georgia Review   GENE ZEIGER

NIGHT SHOW AT THE PLANETARIUM

We have come inside to name the sky,
to follow the changes of the moon,
to mark the cadence of the planets.
The stars look down with their pop eyes and
I make believe it is the fourth grade again
and I am here with Miss O'Ryan,
who has prepared us diligently
for astral adventure:
"Connect the dots, and what do you think?
You can use this ——— to get a big drink!"

After all these years the astronomer
still speaks with the voice of God.
I want to giggle, as I did then with
the joy of swimming in the dark
and fall in love once more with the
silver knight who makes the magic.
"Carl Zeiss, don't you know me?
I am Stella Polaris!"

When it's over, I rise with the false dawn,
move slowly out into the night,
head back to a street tinged with
lights which spell no welcome,
to heavens which seem to be makeshift,
to a sky that is
distant and lackluster.

Yankee   L. L. ZEIGER

THE FASHION DESIGNER

Think of the satisfaction
the shoppers must gather
to be able to buy
my line of nylon pants,

like forty other lines
but distinguished: tighter
in the waist, lighter weight,
not obtrusively bright:

differences that matter
to those who know fashion,
who can discern fine shades
of style, as a blind man

reads shadows behind words,
hears the degrees of force
in steps and breaths taken,
and, weaving all, screens forms.

Some, who can even sense
color by touch, will tell
by the nerves in their fingers
my fabrics' circumspectness:

restrained in their designs
and, though always well refined,
unruffled: therefore most
sincerely defiant.

Imagine what passions
are captured in these pants:
dreams that could not rest dreaming,
nor resist the anxious hand.

The Georgia Review   RICHARD ZENITH

ZIMMER CLOSES HIS FAMILY HOME

How quickly old times empty,
Load after load, fifty years
Hauled out in a day until
Each corner has been violated.

This is the beginning of
A new kind of loneliness.
Now Zimmer has no other home
Except his own. Sometimes
It seems to him that home
Is the simple space around
His body, perhaps his very skin
As he gazes at the moon,
Hoping for a little warmth.

It is small comfort to know
That he will have to bring these
Ancient memories and pieces
Together again, put them back
Where they belong in the old house
Before he turns away to die.

It is wearisome to realize
That home is not where he goes
But where he comes from.

The Georgia Review   PAUL ZIMMER

THE POET'S STRIKE

On the stroke of this midnight
Let us cover our typewriters,
Throw down all pens and papers.

Let there be no more poems,
Not one more metaphor nor image.
No loose nor strict iambics,
No passion, anger, laughter.
Let no one cheat nor scab,
No furtive peeks in notebooks,
No secret scribbling in closets,
Let us dwell together in a void
Removed from truth and beauty.

Then let us see what will happen,
How many trees will blight,
How earth will wobble and fracture,
Words loosen and fall from dictionaries.
People will begin to move through
Life like worms swallowing
And excreting their tedious passage.
They will beg us for one crippled line,
One near rhyme, one feeble dream,
And they will be so sorry
They will pay and pay and pay.

Open Places   PAUL ZIMMER

WATERMELON RIND

(For my father)

Cloves are what I remember
in the watermelon pickles,
floating among the green cubes,
tiny clubs with spiked heads.

Long after he died we ate,
opening the last jars
for Sunday dinner, the way
it used to be—as if

he were still there,
perhaps gone to the kitchen
momentarily. Momentarily.
Oh, we ate the pickles all right,

commenting on them
as if nothing had changed—
the last batch with too much
of something, perhaps cloves;

and while we ate we talked
occasionally of him, the way
one eats pickles here and there,
the way one fills

natural pauses. We finished
the pickles without knowing

it, thinking more were
in the cellar,

surprised, briefly,
that all the jars had been emptied,
cleaned and returned
to the pantry

where they sit awaiting
the next curator of pickles,
though no one has had the ambition.
We throw out the rind now:

it has become summer garbage.
And we talk less of my father,
even on Sundays at dinner.
It seems natural that way.

Oxford Magazine   JAMES A. ZOLLER

THIS, THIS . . .

whenever it is dark in the house
I turn on a light for comfort,
a small light in the kitchen
over the sink.

in winter when the day fades,
I pull a chair to the window
to read by the light of the sunset
news of the distant world,

and the light from the kitchen
collects on the floor in dim puddles.
it reminds me that we are poor.
it reminds me of my mother

cutting sprouts from potatoes,
how she would call when I complained,
"come. look!" water pouring from the tap—
"this, this we have in abundance."

Blueline   JAMES A. ZOLLER

AN ALARM CLOCK RINGS

It's sure to be
a sleepless night.
An alarm clock has awakened somewhere,
rings and rings
and nobody shuts if off.
It shall awaken all the dead.

And where is the hand that turned it on?
A drop of water drips from the faucet and drips—
for whom does it dig a grave
in the long night?

Midstream   RAJZEL ZYCHLINSKA
                                —Translated from the Yiddish
                                        by Aaron Kramer

THE NEED FOR COFFEE BREAK AT LOCKHEED

How could you blame her
if she wandered at ten o'clock
to the end of the company garden
and sat beside a compost pile
that flies of three colors hum over,
each with its peculiar pitch in flight?
Off a shoulder, ceanothus blooming
with its harmonic of honeybees
and a bumblebee's great arcs,
as if held by a thread.

She might finger peatmoss,
steaming and feathery as a nest,
severe terrain for the line of ants
commuting from one unknown to another;
she'd stop at nasturtium's hollow smell
or chew a dandelion stem she pulled.
There in the beds, rank after rank—
calendulas! erupted out of the clay,
out of the dependable seeds—a fiery
quilt so vital she could cry out.

And at ten-fifteen she'd be back
on line, soldering circuits that guide
another Trident's missile home, scraps
from an old song drifting. Hands
prefer to forget their work; but this,
its acrid molten drops—and for what?
So she's glad for these outdoor lulls
and a garden more fertile than hers.
It's the rainy days she begins to distrust.

Southwest Review   CHARLES ATKINSON

FOR ALICE

When we were away at school together
your room was the old cedar closet;
you filled the high cupboards with empty
Smirnoff bottles, their labels gazed
into the backs of shelves.
We sat on a red rug, eating potato chips
and onion dip, and talked late,
listening to Grace Slick.
At Christmas break I waited in the bus
for you to take the seat beside me.
The branches outside breaking under ice—
a black and white frieze.

One summer at Fishers Island
I ate all the crabmeat off your parents' shelves,
unwrapping the flakes from the soaked paper,
inhaling the smell. Nights we stayed up late
drinking White Russians with your brother.
Once, I crept up to the attic with him
and lay on a mattress there. You
and your parents were downstairs, asleep,
and in the damp, under the eaves,
I bent over his stomach.

Our last fight came
after you tried to sleep with Stephen, my lover.
Your shoulders were broader than his; I remember
how your long fingers would draw a glass towards
you with the tips, how definite,
as they spun the tiny wheel on a lighter.
And now, years later, in the deep end of spring,
long past the time when the fields at school
filled with daffodils, their heads bonneted
like your family's portraits, I understand—
whom it was I wanted, looking over those fields,
breathing the opium of that air.

Painted Bride Quarterly   TINA BARR

THE DRUNK'S WIDOW

My cats must think the
housepainter's Landis;
they scatter when he
drags up his ladder.
Today, I'll rummage
in the cellar. Can't
stand this house when
the painter hammers
back the nails that

Landis beat loose for
thirty-five years.
Thirty-five years of
tenpenny nails
torture each other
in a dozen Mason
jars down there, and
a jumbled marriage
of saws and drills
lies rusting in Jim
Beam crates down there.
I've got to forget, as
I dream through his rooms,
how the three Sunday suits
hang empty of him as
they did in his life;
how the dumb boots, split
by his thick ankles,
lean in the hallway. I'll
give them to the painter
if he washes this
whiskey-yellowed house
back to white. When I
pulled in the drive
after morning Mass,
the June sun burned on
the front of the house
and I felt cleansed.
Once Landis and me
were a secret kept
bright behind doors. Then
the howling whiskey-
fits of his rage made
us everyone's talk.
I like this white.
When it flares through me,
my husband's ribs lock
cleanly with mine in
the good and secret
dark again.

Puerto Del Sol   CHARLES BEHLEN

THE SWIMMER

Sometimes when I fall from sleep
Into the cold water of consciousness,
The room awash in shadow,
Rain black and icy on the window,

And find myself diving again
And again for those bright pennies,
Day's sad but necessary coin
That flash always out of reach,

It is enough to float a moment
On my back, breathing slowly
As if everything made perfect sense;
And turning toward you then,

I touch the fine gold hairs
At the nape of your neck—
I the drowning man,
You my dream of shore.

Kansas Quarterly   RICHARD BEHM

SOME SUNDAYS

in the warmer weather we go out for walks
just when nothing moves and the sky is turning
flagstone
we need the clarity of cold
the balm of winter mist
we practice being old and simple
we pick up wood that has fallen into the street
or along other people's sidewalks
it lies lazy
or dead from hard rains or the season or age
the big logs, a cord bought years ago
outlasts the kindling
the twigs, branches, snippets of bark and leaves
we carry them back to replenish the pile
beside the mantle
we know we need to do this to start a fire
when it gets molten cold
as the Upper Peninsula or along vast dark lakes.

The Literary Review   ALICE G. BRAND

ON AN ISLAND

I am like the man
Who suddenly leaves his wife, children,
The row of blank-faced houses
He owns one of,
And disappears . . .

And turns up in some strange place—
Let's say an island—
And keeps himself separate from

The island life,
Responsible only for himself, his hut,
His scrap of garden.
Each day these responsibilities
Become imperceptibly smaller,
And he becomes stronger, more withdrawn.
The handfuls of greens become,
Shall we say, less important, uninteresting,
Abstract piles of leaves and stems.
Each day he sees himself get nearer
To what he saw himself as
All along.

And this business of mine—
Cutting my food down into smaller
And smaller proportions,
Making a game of triangles and circles
And uneaten squares,
Scraping fork against plate—
Is simply that . . .
I'm attracted to that other life,
That isolated life of perfection,
Of narrowing the peripheral vision
So that what is left becomes stronger,
The will dominant,
Shedding its flesh and passing away.

And my reaction would be the same
As that of the man on the island
If suddenly his family would appear,
Having searched him out all those years.
He would sit, detached and staring into the sun,
Having no desire to be saved.

I watch my weight drop off,
My ribs become the savage fans of my desire,
My skin disappears into the beauty
Of frank, imperturbable bone.

The Chattahoochee Review   KIM BRIDGFORD

THE WAY THE LEAVES CRACKLE

(for T. Graham)

The way the leaves crackle, the snow crunches on the ears.
The way the dog scrabbles at the rustling leaves and the snow.
He drags me to smells I cannot sense.
He knows the smell I have and do not know.
Back in the heart of the city,
I swallow pills, sell my book, file my letters, and take
    an old lady's dog out
For a walk.

Once a week, on Wednesdays,
I converse with someone,
Who, selectively, takes notes—
I, as friends tactfully put it,
Am seeing someone.

The Antigonish Review

EUGENE DUBNOV
—*Translated from the Russian*
by the author

THE WALLS OF MY HOUSE

The walls of my house are thin
and full of tiny sounds.
My own skin is thin,
the veins break easily.
My scalp can be bruised by the teeth
of a fine-toothed comb
like the one Mama pulled
through my knots, every schoolmorning,
already late to work,
mumbling *goddamn nasty kid;*
although often, those mornings, she'd stroked
my eyes with wet cotton,
coaxing the gummy lids apart.

Not knowing her children, not dead,
impervious to fear,
my neighbor lies in a coma.
Her daughter waits at her bedside
for permission to leave, or stay.
Through the thin walls, I hear
her waiting; already it's late.
She waits for a half-spoken word,
any blessing or curse,
as though waiting could coax
the sealed refusals open
or loosen the stiffened knots
our fragile bodies hold,

as though we could rise, forgiving,
from all our sleeps, and in partings
be made whole again.

Open Places

MARCIA FALK

WEST TEXAS INTERLUDE

Nine years I've jogged this stretch of unpaved road
at least four days a week and never looked
straight at the house somebody took the time

to piece together out of rock hauled in
from God knows where. Nothing here
but tumbleweeds and scrub mesquite.
A farmer has to be religious
or a fool.

The man who built this house had no choice
about the sand, the only foundation,
but he must have figured rock would settle into place;
all he had to do was look around to know it'd never wash away.
I've heard old timers swear they came here for the view.
Nothing stops the eye. "Ain't nothing gonna sneak up on you"
except this stone house the color of sand, an old woman
hugging the railing, her voice almost lost in the wind:
"He's dead! Help me, Daddy's dead!"

I didn't want to stop. At my age, it's hard to break the pace,
momentum my only motivation. But out here
you can't ignore a cry for help.
No way to rationalize it was meant for someone else.

She was fat and she stank.
What was she doing on this porch crying for her Daddy?
"Ma'am, what's wrong?"
"Oh, God, he's dead! Help me. I'll pay you money."
She pointed past the screen door to the clutter I expected:
dime-store figurines, photographs of soldiers, doilies
yellowed with sweat. A Naugahyde couch. A corpse,
open eyes and mouth. "Is he dead?
Daddy, get up! I'll pay you money."

It was not the first time I had looked into this face,
laid my ear against the chest, heard nothing but my heart.
Asian jungles convince you everyone will wear this grin,
and funeral parlors lie; so who was I to tell somebody's great grandma
after she'd dragged her body along a trail of furniture to the porch
to flag me down when any other day I'd have passed this house
an hour earlier; who was I to be the one to say:
Your Husband's Dead!

So we hugged each other to the kitchen table,
stumbling through a slippery dance to the cold meat
peeking from the Styrofoam containers Meals On Wheels had left
a hundred years ago when I was loosening up, and she was lighter,
and her husband had just come in from the garden for a nap.

TriQuarterly   ROBERT A. FINK

MEYER LEVINE

We placed this gentle, witty, eighty-four-
Year-old, the leader of our family,
Whose mental journeys into the clouded past

And jeopardy of his security
So taxed his wife we feared she might not last,
Into the best old-age facility
That we could find, not many weeks ago,
And have come, since, often to let him know
        We care for him, and more.

Still, what he knows exactly we cannot tell,
Not yet at any rate, for the reports
From personnel vary from "sweet" or "mild"
To "hard to handle" or obscene retorts
To the old man who shares his room, whose wild
Faces, he tells us, put him out of sorts
At mealtime (both have trouble chewing), directed
To mock him, he insists, and is he expected
        To put up with this hell?

We're quite confused, each one of us is torn
Trying to answer that (though the answer's Yes),
For reasons like what happened yesterday:
Strapped to his chair, of which he'd made a mess
(One broken leg), shoving it toward a fray
With the roommate, he then caught sight of us
On our way in, and named each with a smile;
Then begged carfare to go to his job for a while.
        He looked angry, forlorn,

As one of us murmured No, that surely he
Recalled that he could scarcely get around,
And asked a nurse to make a diaper-change.
When this was done, he told us he had found
A new line of hats, which, though a trifle strange,
He thought women would buy, but pressing down
The switch to turn his radio off, so we
Could hear better, proved too much for him;
        Again his eyes grew dim—

This time with tears, as he sighed lucidly
That he wished his green suit for burial,
Told whom we should invite. Another day,
Following many visitors, we all
Wheeled him out in the sun to an out-of-the-way
Corner of the garden, where we fell
(Maybe because of all the talk) quite dumb,
And, piercing the silence, he wept, "I am overcome
        By all my family."

TriQuarterly   DAVID GALLER

ONCE I WAS OLD

Rocks are falling down the mountain, even
as I look up at the peaks and count

the trees turning red and the dying stars
bursting through the grey map of the sky.
Not small stones, which find any excuse to go
their facile way, but boulders, giants of the earth,
immovable permanencies of life which, till now,
have assured me that I, too, am here to stay
for a while, as fixed in place as they.

As I look up today from the cup of autumn, the rain
starts to fall, and blackbirds cry shrilly
for me to go in—today is over for me, they warn.
One even pecks at my eyes.
It wants me to do what I'm told.

Yet today, for no reason, I find myself
fighting the slope. Shrubs tear at clothes,
seeking sensitive skin, then dig deeper,
eager to start in on the underbelly
of this unaccustomed persistence.
Where are my teachers and my peers who
have climbed from the plains before me?
From neighboring heights, they call and wave
instructions, but I cannot make them out.
Am I doing right; do they want me to go on?

I only know that today the rocks
have stirred in the only way they can,
and that, for once, so have I.
March on, I tell my tired feet,
it was yesterday you were old—for but a day.
In the cool of the evening, you shall dance
in the tight hug of star-sweat.
Be still, I purr to my heart,
you shall pour your happy murmurs,
birds breathless from flights of fancy,
into the ears of the troubled and truly old;
and your ragged beats shall be sonatas,
your pills sugar-candy.

The Cape Rock   JUDAH JACOBOWITZ

DONOR

Something set it flowing
far too fast: 300 mL in
less than four minutes.
Surprised, I watched
the spurt as the slack
plastic sack fattened
with amazing swiftness.
I heard alarmed voices
as my vision clouded,

then tunneled: black
all around, then out.

Coming to: a window
opened, the cold air
delicious, delicious
the paper cup of cold
water held to my lips.
The needle nursed out,
a quick deft compress,
then a gauze tourniquet
strangling my arm's neat
pin-prick, and me, having
given, giddily coming back.

Southern Humanities Review   KATE JENNINGS

TALES FROM THE HOLOGRAPH WOODS

Where we walk, the immaculate
images of trees invent themselves—
pine, hemlock, phantom alder   apparitions
of bright air, coherent light.
Listen.   There is wind and bird-song,
orchestrated insect murmur,
the sky cloud-patterned by day,
at night a zodiac glitter.

In the green shimmer of the photon forest
we celebrate the imperishable idea of trees—
arboreal icons mirrored to infinity,
each one discrete and unambiguous.
It is only at the edge of vision
when you turn your head too quickly
that you see the pattern
beginning to repeat itself.

Now imagine a forest
rooted in dark earth
where pale threads grow
knotted, nerve-tangled,
subtle and diffuse as hidden water:
the frail web that in an older physics
held the world together.

Prism International   EILEEN KERNAGHAN

WHERE I LIVED, AND WHAT I LIVED FOR

In my late twenties I discovered that I looked eighteen.
I took a room in the pornographic district,
disowned my family to inaugurate a new

financial chapter: preparation
for my comeback to the academic world.

My undone dissertation haunted me.
My father termed it "your cul-de-sac."
Its subject was these streets, the sexual
recesses of my favorite poets, how each man
drowns in his drunken boat—my boat

the peep-show center stage I grace
in guttering light. I have always loved
sunsets. Among my looseleaf sheets
I was the sunset, a downfall, nude and blunt,
and all my labor of being penetrated

by slow degrees gives me a *déjà vu*
of learning how to read, the picture book
my master, my voyeur. Fragments of the raven's
Nevermore, Nevermore, float back to me
when I striptease: tomorrow I will leave these woods.

Boston Review   WAYNE KOESTENBAUM

BEGINNINGS

Lord, great are Your ways.
Mountains skip like
titanic explosions,
cubic miles of rock clap hands
to welcome You.
Great are Your ways and
beyond the knowledge of
woman.
Lord, all I see is
disaster.
The containment of domestic pressures, the
mending of feelings,
understanding of order moment by
hour by day—
all smashed under Your
leap of mountains.
The dust, Lord, the rubble.
Where to begin?
My vigilant broom
stutters on magnitude.

And now the hills, misbehaving
like lambs.

Beyond rough bones of rock,
I see beginnings
flex
with long eyes of Your creation.
I will discard my broom.

What would I use it
for,
to sweep up singing of the
morning stars,
their hot white glory?

The Malahat Review   ZOE LANDALË

NOTHING WILL COME OF THIS

you say. *Not a thing we can do.* The road falls
fast beneath us to the high bridge,
the gorge. We've done this so often,
driven this same way, toward the same
destination. I peer down at the creek's rocks
as if they had changed. From this height
it seems hardly a creek, it has cut down

so far, breeds such fierce short-lived foam.
But that's how I know it, in glimpses
each week past the rail.
Your hands grip the wheel.
I touch one pale knuckle.
We speed, going uphill.
Next time, I imagine, we'll drive here at night,

the water not visible, sky frost-clear, the stars
alive, cold, white, splendid, unimaginably
deep. We'll give over,
let our wills rest at last.
I'll breathe easy, my muscles slack,
the car warm, your grief
lost in the darkness, in what has not yet come.

Artemis   JEANNE LARSEN

THE CARE AND FEEDING OF POETS

is a noble task (whatever the
feminists may say); it insures

the caretaker a certain immor-
tality (if the poet is a good

one), and it also provides cer-
tain rewards in the here & now,

such as typing manuscripts and
sending poems to magazines and

entertaining the wives of other
poets who come visiting (while

the geniuses sit in the study
drinking beer), and in certain

cases being informed that one
or more ancillary muses are re-

quired to provide inspiration.

The Antigonish Review   JAMES LAUGHLIN

STEEL CLOCK

*(It is appropriate here to recall the brilliant experiment carried
out by Foucault in the Panthéon, in 1851. Unless one denies the
evidence of one's senses, this experiment makes the motion of the
Earth actually visible.)*
—Camille Flammarion

Marble arches glitter and flow, the steel ball
swings in its long curve up to my hand.
I watch my face, suspended there, grow old.
Other faces bulge and swarm, slip to the sides
of my hand as it grows; when it covers the whole ball I feel
a glass sword fall from space burning white with speed:
as it slides down its long parabola closer to earth,
forests and mountains, oceans, cities flow along its blade,
broken and jumbled as it stabs straight down
until it rests on a velvet cushion
in a glass case in the room
where the pendulum loops perpetually
trying to swing in a straight line,
trying to stay between the pegs
that are hours. It brushes against them;
they quiver, rock and fall.
My hand slips away from the side of the arc.
I cannot touch it, just as I cannot touch
my shadow that stretches or squats
because the earth is turning under it;
a wind of light, the moving sun, rushes around me
as I stand between the clock and sword. I know
nothing is fixed, nothing straight,
nothing, even the blade of the sword
that swings and slashes as it falls.

The Antioch Review   EDWARD LENSE

LEONARDO DA VINCI: UOMO UNIVERSALE

Signora, did I know Leonardo?
Ah, yes, I knew him from a letter
that I received sometime ago,
and from the equestrian statue

of my father, done in clay
but never cast in bronze. It
stood mightily as a model
in the courtyard of my palace
in Milan. But then the French
came and used the Sforza statue
as a target for archery practice.
Perhaps it was best that Leonardo
had never finished it—a vice
shadowed by his virtues. I must
admit that he was a man of virtùe.
Perhaps nostalgia deludes
me in my remembrance.
But, pray, let things be:
monumental from a distance.
In truth he is Everyman—
God's Giant of Intelligence.

Arizona Quarterly   DOMINICK J. LEPORE

FULL CIRCLE

For a while, of course,
for your own safety,
they had to tie your thin wrists
to the silver poles of your bed.
For forty-two years your right hand
had held a Lucky Strike; lately,
long past desire, cigarettes
have burned down through your fingers,
through the rough cotton gown
and into your aging skin.
When visitors come, the nurses
untie you, then your hands
hop and jerk like a pair
of mating birds. Once, for me,
you lifted your gown
and patted your flat, wrinkled breasts,
"pies" you smiled, and said, "pies."
Was it in this lifetime, mother,
that you held me to those breasts,
that I rested, however briefly,
my cheek against your skin?
Lately, you have stopped holding
a spoon, a fork, or food.
After so long, we at last
change places: I spoonfeed you.

On the third Sunday of every month
I visit. Today, as I come up the stairs,
gladiolas in my arms, I see you

on the sun porch. They have finally
found something to do with your hands:
you are holding and rocking a plastic
baby-doll, you are cooing
in a voice I've never heard.

Bend close, mother, very close,
to the ear of that child—
whisper everything you might
have forgotten to whisper, I'm listening—
say what it is we both need to hear
so that at last we can both go home.

Tar River Poetry   SUSAN LUZZARO

DINNER AT GRANDPA'S

The tablecloth spreads like a bed sheet between them.
It is as white as the black-whiskered knuckles
the old man holds in front of his face.
But it is the teeth—slashing, luminous white—
which rip at the meat, gouging and tugging,
that the small boy sees. "So eat, eat," the old man says,
stirring the air with glistening fingers,
the teeth still chewing as he speaks.
They gleam like chips of ice behind his lips.
"Can this be our Rochele's son?" the teeth intone,
a hand pointing with a bone as if it were a wand.
"Leave the boy be," the plump old woman says.
Has she been there all along? The old man grunts,
shakes out at her the slippery fingernails
of his other hand as if it were a handkerchief.
She disappears.
                    The boy lifts a meat-heavy bone
and bites, seeing the other mouth pause
as his teeth rip into flesh, shred fibers,
sink through grease and fat.
He is aware at each bite of his jaw's impact,
the hinged weight swinging up like a battering ram.
Below the mask he doesn't remember putting on,
he can sense a blunt bone face he doesn't recognize.
Each jolt, each dental thud, is resonant
and echoes everywhere through his head,
as if his cranium is the dome that surrounds the universe
where black winds snap their tails.
But the dome is cracked; shreds of black membrane
hang and flap like wallpaper from its sides.
A red wingtip stabs through a chink,
clouds of static rumble beyond the rim,
and only by working his teeth until his jaws ache
can the boy keep those clouds backed up
and the universe safe within.

When he looks up, he finds the old man's mouth has stopped,
and with slumping shoulders and a wistful grin,
the old man is smiling across the yards of tablecloth at him.

TriQuarterly   MORTON MARCUS

DEAR MONSTERS

Dear monsters, be patient.
It's sober day, and the world
overflows with light and sound
to its farthest sunny shores.
I go among the crowds, on friendly roads,
gratefully, miraculously
freed of you.
You are distant
as the thud of armies in the streets
heard from within a still, dreamy house;
as silhouettes in remote alleys
glimpsed through a golden haze of lamplight.
Yet something in the gesture, the stride
reminds me that in a strange way
these things are familiar.
Dear monsters, be patient—

because night is coming, and the heart
sick from an old guilt,
defenseless, alone,
hears the approach of footsteps,
hears and waits,
without resisting.

The American Poetry Review   ANNA MARGOLIN
                              —*Translated from the Yiddish*
                                      by Marcia Falk

SPRING?

They call this spring.
This dead sparse grass
lurking on the rims
of ditches, these nights
of mere hoar frost, instead
of frozen storm, because
time is now melting
and we hear its drip;
they call this spring.

They call this spring
because the ice is black
out to the point,

because, under the layers
of navy blue stuffed nylon,
hearts beat against their
cover like trapped birds—
and everyone is
a little mad.

Waves   CARMELITA MCGRATH

CORRESPONDENCE

He finds his place
in Professor Cody's mail-order
rules of punctuation,
licks his pencil as if it needs
to be oiled, and writes, "Dear Jim,"
then nothing for a long time.

Behind him, my mother looks up
from her boiling kettle and tells him
to mention clean clothes
and three squares a day. But this
is his letter. He writes,
"Hope your thumb is better,"
knowing it has been for years.

My aim is no better now
than the time he stood over me,
the wood and my thumb hammered,
and he whispered, "Think, think,"
and tapped my forehead to pound
the message home. When I asked
if thinking was like seeing
in the dark, he said nothing.
"The birds have robbed us blind,"
he writes. "The Cascades are clear."

There's too much paper left.
He fidgets in his chair. Maybe
his back aches from these
ten minutes of nonuse, or my mother
looks over his shoulder
and he remembers my voice
on the far side of his newspaper,
"Dad, dad . . ." Then her yelling
from the kitchen, "He's talking to you!"

He writes, "$10 enclosed for laundry,"
and licking the pencil one more time,
signs, "Love your father,"
the comma left out on purpose
and the last word started

like a ten penny nail,
with three quick strokes driven home.

The Iowa Review   JAMES McKEAN

MILITARY REUNION ON LOWER THIRD AVENUE

We exhaled war memories over warm lager,
Old Timer and I,
I not such a young timer myself.
Saxophones of nostalgia
and marimbas of derring-do
mingled in smoke, mangled
by the strident rise and fall
of saloon clamor as the comic
arm-wrestled the heroic to the beat
of old-fashioned Wurlitzer snare drums
—until laughing, crying shadows
lunged into epitaphs, valor drowned
like the tears for lost comrades
in mahogany puddles of spilled beer.
I don't remember which war it was
and have no way of answering
for my breath, but his was
a World War I gas attack, and just
at the moment the Americans
were about to win,
a pulverizing voice (no serenade)
bellowed CLOSING TIME! Grizzled,
sagging but still full of fight,
Old Timer lurched out the door
into three-in-the-morning Bowery fog
thick as the chlorine yellow air
falling at Ypres that day in 1915.
I wished good luck to his back
as he limped away
like the Spirit of '76
to wage his real war
with the crawling snail of hours;
before dawn bars would open
for another day's campaign.

Studies in Contemporary Satire   JACK McMANIS

A PHOTOGRAPH OF YEATS'S LAPIS LAZULI

Finally she sleeps beside me; to turn the radio off
would wake her and even these pages turning will make her
stir or start up with a shout. So I continue to hold
the open book, one hand hugged in hers

like an infant's toy animal, as she sleeps after screaming
and our third fight of the day, her shoulders shut upon
    themselves.

Perhaps I have enough now to fashion before she wakes
praises of our marriage, to say how some nights
all my talked-up self-esteem peels from me like skin
flashed by a weapon I went blind before I saw.
I don't know why this distance is required
to tell her of the good she's brought,

how we seem sometimes to have grown
from no hard past, no struggle, as if we'd built a ship
and sanded our frames and beams back down into the sea.
What a strained and painful love-speech I make,
like this piece of stone from which our favorite poem
was wrought, the whole so gray and puny

and the facts only half-right. Our past
and parts are never what they were: we change them.
That quarrel, for example, fails in my mind,
a brittle, false substance,
surviving as part of us, not as it was
but better when we are done,

when we have truly worked at it.

The Agni Review   MICHAEL MILBURN

LOVE SONG FOR 23 GREY HAIRS

You're of the same stuff as seagull wings. That
whiteness, that thin curling quality in air.
It's not a lie.
I've seen seagull feathers pierce the sand like forks and
knives, and I've had sympathy for the sand long before this.
My father once told me not to wear the feathers of gulls;
their call is like the cries of women, he'd said.
Now tiny awkward gulls guard my temples, saunter into and through
the darkness of my hair. Now women sadly paddle in the water.
Listen. The water is brown; you can hear them.
It is no use denying it. The ocean is a big place.
At the highschool, the gulls used to fly in from the river,
settle on the asphalt next to the school. It must have been
something in the flat grey texture, in the pebbly grain
of the lot that attracted them. So many straight white lines
were only so many grey hairs on the sea. Seagulls
must get easily confused. Yet, they know a parking lot
from an ocean; they know wood from perch.
I tell you, the ocean is a big place.
And now, like electricity flying from the sky,
like the whiteness of stormy water, I wear seagulls

in my hair; I watch the water of the ocean
in the flatness of my eyes.

The Worcester Review   JAN MORDENSKI

WAKING

In morning the world creates us
as we wake alert, uncertain
of its intent. Trees, roots grappling
the mountain, branches
tossing gravity upward, lean
from the slope. We slept under them,
nylon and canvas holding us up
from the cold which still marks
our knees and thighs. We crouch stiffly
before our small fire, watch bacon
warm and hiss, water become coffee
in the blackened pot. This is good,
our hunger and our pleasure in it.
To live unsheltered, to make fire if
and when we need it, to let it die
because we want it to, to carry
a little food, a plate and fork
on our backs—they give us a kind of power.
This is not our natural way
to live, yet we're at home here
and want nothing but ideas,
printed and bound or recalled,
to give context to our thoughts,
forming, as we seem to be,
from sunwarmed boulders.

Crosscurrents   NONA NIMNICHT

WHITE WILLOW

(Within the balm of trees we walked.)
—Nick Keyes

White willow
of ancient Indian basketweavers, of Jim Link, Potawotomi,
of July windbreaks, of round waterholders,
of well-destroyers, diviners, of European immigrants

Pliant willow of Swedish moonshiners,
of minnow tank protectors, of sauna switches, of smoked suckers,
of spawning walleyes, of cleaned blue-lunged smelt

Water willow of tornado shields, of broken bark,
of caterpillar shelters, of goldfinches crying, of cecropia moths,
of bitching red squirrels, of soon-to-be-shot porcupines

Planted willow of brothers, of tree-climbing Siberian huskies,
of burning moon shadows, of life-and death struggles,
of dead raccoons, of stretched-out guts, of empty eye sockets,
of genital-eating fishers, coyotes, bobcats on the loose

Broken willow of smashed June bugs, of lightning strikes,
of winter freeze-up, of Flicker holes, of blueberry leaves, of feral cats,
of faded wooden swings, of quiet cancer, of women in handcuffs

Fragrant willow of zealous bees, of evening hens roosting,
of bending deer, or white-tailed ballerinas, of Great Horned Owls' talons

Cracking willow of death songs, of marriage songs, of Ed Gein's corpses,
of noisy divorce, of chalky bones, of collapsing buildings, of dead foxes
    in the grass,
of Belgian horses, Babe and Queen leaving

Pregnant willow, blooming willow, first-kiss willow, dead-elm willow,
evening grosbeak willow, willow of screaming bullets—even dead
    you sprout green,

White willow.

CutBank   GENNIE NORD

HOW HISTORY AFFECTS US ALL

            chewing on a sandwich,
            corned beef and cheese,
            you study the moon
            in your German binoculars.
            you've never cared
            for what you saw in the stars.
            the sky is one big
            death camp to you,
            but it's like your grandpa said
            the year after his wife died:
            "you want to know
            how to live alone,
            go take a good look
            at the moon."

            the trees out back raking the sky
            are fingernails on a blackboard.
            the stars are bleeding paint.
            you'd like to believe
            that the last eighty years
            were some fierce mistake,
            but the moon's not helping at all.
            it's the shade of a human skin lamp,
            the mouth of a Nazi oven.
            you can see all the dead
            dancing inside.

            if you'd been the man
            who walked on the moon,

you'd have left
a charge behind,
and blown that moon
right out of the sky,
doing your grandpa one better,
learning how to live alone
from the hole
that's left in the night.

The Chattahoochie Review   CHUCK OLIVEROS

IT WON'T LAST LONG, WE THOUGHT,

this pitcher glazed with bright
naive fish, chasing each other
to breed or devour. It was no Grecian urn
but a cheap Italian import
extracted in some sweatshop
from the last of a line of potters.

I bought it at Woolworth's
for our second wedding anniversary,
that year of anger and birth.
Somehow I presented it
without demeaning you. You laid aside
your petulance to murmur thanks.

Now its rim is chipped
from a thousand usings. We've poured
from it, mixed in it, washed it
for twenty unbroken years. The fish,
forgiving and companionable now,
swim on in their slow annealing

around this made shape of clay
that year by year appears more beautiful.

Passages North   JOHN PALEN

LETTER FROM SPAIN

A letter comes with stamps—
tiny Old Master engravings.
Winter rain blackened the baroque
limestone of the *biblioteca*.
At the end of the long table
near the high weeping window,
the dark man bent over a book
thick as his wrist, traced a line
with a finger like a grandee's,
copied out the words in fine hand.

On the front of the envelope
the address is lined through,
others written in, crossed out,
more names written, a petition
in search of a cause. Unopened,
the letter, like an ugly orphan
passed from the unwilling
to the unknowing, fell to me,
the last, most distant relative.
A professor in Spain asks
with deference and precision
for help in locating an article
printed twenty years ago
in a journal long defunct.
In the forest of shelves it's
always night, nothing breathes.
Dust sleeps without dreams.
The man's hair grows gray
as he traces lines, writes, writes
on a pad of yellowing paper.

The Southern Review　　　M. B. PARRIS

ENDURANCE

I fight with words, then
go up the hill to sleep
and conscience is another word
for all the troubled dreams.
Too much is fading away like leaves
from old limbs that cannot hold green
life, the sap dried into heavy glue,
and fields seem flatter, unrelieved,
as if the grace of reason is impaired.

What is left of love is reluctance,
the stiff selfishness that won't let go,
inside a rented room with all lights on.
It is so dark outside, the world disappears
and a likeness in the window points at me,
a mirrored man moving in past visions,
and I break him with a quick right hand
that shatters a long routine of pain
like a limb snapped in aching cold.
The only voice inside the room is startling:
There is no one here to hurt but you.

Crosscurrents　　　DEAN PHELPS

EPITHALAMION

(For J. F. and D. B.)

The boy who scribbled Smash the State in icing
on his wedding cake has two kids and a coöp,
reads (although pretends not to) the Living Section
and hopes for tenure.

Everything's changed since we played Capture the Red Flag
between Harvard Yard and the river. Which of us dreamed that
History, who grinds men up like meat would
make us her next meal?

But here we are, in a kind of post-imperial
permanent February, with offices and apartments,
balked latecomers out of a Stendhal novel
our brave ambitions

run out into sand: into restaurants and movies,
July at the Cape, where the major source of amusement's
watching middle-aged Freudians snub only just younger
Marxist historians.

And yet if it's true, as I've read, that the starving body
eats itself, it's true, too, it eats the heart last.
We've lost our moment of grandeur, but come on, admit it:
aren't we happier?

And so let's welcome the child already beginning,
who'll laugh, but not cruelly, I hope, at our
    comfy nostalgias,
and praise, friends, praise, this marriage of
    friends and lovers
made in a dark time.

The Atlantic Monthly   KATHA POLLITT

WHAT HAS BEEN TAKEN AND TAKEN BACK

I. What has been denied me:

The freedom to be intense.
To move between your nerves like
spilt mercury, uncaught, running
hot or iced; wild neurons, anarchic
images behind your eyes. To feel
fully and uncensored; tasting all
emotion like honey, licking it, rolling
it over my tongue and lips. To
choreograph all my thoughts, fantasies,
hopes, passions, arguments; and long and
languid solo dance; stalking stages;
strutting down streets, swaggering.
To see my own stars at night; to

sing my own songs and symphonies.
To name my own landmarks and demons;
To harvest my own crops; to stitch and
wave my own colors and flags.

II. What I take back:

Needle and all colored threads;
The secrets of weaving at night.

Crosscurrents   EARL C. PIKE

DAY GOES SHUT

Day goes shut like a morning glory.
(Sorrow, heart, at the lilac edges).
A bluebird whistles his repertory,
Riding the foam of spirea hedges.
    And a plane drifts low
    Like a questing heron;
    From their cherry glow
    How the wings grown barren!
Day goes shut, and night lifts petals:
A black rose where star-dew settles.

The Literary Review   SISTER BERNETTA QUINN

PORTLAND

It came to him riding a subway or bus,
seeing an advertisement for Maine,
the vacation state, a picture meant to
tear at his insides, imagining fresh air,
fresh water. He had once called there
to a girl he knew; he must have been fourteen,
and she in the hospital, just coming to
after some terrible romantic accident
on a horse, and her voice was high
as if because she didn't know who
or where she was. She was drawn to him

over wires and time and several states
through to now, while he rides to work,
her voice: *oh it's you, it's good to hear* . . .
and his: *yes, are you all right—*
as if he had some obligation, or right
to know, to imagine the horse, the road,
the speed of them traveling,
her fall, as if he'd *known* her.

What happens now
in this place that isn't Maine,

in a place that isn't his or anyone's:
the girls are tall and wear their hair
formidably, and their tones are low—
he'd throw it to hell for a childish sound
like the one of the girl in the hospital
in Portland, out for two weeks
with concussion, just coming to when the
telephone rings, and it's him calling,
her voice high and reaching him
at just the right time.

NER/BLQ
(New England Review and Bread Loaf Quarterly)   ELIZABETH RICHARDS

PRAISING HANDS

My mother   visiting
puts her hands to all tasks
cleans the many places
we never think to see
then for occasional diversion lays
her hands on the piano keys.

Watching from the kitchen I
think of all the ancient
instruments she's put
her hands to
tackling stubborn keys
small feet working
the pedals of a piano or pump organ
bought in better times
on islands, in townships,
up on the bench country overlooking
miles of prairie
filling the small structures
of her faith
with music
spreading out from her
working hands filling the places round
the Word.

Now, hearing her complaint she's ancient
and can't play a thing
I smile from the places
that sing with her music:
The church is wherever God's people
are praising.

The Fiddlehead   WILLIAM B. ROBERTSON

EASTER IN BELLAGIO

Even as earth rises here, as jonquils,
hepaticas and crocuses lift skyward,
I am amazed at things that fall: camellia
petals surround the tree in a scarlet wheel;
a cypress sheds dry needles and reveals
lyre-shaped branches. In this country, rain
on the lakes is snow that dazzles mountains.
The south wind brings a phosphorous mist that blends
rock and water into one dull mirror
whose chiseled images cannot be seen.

Master of laurel, craftsman of beginnings,
watercolorist of altering light:
surely as things fade to live, and loss
makes trees grow green, just as the bells
of San Giacomo toll the hours and die,
then echo for miles in harbor towns,
the heart falls, rising. From clay-colored houses
set in these hills, the people stagger down
winding paths only to climb stone steps,
blood-colored at dawn, carrying palms.

The Yale Review   GRACE SCHULMAN

DEATH AS KINDS OF WEATHER

The scent of lemons in the room.
Leaves of the rubber tree
reflect trapezoids of light.

Whereas day paddles predictably
towards evening, there is nothing
more to demonstrate—
                              only those things
eddying in the back of the mind
prod us from our unread books
by the fire onto pristine fields.
                              Are we happy?
One can look down and see few things.
Yet there's every reason to believe
we're engaged in something that matters,
the studious raft carries us
far from where we started.

Except for the topmost branches,
                              snow backs down, and wind
has an easy time maintaining itself.
The ones we loved
are in their graves, we think of them

as part of the lesson

getting around to us.

Southern Humanities Review   SUSAN SONDE

FARMER PLOWS COUNTY TRUNK

"Sitting here, I got to think hard
to get heard. What's buried in this world
wants me off. I mean deep. The dirt's still black
and blue over something, rocks on edge with any
passing disc, worms blind with boredom
to work through. Earplugs, wind screen—I feel like nerves
locked in a tooth. My cap brim's crescent
corners what shade this field lets go
between horizons. John Deere claws earth.
Plow blades gouge furrows, shiny logs
of python, steaming carcass, earthworms, cowbirds.
Fields slide all night under the moon. Where they go,
they get chance and a river to move them?
I tell you, things a guy thinks out here
surprise you. Surprise me, I guarantee!
Wait on skulls of cabbage to crack eyelids
of light. My belly's a bobber some days,
an anchor when wind throws golf balls
of hail through humid nets of air. Lightning-smolder,
compost-steam, grackles think birthday time—
hop around, suck worms, clap wings,
glisten. JD's third wheel nudges country PP's
yellow center line. Traffic backs up so bumpers
unlock hoods. A hoot. How many farmers it takes to steer
3 wheels? Give me a chance, I'll drag out three
townships of dirt. Why they run these roads?
Grackles get here right on time.
Who's gotta get anyplace faster?"

The Spoon River Quarterly   DAVID STEINGASS

THE COLLECTOR

I conceal you
In the cellar
Like a stolen Picasso.
Alone, I go to marvel,
Admire, enjoy.
I have no urge
To boast,
To show you
To the world,
To expose you

To appraising stares.
Not because I fear
Condemnation,
But because someone
Might tell me
That you
Are a forgery.

Crosscurrents   HENRIETTA MOSER THOMPSON

SO FAR OUT OF THE WORLD

(I was living so far out of the world that this
seemed as important a thing to speak of as any
other event whatever.)
Andre Gide, *Fruits of the Earth*

I take the Indian egg basket, its handle worn smooth
with use and wired at one end where the weave has
worked apart. I empty out rotten green tomatoes
wrapped in a hank of burlap, and begin for the last
time this season to fill the basket with fresh
vegetables. I top the turnips, stoop in search of the
last carrots hidden under a light cover of snow.
Digging my fingers down, levering out stubborn
roots. The earth, which all summer has been warm
and yielding, clings to my fingers—numbing them.

As I often did when turning out the heavy rows of
sod left by a late-spring plowing, I straighten to
look over the pasture to the encircling evergreen.
The closeness of summer has retreated. Jays light
in the grizzled apple tree for its prize of frost-
bitten fruit. They rasp. The brook has crested
with the melt of early snow. It bulges coldly above
stones. On the ridge, anemic hardwood.

She looks up from the kitchen sink, sees me bending
down over the rows. She hears my footsteps pause on the
verandah, comes to open the door.

My arms embrace a basketful of roots.

The Fiddlehead   HARRY THURSTON

WINTER OVERNIGHT ON THE MOUNTAIN

From the top in all directions no movement, no man,
no object of his hand. Somewhere across the white
I imagine your fire may roar, perhaps not.
The only glow may be my core within
these layers of wool and weathered shell. My face

flush under this furred mask may be the only
remnant of the sun. When my breath blaze snuffs out
in the wind's instant, it may be the last
mammalian heat.
                              My crampons claw the mountain
like arctic insects. Below a skirt of trees,
a petticoat of tundra splays around a lake's
patch of crust. Water beneath, soft
like skin flows through sluggish fish gills,
swaying like weeds. Will spring come this year
or will these fish shrink below nuclear
cloud? Will the bears that hibernate
mutate into strange shapes and dine on
deer incinerated in pine, or will
the deer leap away? Will we escape?
                                                    If I

sleep and awaken from this coldest night
and sun reappears to draw rice again
from green bogs, will I descend to find you
as I imagine, robed, book in hand,
afghan warming your legs.

Blueline   PARKER TOWLE

MARTHA

Today the flies buzz the kitchen in peace.
Let the coats mend themselves
and the lard gleam on the stove like ice.
Let the lillies wither in the sun
and the dogs yelp at the back door.
Let the priest bind her feet in black rags.
Never mind the safety pin posing as a clasp
or the mismatched button. How much could it matter
if she missed stitching a thread or two
or sang to the dead behind the cemetery fence.
Let them pat someone else's blond rump
and praise their sluggish legs.
Let the spoons shine on their own.
She sat at the window and dreamt of maple trees,
the blue light that inhabited the scoured branches.
To her, maple trees had no pain.
In another year she'd have turned fifty,
in another hour she'll collapse in the mud.
Wish her ghost an afternoon stitched in gold leaves,
a valley scorched clean by wind.
There's bound to be lanes of maples there
to carve her broad fingers into.
Maple trees change colors. They don't seem to want much.

Poetry   JON VEINBERG

RUSSELL ELIAS

Our joints are out of time—
timeless as in a photograph,
an early tintype sandwiched
between glass and wrapped in cheesecloth
inside a strapped watertight chest
found floating on the crest of a flood—
our age not our youth preserved,
arthritic, bent, misshapen.
Who will help an old man cross
the street? He sees in his grandsons
features, muscles, bones, strength to cope,
measure up, match. They fit.
Why remember? Better to totter
on these frail bones back to bed.

2

Our songs are out of tune and blare
at us from public speakers faced
in all directions, turned so high
they shake an old man's dentures loose,
more loud than any truck or plane.
We are wired against our will
and ring like telephones and buzz
like table saws whose teeth are worn
too thin to cut the cheapest wood.
We dial and turn and tune and switch
and overload our eyes and ears.
Plugged in outlets, screwed in sockets,
our lives are shorted out, then thrown away
like bulbs that burned too bright too long.

3

Our times are out of joint and creak from too much strain.
Dull volcanic rumblings shake the world,
and earth erodes from earth to silt our waterways.
Our air's too harsh to breathe and chokes our lungs.
Yoked to all his years, an old man labors
for each breath and knows his end is near.
He looks for brighter days and warmer nights.
Get up and pull your beard. The need is now,
not later. So far forgotten, my life will last
in others' memories, my name its monument.
Let love generate love and live in the root,
not in the stem. All life grows from seeds,
and like a seed, an old man's place is in the ground.
My son, our roots are not in earth alone.

Poem   ROBERT F. WHISLER

THE RED ROOF ON TUCKERMAN AVENUE

I'm lying in bed
looking at the red tiles
that slant in a pyramid
against the sky,

a red roof across the street
that blots out Newport Bay
and the leg of ocean
stretching between me
and the far shore;

there is nothing before me
but roof and sky   yet I know
behind the roof
beneath the sky

expensive houses stand
on generous lawns,
a fisherman's skiff
parts the water,

lovers stroll
along Cliff Walk
observing the mansions,
the picturesque fisherman,

not noticing the red tiled roof
across the inlet
or the little house
where I am hidden
imagining them

The Massachusetts Review   RUTH WHITMAN

FREE AS THE SUN IS FREE

When the sun comes in straight through those windows,
I stand there, or
there, watching the leaves, or
there and drinking sweet wine by myself.
When the color starts to spread into the light,
I listen for my heart to stop beating
and begin holding on to me.

You can die of realization somehow;
You can stand so still
That your muscles will sleep,
And your heart will sleep,
And you will melt all together,
Asleep in the road like a child.

Never did I mean to confuse you
or to make myself a fool in your house.
Wasn't I pretty, though,
pretty like a movie girl—look
how my short hair shone in the light!

But that might not be enough.
Elsewhere they starve, these women, impregnate
as they are with bonus hunger.
There is evil in the sun somewhere,
And it sheets the bed I lie on.
I never meant to be alone like this;
Only I wanted to have freedom in all things.

The Literary Review   NICOLE WILKINSON

LEAVING WICHITA: THE WIND

1.

Settlers knew the prairie
for what it was:
a stopping place.
Looking hard
in every direction,
seeing nothing,
they concluded
there was no place
else to go.

2.

Nothing on the prairie
to slow the wind
but people.
People vanish:
"Wind got him, I guess."
Not bears or wolves—
just wind.

3.

Wide awake at 2 a.m.,
I listen with envy
to the excited chatter
of garbage cans
tumbling down the street
leaving town fast.

Webster Review   DON T. WILLIAMSON

THE BUTTON

My grandmother lifted a button out of her purse.
"This is the future," she said—and cried,
hiding her face in her arms
on the table my mother had built from scrap
at a time after the war when you couldn't buy anything.
In my memory that moment is a white-washed room
where I sit by my mother's table
sewing the button onto the seam of my shirt.
It's the first button I've ever sewn myself,
and my needle moves awkwardly
in and out of the four narrow button holes.
Every time I wait for the needle's silver point
to appear like a dangerous star from a black pit,
I think, "This is the future." And suddenly
I know that being afraid of the future
is being afraid of a thought—
the thought of that needle pricking my finger
the next time it comes out of its hole;
the thought that my missing father
will not return. The thread makes a white cross
between the button holes, a cross that fattens
like a chalk mark in school when we do additions.
The future is an addition, a balloon tied to the wrist,
and without me sitting here thinking,
it wouldn't even exist. Severing the thread with my teeth
I resolve never to forget this moment at my mother's table,
as though I'm born only now and whatever happens to me
from now on will be connected to this moment,
button after button down the front of my shirt.

The American Poetry Review   RENATE WOOD

THE HANGING WAVE

The summer flickered across your eyes.
Elms licked the water
as it shook its skin from the rocks.
Yes, the memory has a small inventory.
Your breasts rakishly promised benevolence
with their frank eyes.

In long greenshot impossible arcs
the wave of summer hung and fell
a long way back into caves of violet ice,
your eyes! And I gladly live with you,
wear you, worn by you, hung out to praise
on all the lines.

Southern Poetry Review   JOHN WOODS

The Indexes

Index of Titles

For alphabetization purposes in this index, the words A,
An and The have been ignored.

Index of First Lines

For alphabetization purposes in this index,
every word has been considered.

642

Books of Poetry by Contributors

*This bibliography is included as an aid for those who
wish to locate additional poetry by authors whose work
appears in the Anthology.*

A

Aal, Katharyn Machan: *Bird On A Wire* (with
Kenneth Winchester). Privately printed, 1970.
—*The Wind In The Pear Tree.* Privately printed,
1972.
—*The Book Of The Raccoon.* Gehry Press, 1977.
—*Looking For The Witches.* Fine-Arts Bluesband
& Poetry Press, 1980.
—*Where The Foxes Say Goodnight.* Scarlet Ibis
Press, 1981.
—*Conversations.* Liberty Press, 1982.
—*Seneca Street Poems.* C.O.P.E., 1982.
—*The Raccoon Book.* McBooks Press, 1982
—*Writing Home* (with Barbara Crooker). Gehry
Press, 1983.
—*Women: A Pocket Book.* Grass Roots Press,
1983.
—*Along The Rain Black Road.* Camel Press,
1986.
—*When She Was The Good-Time Girl.* Signpost
Press, 1987.
—*From Redwing.* Tamarack, 1987.

Ackerman, Diane: *The Planets: A Cosmic Pastoral.*
Morrow, 1976.
—*Wife of Light.* Morrow, 1978.
—*Lady Faustus.* Morrow, 1983.

Acorn, Milton: *In Love And Anger.* 1956.
—*Against A League Of Liars.* 1960.
—*The Brain's The Target.* 1960.
—*Jawbreakers.* 1960.
—*I've Tasted My Blood.* Ryerson Press, 1969.
—*More Poems For People.* N. C. Press, 1972.
—*The Island Means Minago.* N. C. Press, 1975.
—*Jackpine Sonnets.* Steel Rail Publishing Co.,
1977.
—*Captain Neal MacDougal & The Naked God-
dess.* Ragweed Press, 1982.
—*Dig Up My Heart.* McClelland and Stewart,
1983.
—*Whiskey Jack.* H. M. S. Press, 1986.
—*A Stand of Jackpine.* Unfinished Monument
Press, 1987.
—*The Uncollected Acorn.* Deneau, 1987.

Adilman, Mona Elaine: *Beat Of Wings.* Regency
Press, 1972.
—*Cult Of Concrete.* Bonsecours Editions, 1977.

—*Piece Work.* Borealis Press, 1980.
—*Nighty-Knight.* Pierian Press, 1986.

Adler, Carol: *Arioso.* Pentagram Press, 1975.
—*First Reading.* Northwoods Press, 1985.
—*Still Telling.* Northwoods Press, 1987.

Aguero, Kathleen: *Thirsty Day.* Alice James Books,
1977.
—*The Real Weather.* Hanging Loose Press, 1987.

Aleshire, Joan: *Cloud Train.* Texas Tech Press, 1982.
—*This Far.* Quarterly Review of Literature Poetry
Series, 1987.

Allen, Dick: *Anon And Various Time Machine Poems.*
Delacorte and Delta, 1971.
—*Regions With No proper Names.* St. Martin's
Press, 1975.
—*Overnight In The Guest House Of The Mystic.*
Louisiana State University Press, 1984.
—*Flight And Pursuit.* Louisiana State University
Press, 1987.

Allen, Gilbert: *In Everything: Poems 1972-1979.* Lo-
tus Press, 1982.

Almon, Bert: *The Return And Other Poems.* San Mar-
cos press, 1968.
—*Taking Possession.* Solo Press, 1976.
—*Poems For The Nuclear Family.* San Marcos
Press, 1979.
—*Blue Sunrise.* Thistledown Press, 1980.
—*Deep North.* Thistledown Press, 1984.

Amen, Grover: *F. Train Ramble.* Reluctant Buddha
Press, 1982.

Anderson, Maggie: *The Great Horned Owl.* Icarus
Press, 1979.
—*Years That Answer.* Harper & Row, 1980.
—*Cold Comfort.* University of Pittsburgh Press,
1986.

Anson, John: *A Family Album, Sessions & Surround-
ings.* Robert L. Barth, 1983.

Appleman, Philip: *Kites On A Windy Day.* Byron
Press, 1967.
—*Summer Love And Surf.* Vanderbilt University
Press, 1968.
—*Open Doorways.* W. W. Norton, 1976.
—*Darwin's Ark.* Indiana University Press, 1984.
—*Darwin's Beastiary.* Echo Press, 1986.

Astor, Susan: *Dame.* University of Georgia Press,
1980.

Astrada, Etelvina: *Autobiography At The Trigger*

(translated by Timothy J. Rogers). Spanish Literature Publications Co., 1985.
—*Death On The Run* (translated by Timothy J. Rogers). Spanish Literature Publications Co., 1987.
Awad, Joseph: *The Neon Distances.* Golden Quill Press, 1980.

B

Baker, David: *Looking Ahead.* Mid-America Press, 1975.
—*Rivers In The Sea.* Mid-America Press, 1977.
—*Laws Of The Land.* Ahsahta/Boise State University Press, 1981.
—*Summer Sleep.* Owl Creek Press, 1984.
—*Haunts.* Cleveland State University Press, 1985.
Balaban, John: *After Our War.* University of Pittsburgh Press, 1974.
—*Blue Mountain.* Unicorn Press, 1982.
Ball, Angela: *Kneeling Between Parked Cars.* Owl Creek Press, 1987.
—*Recombinant Lives.* Northern Lights Press (England), 1987.
Barnes, Jim: *The Fish On Poteau Mountain.* Cedar Creek Press, 1980.
—*The American Book Of The Dead.* University of Illinois Press, 1982.
—*A Season Of Loss.* Purdue University Press, 1985.
Barnes, Kate: *Talking In Your Sleep.* Blackberry Press, 1986.
Barr, John: *The Other End Of The Couch.* Carthage Press, 1964.
Barr, Tina: *At Dusk On Naskeag Point.* Flume Press, 1984.
Bartlett, Elizabeth: *Poems Of Yes And No.* Editorial Jus (Mexico), 1952.
—*Behold This Dreamer.* Editorial Jus (Mexico), 1959.
—*Poetry Concerto.* Sparrow Poetry Series, 1961.
—*It Takes Practice Not To Die.* Van Riper & Thompson, 1964.
—*Threads.* Unicorn Press, 1968.
—*Twelve-Tone Poems.* Sun Press, 1968.
—*Selected Poems.* Carrefour Books, 1970.
—*The House Of Sleep.* Autograph Editions, 1975.
—*Dialogue Of Dust.* Autograph Editions, 1977.
—*In Search Of Identity.* Autograph Editions, 1977.
—*A Zodiac Of Poems.* Autograph Editions, 1979.
—*Address In Time.* Defour Editions, 1979.
—*Memory Is No Stranger.* Ohio University Press, 1981.
—*The Gemini Poems.* Brandon University Press, 1984.
—*Candles.* Autograph Editions, 1987.
Baxter, Charles: *Chameleon.* New Rivers Press, 1970.
—*The South Dakota Guidebook.* New Rivers Press, 1974.
Beasley, Bruce: *Spirituals.* Wesleyan University Press, 1988.
Behlen, Charles: *Perdition's Keepsake.* Prickly Pear press, 1978.

—*My Grandfather's Hammer.* Mesilla, 1985.
—*Uirsche's First Three Decades.* Firewheel Press, 1987.
Behm, Richard: *Letters From A Cage & Other Poems.* Raspberry Press, 1976.
—*The Book Of Moonlight.* Moonlight Publications, 1978.
—*Simple Explanations.* Juniper Press, 1982.
—*When The Wood Begins To Move.* Jump River Press, 1982.
Benedict, Elinor: *Landfarer.* Hardwood Books, 1978.
—*A Bridge To China.* Hardwood Books, 1984.
Bennett, Bruce: *Coyote Pays A Call.* Bits Press, 1980.
—*The Strange Animal.* State Street Press, 1981.
—*Not Wanting To Write Like Everyone Else.* State Street Press, 1987.
Bennett, Paul: *A Strange Affinity.* Orchard House, 1975.
—*The Eye Of Reason.* Orchard House, 1976.
—*Building A House.* Limekiln Press, 1986.
Bensen, Robert: *Near Misses.* Nocturnal Canary Press, 1979.
—*In The Dream Museum.* Red Herring Press, 1981.
—*Day Labor.* Serpent & Eagle Press, 1984.
—*The Scriptures Of Venus.* Swamp Press, 1987.
Bergamin, Jose: *Rimas Y Sonetos Rezagados.* 1962 (Spain).
—*Duendecitos Y Coplas.* 1963 (Spain).
—*La Claridad Desierta.* 1973 (Spain).
—*Del Otono Y Los Mirlos.* 1975 (Spain).
—*Apartada Orilla.* 1976 (Spain).
—*Velado Desvelo.* 1978 (Spain).
—*Por Debajo Del Sueno.* 1979 (Spain).
—*Poesias Casi Completas.* 1980 (Spain).
—*Esperando La Mano De Nieve.* 1982 (Spain).
Bergman, David: *Cracking The Code.* Ohio State University Press, 1985.
Berry, Wendell: *The Broken Ground.* Harcourt, Brace, 1964.
—*Openings.* Harcourt, Brace, 1966.
—*Findings.* Prairie Press, 1969.
—*Farming: A Handbook.* Harcourt Brace Jovanovich, 1970.
—*The Country Of Marriage.* Harcourt Brace Jovanovich, 1973.
—*Sayings And Doings.* Gnomen Press, 1975.
—*Clearing.* Harcourt Brace Jovanovich, 1977.
—*A Part.* North Point Press, 1980.
—*The Wheel.* North Point Press, 1982.
—*Collected Poems.* North Point Press, 1985.
—*Sabbaths.* North Point Press, 1987.
Bess, Robert: *Domestic Birds.* Center for Design Press, 1986.
Bierds, Linda: *Flights Of The Harvest-Mare.* Ahsahta Press, 1985.
—*Off The Aleutian Chain.* L'Epervier Press, 1985.
Black, Harold: *Heritage.* Black Buzzard Press, 1982.
Blauner, Laurie: *Other Lives.* Owl Creek Press, 1984.
—*Self-Portrait With An Unwilling Landscape.* Owl Creek Press, 1987.
Blomain, Karen: *Black Diamond.* Great Elm Press, 1987.

Blossom, Laurel: *Any Minute.* Greenhouse Review Press, 1979.
—*What's Wrong.* Rowfant Club, 1987.
Blumenthal, Michael: *Sympathetic Magic.* Water Mark Press, 1980.
—*Days We Would Rather Know.* Viking-Penguin, 1984.
—*Laps.* University of Massachusetts Press, 1984.
—*Against Romance.* Viking-Penguin, 1984.
Bogen, Don: *After The Splendid Display.* Wesleyan University Press, 1986.
Bogin, George: *In A Surf Of Strangers.* University Presses of Florida, 1981.
Boland, Eavan: *Introducing Eavan Boland.* Ontario Review Press, 1981.
—*Night Feed.* Arlen House, 1982.
—*The Journey.* Carcanet/Arlen House, 1987.
Bouvard, Marguerite: *Journeys Over Water.* Quarterly Review of Literature Press, 1982.
—*Voices From An Island.* Breitenbush Books, 1985.
Bowers, Neal: *The Golf Ball Diver.* New Rivers Press, 1983.
Bozanic, Nick: *Wood Birds Water Stones.* Barnwood Press Cooperative, 1983.
—*One Place.* Release Press, 1986.
Brand, Alice G.: *As it Happens.* Wampeter Press, 1983.
Brennan, Matthew: *Seeing In The Dark.* Linwood Publishers, forthcoming.
Brett, Peter: *Ghost Rhythms.* Blue Cloud Quarterly, 1978.
—*Gallery.* University of Virginia Press, 1979.
—*Borrowing The Sky.* Kastle Press, 1980.
Brodsky, Louis Daniel: *Trilogy: A Birth Cycle.* Farmington Press, 1974.
—*Monday's Child.* Farmington Press, 1975.
—*The Kingdom Of Gewgaw.* Farmington Press, 1976.
—*Point Of Americas II.* Farmington Press, 1976.
—*Preparing For Incarnations.* Farmington Press, 1976.
—*La Preciosa.* Farmington Press, 1977.
—*Stranded in The Land Of Transients.* Farmington Press, 1978.
—*The Uncelebrated Ceremony Of Pants Factory Fatso.* Farmington Press, 1978.
—*Resume Of A Scapegoat.* Farmington Press, 1980.
—*Birds In Passage.* Farmington Press, 1980.
—*Mississippi Vistas.* University Press of Mississippi, 1983.
Brooks, David: *Narcissism On Rye.* Samisdat Press, 1984.
Brosman, Catharine Savage: *Watering.* University of Georgia Press, 1972.
—*Abiding Winter.* R. L. Barth, 1983.
Broughton, T. Alan: *In The Face Of Descent.* Carnegie-Mellon University Press, 1975.
—*Far From Home.* Carnegie-Mellon University Press, 1979.
—*Dreams Before Sleep.* Carnegie-Mellon University Press, 1982.
—*Preparing to Be Happy.* Carnegie-Mellon University Press, 1987.

Brown, Victor H.: *Eggbox.* Privately printed (England), 1986.
—*If There Be Ghosts.* Aquila Press (England), 1988.
Browne, Michael Dennis: *The Wife Of Winter.* Scribner's, 1970.
—*Sun Exercises.* Red Shadco Press, 1976.
—*The Sun Fetcher.* Carnegie-Mellon University Press, 1978.
—*Smoke From The Fires.* Carnegie-Mellon University Press, 1985.
Bruce, Debra: *Pure Daughter.* University of Arkansas Press, 1983.
—*Sudden Hunger.* University of Arkansas Press, 1987.
Bruchac, Joseph: *Indian Mountain.* Ithaca House, 1971.
—*The Buffalo In The Syracuse Zoo.* Greenfield Review Press, 1972.
—*Great Meadow Poems.* Dustbooks Press, 1973.
—*The Manabozho Poems.* Blue Cloud Quarterly Press, 1973.
—*Flow.* Cold Mountain Press, 1975.
—*This Earth Is A Drum.* Cold Mountain Press, 1976.
—*There Are No Trees Inside The Prison.* Blackberry Press, 1978.
—*Mu'ndu Wi Go: Mohegan Poems.* Blue Cloud Quarterly Press, 1978.
—*Entering Onondaga.* Cold Mountain Press, 1978.
—*The Good Message Of Handsome Lake.* Unicorn Press, 1979.
—*Translator's Son.* Cross Cultural Communications, 1980.
—*Ancestry.* Great Raven Press, 1981.
—*Remembering The Dawn.* Blue Cloud Quarterly Press, 1983.
—*Walking With My Sons.* Landlocked Press, 1985.
—*Tracking.* Ion Books, 1986.
—*Near The Mountains: Selected Poems.* White Pine Press, 1987.
Brush, Thomas: *Opening Night.* Owl Creek Press, 1981.
Bukowski, Charles: *Flower, Fist And Bestial Wail.* 1960.
—*Longshot Poems For Broke Players.* 1962.
—*Run With The Hunted.* 1962.
—*It Catches My Heart In Its Hands.* 1963.
—*Crucifix In A Deathhand.* 1965.
—*Cold Dogs In The Courtyard. 1965.*
—*At Terror Street And Agony Way.* 1968.
—*Poems Written Before Jumping Out Of An 8 Story Window.* 1968.
—The Days Run Away Like Wild Horses Over The Hills, 1969.
—*Mockingbird Wish me Luck.* 1972.
—*Burning In Water, Drowning In Flame. 1974.*
—*Love Is A Dog From Hell.* 1977.
—*Play The Piano Drunk/Like A Percussion Instrument/Until The Fingers Begin To Bleed A Bit.* 1979.
—*Dangling In The Tournefortia.* 1981.

—*War All The Time.* 1984.
—*You Get So Alone At Times That It Just Makes Sense.* 1986.

Burke, Daniel: *Diptych.* Halfpenny Press, 1978.

Burns, Jim: A Way Of Looking At Things. Move Publications (England), 1964.
—*Two For Our Time.* Screeches Publications (England), 1964.
—*Some Poems.* Crank Books, 1965.
—*Some More Poems.* R Books (England), 1966.
—*The Summer Season.* Target Publications (England), 1966.
—*My Sad Story & Other Poems.* New Voice (England), 1967.
—*The Store Of Things.* Phoenix Pamphlets (England), 1969.
—*Types.* Second Aeon Publications (Wales), 1970.
—*A Single Flower.* Andium Press (Jersey), 1972.
—*Leben In Preston.* Palmenpresse (West Germany), 1973.
—*Easter In Stockport.* Rivelin Press (England), 1975.
—*Fred Engels In Woolworths.* Oasis Books (England), 1975.
—*Playing It Cool.* Galloping Dog Press (Wales), 1976.
—*The Goldfish Speaks From Beyond The Grave.* Salamander Imprint (England), 1976.
—*Fred Engels Bei Woolworth.* Rotbuch Verlag (West Germany), 1977.
—*Catullus In Preston.* Cameo Club Alley Press (Wales), 1979.
—*Aristotle's Grill.* Platform Poets (England), 1979.
—*Notes From A Greasy Spoon.* Lettera Press (Wales), 1980.
—*Internal memorandum.* Rivelin Press (England), 1982.
—*Notizen Von Einem Schmierigen Loffel.* Palmenpresse (West Germany), 1982.
—*The Real World.* Purple Heather Publications (England), 1986.
—*The Gift & Other Poems.* Redbeck Press (England), 1987.
—*Out Of The Past: Selected Poems, 1961-1986.* Rivelin-Grapheme Press (England), 1987.

Burns, Ralph: *Us.* Cleveland State University Poetry Center, 1983.
—*Any Given Day.* University of Alabama Press, 1985.

Burroway, Janet: *But To The Season.* Keele University Press (England), 1960.
—*Material Goods.* University Presses of Florida, 1980.

Byer, Kathryn Stripling: *Search Party.* Amicae Press, 1979.
—*Alma.* Phoenix Press, 1983.
—*The Girl In The Midst Of The Harvest.* Texas Tech Press, 1986.

C

Cadnum, Michael: *The Morning Of The Massacre.* Bieler Press, 1982.

—*Wrecking The Cactus.* Salt Lick Press, 1985.
—*Long Afternoons.* State Street Press, 1986.
—*Invisible Mirror.* Ommation Press, 1987.

Cadsby, Heather: *Traditions.* Fiddlehead Poetry Books, 1982.
—*Decoys.* Mosaic Press, 1987.

Cairns, Scott: *Finding The Broken Man.* Window Press, 1982.
—*The Theology Of Doubt.* Cleveland State University Poetry Center, 1985.

Campion, Dan: *Calypso.* Syncline Press, 1981.

Carey, Michael A.: *The Noise The Earth Makes.* Pterodactyl Press, 1987.

Carlile, Henry: *The Rough-Hewn Table.* University of Missouri Press, 1971.
—*The Running Lights.* Dragon Gate Press, 1981.

Carruth, Hayden: *The Crow And The Heart.* Macmillan, 1959.
—*Journey To A Known Place.* New Directions Publishing Corp., 1961.
—*The Norfolk Poems.* Prairie Press, 1962.
—*North Winter.* Prairie Press, 1964.
—*Nothing For Tigers.* Macmillan, 1965.
—*Contra Mortem.* Crow's Mark Press, 1967.
—*The Clay Hill Anthology.* Prairie Press, 1970.
—*For You.* New Directions Publishing Corp., 1970.
—*From Snow And Rock, From Chaos.* New Directions Publishing Corp., 1973.
—*The Bloomingdale Papers.* University of Georgia Press, 1976.
—*Aura.* Janus Press, 1977.
—*Loneliness.* Janus Press, 1978.
—*Brothers, I Loved You All.* Sheep Meadow Press, 1978.
—*Almanach De Printemps Viverois.* Nadja, 1979.
—*The Mythology Of Dark And Light.* Tamarack Press, 1982.
—*The Sleeping Beauty.* Harper & Row, 1983.
—*Working Papers.* University of Georgia Press, 1983.
—*If You Call This Cry A Song.* Countryman Press, 1984.
—*Effluences From The Sacred Caves.* University of Michigan Press.
—*Asphalt Georgics.* New Directions Publishing Corp., 1985.
—*The Oldest Killed Lake In North America.* Salt-Works Press, 1985.
—*Mother.* Tamarack Press, 1985.
—*Lighter Than Air Craft.* Press of Appletree Alley, 1985.
—*Selected Poems.* Macmillan, 1986.
—A book of long-line poems. New Directions Publishing Corp., 1987.
—A sequence of 70 sonnets, 1987.

Carter, Jared: *Early Warning.* Barnwood, 1979.
—*Work, For The Night Is Coming.* Macmillan, 1981.
—*Pincushion's Strawberry.* Cleveland State University Poetry Center, 1984.
—*Fugue State.* Barnwood, 1984.
—*Millennial Harbinger.* Slash & Burn Press, 1986.

Carver, Raymond: *Near Klamath.* 1968.

—*Winter Insomnia*. Kayak Press, 1970.
—*Fires*. Capra Press, 1983.
—*Where Water Comes Together With Other Water*. Random House, 1985.
—*Ultramarine*. Random House, 1986.
—*In A Marine Light: Selected Poems*. Collins Harvill (England), 1987.

Cervo, Nathan: *On The Way To The Hospital*. Rat & Mole, 1973.
—*One Finger Exercises*. Rat & Mole, 1977.

Chandler, Janet Carncross: *The Colors Of A Marriage*. Privately printed, 1982.
—*Poems For Poets And Other Fragile Humans*. Privately printed, 1983.
—*How ARE You? They Ask New Widow*. Privately printed, 1985.

Charach, Ron: *The Big Life Painting*. Quarry Press.

Chichetto, James: *Poems*. Commonwealth Press, 1975.
—*Dialogue:* Emily Dickinson And Christopher Cauldwell. Privately printed, 1977.
—*Stones: A Litany*. Four Zoas Night House, 1980.
—*Gilgemesh And Other Poems*. Four Zoas Night House, 1983.
—*Victims*. Connecticut Poetry Review Press, 1987.

Chitwood, Michael: *The Promised Land*. Iron Mountain Press, 1981.

Choyce, Lesley: *Reinventing The Wheel*. Fiddlehead Poetry Books, 1980.
—*Fast Living*. Fiddlehead Poetry Books, 1982.
—*The End Of Ice*. Fiddlehead Poetry Books, 1985.

Chute, Robert M.: *Quiet Thunder*. Cider Press, 1975.
—*Uncle George Poems*. Cider Press, 1977.
—*Voices Great And Small*. Cider Press, 1977.
—*Thirteen Moons*. Blackberry Press, 1980.
—*Thirteen Moons/Treize Lunes*. Penumbra Press, 1982.
—*Samuel Sewall Sails For Home*. Coyote Love Press, 1986.

Ciardi, John: *Homeward To America*. Henry Holt, 1940.
—*Other Skies*. Little, Brown, 1947.
—*Live Another Day: Poems*. Twayne Publishers, 1949.
—*From Time To Time*. Twayne Publishers, 1951.
—*As If: Poems New And Selected*. Rutgers University Press, 1955.
—*I Marry You: A Sheaf Of Love Poems*. Rutgers University press, 1958.
—*39 Poems*. Rutgers University Press, 1959.
—*In The Stoneworks*. Rutgers University Press, 1961.
—*In Fact*. Rutgers University Press, 1962.
—*Person To Person*. Rutgers University Press, 1964.
—*An Alphabestiary*. Lippincott, 1966.
—*This Strangest Everything*. Rutgers University Press, 1966.
—*A Genesis*. Touchstone Publishers, 1967.
—*Lives Of X*. Rutgers University Press, 1971.
—*The Little That Is All*. Rutgers University Press, 1974.
—*Limericks: Too Gross* (with Isaac Asimov). W.

W. Norton, 1978.
—*For Instance*. W. W. Norton, 1979.
—*A Grossery Of Limericks*. (with Isaac Asimov). W. W. Norton, 1981.
—*Selected Poems*. University of Arkansas Press, 1984.
—*Phonethics: Twenty-Two Limericks For The Telephone*. Palaemon Press, 1985.
—*The Birds of Pompeii*. University of Arkansas Press, 1985.

Citino, David: *Last Rites And Other Poems*. Ohio State University Press, 1980.
—*The Appassionata Poems*. Cleveland State University Poetry Center, 1983.
—*The Appassionata Lectures*. Texas Review Poetry Award Chapbook, 1984.
—*The Gift Of Fire*. University of Arkansas Press, 1986.

Clements, Arthur L.: *Common Blessings*. Lincoln Springs Press, 1987.

Clements, Susan: *The Broken Hoop*. Blue Cloud Press, 1987.

Climenhaga, Joel: *Hawk And Chameleon*. Authors Press of America, 1972.
—*Report On The Progress Of The Bearded One's Homework*. Greenage Enterprises, 1985.
—*Belief In Chaos*. Greenage Enterprises, 1985.
—*The Wind Grieves Easy*. Greenage Enterprises, 1986.
—*Nothing Can Stop The Words*. Greenage Enterprises, 1986.
—*Triangular Aspect Of Confusion*. Greenage Enterprises, 1987.
—*Death Happens Only To Me*. Greenage Enterprises, 1987.

Cofer, Judith Ortiz: *Peregrina*. Riverstone Press, 1986.
—*Terms of Survival*. Arte Publico Press, 1987.
—*Reaching For The Mainland*. Bilingual Press, 1987.

Cogswell, Fred: *The Stunted Strong*. Fiddlehead Poetry Books, 1954.
—*The Haloed Tree*. Ryerson Press, 1956.
—*Descent From Eden*. Ryerson Press, 1958.
—*Lost Dimensions*. Outpost Publications, 1960.
—*Star-People*. Fiddlehead Poetry Books, 1968.
—*Immortal Plowman*. Fiddlehead Poetry Books, 1969.
—*In Praise Of Chastity*. New Brunswick Chapbooks, 1970.
—*The Chains Of Liliput*. Fiddlehead Poetry Books, 1971.
—*The House Without A Door*. Fiddlehead Poetry Books, 1973.
—*Light Bird Of Life*. Fiddlehead Poetry Books, 1974.
—*Against Perspective*. Fiddlehead Poetry Books, 1977.
—*A Long Perspective*. Fiddlehead Poetry Books, 1980.
—*Selected Poems*. Guernica Editions, 1983.
—*Pearls*. Ragweed Press, 1983.
—*Meditations: Fifty Sestinas*. Ragweed Press,

1986.

—*An Edge To Life*. Purple Wednesday Society, 1987.

Coleman, Mary Ann: *Disappearances*. Anhinga Press, 1978.

Coleman, Wanda: *Art In The Court Of The Blue Fag*. Black Sparrow Press, 1977.

—*Mad Dog Black Lady*. Black Sparrow Press, 1979.

—*Imagoes*. Black Sparrow Press, 1983.

—*Heavy Daughter Blues: Poems & Stories (1968-1986)*. Black Sparrow Press, 1987.

Collier, Michael: *The Clasp And Other Poems*. Wesleyan University Press, 1986.

Cook, R. L.: *Hebrides Overture And Other Poems*. Plewlands Press (Scotland), 1948.

—*Within The Tavern Caught*. Hand and Flower Press (England), 1952.

—*Sometimes A Word*. Plewlands Press (Scotland), 1963.

—*Time With A Drooping Hand*. Lomond Press (Scotland), 1978.

Cooley, Peter: *How To Go*. G.S.S.C. Publications, 1968.

—*The Company Of Strangers*. University of Missouri Press, 1975.

—*Miracle, Miracles*. Juniper Press, 1976.

—*The Room Where Summer Ends*. Carnegie-Mellon University press, 1979.

—*Nightseasons*. Carnegie-Mellon University Press, 1983.

—*The Van Gogh Notebook*. Carnegie-Mellon University press, 1987.

—*Canticles And Complaintes*. Ford-Brown Publishers, 1987.

—*One Sparrow, Another, Legion*. Livingston University Press, 1987.

Cooper, Jane: *The Weather Of Six Mornings*. Macmillan, 1969.

—*Maps & Windows*. Macmillan, 1974.

—*Threads: Rosa Luxemburg From Prison*. Flamingo Press, 1979.

—*Scaffolding: New And Selected Poems*. Anvil Press Poetry, 1984.

Cooper, M. Truman: *Substantial Holdings*. Pudding Publications, 1987.

Copeland, Helen M.: *Endangered Specimen And Other Poems From A Lay Naturalist*. St. Andrews Press, 1987.

Cording, Robert: *Life-List*. Ohio State University Press, 1987.

Corey, Stephen: *The Last Magician*. Water Mark Press, 1981.

—*Fighting Death*. State Street Press, 1984.

—*Gentle Iron Lace*. Press of the Night Owl, 1984.

—*Synchronized Swimming*. Swallow's Tale Press, 1985.

Corrigan, Paul: *Waiting For The Spring Freshet*. Blackberry Press, 1984.

Cosier, Tony: *With The Sun And Moon*. Privately printed, 1979.

—*The Verse Master*. Privately printed, 1983.

—*My Youth*. Vesta Publications, 1983.

—*Cubist Ghazals*. Cannon Press, 1986.

—*In The Face Of The Storm*. Anthos Books, 1987.

Crenner, James: *The Aging Ghost*. Golden Quill Press, 1964.

—*The Airplane Burial Ground*. W. W. Hoffstadt & Sons, 1976.

—*My Hat Flies On Again*. L'Epervier Press, 1979.

Crooker, Barbara: *Writing Home*. Gehry Press, 1983.

—*Starting From Zero*. Great Elm Press, 1987.

—*Obbligato*. Linwood Publishers (forthcoming).

—*Moving Poems*. Golden Argosy Press (forthcoming).

Crozier, Lorna: *Inside Is The Sky*. Thistledown Press, 1976.

—*Crow's Black Joy*. NeWest Press, 1978.

—*No Longer Two People* (with Patrick Lane). Turnstone Press, 1979.

—*Humans And Other Beasts*. Turnstone Press, 1980.

—*The Weather*. Coteau Books, 1983.

—*The Garden Going On Without Us*. McClelland & Stewart, 1985.

D

Dana, Robert: *My Glass Brother & Other Poems*. Constance Press, 1957.

—*The Dark Flags Of Waking*. Qara Press, 1964.

—*Journeys From The Skin*. Hundred Pound Press, 1966.

—*Some Versions of Silence*. W. W. Norton & Co., 1967.

—*The Power Of The Visible*. Swallow Press, 1971.

—*In A Fugitive Season*. Swallow Press, 1980.

—*What The Stones Know*. Seamark Press, 1982.

—*Starting Out For The Difficult World*. Harper & Row, 1987.

Daniels, Jim: *On The Line*. Signpost Press, 1981.

—*Places Everyone*. University of Wisconsin Press, 1985.

Darling, Charles: *Things In This Mirror Are Closer Than They Seem*. Andrew Mountain Press, 1986.

David, William Virgil: *One Way To Reconstruct The Scene*. Yale University Press, 1980.

—*The Dark Hours*. Calliope Press, 1984.

Dawber, Diane: *Cankerville*. Borealis Press, 1984.

—*Oatmeal Mittens*. Borealis Press, 1987.

Deahl, James: *Real Poetry*. Unfinished Monument, 1981.

—*In The Lost Horn's Call*. Aureole Point, 1982.

—*No Cold Ash*. Sono Nis, 1984.

—*Blue Ridge*. Aureole Point, 1985.

—*Into This Dark Earth*. Unfinished Monument, 1985.

—*A Stand Of Jackpine*. Unfinished Monument, 1987.

de Andrade, Eugenio: *Inhabited Heart: The Selected Poems Of Eugenio De Andrade* (translated by Alexis Levitin). Perivale Press, 1985.

—*White On White* (translated by Alexis Levitin). QRL Contemporary Poetry Series, 1987.

—*Memory Of Another River* (translated by Alexis

Levitin). New Rivers Press, 1987.

DeFoe, Mark: *Bringing Home Breakfast*. Black Willow Press, 1982.

Dekin, Timothy: *Winter Fruit*. Elpenor Books, 1982.
—*Carnival*. R. L. Barth Press, 1985.

Dempster, Barry: *Fables For Isolated Men*. Guernica Editions, 1982.
—*Globe Doubts*. Quarry Press, 1983.
—*Positions To Pray In*. Guernica Editions, 1988.

Dennis, Carl: *A House Of My Own*. George Braziller, 1974.
—*Climbing Down*. George Braziller, 1976.
—*Signs And Wonders*. Princeton University Press, 1979.
—*The Near World*. William Morrow, 1985.
—*The Outskirts Of Troy*. William Morrow, 1988.

Desy, Peter: *In A Dark Cage*. Samisdat Press, 1986.

Di Cicco, Pier Giorgio: *We Are The Light Turning*. Thunder City Press, 1976.
—*The Sad Facts*. Fiddlehead Poetry Books, 1977.
—*The Circular Dark*. Borealis Press, 1977.
—*Dancing In The House Of Cards*. Three Trees Press, 1978.
—*A Burning Patience*. Borealis Press, 1978.
—*Dolce-Amore*. Papavero Press, 1979.
—*The Tough Romance*. McClelland and Stewart, 1979.
—*A Straw Hat For Everything*. Angelstone Press, 1981.
—*Flying Deeper Into The Century*. McClelland and Stewart, 1982.
—*Dark To Light: Reasons For Humanness*. Intermedia Press, 1983.
—*Women We Never See Again*. Borealis Press, 1984.
—*Post-Sixties Nocturne*. Fiddlehead Poetry Books, 1985.
—*The Tough Romance*. Guernica Editions, 1986.
—*Virgin Science*. McClelland and Stewart, 1986.

Dickson, John: *Victoria Hotel*. Chicago Review Press, 1979.
—*Waving At Trains*. Thorntree Press, 1986.

Dillon, Andrew: *Volkswagen Breakdown And Other Poems*. Flagler College Bookstore, 1975.

Di Piero, W.S.: *The First Hour*. Abattoir Editions, 1983.
—*The Only Dangerous Thing*. Elpenor Books, 1984.
—*Early Light*. University of Utah Press, 1985.

Ditsky, John: *The Katherine Poems*. Killaly Press, 1975.
—*Scar Tissue*. Vesta Publications, 1978.
—*Friend & Lover*. Ontario Review Press.

Djanikian, Gregory: *The Man In The Middle*. Carnegie-Mellon University Press, 1984.

Dobler, Patricia: *Forget Your Life*. University of Nebraska Press, 1982.
—*Talking To Strangers*. University of Wisconsin Press, 1986.

Dobyns, Stephen: *Concurring Beasts*. Atheneum, 1972.
—*Griffon*. Atheneum, 1976.
—*Heat Death*. Atheneum, 1980.

—*The Balthus Poems*. Atheneum, 1982.
—*Black Dog, Red Dog*. Holt, Rinehart and Winston, 1984.
—*Cemetery Nights*. Viking, 1987.

Dorelski, William: *The Testament Of Israel Potter*. Seven Woods Press, 1976.
—*Half Of The Map*. Burning Deck, 1981.

Dorn, Alfred: *Flamenco Dancer And Other Poems*. New Orlando Publications, 1959.
—*Wine In Stone*. New Athenaeum Press, 1959.

Doro, Sue: *Heart, Home & Hard Hats*. Midwest Villages & Voices, 1986.

Dove, Rita: *The Yellow House On The Corner*. Carnegie-Mellon University Press, 1980.
—*Museum*. Carnegie-Mellon University Press, 1983.
—*Thomas And Beulah*. Carnegie-Mellon University Press, 1986.

Doxey, W. S.: *A Winter In The Woods*. Windless Orchard Press, 1976.

Drew, George: *Toads In A Poisoned Tank*. Tamarack Editions, 1986.

Driscoll, Jack: *The Language Of Bone*. Spring Valley Press, 1980.
—*Fishing The Backwash*. Ithaca House, 1984.

Dubnov, Eugene: *Ryzhiye monety (Russet Coins)* (in Russian). Goldfinch Press (England), 1978.
—*Nebom i zemleyu (By Sky And Earth)* (in Russian). Amber Press (England), 1984.

Duddy, Patrick: *10 x 3*. Northeastern University Press, 1975.

Duemer, Joseph: *Fool's Paradise*. Charles Street Press, 1980.
—*The Light Of Common Day*. Windhover Press, 1986.
—*Customs*. University of Georgia Press, 1987.

Duncan, Graham: *The Map Reader*. Great Elm Press, 1987.

Dybek, Stuart: *Brass Knuckles*. University of Pittsburgh Press, 1979.

E

Eberhart, Richard: *A Bravery of Earth*.
—*Reading The Spirit*.
—*Song And Idea*.
—*Poems New And Selected*.
—*Burr Oaks*.
—*Brotherhood Of Men*.
—*An Herb Basket*.
—*Selected Poems*. Oxford University Press, 1951.
—*Undercliff: Poems 1946-1953*.
—*Great Praises*.
—*Collected Poems 1930-1960*. Oxford University Press, 1960.
—*Collected Verse Plays*.
—*The Quarry: New Poems*. Oxford University Press, 1964.
—*Selected Poems 1930-1965*. New Directions Publishing Corp., 1966.
—*Thirty One Sonnets*.
—*Shifts Of Being: Poems*. Oxford University Press, 1968.

—*Fields Of Grace.* Oxford University Press, 1972.
—*Poems To Poets.* Penmaen Press, 1975.
—*To Eberhart From Ginsberg.*
—*Collected Poems 1930-1976.* Oxford University Press, 1976.
—*Ways Of Light.* Oxford University Press, 1980.
—*Survivors.* Boa Editions, 1980.
—*Four Poems.* Palaemon Press, 1980.
—*New Hampshire/Nine Poems.* Pym-Randall Press, 1980.
—*Chocorua.* Nadja Press, 1981.
—*Florida Poems.* Konglomerati Press, 1981.
—*The Long Reach: New & Uncollected Poems 1948-1984.* New Directions Publishing Corp., 1984.
—*Collected Poems 1930-1986.* Oxford University Press, 1987.

Eddy, Gary: *Waking Up, Late.* Slow Loris Press, 1977.

Ehrhart, W. D.: *To Those Who Have Gone Home Tired: New & Selected Poems.* Thunder's Mouth Press, 1984.
—*The Outer Banks & Other Poems.* Adastra Press, 1984.

Elkind, Sue Saniel: *No Longer Afraid.* Lintel Press, 1985.
—*Waiting For Order.* Naked Man Press of Kansas University, 1987.
—*Dinosaurs And Grandparents.* MAF Press, 1988.

Emanuel, Lynn: *Oblique Light.* Slow Loris Press, 1979.
—*Hotel Fiesta.* University of Georgia Press, 1984.
—*The Technology Of Love.* Abattoir Editions, 1987.

Epstein, Daniel Mark: *No Vacancies To Fill.* Liveright/W. W. Norton, 1973.
—*The Follies.* Overlook/Viking Press, 1977.
—*Young Men's Gold.* Overlook/Viking Press, 1978.
—*The Book Of Fortune.* Overlook/Viking Press, 1982.
—*Spirits.* Overlook/Viking press, 1987.

Etter, Dave: *Go Read The River.* University of Nebraska Press, 1966.
—*The Last Train To Prophetstown.* University of Nebraska Press, 1968.
—*Strawberries.* Juniper Press, 1970.
—*Voyages To The Inland Sea* (with John Knoepfle and Lisel Mueller). University of Wisconsin-La Crosse, 1971.
—*Crabtree's Woman.* BkMk Press, 1972.
—*Well You Needn't.* Raindust Press, 1975.
—*Bright Mississippi.* Juniper Press, 1975.
—*Central Standard Time: New And Selected Poems.* BkMk Press, 1978.
—*Alliance, Illinois.* Kylix Press, 1978.
—*Open To The Wind.* Uzzano Press, 1978.
—*Riding The Rock Island Through Kansas.* Wolfsong Press, 1979.
—*Cornfields.* Spoon River Poetry Press, 1980.
—*West Of Chicago.* Spoon River Poetry Press, 1981.
—*Boondocks.* Uzzano Press, 1982.
—*Alliance, Illinois* (complete edition). Spoon River Poetry Press, 1983.

—*Home State.* Spoon River Poetry Press, 1985.
—*Live At The Silver Dollar.* Spoon River Poetry Press, 1986.
—*Selected Poems.* Spoon River Poetry Press, 1987.

Evans, George: *Nightvision.* Pig Press (England), 1983.
—*Space.* Galloping Dog Press (England), 1986.
—*Wrecking.* Shearsman Press (England), 1987.

Ewing, Jim: *Scotland, Texas, Mississippi: Poems.* Colonial Press, 1988.

F

Fagles, Robert: *I, Vincent: Poems From The Pictures Of Van Gogh.* Princeton University Press, 1978.

Fairchild, B. H.: *C&W Machine Works.* Trilobite Press, 1983.
—*Flight.* Devil's Millhopper Press, 1985.
—*The Arrival Of The Future.* Swallow's Tale Press, 1986.

Falk, Marcia: *It Is July In Virginia.* Rara Avis Press, 1984.

Farrar, Winifred Hamrick: *Cry Life.* South & West, Inc., 1968.
—*The Seeking Spirit.* South & West, Inc., 1974.
—*Behind The Ridge.* South & West, Inc., 1987.

Fasel, Ida: *On The Meanings Of Cleave.* Eakin Press, 1979.
—*Thanking The Flowers.* Wings Press, 1981.
—*All Of Us, Dancers.* M. A. F. Press, 1984.
—*Amphora Full Of Light.* Before The Rapture Press, 1985.

Feinstein, Robert N.: *Oysters In Love.* Stronghold Press, 1984.

Fell, Mary: *The Triangle Fire.* Shadow Press, 1983.
—*The Persistence Of Memory.* Random House, 1984.

Ferry, David: *On The Way To The Island.* Wesleyan University Press, 1960.
—*A Letter, And Some Photographs.* Sea Pen Press, 1981.
—*Strangers: A Book Of Poems.* University of Chicago Press, 1983.

Field, Crystal M.: *The Good Woman* (under name of Crystal MacLean). BookMark Press, 1977.
—*My Sister's Leather Bag.* Mid-America Press, 1982.

Finch, Roger: *Winter Sunlight, Summer Rain.* Pierian Press.
—*What Is Written In The Wind.* Sparrow Press, 1984.
—*Suite From The Ivory Rooming House.* South Head Press (Australia), 1987.
—*Animals Fair.* South Head Press (Australia), 1987.

Fincke, Gary: *Breath.* State Street Press, 1984.
—*The Coat In The Heart.* Blue Buildings Press, 1985.
—*The Days Of Uncertain Health.* Lynx House Press, 1987.

Fink, Robert A.: *Azimuth Points.* Texas Review, Sam Houston State University, 1981.

Finley, Jeanne: *Pagan Babies.* Bellevue Press, 1987.
Fishman, Charles: *Aurora.* Tree Books, 1974.
—*Mortal Companions.* Pleasure Dome Press, 1977.
—*Warm-Blooded Animals.* Juniper Press, 1977.
—*The Death Mazurka.* Timberline Press, 1987.
Flanner, Hildegarde: *Young Girl And Other Poems.* Porter Garnett, 1920.
—*This Morning: Poems.* Lantern Press, 1921.
—*Valley Quail.* Ward Ritchie, 1929.
—*Time's Profile.* Macmillan, 1929.
—*If There Is Time.* New Directions Publishing Corp., 1942.
—*In Native Light.* James Beard, 1970.
—*The Hearkening Eye.* Ahsahta Press, 1979.
—*A Vanishing Land.* No Dead Lines, 1980.
—*Brief Cherishing: A Napa Valley Harvest.* John Daniel, 1985.
—*At The Gentle Mercy Of Plants.* John Daniel, 1986.
Flook, Maria: *Reckless Wedding.* Houghton Mifflin, 1982.
Folsom, Eric: *Brewed For Ontario.* Imaginary Press, 1981.
Fowler, Jay Bradford, Jr.: *Psalmbook For The White Butterfly.* Orchises Press, 1985.
—*Writing Down The Light.* Orchises Press, 1987.
Franklin, Walt: *Talking To The Owls.* Great Elm Press, 1984.
—*Topographies.* M.A.F. Press, 1985.
—*The Glass Also Rises.* Great Elm Press, 1985.
—*Little Water Company.* White Pine Press, 1986.
—*Ekos: A Journal Poem.* Great Elm Press, 1986.
—*Earthstars, Chanterelles, Destroying Angels.* Garall Press, 1987.
—*The Ice Harvest.* (forthcoming).
—*The Stewbone Chronicles.* (forthcoming).
Friman, Alice: *A Question Of Innocence.* Raintree Press, 1978.
—*Song To My Sister.* Indiana Writers' Center Press, 1979.
—*Reporting From Corinth.* Barnwood Press, 1984.
Frost, Carol: *The Salt Lesson.* Graywolf Press, 1976.
—*Liar's Dice.* Ithaca House, 1978.
—*Cold Frame.* Owl Creek Press, 1982.
—*The Fearful Child.* Ithaca House, 1983.
—*Day Of The Body.* Ion Books, 1987.
Frumkin, Gene: *The Hawk & The Lizard.* Swallow Press, 1963.
—*The Orange Tree.* Cyfoeth Press, 1965.
—*The Rainbow-Walker.* Grasshopper Press, 1969.
—*Dostoevsky & Other Nature Poems.* Solo Press, 1972.
—*Locust Cry: Poems 1958-65.* San Marcos Press, 1973.
—*The Mystic Writing-Pad.* Red Hill Press, 1977.
—*Loops.* San Marcos Press, 1978.
—*Clouds And Red Earth.* Swallow/Ohio University Press, 1982.
—*A Lover's Quarrel With America.* Automatic Press, 1985.
—*A Sweetness In The Air.* Solo Press, 1987.
Funkhouser, Erica: *Natural Affinities.* Alice James Books, 1983.

G

Gallagher, Joseph: *Painting On Silence: An Orchestra of Poems.* Exposition Press, 1973.
Galler, David: *Walls And Distances.* Macmillan, 1959.
—*Leopards In The Temple.* Macmillan, 1968.
—*Third Poems: 1965-1978.* Quarterly Review of Literature Press, 1979.
Galvin, Brendan: *The Narrow Land.* Northeastern University Press, 1971.
—*The Salt Farm.* Fiddlehead Poetry Books, 1972.
—*No Time For Good Reasons.* University of Pittsburgh Press, 1974.
—*The Minutes No One Owns.* University of Pittsburgh Press, 1977.
—*Atlantic Flyway.* University of Georgia Press, 1980.
—*Winter Oysters.* University of Georgia Press, 1983.
—*A Birder's Dozen.* Ampersand Press, 1984.
—*Seals In The Inner Harbor.* Carnegie-Mellon University Press, 1986.
Galvin, James: *Imaginary Timber.* Doubleday, 1980.
—*God's Mistress.* Harper & Row, 1984.
Garrison, David: *Blue Oboe.* Wyndham Hall Press, 1984.
Genega, Paul: *Perhaps.* Ardearum Workshop, 1985.
George, David: *The Flamenco Guitar.* Society of Spanish Studies, 1969.
—*Lamentation For Emmanuel: An Elegy For The Gypsy Flamenco Singer, Manolito De La Maria De Alcala.* Wooden Angel Press, 1987.
Gernes, Sonia: *The Mutes Of Sleepy Eye.* Inchbird Press, 1981.
—*Brief Lives.* University of Notre Dame Press, 1982.
Ghiradella, Robert: *Fragments.* Apple-wood Press, 1980.
Gibb, Robert: *Whalesongs.* Turkey Press, 1979.
—*The Margins.* White Bear Books, 1979.
—*The Names Of The Earth In Summer.* Stone Country, 1983.
—*The Winter House.* University of Missouri Press, 1984.
—*Entering Time.* Barnwood, 1986.
—*A Geography of Common Names.* Devil's Millhopper, 1987.
—*Momentary Days.* Walt Whitman Center, 1988.
Gilbert, Celia: *Queen of Darkness.* Viking Press, 1977.
—*Bonfire.* Alice James Books, 1983.
Gilbert, Sandra M.: *In The Fourth World.* University of Alabama Press, 1979.
—*The Summer Kitchen.* Heyeck Press, 1984.
—*Emily's Bread.* W. W. Norton, 1985.
Gildner, Gary: *First Practice.* University of Pittsburgh Press, 1969.
—*Digging For Indians.* University of Pittsburgh Press, 1971.
—*Eight Poems.* Bredahl, 1973.
—*Nails.* University of Pittsburgh Press, 1976.
—*Letters From Vicksburg.* Unicorn Press, 1976.
—*The Runner.* University of Pittsburgh Press, 1978.

—*Jabon*. Breitenbush Books, 1981.
—*Blue Like The Heavens*. University of Pittsburgh Press, 1984.

Gioia, Dana: *Daily Horoscope*. Graywolf Press, 1986.

Glaser, Elton: *Relics*. Wesleyan University Press, 1984.
—*Tropical Depressions*. University of Iowa Press, 1988.

Glass, Malcolm: *Bone Love*. University Presses of Florida, 1979.
—*Wiggins Poems*. Bucksnort Press, 1984.
—*In The Shadow Of The Gourd*. New Rivers Press, 1987.

Glazner, Greg: *Walking Two Landscapes*. State Street Press, 1984.

Goldberg, Barbara: *Berta Broadfoot And Pepin The Short: A Merovingian Romance*. Word Works, 1986.

Goldman, Judy: *Holding Back Winter*. St. Andrews Press, 1987.

Gom, Leona: *Kindling*. Fiddlehead Poetry Books, 1972.
—*The Singletree*. Sono Nis, 1975.
—*Land Of The Peace*. Thistledown Press, 1980.
—*North Bound*. Thistledown Press, 1984.
—*Private Properties*. Sono Nis, 1986.

Goodenough, J. B.: *Dower Land*. Cleveland State University Press, 1984.
—*Homeplace*. St. Andrews Press, 1987.

Goodman, Miriam: *Permanent Wave*. Alice James Books, 1978.
—*Signal: Noise*. Alice James Books, 1982.

Goodman, Ryah Tumarkin: *Toward The Sun*. Bruce Humphries, 1970.
—*Suddenly It's Evening*. William L. Bauhan, 1977.
—*New & Selected Poems*. William L. Bauhan, 1985.

Gourlay, Elizabeth: *Motions, Dreams and Aberrations*. Morris, 1969.
—*Songs And Dances*. Caitlin, 1981.
—*M Poems*. Fiddlehead Poetry Books, 1983.

Graham, David: *Magic Shows*. Cleveland State University Poetry Center, 1986.
—*Common Waters*. Flume Press, 1986.

Gray, Patrick Worth: *Disapearances*. University of Nebraska Press, 1979.
—*Spring Comes Again To Arnett*. Mr. Cogito Press, 1987.

Green, Connie J.: *A Peopled Garden*. (thesis, available from University of Tennessee Library, Knoxville), 1987.

Greenberg, Alvin: *The Metaphysical Giraffe*. New Rivers Press, 1968.
—*The House Of The Would-Be Gardener*. New Rivers Press, 1972.
—*Dark Lands*. Ithaca House, 1973.
—*Metaform*. University of Massachusetts Press, 1975.
—*In/Direction*. David R. Godine, 1978.
—*And Yet*. Juniper Press, 1981.

Greenway, William: *Pressure Under Grace*. Breitenbush Books, 1982.
—*Where We've Been*. Breitenbush Books, 1987.

Gregg, Linda: *Too Bright To See*. Graywolf Press, 1981.
—*Eight Poems*. Graywolf Press, 1982.
—*Alma*. Random House, 1986.

Grennan, Eamon: *Wildly For Days*. Gallery Press (Ireland), 1983.
—*What Light There Is*. Gallery Press (Ireland), 1987.

Guernsey, Bruce: *Shelled Flesh*. Back Door Press, 1971.
—*Hour Of The Wolf*. Penyeach Press, 1972.
—*Biological Clock*. Ktaadn Poetry Series, 1973.
—*Lost Wealth*. Basilisk Press, 1974.
—*Genesis*. Puddingstone Press, 1975.
—*Canoe/The Nest/The Apple*. Ives Street Press, 1982.
—*January Thaw*. University of Pittsburgh Press, 1982.
—*The Death Of The Ventriloquist*. Stormline Press, 1988.

Gunn, Thom: *Moby And My Sad Captains*. Farrar, Straus & Giroux, 1971.
—*Jack Straw's Castle*. Farrar, Straus & Giroux, 1976.
—*Selected Poems*. Farrar, Straus & Giroux, 1979.
—*The Passages of Joy*. Farrar, Straus & Giroux, 1982.

Gustafson, Lars: *Selected Poems* (translated by Robin Fulton). New Rivers Press, 1972.
—*Warm Rooms And Cold* (translated by Sundstrom). Copper Beech Press, 1975.
—*QRL Poetry Series IV* (translated by Philip Martin). Quarterly Review of Literature Press, 1982.
—*Selected Poems* (edited by Christopher Middleton). New Directions Publishing Corp., 1988.

H

Hadas, Rachel: *Starting From Troy*. David R. Godine, 1975.
—*Slow Transparency*. Wesleyan University Press, 1983.
—*A Son From Sleep*. Wesleyan University Press, 1987.

Hall, James B.: *The Hunt Within*. Louisiana State University Press, 1973.

Hall, Jim: *Lady From The Dark Green Hills*. Carnegie-Mellon University Press, 1976.
—*The Mating Reflex*. Carnegie-Mellon University Press, 1981.
—*False Statements*. Carnegie-Mellon University Pess, 1986.

Halpern, Daniel: *Traveling On Credit*. Viking/Compass, 1972.
—*Street Fire*. Viking Press, 1975.
—*Life Among Others*. Viking/Penguin, 1978.
—*Seasonal Rights*. Viking/Penguin, 1983.
—*Tango*. Viking/Peguin, 1987.

Hamilton, Fritz: *The Street And The Joint*. Gyro Press, 1969.
—*The Plunge*. Zetetic Press, 1972.
—*Redman is Redman's Mommy*. Downtown Poets, 1977.

—*Sores and Roses*. Downtown Poets, 1980.
—*A Father At A Soldier's Grave*. Downtown Poets, 1980.
—*No Difference*. Trout Creek Press, 1987.
—*Beneath The Rags*. Minotaur Press, 1987.
Handy, Nixeon Civille: *Do Not Disturb The Dance: Enter It*. Creative Aids, 1973.
—*Earth House*. Creative Aids, 1977.
Hankla, Cathryn: *Phenomena*. University of Missouri Press, 1983.
Harjo, Joy: *The Last Song*. Puerto Del Sol Press, 1975.
—*What Moon Drove Me To This*. I. Reed Books, 1980.
—*She Had Some Horses*. Thunder's Mouth Press, 1983.
Harper, Michael S.: *Dear John, Dear Coltrane*. University of Pittsburgh Press, 1970.
—*History Is Your Own Heartbeat*. University of Illinois Press, 1971.
—*History As Apple Tree*. Scarab Press, 1972.
—*Song: I Want A Witness*. University of Pittsburgh Press, 1972.
—*Debridement*. Doubleday, 1973.
—*Nightmare Begins Responsibility*. University of Illinois Press, 1975.
—*Images of Kin*. University of Illinois Press, 1977.
—*Healing Song For The Inner Ear*. University of Illinois Press, 1985.
Harrison, Jeffrey: *The Singing Underneath*. E. P. Dutton, 1988.
Harrison, Richard: *Fathers Never Leave You*. Mosaic Press, 1987.
Hashmi, Alamgir: *The Oath And Amen*. Dovers, 1976.
—*An Old Chair*. Xenia Press, 1979.
—*America Is A Punjabi Word*. Karakorum Range, 1979.
—*My Second In Kentucky*. Vision Press, 1981.
—*This Time In Lahore*. Vision Press, 1983.
—*Neither This Time/Nor That Place*. Vision Press, 1984.
Haskins, Lola: *Planting The Children*. University Presses of Florida, 1983.
—*Castings*. Countryman Press, 1984.
Hasselstrom, Linda M.: *Caught By One Wing*. Julie D. Holcomb, 1984.
—*Roadkill*. Spoon River Poetry Press, 1987.
Hathaway, James: *Foraging*. Ithaca House, 1978.
Haug, James: *Staying Overnight In A Strange House*. La Huerta Press, 1979.
Hayford, James: *At Large On The Land*. Oriole Books, 1983.
Hedin, Robert: *Snow Country*. Copper Canyon Press, 1975.
—*At The Home-Altar*. Copper Canyon Press, 1978.
—*On The Day Of Bulls*. Jawbone Press, 1980.
—*County O*. Copper Canyon Press, 1984.
—*Tornadoes*. Dooryard Press, 1987.
Helwig, Maggie: *Walking Through Fire*. Turnstone Press, 1981.
—*Tongues Of Men And Angels*. Oberon Press, 1985.

—*Eden*. Oberon Press, 1987.
—*Because The Gunman*. Lowlife Press, 1987.
Henrikson, Carol: *The Well*. Vermont Council on the Arts, 1976.
Heyen, William: *Depth Of Field*. Louisiana State University Press, 1970.
—*Noise In The Trees*. Vanguard Press, 1974.
—*The Swastika Poems*. Vanguard Press, 1977.
—*Long Island Light*. Vanguard Press, 1979.
—*My Holocaust Songs*. William B. Ewert, 1980.
—*The City Parables*. Croissant & Co., 1980.
—*Lord Dragonfly: Five Sequences*. Vanguard Press, 1981.
—*The Trains*. Metacom Press, 1981.
—*Along This Water*. Tamarack Editions, 1983.
—*Erika: Poems Of The Holocaust*. Vanguard Press, 1984.
—*The Chestnut Rain: A Poem*. Ballantine/Available Press, 1986.
Hicks, John V.: *Now Is A Far Country*. Thistledown Press, 1978.
—*Winter Your Sleep*. Thistledown Press, 1980.
—*Silence Like The Sun*. Thistledown Press, 1983.
—*Rootless Tree*. Thistledown Press, 1985.
—*Fives And Sixes*. Porcupine's Quill, 1986.
—*Side Glances: Notes On The Writer's Craft*. Thistledown Press, 1987.
Hill, Gerald: *Heartwood*. Thistledown Press, 1985.
Hilles, Robert: *Look The Lovely Animal Speaks*. Turnstone Press, 1980.
—*The Surprise Element*. Sidereal Press, 1982.
—*An Angel In The Works*. Oolichan Books, 1983.
—*A Breath At A Time*. Oolichan Books, forthcoming.
Hirsch, Edward: *For The Sleepwalkers*. Knopf, 1981.
—*Wild Gratitude*. Knopf, 1986.
Hoeft, Robert D.: *Exhibits At A Retirement Home*. Wings Press, 1982.
—*Tools*. Mosaic Press, 1982.
—*Out Of Work*. Winewood Publishing, 1983.
—*What Are You Doing?* Trout Creek Press, 1987.
Hoey, Allen: *Evening In The Antipodes*. Banjo Press, 1977.
—*Cedar Light*. Street Press, 1980.
—*Hymns To A Tree*. Tamarack Editions, 1984.
—*New Year*. Liberty Street Books, 1986.
—*Work The Tongue Could Understand*. State Street Press, 1987.
—*A Fire In The Cold House Of Being*. Walt Whitman Center, 1987.
Hoffman, Daniel: *An Armada Of Thirty Whales*. Yale University Press, 1954.
—*A Little Geste & Other Poems*. Oxford University Press, 1960.
—*The City Of Satisfactions*. Oxford University Press, 1963.
—*Striking The Stones*. Oxford University Press, 1968.
—*Broken Laws*. Oxford University Press, 1970.
—*The Center Of Attention*. Random House, 1974.
—*Able Was I Ere I Saw Elba*. Hutchinson (England), 1977.
—*Brotherly Love*. Random House, 1982.

—*Hang-Gliding From Helicon: New & Selected Poems 1948-1988*. Louisiana State University Press, 1988.

Holden, Jonathan: *Design For A House*. University of Missouri Press, 1972.
—*Leverage*. University Press of Virginia, 1983.
—*Falling From Stardom*. Carnegie-Mellon University Press, 1984.
—*The Names Of The Rapids*. University of Massachusetts Press, 1985.

Holt, Rochelle Lynn: *Timelapse*. Lunchroom Press, 1981.
—*The Blue Guitar*. Northwoods Press, 1984.
—*Haiku Of Desire*. Merging Media, 1984.
—*Extended Family*. American Studies Press, 1985.
—*Prescriptons For Psyche*. Timberline Press, 1986.
—*The Suicide Chap*. Willow Bee House, 1987.
—*The Elusive Rose*. Aquila Press, 1987.
—*Stream Of Consciousness*. Kindred Spirit Press, 1987.
—*In The Mist & Fog*. Kindred Spirit Press, 1988.

Homer, Art: *What We Did After The Rain*. Abattoir Editions, 1984.
—*Tattoos*. Green Tower Press, 1986.
—*Skies Of Such Valuable Glass*. Owl Creek Press, 1988.

Hood, Michael: *Lighter Confrontations*. New Leaves Press, 1980.

Hooper, Patricia: *Other Lives*. Elizabeth Street Press, 1984.
—*A Bundle Of Beasts*. Houghton Mifflin, 1987.

Horne, Lewis: *The Seventh Day*. Thistledown Press, 1982.

Howard, Ben: *Father of Waters*. Abattoir Editions, 1979.
—*Northern Interior: Poems 1976-1982*. Cummington Press, 1986.
—*Lenten Anniversaries: Poems 1982-1985*. Cummington Press, 1988.

Howell, Christopher: *The Crime Of Luck*. Panache Books, 1976.
—*Why Shouldn't I*. L'Epervier Press, 1977.
—*Through Silence: The Ling Wei Texts*. L'Epervier Press, 1981.
—*Sea Change*. L'Epervier Press, 1985.

Hudgins, Andrew: *Saints And Strangers*. Houghton Mifflin, 1985.
—*After The Lost War*. Houghton Mifflin, 1988.

I

Iddings, Kathleen: *The Way Of Things*. West Anglia Publications, 1984.
—*Invincible Summer*. West Anglia Publications, 1985.
—*Promises To Keep: Poetry And Photographs*. West Anglia Publications, 1987.

J

Jackson, Reuben M.: *Potentially Yours*. Mom Press, 1986.

Jackson, Richard: *Part Of The Story*. Grove Press, 1983.
—*Worlds Apart*. University of Alabama Press, 1987.

James, David: *A Heart Out Of This World*. Carnegie-Mellon University Press, 1984.

Janzen, Jean: *Words For The Silence*. Center for Mennonite Studies, 1984.
—*Three Mennonite Poets* (with Yorifumi Yaguchi and David Waltner-Toews). Good Books, 1986.

Jenkins, Louis: *The Well Digger's Wife*. Minnesota Writers' Publishing House, 1973.
—*The Wrong Tree*. Scopcraeft Press, 1980.
—*The Water's Easy Reach*. White Pine Press, 1985.
—*An Almost Human Gesture*. Eighties Press, 1987.

Johnson, Robert K.: *Blossoms Of The Apricot*. Helix House, 1977.
—*The Wheel Of Daily Life*. M.A.F. Press, 1988.

Johnston, Gordon: *Inscription Rock*. Penumbra Press, 1981.

Jones, Richard: *Windows And Walls*. Adastra Press, 1982.
—*Innocent Things*. Adastra Press, 1985.
—*Walk On*. Alderman Press, 1986.
—*Country Of Air*. Copper Canyon Press, 1986.

K

Kamenetz, Roger: *The Missing Jew*. Dryad Press, 1980.
—*Nympholepsy*. Dryad Press, 1985.
—*Terra Infirma*. University of Arkansas, 1986.

Kasdorf, Julia Spicher: *Moss Lotus*. Pinchpenny Press, 1984.

Keefer, Janice Kulyk: *White Of The Lesser Angels*. Ragweed Press, 1986.

Keeler, Greg: *Spring Catch*. Confluence Press, 1982.
—*The Far Bank*. Confluence Press, 1985.
—*American Falls*. Confluence Press, 1987.

Keller, David: *New Room*. Quarterly Review of Literature Press, 1987.

Kelly, Dave: *The Night Of The Terrible Ladders*. Hors Commerce Press, 1966.
—*Dear Nate*. Runcible Spoon Press, 1969.
—*Summer Study*. Runcible Spoon Press, 1969.
—*All Here Together*. Lillabulero Chapbook Series, 1969.
—*At A Time: A Dance For Voices*. Basilisk Press, 1972.
—*Instructions For Viewing A Solar Eclipse*. Wesleyan Univesity Press, 1972.
—*Did You Hear They're Beheading Bill Johnson Today?* Stone Press, 1974.
—*In These Rooms*. Red Hill Press, 1976.
—*The Flesh-Eating Horse And Other Sagas*. Bartholomew's Cobble, 1976.
—*Poems In Season*. Texas Portfolio Editions, 1977.
—*Filming Assassinations*. Ithaca House, 1979.

—*Nothern Letter*. Nebraska Review Chapbook Series, 1980.

—*Great Lakes Cycle*. Steps Inside Press, 1981.

Kessler, Milton: *A Road Came Once*. Ohio State University Press, 1963.

—*Woodlawn North*. Impressions Workshop, 1970.

—*Sailing Too Far*. Harper & Row, 1974.

Kilgore, James C.: *The Big Buffalo*. 1969.

—*Midnight Blast*. 1970.

—*A Time Of Black Devotion*. 1971.

—*Night Song*. 1974.

—*Let It Pass*. 1976.

—*A Black Bicentennial*. 1976.

—*Until I Met You*. 1978.

—*African Violet*. 1982.

—*I've Been In The Storm So Long*. 1983.

—*During Aribica lunch*. 1986.

Kinzie, Mary: *The Threshold Of The Year*. University of Missouri Press, 1982.

Kirby, David: *Sarah Bernhardt's Leg*. Cleveland State University Poetry Center, 1983.

—*Saving The Young Men Of Vienna*. University of Wisconsin Press, 1987.

Kitchen, Judith: *Upstairs Window*. Tamarack Editions, 1983.

—*Perennials*. Anhinga Press, 1986.

Klavan, Andrew: *The Suicide Hotline*. Cadmus Editions, forthcoming.

Kleinschmidt, Edward: *Magnetism*. Heyeck Press, 1987.

Kormos, Charles: *Pawn And Prophet*. ARC Books (Israel), 1987.

Korwin, Yala: *To Tell The Story—Poems Of The Holocaust*. Holocaust Library, 1987.

Kumin, Maxine: *Halfway*. Holt, Rinehart & Winston, 1961.

—*The Privilege*. Harper & Row, 1965.

—*The Nightmare Factory*. Harper & Row, 1970.

—*Up Country*. Harper & Row, 1972.

—*House, Bridge, Fountain, Gate*. Viking/Penguin, 1975.

—*The Retrieval System*. Viking/Penguin, 1978.

—*Our Ground Time Here Will Be Brief: New & Selected Poems*. Viking/Penguin, 1982.

—*The Long Approach*. Viking/Penguin, 1985.

Kunitz, Stanley: *Intellectual Things*. 1930.

—*Passport To The War*. 1944.

—*Selected Poems 1928-1958*. 1958.

—*The Testing-Tree*. 1971.

—*The Poems Of Stanley Kunitz, 1928-1978*. Atlantic Monthly Press, 1979.

—*The Wellfleet Whale And Companion Poems*. Sheep Meadow Press, 1984.

Kuzma, Greg: *Sitting Around*. Lillabulero Press, 1969.

—*Something At Last Visible*. Zeitgeist, 1969.

—*Eleven Poems*. Portfolio Press, 1971.

—*The Bosporus*. Hellric Publishing, 1971.

—*Harry's Things*. Apple, 1971.

—*Poems*. Three Sheets, 1971.

—*Song For Someone Going Away And Other Poems*. Ithaca House, 1971.

—*Good News*. Viking, 1973.

—*What Friends Are For*. Best Cellar, 1973.

—*A Problem Of High Water*. West Coast Poetry Review, 1973.

—*The Buffalo Shoot*. Basilisk Press, 1974.

—*The Obedience School*. Three Rivers Press, 1974.

—*A Day In The World*. Abattoir Editions, 1976.

—*Nebraska: A Poem*. Best Cellar Press, 1977.

—*Adirondacks*. Bear Claw Press, 1978.

—*Village Journal*. Best Cellar Press, 1978.

—*For My Brother*. Abattoir Editions, 1981.

—*Everyday Life*. Spoon River Poetry Press, 1983.

—*A Horse Of A Different Color*. Illuminati, 1983.

—*Of China And Of Greece*. Sun, 1984.

L

LaBombard, Joan: *Calendar*. Orirana Press, 1985.

Lagomarsino, Nancy: *Sleep Handbook*. Alice James Books, 1987.

Lahey-Dolega, Christine: *Sticks And Stones*. Urban Despair Press, 1980.

Lake, Paul: *Bull Dancing*. New Poets Series, 1978.

—*Catches*. R. L. Barth, 1986.

Lally, Margaret: *Juliana's Room*. Bits Press, 1988.

Larsen, Jeanne: *James Cook In Search of Terra Incognita*. University Press of Virginia, 1979.

Lattimore, Richard: *Poems*. University of Michigan Press, 1957.

—*Sestina For A Far-Off Summer*. University of Michigan Press, 1962.

—*The Stride Of Time*. University Of Michigan Press, 1966.

—*Poems From Three Decades*. Charles Scribner's Sons, 1972.

—*Continuing Conclusions*. Louisiana State University Press, 1983.

Laughlin, James: *The River*. New Directions Publishing Corp., 1938.

—*Some Natural Things*. New Directions Publishing Corp., 1945.

—*Skiing East And West*. Hastings House, 1946.

—*Report On A Visit To Germany*. Henri Held (Switzerland), 1948.

—*A Small Book Of Poems*. New Directions Publishing Corp., 1948.

—*The Wild Anemone & Other Poems*. New Directions Publishing Corp., 1957.

—*Selected Poems*. New Directions Publishing Corp., 1959.

—*The Pig*. Perishable Press, 1970.

—*In Another Country: Poems 1935-1975*. City Lights Books, 1978.

—*Gists & Piths: A Memoir Of Ezra Pound*. Windhover Press, 1982.

—*Stolen & Contaminated Poems*. Turkey Press, 1985.

—*The Deconstructed Man*. Windhover Press, 1985.

—Selected Poems 1935-1985. City Lights Books, 1986.
—The House Of Light. Grenfell Press, 1986.
—The Owl Of Minerva. Copper Canyon Press, 1987.

Layton, Irving: *Here And Now*. 1945.
—Now Is The Place. 1948.
—The Black Huntsman. 1951.
—Cerberus. 1952.
—Love The Conqueror Worm. 1953.
—In The Midst Of My Fever. 1954.
—The Long Pea-Shooter. 1954.
—The Cold Green Element. 1955.
—The Blue Propeller. 1955.
—The Bull Calf And Other Poems. 1956.
—Music On A Kazoo. 1956.
—A Laughter In The Mind. 1958.
—Red Carpet For The Sun. 1959.
—The Swinging Flesh. 1961.
—Balls For A One-Armed Juggler. 1963.
—The Laughing Rooster. 1964.
—Collected Poems. 1965.
—Periods Of The Moon. 1967.
—The Shattered Plinths. 1968.
—The Whole Bloody Bird. 1969.
—Selected Poems. 1969.
—Nail Polish. 1971.
—Collected Poems. 1971.
—Lovers And Lesser Men. 1973.
—The Pole Vaulter. 1974.
—Seventy-Five Greek Poems. 1974.
—The Darkening Fire: Selected Poems, 1945-1968. 1975.
—Selected Poems, 1969-1975. 1979.
—For My Brother Jesus. McClelland & Stewart, 1976.
—The Covenant. McClelland & Stewart, 1977.
—Selected Poems. 1977.
—The Tightrope Dancer. McClelland & Stewart, 1978.
—The Love Poems Of Irving Layton. 1978.
—Droppings From Heaven. McClelland & Stewart, 1979.
—For My Neighbours In Hell. Mosaic Press, 1980.
—Europe And Other Bad News. McClelland & Stewart, 1981.
—A Wild Peculiar Joy: Selected Poems 1945-1982. McClelland & Stewart, 1982.
—The Gucci Bag. McClelland & Stewart, 1983.
—With Reverence And Delight. Mosaic Press, 1984.
—Dance With Desire. McClelland & Stewart, 1986.
—Final Reckoning: Poems 1982-1986. Mosaic Press, 1987.
—Fortunate Exile. McClelland & Stewart, 1987.

Lefcowitz, Barbara F.: *A Risk Of Green*. Gallimaufry, 1978.
—The Wild Piano. Dryad, 1981.
—The Queen Of Lost Baggage. Washington Writers' Publishing House, 1986.

Lense, Edward: *Buried Voices*. Logan Elm Press, Ohio State University, 1982.

Lepore, Dominick J.: *The Praise And The Praised*. Bruce Humphries, 1955.
—Within His Walls. Branden Press, 1968.

Levett, John: *Changing Sides*. Peterloo Poets (England), 1983.
—Skedaddle. Peterloo Poets (England), 1987.

Levine, Philip: *On The Edge*. Stone Wall Press, 1963.
—Not This Pig. Wesleyan University Press, 1968.
—Red Dust. Kayak Press, 1971.
—Pili's Wall. Unicorn Press, 1971.
—They Feed The Lion. Atheneum, 1972.
—1933. Atheneum, 1974.
—The Names Of The Lost. Atheneum, 1976.
—Ashes. Atheneum, 1979.
—7 Years From Somewhere. Atheneum, 1979.
—One For The Rose. Atheneum, 1981.
—Selected Poems. Atheneum, 1984.
—Sweet Will. Atheneum, 1985.
—A Walk With Tom Jefferson. 1988.

Levy, Robert J.: *The Glitter Bait*. Arts-Wayland Foundation, 1986.
—Whistle Maker. Anhinga Press, 1987.

Lieberman, Laurence: *The Unblinding*. Macmillan, 1968.
—The Osprey Suicides, Macmillan, 1973.
—God's Measurements. Macmillan, 1980.
—Eros At The World Kite Pageant. Macmillan, 1983.
—The Mural Of Wakeful Sleep. Macmillan, 1985.
—The Creole Mephistopheles. Macmillan, 1988.

Liotta, Peter H.: *Solstice*. Pathos Press, 1986.
—Tellurion. Cornell University Council for the Creative and Performing Arts, 1988.

Lipsitz, Lou: *Cold Water*. Wesleyan University Press, 1967.
—Reflections On Samson. Kayak Press, 1977.

Logue, Christopher: *War Music*. F. S. & G. (England), 1987.
—Ode To The Dodo. Jonathan Cape (England), 1987.

Lohmann, Jeanne: *Bonnie Jeanne* (with Harry A. Ackley). Privately printed, 1971.
—Where The Field Goes. Privately printed, 1976.
—Steadying The Landscape. Privately printed, 1982.

Long, Virginia: *Song Of America*. Aquarian Truth Press, 1976.
—The Armadillo From Amarillo. Image Press, 1980.

Loots, Barbara: *The Bride's Mirror Speaks*. Rockhill Press, 1986.

Lott, Rick: *Digging For Shark Teeth*. Anhinga Press, 1984.
—The Patience Of Horses. Livingston University Press, 1987.

Low, Denise: *Dragon Kite*. BkMk Press, 1981.
—Spring Geese. University of Kansas Museum of Natural History, 1984.
—Quilting. Holiseventh Press, 1984.

—Learning The Language of Rivers. Midwest Quarterly, 1987.

Lunde, David: *Ironic Holidays.* Sariya Press, 1965.
—Les Papillons. Lupo Press, 1967.
—Sludge Gulper 1. Basilisk Press, 1971.
—Calibrations. Allegany Mountain Press, 1981.

Lux, Thomas: *Memory's Handgrenade.*
—The Glassblower's Breath.
—Sunday.
—Half Promised Land.

M

Madson, Arthur: *Find My Pelvis.* Plaxis Press, 1982.
—Because It's Sprung An Oooze. Plaxis Press, 1982.

Magarrell, Elaine: *On Hogback Mountain.* Washington Writer's Publishing House, 1985.

Mahapatra, Jayanta: *Close The Sky, Ten By Ten.* Dialogue (India), 1971.
—Svayamvara & Other Poems. Writers' Workshop (India), 1971.
—A Father's Hours. United Writers (India), 1976.
—A Rain Of Rites. University of Georgia Press, 1976.
—Waiting. Samkaleen Prakashan (India), 1979.
—The False Start. Clearing House (India), 1980.
—Relationship. Greenfield Review Press, 1980.
—Life Sighs. Oxford University Press (India), 1983.
—Dispossessed Nests. Nirala Publications (India), 1986.
—Burden Of Waves And Fruit. Three Continents Press, 1986.
—Selected Poems. Oxford University Press (India), 1987.

Maino, Jeannette: *Speeding Into Lost Landscapes.* Dry Creek Books, 1977.
—Islands. Dry Creek Books, 1982.

Makuck, Peter: *Where We Live.* BOA Editions, 1982.
—Pilgrims. Ampersand Press, 1987.

Male, Belkis Cuza: *El Viento En La Pared.* Universidad de Oriente (Cuba), 1962.
—Tiempos De Sol. Ediciones El Puente (Cuba), 1963.
—Cartas A Ana Frank. Cuadernos Union (Cuba), 1966.
—Woman On The Front Lines. Unicorn Press, 1987.

Mandel, Charlotte: *A Disc Of Clear Water.* Saturday Press, 1981.
—Doll. Salt-Works Press, 1986.

Margolis, Gary: *The Day We Still Stand Here.* University of Georgia Press, 1983.
—Falling Awake. University of Georgia Press, 1986.

Marshall, Margaret: *Intermezzo.* Outposts Publications, 1972.

Martin, Charles: *Room For Error.* University of Georgia Press, 1978.
—Passages From Friday. Abattoir Editions, 1983.
—Steal The Bacon. Johns Hopkins University Press, 1987.

Mason, Julian: *Search Party.* Pageant Press, 1953.

Masters, Marcia Lee: *Intent On Earth.* Candlelight Press, 1965.
—Wind Around The Moon. Dragon's Teeth Press, 1986.

Matthews, William: *Ruining The New Road.* Random House, 1970.
—Sleek For The Long Flight. Random House, 1972.
—Sticks & Stones. Pentagram, 1975.
—Rising And Falling. Atlantic, Little Brown, 1979.
—Flood. Atlantic, Little Brown, 1984.
—A Happy Childhood. Atlantic, Little Brown, 1984.
—A Happy Childhood (British edition). Secker & Warburg, 1985.
—Foreseeable Futures. Houghton Mifflin, 1987.

Maura, Sister: *Initiate The Heart.* Macmillan, 1946.
—The Word Is Love. Macmillan, 1958.
—Bell Sound And Vintage. Contemporary Poetry, 1966.
—Walking On Water. Paulist/Newman, 1972.
—What We Women Know. Sparrow Press, 1980.
—A Word, A Tree: Christmas Poems. Franciscan Graphics, 1980.
—The Flowering Of The Word Of God. Franciscan Graphics, 1985.

Mayhall, Jane: *Ready For The Ha-Ha.* Eakins Press, 1966.
—Givers & Takers 1. Eakins Press, 1968.
—Givers & Takers 2. Eakins Press, 1973.

Mazur, Gail: *Nightfire.* David R. Godine, 1978.
—The Pose of Happiness. David R. Godine, 1986.

Mazzaro, Jerome: *Changing The Windows: Poems.* Ohio University Press, 1966.
—The Caves Of Love. Jazz Press, 1985.
—Rubbings. Quiet Hills Press, 1985.

McAdam, Rhona: *Life In Glass.* Longspoon Press, 1984.
—Hour Of The Pearl. Thistledown Press, 1987.

McCann, Janet: *How They Got Here.* Pudding Publications, 1985.

McCue, Edward Patrick: *Observer.* Lorrah & Hitchcock Publishers, 1987.

McCurdy, Harold: *A Straw Flute.* Meredith College, 1946.
—The Chastening Of Narcissus. Blair, 1970.
—Novus Ordo Seclorum. Privately printed, 1981.
—And Then The Sky Turned Blue. Briarpatch Press, 1982.

McDonald, Walter: *Caliban In Blue.* Texas Tech Press, 1976.
—One Thing Leads To Another. Cedar Rock Press, 1978.
—Anything, Anything. L'Epervier Press, 1980.

—*Working Against Time*. Calliope Press, 1981.

—*Burning The Fence*. Texas Tech Press, 1981.

—*Witching On Hardscrabble*. Spoon River Poetry Press, 1985.

—*The Flying Dutchman*. Ohio State University Press, 1987.

—*After The Noise Of Saigon*. University of Massachusetts Press, 1987.

McElroy, Colleen J.: *Music From Home: Selected Poems*. Southern Illinois University Press, 1976.

—*Winters Without Snow*. I. Reed Publishing, 1979.

—*Lie And Say You Love Me*. Circinatum Press, 1981.

—*Queen Of The Ebony Isles*. Wesleyan University Press, 1984.

—*Bone Flames*. Wesleyan University Press, 1987.

McFadden, David: *The Poem Poem*. Weed/Flower Press, 1967.

—*Letters From The Earth To The Earth*. Coach House Press, 1968.

—*The Saladmaker*. Imago Books, 1968.

—*Poems Worth Knowing*. Coach House Press, 1971.

—*Intense Pleasure*. McClelland and Stewart, 1972.

—*The Ova Yogas*. Ganglia Press, 1972.

—*A Knight In Dried Plums*. McClelland and Stewart, 1975.

—*The Great Canadian Sonnet*. Coach House Press, 1975.

—*I Don't Know*. Cross Country Press, 1977.

—*The Saladmaker* (revised edition). Cross Country Press, 1977.

—*The Poet's Progress*. Coach House Press, 1977.

—*On The Road Again*. McClelland and Stewart, 1978.

—*A Trip Around Lake Huron*. Coach House Press, 1981.

—*A Trip Around Lake Erie*. Coach House Press, 1981.

—*My Body Was Eaten By Dogs: Selected Poems*. McClelland and Stewart, 1981.

—*Three Stories And Ten Poems*. Identity Press, 1982.

—*Country Of The Open Heart*. Longspoon Press, 1982.

—*A Pair of Baby Lambs*. Front Press, 1983.

—*Animal Spirits*. Coach House Press, 1983.

—*The Art Of Darkness*. McClelland and Stewart, 1984.

—*Canadian Sunset*. Black Moss Press, 1986.

—*Gypsy Guitar: A Hundred Poems Of Romance And Betrayal*. Talon Books, 1987.

—*A Trip Around Lake Ontario*. Coach House Press, 1988.

McFarland, Ron: *Certain Women*. Confluence Press, 1977.

—*Composting At Forty*. Confluence Press, 1984.

McGuinn, Rex: *Seasons Of Acceptance*. Cairn Press, 1973.

McKain, David: *In Touch*. Ardis Books, 1975.

—*The Common Life*. Alice James Books, 1982.

McKean, James: *Headlong*. University of Utah Press, 1987.

McKee, Louis: *Schuylkill County*. Wampeter Press, 1982.

—*The True Speed Of Things*. Slash & Burn Press, 1984.

—*Safe Water*. Slash & Burn Press, 1986.

—*No Matter*. Pig in the Poke Press, 1987.

McLean, Anne: *Lil*. New Delta, 1977.

—*A Nun's Diary*. Vehicule Press, 1984.

Meek, Jay: *The Week The Dirigible Came*. Carnegie-Mellon University Press, 1976.

—*Drawing On The Walls*. Carnegie-Mellon University Press, 1980.

—*Earthly Purposes*. Carnegie-Mellon University Press, 1986.

—*Stations*. Carnegie-Mellon University Press, 1988.

Meinke, Peter: *Lines From Neuchatel*. Konglomerati Press, 1974.

—*The Rat Poems*. Bits Press, 1977.

—*The Night Train & The Golden Bird*. University of Pittsburgh Press, 1977.

—*Trying To Surprise God.*. University of Pittsburgh Press, 1981.

—*Underneath The Lantern*. Heatherstone Press, 1987.

—*Night Watch On The Chesapeake*. University of Pittsburgh Press, 1987.

Meissner, Bill: *Learning To Breathe Underwater*. Ohio University Press, 1979.

Menashe, Samuel: *The Many Named Beloved*. Victor Gollancz, Ltd., 1961.

—*No Jerusalem But This*. October House, 1971.

—*Fringe Of Fire*. Victor Gollancz, Ltd., 1973.

—*To Open*. Viking Press, 1974.

—*Collected Poems*. National Poetry Foundation, 1986.

Miller, Leslie Adrienne: *Hanging On The Sunburned Arm Of Some Homeboy*. Domino Impressions, 1982.

—*No River*. St. Louis Poetry Center, 1987.

Miller, Michael: *Jackhammer*. Helikon Press, 1972.

Miller, Philip: *Cats In The House*. Woodley Press, 1987.

—*George Grand*. Samisdat Press, 1987.

Milosz, Czeslaw: *The Captive Mind*. 1953.

—*Native Realm*. 1968.

—*Selected Poems*. 1972.

—*Bells In Winter*. 1978.

—*The Issa Valley*. 1981.

—*Separate Notebooks*. 1984.

—*The Land Of Ulro.*. 1984.

—*The Unattainable Earth*. 1985.

Minar, Scott: *The Nexus Of Rain*. Ohio Review Books, 1986.

Minton, Helena: *The Canal Bed*. Alice James Books, 1985.

Mitcham, Judson: *Notes For A Prayer In June*. State Street Press, 1986.

Montesi, Albert J.: *Micrograms*. Maryhurst Press, 1967.
—*Windows And Mirrors*. Cornerstone Press, 1977.
—*Five Dinners To Cheap Cuts*. Toulouse Press (England), 1980.
—*Robots And Gardens*. Cornerstone Press, 1984.
Moore, Barbara: *The Passionate City*. Hoffstadt Press, 1979.
Moore, Richard: *A Question Of Survival*. University of Georgia Press, 1971.
—*Word From The Hills: A Sonnet Sequence In Four Movements*. University of Georgia Press, 1972.
—*Empires*. Ontario Review Press, 1981.
—*The Education Of A Mouse*. Countryman Press, 1983.
Moran, Ronald: *So Simply Means The Rain*. Claitor's Book Store, 1965.
Morgan, Robert: *Zirconia Poems*. Lillabulero Press, 1969.
—*Red Owl*. W. W. Norton, 1972.
—*Land Diving*. Louisiana State University Press, 1976.
—*Trunk & Thicket*. L'Epervier Press, 1978.
—*Groundwork*. Gnomen Press, 1979.
—*Bronze Age*. Iron Mountain Press, 1981.
—*At The Edge Of The Orchard Country*. Wesleyan University Press, 1987.
Moritz, A. F.: *New Poems*. Swan Song Books, 1974.
—*Here*. Contraband Press, 1975.
—*Catalogue Of Bourgeois Objects*. Some, 1976.
—*Water Follies*. Killaly Press, 1977.
—*The Death Of Francisco Franco*. Blackfish Press, 1979.
—*Signs And Certainties*. Villeneuve Press, 1979.
—*Keats In Rome*. L1 Editions, 1979.
—*Music And Exile*. Dreadnaught Press, 1980.
—*Black Orchid*. Dreadnaught Press, 1981.
—*Between The Root And The Flower*. Blackfish Press, 1982.
—*The Visitation*. Aya Press, 1983.
—*Putting Up For The Night*. Northern Lights (England), 1985.
—*The Tradition*. Princeton University Press, 1986.
Morrison, Lillian: *The Ghosts Of Jersey City*. T. Y. Crowell, 1967.
—*Miranda's Music* (with Jean Boudin). T. Y. Crowell, 1968.
—*The Sidewalk Racer*. Lothrop, Lee & Shepard, 1977.
—*Who Would Marry A Mineral?* Lothrop, Lee & Shepard, 1978.
—*Overheard In A Bubble Chamber*. Lothrop, Lee & Shepard, 1981.
—*The Break Dance Kids*. Lothrop, Lee & Shepard, 1985.
Morrow, M.E.: *Ghosts On The Run*. Merton Press, 1984.
Morton, Colin: *In Transit*. Thistledown Press, 1981.

—*Printed Matter*. Sidereal Press, 1982.
—*This Won't Last Forever*. Longspoon Press, 1985.
—*The Merzbook*. Quarry Press, 1987.
Murphy, Kay: *The Autopsy*. Spoon River Poetry Press, 1985.
Murray, G. E.: *A Mile Called Timothy*. Ironwood Press, 1972.
—*Holding Fast*. Bonewhistle Press, 1974.
—*Gasoline Dreams*. Red Hill Press, 1978.
—*Repairs*. University of Missouri Press, 1980.

N

Nash, Valery: *The Narrows*. Cleveland State University Poetry Center, 1980.
Nelson, Eric: *On Call*. Moonsquilt Press, 1983.
—*The Light Bringers*. Washington Writers' Publishing House, 1984.
Newlove, John: *Black Night Window*. McClelland and Stewart, 1968.
—*The Cave*. McClelland and Stewart, 1970.
—*Lies*. McClelland and Stewart, 1972.
—*The Fat Man: Selected Poems 1962-1972*. McClelland and Stewart, 1977.
—*Moving In Alone*. Oolichan Books, 1977.
—*The Night The Dog Smiled*. ECW Press, 1986.
Newman, P. B.: *The Cheetah And The Fountain*. South and West, 1968.
—*Dust Of The Sun*. South and West, 1969.
—*The Ladder Of Love*. Smith-Horizon Press, 1970.
—*Paula*. Dragon's Teeth Press, 1975.
—*The House On The Saco*. William L. Bauhan, 1977.
—*The Light Of The Red Horse*. Carolina Wren Press, 1981.
—*The G. Washington Poems*. Briarpatch Press, 1986.
Niditch, B. Z.: *Freedom Trail*. Wings Press, 1980.
—*Elements*. MO.O.P. Press, 1980.
—*A Boston Winter*. Realities Library, 1982.
—*Unholy Empire*. Ptolemy/Browns Mills Review, 1982.
—*A Musical Collection*. M.A.F. Press, 1984.
—*In Dreams*. Parvenu Press, 1986.
Nielsen, Nancy L.: *Living On Salt And Stone*. 1984.
—*Blackberries And Dust*. 1984.
—*East Of The Light*. 1985.
Nimnicht, Nona: *In The Museum Naked*. Second Coming Press, 1978.
Nims, John Frederick: *The Iron Pastoral*. William Sloane Associates, 1947.
—*A Fountain In Kentucky*. William Sloane Associates, 1950.
—*Knowledge Of The Evening*. Rutgers University Press, 1960.
—*Of Flesh And Bone*. Rutgers University Press, 1967.
—*Selected Poems*. University of Chicago Press, 1982.

—The Kiss: Jambalaya. Houghton Mifflin, 1982.

Nonagase, Masao: *Flowers Bloomed In The Prison Yard.* 1927 (Japan).
—Sorrowful Bread. 1929 (Japan).
—Poems For Home Country. 1941 (Japan).
—Yamato Yoshino. 1960 (Japan).
—Lyrics Of Japan. 1965 (Japan).
—TheSky Of That Day Was Blue. Kin-no-hoshi Publishing Co. (Japan), 1970.
—Old Age Lyrics. Kin-no-hoshi Publishing Co. (Japan), 1971.
—My Little House. Kodansha (Japan), 1976.
—A Boy Crossed The River. PHP-Kenkyusho (Japan), 1977.
—Songs Of Tender Love. Kin-no-hoshi Publishing Co. (Japan), 1979.
—Old Age Blues In The Sunset. Kado Sobo (Japan), 1981.

Nord, Gennie: *Greene's Barn.* Valhalla Publications, 1986.

Norris, Ken: *Vegetables.* Vehicule Press, 1975.
—Autokenesis. Cross Country Press, 1980.
—To Sleep, To Love. Guernica Editions, 1982.
—Whirlwinds. Guernica Editions, 1983.
—The Better Part Of Heaven. Coach House Press, 1984.
—One Night. Black Moss Press, 1985.
—In The Spirit Of The Times. Muses' Co., 1986.
—Report On The Second Half Of TheTwentieth Century. Guernica Editions, 1987.

Nye, Naomi Shihab: *Different Ways To Pray.* Breitenbush Books, 1980.
—Hugging The Jukebox. E. P. Dutton, 1982.
—Yellow Glove. Breitenbush Books, 1986.

O

Ochester, Ed: *Dancing On The Edges Of Knives.* University of Missouri Press, 1973.
—The End Of The Ice Age. Slow Loris Press, 1977.
—A Drift Of Swine. Thunder City Press, 1981.
—Miracle Mile. Carnegie-Mellon University Press, 1984.
—Weehawken Ferry. Juniper Press, 1985.
—Changing The Name To Ochester. Carnegie-Mellon University Press, 1987.

Older, Julia: *Conts And Others.* Unicorn Press, 1982.
—A Little Wild. Typographeum Press, 1987.

Olds, Sharon: *Satan Says.* University Of Pittsburgh Press, 1980.
—The Dead And The Living. Knopf, 1984.
—The Gold Cell. Knopf, 1987.

Oliveros, Chuck: *The Pterodactyl In The Wilderness.* Dead Angel Press, 1983.

Orr, Gregory: *Burning The Empty Nests.* Harper & Row, 1973.
—Gathering The Bones Together. Harper & Row, 1975
—The Red House. Harper & Row, 1980.
—We Must Make A Kingdom Of It. Wesleyan University Press, 1986.
—New And Selected Poems. Wesleyan University Press, 1987.

Orth, Kevin: *The Other Life.* Plaice Press, 1987.

Osers, Ewald: *Wish You Were Here.* Hub Publications (England), 1976.
—Anamneza. Odeon Publishing House (Czechoslovakia), 1986.

Owen, Sue: *Nursery Rhymes For The Dead.* Ithaca House, 1980.

P

Pacernick, Gary: *Credence.* Quinn Press, 1974.
—Wanderers. Prasada Press, 1985.
—The Jewish Poems. Wright State University Monographs, 1985.

Pacey, Michael: *Anonymous Mesdemoiselles.* New Brunswick Chapbooks, 1972.
—Birds Of Christmas. Three Trees Press, 1987.

Page, Wiliam: *Clutch Plates.* Branden Press, 1976.
—The Gatekeeper. Ion/Raccoon Books, 1982.
—Bodies Not Our Own. Memphis State University Press, 1986.

Palen, John: *To Coax A Fire.* Green River Press, 1984.

Pape, Greg: *Little America.* Maguey Press, 1976.
—Border Crossings. University of Pittsburgh Press, 1978.
—Black Branches. University of Pittsburgh Press, 1984.

Parini, Jay: *Singing In Time.* 1972.
—Anthracite Country. Random House, 1982.
—Town Life. Holt, 1988.

Pass, John: *Taking Place.* Talonbooks, 1971.
—The Kenojuak Prints. Caledonia Writing Series, 1973.
—AIR 18. Airbooks, 1973.
—Port Of Entry. Repository Press, 1975.
—Love's Confidence. Caledonia Writing Series, 1976.
—Blossom: An Accompaniment. Cobblestone Press, 1978.
—There Go The Cars. Sesame Press, 1979.
—An Arbitrary Dictionary. Coach House Press, 1984.

Pastan, Linda: *A Perfect Circle Of Sun.* Swallow Press, 1971.
—Aspects Of Eve. Liveright/Norton, 1975.
—The 5 Stages Of Grief. W. W. Norton, 1978.
—Setting The Table. Druad Press, 1980.
—Even As We Sleep. Croissant Press, 1980.
—Waiting For My Life. W. W. Norton, 1981.
—PM/AM: New & Selected Poems. W. W. Norton, 1982.
—A Fraction Of Darkness. W. W. Norton, 1985.
—The Imperfect Paradise. W. W. Norton, forthcoming.

Peacock, Molly: *And Live Apart.* University of Missouri Press, 1980.
—Raw Heaven. Random House, 1984.

Perel, Jane Lunin: *The Lone Ranger And The Neo-American Church.* Archival Press, 1975.

—*The Fishes*. Providence College Press, 1977.
—*Blowing Kisses To The Sharks*. Copper Beech Press, 1978.

Perlberg, Mark: *The Burning Field*. William Morrow, 1970.
—*The Feel Of The Sun*. Swallow/University of Ohio Press, 1981.

Petrie, Paul: *Confessions Of A Non-Conformist*. Hillside Press, 1963.
—*The Race With Time And The Devil*. Golden Quill Press, 1965.
—*From Under The Hell Of Night*. Vanderbilt University Press, 1969.
—*The Academy Of Goodbye*. University Press of New England, 1974.
—*Light From The Furnace Rising*. Copper Beech Press, 1978.
—*Not Seeing Is Believing*. Juniper Press, 1983.
—*Strange Gravity*. Tidal Press, 1984.

Pettit, Michael: *American Light*. University of Georgia Press, 1984.

Pfingston, Roger: *Stoutes Creek Road*. Raintree Press, 1976.
—*Nesting*. Sparrow Press, 1978.
—*The Presence Of Trees*. Raintree Press, 1979.
—*Hazards Of Photography*. Writers' Center Press, 1980.
—*The Circus Of Unreasonable Acts*. Years Press, 1982.
—*Something Iridescent*. Barnwood Press, 1987.

Phelps, Dean: *When The Morning Comes*. Harpoon Press, 1974.
—*Shoshoni River Witching Hour*. Holmgangers Press, 1975.
—*The Serum Of The Water*. Holmgangers Press, 1978.

Phillips, Robert: *Inner Weather*. Golden Quill Press, 1966.
—*The Pregnant Man*. Doubleday, 1978.
—*Running On Empty*. Doubleday, 1981.
—*Personal Acounts: New & Selected Poems, 1966-1986*. Ontario Review Press, 1986.
—*The Wounded Angel*. Brighton Press, 1987.

Pijewski, John: *Dinner With Uncle Jozef*. Wesleyan University Press, 1982.

Pinsker, Sanford: *Still Life And Other poems*. Greenfield Review Press, 1975.
—*Memory Breaks Off And Other Poems*. Northwoods Press, 1984.
—*Whales At Play And Other Poems Of Travel*. Northwoods Press, 1986.

Pollitt, Katha: *Antarctic Traveller*. Alfred A. Knopf, 1982.

Polson, Don: *Wakening*. Fiddlehead Poetry Books, 1971.
—*Brief Evening In A Catholic Hospital*. Fiddlehead Poetry Books, 1972.
—*In Praise of Young Thieves*. Alive Press, 1975.
—*Lone Travellers*. Fiddlehead Poetry Books, 1979.
—*Moving Through Deep Snow*. Thistledown Press, 1984.
—*And Though It Is Not Death*. Wee Giant Press, 1986.

Powell, Joseph: *Counting The Change*. Quarterly Review of Literature Press, 1986.

Powell, Susan: *An Act Of Leaving*. San Pedro Press, 1983.

Pratt, Charles W.: *In The Orchard*. Tidal Press, 1986.

Privett, Katharine: *The Poet-People*. San Marcos Press, 1976.
—*The Dreams Of Exiles*. Holmgangers Press, 1982.
—*Two Figures In Circular Dance*. Samisdat, 1986.

Pulley, Nancy L.: *Desert And Hibiscus*. Writer's Center Press, 1985.

R

Raborg, Frederick A.: *Why Should The Devil Have All The Good Tunes?* Parvenu Press, 1972.
—*Tule*. Amelia, 1986.
—*Hakata*. Amelia, 1987.

Radu, Kenneth: *Letter To A Distant Father*. Brick Books, 1987.

Ragan, James: *In The Talking Hours*. Eden-Hall, 1979.

Ramke, Bin: *The Difference Between Night And Day*. Yale University Press, 1978.
—*White Monkeys*. University of Georgia Press, 1981.
—*The Language Student*. Louisiana State University Press, 1986.

Ramsey, Jarold: *The Space Between Us*. Adam Press (England), 1970.
—*Love In An Earthquake*. University of Washington Press, 1973.
—*Dermographia*. Cornstalk Press, 1982.

Rankin, Paula: *By The Wreckmaster's Cottage*. Carnegie-Mellon University Press, 1977.
—*Augers*. Carnegie-Mellon University Press, 1981.
—*To The House Ghost*. Carnegie-Mellon University Press, 1985.

Ray, David: *X-Rays: A Book Of Poems*. Cornell University Press, 1965.
—*Dragging The Main And Other Poems*. Cornell University Press, 1968.
—*A Hill In Oklahoma*. BkMk Press, 1972.
—*Gathering Firewood: New Poems And Selected*. Wesleyan University Press, 1974.
—*Enough Of Flying: Poems Inspired By The Ghazals Of Ghalib*. Writers Workshop (India), 1977.
—*The Tramp's Cup*. Chariton Review Press, 1978.
—*The Touched Life*. Scarecrow Press, 1982.
—*Not Far From The River: Transcreations From The Gatha-Saptasati*. Prakrit Society (India), 1984.
—*On Wednesday I Cleaned Out My Wallet*. Pancake Press, 1984.
—*Sam's Book*. Wesleyan University Press, 1987.

—The Maharani's New Wall. Wesleyan University Press, 1989.

Ray, Judy: *Pebble Rings.* Greenfield Review Press, 1980.

Reed, Alison: *The First Movement.* Dragon's Teeth Press, 1976.

—Bid Me Welcome. Golden Quill Press, 1978.

Rees, Ennis: *Selected Poems.* University of South Carolina Press, 1973.

Reiss, James: *The Breathers.* Ecco Press/Viking, 1974.

—Express. University of Pittsburgh Press, 1983.

Revell, Donald: *From The Abandoned Cities.* Harper & Row, 1983.

Ridl, Jack: *The Same Ghost.* Dawn Valley Press, 1984.

Rigsbee, David: *Stamping Ground.* Ardis Publishers, 1976.

—The Hopper Light. L'Epervier Press, 1987.

—Memory Annex. Thunder City Press, 1987.

Rivers, J. W.: *From The Chicago Notebook.* Spoon River Poetry Press, 1979.

—Proud And On My Feet. University of Georgia Press, 1983.

—When The Owl Cries, Indians Die. Associated University Presses, 1986.

Rizzuto, Helen Morrissey: *Evening Sky On A Japanese Screen.* Lintel, 1978.

—A Bird In Flight. Lintel, 1986.

Robbins, Richard: *Toward New Weather.* Frontier Award Committee, 1979.

—The Invisible Wedding. University of Missouri Press, 1984.

Roberts, Len: *Cohoes Theater.* Momentum Press, 1981.

—From The Dark. State University of New York Press, 1984.

—Sweet Ones. Milkweed Editions, 1987.

Robertson, William B.: *Standing On Our Own Two Feet.* Coteau Books, 1986.

Root, Judith: *Weaving The Sheets.* Abattoir Editions, 1985.

Rosberg, Rose: *Trips—Without LSD.* Fiddlehead Poetry Books, 1969.

Rosenberg, Liz: *The Fire Music.* University of Pittsburgh Press, 1986.

Rosenberger, F. C.: *The Virginia Poems.* University of Virginia Press, 1943.

—XII Poems. University of Virginia Press, 1946.

—One Season Here. University of Virginia Press, 1976.

—An Alphabet. University of Virginia Press, 1978.

—The Visit. Honeybrook Press, 1984.

—Pattern & Variation. Honeybrook Press, 1986.

Ruark, Gibbons: *A Program For Survival.* University Press of Virginia, 1971.

—Reeds. Texas Tech Press, 1978.

—Keeping Company. Johns Hopkins University Press, 1983.

—Small Rain. Center for Edition Works, SUNY-Purchase, 1984.

Rubin, Larry: *The World's Old Way.* University of

Nebraska Press, 1963.

—Lanced In Light. Harcourt, Brace & World, 1967.

—All My Mirrors Lie. Godine Press, 1975.

Ruffin, Paul: *Lighting The Furnace Pilot.* Spoon River Poetry Press, 1980.

—Our Women. Abbott House Press, 1982.

—The Storm Cellar. Ceder Creek Press, 1985.

Russ, Lawrence: *The Burning-Ground.* Owl Creek Press, 1981.

Rutsala, Vern: *The Window.* Wesleyan University Press, 1965.

—Laments. New Rivers Press, 1975.

—The Journey Begins. University of Georgia Press, 1976.

—Paragraphs. Wesleyan Univesity Press, 1978.

—Walking Home From The Icehouse. Carnegie-Mellon University Press, 1981.

—Backtracking. Story Line Press, 1985.

—Ruined Cities. Carnegie-Mellon University Press, 1987.

Ryan, Kay: *Strangely Marked Metal.* Copper Beech Press, 1985.

S

Sadoff, Ira: *Settling Down.* Houghton Mifflin, 1975.

—Palm Reading In Winter. Houghton Mifflin, 1978.

—Maine: Nine Poems. Pym-Randall, 1981.

—A Northern Calendar. David Godine, 1982.

—Emotional Traffic. David Godine, 1988.

Sargent, Robert: *Now Is Always The Miraculous Time.* Washington Writers' Publishing House, 1977.

—A Woman From Memphis. Word Works, 1979.

—Aspects Of A Southern Story. Word Works, 1983.

Sarton, May: *Encounter In April.* Houghton Mifflin, 1937.

—Inner Landscape. Houghton Mifflin, 1939.

—The Lion And The Rose. Rinehart & Co., 1948.

—The Leaves Of The Tree. Cornell Chapbook, 1950.

—The Land Of Silence. Rinehart & Co., 1953.

—In Time Like Air. Rinehart & Co., 1957.

—Cloud, Stone, Sun, Vine. W. W. Norton, 1961.

—A Private Mythology. W. W. Norton, 1966.

—As Does New Hampshire. Richard R. Smith, 1967.

—Plant Dreaming Deep. W. W. Norton, 1968.

—Kinds Of Love. W. W. Norton, 1970.

—Bridge of Years. W. W. Norton, 1971.

—A Grain Of Mustard Seed. W. W. Norton, 1971.

—Faithful Are The Wounds. W. W. Norton, 1972.

—A Durable Fire. W. W. Norton, 1972.

—As We Are Now. W. W. Norton, 1973.

—Collected Poems, 1930-1973. W. W. Norton, 1974.

—*Crucial Conversations.* W. W. Norton, 1975.

—*The Small Room.* W. W. Norton, 1976.

—*A Walk Through The Woods.* Harper & Row, 1976.

—*A World Of Light.* W. W. Norton, 1976.

—*Selected Poems Of May Sarton* (edited by Serena Sue Hilsinger and Lois Byrnes). W. W. Norton, 1978.

—*A Reckoning.* W. W. Norton, 1978.

—*A Fur Person.* W. W. Norton, 1979.

—*A Shower Of Summer Days.* W. W. Norton, 1979.

—*Halfway To Silence.* W. W. Norton, 1980.

—*A Winter Garland.* William B. Ewert, 1982.

Savishinsky, Joel: *The Trail Of The Hare.* Gordon and Breach, 1978.

Scheier, Libby: *The Larger Life.* Black Moss Press, 1983.

—*Second Nature.* Coach House Press, 1986.

Schloss, David: *The Beloved.* Ashland Poetry Press, 1973.

—*Legends.* Windmill Press, 1976.

Schorb, E. M.: *The Poor Boy And Other Poems.* Dragon's Teeth Press, 1975.

—*50 Poems.* Hill House New York, 1987.

Schulman, Grace: *Burn Down The Icons.* Princeton University Press, 1976.

—*Hemispheres.* Sheep Meadow Press, 1984.

Schultz, Robert: *Vein Along The Fault.* Laueroc Press, 1979.

Schwartz, Hillel: *Phantom Children.* State Street Press, 1982.

Seifert, Jaroslav: *The Plague Column* (translated by Ewald Osers). Terra Nova Editions, 1979.

—*An Umbrella From Piccadilly* (translated by Ewald Osers). London Magazine Editions (England), 1983.

—*The Selected Poetry Of Jaroslav Seifert* (translated by Ewald Osers). Macmillan, 1986.

—*Women* (translated by Ewald Osers). 1986 (Netherlands).

Sexton, Tom: *Terra Incognita.* Solo Press, 1974.

Shapiro, Harvey: *The Eye.* Swallow Press, 1953.

—*Mountain, Fire, Thornbush.* Swallow Press, 1961.

—*Battle Report.* Wesleyan University Press, 1966.

—*This World.* Wesleyan University Press, 1971.

—*Lauds & Nightsounds.* Sun, 1978.

—*The Light Holds.* Wesleyan University Press, 1984.

—*National Cold Storage Company: New And Selected Poems.* Wesleyan University Press, 1988.

Shattuck, Roger: *Half Tame.* University of Texas Press, 1964.

Shaw, Robert B.: *Comforting The Wilderness.* Wesleyan University Press, 1977.

Sheck, Laurie: *Amaranth.* University of Georgia Press, 1981.

Sher, Steven: *Nickelodeon.* Gull Books, 1978.

—*Persnickety.* Seven Woods Press, 1979.

—*Caught In The Revolving Door.* Love Street Books, 1980.

—*Trolley Lives.* Wampeter Press, 1985.

Sherman, Kenneth: *Snake Music.* Mosaic Press, 1978.

—*The Cost Of Living.* Mosaic Press, 1981.

—*Words For Elephant Man.* Mosaic Press, 1983.

—*Black Flamingo.* Mosaic Press, 1985.

—*The Book Of Salt.* Oberon Press, 1987.

Shirley, Aleda: *Chinese Architecture.* University of Georgia Press, 1986.

Shuttleworth, Paul: *Moaning Woman Wind.* Lazy Ears Press, 1971.

—*Lanterns Searching Night.* Caledonia Writing Series, 1975.

—*Say That Again And I'll Kick Your Teeth In.* Caledonia Writing Series, 1975.

—*Sucking On Rattlesnake Bones.* Texas Portfolio Press, 1976.

—*Before It's Meant To Be That Way.* Texas Portfolio Press, 1977.

—*Poems To The Memory Of Benny Kid Paret.* Sparrow Press, 1978.

—*Refractions.* Impact Foundation Press, 1978.

—*Always Autumn.* Nebraska Review Chapbooks, 1980.

—*Bullpen Catcher.* Samisdat Press, 1984.

—*Over The Precipice.* Broncho Press, 1985.

—*Bullpen Catcher And Friends.* Samisdat Press, 1985.

—*Living And Sinning For Them.* Signport Press, 1986.

—*Hurrahing The Town.* Pterodactyl Press, 1988.

Sidney, Joan Seliger: *Deep Between The Rocks.* Andrew Mountain Press, 1985.

Siegel, Robert: *The Beasts & The Elders.* University Press of New England, 1973.

—*In A Pig's Eye.* University Presses of Florida, 1980.

Simmerman, Jim: *Home.* Dragon Gate, 1983.

Simon, Maurya: *The Enchanted Room.* Copper Canyon Press, 1986.

Simpson, Louis: *The Arrivistes: Poems 1940-49.* Fine Editions Press, 1949.

—*A Dream Of Governors.* Wesleyan University Press, 1959.

—*At The End Of The Open Road.* Wesleyan University Press, 1963.

—*Selected Poems.* Harcourt, Brace and World, 1965.

—*Adventures Of The Letter I.* Harper & Row, 1971.

—*Searching For The Ox.* William Morrow, 1976.

—*Armidale.* BOA Editions, 1979.

—*Out Of Season.* Deerfield Press, 1979.

—*Caviare At The Funeral.* Franklin Watts, 1980.

—*The Best Hour Of The Night.* Ticknor and Fields, 1983.

—*People Live Here: Selected Poems 1949-83.* BOA Editions, 1983.

Simpson, Nancy: *Across Water.* State Street Press, 1983.

—*Night Student.* State Street Press, 1985.

Singleton, Martin: *Difficult Magic.* Wolsak & Wynn, 1984.

Skeen, Anita: *Each Hand A Map.* Naiad Press, 1986.

Skillman, Judith: *The Worship Of The Visible Spectrum.* Breitenbush Books, 1987.

Skloot, Floyd: *Rough Edges.* Chowder Chapbooks, 1979.
—*Kaleidoscope.* Silverfish Review Press, 1986.

Skov-Nielsen, Kurt: *Snowed In.* The Purple Wednesday Society, 1987.

Smith, R. T.: *Walking Under Snow.* Cold Mountain Press, 1975.
—*Good Water.* Banjo Press, 1979.
—*Rural Route.* Tamarack Editions, 1981
—*Beasts Did Leap.* Tamarack Editions, 1982.
—*Finding The Path.* Black Willow Press, 1983.
—*From The High Dive.* Water Mark Press, 1983.
—*Roosevelt Unbound.* Tamarack Editions, 1985.
—*The Hollow Log Lounge.* Texas Review Press, 1986.
—*Birch-Light.* Tamarack Editions, 1986.
—*Banish Misfortune.* Livingston University Press, 1987.

Smith, Stephen E.: *The Bushnell Hamp Poems.* Green River Press, 1980.

Smith, Virginia E.: *Lion Rugs From Fars.* Northwoods/Dan River Press, 1982.
—*Inhale, Exhale, Hold.* Northwoods/Dan River Press, 1985.

Snively, Susan: *Voices In The House.* University of Alabama Press, 1988.

Solway, David: *In My Own Image.* McGill Poetry Series, 1961.
—*The Crystal Theatre.* Fiddlehead Poetry Books, 1971.
—*Paximalia.* Fiddlehead Poetry Books, 1972.
—*The Egyptian Airforce.* Fiddlehead Poetry Books, 1973.
—*The Road To Arginos.* Delta Canada, 1976.
—*Anacrusis.* Fiddlehead Poetry Books, 1977.
—*Mephistopheles And The Astronaut.* Mosaic Press, 1979.
—*The Mulberry Man.* Vehicule Press, 1982.
—*Selected Poetry.* Vehicule Press, 1982.
—*Stones In Water.* Mosaic Press, 1983.
—*Modern Marriage.* Vehicule Press, 1987.

Somoza, Joseph: *Greyhound.* Grande Ronde Press, 1968.
—*Olive Woman.* San Marcos Press, 1976.
—*Backyard Poems.* Cinco Puntos Press, 1986.

Sonde, Susan: *Inland Is Parenthetical.* Dryad Press, 1979.

Spacks, Barry: *The Company Of Children.* Doubleday, 1968.
—*Something Human.* Harper's Magazine Press, 1972.
—*Teaching The Penguins To Fly.* Godine, 1975.
—*Imagining A Unicorn.* University of Georgia Press, 1978.
—*Spacks Street: New And Selected Poems.* Johns Hopkins University Press, 1982.

Speer, Laurel: *A Bit Of Wit.* Gusto Press, 1979.
—*Lovers & Others.* Truedog Press, 1980.
—*Don't Dress Your Cat In An Apron.* Adastra Press, 1981.
—*Hokum/Visions Of A Gringa.* Seven Buffaloes Press, 1982.
—*The Hobbesian Apple.* Signpost Press, 1982.
—*T. Roosevelt Tracks The Last Buffalo.* Rhiannon Press, 1982.
—*I'm Hiding From The Cat.* Geryon Press, 1983.
—*One Lunch.* Geryon Press, 1984.
—*Weird Sister 1.* Geryon Press, 1984.
—*Vincent Et Al.* Geryon Press, 1985.
—*The Scandal Of Her Bath.* Geryon Press, 1986.
—*Second Thoughts Over Bourget.* Geryon Press, 1987.

Spence, Michael: *The Spine.* Purdue University Press, 1987.

Stafford, Kim R.: *A Gypsy's History Of The World.* Copper Canyon Press, 1976.
—*Braided Apart* (with William E. Stafford). Confluence Press, 1976.
—*The Granary.* Carnegie-Mellon University Press, 1982.
—*Places & Stories.* Carnegie-Mellon University Press, 1987.

Stafford, William: *Braided Apart* (with Kim R. Stafford). Confluence Press, 1976.
—*Smoke's Way.* Graywolf Press, 1978.
—*Stories That Could Be True: New And Collected Poems.* Harper & Row, 1978.
—*Things That Happen Where There Aren't Any People.* BOA Editions, 1980.
—*Sometimes Like A Legend.* Copper Canyon Press, 1981.
—*A Glass Face In The Rain.* Harper & Row, 1982.
—*Roving Across Fields.* Barnwood Press, 1983.
—*Segues: A Correspondence In Poetry* (with Marvin Bell). David R. Godine, 1983.
—*Listening Deep.* Penmaen Press, 1984.
—*Stories And Storms And Strangers.* Honeybrook Press, 1984.
—*An Oregon Message.* Harper & Row, 1987.

Standing, Sue: *Amphibious Weather.* Zephyr Press, 1981.
—*Deception Pass.* Alice James Books, 1984.

Steele, Timothy: *Uncertainties And Rest.* Louisiana State University Press, 1979.
—*Sapphics Against Anger And Other Poems.* Random House, 1986.

Steinbergh, Judith: *Marshmallow Worlds.* Grosset and Dunlap, 1972.
—*Lillian Bloom, A Separation.* Wampeter Press, 1980.
—*Motherwriter.* Wampeter Press, 1983.

Steingass, David: *Body Compass.* University of Pittsburgh Press, 1969.
—*American Handbook.* University of Pittsburgh Press, 1975.

Stern, Gerald: *Rejoicings.* Fiddlehead Poetry Books, 1972.
—*Lucky Life.* Houghton Mifflin, 1977.
—*The Red Coal.* Houghton Mifflin, 1981.
—*Paradise Poems.* Random House, 1984.
—*Lovesick.* Harper & Row, 1987.

Sternlieb, Barry: *Fission*. Adastra Press, 1986.
Stewart, Frank: *The Open Water*. Floating Island Publications, 1982.
—*Reunion*. Paper Press, 1986.
—*Flying The Red Eye*. Floating Island Publications, 1986.
Still, James: *Hounds On the Mountain*. Viking Press, 1937.
—*The Wolfpen Poems*. Berea College Press, 1986.
Stone, John: *The Smell Of Matches*. Rutgers University Press, 1972.
—*In All This Rain*. Louisiana State University Press, 1980.
—*Renaming The Streets*. Louisiana State University Press, 1985.
Stone, Ruth: *In An Iridescent Time*. Harcourt Brace Jovanovich, 1960.
—*Topography And Other Poems*. Harcourt Brace Jovanovich, 1971.
—*Unknown Messages*. Nemesis Press, 1973.
—*Cheap*. Harcourt Brace Jovanovich, 1975.
—*American Milk*. From Here Press, 1986.
—*Second Hand Coat*. David R. Godine, 1987.
Stout, Robert Joe: *The Trick*. Juniper Press, 1975.
—*Moving Out*. Road Runner Press, 1975.
—*Swallowing Dust*. Red Hill Press, 1976.
Strahan, B. R.: *Love Songs For An Age Of Anxiety*. Black Buzzard Press, 1980.
—*Poems*. Black Buzzard Press, 1981.
—*A Visit With Crocodile Man*. The Smith, 1988.
Struthers, Ann: *Stoneboat*. Pterodactyl Press, 1987.
Sullivan, Rosemary: *The Space A Name Makes*. Black Moss Press, 1986.
—*First Person Plural*. Black Moss Press, 1987.
Swanger, David: *Lemming Song*. Jazz, 1976.
—*The Shape Of Waters*. Ithaca House, 1978.
—*Inside The Horse*. Ithaca House, 1981.
Swann, Brian: *The Whale's Scars*. New Rivers Press, 1974.
—*Roots*. New Rivers Press, 1976.
—*Living Time*. Quarterly Review of Literature Press, 1978.
—*The Middle Of The Journey*. University of Alabama Press, 1983.
Swenson, Karen: *An Attic Of Ideals*. Doubleday, 1974.
—*East-West*. Confluence Press, 1980.
Swift, Joan: *This Element*. Alan Swallow, 1965.
—*Parts Of Speech*. Confluence Press, 1978.
—*The Dark Path Of Our Names*. Dragon Gate, 1985.
Sze, Arthur: *The Willow Wind*. Tooth of Time, 1981.
—*Two Ravens*. Tooth of Time, 1984.
—*Dazzled*. Floating Island Publications, 1982.
—*River River*. Lost Roads Publishers, 1987.

T

Tall, Deborah: *Eight Colors Wide*. London Magazine Editions, 1974.

—*Ninth Life*. Ithaca House, 1982.
Tana, Patti: *How Odd This Ritual Of Harmony* (under the name of Patti Renner-Tana). Gusto Press, 1981.
—*Ask The Dreamer Where Night Begins*. Kendall/Hunt Publishing Co., 1986.
Taylor, Bruce: *Everywhere The Beauty Gives Itself Away*. Red Weather Press, 1976.
—*Idle Trade: Early Poems*. Wolfsong Press, 1979.
—*The Darling Poems: A Romance*. Red Weather Press, 1984.
Taylor, James: *The Dreams*. Dolphin-Moon Press, 1978.
—*Tigerwolves*. Dolphin-Moon Press, 1982.
—*Baltimore-A City In Four Poems*. Dolphin-Moon Press, 1984.
—*Tricks Of Vision*. 7th Son Press, 1985.
Taylor, Sally: *A Little Light At The Edge Of Day*. Press Publishing Co., 1984.
Thompson, Gary: *Hold Fast*. Confluence Press, 1984.
Thompson, Phyllis Hoge: *Artichoke & Other Poems*. University Press of Hawaii, 1969.
—*The Creation Frame*. University of Illinois Press, 1973.
—*The Serpent Of The White Rose*. Petronium, 1976
—*What The Land Gave*. QRL Series III, 1981.
—*The Ghosts Of Who We Were*. University of Illinois Press, 1986.
Thurston, Harry: *Barefaced Stones*. Fiddlehead Poetry Books, 1980.
—*Clouds Flying Before The Eye*. Fiddlehead Poetry Books, 1985.
Timmerman, William: *Brain Coral*. Pineturn Press, 1982.
Towle, Parker: *Search For Doubloons*. Wings Press, 1984.
Trethewey, Eric: *In The Traces*. Inland Boat Pamphlet Series, 1980.
—*Dreaming Of Rivers*. Cleveland State University Poetry Center, 1984.
Trowbridge, William: *The Book Of Kong*. Iowa State University Press, 1986.

U

Uceda, Julia: *Mariposa En Cenizas*. Alcaravan (Spain), 1959.
—*Extrana Juventud*. Rialp (Spain), 1962.
—*Sin Mucha Esperanza*. Agora (Spain), 1966.
—*Poemas De Cherry Lane*. Agora (Spain), 1968.
—*Campanas En Sansuena*. Dulcinea (Spain), 1977.
—*Viejas Voces Secretas De La Noche*. Esquio-Ferrol (Spain), 1981.
Ullman, Leslie: *Natural Histories*. Yale University Press, 1979.
—*Dreams By No One's Daughter*. University of Pittsburgh Press, 1987.
Unterecker, John: *The Dreaming Zoo*. Henry Z.

Walck, 1965.
—*Dance Sequence*. Kayak Books, 1975.
—*Stone*. University of Hawaii Books, 1977.
Updike, John: *The Carpentered Hen*. Harper and Bros., 1958.
—*Telephone Poles*. Knopf, 1963.
—*Midpoint And Other Poems*. Knopf, 1969.
—*Tossing And Turning*. Knopf, 1977.
—*Facing Nature*. Knopf, 1985.
Urdang, Constance: *Charades & Celebrations*. October House, 1965.
—*The Picnic In The Cemetery*. Braziller, 1975.
—*The Lone Women And Others*. Pitt Poetry Series, 1981.
—*Only The World*. Pitt Poetry Series, 1983.

V

Van Brunt, Lloyd: *Uncertainties*. The Smith, 1968.
—*Indian Territory And Other Poems*. The Smith, 1974.
—*Feral: Crow-Breath & Caw*. Conspiracy Press, 1976.
—*For Luck: Poems 1962-1977*. Carnegie-Mellon University Press, 1978.
—*And The Man Who Was Traveling Never Got Home*. Carnegie-Mellon University Press, 1980.
—*Working Firewood For The Night*. 1988.
Van Duyn, Mona: *Valentines To The Wide World*. Cummington Press, 1959.
—*A Time Of Bees*. University of North Carolina Press, 1964.
—*To See, To Take*. Atheneum Publishers, 1970.
—*Bedtime Stories*. Ceres Press, 1972.
—*Merciful Disguises: Published And Unpublished Poems*. Atheneum Publishers, 1973.
—*Letters From A Father And Other Poems*. Atheneum Publishers, 1982.
Veinberg, Jon: *An Owl's Landscape*. Vanderbilt University Press, 1987.
Viereck, Peter: *Terror And Decorum*. 1948.
—*Strike Through The Mask: New Lyrical Poems*. 1950.
—*New Lyrical Poems*. 1950.
—*The First Morning: New Poems*. 1952.
—*The Persimmon Tree*. 1956.
—*Inner Liberty*.
—*The Stubborn Grit In The Machine*. 1957.
—*The Tree Witch: A Verse Drama*. 1961.
—*New And Selected Poems, 1932-67*. 1967.
—*Archer In The Marrow: The Applewood Cycles, 1967-1987*. W. W. Norton.
Vinz, Mark: *Winter Promises*. BkMk Press, 1975.
—*Letters To The Poetry Editor*. Capra Press, 1975.
—*Red River Blues*. Poetry Texas, 1977.
—*Songs For A Hometown Boy*. Solo Press, 1977.
—*Contingency Plans*. Ohio Review, 1978.
—*Deep Water, Dakota*. Juniper Press, 1980.
—*Climbing The Stairs*. Spoon River Poetry Press, 1983.
—*The Weird Kid*. New Rivers Press, 1983.
—*Minnesota Gothic*. Barnwood Press, 1987.

W

Walker, Jeanne Murray: *Nailing Up The Home Sweet Home*. Cleveland State University Poetry Center, 1980.
—*Fugitive Angels*. Dragon Gate Press, 1985.
Wallace, Robert: *This Various World And Other Poems*. Scribner's, 1957.
—*Views From A Ferris Wheel*. Dutton, 1965.
—*Ungainly Things*. Dutton, 1968.
—*Critters*. Bits Press, 1978.
—*Swimmer In The Rain*. Carnegie-Mellon University Press, 1979.
—*Charlie Joins The Circus*. Bits Press, 1980.
—*The Author*. Bits Press, 1983.
—*Girlfriends And Wives*. Carnegie-Mellon University Press, 1984.
—*The Lost History Of Everything*. Carnegie-Mellon University Press, 1987.
Wallace, Ronald: *Installing The Bees*. Chowder Chapbooks, 1977.
—*Cucumbers*. Pendle Hill Press, 1977.
—*The Facts Of Life*. Mary Phillips, 1979.
—*Plums, Stones, Kisses & Hooks*. University of Missouri Press, 1981.
—*Tunes For Bears To Dance To*. University of Pittsburgh Press, 1983.
—*People And Dog In The Sun*. University of Pittsburgh Press, 1987.
Warren, Robert Penn: *Eleven Poems On The Same Theme*. New Directions Publishing Corp., 1942.
—*Promises: Poems 1954-1956*. Random House, 1957.
—*You, Emperors, and Others: Poems 1957-1960*. Random House, 1960.
—*Selected Poems, New And Old 1923-1966*. Random House, 1966.
—*Incarnations: Poems 1966-1968*. Random House, 1968.
—*Audubon, A Vision*. Random House, 1969.
—*Or Else: Poems 1968-1974*. Random House, 1974.
—*Selected Poems: 1923-1975*. Random House, 1976.
—*Now And Then 1976-1978*. Random House, 1978.
—*Brother To Dragons*. Random House, 1979.
—*Life Is A Fable: Poetry, 1978-1980*. Random House, 1980.
—*A Robert Penn Warren Reader*. Random House, 1987.
Waters, Mary Ann: *The Exact Place*. Confluence Press, 1987.
Waters, Michael: *Fish Light*. Ithaca House, 1975.
—*Not Just Any Death*. BOA Editions, 1979.
—*Anniversary Of The Air*. Carnegie-Mellon University Press, 1985.
Waugaman, Charles A.: *Patterns Of Passing*. Privately printed, 1963.
—*A Harvest Of Willow*. Partridge Press, 1967.
—*The Fabric Of Truth*. Partridge Press, 1970.
—*Fruit By The Sea*. Partridge Press, 1976.
—*Sweet Valley Of Shadow*. Partridge Press,

1979.
—*Moments In The Sun*. B & R Printing Co., 1981.
—*Myrrh For My Birthday*. B & R Printing Co., 1986.

Weeks, Robert Lewis: *To The Maker Of Globes And Other Poems*. South & West, 1964.
—*For Those Who Waked Me And Other Poems*. South & West, 1969.
—*A Master of Clouds*. Northeast/Juniper Books, 1972.

Weigl, Bruce: *A Sack Full Of Old Quarrels*. Cleveland State University Poetry Center, 1976.
—*The Executioner*. Ironwood Press, 1977.
—*A Romance*. University of Pittsburgh Press, 1979.
—*The Monkey Wars*. University of Georgia Press, 1985.

Weingarten, Roger: *What Are Birds Worth*. Cummington Press, 1975.
—*Ethan Benjamin Boldt*. Knopf, 1975.
—*The Vermont Suicides*. Knopf, 1978.
—*The Love & Death Boy*. W. D. Hoffstadt & Sons, 1981.
—*Tables Of The Meridian*. Blue Buildings Press, 1982.
—*Shadow Shadow*. David R. Godine, 1986.
—*Ethan Benjamin Boldt*. Story Line Press, 1987.

Westerfield, Nancy G.: *Welded Women*. Kearney State College Press, 1983.

Wetteroth, Bruce: *Words Like These*. Ohio Review Books, 1986.

Wheatley, Pat: *A Hinge Of Spring* (under Patience Wheatley). Fiddlehead Poetry Books/Goose Lane Editions, 1986.

White, Gail: *Pandora's Box*. Samisdat Press, 1977.
—*Irreverent Parables*. Border-Mountain Press, 1980.
—*Fishing For Leviathan*. Wings Press, 1982.
—*All Night In The Churchyard*. Proof-Rock Press, 1986.

White, J. P.: *In Pursuit Of Wings*. Panache Books, 1978.
—*The Pomegranate Tree Speaks From The Dictator's Garden*. Holy Cow! Press, 1988.

Whitman, Ruth: *Blood & Milk Poems*. Clarke & Way, 1963.
—*The Marriage Wig And Other Poems*. Harcourt Brace Jovanovich, 1968.
—*The Passion Of Lizzie Borden: New And Selected Poems*. October House, 1973.
—*Permanent Address: New Poems 1973-1980*. Alice James Books, 1977.
—*The Testing Of Hannah Senesh*. Wayne State University Press, 1986.

Wiggins, Jean: *Half Moon*. Linwood Publishers, forthcoming.

Wild, Peter: *The Good Fox*. Goodly Company, 1967.
—*Sonnets*. Cranium Press, 1967.
—*The Afternoon In Dismay*. Art Association of Cincinnati, 1968.
—*Mica Mountain Poems*. Lillabulero Press, 1968.
—*Love Poems*. Lillabulero Press, 1969.
—*Poems*. Prensa de Lagar, 1969.
—*Fat Man Poems*. Hellric Publications, 1970.
—*Terms And Renewals*. Two Windows Press, 1970.
—*Peligros*. Ithaca House, 1971.
—*Dilemma: Being An Account Of The Wind That Blows The Ship Of The Tongue*. Back Door Press, 1971.
—*Wild's Magical Book Of Cranial Effusions*. New Rivers Press, 1971.
—*Grace*. Stone Press, 1971.
—*New And Selected Poems*. New Rivers Press, 1973.
—*Cochise*. Doubleday & Co., 1973.
—*The Cloning*. Doubleday & Co., 1973.
—*Tumacacori*. Two Windows Press, 1974.
—*Health*. Two Windows Press, 1974.
—*The Island Hunter*. Tideline Press, 1976.
—*Pioneers*. Tideline press, 1976.
—*The Cavalryman*. Tideline Press, 1976.
—*Chihuahua*. Doubleday & Co., 1976.
—*House Fires*. Greenhouse Review Press, 1977.
—*Gold Mines*. Wolfsong Press, 1978.
—*Barn Fires*. Floating Island Publications, 1978.
—*Zuni Butte*. San Pedro Press, 1978.
—*The Lost Tribe*. Wolfsong Press, 1979.
—*Jeanne D'Arc*. St. Luke's Press, 1980.
—*Rainbow*. Blue Buildings Press, 1980.
—*Wilderness*. New Rivers Press, 1980.
—*Heretics*. Ghost Pony Press, 1981.
—*Bitterroots*. Blue Moon Press, 1982.
—*The Light On Little Mormon Lake*. Floating Island Publications, 1983.
—*The Peaceable Kingdom*. Adler Press, 1983.
—*Getting Ready For A Date*. Abraxas Press, 1984.

Williams, C. K.: *Lies*. Houghton Mifflin, 1969.
—*I Am The Bitter Name*. Houghton Mifflin, 1972.
—*With Ignorance*. Houghton Mifflin, 1977.
—*Tar*. Random House, 1983.
—*Flesh And Blood*. Farrar, Straus & Giroux, 1987.

Williams, Miller: *A Circle Of Stone*. Louisiana State University Press, 1964.
—*So Long At The Fair*. E. P. Dutton, 1968.
—*The Only World There Is*. E. P. Dutton, 1971.
—*Halfway From Hoxie: New & Selected Poems*. Louisiana State University Press, 1973.
—*Why God Permits Evil*. Louisiana State University Press, 1977.
—*Distractions*. Louisiana State University Press, 1981.
—*Imperfect Love*. Louisiana State University Press, 1986.

Williams, Philip Lee: *New Seeds*. Madisonian Press, 1972.

Wood, Renate: *Points Of Entry*. Riverstone Press, 1981.

Woods, John: *The Deaths At Paragon, Indiana*. Indiana University Press, 1955.

—*On The Morning Of Color.* Indiana University Press, 1961.
—*The Cutting Edge.* Indiana University Press, 1966.
—*Keeping Out Of Trouble.* Indiana University Press, 1968.
—*The Knees Of Widows.* Westigan Review Press, 1971.
—*Turning To Look Back: Poems, 1955-1970.* Indiana University Press, 1972.
—*Alcohol.* Pilot Press Broadsheet, 1973.
—*Bone Flicker.* Juniper Press, 1973.
—*Striking The Earth.* Indiana University Press, 1976.
—*Thirty Years On The Force.* Juniper Press, 1977.
—*The Night Of The Game.* Raintree Press, 1982.
—*The Valley Of Minor Animals.* Dragon Gate, 1982.
—*The Salt Stone: Selected Poems.* Dragon Gate, 1984.
Wormser, Baron: *The White Words.* Houghton Mifflin, 1983.
—*Good Trembling.* Houghton Mifflin, 1985.
Wrigley, Robet: *The Sinking Of Clay City.* Copper Canyon Press, 1979.
—*The Glow.* Owl Creek Press, 1982.
—*Moon In A Mason Jar.* University of Illinois Press, 1986.

Z

Zander, William: *Distances.* Solo Press, 1979.
Zanes, John P.: *Athena And High Voltage.* New Brunswick Chapbooks, 1968.
—*Uncle John's Frigate.* Fiddlehead Poetry Books, 1972.
Zarzyski, Paul: *Call Me Lucky.* Confluence Press, 1981.
—*The Make-Up Of Ice.* University of Georgia Press, 1984.
Zeiger, Gene: *Sudden Dancing.* Amherst Writers and Artists, 1987.
Zeiger, L. L.: *The Way To Castle Garden.* State Street Press, 1982.
Zimmer, Paul: *The Ribs Of Death.* October House, 1967.
—*The Republic Of Many Voices.* October House, 1969.
—*The Zimmer Poems.* Dryad Press, 1976.
—*With Wanda: Town And Country Poems.* Dryad Poems, 1980.
—*The Ancient Wars.* Slow Loris Press, 1981.
—*Earthbound Zimmer.* Chowder Chapbooks, 1981.
—*Family Reunion: Selected And New Poems.* University of Pittsburgh Press, 1983.
—*The American Zimmer.* Press of the Night Owl, 1984.

PART TWO

Yearbook
of American Poetry

The Yearly Record

The following bibliography lists books of and about poetry that were published, copyrighted, officially announced, distributed or otherwise appeared in the United States and Canada during 1987

(1) COLLECTIONS OF POETRY BY INDIVIDUAL AUTHORS
(Listed alphabetically by author)

A

Aal, Katharyn Machan—*When She Was The Good-Time Girl*. Signpost Press
—*From Redwing*. Tamarack
Ackerman, Diane—*On Extended Wings: An Adventure In Flight*. Scribner's
Ackroyd, Peter—*The Diversions of Purley And Other Poems*. David & Charles
Acorn, Milton—*A Stand Of Jackpine*. Unfinished Monument Press
—*The Uncollected Acorn*. Deneau
—*Whiskey Jack*. HMS Press
Adcock, Fleur—*The Incident Book*. Oxford University Press
Adler, Carol—*Still Telling*. Northwoods Press
Adnan, Etel—*The Indian Never Had A Horse And Other Poems*. Post-Apollo Press
Agha, Shahid Ali—*The Half-Inch Himalayas*. Wesleyan University Press
Agoos, Julie—*Above The Land*. Yale University Press
Aguero, Kathleen—*The Real Weather*. Hanging Loose Press
Ai—*Cruelty; Killing Floor*. Thunder's Mouth Press
—*Sin*. Houghton Mifflin
Aleixandre, Vicente—*Shadow Of Paradise* (translated by Hugh A. Harter). University of California Press
Aleshire, Joan—*This Far*. Quarterly Review of Literature Poetry Series
Ali, Agha Shahid—(see listing for Agha, Shahid Ali, above)
Allen, Dick—*Flight And Pursuit: Poems*. Louisiana State University Press
Allen, William—*The Man On The Moon: Poems*. New York University Press
Allman, Ethel—*Moments*. Todd & Honeywell
Amichai, Yehuda—*Amen* (translated by Yehuda Amichai and Ted Hughes). Milkweed Editions
Ammons, A. R.—*Sumerian Vistas: Poems*. W. W. Norton
—*The Selected Poems*. W. W. Norton

Amos, Winsom—*Surprise*. Soma Press
Anderson, Barbara—*Junk City: Poems*. Persea Books
Anderson, Wendy—*Wild Things In The Yard*. Thorntree Press
Andrade, Carlos Drummond de—*Travelling In The Family: Selected Poems Of Carlos Drummond De Andrade* (edited by Thomas Colchie; translated by Elizabeth Bishop). Random House
Angelou, Maya—*How Sheba Sings The Song*. Dutton/Hillside
Anglund, Joan Walsh—*The Song Of Love*. Scribner's
Ashbery, John—*April Galleons: Poems*. Viking Press
—*Three Poems*. Penguin
—*Selected Poems*. Penguin
Astrada, Etelvina—*Death On The Run* (translated by Timothy J. Rogers). Spanish Literature Publications Co.

B

Baca, Jimmy Santiago—*Martin; And Meditations On The South Valley*. New Directions Publishing Corp.
Bachelard, Gaston—*On Poetic Imagination And Reverie: Selections From Gaston Bachelard* (translated by Colette Gaudin). Spring Publications
Bagliore, Virginia—*Oracles Of Light*. Pella Publishing Co.
Baker, Milton—*Poems By The Summer Eve*. Privately printed
Balam, Chilam—*The Destruction Of The Jaguar: Poems From The Books Of Chilam Balam* (translated by Christopher Sawyer-Lucanno). City Lights Books
Ball, Angela—*Kneeling Between Parked Cars*. Owl Creek Press
Barnard, Mary—*Time And The White Tigress*. Breitenbush Books
Barney, William D.—*Long Gone To Texas*. Nortex Press

Barnstone, Willis—*5 A.M. In Beijing: Poems Of China*. Sheep Meadow Press

Barresi, Dorothy—*The Judas Clock*. Devil's Mill-hopper Press

Bartlett, Elizabeth—*Candles*. Autograph Editions

Bateman, James A.; Chambers, Henry Tim—*One/1*. Privately printed

Bauer, Bill—*The Eye Of The Ghost: Vietnam Poems*. BkMk Press

Beaver, Bruce—*Headlands*. University of Queensland Press

Behlen, Charles–*Uirsche's First Three Decades*. Firewheel Press

Belitt, Ben—*Possession: New And Selected Poems (1938-1985)*. David R. Godine

Bell, Doris—*Strings*. Schubert Club

Bell, Marvin—*New And Selected Poems*. Atheneum

Belloc, Hilaire—*The Bad Child's Pop-Up Book Of Beasts*. Putnam

Benn, Gottfried—*Prose, Essays, Poems* (edited by Richard Paul Becker and Volkmar Sander). Continuum

Bennett, Bruce—*Not Wanting To Write Like Everyone Else*. State Street Press

Bennett, W. C.—*Anti-Maud*. Garland Publishing Co.

Bensen, D. R.—*Biblical Limericks: Old Testament Stories Reversed*. Ballantine Books

Bensen, Robert—*The Scriptures Of Venus*. Swamp Press

Berry, Wendell—*Sabbaths*. North Point Press
—*Collected Poems: 1957-1982*. North Point Press

Bidgood, Ruth—*Kindred*. Poetry Wales Press/Dufour Editions

Bivona, Francesco—*The Sciaccatan*. Privately printed

Black, H. D.—*Ion: A Play After Euripides*. Black Swan Books

Blackburn, Paul—*The Parallel Voyages* (selected and edited by Clayton Eshelman). SUN/gemini Press

Blake, William—*An Island In The Moon*. Cambridge University Press
—*The Essential Blake* (selected by Stanley Kunitz). Ecco Press
—*William Blake* (edited by Peter Porter). C. N. Potter

Blauner, Laurie—*Self-Portrait With An Unwilling Landscape*. Owl Creek Press

Blessington, Francis—*Lantskip*. W. L. Bauhan

Blomain, Karen—*Black Diamond*. Great Elm Press

Blondeau, Don—*The Spell Of The Cosmos And Other Transcending Poems*. Privately printed
—*Undared Unhappened Things And Other Nuclear Times Peace Poems*. Privately printed

Blossom, Laurel—*What's Wrong*. Rowfant Club

Blount, Roy, Jr.—*Soupsongs; Webster's Ark*. Houghton Mifflin

Blumenthal, Michael—*Against Romance: Poems*. Viking Press

Bly, Robert—*Loving A Woman In Two Worlds*. Harper & Row

Bodecker, N. M.—*Hurry, Hurry, Mary Dear! And Other Nonsense Poems*. Margaret K. McElderry Books

Boe, Deborah—*Mojave*. Hanging Loose Press.

Boland, Eavan—*The Journey And Other Poems*. Carcanet

Bosley, Keith—*A Chiltern Hundred*. Anvil Press Poetry

Boss, Laura—*On The Edge Of The Hudson*. Cross-Cultural Communications

Bottoms, David—*Under The Vulture-Tree*. Morrow

Bowie, Robert—*Wintermost*. Scop Publications

Boyle, David—*Idioms*. Three Island Press

Bradley, George—*Terms To Be Met*. Yale University Press

Brathwaite, Edward Kamau—*X/Self*. Oxford University Press

Breckenridge, Jill—*Civil Blood: Poems And Prose*. Milkweed Editions

Bremser, Ray—*Poems Of Madness; & Angel*. Water Row Press

Breuer, Lee—*Sister Suzie Cinema: Collected Poems And Performances, 1976-1986*. Theatre Communications Group

Bringhurst, Robert—*Pieces Of Map, Pieces Of Music*. Copper Canyon Press

Brito, S. J.—*Red Cedar Warrior: Collected Poems*. Jelm Mountain Publications

Brody, Harry—*Fields*. Ion Books

Bronk, William—*Manifest; And Furthermore*. North Point Press

Brook, Sebastian—*Tid-Bits By The Bard Of Brooklyn: A Collection of Epigrams, Aphorisms And Poems*. Branden Publishing Co.

Brooks, Gwendolyn—*The Near-Johannesburg Boy And Other Poems*. David Co.

Broughton, T. Alan—*Preparing To Be Happy*. Carnegie-Mellon University Press

Brown, Kathryn—*Death Of The Plankton Bar & Grill*. New Rivers Press

Browning, Robert—*Browning* (compiled by Patricia Machin). Salem House

Bruce, Debra—*Sudden Hunger*. University of Arkansas Press

Bruchac, Joseph—*Near The Mountains: Selected Poems*. White Pine Press

Brundage, Burr C.—*The King Who Cast No Shadow*. University Press of America

Bryan, Sharon—*Objects Of Affection*. Wesleyan University Press

Buchman, Marion—*In His Pavilion*. Haskell House Publishers

Buck, Heather—*The Sign Of The Water Bearer*. Anvil Press Poetry

Buckley, Christopher—*Dust Light*. Vanderbilt University Press

Burkard, Michael—*The Fires They Kept: Poems*. Metro Book Co.

Byer, Kathryn Stripling—*The Girl In The Midst Of The Harvest*. Texas Tech Press

Byrd, Bobby—*Get Some Fuses For The House: Householder Poems*. North Atlantic Books

Byrd, Don—*The Great Dimestore Centennial*. Station Hill Press

Byron, Lord—*Poems In The Autograph of Lord Byron Once In The Possession Of The Countess Guiccioli* (edited by Alice Levine and Jerome J. McGann). Garland Publishing Co.

C

Cadnum, Michael—*Invisible Mirror*. Ommation Press

Cadsby, Heather—*Decoys*. Mosaic Press

Calmenson, Stephanie; Cole, Joanna—*The Laugh Book* (part poetry). Doubleday

Cardenal, Ernesto—*From Nicaragua With Love: Poems, 1979-1986* (translated by Jonathan Cohen). City Lights Books

Carey, Michael A.—*The Noise The Earth Makes*. Pterodactyl Press

Carroll, Paul—*The Garden Of Earthly Delights*. Chicago Office of Fine Arts

Carver, Raymond—*Ultramarine*. Random House

Cassedy, Sylvia—*Roomrimes: Poems*. Crowell

Cavafy, Constantine—*The Greek Poems Of C. P. Cavafy* (translated by Memas Kolaitis). A. D. Caratzas

Cavalieri, Grace—*Bliss*. H. Roberts Publishing Co.

Celan, Paul—*Last Poems* (translated by Katharine Washburn and Margret Guillemin). North Point Press

Cendrars, Blaise—*Shadow* (translated by Marcia Brown). Aladdin Books

Chambers, Henry Tim; Bateman, James A.—*One/1*. Privately printed

Charach, Ron—*The Big Life Painting*. Quarry Press

Chase-Riboud, Barbara—*Portrait Of A Nude Woman As Cleopatra*. Morrow

Chaucer, Geoffrey—*The Physician's Tale* (edited by Helen Storm Corsa). University of Oklahoma Press
—*The Canterbury Tales* (notes by David Wright). Oxford University Press
—*The Pierpont Morgan Library Manuscript M.817: A Facsimile*. Pilgrim Books
—*The Legend Of Good Women* (translated by Ann McMillan). Rice University Press

Cheatwood, Kiarri T.-H.—*Bloodstorm: Five Books Of Poems And Docupoems: Towards Liberation*. University Press of America

Chesterton, G. K.—*Collected Nonsense And Light Verse*. Dodd, Mead

Chin, Marilyn—*Dwarf Bamboo*. Greenfield Review Press

Chretien de Troyes—*Yvain: The Knight Of The Lion* (translated by Burton Raffel). Yale University Press

Chichetto, James—*Victims*. Connecticut Poetry Review Press

Christopher, Nicholas—*A Short History Of The Island Of Butterflies: Poems*. Viking Press

Ciardi, John—*You Read To Me, I'll Read To You*. Harper & Row

Citino, David—*The Appassionata Doctrines*. Cleveland State University Poetry Center
—*The Gift Of Fire*. University of Arkansas Press

Clampitt, Amy—*Archaic Figure: Poems*. Knopf

Clare, John—*John Clare: Selected Poems And Prose* (edited by Merryn and Raymond Williams). Methuen

Clark, Tom—*Disordered Ideas*. Black Sparrow Press

Clarke, Cheryl—*Living As A Lesbian: Poetry*. Firebrand Books

Clements, Arthur L.—*Common Blessings*. Lincoln Springs Press

Clements, Susan—*The Broken Hoop*. Blue Cloud Press

Climenhaga, Joel—*Triangular Aspects Of Confusion*. Greenage Enterprises
—*Death Happens Only To Me*. Greenage Enterprises

Clough, Arthur Hugh—*The Poems Of Arthur Hugh Clough* (edited by A. L. P. Norrington). Oxford University Press

Cofer, Judith Ortiz—*Terms Of Survival*. Arte Publico Press
—*Reaching For The Mainland*. Bilingual Press

Cogswell, Fred—*An Edge To Life*. Purple Wednesday Society

Cohen, William S.—*Of Sons And Seasons*. Hamilton Press

Colby, Joan—*The Lonely Hearts Killers*. Spoon River Poetry Press

Cole, Joanna; Calmenson, Stephanie—*The Laugh Book* (part poetry). Doubleday

Coleman, Wanda—*Heavy Daughter Blues: Poems & Stories, 1968-1986*. Black Sparrow Press

Coley, John Smartt (translator)—*The Story Of Thebes*. Garland Publishing Co.

Collier, Michael—*The Clasp And Other Poems*. Wesleyan University Press

Colvill, Robert—*Atlanta; And Savannah: Facsimile Reproductions*. Scholars' Facsimiles & Reprints

Confar, Carole Frances—*Partly Cloudy*. Pelican Poems

Connor, Tony—*Spirits Of The Place*. Anvil Press Poetry

Conoley, Gillian—*Some Gangster Pain*. Carnegie-Mellon University Press

Conquest, Robert—*New And Collected Poems*. C. Schlacks, Jr.

Cooley, Peter—*The Van Gogh Notebook*. Carnegie-Mellon University Press
—*Canticles And Complaintes*. Ford-Brown Publishers
—*One Sparrow, Another, Legion*. Livingston University Press

Cooper, Marsha Freeman—*Substantial Holdings*. Pudding Publications

Cooper, Vincent O.; Parris, Trevor; Lisowski, Joseph—*Three Islands*. University of the Virgin Islands

Cope, David—*On The Bridge*. Humana Press

Copeland, Helen M.—*Endangered Specimen And Other Poems From A Lay Naturalist*. St. Andrews Press

Cording, Robert—*Life-List*. Ohio State University Press

Corneille, Pierre—*Le Cid: A Translation In Rhymed Couplets* (translated by Vincent J. Cheng). University of Delaware Press

Cornford, Adam—*Animations*. City Lights Books

Cosier, Tony—*In The Face Of The Storm*. Anthos Books

Coursen, H. R.—*Rewriting The Book*. Cider Mill Press

Cramer, Steven—*The Eye That Desires To Look Up-

ward: Poems. Galileo Press

Crooker, Barbara—*Starting From Zero.* Great Elm Press

Cummings, E. E.—*Little Tree.* Crown Publishers

Cummings, Michael—*I Know Why Parents Eat Their Children: Poems.* American Studies Press

Cunningham, J. V.—*Let Thy Words Be Few.* Symposium Press

Curnow, Allen—*The Loop In The Lone Kauri Road: Poems 1983-1985.* Aukland University Press/Oxford University Press

D

Dacey, Philip—*The Man With Red Suspenders: Poems.* Milkweed Editions

Dana, Robert—*Starting Out For The Difficult World.* Harper & Row

Dangel, Leo—*Old Man Brunner Country.* Spoon River Poetry Press

Dante Alighieri—*The Divine Comedy* (translated and edited by Thomas G. Bergin). H. Davidson

Darweesh, Mahmoud—*Sand And Other Poems* (edited and translated by Rana Kabbani). Methuen

Dass, Nirmal—*The Avowing Of King Arthur: A Modern Verse Translation.* University Press of America

Dauenhauer, Richard—*Frames Of Reference: Poems.* Black Current Press

Dawber, Diane—*Oatmeal Mittens.* Borealis Press

Deahl, James—*A Stand Of Jackpine.* Unfinished Monument Press

de Andrade, Eugenio—*White On White* (translated by Alexis Levitin). QRL Contemporary Poetry Series
—*Memory Of Another River* (translated by Alexis Levitin). New Rivers Press

de Regniers, Beatrice Schenk—*A Week In The Life Of Best Friends, And Other Poems Of Friendship.* Atheneum

Derry, Anne—*Stages Of Twilight.* Breitenbush Books

Dhurjati—*For The Lord Of The Animals: Poems From The Telugu: The Kalahastisvara Satakamu Of Dhurjati* (translated by Hank Heifetz and Velcheru Narayana Rao). University of California Press

Diamond, Stanley-*Going West.* Hermes House Press

Dickey, James—*Bronwen, The Traw, And The Shape-Shifter: A Poem In Four Parts.* Harcourt Brace Jovanovich

Dickey, William—*The King Of The Golden River.* Pterodactyl Press

Dickinson, Emily—*Emily Dickinson* (edited by Geoffrey Moore). Clarkson N. Potter

Dickinson, Paul; Dolan, Scott—*The Ony Son Of Everything.* Wicked Mule Poetry Alliance

Dickson, John—*Waving At Trains.* Thorntree Press

Dienstfrey, Patricia—*Small Salvations.* Kelsey Street Press

Dion, Marc—*To Veronica's New Lover.* BkMk Press

Disch, Thomas M.—*The Tale Of Dan De Lion.* Coffee House Press

Dobler, Patricia—*Talking To Strangers.* University of Wisconsin Press

Dobyns, Stephen—*Cemetery Nights.* Viking/Penguin

Dolan, Scott (see Dickinson, Paul)

Donegan, Patricia—*Bone Poems (Mini-Cantos).* Chinook Press

Donne, John—*Selected Poetry And Prose* (edited by T. W. and R. J. Craik). Methuen

Doty, Mark—*Turtle, Swan.* David R. Godine

Drake, Barbara—*What We Say To Strangers: Poems.* Breitenbush Books

Drew, George—*Toads In A Poisoned Tank.* Tamarack Editions

Dryden, John—*Absalom And Achitophel* (edited by Robert W. McHenry). Archon Books

Duemer, Joseph—*Customs.* University of Georgia Press

Dumars, Denise—*Sheet Lightning.* Terata Publications

Duncan, Graham—*The Map Reader.* Great Elm Press

Dunn, Douglas—*Selected Poems: 1964-1983.* Faber and Faber

E

Eaton, Charles Edward—*New And Selected Poems: 1942-1987.* Cornwall Books

Ebensen, Barbara Juster—*Words With Wrinkled Knees: Animal Poems.* Crowell

Eberhart, Richard—*Collected Poems, 1930-1986.* Oxford University Press

Egerton, Sarah Fyge—*Poems On Several Occasions (1703).* Scholars' Facsimiles & Reprints

Ekkens, Thomas A.—*Collected Poetry Of Thomas A. Ekkens: Early Works.* Backspace Ink.

Eliraz, Israel—*Via Bethlehem: Poems* (translated by the author and Beate Hein Bennett). Micah Publications

Elkind, Sue Saniel—*Waiting For Order.* Naked Man Press of Kansas University

Eluard, Paul—*Selected Poems* (translated by Gilbert Bowen). Riverrun Press

Emanuel, Lynn—*The Technology Of Love.* Abattoir Editions

Engler, Robert Klein—*Sonnets By Degree.* Alphabeta Press
—*Loose Change.* Alphabeta Press

Engles, John—*Cardinals In The Ice Age.* Graywolf Press

Enright, D. J.—*Collected Poems, 1987.* Oxford University Press

Epstein, Daniel Mark—*Spirits.* Overlook Press

Etter, David—*Selected Poems.* Spoon River Poetry Press
—*Alliance, Illinois.* Spoon River Poetry Press

Ewald, Mary—*Weapons Against Chaos.* Devin-Adair

Ewart, Gavin—*The Gavin Ewart Show: Selected Poems, 1939-1985.* Bits Press

F

Farrar, Winifred Hamrick—*Behind The Ridge*. South & West, Inc.

Farrell, John P.—*Voices Behind The Wall: Ninety Prison Stories*. Henry Holt and Co.

Feldman, Irving—*All Of Us Here And Other Poems*. Viking Press

Feldman, Ruth—*To Whom It May Concern*. Bauhan

Field, Edward—*New And Selected Poems*. Sheep Meadow Press

Finch, Anne—*Selected Poems* (edited by Denys Thompson). Carcanet

Finch, Peter—*Selected Poems*. Poetry Wales Press/ Dufour Editions

Fink, Eloise Bradley—*Girl In The Empty Nightgown*. Thorntree Press

Fincke, Gary—*The Days Of Uncertain Health*. Lynx House Press

Finkel, Donald—*Selected Shorter Poems*. Atheneum

Finkelstein, Caroline—*Windows Facing East*. Dragon Gate

Finley, Jeanne—*Pagan Babies*. Bellevue Press

Fish, Karen—*The Cedar Canoe: Poems*. University of Georgia Press

Fisher, Aileen—*Holiday Programs For Boys And Girls* (part poetry). Plays, Inc.

Fishman, Charles—*The Death Mazurka*. Timberline Press

FitzPatrick, Kevin—*Down On The Corner: Poems*. Midwest Villages and Voices

Foix, J. V.—*As For Love: Poems And Translations*. Oxford University Press

Ford, Ford Madox—*The Ford Madox Ford Reader* (edited by Sondra J. Stang). Ecco Press

Foster, Frances A. (editor)—*A Stanzaic Life Of Christ: Compiled From Hidgen's Polychronicon And The Legends Aura*. Kraus Reprint

Foster, Robert—*Nipping Leaves*. Tenth Muse Press

Fowler, Jay Bradford, Jr.—*Writing Down The Light*. Orchises Press

Fox, Connie—*Ten Questions*. Trout Creek Press

Franklin, Walt—*Earthstars, Chanterelles, Destroying Angels*. Garall Press

Frost, Carol—*Day Of The Body*. Ion Books

Frost, Robert—*Robert Frost* (edited by Geoffrey Moore). Clarkson N. Potter

Frumkin, Gene—*A Sweetness In The Air*. Solo Press

Fuller, John—*Selected Poems 1954-1982*. Secker & Warburg

Funk, Allison—*Forms Of Conversation*. Alice James Books

Furman, Watkins—*Poems*. Ursus Press

Furnivall, F. J. (editor)—*The Minor Poems Of The Vernon MS*. Kraus Reprint

G

George, David—*Lamentation For Emmanuel: An Elegy For The Gypsy Flamenco Singer, Manolito De La Maria De Alcala*. Wooden Angel Press

George, Emery—*The Boy And The Monarch*. Ardis
—*Voiceprints*. Ardis

Gibb, Robert—*A Geography Of Common Names*. Devil's Millhopper
—*Evening Time*. Barnwood Press

Gillespie, Jane Baldwin—*Susurrus: Poems*. W. L. Bauhan

Ginsberg, Allen—*Howl*. Harper & Row
—*White Shroud: Poems, 1980-1985*. Harper & Row

Glass, Malcolm—*In The Shadow Of The Gourd*. New Rivers Press

Glen, Emilie—*Hope Of Amethyst: Poems*. North American Editions

Goedicke, Barbara—*Listen, Love*. Barnwood Press

Goldbarth, Albert—*Arts & Sciences*. Ontario Review Press

Goldberg, Barbara—*Berta Broadfoot And Pepin The Short: A Merovingian Romance*. Word Works

Goldman, Judy—*Holding Back Winter*. St. Andrews Press

Goldstein, Laurence—*The Three Gardens*. Copper Beech Press

Goodenough, J. B.—*Homeplace*. St. Andrews Press

Goodman, Barry—*You Are Involved In A Fable*. Thorntree Press

Goshe, Frederick—*Collected Poems*. Harlo

Goswami, Satsvarupa Dasa—*The Dust Of Vrindaban*. Gita-Nagari Press

Graham, David—*Magic Shows*. Cleveland State University Poetry Center
—*Common Waters*. Flume Press

Graham, Jorie—*The End Of Beauty*. Ecco Press

Graves, Roy Neil—*Somewhere On The Interstate*. Ion Books/Raccoon

Gray, Patrick Worth—*Spring Comes Again To Arnett*. Mr. Cogito Press

Green, Joseph—*His Inadequate Vocabulary*. Signpost Press

Green, Melissa—*The Squanicook Eclogues*. W. W. Norton

Greenway, William—*Where We've Been: Poems*. Breitenbush Books

Greer, Jane—*Bathsheba On The Third Day*. Cummington Press

Griffin, Larry D.—*The Blue Water Tower*. Poetry Around Press

Griffin, Susan—*Unremembered Country*. Copper Canyon Press

Grigson, Geoffrey—*Persephone's Flowers And Other Poems*. Secker & Warburg

Grillo, Peter R. (editor)—*La Prise d'Acre; La Mort Godefroi; And, La Chanson Des Rois Baudoin*. University of Alabama Press

Grossman, Bruce Alan—*The Art Of Dada And Other Decompositions*. Privately printed

Guenther, Charles—*The Hippopotamus: Selected Translations, 1945-1985*. BkMk Press

Guillaume de Machaut—*Le Jugement Du Roy De Behaigne; And Remede De Fortune* (edited by James I. Wimsatt and William W. Kibler). University of Georgia Press

Gullar, Ferreira—*Sullied Poems* (translated by Leland Guyer). Associated Faculty Press

Gundy, Jeff—*Surrendering To The Real Thing*. Pikestaff Press

I

Ibsen, Henrik—*Ibsen's Poems* (translated by John Northam). Oxford University Press

Iddings, Kathleen—*Promises To Keep: Poetry And Photographs*. West Anglia Publications

Irwin, Mark—*The Halo Of Desire: Poems*. Galileo Press

J

Jackson, Angela—*The Man With The White Liver: Poems*. Contact II Publications

Jackson, Richard—*Worlds Apart*. University of Alabama Press

Jacob, John—*Wooden Indian: Poems*. Holmgangers Press

Jacobsen, Josephine—*The Sisters: New And Selected Poems*. Bench Press

Jaffe, Dan—*Seasons Of The River*. BkMk Press

James, Sibyl—*The White Junk Of Love, Again*. Calyx Books

Janowitz, Phyllis—*Temporary Dwellings*. University of Pittsburgh Press

Jansen, Matthew—*Clearing*. Kutenai Press

Jenkins, Louis: An Almost Human Gesture. Eightees Press

Jenkins, Mike—*Invisible Times*. Poetry Wales Press/Dufour Editions

Jennings, Elizabeth—*Collected Poems*. Carcanet

Jimenez, Juan Ramon—*God Desired And Desiring* (translated by Antonio T. deNicolas). Paragon House

Johnson, Albert—*Once Upon A Planet: Poems*. J. Daniel

Johnson, Ann—*Miryam Of Judah: Witness In Truth & Tradition*. Ave Maria Press

Johnson, Kate Knapp-*When Orchids Were Flowers*. Dragon Gate

Joron, Andrew—*Force Fields*. Starmont House

Juan Ines de la Cruz, Sor—*Three Women Poets: Renaissance And Baroque: Louise Labe, Gaspara Stampa And Sor Juan Ines De La Cruz* (selected and translated by Frank J. Warnke). Bucknell University Press

Judd, Kirk—*Field Of Vision*. Aegina Press

Juergensen, Hans—*The Ambivalent Journey: Return Of A Refugee*. American Studies Press

H

Hacker, Marilyn—*Love, Death, And The Changing Of The Seasons*. Arbor House

Hadas, Rachel—*A Son From Sleep*. Wesleyan University Press

Hafiz—*Hafiz: Dance Of Life* (translated by Michael Boylan). Mage Publishers

Haislip, John—*Seal Rock*. Barnwood Press

Halley, Robin—*Parts Of The Heart*. Park Row Press

Halliday, Mark—Little Star: Poems. William Morrow

Halpern, Daniel—*Tango: Poems*. Viking

Hamill, Sam—*The Nootka Rose*. Breitenbush Books

Hamilton, Fritz—*No Difference*. Trout Creek Press
—*Beneath The Rags*. Minotaur Press

Hammer, Louis—*The Mirror Dances*. Intertext

Hampl, Patricia—Spillville. Milkweed Editions

Hansen, Matthew—*Clearing*. Kutenai Press

Harper, Michael S.—*Dear John, Dear Coltrane*. University of Pittsburgh Press

Harrison, Richard—*Fathers Never Leave You*. Mosaic Press

Harrison, Tony—*Selected Poems*. Random House

Harteis, Richard—*Internal Geography*. Carnegie-Mellon University Press

Hartley, Marsden—*The Collected Poems Of Marsden Hartley* (edited by Gail R. Scott). Black Sparrow Press

Hartnett, Michael—*Collected Poems: Vol. 2*. Raven Arts Press/Dufour Editions

Hasselstrom, Linda M.—*Roadkill*. Spoon River Poetry Press

Haxton, Brooks—*Dominion: Poems*. Knopf

Hayes, Dorsha—*Hold Back The Night: Late Poems From The Bell-Branch*. Dragon's Teeth Press

Hedin, Robert—*Tornadoes*. Dooryard Press

Helfman, Suzanne—*Night Driving*. San Francisco State University

Heggie, Esther—Sensual Rhythms & Purple Bats. Shu Publishing Co.

Heine, Heinrich—*Selected Verse* (selected and translated by Peter Branscombe). Penguin
—*Deutschland*. Angel Books/Dufour Editions

Helfgott Hyett, Barbara—*In Evidence: Poems Of The Liberation Of Nazi Concentration Camps*. University of Pittsburgh Press

Helwig, Maggie—*Eden*. Oberon Press
—*Because The Gunman*. Lowlife Publishing

Henri, Adrian—*Collected Poems, 1967-85*. Allison & Busby

Herbert, George—*The Essential Herbert* (selected by Anthony Hecht). Ecco Press

Hewitt, John—*Freehold, And Other Poems*. Blackstaff Press

Hicks, John V.—*Side Glances: Notes On The Writer's Craft*. Thistledown Press

Hikmet, Nazim—*Selected Poetry* (translated by Randy Blasing and Mutlu Konuk). Persea Books

Hill, Geoffrey—*Collected Poems*. Oxford University Press

Hill, Hyacinthe—*Poetry And The Stars*. Scop and Gleeman Publishers

Hodgson, Harriet W.—*My First Fourth Of July Book*. Childrens Press

Hoeft, Robert D.—*What Are You Doing?* Trout Creek Press

Hoey, Allen—*A Fire In The Cold House Of Being*. Walt Whitman Center
—*Work The Tongue Could Understand*. State Street Press

Hofmann, Michael—*Acrimony*. Faber and Faber

Holderlin, Friedrich—*Holderlin: Selected Verse* (edited by Michael Hamburger). Anvil Press Poetry

Hollander, Jean—*Crushed Into Honey.* Saturday Press

Hollander, John—*In Time And Place.* Johns Hopkins University Press

Hollis, Jocelyn—*Poems Of The Vietnam War* (revised edition). American Poetry and Literature Press

—*Collected Poems.* American Poetry and Literature Press

Holmes, Philip—*The Green Road.* Anvil Press Poetry

Holt, Rochelle Lynn—*The Suicide Chap.* Willow Bee House

—*The Elusive Rose.* Aquila Press

—*Stream Of Consciousness.* Kindred Spirit Press

Homer—*Homer's Iliad* (edited by Harold Bloom). Chelsea House Publishers

—*The Homeric Hymns* (translated by Charles Boer). Spring Publications

Hooper, Patricia—*A Bundle Of Beasts.* Houghton Mifflin

Hopper, Stanley Romaine—*Why Persimmons And Other Poems: Transformations Of Theology In Poetry.* Scholars Press

Howe, Fanny—*The Lives Of A Spirit.* Sun & Moon Press

Howell, Anthony—*Why I May Never See The Walls Of China.* Anvil Press Poetry

Hudgins, Andrew—*After The Lost War.* Houghton Mifflin

Hull, Lynda—*Ghost Money.* University of Massachusetts Press

Humes, Harry—*Throwing Away The Compass.* Silverfish Review

Hummer, T. R.—*Lower-Class Heresy: Poems.* University of Illinois Press

Huppe, Bernard F. (translator)—*Beowulf: A New Translation.* Medieval & Renaissance Texts & Studies

K

Karr, Mary—*Abacus.* Wesleyan University Press

Kashtan, Rivka—*Wild Variations On A Theme Of The Garden Of Eden & Other Poems From Those Troubled Times.* Shapolsky Publishers

Katrovas, Richard—*Snug Harbor.* Wesleyan University Press

Keats, John—*The Essential Keats* (selected by Philip Levine). Ecco Press

—*Keats* (compiled by Patricia Machin). Salem House

Keeler, Greg—*American Falls.* Confluence Press

Keithley, George—*To Bring Spring: Poems.* Holmgangers Press

Keller, David—*New Room.* Quarterly Review of Literature Press

Kelly, Kate—*Barking At Sunspots And Other Poems.* Justin Books

Kennedy, Charles W.—*Poems: Mostly Occasional.* Privately printed

Kenny, Maurice—*Blackrobe: Isaac Jogues, b. March 11, 1607, d. October 18, 1646: Poems.* Chauncy Press

—*Greyhounding This America: Poems And Dialogue.* Heidelberg Graphics

Kenyon, Jane—*The Boat Of Quiet Hours.* Graywolf Press

Khlebnikov, Velimir—*Collected Works Of Velimir Khlebnikov* (translated by Paul Schmidt). Harvard University Press

Kicknosway, Faye—*All These Voices: New And Selected Poems.* Coffee House Press

Kimmet, Gene—*In Fee Simple.* Stormline Press

Kirby, David—*Saving The Young Men Of Vienna.* University of Wisconsin Press

Kirstein, Lincoln—*The Poems Of Lincoln Kirstein.* Atheneum

Kiskaddon, Bruce—*Rhymes Of The Ranges: A New Collection Of The Poems Of Bruce Kiskaddon* (edited by Hal Cannon). Peregrine Smith Books

Kizer, Carolyn—*The Nearness Of You.* Copper Canyon Press

Kleinschmidt, Edward—*Magnetism.* Heyeck Press

Kloss, Phillips—*The Stronghold.* Sunstone Press

Knight, Etheridge—*The Essential Etheridge Knight.* University of Pittsburgh Press

Koch, Kenneth—*Seasons On Earth.* Penguin Books

Kofalk, Marriet—*Rainbows: A Collection Of Haiku.* Friends of Wisdom Press

Kolumban, Nicholas—*Reception At The Mongolian Embassy.* New Rivers Press

Komunyakaa, Yusef—*I Apologize For The Eyes In My Head.* Wesleyan University Press

Kooser, Ted—*The Blizzard Voices.* Bieler Press

Korty, Margaret Barton—*God's Mundane World In Risible Rhyme.* Church Library Council

Korwin, Yala—*To Tell The Story-Poems Of The Holocaust.* Holocaust House

Krampf, Thomas—*Subway Prayer And Other Poems Of The Inner City.* American Poets Co-operative Publications

—*Satori West.* Ischua Books

Kumin, Maxine—*The Long Approach.* Penguin

Kuppner, Frank—*The Intelligent Observation Of Naked Women.* Carcanet

L

Labe, Louise—*Three Women Poets: Renaissance And Baroque: Louise Labe, Gaspara Stampa And Sor Juan Ines De La Cruz* (selected and translated by Frank J. Warnke). Bucknell University Press

LaGattuta, Margo; Reising, Chris—*Noedgelines.* Earhart Press

Lagomarsino, Nancy—*Sleep Handbook.* Alice James Books

Larrea, Juan—*A Tooth For A Tooth: Selected Poems Of Juan Larrea* (translated by David Bary). University Press of America

Larsen, Wendy Wilder; Tran Thi Nga—*Shallow Graves: Two Women And Vietnam.* Harper & Row

Laughin, James—*The Owl Of Minerva.* Copper Canyon Press

Lauter, Ken—*Before The Light*. BkMk Press

Lauterbach, Ann—*Before Recollection*. Princeton University Press

Layton, Irving—*Final Reckoning: Poems 1982-1986*. Mosaic Press

—*Fortunate Exile*. McClelland & Stewart

Lea, Sydney—*No Sign*. University of Georgia Press

Lear, Edward—*The Owl And The Pussy-Cat*. Harper & Row

—*The Owl & The Pussycat & Other Nonsense*. Silver Burdett Co.

LeBlanc, Liz—*Cheap Entertainment*. Ommation Press

Lee, Li-Young—*Rose*. BOA Editions

Le Guin, Ursula K.—*Wild Oats And Fireweed*. Harper & Row

Lehman, David—*An Alternative To Speech*. Princeton University Press

Lengyel, Cornel—*El Dorado Forest: Selected Poems 1935-1985*. Hillside Press

Leopardi, Giacomo—*Leopardi: Poems And Prose* (edited by Angel Flores). Greenwood Press

Lerner, Laurence—*Rembrandt's Mirror*. Vanderbilt University Press

Leventhal, Ann Z.—*Life-Lines*. Magic Circle Press

Levertov, Denise—*Breathing The Water*. New Directions Publishing Corp.

—*Poems 1968-1972*. New Directions Publishing Corp.

Levy, Robert J.—*Whistle Maker*. Anhinga Press

Lewis, Claudia—*Long Ago In Oregon*. Harper & Row

Lietz, Robert—*The Lindbergh Half-Century*. L'Epervier Press

Lifshin, Lyn—*Dance Poems*. Ommation Press

Lindbergh, Reeve—*The Midnight Farm*. Dial Books For Young Readers

Lindo, Hugo—*The Ways Of Rain And Other Poems* (translated by Elizabeth Gamble Miller). Latin American Literary Review Press

Linthicum, John—*Love Poems: 1976-1986*. Spheric House

Lisowski, Joseph (see Cooper, Vincent)

Little, Geraldine C.—*Strong Against The Frost*. Green Glens Press

Livingston, Myra Cohn—*Valentine Poems*. Holiday House

Llewellyn, Chris—*Fragments From The Fire*. Viking/Penguin

Lloyd, D. H.—*Bible Bob Responds To A Jesus Honker And Other Poems*. Applezaba Press

Longo, Perie—*Milking The Earth*. John Daniel, Publisher

Lott, Rick—*The Patience Of Horses*. Livingston University Press

Low, Denise—*Learning The Language Of Rivers*. Midwest Quarterly

Ludvigson, Susan—*The Beautiful Noon Of No Shadow*. Louisiana State University Press

Lydgate, John—*Lydgate's Minor Poems: The Two Nightingale Poems* (edited by Otto Glauning). Kraus Reprint

Lynch, Thomas—*Skating With Heather Grace*. Knopf

M

MacBeth, George—*The Cleaver Garden*. Secker & Warburg

MacGill-Eain, Somhairle—*Poems 1932-82*. Iona Foundation

Machado, Antonio—*Solitudes, Galleries And Other Poems* (translated by Richard L. Predmore). Duke University Press

Mackey, Mary—*The Dear Dance Of Eros*. Fjord Press

Madeleva, Sister M.—*The Four Last Things: Collected Poems*. Saint Mary's College

Makuck, Peter—*Pilgrims*. Ampersand Press

Male, Belkis Cuza—*Woman On The Front Lines*. Unicorn Press

Mandelstam, Osip—*Tristia: Poems* (translated by Bruce McClelland). Station Hill Press

Manhire, Bill—*Zoetropes: Poems 1972-83*. Carcanet

Manning, Nichola—*Save Save Save And Other Poems*. Applezaba Press

Mao Tse-tung—*Snow Glistens On The Great Wall* (translated by May Wen-yee). Santa Barbara Press

Markham, E. A.—*Living In Disguise*. Anvil Press Poetry

Marshall, Jack—*Arabian Nights*. Coffee House Press

Martin, Charles—*Steal The Bacon*. Johns Hopkins University Press

Marton, Charles—*Steal The Bacon*. Johns Hopkins University Press

Marvell, Andrew—*Selected Poetry And Prose* (edited by Robert Wilcher). Methuen

Mason, Herbert—*A Legend Of Alexander And The Merchant And The Parrot*. Notre Dame University Press

Masters, Marcia Lee—*Wind Around The Moon: New And Collected Poems*. Dragon's Teeth Press

Matthews, Harry—*Armenian Papers: Poems, 1954-1984*. Princeton University Press

Matthews, William—*Foreseeable Futures*. Houghton Mifflin

Matthias, John; Vuckovic, Vladeta (translators)—*The Battle Of Kosovo*. Swallow Press

Mazur, Gail—*The Pose Of Happiness: Poems*. David R. Godine

McAdam, Rhona—*Hour Of The Pearl*. Thistledown Press

McClatchy, J. D.—*Stars Principal: Poems*. Collier Books

McCollum, Bernice Claire—*Mosaic Of Poems: Here And There, Then And Now*. Golden Quill Press

McCue, Edward Patrick—*Observer*. Lorrah & Hitchcock Publishers

McDonald, Walter—*The Flying Dutchman*. Ohio State University Press

—*After The Noise Of Saigon*. University of Massachusetts Press

McDougall, Jo—*The Woman In The Next Booth*. BkMk Press

McDowell, Robert—*Quiet Money*. Henry Holt

McElroy, Colleen J.—*Bone Flames*. Wesleyan University Press

McFadden, David—*Gypsy Guitar: A Hundred Poems Of Romance And Betrayal*. Talon Books

McFerren, Martha—*A Contour For Ritual: Poems*. Louisiana State University Press

McGarry, Jean—*The Very Rich Hours*. Johns Hopkins University Press

McHugh, Heather—*To The Quick*. Wesleyan University Press

McKee, Louis—*No Matter*. Pig in the Poke Press

McKeon, James—*Headlong*. University of Utah Press

McKeown, Tom—*Invitation Of The Mirrors*. Wisconsin Review Press

McKuen, Rod—*Valentines*. Harper & Row

McNamara, Eugene—*The Moving Light*. Wolsak & Wynn

McNamara, Hugh—*The Potlatch Moon*. Macaw

Meinke, Peter—*Underneath The Lantern*. Heatherstone Press
—*Night Watch On The Chesapeake*. University of Pittsburgh Press

Meissner, Bill—*The Sleepwalker's Son*. Ohio University Press/Swallow Press

Mellichamp, Leslie—*We Thought At Least The Roof Would Fall*. Pocahontas Press

Melville, Herman—*The Essential Melville* (selected by Robert Penn Warren). Ecco Press

Menashe, Samuel—*Collected Poems*. National Poetry Foundation

Meredith, William—*Partial Accounts: New And Selected Poems*. Knopf

Merriam, Eve—*Halloween A B C*. Macmillan
—*Fresh Paint*. Macmillan

Merrifield, Gladys—*Windows On Manhattan*. Dragon's Teeth Press

Micheline, Jack—*River Of Red Wine And Other Poems*. Water Row Press

Middleton, Christopher—*Two-Horse Wagon Going By*. Carcanet

Miller, Leslie Adrienne—*No River*. St. Louis Poetry Center

Miller, Philip—*Cats In The House*. Woodley Press
—*George Grand*. Samisdat Press

Millett, John—*Blue Dynamite: A Narrative*. South Head Press/Elliott Bay Book Co.

Mills, Ralph J., Jr.—*Each Branch: Poems, 1976-1985*. Spoon River Poetry Press

Mills, Robert—*Kindly Angel: New And Selected Poems*. Spoon River Poetry Press

Minthorn, Philip—*Vigil Of The Wounded*. Contact II Publications

Mirikitani, Janice—*Shedding Silence: Poetry And Prose*. Celestial Arts

Mitchell, Roger—*A Clear Space On A Cold Day*. Cleveland State University Poetry Center

Mitchell, Stephen (translator)—*The Book Of Job*. North Point Press

Molloy-Olund, Barbara—*In Favor Of Lightning*. Wesleyan University Press

Montale, Eugenio—*The Occasions* (translated by William Arrowsmith). Norton

Moore, Alan—*Opia*. Anvil Press Poetry

Moore, Clement C.—*The Night Before Christmas*. Troll Associates

Morgan, Frederick—*Poems: New And Selected*. University of Illinois Press

Morgan, Robert—*At The Edge Of The Orchard Country*. Wesleyan University Press

Morton, Colin—*The Merzbook*. Quarry Press

Moss, Sylvia—*Cities In Motion: Poems*. University of Illinois Press

Mott, Michael—*Corday*. Beacham Publishing

Mueller, Lisel—*Second Language: Poems*. Louisiana State University Press

Muldoon, Paul—*Selected Poems, 1968-1986*. Ecco Press
—*Meeting The British*. Wake Forest University Press

Mulhern, Maureen—*Parallax*. Wesleyan University Press

Muth, Marcia—*Thin Ice And Other Poems*. Sunstone Press

Mycue, Edward—*Edward*. Primal Publishing

Myers, Jack—*As Long As You're Happy*. Graywolf Press

N

Nash, Ogden—*Ogden Nash's Zoo* (edited by Roy Finamore). Stewart, Tabori & Chang

Nemerov, Howard—*War Stories: Poems About Long Ago And Now*. University of Chicago Press

Newlin, Margaret—*Collected Poems, 1963-1985*. Ardis

Newman, P. B. (Paul Baker)—*The G. Washington Poems*. Briarpatch Press

Nichol, B. P.—*Once, A Lullaby*. Greenwillow Books

Nordhaus, Jean—*A Bracelet Of Lies*. Washington Writers' Publishing House

Norris, Ken—*Report On The Second Half Of The Twentieth Century*. Guernica Editions

Norse, Harold—*The Love Poems: 1940-1985*. Crossing Press

Nye, Naomi Shihab—*Yellow Glove*. Breitenbush Books

Nyhart, Nina—*French For Soldiers*. Alice James Books

O

Ochester, Ed—*Changing The Name To Ochester*. Carnegie-Mellon University Press

O'Connell, Richard—*Hanging Tough*. Atlantis Editions

O'Driscoll, Dennis—*Hidden Extras*. Anvil Press Poetry

Older, Julia—*A Little Wild*. Typographeum Press

Olds, Sharon—*The Gold Cell: Poems*. Knopf

Olson, Charles—*The Collected Poems Of Charles Olson* (edited by Charles F. Butterick). University of California Press

Ormond, John—*Selected Poems*. Poetry Wales Press/Dufour Editions

Ormsby, Frank—*A Northern Spring*. William Heinemann

Orr, Gregory—*New And Selected Poems*. Wesleyan University Press

Orth, Kevin—*The Other Life*. Plaice Press

Ortner-Zimmerman, Toni—*The House In The Woods*. Linwood

Ostriker, Alicia—*The Imaginary Lover*. University of Pittsburgh Press

Otis, Alicia—*Spiderwoman's Dream*. Sunstone Press

Ottewell, Guy—*Language*. Kala

Owen, Wilfred—*The Poems Of Wilfred Owen* (edited by Jon Stallworthy). W. W. Norton

Owens, Rochelle—*W. C. Fields In French Light*. Contact II Publications

P

Pacey, Michael—*Birds Of Christmas*. Three Trees Press

Pacheco, Jose Emilio—*Selected Poems* (edited by George McWhirter; translated by Thomas Hoeksema). New Directions Publishing Corp.

Pack, Robert—*Clayfeld Rejoices, Clayfeld Laments: A Sequence Of Poems*. David R. Godine

Page, William—*Bodies Not Our Own: Poems*. Memphis State University Press

Parker, Lewis—*Serpentine Futures*. University of Queensland Press

Parris, Trevor (see Cooper, Vincent)

Pasolini, Pier Paolo—*Roman Poems* (translated by Lawrence Ferlinghetti and Francesca Valente). City Lights Books

Paz, Octavio—*The Collected Poems Of Octavio Paz, 1957-1987* (edited and translated by Eliot Weinberger). New Directions Publishing Corp.

Peckenpaugh, Angela—*Refreshing The Fey*. Sackbut Press

Persius—*The Satires Of Persius: The Latin Text With A Verse Translation* (by Guy Lee). Francis Cairns

Pessoa, Fernando—*The Surprise Of Being*. Angel Books/Dufour Editions

Peterfreund, Stuart—*Interstatements*. Curbstone Publishing Co.

Petrarch—*For Love Of Laura: Poetry Of Petrarch* (selected and translated by Marion Shore). University of Arkansas Press

Pfingston, Roger—*Something Iridescent*. Barnwood Press

Phillips, Michael Joseph—*Selected Concrete Poems*. Cambric Press
—*Adornings*. World Poetry Center
—*Imaginary Women*. Cambric Press

Phillips, Robert—*The Wounded Angel*. Brighton Press

Piccione, Anthony—*Seeing It Was So*. BOA Editions

Pike, Albert—*Prose Sketches And Poems Written In The Western Country* (edited by David J. Weber). Texas A&M University Press

Pintonelli, Deborah—*Meat And Memory*. Erie Street Press

Plutzik, Hyam—*Hyam Plutzik: The Collected Poems*. BOA Editions

Pollack, Felix—*Benefits Of Doubt*.

Pollack, Frederick—*The Adventure*. Story Line Press

Pomerance, Bernard—*We Need To Dream All This Again*. Viking

Ponce, Manuel—*Manuel Ponce: Some of My Poems* (translated by Maria Luisa Rodriguez Lee). Latin American Literary Review Press

Popa, Vasko—*Homage To The Lame Wolf: Selected Poems* (translated by Charles Simic). Oberlin College Press

Pope, Alexander—*The Poetry Of Pope: A Collection* (edited by M. H. Abrams). H. Davidson

Poulin, A., Jr.—*A Momentary Order*. Graywolf Press

Pound, Omar—*Pissle And The Holy Grail*. Woolner, Brotherson, Ltd.

Prelutsky, Jack—*Ride A Purple Pelican*. Greenwillow Books

Presley, John Woodrow—*How Like A Life*. Blue Cloud Quarterly

Prevert, Jacques—*Selected Poems Of Jacques Prevert* (translated by Harriet Zinnes). Schocken Books

Price, Reynolds—*The Laws Of Ice*. Atheneum

Provost, Foster—*Columbus: Dream And Act: A Tragic Suite*. John Carter Brown Library

Pugh, Sheenagh—*Beware Falling Tortoises*. Poetry Wales Press/Dofour Editions

Purdy, James—*The Brooklyn Branding Parlors: Poems*. Contact II Publications

Pushkin, Alexander—*Tainye Zapiski 1836-1837 Godov*. M.I.P.

R

Raab, Lawrence—*Other Children*. Carnegie-Mellon University Press

Raborg, Frederick A., Jr.—*Hakata*. Amelia

Racine, Jean—*Phaedra* (translated by Richard Wilbur). Harcourt Brace Jovanovich

Radauskas, Henrikas—*Chimeras In The Tower* (translated by Jonas Zdanys). Wesleyan University Press

Radu, Kenneth—*Letter To A Distant Father*. Brick Books

Rakosi, Carl—*Collected Poems Of Carl Rakosi*. National Poetry Foundation

Ramanujan, A. K.—*Second Sight*. Oxford University Press

Ramke, Bin—*The Language Student*. Louisiana State University Press

Randall, Julia—*Moving In Memory: Poems*. Louisiana State University Press

Randell, Elaine—*Beyond All Other*. Pig Press

Rank, Duke—*Sea Of Cortez: 36 Exposures*. Privately printed

Ratushinskaya, Irina—*Beyond The Limit: Poems* (translated by Frances Padorr Brent and Carol J. Avins). Northwestern University Press

Ray, David—*Sam's Book*. Wesleyan University Press

Reid, Colin Way—*Open Secret*. Dufour Editions

Reising, Chris; LaGattuta, Margo—*Noedgelines.* Earhart Press

Rice, Eve—*City Night.* Greenwillow Books

Rice, Helen Steiner—*Celebrations Of The Heart.* F. H. Revell Co.

—*A Time To Love.* F. H. Revell

Richardson, Dorothy Lee—*The Invisible Giant.* William L. Bauhan

Rigsbee, David—*The Hopper Light.* L'Epervier Press

—*Memory Annex.* Thunder City Press

Rilke, Rainer Maria—*The Complete French Poems Of Rainer Maria Rilke* (translated by A. Poulin). Graywolf Press

—*Sonnets To Orpheus* (translated by David Young). Wesleyan University Press

Rimbaud, Arthur—*Collected Poems.* Penguin

Ritchey, Joseph—*Riding The Big Earth: Poems 1980-86.* National Poetry Foundation

Robbins, Mary Susannah—*Amelie.* Ommation Press

Roberts, Len—*Sweet Ones.* Milkweed Editions

Rogers, Del Marie—*Origins.* Firewheel Press

Rogers, Pattiann—*The Tattooed Lady In The Garden.* Wesleyan University Press

—*Legendary Performances.* Ion Books

Romer, Stephen—*Idols.* Oxford University Press

Roosevelt, Caleb—*I Know Some Spinners Weave My End: Poems.* Dogsbody Press

Rosen, Michael—*Smelly Jelly Smelly Fish.* Prentice Hall

Rosenberg, Leon J.—*Annie.* Equity Press

Rosenberg, Liz—*The Fire Music.* University of Pittsburgh Press

Rosenthal, M. L.—*As For Love: Poems And Translations.* Oxford University Press

Rosetti, Christina—*Christina Rosetti* (edited by Peter Porter). Clarkson N. Potter

Rothenberg, Jerome—*New Selected Poems, 1970-1985.* New Directions Publishing Corp.

Rotstein, Nancy-Gay—*China: Shockwaves.* Dodd, Mead

Roy, Wayne—*Uketorinin: Haiku.* Hamilton Haiku Press

Rua, Antonio—*Open Fire And Other Poems.* First Circle Press

Rudman, Mark—*My Contraries And Other Poems.* National Poetry Foundation

Ruefle, Mary—*Life Without Speaking.* University of Alabama Press

Russell, Frank—*Dinner With Dr. Rocksteady: Poems.* Ion Books/Raccoon

Rutsala, Vern—*Ruined Cities.* Carnegie-Mellon University Press

S

Sacks, Peter—*In These Mountains.* Collier Books

Sadlowski, Anne—*Rising Storm.* International Publishers

Salinas, Luis Omar—*The Sadness Of Days: Selected And New Poems.* Arte Publico Press

Sanchez, Sonia—*Under A Soprano Sky.* Thunder's Mouth Press

Sanders, Edward—*Thirsting For Peace In A Raging Century: Selected Poems, 1960-1985.* Coffee House Press

Sandy, Stephen—*Man In The Open Air.* Knopf

Sapia, Yvonne—*Valentino's Hair.* Northeastern University Press

Sappho—*Greek Lyric Poetry: Including The Complete Poetry Of Sappho* (translated by Willis Barnstone). Schocken Books

Sariban, Michael—*A Formula For Glass.* University of Queensland Press

Sauls, Roger—*Hard Weather.* Bench Press

Schevill, James—*Ambiguous Dancers Of Fame: Collected Poems, 1945-1985.* Swallow Press

Schneider, Fred—*Fred Schneider And Other Unrelated Works.* Arbor House

Schoenberger, Nancy—*Girl On A White Porch: Poems.* University of Missouri Press

Sholl, Betsy—*Rooms Overhead.* Alice James Books

Schorb, E. M.—*50 Poems.* Hill House New York

Schreck, Daniel Wells—*The Signature Of The Spiral.* Sunstone Press

Scott, John A.—*St. Clair: Three Narratives.* University of Queensland Press

Sears, Peter—*Tour: New & Selected Poems.* Breitenbush Books

Segalen, Victor—*Steles* (translated by Michael Taylor). Lapis Press

Sellers, Bettie—*Liza's Monday And Other Poems.* Appalachian Consortium Press

Service, Robert W.—*Dan McGrew, Sam McGee And Other Great Service: The Rugged And Romantic Poems Of Robert Service.* Taylor Publishing Co.

Seth, Vikram—*The Golden Gate.* Random House

Shabistari, Mahmud ibn—*The Secret Rose Garden of Sa'd un Din Mahmud Shabistari* (translated by Florence Lederer). Phanes Press

Shakespeare, William—*The Complete Works* (edited by Stanley Wells and Gary Taylor). Clarendon Press

—*Under The Greenwood Tree: Shakespeare For Young People* (edited by Barbara Holdridge). Stemmer House

—*Shakespeare* (compiled by Patricia Machin). Salem House

—*The Sonnets; And, A Lover's Complaint* (edited by John Kerrigan). Viking Press

Shapcott, Thomas—*Travel Dice.* University of Queensland Press

Shapiro, Alan—*Happy Hour.* University of Chicago Press

Shapiro, David—*To An Idea: A Book Of Poems.* Overlook Press

Shapiro, Karl—*New & Selected Poems, 1940-1986.* University of Chicago Press

Shartle, Gretchen—*On Earth And In Heaven.* Illuminations Press

Shelley, Percy Bysshe—*Shelley* (compiled by Patricia Machin). Salem House

Shelton, Patricia—*The Dragon's Sceptre.* Charles E. Tuttle

Shepard, Andrea J.—*Sing A New Song: Healing The

Hurt Of Divorce. Zondervan Publishing House

Sherman, Alana—*Glue*. Alms House Press

Sherman, Kenneth—*The Book Of Salt*. Oberon Press

Shirley, Aleda—*Chinese Architecture*. University of Georgia Press

Sholevar, Bahman—*Rooted In Volcanic Ashes*. Concourse Press

Sholl, Betsy—*Rooms Overhead*. Alice James Books

Shore, Jane—*The Minute Hand*. University of Massachusetts Press

Siegelman, Ken—*Clusters and Panicles*. Modern Images

Silkin, Jon—*The Ship's Pasture*. Routledge & Kegan Paul

Simic, Charles—*Unending Blues*. Harcourt Brace Jovanovich

Simon, Maurya—*The Enchanted Room: Poems*. Copper Canyon Press

Singer, Sarah—*Of Love And Shoes*. Bauhan

Skellings, Edmund—*Living Proof*. Florida International University Press

Skillman, Judith—*The Worship Of The Visible Spectrum*. Breitenbush Books

Sklarew, Myra—*Altamira*. Washington Writers' Publishing House

Skov-Nielsen, Kurt—*Snowed In*. Purple Wednesday Society

Smith, Charlie—*Red Roads*. E. P. Dutton

Smith, R. T.—*Banish Misfortune*. Livingston University Press
—*Birch-Light*. Tamarack Editions

Snodgrass, W. D.—*Selected Poems: 1957-1987*. Soho Press

Snyder, Gary—*Left Out In The Rain: New Poems, 1947-1985*. North Point Press

Solway, David—*Modern Marriage*. Vehicle Press

Sordello of Goito—*The Poetry Of Sordello* (edited and translated by James J. Wilhelm). Garland Publishing Co.

Soto, Gary—*Lesser Evils: Ten Quartets*. Arte Publico Press

Spears, Heather—*How To Read Faces*. Wolsak & Wynn

Speer, Laurel—*Second Thoughts Over Bourget*. Geryon Press

Spence, Michael—*The Spine*. Purdue University Press

Spicer, David—*Everybody Has A Story*. St. Luke's Press

Spivack, Kathleen—*The Beds We Lie In: Selected And New Poems*. Scarecrow Press

Stafford, Kim R.—*Places & Stories*. Carnegie-Mellon University Press

Stafford, William—*An Oregon Message*. Harper & Row

Stampa, Gaspara—*Three Women Poets: Renaissance And Baroque: Louise Labe, Gaspara Stampa And Sor Juan Ines De La Cruz* (selected and translated by Frank J. Warnke). Bucknell University Press

Steele, Timothy—*Sapphics Against Anger And Other Poems*. Random House

Stein, Kevin—*A Field Of Wings*. Illinois Writers, Inc.

Stern, Gerald—*Lovesick: Poems*. Harper & Row

Stevens, Wallace—*The Palm At The End Of The Mind: Selected Poems And A Play* (edited by Holly Stevens). Archon Books

Stevenson, Anne—*Selected Poems*. Oxford University Press

Stevenson, Robert Louis—*Poems From A Child's Garden Of Verses*. Harper & Row

Stewart, Frank—*Reunion*. Paper Press
—*Flying The Red Eye*. Floating Island Publications

Stewart, Susan—*The Hive*. University of Georgia Press

Still, James—*The Wolfpen Poems*. Berea College Press

Stone, Ruth—*Second Hand Coat*. David R. Godine

Storace, Patricia—*Heredity*. Beacon Press

Stringer, A. E.—*Channel Markers*. Wesleyan University Press

Stripling, Kathryn Byer—*The Girl In The Midst Of The Harvest*. Texas Tech Press

Struthers, Ann—*Stoneboat*. Pterodactyl Press

Stryk, Lucien—*Bells Of Lombardy*. Northern Illinois University Press

Stuart, Dabney—*Don't Look Back: Poems*. Louisiana State University Press

Stuart, Jesse—*Songs Of A Mountain Plowman* (edited by Jim Wayne Miller). Morehead State University

Suvin, Darko R.—*The Long March: Notes On The Way, 1981-1984*. Hounslow Press

Swenson, May—*In Other Words: New Poems*. Multnomah Press

Sze, Arthur—*River River*. Lost Roads Publishers

Szirtes, George—*The Photographer In Winter*. Secker and Warburg

T

Tandori, Dezso—*Birds And Other Relations: Selected Poetry Of Dezso Tandori* (translated by Bruce Berlind). Princeton University Press

Tasso, Torquato—*Jerusalem Delivered* (translated and edited by Ralph Nash). Wayne State University Press

Tate, James—*Reckoner*. Wesleyan University Press

Taylor, Andrew—*Travelling*. University of Queensland Press

Tennyson, Alfred—*Tennyson* (compiled by Patricia Machin). Salem House
—*Tennyson: The Harvard Manuscripts* (edited by Christopher Ricks and Aidan Day). Garland Publishing Co.

Thaddeus, Janice—*Lot's Wife*. Saturday Press

Thayer, Ernest L.—*The Illustrated Casey At The Bat*. Workman Publishers

Thomas, Barbara Jean—*Proverbs II*. Landsberry Press

Thomas, R. S.—*Welsh Airs*. Poetry Wales Press/ Dufour Editions

Thompson, Sue Ellen—*This Body Of Silk*. Northeastern University Press

Thoreau, Henry David—*The Winged Life* (edited by Robert Bly). Sierra Club

Tipping, Richard Kelly—*Nearer By Far*. University of Queensland Press

Tomlinson, Charles—*Collected Poems*. Oxford University Press

Toney, Mitchell—*The Matter With Stars*. Lynx House Press

Tootell, Jack—*Lightly The Harper*. Blue Dolphin Publishers

Tran Thi Nga; Larsen, Wendy Wilder—*Shallow Graves: Two Women And Vietnam*. Harper & Row

Transtromer, Tomas—*Tomas Transtromer: Selected Poems 1954-1986* (translated by Robert Bly; edited by Robert Hass). Ecco Press

Trungpa, Chogyam—*Mudra*. Shambhala

U

Ullman, Leslie—*Dreams By No One's Daughter*. University of Pittsburgh Press

Umpierre-Herrera, Luz—*And Other Misfortunes*. Third Woman Press

Unger, Barbara—*Inside The Wind*. Linwood Publishers

V

Van Houten, Lois—*Coming To Terms With Geese*. Lincoln Springs Press

Van Peenen, John—*A Family Album* (part poetry). Goat Foot Press

Vantuono, William (editor)—*The Pearl Poem In Middle And Modern English*. University Press of America

Veinberg, Jon—*An Owl's Landscape*. Vanderbilt University Press

Viereck, Peter—*Archer In The Marrow: The Applewood Cycles, 1967-1987*. W. W. Norton

Vigil-Pinon, Evangelina—*The Computer Is Down*. Arte Publico Press

Vinz, Mark—*Minnesota Gothic*. Barnwood Press

Viorst, Judith—*When Did I Stop Being Twenty And Other Injustices: Selected Poems From Single To Mid-Life*. Simon and Schuster

Virgil—*The Aeneid* (translated by C. H. Sisson). Carcanet

Voight, Ellen Bryant—*The Lotus Flowers*. Norton

Voznesensky, Andrei—*An Arrow In The Wall: Selected Poetry And Prose* (edited by William Jay Smith and F. D. Reeve). Henry Holt & Co.

W

Wagoner, David—*Through The Forest: New And Selected Poems*. Atlantic Monthly Press

Walcott, Derek—*The Arkansas Testament*. Farrar, Straus & Giroux

Waldrop, Rosemarie—*The Reproduction Of Profiles*. New Directions Publishing Corp.

Wallace, Robert—*The Lost History Of Everything*. Carnegie-Mellon University Press

Wallace, Ron—*People And Dog In The Sun*. University of Pittsburgh Press

Walmsley, Gordon—*Visions For Lack Of A Better Word, Or, Oxidized Virgin*. Bridgehead Press

Wangerin, Walter, Jr.—*A Miniature Cathedral And Other Poems*. Harper & Row

Ward, Robert—*Camera Obscura*. Silverfish Review

Warren, Robert Penn—*A Robert Penn Warren Reader*. Random House

Waterman, Andrew—*Selected Poems*. Carcanet/Harper & Row

Waters, Mary Ann—*The Exact Place*. Confluence Press

Weaver, Francis K.—*Posy Of A Ring*. Dragon's Teeth Press

Weems, Ann—*Kneeling In Bethlehem*. Westminster Press

Weil, James L.—*Houses Roses*. Sparrow Press

Weingarten, Roger—*Ethan Benjamin Boldt*. Story Line Press

Weisbort, Daniel—*Leaseholder: New And Selected Poems, 1965-1985*. Carcanet

Wells, Robert—*Selected Poems*. Carcanet/Harper & Row

Wendt, Ingrid—*Singing The Mozart Requiem*. Breitenbush Books

Westerback, Arnold J.—*Sixfold Symmetry: Six Complete Volumes Of Poetry*. Samara

Wetteroth, Bruce—*Words Like These*. Ohio Review Books

Wheatley, Phillis—*The Collected Works Of Phillis Wheatley* (edited by John Shields). Oxford University Press

Whitehead, James—*Local Men; And, Domains: Two Books Of Poetry*. University of Illinois Press

Whitlow, Carolyn Beard—*Wild Meat*. Lost Roads

Whitman, Ruth—*The Testing Of Hanna Senesh*. Wayne State University Press

Williams, C. K.—*Flesh And Blood*. Farrar, Straus & Giroux

Williams, Miller—*Imperfect Love*. Louisiana State University Press

Williams, Susan—*Dying Old And Dying Young*. New Rivers Press

Williams, William Carlos—*The Collected Poems Of William Carlos Williams, Volume 1: 1909-1939* (edited by A. Walton Litz and Christopher MacGowan). New Directions Publishing Corp.

Wilson, Robley, Jr.—*Kingdoms Of The Ordinary*. University of Pittsburgh Press

Woessner, Warren—*Storm Lines: A Collection Of Poems*. New Rivers Press

Wojahn, David—*Glassworks*. University of Pittsburgh Press

Wordsworth, William—*Wordsworth* (compiled by Patricia Machin). Salem House
—*Wordsworth's Poems Of 1807* (edited by Alun R. Jones). Humanities Press International

Worth, Douglas—*Once Around Bullough's Pond: A Native American Epic*. W. L. Bauhan

Worth, Valerie—*small poems again*. Farrar, Straus

& Giroux

Wright, Jay—*Selected Poems Of Jay Wright* (edited by Robert B. Stepto). Princeton University Press

Wrigley, Robert—*Moon In A Mason Jar: Poems.* University of Illinois Press

X

Xue Tao—*Brocade River Poems: Selected Works Of The Tang Dynasty Courtesan Xue Tao* (translated by Jeanne Larsen). Princeton University Press

Y

Yates, J. Michael—*The Completely Collapsible Portable Man: Selected Shorter Lyrics.* Mosaic Press
—*Fugue Brancusi.* Sono Nis Press
—*Schedules Of Silence: The Collected Longer Poems, 1960-1986.* Pulp Press

Yeats, William Butler—*Selected Poems And Three Plays Of William Butler Yeats* (edited by M. L. Rosenthal). Collier Books

Yevtushenko, Yevgeny—*Almost At The End of The World* (translated by Antonina W. Bouis, Albert C. Todd and Yevgeny Yevtushenko). Henry Holt and Co.

Yolen, Jane—*The Three Bears Rhyme Book.* Harcourt Brace Jovanovich

Yosano, Akiko—*Tangled Hair: Selected Tanka From Midaregami.* Charles Tuttle

Yoshimasu, Gozo—*A Thousand Steps—And More: Selected Poems And Prose* (translated by Richard Arno, Brenda Barrows and Takato Lento). Katydid Books

Z

Zadravec, Katharine—*How To Travel.* Scop Publications

Zahn, Curtis—*The Plight Of The Lesser Sawyer's Cricket: Plays, Prose And Poems.* Capra Press

Zahniser, Ed—*The Way To Heron Mountain.* Night Tree Press

Zawadiwsky, Christina—*The Hand On The Head Of Lazarus.* Ion Books/Raccoon

Zeiger, Gene—*Sudden Dancing.* Amherst Writers and Artists

Zimmerman, Irene—*For-Giving Ground: Poems For Living And Praying.* Franciscan Herald Press

(2) ANTHOLOGIES

(listed alphabetically by title)

American Yiddish Poetry (edited by Benjamin and Barbara Harshav). University of California Press

The Anthology Of Twentieth Century New Zealand Poetry (Third Edition) (edited by Vincent O'Sullivan). Oxford University Press

The Bakchesarian Fountain (by Alexander Pushkin and other poems by various authors; translated by William D. Lewis). Ardis Publishers

Bennett Cerf's Out On A Limerick: A Collection Of Over 300 Of The World's Best Printable Limericks (assembled by Bennett Cerf). Perennial Library

A Book Of Love Poetry (edited by John Stallworthy). Oxford University Press

Cat Poems (selected by Myra Cohn Livingston). Holiday House

Cat Will Rhyme With Hat: A Book Of Poems (compiled by Jean Chapman). Scribner

The Children's Book Of Rhymes (collected by Cicely Mary Barker). Bedrick

Click, Rumble, Roar: Poems About Machines (selected by Lee Bennett Hopkins). T. Y. Crowell

The Columbia Book Of Later Chinese Poetry: Yuan, Ming And Ch'ing Dynasties (1279-1911) (edited and translated by Jonathan Chaves). Columbia University Press

Contemporary Religious Poetry (edited by Paul Ramsey). Paulist Press

The Cooke Book: A Seasoning Of Poets (edited by Michael S. Glaser). Scop Publications

Dinosaurs: Poems (selected by Lee Bennett Hopkins). Harcourt Brace Jovanovich

The Faber Book Of Contemporary Irish Poetry (edited by Paul Muldoon). Faber and Faber

The Faber Book Of 20th Century Women's Poetry (edited by Fleur Adcock). Faber and Faber

First Lines: Poems Written In Youth, From Herbert To Heaney (edited by Jon Stallworthy). Carcanet

First Person Plural. Black Moss Press

For Cowboys, Campers, An' Common Folk: If You Ain't One Of These, Don't Buy It!: A Collection Of Some Of The Original Poetry Of Charles E. "Charlie" Hunt With Selected Poems From Other Cowboy Poets. Old West Publishing Co.

German Poetry: An Anthology From Klopstock To Enzensberger (edited by Martin Swales). Cambridge University Press

Going Over To Your Place: Poems For Each Other (edited by Paul B. Janeczko). Bradbury Press

The Golden Treasury Of The Best Songs & Lyrical Poems In The English Language (selected by Francis Turner Palgrave; updated by John Press). Oxford University Press

The Greek Anthology (edited by Donya Lida Taran). Garland Publishing Co.

Greek Lyric Poetry: Including The Complete Poetry Of Sappho (translated by Willis Barnstone).

Schocken Books

The Heart Of Love (edited by Priscilla Young). Harper & Row

The Hidden Italy: A Bilingual Edition Of Italian Dialect Poetry (translated by Hermann W. Haller). Wayne State University Press

How We Are Islanded Together: Poetry And Other Writing (by Kauai, Hawaii, writers). Magic Fishes Press

I Like You, If You Like Me: Poems Of Friendship (selected and edited by Myra Cohn Livingston). Margaret K. McElderry Books

I'll Be Here When You Need Me: A Collection Of Poems (edited by Susan Polis Schutz). Blue Mountain Press

In Praise Of Sailors: A Nautical Anthology Of Art, Poetry and Prose (compiled and edited by Herbert W. Warden III). Abradale Press

Japanese Death Poems (edited by Yoel Hoffman). Charles E. Tuttle Co.

Jump All The Morning: A Child's Day In Verse (selected by P. K. Roche). Puffin Books

Keener Sounds: Selected Poems From The Georgia Review (edited by Stanley W. Lindberg and Stephen Corey). University of Georgia Press

Language Poetries: An Anthology (edited by Douglas Messerli). New Directions Publishing Corp.

The Long Embrace: Twentieth-Century Irish Love Poems (edited by Frank Ormsby). Blackstaff Press

Long Island Poets: An Anthology (edited by Robert Long). Permanent Press

Love In Mid-Winter Night: Korean Sijo Poetry (translated by Chung Chong-wha). KPI

Love Poems From Spain And Spanish America (selected and translated by Perry Higman). City Lights Books

The Made Thing: An Anthology Of Contemporary Southern Poetry (edited by Leon Stokesbury). University of Arkansas Press

Marriage Poems And Satires, 1670-1800: Facsimile Reproductions (selected by William C. Horne). Scholars' Facsimiles & Reprints

Modern American Poets: Their Voices And Visions (collected by Robert DiYanni). Random House

Modern Arabic Poetry: An Anthology (edited by Salma Khadra Jayyusi). Columbia University Press

Modern Poetry Of The Arab World (edited and translated by Abdullah al-Udhari). Penguin

More Surprises (selected by Lee Bennett Hopkins). Harper & Row

My Christian Reader: 52 Stories And Poems For Children Ages 7 to 10. Concordia Publishing House

New Directions 50 (part poetry) (edited by J. Laughlin). New Directions Publishing Corp.

The New Oxford Book Of Victorian Verse (edited by Christopher Ricks). Oxford University Press

New Songs From A Jade Terrace: An Anthology Of Early Chinese Love Poems (edited and translated by Anne Birrell). Penguin

New Year's Poems (selected by Myra Cohn Livingston). Holiday House

The Nobel Reader: Short Fiction, Poetry And Prose

By Nobel Laureates In Literature (edited by Jonathan Eisen and Stuart Troy). C. N. Potter

North Carolina's 400 Years: Signs Along The Way: An Anthology Of Poems By North Carolina Poets To celebrate North Carolina's 400th Anniversary (edited by Ronald H. Bayes). Acorn Press

On This Crust Of Earth: A Gathering Of Poets From Fairfield County, Connecticut (edited by Ralph Nazareth and Lynda Sorensen). Yuganta Press

100 Poems By 100 Poets: An Anthology (selected by Harold Pinter, Geoffrey Godbert and Anthony Astbury). Grove Press

The Oxford Book Of Local Verse (chosen by John Holloway). Oxford University Press

The Oxford Book Of Travel Verse (chosen and edited by Kevin Crossley-Holland). Oxford University Press

A Paper Zoo: A Collection Of Animal Poems (selected by Renee Karol Weiss). Macmillan

P.E.N. New Poetry I (edited by Robert Nye). Quartet Books

The Penguin Book Of Caribbean Verse In English (selected and edited by Paula Burnett). Penguin Books

The Penguin Book Of Lieder (edited and translated by S. S. Prawer). Penguin

The Penguin Book Of Modern Urdu Poetry (edited and translated by Mahmood Jamal). Penguin

The Penguin Book Of Modern Yiddish Verse (edited by Irving Howe, Ruth R. Wisse and Khone Shmeruk). Viking Press

Piecework: 19 Fresno Poets (edited by Jon Veinberg and Ernesto Trejo). Silver Skates Publishing

The Ploughshares Poetry Reader (edited by Joyce Peseroff). New American Library

Poetry Connoisseur's Fifty Prizewinning Poems (edited by Robert Travis). Aesthetics West

Poetry Worth Remembering: An Anthology Of Poetry (compiled by Roy W. Watson). Brunswick

Poets For Africa: An International Anthology For Hunger Relief (edited by Susann Flammang). Family of God

Proensa: An Anthology Of Troubador Poetry (edited by George Economou; translated by Paul Blackburn). Paragon House Publishers

Read Aloud Rhymes For The Very Young (selected by Jack Prelutsky). Knopf

Slow Chrysanthemums: Classical Korean Poems In Chinese (translated by Kim Jong-gil). Anvil Press

Snowy Day: Stories And Poems (edited by Caroline Feller Bauer). Lippincott

Sound And Light: Poets Club Of Chicago, 1937-1987, 50th Anniversary Anthology. Lake Shore Publishing

Themes, Thoughts And Treasures: An Anthology Of Poetry, Volumes 1-2 (edited by Jimmy L. Gravely). Certified Feelings

These Small Stones (selected by Myra Cohn Livingston). Harper & Row

Tilted Planet Poems: Hearts And Souls From Austin And Central Texas (edited by Robin Cravey). Tilted Planet Press

To Father With Love (edited by Betty Sullivan).

Harper & Row
Tongues Of Fire: An Anthology Of Religious And Poetic Experience (edited by Karen Armstrong). Penguin
The Twenties: An Anthology (part poetry) (edited by Carl Ellendea Proffer). Ardis
Waiting For The Unicorn: Poems And Lyrics Of China's Last Dynasty, 1644-1911) (edited by Irving Ucheng Lo and William Schultz). Indiana University Press

Welsh Verse (compiled by Tony Conran). Poetry Wales Press/Dufour Editions
Wine, Women & Death: Medieval Hebrew Poems On The Good Life (compiled by Raymond P. Scheindlin). Jewish Publication Society
Wynken, Blynken And Nod, And Other Bedtime Poems. Golden Books
Yaqui Deer Songs, Maso Bwikam: A Native American Poetry (edited by Larry Evers And Felipe S. Molina). Sun Tracks/University of Arizona Press

(3) BIOGRAPHY AND COMMENT ON SPECIFIC POETS
(listed alphabetically by subject)

Ammons, A. R.—*A. R. Ammons* (edited by Harold Bloom). Chelsea House Publishers
Angelou, Maya—*All God's Children Need Traveling Shoes* (by Maya Angelou). Vintage Books
Ariosto, Ludovico—*Ariosto's Bitter Harmony: Crisis And Evasion In The Italian Renaissance* (by Albert Russell Ascoli), Princeton University Press
—*The Poetics Of Ariosto* (by Marianne Shapiro). Wayne State University Press
—*Ariosto And Boiardo: The Origins Of Orlando Furioso* (by Peter V. Marinelli). University of Missouri Press
Aristotle—*The Poetics Of Aristotle: Translation And Commentary* (by Stephen Halliwell). University of North Carolina Press
Atwood, Margaret—*Margaret Atwood* (by Barbara Hill Rigney). Barnes & Noble Books
Auden, W. H.—*W. H. Auden* (edited by Harold Bloom). Chelsea House Publishers
Baudelaire, Charles—*Baudelaire And Le Spleen De Paris* (by J. A. Hiddleston). Clarendon Press
—*Poetic Principles And Practices: Occasional Papers On Baudelaire, Mallarme And Valery* (by Lloyd Austin). Cambridge University Press
—*Charles Baudelaire: Une Micro-Histoire* (by Raymond P. Poggenburg). Vanderbilt University Press
—*Charles Baudelaire* (edited by Harold Bloom). Chelsea House Publishers
Bennett, Paula—*My Life A Loaded Gun: Female Creativity And Female Poetics.* Beacon Press
Berryman, John—*Berryman And Lowell: The Art Of Losing* (by Stephen Matterson). Barnes & Noble Books
—*The Middle Generation: The Lives And Poetry of Delmore Schwartz, Randall Jarrell, John Berryman And Robert Lowell* (by Bruce Bawer). Archon Books
—*Manic Power: Robert Lowell And His Circle* (by Jeffrey Meyers). Arbor House
—*The Berryman Gestalt: Therapeutic Strategies In The Poetry Of John Berryman* (by Joseph Mancini, Jr.). Garland Publishing Co.
Bishop, Elizabeth—*That Sense Of Constant Readjustment: Elizabeth Bishop's North & South* (by Lloyd Schwartz). Garland Publishing Co.
—*Elizabeth Bishop* (edited by Harold Bloom). Chelsea House Publishers
Blackmur, R. P.—*The Legacy Of R. P. Blackmur: Essays, Memoirs, Texts* (edited by Edward T. Cone, Joseph Frank and Edmund Keeley). Ecco Press
Blake, William—*The Paintings Of William Blake* (by Raymond Lister). Cambridge University Press
—*Songs Of Innocence And Experience* (edited by Harold Bloom). Chelsea House Publishers
—*The Four Zoas By William Blake: A Photographic Facsimile Of The Manuscript With Commentary On The Illuminations* (by Cettina Tramontane Magno and David V. Erdman). Bucknell University Press
Bly, Robert—*Robert Bly* (by Richard P. Sugg). Twayne Publishers
Boethius—*Boethian Apocalypse: Studies In Middle English Vision Poetry* (by Michael D. Cherniss). Pilgrim Books
Bogan, Louise—*Louise Bogan's Aesthetic of Limitation* (by Gloria Bowles). Indiana University Press
Borges, Jorge Luis—*The Poetry And Poetics Of Jorge Luis Borges* (by Paul Chesalka). P. Lang
—*Critical Essays On Jorge Luis Borges* (by Jaime Alazraki). G. K. Hall
Brooke, Rupert—*Letters From America* (by Rupert Brooke). Beaufort Books
—*The Neo-Pagans: Rupert Brooke And The Ordeal Of Youth* (by Paul Delany). Free Press
Brooks, Gwendolyn—*A Life Distilled: Gwendolyn Brooks, Her Poetry And Fiction* (edited by Maria K. Mootry and Gary Smith). University of Illinois Press
—*Gwendolyn Brooks: Poetry And The Heroic Voice* (by D. H. Melhem). University Press of Kentucky
Browning, Elizabeth Barrett—*The Courtship Of Robert Browning And Elizabeth Barrett* (by Daniel Karlin). Oxford University Press
Browning, Robert—*The Courtship Of Robert Browning And Elizabeth Barrett* (by Daniel Karlin). Oxford University Press
—*History And The Prism Of Art: Browning's Poetic Experiments* (by Mary Ellis Gibson). Ohio

State University Press

Bryant, William Cullen—*Under Open Sky: Poets On William Cullen Bryant* (edited by Norbert Krapf). Fordham University Press

Burns, Robert—*Robert Burns* (by Raymond Bentman). Twayne Publishers

Byron, Lord—*Lord Byron's Don Juan* (edited by Harold Bloom). Chelsea House Publishers
—*Byron* (by Angus Calder). Open University Press
—*Byron's Politics* (by Malcolm Kelsall). Barnes & Noble Books
—*Social Relations In Byron's Eastern Tales* (by Daniel P. Watkins). Fairleigh Dickinson University Press
—*At The Titan's Breakfast: Three Essays On Byron's Poetry* (by Robert Polito). Garland Publishing Co.
—*Byron And Tragedy* (by Martyn Corbett). St. Martin's Press

Cesaire, Aime—*Engagement And The Language Of The Subject In The Poetry Of Aime Cesaire* (by Ronnie Leah Scharfman). University Presses of Florida

Chatterton, Thomas—*The Family Romance Of The Imposter-Poet Thomas Chatterton* (by Louise J. Kaplan). Atheneum

Chaucer, Geoffrey—*Geoffrey Chaucer* (by Stephen Knight). B. Blackwell
—*The Canterbury Tales And The Good Society* (by Paul A. Olson). Princeton University Press
—*The Cambridge Chaucer Companion* (edited by Piero Boitani and Jill Mann). Cambridge University Press
—*Chaucer: The Earlier Poetry: A Study In Poetic Development* (by Derek Traversi). University of Delaware Press
—*A Critical Edition Of The Isle Of Ladies* (edited by Vincent Daly). Garland Publishing Co.
—*Earnest Games: Folkloric Patterns In The Canterbury Tales* (by Carl Lindahl). Indiana University Press
—*Chaucer: His Works, His World* (by Donald R. Howard). E. P. Dutton
—*Chaucer's Frame Tales: The Physical And Metaphysical* (edited by Joerg O. Fichte). Boydell and Brewer
—*Geoffrey Chaucer: An Introduction To His Narrative Poetry* (by Dieter Mehl). Cambridge University Press
—*Chaucer Aloud: The Varieties Of Textual Interpretation* (by Betsy Bowden). University of Pennsylvania Press
—*Scott, Chaucer And Medieval Romance: A Study In Sir Walter Scott's Indebtedness To The Literature Of The Middle Ages) (by Jerome Mitchell). University of Kentucky Press*

Ciardi, John—*John Ciardi: Measure Of The Man* (edited by Vince Clemente). University of Arkansas Press

Coleridge, Samuel Taylor—*A Complete Concordance To The Lyrical Ballads Of Samuel Taylor*

Coleridge And William Wordsworth: 1798 And 1800 Editions (by Thomas F. Beckwith and Patricia A. McEahern). Garland Publishing Co.
—*The Singing Of Mount Abora: Coleridge's Use Of Biblical Imagery And Natural Symbolism In Poetry And Philosophy* (by H. W. Piper). Fairleigh Dickinson University Press
—*Samuel Taylor Coleridge* (edited by Harold Bloom). Chelsea House Publishers
—*Samuel Taylor Coleridge: The Rime Of The Ancient Mariner* (edited by Harold Bloom). Chelsea House Publishers
—*Coleridge* (by W. Jackson Bate). Harvard University Press
—*Coleridge's Philosophy Of Language* (by James C. McKusick). Yale University Press

Corman, Cid—*Between Your House And Mine: The Letters Of Lorine Neidecker To Cid Corman 1960-1970* (edited by Lisa Pater Faranda). Duke University Press

Cowley, Abraham—*A Critical Edition Of Abraham Cowley's Davideis* (edited by Gayle Shadduck). Garland Publishing Co.

Crane, Hart—*Voyager: A Life Of Hart Crane* (by John Unterecker). Liveright Publishing Corp.
—*Unfractioned Idiom: Hart Crane And Modernism* (by Maria F. Bennett). P. Lang
—*Transmemberment Of Song: Hart Crane's Anatomies Of Rhetoric And Desire* (by Lee Edelman). Stanford University Press

Cummings, E. E.—*Poet And Painter: The Aesthetics Of E. E. Cummings's Early Works* (by Milton A. Cohen). Wayne State University Press

Dante Alighieri—*The Reader's Companion To Dante's Divine Comedy* (by Angelo A. De Gennaro). Philosophical Library
—*Dante: The Divine Comedy* (by Robin Kirkpatrick). Cambridge University Press
—*Dante And The Empire* (by Donna Mancusi-Ungaro). P. Lang

Davenant, William—*Rare Sir William Davenant: Poet Laureate, Playwright, Civil War General, Restoration Theatre Manager* (by Mary Edmond). St. Martin's Press

Davies, Hugh Sykes—*Wordsworth And The Worth Of Words*. Cambridge University Press

Dickey, James—*James Dickey And The Gentle Ecstasy Of Earth: A Reading Of The Poems* (by Robert Kirschten). Louisiana State University Press

Dickinson, Emily—*Emily Dickinson* (by Cynthia Griffin Wolff). Knopf
—*Emily Dickinson: Looking To Canaan* (by John Robinson). Faber and Faber
—*Emily Dickinson: The Poet On The Second Story* (by Jerome Loving). Cambridge University Press
—*Emily Dickinson: A Poet's Grammar* (by Christiane Miller). Harvard University Press
—*Lunacy Of Light: Emily Dickinson And The Experience Of Metaphor* (by Wendy Barker). Southern Illinois University Press
—*The Language Of Exclusion: The Poetry Of*

Emily Dickinson And Christina Rossetti (by Sharon Leder with Andrea Abbott). Greenwood Press

Docherty, Thomas—*John Donne Undone.* Methuen

Donne, John—*John Donne, Undone* (by Thomas Docherty). Methuen

Doolittle, Hilda—*H. D.: Woman And Poet* (by Michael King). National Poetry Foundation

Dracontius, Blossius Aemilius—*The Miniature Epic In Vandal Africa* (by David F. Bright). University of Oklahoma Press

Dryden, John—*John Dryden: Dramatist, Satirist, Translator* (by William Frost). AMS Press
—*John Dryden And His World* (by James Anderson Winn). Yale University Press
—*John Dryden* (edited by Harold Bloom). Chelsea House Publishers

Eliot, T. S.—*He Do The Police In Different Voices: The Waste Land And Its Protagonist* (by Calvin Bedient). University Of Chicago Press
—*T. S. Eliot: The Waste Land* (edited by Harold Bloom). Chelsea House Publishers
—*The Waste Land And Ash Wednesday* (by Arnold P. Hinchliffe). Humanities Press
—*T. S. Eliot And The Politics Of Voice: The Argument Of The Waste Land* (by John Xiros Cooper). UMI Research Press
—*Eliot, Joyce And Company* (by Stanley Sultan). Oxford University Press
—*Modernist Poetics Of History: Pound, Eliot, And The Sense Of The Past* (by James Longenbach). Princeton University Press
—*A T. S. Eliot Companion: Life And Works* (by F. B. Pinion). Barnes & Noble Books
—*Discovering Modernism: T. S. Eliot And His Context* (by Louis Menand). Oxford University Press
—*T. S. Eliot, Wallace Stevens, And The Discourses Of Difference* (by Michael Beehler). Louisiana State University Press
—*A Preface To T. S. Eliot* (by Ronald Tamplin). Longman
—*The Poetics Of Impersonality: T. S. Eliot And Ezra Pound* (by Maud Ellmann). Harvard University Press

Everson, William—*The Life Of Brother Antoninus* (by Lee Bartlett). New Directions Publishing Corp.

Farrokhzad, Forugh—*A Lonely Woman: Forugh Farrokhzad And Her Poetry* (by Michael C. Hillmann). Three Continents Press

Ford, Ford Madox—*Ford Madox Ford And His Relationship To Stephen Crane And Henry James* (by Brita Lindberg-Syersted). Humanities Press Intl.

Francis, Robert—*Travelling In Amherst: A Poet's Journal, 1931-1954* (by Robert Francis). Rowan Tree Press

Frost, Robert—*Robert Frost* (edited by Harold Bloom). Chelsea House Publishers
—*Robert Frost Himself* (by Stanley Burnshaw). George Braziller
—*Robert Frost's Emergent Design: The Truth Of The Self In-Between Belief And Unbelief* (by Jo-

hannes Kjorven). Humanities Press International

Garth, Samuel—*The Best-Natured Man: Sir Samuel Garth, Physician And Poet* (by John F. Sena). AMS Press

Gezelle, Guido—*Guido Gezelle: Flemish Poet-Priest* (by Hermine J. van Nuis). Greenwood Press

Gidlow, Elsa—*Elsa, I Come With My Songs: The Autobiography Of Elsa Gidlow.* Booklegger Press

Guillens, Nicolas—*Against The American Grain: Myth And History In William Carlos Williams, Jay Wright And Nicolas Guillens* (by Vera Kutzinski). Johns Hopkins University Press

H. D.—see Doolittle, Hilda

Hall, Donald—*Seasons At Eagle Pond* (by Donald Hall). Ticknor & Fields

Hayden, Robert—*A Critical Analysis Of The Poetry Of Robert Hayden, 1940-78* (by Pontheolla T. Williams). University Of Illinois Press

Heaney, Seamus—*Seamus Heaney (by Neil Corcoran). Faber and Faber*
—*Seamus Heaney* (edited by Harold Bloom). Chelsea House Publishers

Herbert, George—*George Ryley, Mr. Herbert's Temple And Church Militant Explained And Improved: Bodleian MS Rawl. D. 199* (edited by Maureen Boyd and Cedric C. Brown). Garland Publishing Co.

Herbert, Zbigniew—*A Fugitive From Utopia: The Poetry Of Zbigniew Herbert* (by Stanislaw Baranczak). Harvard University Press

Herrick, Robert—*Fantasy, Fashion And Affection: Editions Of Robert Herrick's Poetry For The Common Reader, 1810-1968* (by Jay A. Gertzman). Bowling Green State University Popular Press

Hill, Geoffrey—*The Uncommon Tongue: The Poetry And Criticism Of Geoffrey Hill* (by Vincent Sherry). University of Michigan Press

Holderlin, Friedrich—*Agnostic Poetry: The Pindaric Mode In Pindar, Horace, Holderlin, And The English Ode* (by William Fitzgerald). University of California Press
—*Keats, Leopardi And Holderlin: The Poet As Priest Of The Absolute* (by Ray Fleming). Garland Publishing Co.

Holm, Bill—*Prairie Days* (by Bill Holm). Saybrook Publishing Co./W. W. Norton

Homer—*Odysseus Polutropos: Intertextual Readings In The Odyssey And The Iliad* (by Pietro Pucci). Cornell University Press
—*Homer: Poet Of the Iliad* (by Mark W. Edwards). Johns Hopkins University Press
—*War Music* (an account of books 16-19 of Homer's Iliad) (by Christopher Logue). Farrar, Straus & Giroux
—*Homeric Researches* (by Johannes Th. Kakridis). Garland Publishing Co.
—*Approaches To Teaching Homer's Illiad And Odyssey* (edited by Kostas Myrsiades). Modern Language Association of America
—*Epos: Word, Narrative And The Iliad* (by Michael Lynn-George). Humanities Press

—*The Making Of Homeric Verse: The Collected Papers Of Milman Parry* (edited by Adam Parry). Oxford University Press

—*From Delos To Delphi: A Literary Study Of The Homeric Hymn To Apollo* (by Andrew M. Miller). E. J. Brill

—*Homer's The Odyssey* (edited by Harold Bloom). Chelsea House Publishers

—*Critical Essays On Homer* (edited by Kenneth Atchity). G. K. Hall

Hopkins, Gerard Manley—*Gerard Manley Hopkins* (edited by Harold Bloom). Chelsea House Publishers

—*Created To Praise: The Language Of Gerard Manley Hopkins* (by Margaret R. Ellsberg). Oxford University Press

Horace—*Agnostic Poetry: The Pindaric Mode In Pindar, Horace, Holderlin, And The English Ode* (by William Fitzgerald). University of California Press

—*Horace's Poetic Journey: A Reading Of Odes 1-3* (by David H. Porter). Princeton University Press

Hughes, Langston— *I Wonder As I Wander: An Autobiographical Journey* (by Langston Hughes). Thunder's Mouth Press

—*The Life Of Langston Hughes: Volume I, 1902-1941* (by Arnold Rampersad). Oxford University Press

Huysmans, J.-K.—*J.-K. Huysmans: Novelist, Poet And Art Critic* (by Annette Kahn). UMI Research Press

Iqbal, Muhammad—*Iqbal: Poet-Patriot Of India* (by S. M. H. Burney) (translated by Syeda Saiyidain Hameed). Vikas Publishing House

Jarrell, Randall—*The Middle Generation: The Lives And Poetry Of Delmore Schwartz, Randall Jarrell, John Berryman And Robert Lowell* (by Bruce Bawer). Archon Books

—*Manic Power: Robert Lowell And His Circle* (by Jeffrey Meyers). Arbor House

Jeffers, Robinson—*Robinson Jeffers: Poet Of California* (by James Karman). Chronicle Books

Jonson, Ben—*Ben Jonson* (edited by Harold Bloom). Chelsea House Publishers

Keats, John—*Keats, Leopardi And Holderlin: The Poet As Priest Of The Absolute* (by Ray Fleming). Garland Publishing Co.

—*John Keats* (by John Barnard). Cambridge University Press

—*The Odes Of Keats* (edited by Harold Bloom). Chelsea House Publishers

—*Keats As A Reader Of Shakespeare* (by R. S. White). University of Oklahoma Press

Kinnell, Galway—*Intricate And Simple Things: The Poetry Of Galway Kinnell* (by Lee Zimmerman). University of Illinois Press

Langland, William—*The Clerkly Maker: Langland's Poetic Art* (by A. V. C. Schmidt). D. S. Brewer/Longwood

Lawrence, D. H.—*A Study Of The Poems Of D. H. Lawrence: Thinking In Poetry* (by M. J. Lockwood). St. Martin's Press

Leopardi, Giacomo—*Keats, Leopardi And Holderlin: The Poet As Priest Of The Absolute* (by Ray Fleming). Garland Publishing Co.

Lindbergh, Anne Morrow—*Anne Morrow Lindbergh: Pilot And Poet* (by Roxane Chadwick). Lerner Publications Co.

Longfellow, Henry Wadsworth—*Henry Wadsworth Longfellow: His Poetry & Prose* (by Edward Wagenknecht). Ungar

Lowell, Robert—*The Middle Generation: The Lives And Poetry Of Delmore Schwartz, Randall Jarrell, John Berryman And Robert Lowell* (by Bruce Bawer). Archon Books

—*Manic Power: Robert Lowell And His Circle* (by Jeffrey Meyers). Arbor House

—*Berryman And Lowell: The Art Of Losing* (by Stephen Matterson). Barnes & Noble Books

—*Robert Lowell: Essays On The Poetry* (edited by Steven Gould Axelrod And Helen Deese). Cambridge University Press

MacNeice, Louis—*Selected Literary Criticism Of Louis MacNeice* (edited by Alan Heuser). Oxford University Press

Mallarme, Stephane—*Eros Under Glass: Psychoanalysis And Mallarme's Herodiade* (by Mary Ellen Wolf). Ohio State University Press

—*Poetic Principles And Practices: Occasional Papers On Baudelaire, Mallarme And Valery* (by Lloyd Austin). Cambridge University Press

—*Patterns Of Thought In Rimbaud And Mallarme* (by John Porter Houston). French Forum

—*Mallarme, Or, The Poet Of Nothingness* (by Jean-Paul Sartre) (translated by Ernest Sturm). Pennsylvania State University Press

—*Stephane Mallarme* (edited by Harold Bloom). Chelsea House Publishers

Mandelstam, Osip—*Essay On The Poetry Of Osip Mandelstam: God's Grateful Guest* (by Ryszard Przybylski; translated by Madeline G. Levine). Ardis

Marie de France—*The Lais Of Marie de France: Text And Context* (by Glyn S. Burgess). University of Georgia Press

Masefield, John—*John Masefield* (by June Dwyer). Ungar

Mayakovsky, Vladimir—*Love Is The Heart Of Everything: Correspondence Between Vladimir Mayakovsky And Lily Brik* (edited by Bengt Jangfeldt). Grove Press

Melville, Herman—*Poet Of A Morning: Herman Melville And The Redburn Poem* (by Jeanne C. Howes). University Press of America

Meredith, George—*George Meredith* (by Renate Muendel). Twayne Publishers

Merrill, James—*The Consuming Myth: The Work Of James Merrill* (by Stephen Yenser). Harvard University Press

Merwin, M. S.—*M. S. Merwin: Essays On Poetry* (edited by Cary Nelson and Ed Folsom). University of Illinois Press

Milosz, Czeslaw—*Conversations With Czeslaw Milosz* (by Ewa Czarnecka and Aleksander Fiut) (translated by Richard Lourie). Harcourt Brace

Jovanovich
—*Czeslaw Milosz And The Insufficiency Of Lyric* (by Donald Davie). University of Tennessee Press

Milton, John—*Milton And Free Will* (by William Myers). Croom Helm
—*Milton And The Paradoxes Of Renaissance Heroism* (by John M. Steadman). Louisiana State University Press
—*Milton: Poet Of Exile* (by Louis L. Martz). Yale University Press
—*Cannibals, Witches And Divorce: Estranging The Renaissance* (edited by Marjorie Garber). Johns Hopkins University Press
—*Before And After The Fall: Contrasting Modes In Paradise Lost* (by Kathleen M. Swaim). University of Massachusetts Press
—*A Preface to Milton* (by Lois Potter). Longman—
Matter Of Glory: A New Preface To Paradise Lost (by John Peter Rumrich). University of Pittsburgh Press
—*John Milton's Paradise Lost* (edited by Harold Bloom). Chelsea House Publishers

Mistral, Frederic—*The Memoirs Of Frederic Mistral* (translated by George Wickes). New Directions Publishing Corp.

Montale, Eugenio—*Eugenio Montale* (by Jared Becker). Twayne Publishers

Moore, Marianne—*Marianne Moore: Subversive Modernist* (by Taffy Martin). University of Texas Press
—*Marianne Moore: The Poetry of Engagement* (by Grace Schulman). University of Illinois Press

Neidecker, Lorine—*Between Your House And Mine: The Letters Of Lorine Neidecker To Cid Corman, 1960-1970* (edited by Lisa Pater Faranda). Duke University Press

Nemesianus, Marcus Aurelius Olympius—*The Eclogues And Cynegetica Of Nemesianus* (edited by Heather J. Williams). E. J. Brill

Nietzsche, Friedrich—*The Poetry Of Friedrich Nietzche* (by Philip Grundlehner). Oxford University Press

Oates, Joyce Carol—*Joyce Carol Oates* (edited by Harold Bloom). Chelsea House Publishers
—*Joyce Carol Oates: Artist In Residence* (by Eileen Teper Bender). Indiana University Press

O'Sullivan, Seumas—*James Starkey/Seumas O'Sullivan: A Critical Biography* (by Jane Russell). Fairleigh Dickinson University Press

Pindar—*Agnostic Poetry: The Pindaric Mode In Pindar, Horace, Holderlin, And The English Ode* (by William Fitzgerald). University of California Press
—*Studia Pindarica* (by Elroy L. Bundy). University of California Press

Plath, Sylvia—*A Concordance To The Selected Poems Of Sylvia Plath* (edited by Richard M. Matovich). Garland Publishing Co.
—*Sylvia Plath: A Biography* (by Linda Wagner-Martin). Simon and Schuster

Poe, Edgar Allan—*Edgar Allan Poe: The Critical Heritage (edited by I. M. Walker). Routledge & Kegan Paul*

Pope, Alexander—*Alexander Pope* (edited by Harold Bloom). Chelsea House Publishers
—*Alexander Pope: The Poetry Of Allusion* (by Reuben A. Brower). Clarendon Press

Pound, Ezra—*Modernist Poetics of History: Pound, Eliot, And The Sense Of The Past* (by James Longenbach). Princeton University Press
—*Digging For The Treasure: Translation After Pound* (by Ronnie Apter). Paragon House
—*Ezra Pound: The Solitary Volcano* (by John Tytell). Anchor Press
—*The Masters Of Those Who Know: Ezra Pound* (by James Laughlin). City Lights Books
—*Ezra Pound & Japan: Letters And Essays* (edited by Sanehide Kodama). Black Swan Books.
—*Pound As Wuz: Essays And Lectures On Ezra Pound* (by James Laughlin). Graywolf Press
—*The Poetics Of Impersonality: T. S. Eliot And Ezra Pound* (by Maud Ellmann). Harvard University Press

Pulci, Luigi—*Pulci's Morgante: Poetry And History In Fifteenth-Century Florence* (by Constance Jordan). Folger Shakespeare Library

Pushkin, Alexander—*Alexander Pushkin* (edited by Harold Bloom). Chelsea House Publishers

Rexroth, Kenneth—*Revolutionary Rexroth: Poet Of East-West Wisdom* (by Morgan Gibson). Archon Books

Rimbaud, Arthur—*Rimbaud* (by Pierre Petitfils; translated by Alan Sheridan). University Press of Virginia
—*Patterns Of Thought In Rimbaud And Mallarme* (by John Porter Houston). French Forum
—*Arthur Rimbaud* (edited by Harold Bloom). Chelsea House Publishers

Robinson, Edwin Arlington—*Edwin Arlington Robinson* (edited by Harold Bloom). Chelsea House Publishers
—*Edwin Arlington Robinson: Stages In A New England Poet's Search* (by David H. Burton). E. Mellen Press

Roethke, Theodore—*Theodore Roethke* (edited by Harold Bloom). Chelsea House Publishers
—*Theodore Roethke: The Poet And His Critics* (by Randall Stiffler). American Library Association
—*Manic Power: Robert Lowell And His Circle* (by Jeffrey Meyers). Arbor House
—*Understanding Theodore Roethke* (by Walter B. Kalaidjian). University of South Carolina Press

Rossetti, Christina—*The Language Of Exclusion: The Poetry Of Emily Dickinson And Christina Rossetti* (by Sharon Leder with Andrea Abbott). Greenwood Press
—*Christina Rossetti: The Poetry Of Endurance* (by Delores Rosenblum). Southern Illinois University Press

Sandburg, Carl—*Carl Sandburg: His Life And Works* (by North Callahan). Pennsylvania State University Press
—*The Poet And The Dream Girl: The Love Letters Of Lilian Steichen And Carl Sandburg* (edited by Margaret Sandburg). University of Illinois Press

Schwartz, Delmore—*The Middle Generation: The*

Lives And Poetry of Delmore Schwartz; Randall Jarrell, John Berryman And Robert Lowell (by Bruce Bawer). Archon Books
—*Portrait Of Delmore: Journals And Notes Of Delmore Schwartz, 1939-1959* (edited by Elizabeth Pollet). Farrar, Straus & Giroux

Sexton, Anne—*Oedipus Anne: The Poetry Of Anne Sexton* (by Diana Hume George). University Of Illinois Press

Shakespeare, William—*Shakespeare's Verse: Iambic Pentameter And The Poet's Idiosyncrasies* (by Marina Tarlinskaja). P. Lang
—*A Reading Of Shakespeare's Sonnets* (by David K. Weiser). University of Missouri Press
—*Captive Victors: Shakespeare's Narrative Poems And Sonnets* (by Heather Dubrow). Cornell University Press

Shelley, Percy Bysshe—*Pieracci And Shelley: An Italian Un-Cenci* (by George Yost). Scripta Humanistica
—*Shelley's Venomed Melody* (by Nora Crook and Derek Guiton). Cambridge University Press

Sidney, Philip—*Essential Articles For The Study Of Sir Philip Sidney* (edited by Arthur F. Kinney). Archon Books

Skelton, John—*A Concordance To The Complete English Poems Of John Skelton* (edited by Alistair Fox and Gregory Waite). Cornell University Press
—*John Skelton, Priest As Poet: Seasons Of Discovery* (by Arthur F. Kinney). University of North Carolina Press

Smith, Stevie—*Stevie: A Biography Of Stevie Smith* (by Jack Barbera and William McBrien). Oxford University Press

Spenser, Edmund—*The Sacred Marriage: Psychic Integration In The Faerie Queen* (by Benjamin G. Lockerd, Jr.). Bucknell University Press
—*John Upton: Notes On The Fairy Queen* (edited by John G. Radcliffe). Garland Publishing Co.
—*Cannibals, Witches And Divorce: Estranging The Renaissance* (edited by Marjorie Garber). Johns Hopkins University Press

Starkey, James—see O'Sullivan, Seumas

Stevens, Wallace—*Secretaries Of The Moon: The Letters Of Wallace Stevens And Jose Rodriguez Feo* (edited by Beverly Coyle and Alan Filreis). Duke University Press
—*Wallace Stevens And Poetic Theory: Conceiving The Supreme Fiction* (by B. J. Leggett). University of North Carolina Press
—*The Poetry Of Wallace Stevens* (by Robert Rehder). St. Martin's Press
—*T. S. Eliot, Wallace Stevens, And The Discourses Of Difference* (by Michael Beehler). Louisiana State University Press
—*The Skepticism And Animal Faith Of Wallace Stevens* (by Richard N. Sawaya). Garland Publishing Co.

Stevenson, Robert Louis—*The Voyage Of The Ludgate Hill: Travels With Robert Louis Stevenson* (by Nancy Willard).

Symons, Arthur—*Arthur Symons: A Life* (by Karl Beckson). Clarendon Press

Tagore, Rabindranath—*Tagore's Vision Of A Global Family* (by Vivek Ranjan Bhattacharya). Enkay Publishers/Advent Books

Tall, Deborah—*The Island Of The White Cow: Memories Of An Irish Island* (by Deborah Tall). Atheneum

Taylor, Edward—*Saint And Singer: Edward Taylor's Typology And The Poetics Of Meditation* (by Karen E. Rowe). Cambridge University Press

Teasdale, Sara—*Sara Teasdale* (by Carol B. Schoen). Twayne Publishers

Tennyson, Alfred—*The Poetry Of Tennyson* (by Alastair W. Thomson). Routledge & Kegan Paul
—*A Circle Of Friends: The Tennysons And The Lushingtons* (by John O. Waller). Ohio State University Press
—*Tennyson's Maud Vindicated* (by Robert James Mann). Garland Publishing Co.

Thomas, Edward—*The Imagination Of Edward Thomas* (by Michael Kirkham). Cambridge University Press

Valery, Paul—*Poetic Principles And Practice: Occasional Papers On Baudelaire, Mallarme And Valery* (by Lloyd Austin). Cambridge University Press

Van Doren, Mark—*The Selected Letters Of Mark Van Doren* (edited by George Hendrick). Louisiana State University Press

Vaughan, Henry—*Essential Articles For The Study Of Henry Vaughan* (edited by Alan Rundrum). Archon Books

Verwey, Albert—*Vision And Form In The Poetry Of Albert Verwey* (by Theodoor Weevers). Athlone Press

Virgil—*Virgil's Elements: Physics And Poetry In The Georgics* (by David O. Ross, Jr.). Princeton University Press
—*Virgil* (by Jasper Griffin). Oxford University Press
—*The Aeneid Of Thomas Phaer And Thomas Twyne: A Critical Edition Introducing Renaissance Metrical Typography* (edited by Steven Lally). Garland Publishing Co.
—*Further Voices In Virgil's Aeneid* (by R. O. A. M. Lyne). Oxford University Press
—*Virgil* (edited by Harold Bloom). Chelsea House Publishers
—*The Art of Virgil: Image And Symbol In the Aeneid* (by Viktor Poschl; translated by Gerda Seligson). Greenwood Press
—*Virgil's Aeneid* (edited by Harold Bloom). Chelsea House Publishers
—*Virgil At 2000: Commemorative Essays On The Poet And His Influence* (edited by John D. Bernard). AMS Press

Warren, Robert Penn—*Time's Glory: Original Esays On Robert Penn Warren* (edited by James A. Grimshaw, Jr.). University of Central Arkansas Press

Wheatley, Phillis—*Phillis Wheatley: Negro Slave Of Mr. John Wheatley Of Boston* (by Marilyn Jenses). Lion Books

Whitman, Walt—*The Literary Reputation Of Walt Whitman In France* (by Oreste F. Pucciani). Garland Publishing Co.
—*The Lunar Light Of Whitman's Poetry* (by M. Wynn Thomas). Harvard University Press

Williams, William Carlos—*Virgin And Whore: The Image Of Women In The Poetry Of William Carlos Williams* (by Audrey T. Rodgers). McFarland & Co.
—*William Carlos Williams* (edited by Harold Bloom). Chelsea House Publishers
—*Against The American Grain: Myth And History In William Carlos Williams, Jay Wright And Nicolas Guillens* (by Vera M. Kutzinski). Johns Hopkins University Press
—*The Early Politics And Poetics Of William Carlos Williams* (by David Frail). UMI Research Press

Wordsworth, William—*Subject-Object Relations In Wordsworth And Lawrence* (by Donald Gutierrez). UMI Research Press
—*A Complete Concordance To The Lyrical Ballads Of Samuel Taylor Coleridge And William Wordsworth: 1798 And 1800 Editions* (by Thomas F. Beckwith and Patricia A. McEahern). Garland Publishing Co.
—*Wordsworth's Art Of Allusion* (Edwin Stein). Pennsylvania State University Press
—*Wordsworth's Informed Reader: Structures Of Experience In His Poetry* (by Susan E. Meisenhelder). Vanderbilt University Press
—*Radical Literary Education: A Classroom Experiment With Wordsworth's Ode* (by Jeffrey C. Robinson). University of Wisconsin Press
—*William Wordsworth And The Age Of English Romanticism* (by Jonathan Wordsworth, Michael C. Jaye and Robert Woof). Rutgers University Press

Wright, James Arlington—*James Wright* (by David C. Dougherty). Twayne Publishers

Wright, Jay—*Against The American Grain: Myth And History In William Carlos Williams, Jay Wright And Nicolas Guillens* (by Vera Kutzinski). Johns Hopkins University Press

Wu Wen-ying—*Wu Wen-ying And The Art Of Southern Song Ci Poetry* (by Grace S. Fong). Princeton University Press

Yeats, William Butler—*Stylistic Arrangements: A Study Of William Butler Yeats' A Vision* (by Barbara L. Croft). Bucknell University Press
—*Singing In Chains: Yeats's Interactions With Tradition* (by Patrick J. Keane). University of Missouri Press
—*Towards A Mythology: Studies In The Poetry Of W. B. Yeats* (by Peter Ure). Greenwood Press
—*The Poetry Of William Butler Yeats: An Introduction* (by William H. O'Donnell). Ungar
—*Yeats And The Poetics Of Hate* (by Joseph M. Hassett). St. Martin's Press
—*A Terrible Beauty: The Easter Rebellion And Yeats's Great Tapestry* (by Carmel Jordan). Bucknell University Press
—*Yeats' Myth Of Self: The Autobiographical Prose* (by David G. Wright). Barnes & Noble Books
—*The Making Of Yeats's A Vision: A Study Of The Automatic Script* (by George Mills Harper). Southern Illinois University Press
—*The Collected Letters Of W. B. Yeats* (edited by John Kelly). Oxford University Press
—*Yeats And Politics In The 1930s* (by Paul Scott Stanfield). St. Martin's Press
—*Mask And Tragedy: Yeats And Nietzsche, 1902-10* (by Frances Nesbitt Oppel). University Press of Virginia
—*Yeats And The Beginning Of The Irish Renaissance* (by Phillip L. Marcus). Syracuse University Press
—*Four Dubliners: Wilde, Yeats, Joyce And Beckett* (by Richard Ellmann). George Braziller
—*Yeats And The Visual Arts* (by Elizabeth Bergmann Loizeaux). Rutgers University Press

COMMENT, CRITICISM AND REFERENCE

(listed alphabetically by author)

Aguero, Kathleen (see listing for Harris, Marie).

Aristotle—*Poetics* (translated by Richard Janko). Hackett Publishing Co.

Bartlett, Lee (compiler)—*Talking Poetry: Conversations In The Workshop With Contemporary Poets*. University of New Mexico Press

Blasing, Multu Konuk—*American Poetry: The Rhetoric Of Its Forms*. Yale University Press

Bloom, Harold (editor)—*Beowulf*. Chelsea House Publishers
—*French Poetry: The Renaissance Through 1915*. Chelsea House Publishers
—*Modern German Poetry*. Chelsea House Publishers
—*American Poetry, 1915-1945*. Chelsea House Publishers
—*American Poetry, 1946-1965*. Chelsea House Publishers
—*Contemporary Poets*. Chelsea House Publishers
—*English Romantic Poets*. Chelsea House Publishers
—*Poets Of Sensibility And The Sublime*. Chelsea House Publishers

Bohn, Willard—*The Aesthetics Of Visual Poetry, 1914-1928*. Cambridge University Press

Breslin, Paul—*The Psycho-Political Muse: American Poetry Since The Fifties*. University of Chicago Press

Bruchac, Joseph—*Survival This Way: Interviews With American Indian Poets.* University of Arizona Press

Buckley, Jerome H. (editor)—*The Pre-Raphaelites.* Academy Chicago

Buja, Maureen E.—*Italian Renaissance Poetry: A First-Line Index To Petrarch, Ariosto, Tasso And Others.* Garland Publishing Co.

Carpenter, John—*Creating The World: Poetry, Art And Children.* University of Washington Press

Carter, Steven D.—*The Road To Komatsubara: A Classical Reading Of The Renga Hyakuin.* Harvard University Press

Chandra, Sansar—*Some Prominent Muslim Hindi Poets.* Atma Ram/South Asia Books

Chinweizu, et al.—*Toward The Decolonization Of African literature: African Fiction And Poetry And Their Critics.* Routledge & Kegan Paul

Cook, Elizabeth—*Seeing Through Words: The Scope Of Late Renaissance Poetry.* Yale University Press

Cutler, Norman—*Songs Of Experience: The Poetics Of Tamil Devotion.* Indiana University Press

Dauster, Frank—*The Double Strand: Five Contemporary Mexican Poets.* University Press of Kentucky.

Davidoff, Judith M.—*Beginning Well: Framing Fictions In Late Middle English Poetry.* Fairleigh Dickinson University Press

Dobay. Rifelj, Carol de—*Word And Figure: The Language Of Nineteenth-Century French Poetry.* Ohio State University Press

Dove, Mary—*The Perfect Age Of Man's Life.* Cambridge University Press

Eliot, T. S.—*The Use Of Poetry And The Use Of Criticism: Studies In The Relation Of Criticism To Poetry In England.* Harvard University Press

Else, Gerald F.—*Plato And Aristotle On Poetry.* University of North Carolina Press

Estes, Glenn E. (editor)—*American Writers For Children Since 1960: Poets, Illustrators And Nonfiction Authors.* Gale Research Co.

Everett, Barbara (editor)—*Poets In Their Time: English Poetry From Donne To Larkin.* Faber and Faber

Flanner, Hildegarde—*Portraits Of Remarkable People.* J. Daniel

Fraistat, Neil (editor)—*Poems In The Place: Intertextuality And Order Of Poetic Collections.* University of North Carolina Press

Fredeman, William E.—*Victorian Prefaces And Introductions: A Facsimile Collection.* Garland Publishing Co.

Gallagher, Tess—*A Concert Of Tenses: Essays On Poetry.* University of Michigan Press

Gallatin, Michael D.—*The Ineffability Of The Ideal: Tragedy And The Modern World In Poetry, Fiction And Drama.* Q.E.D. Press

Gardner, John—*Jason And Medeia.* Vintage Books (reprint)

Garratt, Robert F.—*Modern Irish Poetry: Tradition And Continuity From Yeats To Heaney.* University of California Press

Garrett, John—*British Poetry Since The Sixteenth Century.* Barnes & Noble

Guilhamet, Leon—*Satire And The Transformation Of Genre.* University of Pennsylvania Press

Harap, Louis—*Dramatic Encounters: The Jewish Presence In Twentieth-Century American Drama, Poetry And Humor And The Black-Jewish Literary Relationship.* Greenwood Press

Harris, Marie; Aguero, Kathleen (editors)—*A Gift Of Tongues: Critical Challenges In Contemporary American Poetry.* University of Georgia Press

Higgins, Dick—*Pattern Poetry: Guide To An Unknown Literature.* State University of New York Press

Huot, Sylvia—*From Song To Book: The Poetics Of Writing In Old French Lyric And Lyrical Narrative Poetry.* Cornell University Press

Kennedy, X. J. (compiler)—*Literature: An Introduction To Fiction, Poetry And Drama.* Little, Brown

Knight, Philip—*Flower Poetics In Nineteenth-Century France.* Oxford University Press

Kramer, Lawrence—*Music And Poetry.* University of California Press

Langbaum, Robert—*The Word From Below: Essays On Modern Literature And Culture.* University of Wisconsin Press

Leeming, Glenda—*Poetic Drama.* St. Martin's Press

Lord, George deForest—*Classical Presences In Seventeenth-Century English Poetry.* Yale University Press

Machin, Richard; Norris, Christopher (editors)—*Post-Structuralist Readings Of English Poetry.* Cambridge University Press

Magill, Frank N. (editor)—*Critical Survey Of Poetry.* Salem Press

Mandel, Jerome—*Alternative Readings In Old English Poetry.* P. Lang

Meisami, Julie Scott—*Medieval Persian Court Poetry.* Princeton University Press

Miller, Jacqueline T.—*Poetic License: Authority And Authorship In Medieval And Renaissance Contexts.* Oxford University Press

Monroe, Jonathan—*A Poverty Of Objects: The Prose Poem And The Politics Of Genre.* Cornell University Press

Muscatine, Charles—*The Old French Fabliaux.* Yale University Press

Norris, Christopher—see Machin, Richard

Packard, William (editor)—*The Poet's Craft: Interviews From The New York Quarterly.* Paragon House

Padgett, Ron (editor)—*The Teachers & Writers Handbook Of Poetic Forms.* Teachers & Writers Collaborative

Parini, Jay—*An Invitation To Poetry.* Prentice-Hall

Parkinson, Thomas—*Poets, Poems, Movements.* UMI Research Press

Paz, Octavio—*On Poets And Others.* Seaver Books/Henry Holt

Pelen, Marc M.—*Latin Poetic Irony In The Roman De La Rose.* F. Cairns

Perkins, David—*A History Of Modern Poetry: Modernism And After.* Belknap Press

Persin, Margaret H.—*Recent Spanish Poetry And

The Role Of The Reader. Bucknell University Press

Peters, Robert—*The Great American Poetry Bake-Off: Third Series.* Scarecrow Press

Plotz, Judith A.—*Ideas Of The Decline Of Poetry: A Study In English Criticism From 1700 To 1830.* Garland Publishing Co.

Preminger, Alex (editor)—*Princeton Handbook Of Poetic Terms.* Princeton University Press

Quartermain, Peter (editor)—*American Poets, 1880-1945: Third Series, Part 1-2.* Gale Research Co.

Reiman, Donald H.—*Romantic Texts And Contexts.* University of Missouri Press

Roberts, Sheila—*Still The Frame Holds: Women Poets And Writers.* Borgo Press

Roe, Sue (editor)—*Women Reading Women's Writing.* St. Martin's Press

Rolleston, James—*Narratives Of Ecstasy: Romantic Temporality In Modern German Poetry.* Wayne State University Press

Ross, Andrew—*The Failure Of Modernism: Symptoms Of American Poetry.* Columbia University Press

Russell, Charles—*Poets, Prophets And Revolutionaries: The Literary Avant-Garde From Rimbaud Through Postmodernism.* Oxford University Press

Sanchez, Marta Ester—*Contemporary Chicana Poetry: A Critical Approach To An Emerging Literature.* University of California Press

Scott, Clive—*A Question Of Syllables: Essays On Nineteenth-Century French Verse.* Cambridge University Press

Shavit, Zohar—*The Poetics Of Children's Literature.* University of Georgia Press

Singh, Charu Sheel—*Auguries Of Evocation: British Poetry During And After The Movement.* Advent Books

Stafford, William—*You Must Revise Your Life.* University of Michigan Press

Stasny, John F. (editor)—*Victorian Poetry: A Collection Of Essays From The Period.* Garland Publishing Co.

Stead, C. K.—*The New Poetic: Yeats To Eliot.* University of Pennsylvania Press

Steinman, Lisa M.—*Made In America: Science, Technology, And American Modernist Poetry.* Yale University Press

Summers, Claude J.; Pebworth, Ted-Larry (editors)—*Bright Shootes Of Everlastingnesse: The Seventeenth-Century Religious Lyric.* University of Missouri Press

Taylor, Andrew—*Reading Australian Poetry.* University of Queensland Press

Turco, Lewis—*The New Book Of Forms: A Handbook Of Poetics.* University Press of New England

Vance, Eugene—*From Topic To Tale: Logic And Narrativity In The Middle Ages.* University of Minnesota Press

Vendler, Helen (editor)—*Voices And Visions: The Poet In America.* Vintage Books

von Hallberg, Robert (editor)—*Politics & Poetic Value.* University of Chicago Press

Walker, Steven F.—*A Cure For Love: A Generic Study Of The Pastoral Idyll.* Garland Publishing Co.

Waller, Christopher—*Expressionist Poetry And Its Critics.* University of London/Humanities Press

Ward, Aileen—*The Unfurling Of Entity: Metaphor In Poetic Theory.* Garland Publishing Co.

Williams, Miller—*Patterns Of Poetry: An Encyclopedia Of Forms.* Louisiana State University Press

Wilson, Colin—*Poetry & Mysticism.* City Lights Books

Wolff, Hope Nash—*A Study In The Narrative Of Three Epic Poems: Gilgamesh, The Odyssey, Beowulf.* Garland Publishing Co.

York, R. A.—*The Poem As Utterance.* Methuen

Yu, Pauline—*The Reading Of Imagery In The Chinese Poetic Tradition.* Princeton University Press

Zanker, Graham—*Realism In Alexandrian Poetry: A Literature And Its Audience.* Croom Helm

Book Publishers Publishing Poetry

Following is a directory of U.S. and Canadian publishers who issued at least one book of current original poetry during 1987; it is based on publishers represented in Section 1 of The Yearly Record. *Not included are subsidy (vanity) publishers. The directory is for information purposes only; it does not indicate recommendation of any publisher listed.*

A

Abattoir Editions, University of Nebraska, Omaha, NE 68182
Aegina Press, 4937 Humphrey Rd., Huntington, WV 25704
Alice James Books, 138 Mt. Auburn St., Cambridge, MA 02138
Allison & Busby, New York, NY
Alms House Press, New York, NY
Alphabeta Press, Chicago, IL
Amelia, Box 2385, Bakersfield, CA 93303
American Poetry and Literature Press, Box 2013, Upper Darby, PA 19082
American Studies Press, 13511 Palmwood Lane, Tampa, FL 33624
Ampersand Press, Roger Williams College, Bristol, RI 02809
Anhinga Press, Box 10423, Tallahassee, FL 30302
Anvil Press Poetry, 27 S. Main St., Wolfeboro, NH 03894
Appalachian Consortium Press, 202 Appalachian St., Boone, NC 28607
Applezaba Press, Box 4134, Long Beach, CA 90804
Arbor House Publishing Co., 105 Madison Ave., New York, NY 10016
Archon Books, Hamden, CT 06514
Ardis Publishers, 2901 Heatherway, Ann Arbor, MI 48104
Arte Publico Press, University of Houston, Houston, TX 77004
Associated Faculty Press, Rt. 100, Millwood, NY 10546
Atheneum Publishers, 115 Fifth Ave., New York, NY 10003
Atlantic Monthly Press, 420 Lexington Ave., New York, NY 10170
Atlantis Editions, Box 18326, Philadelphia, PA 19120
Ave Maria Press, Notre Dame, IN 46556

B

Backspace Ink., 372 Second Ave., San Francisco, CA 94118
Barnwood Press, RR2, Box 11C, Daleville, IL 47334
W. L. Bauhan, Publisher, Old Country Rd., Dublin, NH 03444
Beacham Publishing, Washington, DC
Beacon Press, 25 Beacon St., Boston, MA 02108
Bellevue Press, 60 Schubert St., Binghamton, NY 13905
Bench Press, 1355 Raintree Drive, Columbia, SC 29210
Berea College Press, Berea, KY 40404
Bieler Press, Box 3856, St. Paul, MN 55165
Bilingual Press, Hispanic Research Center, Arizona State University, Tempe, AZ 85287
Bits Press, Case Western University, Dept. of English, Cleveland, OH 44106
BkMk Press, University of Missouri, 5725 Wyandotte, Kansas City, MO 64113
Black Current Press, Box 1149, Haines, AK 99827
Black Sparrow Press, Box 3993, Santa Barbara, CA 93130

Black Swan Books, Box 327, Redding Ridge, CT 06876
Blackstaff Press, Dover, NH 03820
Blue Cloud Press, Blue Cloud Abbey, Box 98, Marvin, SD 57251
Blue Dolphin Publishers, Nevada City, CA 95959
BOA Editions, Ltd., 92 Park Ave., Brockport, NY 14420
Borealis Press, 9 Ashburn Drive, Ottawa, Ont. K2E 6N4, Canada
Branden Publishing Co., Box 843, Brookline Village, MA 02147
Breitenbush Books, Box 02137, Portland, OR 97202
Briarpatch Press, Box 148, Davidson, NC 28036
Brick Books, Box 219, Ilderton, Ont. N0M 2A0, Canada
Bridgehead Press, New Orleans, LA
John Carter Brown Library, Box 1894, Providence, RI 02901

C

Francis Cairns, Wolfeboro, NH 03894
Calyx Books, Box B, Corvallis, OR 97335
Cambric Press, 912 Strowbridge Drive, Huron, OH 44839
Capra Press, Box 2068, Santa Barbara, CA 93120
Carnegie-Mellon University Press, Pittsburgh, PA 15213
Celestial Arts, 231 Adrian Rd., Millbrae, CA 94030
Chauncy Press, Turtle Pond Rd., Saranac Lake, NY 12983
Childrens Press, 1224 W. Van Buren St., Chicago, IL 60607
Church Library Council, 4748 Eastern Ave. N.E., Washington, DC 20017
Cider Mill Press, Box 211, Stratford, CT 06497
City Lights Books, 261 Columbus Ave., San Francisco, CA 94133
Cleveland State University Poetry Center, Cleveland, OH 44115
Coffee House Press, Box 10870, Minneapolis, MN 55440
Mr. Cogito Press, U.C. Box 627, Pacific University, Forest Grove, OR 97116
Collier Books, 866 Third Ave., New York, NY 10022
Concourse Press, Philadelphia, PA
Confluence Press, Lewis-Clark State College, Spalding Hall, Lewiston, ID 83501
Connecticut Poetry Review Press, Box 3783, New Haven, CT 06525
Contact II Publications, Box 451, Bowling Green Sta., New York, NY 10004
Copper Beech Press, Box 1852, Brown University, Providence, RI 02912
Copper Canyon Press, Box 271, Port Townsend, WA 98368
Cornwall Books, 4 Cornwall Drive, East Brunswick, NJ 08816
Cross-Cultural Communications, Merrick, NY 11566
Crossing Press, 17 W. Main St., Box 640, Trumansburg, NY 14886
Thomas Y. Crowell, 10 E. 53rd St., New York, NY 10022
Crown Publishers, 1 Park Ave., New York, NY 10016
Curbstone Publishing Co., Box 7445, U.T. Sta., Austin, TX 78712

D

J. Daniel, Publisher, Box 21922, Santa Barbara, CA 93121
David Co., Chicago, IL
Devil's Millhopper Press, Rt. 3, Box 29, Elgin, SC 29045
Devin-Adair, 6 N. Water St., Greenwich, CT 06830
Dial Press, 2 Park Ave., New York, NY 10016
Dodd, Mead & Co., 71 Fifth Ave., New York, NY 10003
Dogsbody Press, Box 27, Cabin John, MD 20818
Dooryard Press, Box 221, Story, WY 82842
Doubleday & Co., Garden City, NY 11530
Dragon Gate, 6532 Phinney Ave. N., Seattle, WA 98103
Dragon's Teeth Press, El Dorado National Forest, Georgetown, CA 95634
Dufour Editions, Box 449, Chester Springs, PA 19425
Duke University Press, Box 6697, College Sta., Durham, NC 27706
E. P. Dutton/Hillside, 2 Park Ave., New York, NY 10016

E

Earhart Press, 424 Hilldale, Ann Arbor, MI 48105
Ecco Press, 26 W. 17th St., New York, NY 10011
Equity Press, Bethesda, MD 20815
Erie St. Press, 221 S. Clinton, Oak Park, IL 60302

F

Faber and Faber, 39 Thompson St., Winchester, MA 01890
Farrar, Straus & Giroux, 19 Union Square W., New York, NY 10003
Firebrand Books, 141 The Commons, Ithaca, NY 14850
First Circle Press, 807 Foothill Boulevard, No. 12, Oakland, CA 94606
Fjord Press, Box 16501, Seattle, WA 98116
Floating Island Publications, Box 516, Point Reyes Sta., CA 94596
Florida International University Press, Tamiami Trail & 107th Ave., Miami, FL 33199
Flume Press, 646 Citrus Ave., Chico, CA 95926
Ford-Brown Publishers, Box 600574, Houston, TX 77260
Franciscan Herald Press, 1434 W. 51st St., Chicago, IL 60609

G

Galileo Press, 15201 Wheeler Lane, Sparks, MD 21152
Garland Publishing Co., 136 Madison Ave., New York, NY 10016
Geryon Press, Box 770, Tunnel, NY 13848
Goat Foot Press, Tacoma, WA
David R. Godine, Publisher, 300 Massachusetts Ave., Boston, MA 02115
Golden Quill Press, RFD #1, Avery Rd., Francestown, NH 03043
Graywolf Press, Box 142, Port Townsend, WA 98368
Great Elm Press, RD2, Box 37, Rexville, NY 14877
Green Glens Press, Hainesport, NJ 08036
Greenfield Review Press, RD 1, Box 80, Greenfield Center, NY 12833
Greenwillow Books, 105 Madison Ave., New York, NY 10016
Greenwood Press, Box 5007, 88 Post Rd. W., Westport, CT 06881
Guernica Editions, Box 633, Sta. NDG, Montreal, Que. H4A 3R1, Canada

H

Hamilton Haiku Press, Hamilton, Ont., Canada
Hamilton Press, 4720 Boston Way, Lanham, MD 20706
Hanging Loose Press, 231 Wyckoff St., Brooklyn, NY 11217
Harcourt Brace Jovanovich, 1250 Sixth Ave., San Diego, CA 92101
Harlo Press, 50 Victor, Detroit, MI 48203
Harper & Row Publishers, 10 E. 53rd St., New York, NY 10022
Haskell House Publishers, Box 420, Blythebourne Sta., Brooklyn, NY 11219
Heidelberg Graphics, 1116-D Wendy Way, Chico, CA 95926
Heyeck Press, 25 Patrol Court, Woodside, CA 94062
Henry Holt & Co., 521 Fifth Ave., New York, NY 10175
Hermes House Press, 39 Adare Place, Northampton, MA 01060
Hill House New York, Box 1087, Rockefeller Center Sta., New York, NY 10185
Hillside Press, San Francisco, CA
HMS Press, 204-100 Dundalk, Scarborough, Ont. M1P 4V2, Canada
Holiday House, 18 E. 53rd St., New York, NY 10022
Holmgangers Press, 95 Carson Court, Shelter Cove, Whitehorn, CA 95489
Houghton Mifflin Co., 1 Beacon St., Boston, MA 02108
Hounslow Press, 124 Parkview Ave., Willowdale, Ont. M2N 3Y5, Canada
Humana Press, Box 2148, Clifton, NJ 07015

I

International Publishers, 381 Park Ave. S., New York, NY 10016
Intertext, 2633 E. 17th Ave., Anchorage, AK 99508
Ion Books, 3387 Poplar Ave., Memphis, TN 38111
Illuminations Press, 2110 9th St., Berkeley, CA 94710
Ischua Books, Bonaventure, NY

J

Jelm Mountain Publications, c/o Green Mountain Book Co., Box 338, Markleeville, CA 96120
Johns Hopkins University Press, Baltimore, MD 21211
Justin Books, New York, NY

K

Kala, Traveler's Rest, SC
Katydid Books, Oakland University, Dept. of English, Rochester, MN 48063
Kelsey St. Press, Box 9235, Berkeley, CA 94709
Kindred Spirit Press, Route 2, Box 111, St. John, KS 67576
Alfred A. Knopf, Inc., 201 E. 50th St., New York, NY 10022
Kutenai Press, 515 Stephens Ave., Missoula, MT 59801

L

Landsberry Press, Washington, DC
Lapis Press, 2056 Broadway, Santa Monica, CA
Latin American Literary Review Press, Box 8385, Pittsburgh, PA 15218
L'Epervier Press, 4522 Sunnyside N., Seattle, WA 98103
Lincoln Springs Press, Box 269, Franklin Lakes, NJ 07417
Linwood Publishers, Box 70152, North Charleston, SC 29415
Livingston University Press, Livingston, AL 35470
Lorrah & Hitchcock Publishers, 301 S. 15th St., Murray, KY 42071
Lost Roads Publishers, Box 5848, Providence, RI 02902
Louisiana State University Press, Baton Rouge, LA 70893
Lynx House Press, Box 800, Amherst, MA 01004

M

Macmillan Publishing Co., 866 Third Ave., New York, NY 10022
Magic Circle Press, 10 Hyde Ridge Rd., Weston, CT 06883
McClelland & Stewart Ltd., 481 University Ave., Toronto, Ont. M4B 3G2, Canada
Margaret K. McElderry Books, New York, NY
Memphis State University Press, Memphis, TN 38152
Methuen, Inc., 29 W. 35th St., New York, NY 10001
Metro Book Co., Los Angeles, CA
Midwest Villages and Voices, 3220 Tenth Ave. S., Minneapolis, MN 55407
Milkweed Editions, Box 24303, Minneapolis, MN 55424
M.I.P. Co., Box 27484, Minneapolis, MN 55427
Modern Images, Box 912, Mattoon, IL 61938
William Morrow & Co., 105 Madison Ave., New York, NY 10016
Mosaic Press, Box 1032, Oakville, Ont. L6J 5E9, Canada
Multnomah Press, 10209 S.E. Division St., Portland, OR 97266

N

Naked Man Press, 1128 Rhode Island, Bowling Green, KS 66044
National Poetry Foundation, University of Maine, 305 EM Bldg., Orono, ME 04469

New Directions Publishing Corp., 80 Eighth Ave., New York, NY 10011
New Rivers Press, 1602 Selby Ave., St. Paul, MN 55104
New York University Press, 70 Washington Sq. South, New York, NY 10012
Night Tree Press, 414 W. Thomas St., Rome, NY 13440
Nortex Press, Austin, TX
North American Editions, 101 Phillips Rd., Holden, MA 01520
North Atlantic Books, 2320 Blake St., Berkeley, CA 94704
North Point Press, Box 6275, Berkeley, CA 94706
Northeastern University Press, 360 Huntington Ave., Boston, MA 02115
Northern Illinois University Press, De Kalb, IL 60115
Northwestern University Press, Box 1093X, 1735 Benson Ave., Evanston, IL 60201
Northwoods Press, Box 88, Thomaston, ME 04861
W. W. Norton & Co., 500 Fifth Ave., New York, NY 10110
Notre Dame University Press, Notre Dame, IN 46556

O

Ohio Review Books, Ohio University, Ellis Hall, Athens, OH 45701
Ohio State University Press, 1050 Carmack Rd., Athens, OH 43210
Ommation Press, 5548 N. Sawyer, Chicago, IL 60625
Ontario Review Press, 9 Honey Brook Drive, Princeton, NJ 08540
Orchises Press, Box 20602, Alexandria, VA 22313
Overlook Press, Route 212, Box 427, Woodstock, NY 12498
Owl Creek Press, Box 2248, Missoula, MT 59806
Oxford University Press, 200 Madison Ave., New York, NY 10016; 70 Wynford Drive,
    Don Mills, Ont. M3C 1J9, Canada

P

Paper Press, Honolulu, HI
Park Row Press, 1418 Park Row, San Diego, CA 92037
Pelican Poems, Santa Barbara, CA
Penguin Books, 40 W. 23rd St., New York, NY 10010
Peregrine Smith Books, Box 667, Layton, UT 84041
Persea Books, 225 Lafayette St., New York, NY 10012
Pig in a Poke Press, Box 19426, Pittsburgh, PA 15273
Pikestaff Press, Box 127, Normal, IL 61761
Pocahontas Press, 2805 Wellesley Court, Blacksburg, VA 24060
Poetry Around Press, 436 Elm, Norman, OK 73069
Post-Apollo Press, 35 Marie St., Sausalito, CA 94965
Clarkson N. Potter, Inc., 225 Park Ave. S., New York, NY 10003
Prentice Hall Press, Englewood Cliffs, NJ 07632
Primal Publishing Co., East Cambridge, MA
Princeton University Press, Princeton, NJ 08540
Pterodactyl Press, Box 125, Cumberland, IA 50843
Pudding Publications, 2384 Hardesty Dr. S., Columbus, OH 43204
Pulp Press, 986 Homer St., Vancouver, B.C. U6B 2W7, Canada
Purdue University Press, West Lafayette, IN 47907
Purple Wednesday Society, Saint John, N.B., Canada
G. P. Putnam's Sons, 200 Madison Ave., New York, NY 10016

Q

Quarry Press, Box 1061, Kingston, Ont. K7L 4Y5, Canada
Quarterly Review of Literature Poetry Series, 26 Haslet Ave., Princeton, NJ 08540

R

Random House, Inc., 201 E. 50th St., New York, NY 10022
F. H. Revell, Old Tappan, NJ 07675

Riverrun Press, 1170 Broadway, New York, NY 10001
H. Roberts Publishing Co., York, PA
Routledge & Kegan Paul, Ltd., 9 Park St., Boston, MA 02108
Rowfant Club, Cleveland, OH

S

Sackbut Press, 2513 E. Webster Place, Milwaukee, WI 53211
St. Andrews Press, St. Andrews College, Laurinburg, NC 28352
St. Luke's Press, 1407 Union Ave., Memphis, TN 38104
Samara, Racine, WI
San Francisco State University Press, 1630 Holloway Ave., San Francisco, CA 94132
Saturday Press, Box 884, Upper Montclair, NJ 07043
Scarecrow Press, 52 Liberty St., Box 656, Metuchen, NJ 08840
Scop Publications, Box 376, College Park, MD 20740
C. Schlacks, Jr., Box 5001, Irvine, CA 92716
Schocken Books, 200 Madison Ave., New York, NY 10016
Scholars Press, Box 1608, Decatur, GA 30031
Schubert Club, 75 W. 5th St., St. Paul, MN 55102
Scop and Gleeman Publishers, Putnam Valley, NY 10579
Scop Publications, College Park, MD 20740
Shapolsky Publishers, 56 E. 11th St., New York, NY 10003
Charles Scribner's Sons, 115 Fifth Ave., New York, NY 10003
Shambhala Publications, Inc., 314 Dartmouth St., Boston, MA 02116
Sheep Meadow Press, Box 1345, Riverdale-on-Hudson, NY 10471
Shu Publishing Co., 218 Dewey St., Worcester, MA 01610
Signpost Press, 412 N. State St., Bellingham, WA 98225
Silver Burdett Co., 250 James St., Morristown, NJ 07960
Silverfish Review Press, Box 3541, Eugene, OR 97403
Simon and Schuster, 1230 Ave. of the Americas, New York, NY 10020
Soho Press, 1 Union Square, New York, NY 10003
Solo Press, Atascadero, CA 93422
Solo Press, 578 Broadway, New York, NY 10012
Sono Nis Press, 1745 Blanshard St., Victoria, B.C. V8W 2J8, Canada
South Head Press/Elliott Bay Book Co., Seattle, WA
Sparrow Press, 103 Waldron St., West Lafayette, IN 47906
Spheric House, Tucson, AZ
Spoon River Poetry Press, Box 1443, Peoria, IL 61655
Starmont House, Box 851, Mercer Island, WA 98040
State St. Press, 67 State Street, Pittsford, NY 14534
Station Hill Press, Station Hill Rd., Barrytown, NY 12507
Stormline Press, Box 593, Urbana, IL 61801
Sun/gemini Press, P. O. Box 42170, Tucson, AZ 85733
Sun & Moon Press, Box 481170, Los Angeles, CA 90048
Sunstone Press, Box 2321, Santa Fe, NM 87504
Swallow Press, c/o Ohio University Press, Scott Triangle, Athens, OH 45701
Swamp Press, 323 Pelham Rd., Amherst, MA 01002
Symposium Press, 1620 Greenfield, Los Angeles, CA 90025

T

Talon Books, 201/1019 E. Cordova St., Vancouver, B.C. V6A 1M8, Canada
Tamarack Editions, 128 Benedict Ave., Syracuse, NY 13210
Tenth Muse Press, Elgin, IL 60120
Terata Publications, Hawthorne, CA 90250
Texas Tech Press, Texas Tech University, Box 4240, Lubbock, TX 79409
Theatre Communications Group, 355 Lexington Ave., New York, NY 10017
Third Woman Press, c/o Chicano-Riqueno Studies, BH849, Indiana University, Bloomington, IN 47405
Thistledown Press, Ltd., 668 East Place, Saskatoon, Sask. S7J 2Z5, Canada
Thorntree Press, 547 Hawthorn Lane, Winnetka, IL 60093
Three Island Press, New York, NY

Thunder City Press, Box 600574, Houston, TX 77260
Thunder's Mouth Press, 93 Greene St., New York, NY 10012
Timberline Press, Box 327, Fulton, MO 65251
Todd & Honeywell, New York, NY
Trout Creek Press, 5976 Billings Rd., Parkdale, OR 97041
Charles E. Tuttle, Co., Inc., 28 S. Main St., Rutland, VT 05701
Typographeum Press, Francestown, NH 03043

U

Unicorn Press, Box 3307, Greensboro, NC 27402
University of Alabama Press, Box 2877, University, AL 35486
University of Arkansas Press, McIlroy House, 201 Ozark St., Fayetteville, AR 72701
University of California Press, 2120 Berkeley Way, Berkeley, CA 94720
University of Chicago Press, 5801 Ellis Ave., Chicago, IL 60637
University of Georgia Press, Waddell Hall, Athens, GA 30602
University of Illinois Press, 54 E. Gregory Drive, Champaign, IL 61820
University of Massachusetts Press, Amherst, MA 01003
University of Missouri Press, 200 Lewis Hall, Columbia, MO 65211
University of Pittsburgh Press, 127 N. Bellefield Ave., Pittsburgh, PA 15260
University Press of America, 4720 Boston Way, Lanham, MD 20706
University of Queensland Press, Box 1365, New York, NY 10023
University of Utah Press, Salt Lake City, UT 84112
University of Wisconsin Press, Madison, WI 53706
Ursus Press, San Diego, CA

V

Vanderbilt University Press, 1211 18th Ave. S., Nashville, TN 37212
Vehicule Press, Box 125, Place du Parc Sta., Montreal, Que. H2W 2M9, Canada
Viking Press, 40 W. 23rd St., New York, NY 10010

W

Wake Forest University Press, Box 7333, Winston-Salem, NC 27109
Washington Writers' Publishing House, Box 50068, Washington, DC 20004
Water Row Press, Box 438, Sudbury, MA 01776
Wesleyan University Press, 110 Mt. Vernon St., Middletown, CT 06457
West Anglia Publications, Box 2683, La Jolla, CA 92038
Westminster Press, 925 Chestnut St., Philadelphia, PA 19107
White Pine Press, 73 Putnam St., Buffalo, NY 14213
Walt Whitman Center, c/o Frederick Missimer, 2nd and Cooper Sts., Camden, NJ 08102
Wisconsin Review Press, Box 158, Radford Hall, University of Wisconsin, Oshkosh, WI 54901
Wolsak & Wynn, Ltd., 43 Eglinton Ave. E., Toronto, Ont. M4P 1A2, Canada
Woodley Press, Washburn University, Topeka, KS 66621
Woolner, Brotherson, Ltd., Revere, PA 18953
World Poetry Center, Bloomington, IN 47401
Word Works, Box 42164, Washington, DC 20015

Y

Yale University Press, 92A Yale Sta., New Haven, CT 06520

Z

Zondervan Publishing House, 1415 Lake Dr. S.E., Grand Rapids, MI 49506

Magazines Publishing Poetry

The following is a select list of magazines and journals which regularly publish contemporary poetry and which form the basic core of source material for this Anthology. All poems contained in this edition of the Anthology originally appeared in many of the publications on this list. Not all the magazines and journals listed here are represented in this particular edition due to space limitations and editorial considerations, but they do denote a wide and diverse range of literary views, cultures and policies for serious poets seeking appropriate markets for their work; they are active publications, regularly publishing quality poetry and which are eager to consider material submitted to them.

A

The Agni Review, Box 660, Amherst, MA 01004

Amelia, 329 "E" St., Bakersfield, CA 93304

America, 106 W. 56th St., New York, NY, 10019

The American Scholar, 1811 Q St., NW, Washington, DC 20009

The American Poetry Review, Temple University Center City, 1616 Walnut St., Philadelphia, PA 19103

Anima, 1053 Wilson Ave., Chambersburg, PA 17201

Antaeus, 18 W. 30th St., New York, NY 10001

The Antigonish Review, St. Francis Xavier University, Antigonish, N. S., Canada B26 1CO

The Antioch Review, Box 148, Yellow Springs, OH 45387

Apalachee Quarterly, Box 20106, Tallahassee, FL 32316

A Poem in a Pamphlet, Box 14353, Hartford, CT 06114

Ararat, 625 Second Ave., New York, NY 10016

Arc, English Dept., Carleton University, Ottawa, Ont., Canada K1S 5B6

Ariel, English Dept., University of Calgary, Calgary, Alta., Canada T2N 1N4

Arizona Quarterly, Main Library, B-541, University of Arizona, Tucson, AZ 85721

Artemis, Box 945, Roanoke, VA 24005

The Arts Journal, 324 Charlotte St., Asheville, NC 28801

Arts Manitoba, 360 Princess St., Winnipeg, Man., Canada R3B 1K9

Ascent, English Dept., University of Illinois, Urbana, IL 61801

The Atlantic Advocate, Gleaner Bldg., Phoenix Sq., Fredericton, N. B., Canada. E3B 5A2

The Atlantic Monthly, 8 Arlington St., Boston, MA 02116

B

Ball State University Forum, Ball State University, Muncie, IN 47306

The Bellingham Review, 412 N. State, Bellingham, WA 98225

Beloit Poetry Journal, RFD 2, Box 154, Ellsworth, ME 04605

Berkeley Poets Cooperative, Box 459, Berkeley, CA 94701

Bitterroot, PO Box 489, Spring Glen, NY 12483

Black American Literature Forum, Parsons Hall 237, Indiana State University, Terre Haute, IN 47809

Black Warrior Review, University of Alabama, PO Box 2936, University, AL 35486

The Bloomsbury Review, PO Box 8928, Denver, CO 80201

Blue Unicorn, 22 Avon Rd., Kensington, CA 94707

Blueline, Blue Mountain Lake, NY 12812

Boston Review, 33 Harrison Ave., Boston, MA 02111

Boulevard, 4 Washington Square Village, New York, NY 10012

The Brooklyn College Alumni Literary Review, Brooklyn College, Brooklyn, NY 11210

Brooklyn Review, English Dept. Brooklyn College, Brooklyn, NY 11210

Buffalo Spree, 4511 Harlem Rd., Buffalo NY 14226

C

CV/11, Box 30, University Centre, University of Manitoba, Winnipeg, Man., Canada R3T 9Z9

California Quarterly, 100 Sproul Hall, University of California-Davis, Davis, CA 95616

California State Poetry Society Quarterly, 526 W. 19th St., Santa Ana, CA 92706

Calliope, Creative Writing Program, Roger Williams College, Bristol, RI 02809

Calyx, PO Box B, Corvallis, OR 97335

Canadian Author & Bookman, 70 Champlain Ave., Welland, Ont., Canada L3C 2L7

Canada Forum, 20 The Esplanade, Third Floor, Toronto, Ont., Canada M3E 9Z9

Canadian Literature, 2029 West Mall, University of British Columbia, Vancouver, B.C., Canada V6T 1W5

Canadian Poetry, English Dept., University of Western Ontario, London, Ont., Canada. N6A 3K7

Canadian Woman Studies, York University, 204 Founders College, Downsview, Ont., Canada. M3J 1P3

The Cape Rock, English Dept., Southeast Missouri State University, Cape Girardeau, MO 63701

The Capilano Review, 2055 Purcell Way, North Vancouver, BC, Canada V7J 3H5

Capper's Weekly, 616 Jefferson St., Topeka, KS 66607

Carnegie-Mellon Magazine, Carnegie-Mellon University, Pittsburgh, PA 15213

Carolina Quarterly, Greenlaw Hall 066A, University of North Carolina, Chapel Hill, NC 27514

Casper State Tribune Arts Section, Casper State Tribune, Casper, WY 82601

The Centennial Review, 110 Morrill Hall, Michigan State University, East Lansing, MI 48824

Chaminade Literary Review, Chaminade University, 3140 Waialae Ave., Honolulu, HI 96816

The Chariton Review, Northeast Missouri State University, Kirksville, MO 63501

The Chattahoochee Review, DeKalb Community College, North Campus, 2101 Womack Rd., Dunwoody, GA 30338

Chelsea, PO Box 5880, Grand Central Sta., New York, NY 10017

Chicago Review, University of Chicago, 5700 So. Ingleside, Box C, Chicago, IL 60637

The Chowder Review, PO Box 33, Wollaston, MA 02170

The Christian Century, 407 S. Dearborn, Chicago, IL 60605

Cimmaron Review, 208 Life Science East, Oklahoma State University, Stillwater, OK 74078

Cincinnati Poetry Review, English Dept., University of Cincinnati, Cincinnati, OH 45221

The Classical Outlook, Dept. of Classics, Park Hall, University of Georgia, Athens, GA 30602

Mr. Cogito, Box 627, Pacific University, Forest Grove, OR 97116

Cold Mountain Review, English Dept., Appalachian State College, Boone, NC 28608

College English, English Dept., University of Alabama, Drawer AL, University, AL 35486

Colorado State Review, English Dept., Colorado State University, 350 W.O. Eddy Bldg., Fort Collins, CO 80523

Columbia, 404 Dodge Hall, Columbia University, New York, NY 10027

Commonweal, 232 Madison Ave., New York, NY 10016

Concerning Poetry, English Dept., Western Washington University, Bellingham, WA 98225

Confrontation, English Dept., Long Island University, Greenvale, NY 11548

The Connecticut Poetry Review, PO Box 3783, New Haven, CT 06525

Contact, PO Box 451, Bowling Green Sta., New York, NY 10004

Cornfield Review, Ohio State University, 1465 Mt. Vernon Ave., Marion, OH 43302

Corona, Dept. of History & Philosophy, Montana State University, Bozeman, MT 59717

Cosmopolitan, 224 W. 57th St., New York, NY 10019

Cottonwood, Box J, Kansas Union, University of Kansas, Lawrence, KS 66045

The Creative Woman, Governors State University, University Park, IL 60466

Cross-Canada Writers' Quarterly, PO Box 277, Station F, Toronto, Ont., Canada M4Y 2L7

Crosscurrents, 2200 Glastonbury Rd., Westlake Village, CA 91361

Croton Review, PO Box 277, Croton-on-Hudson, NY 10520

CutBank., English Dept., University of Montana, Missoula, MT 59812

D

The Dalhousie Review, Dalhousie University, Halifax, N.S., Canada B3H 4H8

Dandelion, 922-9th Ave., SE, Calgary, Alta., Canada T2G 0S4

DeKalb Literary Arts Journal, 555 No. Indian Creek Dr., Clarkson, GA 30021

Denver Quarterly, University of Denver, Denver, CO 80208

Descant, English Dept., Texas Christian University, TCU Sta., Fort Worth, TX 76129

Descant (Canada), PO Box 314, Sta. P., Toronto, Ont., Canada M5S 258

Dialogue, 202 W. 300, No., Salt Lake City, Utah 84103

Dimension, PO Box 26673, Austin, TX 78755

E

Educational Studies, 331 De Garno Hall, Illinois State University, Normal, IL 61761

Elkhorn Review, Northeast Community College, Norfolk, NE 68701

The Emrys Journal, PO Box 8813, Greenville, SC 29604

Encore, 1121 Major Ave., NW, Albuquerque, NM 87107

Envy's Sting, Green Tower Press, English Dept., Northwest Missouri State University, Maryville, MO 64468

Epoch, 251 Goldwin Smith, Cornell University, Ithaca, NY 14853

Eureka Review, English Dept., University of Cincinnati, Cincinnati, OH 45221

Event, PO Box 9030, Surrey, B.C. Canada V3T 5H8

F

The Falcon, Mansfield State College, Mansfield, PA 16933

Family Circle, 110-5th Ave., New York, NY 10011

Farm Wife News, 733 N. Van Buren, Milwaukee, WI 53202

Farmer's Market, PO Box 1272, Galesburg, IL 61402

Feminist Studies, University of Maryland, College Park, MD 20742

The Fiddlehead, The Observatory, University of New Brunswick, Fredericton, N. B., Canada E3B 5A3

Field, Rice Hall, Oberlin College, Oberlin, OH 20742

Fireweed, PO Box 279, Sta. B, Toronto, Ont., Canada M5T 2W2

Folio, Dept. of Literature, Gray Hall, American University, Washington, DC 20016

Firelands Arts Review, Firelands Campus, Bowling Green State University, Huron, OH 44839

Footwork Magazine, Passaic County Community College, Paterson, NJ 07503

Four Quarters, La Salle College, Olney Ave. at 20th St., Philadelphia, PA 19191

Frank, Mixed General Delivery, APO New York 09777

Free Lance, 6005 Grand Ave., Cleveland, OH 44104

Frontiers, c/o Women's Studies, University of Colorado, Boulder, CO 80309

G

Gamut, 238 Davenport Rd., Toronto, Ont., Canada M5R 1J6

Gargoyle, 160 Boylston St. (No.3), Jamaica Plain, MA 02130

The Georgia Review, University of Georgia, Athens, GA 30602

Germination, 428 Yale Ave., Riverview, N.B., Canada, E1B 2B5

Good Housekeeping, 959-8th Ave., New York, NY 10019

Graham House Review, PO Box 489, Englewood, NJ 07631

Grain, PO Box 1154, Regina, Sask., Canada S4P SB4

The Gramercy Review, PO Box 15362, Los Angeles, CA 90015

Grand Street, 50 Riverside Drive, New York, NY 10024

Great Lakes Review, Northeastern Illinois University, Chicago, IL 60625

Green Mountain Quarterly, 460 N. Main St., Oshkosh, WI 54901

Green River Review, SVSC, Box 56, University Center, MI 48710

The Greenfield Review, PO Box 80, Greenfield Center, NY 12833

Greenhouse Review, 126 Escalona Dr., Santa Cruz, CA 95060

Green's Magazine, PO Box 3236, Regina, Sask., Canada S4P 3H1

Greensboro Review, English Dept., North Carolina University, Greensboro, NC 27412

Grit, 208 W. 3rd St., Williamsport, PA 17701

Gryphon, Dept. of Humanities-LE3-370, The University of South Florida, Tampa, FL 33620

H

The Hampden-Sydney Poetry Review, PO Box 126, Hampton-Sydney, VA 23943

Hanging Loose, 231 Wyckoff St., Brooklyn, NY 11217

The Harbor Review, English Dept., University of Massachusetts at Boston, Boston, MA 02125

Harlequin, 240 Duncan Mill Rd., Don Mills, Ont., Canada M3B 1Z4

Harmony, M.V.B., Room 155, University of New Hampshire, Durham, NH 03824

The Harvard Advocate, Advocate House, 21 South St., Cambridge, MA 02138

Hawaii Review, English Dept., University of Hawaii, Honolulu, HI 96822

Helicon Nine, PO Box 22412, Kansas City, MO 64113

Higginson Journal of Poetry, 4508-38th St., Brentwood, MD 20722

The Hiram Poetry Review, PO Box 162, Hiram, OH 44234

The Hollins Critic, Hollins College, Hollins College, VA 24020

Home Education Magazine, PO Box 218, Tonasket, WA 98855

The Hudson Review, 684 Park Ave., New York, NY 10021

The Humanist, 928 Kensington Ave., Buffalo, NY 14215

Humanist in Canada, PO Box 2007, Postal Sta. D, Ottawa., Ont., Canada K1P 5W3

Huron Review, 423 S. Franklin Ave., Flint, MI 48503

Hyperion, c/o Hogan/Chase Park 2-D, Chapel Hill, NC 27514

Hysteria, PO Box 2481, Sta. B, Kitchener, Ont., Canada N2B 6M3

I

Indentity, 336 Queen St., E., Toronto, Ont., Canada M5A 1S8

Illuminations, 1900-9th St., (No.8), Berkeley, CA 94710

Image Magazine, PO Box 24048, St. Louis, MO 63119

Images, English Dept., Wright State University, Dayton, OH 45435

Impact, PO Box 61297, Sunnyvale, CA 94088

Indiana Review, 316 N. Jordan Ave., Bloomington, IN 47405

Indiana Writes, 321 Goodbody Hall, Bloomington, IN 47401

Inlet, English Dept., Virginia Wesleyan University, Norfolk, VA 23502

Insight, 6856 Eastern Ave., Washington, DC 20012

Interim, English Dept., University of Nevada, Las Vegas, NV 89154

Interior Voice, PO Box 117, Kelowna, B.C., Canada V1Y 7N2

International Poetry Forum, PO Box 91, Waynesboro, TN 38485

International Poetry Review, PO Box 2047, Greensboro, NC 27402

Intertext, 2633 E. 17th Ave., Anchorage, AK 99508

The Iowa Review, EPB 321, University of Iowa, Iowa City, IA 53342

Ironwood, PO Box 40907, Tucson, AZ 85717

Isaac Asimov's Science Fiction Magazine, 380 Lexington Ave., New York, NY 10017

J

Jacksonville Poetry Quarterly, 5340 Weller Ave., Jacksonville, FL 32211

Jeopardy, Humanities 350, Western Washington University, WWU, Bellingham, WA 98225

Jewish Currents, 22 E. 17th St., New York, NY 10003

The Jewish Spectator, PO Box 2016, Santa Monica, CA 90406

The Journal, Ellis Hall, Ohio University, Athens, OH 45701-2979

Journal of Canadian Poetry, 9 Ashburn Dr., Nepean, Ont., Canada

Journal of Irish Literature, PO Box 361, Newark, DE 19711

Journal of New Jersey Poets, English Dept., Fairleigh Dickinson University, Madison, NJ 07940

Journal of Reading, 600 Barksdale Rd., Newark, DE 19711

Journal of World Education, 530 E. 86th St., New York, NY 10028

Jubilee (Canadian material only), 332 Minnic St., Wingham, Ont., Canada NOG 2WO

K

Kaldron, 441 N. 6th St., Grover City, CA 93433

Kansas Quarterly, Eng. Dept./Denison Hall, Kansas State University, Manhattan, KS 66506

Karamus, English Dept., Eastern Illinois University, Charleston, IL 61920

Kayak, 325 Ocean View Ave., Santa Cruz, CA 95062

Kentucky Poetry Review, 1568 Cherokee Rd., Louisville, KY 40205

The Kenyon Review, Kenyon College, Gambier, OH 43022

The Kindred Spirit, 808 Maple, Great Bend, KS 67530

Konglomerati, 5719-29th Ave., So. Gulfport, FL 33707

Kosmos, 130 Eureka, San Francisco, CA 94114

Kudzu, PO Box 65, Cayce, SC 29033

L

Ladies' Home Journal, 3 Park Ave., New York, NY 10016

The Lake Street Review, PO Box 7188, Minneapolis, MN 55407

The Lake Superior Review, PO Box 724, Ironwood, MI 49938

Latin-American Literary Review, Dept. of Modern Languages, Carnegie-Mellon University, Pittsburgh, PA 15213

The Laurel Review, English Dept., West Virginia Wesleyan College, Buckhannon, WV 26201

The Limberlost Review, English Dept., Idaho State University, Pocatello, ID 83209

The Literary Review, Fairleigh Dickinson University, 285 Madison Ave., Madison, NJ 07940

The Little Review, English Dept., Marshall University, Huntington, WV 25701

Long Island Review, 360 W. 21st St., New York, NY 10011

Long Pond Review, English Dept., Suffolk Community College, Selden, NY 11784

The Lookout, 15 State St., New York, NY 10004

The Lutheran Journal, 7317 Cahill Rd., Edina, MN 55435

Lutheran Women, 2900 Queen Lane, Philadelphia, PA 19129

The Lyric, 307 Dunton Dr., SW., Blacksburg, VA 24060

M

Madamoiselle, 350 Madison Ave., New York, NY 10017

The Madison Review, English Dept., Helen C. White Hall, University of Wisconsin, 600 N. Park St., Madison, WI 53706

The Mainstreeter, English Dept., University of Wisconsin, Stevens Point, WI 54481

The Malahat Review, University of Victoria, PO Box 1700, Victoria, B.C. Canada V8W 2Y2

The Manhattan Review, 304-3rd Ave., New York, NY 10010

The Massachusetts Review, Memorial Hall, University of Massachusetts, Amherst, MA 01002

Matrix, PO Box 510, Lennoxville, Que., Canada J0M 1Z6

Memphis State Review, English Dept., Memphis State University, Memphis, TN 38152

Michigan Quarterly Review, 3032 Rackham Bldg., University of Michigan, Ann Arbor, MI 48109

Mid-American Review, English Dept., Bowling Green State University, Bowling Green, OH 43403

The Midatlantic Review, PO Box 398, Baldwin Place, NY 10505

Midstream, 515 Park Ave., New York, NY 10022

Midwest Chaparral, 5508 Osage, Kansas City, KS 66106

Midwest Poetry Review, PO Box 776, Rockland, IL 61202

The Midwest Quarterly, Pittsburg State University, Pittsburg, KS 66762

The Minnesota Review, PO Box 211, Bloomington, IN 47401

The Minetta Review, 21 Washington Pl., Box 65, New York, NY 10003

The Miraculous Medal, 475 E. Chelten Ave., Philadelphia, PA 19144

Mississippi Poetry Journal, PO Box 875, Hazlehurst, MS 39083

Mississippi Review, Center for Writers, Univerity of Southern Mississippi, PO Box 37/Southern Sta., Hattiesburg, MS 39401

Mississippi Valley Review, English Dept., Western Illinois University, Macomb, IL 61455

Missouri Review, University of Missouri, 231 Arts & Science, Columbia, MO 65211

Modern Haiku, 260 Vista Marina, San Clemente, CA 92672

Modern Maturity, 215 Long Beach Blvd., Long Beach, CA 10810

Moosehead Review, PO Box 169, Ayer's Cliff, Que., Canada J0B 1C0

The Morningside Review, University of Missouri, 231 Low Library, Columbia University, New York, NY 10027

Moving Out, Wayne County State University, Detroit, MI 48202

Ms Magazine, 119 W. 40th St., New York, NY 10018

Mss, State University of New York at Binghamton, Binghamton, NY 13901

N

Nantucket Review, Po Box 1234, Nantucket, MA 02554

The Nation, 72-5th Ave., New York, NY 10011

National Forum, East Tennessee University, PO Box 19420A, Johnson City, TN 37601

Nebo, English Dept., Arkansas Technical University, Russellville, AR 72801

Nebula, 970 Copeland St., North Bay, Ont., Canada P1B 3E4

Negative Capability, 6116 Timberly Rd., No., Mobile, AL 36609

New America, Humanities, Room 324, University of New Mexico, Albuquerque, NM 87131

NER/BLQ., PO Box 170, Hanover, NH 03755

New Catholic World, 1865 Broadway, New York, NY 10023

The New Criterion, 850-7th Ave., New York, NY 10019

New Directions, Dept. of Human Relations and Publications, Howard University, Washington, DC 20059

New Jersey Poetry Monthly, PO Box 824, Saddle Brook, NJ 07662

The New Kent Quarterly, 239 Student Center, Kent State University, Kent, OH 44240

The New Laurel Review, PO Box 1083, Chalmette, LA 70044

The New Leader, 275-7th Ave., New York, NY 10001

New Letters, University of Missouri, 5346 Charlotte, Kansas City, MO 64110

New Mexico Humanities Review, Box A, New Mexico Institute of Mining and Technology, Socorro, NM 87801

New Oregon Review, 537 NE Lincoln St., Hillsboro, OR 97124

New Orleans Review, Loyola University, New Orleans, LA 70118

New Quarterly, University of Waterloo, Waterloo, Ont., Canada N2L 3G1

The New Republic, 1220-19th St., NW, Washington, DC 20036

New York Arts Journal, 560 Riverside Drive, New York, NY 10027

New York Quarterly, PO Box 693, Old Chelsea Station, New York, NY 10113

The New York Smith, 5 Beekman St., New York, NY 10038

The New Yorker, 25 W. 43rd St., New York, NY 10036

Nexus, 006 University Center, Wright State University, Dayton, OH 45435

Nimrod, Arts & Humanities Council of Tulsa, 2210 S. Main St., Tulsa, OK 74114

North American Mentor Magazine, 1745 Madison St., Fennimore, WI 53809

The North American Review, University of Northern Iowa, Cedar Falls, IA 50614

The North Carolina Review, 3329 Granville Dr., Raleigh, NC 27609

North Dakota Quarterly, University of North Dakota, PO Box 8237, Grand Forks, ND 58202

Northeast Journal, Providence College, Box 217, Kingston, RI 02881

Northern Light, University of Manitoba, 605 Fletcher Argus Bldg.,Winnipeg, Man., Canada R3T 2N2

Nothern New England Review, Franklin Pierce College, PO Box 825, Ridge, NH 03461

Northwest Magazine, 1320 SW Broadway, Portland, OR 97201

Northwest Review, 369 P. L. C., University of Oregon, Eugene, OR 97405

O

Obsidian, English Dept., Wayne State University, Detroit, MI 48202

Occident, University of California-Berkeley, 103 Sproul Hall, Berkeley, CA 94720

The Ohio Review, Ellis Hall, Ohio University, Athens, OH 45701-2979

The Ontario Review, 9 Honey Brook Dr., Princeton, NJ 08540

Open Letter, 104 Lyndhurst Ave., Toronto, Ont.,

Canada M5R 2Z7

Open Places, Stephens College, PO Box 2085, Columbia, MO 65215

Orphic Lute, 1021 E. Little Black River Rd., Hampton, VA 23669

Osiris, PO Box 297, Deerfield, MA 01342

Our Family, PO Box 249, Battlefort, Sask., Canada SOM OFO

Outerbridge, English A323, The College of Staten Island, 715 Ocean Terr., Staten Island, NY 10301

Oxford Magazine, Miami (Ohio) University, Oxford, OH 45056

P

Pacific Northwest Review of Books, PO Box 21566, Seattle, WA 98111

Pacific Poetry & Fiction Review, English Office, San Diego State University, San Diego, CA 92182

Pacific Quarterly, 626 Coate Rd., Orange, CA 92669

Padam Aram, 52 Dunster St., Harvard University, Cambridge, MA 02138

Paintbrush, English Dept., Northeastern University, Boston, MA 02115

Painted Bride Quarterly, 230 Vine St., Philadelphia, PA 19106

Pan American Review, 1101 Tori Lane, Edinburg, TX 78539

The Panhandler, Writers Workshop, English Dept., University of West Florida, Pensacola, FL 32504

The Paris Review, 45-39—171st Place, Flushing, NY 11358

Parnassus Literary Journal, PO Box 1384, Forest Park, GA 30051

Partisan Review, Boston University, 141 Bay State Rd., Boston, MA 02215

Passages North, William Bonifas Fine Arts Center, 7th St. & 1st Ave., So., Escanaba, MI 49829

Passaic Review, c/o Forstmann Library, 195 Gregory Ave., Passaic, NJ 07055

Pembroke Magazine, Pembroke State University, Pembroke, NC 28372

Pentecostal Evangel, 1445 Boonville, Springfield, MO 65802

Permafrost Magazine, University of Alaska, Fairbanks, AK 99701

Perspectives, English Dept., West Virginia University, Morgantown, WV 26506

Phoebe, 4400 University Dr., Fairfax, VA 22032

Pieran Spring, Brandon University Press, Brandon, Man., Canada R7A 6A9

Piedmont Literary Review, PO Box 3656, Danville, VA 24543

The Pikestaff Forum, PO Box 127, Normal, IL 61761

Pinchpenny, 4851 Q St., Sacramento, CA 95819

Plains Poetry Jounal, PO Box 2337, Bismarck, ND 58502

Ploughshares, PO Box 529, Cambridge, MA 02139

Poem, PO Box 919, Huntsville, AL 35804

The Poet, Fine Arts Society, 2314 W. 6th St., Mishawaka, IN 46544-1594

Poet & Critic, English Dept., Iowa State University, 203 Ross Hall, Ames, IA 50011

Poet International, 208 W. Latimer Ave., Campbell, CA 95008

Poet Lore, 7815 Old Georgetown Rd., Bethesda, MD 20814-2415

Poetry, PO Box 4348, Chicago, IL 60680

Poetry Canada Review, 307 Coxwell Ave., Toronto, Ont., Canada M4L 3B5

Poetry East, English Dept., DePaul University, 802 W. Belden Ave., Chicago, IL 60614

Poetry/LA, PO Box 84271, Los Angeles, CA 90073

Poetry Miscellany, English Dept., University of Tennessee, Chattanooga, TN 37403

Poetry North Review, 3809 Barbara Dr., Anchorage, AK 99503

Poetry Northwest, University of Washington, 4045 Brooklyn, NE, Seattle, WA 98195

Poetry Northwest Magazine, The Oregonian, Portland, OR 97201

Poetry Now, 3118 K St., Eureka, CA 95501

Poetry Review, Poetry Society of America, 15 Gramercy Park, So.,New York, NY 10003

Poetry Texas, Div. of Humanities, College of the Mainland, Texas City, TX 77590

Poetry Today Magazine, PO Box 20822, Portland, OR 97220

Poetry Toronto, 217 Northwood Dr., Willowdale, Ont., Canada, M2M 2K5

Poets On, PO Box 255, Chaplin, CT 06235

Poets & Writers Newsletter, 201 W. 54th St., New York, NY 10019

Pontchartrain Review, PO Box 1065, Chalmette, LA 70044

Portland Review, PO Box 751, Portland, OR 97207

Pottersfield Portfolio, RR 2, Porters Lake, N.S., Canada BOJ 2SO

Prairie Fire, 374 Donald St., Winnipeg, Man., Canada R3B 2J2

Prairie Schooner, 201 Andrews, University of Nebraska, Lincoln, NE 68588

Primavera, 1212 E. 59th St., Chicago, IL 60637

Prism International, Dept. of Creative Writing, University of British Columbia, Vancouver, B.C. Canada V6T 1W5

Puerto Del Sol, New Mexico State University, Box 3E, Las Cruces, NM 88003

Q

Quarry, PO Box 1061, Kingston, Ont., Canada K7L 4Y5

Quarry West, Porter College, University of California-Santa Cruz, Santa Cruz, CA 95064

Quarterly Review of Literature, 26 Haslet Ave., Princeton, NJ 08540

Quarterly West, 312 Olpin Union, University of Utah, Salt Lake City, UT 84112

Queen's Quarterly, John Watson Hall, Queen's University, Kingston, Ont., Canada K7L 3N6

R

Rackham Journal, University of Michigan, MLB-4024, Ann Arbor, MI 48109

Red Cedar Review, English Dept., Michigan State University, East Lansing MI 48825

Review, 680 Park Ave., New York, NY 10021

Rhino, 3915 Foster St., Evanston, IL 60203

Rhode Island Review, 85 Preston St., Providence, RI 02906

River City Review, Box 34275, Louisville, KY 40232

River Styx, 7420 Cornell Ave., St. Louis, MO 63130

Riverside Quarterly, PO Box 14451, University Sta., Gainesville, FL 32604

Riverside Quarterly, 13931 N. Central Expressway, Dallas, TX 75243

Roanoke Review, Roanoke College, Salem, VA 24153

The Rockford Review, PO Box 858, Rockford, IL 61105

Rocky Mountain Review, English Dept., Arizona State University, Tempe, AZ 85281

Room of One's Own, PO Box 46160, Sta. G, Vancouver, B.C., Canada V6R 4G5

The Round Table, 206 Sherman St., Wayne, NE 68787

Rubicon, McGill University, 853 Sherbrooke, Montreal, Que., Canada H3A 2T6

S

Sackbut Review, 2513 E. Webster, Milwaukee, WI 53211

St. Andrews Review, St. Andrews Presbyterian College, Laurinburg, NC 28352

St. Anthony Messenger, 1615 Republic St., Cincinnati, OH 45210

Salmagundi, Skidmore College, Saratoga Springs, NY 12866

Sam Houston Literary Review, Sam Houston State University, Huntsville, TX 77346

Samisdat, PO Box 129, Richford, VT 05476

San Fernando Poetry Journal, 18301 Halstead St., Northridge, CA 91325

San Jose Studies, San Jose State University, San Jose, CA 95192

Sanctum Quarterly, 9123-C Fargo Dr., Richmond, VA 23229

The Saturday Evening Post, 1100 Waterway Blvd., Indianapolis, IN 46202

Saturday Night, 70 Bond St., Suite 500, Toronto, Ont., Canada M5B 2J3

Scandinavian Review, 127 E. 73rd St., New York, NY 10021

Scholia Satyrica, English Dept., University of South Florida, Tampa, FL 33620

Science, 1101 Vermont Ave., NW, Washington, DC 20005

Scrivener, Arts B-20, McGill University, 853 Sherbrooke St. W., Montreal, Que., Canada H3A 2T6

The Seattle Review, University of Washington, Padelford Hall, Seattle, WA 98195

Seems, English Dept., University of Northern Iowa, Cedar Falls, IA 50613

The Seneca Review, Hobart & William Smith Colleges, Geneva, NY 14456

Separate Doors, 911 WT, Canyon, TX 79106

Sequoia: Stanford Literary Magazine, Storke Publications Bldg., Stanford, CA 94305

Seventeen, 850-3rd Ave., New York, NY 10022

Sewanee Review, University of the South, Sewanee, TN 37375

Shankpainter, The Fine Arts Work Center, 24 Pearl St., Box 565, Provincetown, MA 02657

Sharing, PO Box 1470, Yuma, AZ 85364

Shenandoah, PO Box 722, Lexington, VA 24450

Sing, Heavenly Muse, PO Box 13299, Minneapolis, MN 55101

The Slackwater Review, Lewis-Clark Campus, Lewiston, ID 83501

The Small Pond Magazine, PO Box 664, Stratford, CT 06497

The Smith, 5 Beekman St., New York, NY 10038

Snapdragon, English Dept., University of Idaho, Moscow, ID 83843-4198

Sojourner, 143 Albany St., Cambridge, MA 02139

Sonoma Mandala, Sonoma State University, English Dept., Rohnert Park, CA 94928

Sonora Review, English Dept., University of Arizona, Tucson, AZ 85721

Soundings/East, English Dept., Salem State College, Salem, MA 01970

South Atlantic Quarterly, PO Box 6697, College Station, Durham, NC 27708

The South Carolina Review, English Dept., Clemson University, Clemson, SC 29631

South Dakota Review, Box 111, University Exchange, Vermillion, SD 57069

The South Florida Poetry Review, PO Box 7072, Hollywood, FL 33081

South Western Ontario Poetry, 396 Berkshire Dr., London, Ont., Canada N6J 3S1

Southern Exposure, PO Box 531, Durham, NC 27702

Southern Humanities Review, 9090 Haley Center, Auburn University, Auburn IL 36830

Southern Poetry Review, English Dept., University of North California, UNCC Station, Charlotte, NC 28223

The Southern Review, Drawer D, University Sta., Baton Rouge, LA 70893

Southwest Review, Southern Methodist University, Dallas, TX 75275

Sou'Wester, English Dept., Southern Illinois University, Edwardsville, IL 62025

The Spirit That Moves Us, PO Box 1585, Iowa City, IA 52244

The Spoon River Quarterly, PO Box 1443, Peoria, IL 61655

State of the Arts Magazine, Connecticut Commission on the Arts, 190 Trumbull St., 4th floor, Hartford, CT 06103-2206

Stone Country, PO Box 132, Menemsha, MA 02552

Stone Drum, PO Box 233, Valley View, TX 76272

Studia Mystica, California State University, Sacramento, CA 95819

Studies in Poetry, English Dept., Texas Tech University, Lubbock, TX 79409

Sulfur Magazine, 852 S. Bedford St., Los Angeles, CA 90035

The Sun, 412 W. Rosemary St., Chapel Hill, NC 27514

Swallow's Tale Magazine, PO Box 4328, Tallahassee, FL 32315

T

Tamarack, 909 Westcott St., Syracuse, NY 13210

Tamarisk, 319 S. Juniper St., Philadelphia, PA 19107

Tar River Poetry, English Dept., East Carolina University, Austin Bldg., Greenville, NC 27834

Taurus, PO Box 28, Gladstone, OR 97027-0028

Tendril, PO Box 512, Green Harbor, MA 02041

The Texas Arts Journal, PO Box 7458, Dallas, TX 75209

The Texas Review, English Dept., Sam Houston State University, Huntsville, TX 77341

Texas Quarterly, PO Box 7517, University Sta., Austin, TX 78712

Theology Today, PO Box 29, Princeton NJ 08540

This Magazine, 70 The Esplanade, Toronto, Ont., Canada M5E 1R2

Thoreau Journal Quarterly, 355 Ford Hall, University of Minnesota, 224 Church St., S.E., Minneapolis, MN 55455

Thought: The Quarterly of Fordham University, Box L, Fordham University, Bronx, NY 10458

Three Rivers Poetry Journal, Carnegie-Mellon University, PO Box 21, Pittsburgh, PA 15213

The Threepenny Review, PO Box 9131, Berkeley, CA 94709

Toronto South Asian Review, PO box 6996, Sta. A., Toronto, Ont., Canada M5W 1X7

Touchstone, English Dept., Kansas State University, Manhattan, KS 66502

Tower Poetry Magazine, c/o Dundas Public Library, 18 Ogilvie St., Dundas, Ont., Canada L9H 2S2

Translation, Columbia University, 307A Mathematics, New York, NY 10027

Trinity Review, Trinity University, 715 Stadium Dr., San Antonio, TX 78284

TriQuarterly, 1735 Benson Ave., Evanston, IL 60201

Tyuonyl, Institute of American Indian Arts, College of Santa Fe Campus, St. Michael's Dr., Santa Fe, NM 87501

U

UT Review, University of Tampa, Tampa, FL 33606

Unicorn, 4501 No. Charles St., Baltimore, MD 21210

Unicorn: A Miscellaneous Journal, 345 Harvard St.

(3B), Cambridge, MA 02138

The United Methodist Reporter, PO Box 660275, Dallas, TX 75266-0275

Unity, Unity Village, MO 64065

Universal Unitarian Christian, 5701 So. Woodlawn Ave., Chicago, IL 60637

University of Portland Review, 5000 No. Willamette, Portland, OR 97203

University of Windsor Review, University of Windsor, Windsor, Ont., Canada N9B 3P4

The Upper Room, Alive Now!, 1908 Grand Box 189, Nashville, TN 37212

Urobos, 111 No. 10th St., Olean, NY 14760

V

Valley Spirit, 433 F St., Davis, CA 95616

Vantage Point, Centre College, Danville, KY 40422

Velocities, 1509 Le Roy Ave., Berkeley, CA 94708

Verse & Universe, 1780 McKinley (#3), Wyandotte, MI 48192

The Villager, 135 Midland Ave., Bronxville, NY 10707

Vintage, PO Box 266, Orinda, CA 94563

The Virginia Quarterly Review, 1 West Range, Charlottesville, VA 22903

Visions, 4705 So. 8th Rd., Arlington, VA 22204

Voices International, 1115 Gillete Dr., Little Rock, AR 72207

VOL No. Magazine, 24721 Newhall Ave., Newhall, CA 91321

W

Wascana Review, University of Regina, Regina, Sask., Canada S4S OA2

The Washington Dossier, 3301 New Mexico Ave., NW, Washington, DC 20016

Washington Review, PO Box 50132, Washington, DC 20004

The Washingtonian Magazine, 1828 L St., NW, Washington, DC 20036

Waterways, 799 Greenwich St., New York, NY 10014

Waves, 79 Denham Dr., Richmond Hill, Ont., Canada L4C 6H9

Waves, Room 357/Stong College, York University, 4700 Keele ST., Downsview, Ont., Canada M3J 1P3

Webster Review, Webster College, Webster Groves, MO 63119

The Wierdbook Sampler, PO Box 149, Amherst Sta., Buffalo, NY 14226

Wellspring, 321 O'Connor St., Menlo Park, CA 94025

West Branch, English Dept., Bucknell University, Lewisburg, PA 17837

West Coast Poetry Review, 1335 Dartmouth Dr., Reno, NV 89507

West Coast Review, Simon Fraser University, Burnaby, B.C., Canada MSA 156

West Hills Review, Walt Whitman Birthplace Assoc., 246 Walt Whitman Rd., Huntington Station, NY 11746

Western Humanities Review, University of Utah, Salt Lake City, UT 84112

Whiskey Island Magazine, Cleveland State University—UC7, Cleveland, OH 44115

The White Rock Review, 16W481 Second Ave., Bensenville, IL 60106

White Walls, PO Box 8204, Chicago, IL 60680

Wide Open, 326 I St., Eureka, CA 95501

Willow Springs Magazine, PO Box 1063, Eastern Washington University, Cheney, WA 99004

Wind/A Literary Journal, RFD, Rte 1, Box 809K, Pikeville, KY 41501

Windfall, English Dept., University of Wisconsin, Whitewater, WI 53190

The Windless Orchard, English Dept., Indiana University, Fort Wayne, IN 46805

Wisconsin Academy Review, 1922 University Ave., Madison, WI 53705

Wisconsin Review, Box 158, Radford Hall, University of Wisconsin, Oshkosh, WI 54901

Woman of Power, PO Box 827, Cambridge, MA 02238-0827

Woman: A Journal of Liberation, 3028 Greenmount Ave., Baltimore, MD 21218

Woman's Quarterly Review, 900 West End Ave., New York, NY 10025

The Wooster Review, The College of Wooster, Wooster, OH 44691

The Worcester Review, PO Box 687, West Side Sta., Worcester, MA 01602

World Liberation Today, 630 Parrington Oval, Room 110, Norman, OK 73019

The Wormwood Review, Box 8840, Stockton, CA 95208-0840

Writer's Digest, 9933 Alliance Road, Cincinnati, OH 45242

Writers Forum, University of Colorado, Colorado Springs, CO 80907

Writer's Lifeline, PO Box 1641, Cornwall, Ont., Canada K6H 5V6

Writer's News Manitoba, 304 Parkview St., Winnipeg, Man., Canada

X

Xanadu, PO Box 773, Huntington, NY 11743

X-It Magazine, PO Box 102, St. John's, Newfoundland, Canada A1C 5H5

Y

The Yale Literary Magazine, PO Box 243-A, Yale Sta., New Haven, CT 06520

The Yale Review, 1902A Yale Sta., New Haven, CT 06520

Yankee, Dublin, NH 03444

Yarrow: A Journal of Poetry, English Dept., Kutztown State College, Lytle Hall, Kutztown, PA 19530

The Yellow Butterfly, 835 W. Carolina St., Lebanon, OR 97355

The Yellow Mountain Review, PO Box 557, New Hartford, CT 06057

Yellow Silk, PO Box 6374, Albany, CA 94706

Yet Another Small Magazine, PO Box 14353, Hartford, CT

Z

Zephyr, PO Box 216, Central Islip, NY 11722

Zest, PO Box 339, Sta. P, Toronto, Ont., Canada M5S 2S8

Poetry Associations, Organizations and Clubs

This directory lists organizations in the United States and Canada devoted to poetry. An asterisk (*) denotes affiliation with the National Federation of State Poetry Societies.

ALABAMA
Alabama State Poetry Societies*, Dr. Sue Walker, President, 6116 Timberly Rd., Mobile, AL 36609

ARIZONA
Arizona State Poetry Society*, Olive Merchant, President, 3840W New York Ave., Tucson, AZ 85705
First Friday Poets, c/o Changing Hands Bookstore, 411 Mill Ave., Tempe, AZ 85281
Phoenix Poetry Society, c/o Pauline Mounsey, 6511 W. Osborn, Phoenix, AZ 85033
University of Arizona Poetry Center, c/o Lois Shelton, 1086 N. Highland, Tucson, AZ 85721

ARKANSAS
Poets Roundtable of Arkansas*, Akers Pence-Moore, President, Rivercliff Apt. #326, 2000 Magnolia Dr., Little Rock, AR 72202

CALIFORNIA
Alchemedias Poets Circle, c/o Stephanie Buffington, 1005 Buena Vista St., South Pasadena, CA 91030
American Poetry Association, 1620 Seabright Ave., Santa Cruz, CA 95063
California Federation of Chapparal Poets, 1422 Ashland Ave., Claremont, CA 91711
California Poetry Reading Circuit, c/o James McMichael, University of California, Dept. of English, Irvine, CA 92664
California Poets-in-the-Schools, c/o J. O. Simon, San Francisco State University, 1600 Holloway (HLL Bldg.), San Francisco, CA 94132
California State Poetry Society*, Helen Shanley, President, 6601 Eucalyptus Ave., #97, Bakersfield, CA 93306
College of San Mateo Poetry Center, c/o Jean Pumphrey, 1700 W. Hillsdale Blvd., San Mateo, CA 94402
Grand Piano Poetry Readings, c/o Steve Benson and Carla Harryman, 1607 Haight St., San Francisco, CA 94117
Intersection Poets and Writers Series, c/o Jim Hartz, 756 Union St., San Francisco, CA 94133
Poetry Center, San Francisco State University, 1600 Holloway, San Francisco, CA 94132
Poetry Therapy Institute, P. O. Box 70244, Los Angeles, CA 90070
Poets Place, c/o Beverly Michaels-Cohn, Hyperion Theatre, 1835 Hyperion Ave., Los Angeles, CA 90027
Poets of the Vineyard, c/o Winnie E. Fitzpatrick, P. O. Box 77, Kenwood, CA 95452
Southern California Poets, c/o J. P. Watson, P. O. Box 77, Kenwood, CA 95452
World Order of Narrative Poets, P. O. Box 2085, Walnut Creek, CA 94596
World Poetry Society, c/o E. A. Falkowski, 208 W. Latimer Ave., Campbell, CA 95008
Yuki Teikei Haiku Society, c/o Haiku Journal, Kiyoshi Tokutomi, 1020 S. 8th St., San Jose, CA 95112

COLORADO
Columbine Poets, c/o Veda Steadman, 631 S. Grant Ave., Fort Collins, CO 80521
League of Colorado Poets*, Lois Leonard, President, 804 Garfield, Fort Collins, CO 80524
Poets of the Foothills Art Center, 809 15th St., Golden, CO 80401

CONNECTICUT
Connecticut Poetry Circuit, c/o Jean Maynard, The Honors College, Wesleyan University, Middletown, CT 06457
Connecticut Poetry Society*, Gerald Coulombe, President, 1816 Jennings Rd., Fairfield, CT 06430
Golden Eagle Poetry Club, P. O. Box 1314, New Milford, CT 06776

DELAWARE
First State Writers*, Margaret H. Rowe, President, 400 W. 24th St., Wilmington, DE 19802

DISTRICT OF COLUMBIA
Federal Poets of Washington, D.C.*, Craig Reynolds, President, P. O. Box 65400, Washington Square, Washington, DC 20035

Federation of International Poetry Associations, P. O. Box 39072, Washington, DC 20016

FLORIDA
Audio-Visual Poetry Foundation, 400 Fish Hatchery Rd., Marianna, FL 32446
Florida State Poetry Association, 1110 N. Venetian Dr., Miami, FL 33139
Florida State Poets Association*, Madelyn Eastlund, President, 310 S. Adams, Beverly Hills, FL 32665
National Federation of State Poetry Societies, Henrietta Kroah, President, 92 Claimont Ave., DeBarry, FL 32713
Poetry Society of Jacksonville, c/o Carlota Fowler, 4411 Charles Bennett Dr., Jacksonville, FL 32225

GEORGIA
Atlanta Poetry Society, c/o Robert Manns, 1105-E N. Jamestown Rd., Decatur, GA 30033
Georgia State Poetry Society*, Dr. E. Jerome Zeller, President, 3450 Evans Rd., #139-A, Atlanta, GA 30340
Poetry at Callanwolde, c/o Gene Ellis, 980 Briarcliff Rd., N.E., Atlanta, GA 30306

HAWAII
Hawaii Writers Club*, Marie Fujii, President, 916-15th Ave., Honolulu, HI 96816

IDAHO
Idaho Poets-in-the-Schools, c/o Keith Browning, Lewis & Clark State College, Dept. of English, Lewiston, ID 83501

ILLINOIS
Apocalypse Poetry Association, c/o Rose Lesniak, Creative Writing Center, 3307 Bryn Mawr, Chicago, IL 60625
Modern Poetry Association, P. O. Box 4348, Chicago, IL 60680
Poetry Center, c/o Paul Hoover, Museum of Contemporary Art, 237 E. Ontario, Chicago, IL 60611
Poets Club of Chicago, c/o Nolan Boiler Co., 8531 S. Vincennes Ave., Chicago, IL 60620
Poets and Patrons of Chicago, c/o Mary Mathison, 13924 Keeler Ave., Crestwood, IL 60445

INDIANA
Indiana State Federation of Poetry Clubs*, Glenna Jenkins, President, 808 E. 32nd St., Anderson, IN 46014
Poets' Study Club of Terre Haute, 826 S. Center St., Terre Haute, IN 47807

IOWA
Ellsworth Poetry Project, c/o Daniel M. McGuiness, Ellsworth College, 1100 College Ave., Iowa Falls, IA 50126
Iowa Poetry Association*, Ralph Speer, President, English Dept., Grandview College, Des Moines, IA 50312

KANSAS
Kansas Poetry Society*, Sister Mary Faith Schuster, President, 302 N. 5th St., Atchison, KS 66002

KENTUCKY
Appalachian Poetry Association, Box 1358, Middlesboro, KY 40965
Kentucky State Poetry Society*, R. Franklin Pate, President, 5018 Wabash Place, Louisville, KY 40214

LOUISIANA
Louisiana State Poetry Society*, Dr. Glenn Swetman, President, P. O. Box 1162, Thibodaux, LA 70302
New Orleans Poetry Forum, c/o Garland Strother, 76 Marcia Dr., Luling, LA 70070

MAINE
National Poetry Foundation, University of Maine, Orono, ME 04469

MARYLAND
Howard County Poetry and Literature Society, c/o Ellen C. Kennedy, 10446 Waterfowl Terrace, Columbia, MD 21044
Maryland State Poetry Society*, Charles Streckfus, President, 402 Hemingway Dr., Bel-Air, MD 21014

MASSACHUSETTS
Blacksmith House Poetry Program, c/o Gail Mazur, 5 Walnut Ave., Cambridge, MA 02140
Longfellow Poetry Society, c/o Longfellow's Wayside Inn, Wayside Inn Rd., Sudbury, MA 01776
Massachusetts State Poetry Society*, Jeanette Maes, President, 64 Harrison Ave., Lynn, MA 01905
New England Poetry Club, c/o Diana Der Hovanessian, 2 Farrar St., Cambridge, MA 02138

MICHIGAN
Miles Modern Poetry Committee, c/o Steve Tudor, Wayne State University, Dept. of English, Detroit, MI 48202
Poetry Resource Center of Michigan, 743 Beaubien, Detroit, MI 48226

Michigan State Poetry Society*, Vonnie Thomas, President, 8757 Berridge Rd., Greenville, MI 49307
Rhyme Space and West Park Poetry Series, c/o Carolyn Holmes Gregory, 709 W. Huron, Ann Arbor, MI 48103

MINNESOTA
Hungry Mind Poetry Series, c/o Jim Sitter, Hungry Mind Bookstore, 1648 Grand Ave., St. Paul, MN 55105
League of Minnesota Poets*, Wilfred Johnson, President, 732 Garfield Ave., North Mankato, MN 56001
University Poets' Exchange of Minnesota, c/o William Elliott, Bemidji State University, Dept. of English, Bemidji, MN 56601

MISSISSIPPI
Mississippi Poetry Society*, Mildred Henderson, President, 907 Canal St., Pascagoula, MS 39567

MISSOURI
American Poets Series and Poetry Programs, c/o Gloria Goodfriend, Jewish Community Center of Kansas City, 8201 Holmes Rd., Kansas City, MO 64131
St. Louis Poetry Center, c/o Leslie Konnyu, 5410 Kerth Rd., St. Louis, MO 63128

NEBRASKA
Nebraska Poets Association*, Nancy Goodrich Jay, President, 4340 Parker St., Omaha, NE 68111

NEVADA
Nevada Poetry Society*, Dr. Margaret P. McCarran, President, McCarran Ranch via Sparks, NV 89431

NEW HAMPSHIRE
The Frost Place, c/o Donald Sheehan, Ridge Rd., Box 74, Franconia, NH 03580

NEW JERSEY
Kilmer House Poetry Center, c/o Robert Truscott, 88 Guilden St., New Brunswick, NJ 08901
New Jersey Poetry Society*, Constance Alexander, President, 36 Deborah Dr., Piscataway, NJ 08854
Poets & Writers of New Jersey, P. O. Box 852, Upper Montclair, NJ 07043
Walt Whitman International Poetry Center, c/o Frederick W. Missimer, 2nd and Cooper Sts., Camden, NJ 08102

NEW MEXICO
New Mexico State Poetry Society*, Beverly Merrick, President, 655 Spur Rd., Rio Rancho, NM 87114

NEW YORK
Academy of American Poets, 177 E. 87th St., New York, NY 10128
Bronx Poets and Writers Alliance, 5800 Arlington Ave., Bronx, NY 10471
Columbia Street Poets, c/o Emilie Glen, 77 Barrow St., New York, NY 10014
Committee for Spiritual Poetry, 86-16 Parsons Blvd., Jamaica, NY 11432
Haiku Society of America, Japan House, 333 E. 47th St., New York, NY 10017
Ithaca Community Poets, c/o Katharyn Machan Aal, 432-B E. Seneca St., Ithaca, NY 14850
National Association for Poetry Therapy, c/o Beverly Bussolati, 1029 Henhawk Rd., Baldwin, NY 11510
New York Poetry Forum*, Dr. Dorothea Neale, President, 3064 Albany Crescent, Apt. 54, Bronx, NY 10463
New York State Poets-in-the-Schools, c/o Myra Klahr, 24 N. Greeley Ave., Chappaqua, NY 10514
Noho for the Arts Poetry Forum, c/o Palmer Hasty, 542 La Guardia Place, New York, NY 10012
Nuyorican Poet's Cafe, c/o Miguel Algarin, 524 E. 6th St., New York, NY 10003
Outriders Poetry Program, c/o Max A. Wickert, 182 Colvin Ave., Buffalo, NY 14216
Poetry Center, 92nd St. YM-YWHA, 1395 Lexington Ave., New York, NY 10028
Poetry Society of America, 15 Gramercy Park, New York, NY 10003
Poets Union, c/o Lester Von Losberg, Jr., 315 6th Ave., Brooklyn, NY 11215
Poets & Writers, Inc., 201 W. 54th St., New York, NY 10019
C. W. Post Poetry Center, Dept. of English, C. W. Post Center, Long Island University, Greenvale, NY 11548
Rochester Poetry Central, c/o Jim LaVilla-Havelin, 322 Brooks Ave., Rochester, NY 14619
Rochester Poetry Society, c/o Dale Davis, 155 S. Main St., Fairport, NY 14450
St. Mark's Poetry Project, c/o Maureen Owen or Paul Violi, 2nd Ave. and 10th St., New York, NY 10003
Shelley Society of New York, c/o Annette B. Feldmann, 144-20 41st Ave., Apt. 322, Flushing, NY 11355
World Order of Narrative Poets, c/o Dr. Alfred Dorn, P. O. Box 174, Sta. A, Flushing, NY 11358

NORTH CAROLINA
North Carolina Poetry Society*, Gladys Hughes, President, Box 111, Elon College, NC 27240

OHIO
Cleveland State University Poetry Center, Cleveland, OH 44115
George Elliston Poetry Foundation, University of Cincinnati, Cincinnati, OH 45221
Kenyon Poetry Society, c/o George C. Nelson, Kenyon College, Gambier, OH 43011
Ohio Poetry Day Association, c/o Evan Lodge, 1506 Prospect Rd., Hudson, OH 44236

Poetry Circuit of Ohio, c/o R. W. Daniel, P. O. Box 247, Gambier, OH 43022
Poets League of Greater Cleveland, P. O. Box 6055, Cleveland, OH 44101
Toledo Poets Center, c/o Joze Lipman, UH-507-C, University of Toledo, Toledo, OH 43606
Verse Writers Guild of Ohio*, June Gilbaugh, President, 5275 Antique Rd. S.W., Sherrodsville, OH 44675
Yellow Pages Poets, c/o Jack Roth, P. O. Box 8041, Columbus, OH 43201

OKLAHOMA
Poetry Society of Oklahoma*, Edith Roper, President, 3816 E. Clyde, Oklahoma City, OK 73111

OREGON
Western World Haiku Society, 4102 N.E. 130th Place, Portland, OR 97230

PENNSYLVANIA
American Physicians Poetry Association, 230 Toll Dr., Southampton, PA 18966
Homewood Poetry Forum, Inner City Services, Homewood Branch, Carnegie Library, 7101 Hamilton Ave.,
    Pittsburgh, PA 15206
International Poetry Forum, c/o Dr. Samuel Hazo, 4400 Forbes Ave., Pittsburgh, PA 15213
Pennsylvania Poetry Society*, Dorman Grace, President, 623 N. 4th St., Reading, PA 19601
Y Poetry Center/Workshop, YM-YWHA Branch of JYC, Broad & Pine Sts., Philadelphia, PA 19147

RHODE ISLAND
Rhode Island Poetry Society*, Sharon Lonergan, President, 117 Park Dr., Riverside, RI 02915

SOUTH DAKOTA
Fireside Poetry Group, c/o Isabel Ackley, 416 S. Kline St., Aberdeen, SD 57401
South Dakota State Poetry Society*, Carol Hardwick, President, 104 E. 38th, Sioux Falls, SD 57105

TENNESSEE
Poetry Society of Tennessee*, Frances Cawden, President, 1349 Rolling Oaks Dr. E., Memphis TN 38119
Poets for Christ, c/o George Rickett, Rt. 6, Box 266, Tennessee Dr., Seymour, TN 37865

TEXAS
American Poetry League, 3915 S.W. Military Dr., San Antonio, TX 79601
Hyde Park Poets, c/o Albert Huffstickler, 609 E. 45th St., Austin, TX 78751
National Federation of State Poetry Societies, c/o Jack Murphy, 10436 Creekmere Dr., Dallas, TX 75218
Poetry Society of Texas*, Marvin Hirsh, President, 3232 Broadway Blvd. S., Garland, TX 75093
Stella Woodall Poetry Society, P. O. Box 253, Junction, TX 76849

UTAH
Utah State Poetry Society*, Dr. LaVon B. Carroll, President, 1742 25th St., Ogden, UT 84401

VERMONT
Vermont Poetry Society*, Susan Anthony, President, 151 Main St., Windsor, VT 05089

VIRGINIA
Pause for Poetry, c/o Margaret T. Rudd, 6925 Columbia Pike, Annandale, VA 22003

WASHINGTON
Poetry League of America, 5603 239th Place, S.W., Mountain Terrace, WA 98043

WEST VIRGINIA
Morgantown Poetry Society, 673 Bellaire Dr., Morgantown, WV 26505
West Virginia Poetry Society*, Calvert Estill, President, One Morris St., #806, Charleston, WV 25249

WISCONSIN
Wisconsin Fellowship of Poets*, Loretta Strehlow, President, N76 W. 7292 Lindon, Cedarburg, WI 53012

WYOMING
Poetry Programs of Wyoming, c/o David J. Fraher, P. O. Box 3033, Casper, WY 82602
Poets of Wyoming Writers*, Lou Layman, President, 7125 Salt Creek Route, Box 13, Casper, WY 82601

CANADA
League of Canadian Poets, 24 Ryerson Ave., Toronto, Ont. M5T 2P3

Poets Laureate

Numerous states recognize the excellence and stature of particular poets residing within their borders by officially designating a state poet laureate or poets laureate. Although the specifics of the appointments vary somewhat among the states, the title is usually bestowed by the Governor and is frequently for the life of the poet. The United States now also has an official poet laureate.

UNITED STATES: Richard Wilbur
ALABAMA: Morton D. Prouty, Jr.
ALASKA: Richard Dauenhauer
ARIZONA: None
ARKANSAS: Lily Peter
CALIFORNIA: Charles B. Garrigus
COLORADO: Thomas Hornsby Ferril
CONNECTICUT: James Merrill
DELAWARE: None
FLORIDA: Edmund Skellings
GEORGIA: John Ransom Lewis, Jr.
HAWAII: None
IDAHO: Robert Wrigley (Writer-In-Residence)
ILLINOIS: Gwendolyn Brooks
INDIANA: None
IOWA: None
KANSAS: None
KENTUCKY: Lowell Allen Williams; Lillie D. Chaffin; Agnes O'Rear; Lee Pennington; Clarence Henry "Soc" Clay; Paul Salyers; Henry E. Pilkenton; Dale Faughn; Jim Wayne Miller
LOUISIANA: Henry Thomas Voltz
MAINE: None
MARYLAND: Lucille Clifton
MASSACHUSETTS: None
MICHIGAN: None
MINNESOTA: None
MISSISSIPPI: Winifred Hamrick Farrar
MISSOURI: None
MONTANA: None
NEBRASKA: William C. Kloefkorn (Nebraska State Poet)
NEVADA: None
NEW HAMPSHIRE: Donald Hall
NEW JERSEY: None
NEW MEXICO: None
NEW YORK: Stanley Kunitz (New York State Poet)
NORTH CAROLINA: Sam Ragan
NORTH DAKOTA: None
OHIO: None
OKLAHOMA: Maggie Culver Fry
OREGON: William Stafford

PENNSYLVANIA: None
RHODE ISLAND: None
SOUTH CAROLINA: Bennie Lee Sinclair
SOUTH DAKOTA: Audrae Visser
TENNESSEE: Richard M. "Pek" Gunn
TEXAS: None
UTAH: None
VERMONT: None
VIRGINIA: None
WASHINGTON: None
WEST VIRGINIA: Louise McNeill Pease
WISCONSIN: None
WYOMING: Peggy Simson Curry (recently deceased; succesor to be announced).

Awards and Prizes for Poetry / The 1987 Winners

For the purpose of this list, 1987 winners are those announced during the calendar year 1987; they are arranged alphabetically by name of sponsor.

Academy of American Poets
177 E. 87 St.
New York, NY 10128
   Walt Whitman Award: Judith Baumel, for "The Weight of Numbers."
   Lavan Younger Poet Awards: Jon Davis; Debora Greger, Norman Williams.
   Harold Morton Landon Translation Award: Mark Anderson, for "In The Storm Of Roses," by Ingeborg Bachmann.
   Lamont Poetry Selection: Garrett Kaoru Hongo, for "The River Of Heaven."
   AAP Fellowship: Josephine Jacobsen.

Alabama State Poetry Society
c/o Sue Walker, President
6116 Timberly Rd., N.
Mobile, AL 36609
   Ralph Hammond Contest: First—Carl Morton, for "Poets Lie A Lot"; Second—R. T. Smith, for "Walking to Work; Third—Mary Kroncke, for "How These Burning Winters."
   Alabama State Poetry Society Annual Contest: First—Dorothy W. Worth, for "Overture"; Second—Andrew Dillow, for "Father & Son"; Third—Ann Gasser, for "Twin Sonnets To A Vanishing Wilderness."
   Mary Ward Memorial Contest: First—Elaine McDermott, for "Prelude To The Hunt"; Second—Grace Haynes Smith, for "The Long Dash"; Third—Ann Gasser, for "A Message To Steve From Christa."
   Isabel Morton Poetry Award: First—Glenna Holloway, for "Bee Hive By Night"; Second—Verna Lee Hinegardner, for "Feed Sack To Silk"; Third—Betty Brown Hicks, for "Epistle To Poets."
   Vivian Smallwood Contest: First—Elizabeth House, for "Zip Code Efficiency"; Second—Virginia Julavits, for "New England Sampler"; Third—Kathleen Thompson, for "Borrowed Time."
   Spring Season Contest: First—Grace Haynes Smith, for "The Turtle's Voice"; Second—Lucille Morgan Wilson, for "The Morning Af-ter"; Third—Morton D. Prouty, Jr., for "Raging With Life."
   Brannan Memorial Poetry Contest: First—Grace Haynes Smith, for "Pigeon Sanctuary"; Second—Phillip O'Hern, for "Mute Hands"; Third—Billie Marsh, for "Soap Bubbles."
   Dr. Leslie Lee Gwaltney Memorial Contest: First—Ruth Halbrooke, for "Omnipresence"; Second—Verna Lee Hinegardner, for "Diamond Of Hope"; Third—James W. Proctor, for "When Momma Played."
   William Young Elliott Poetry Contest: First— Helen F. Blackshear, for "Search And Destiny"; Second—Jessie Ruhl Miller, for "On the Edge of Nowhere"; Third—Vivian Smallwood, for "First Love."
   Onzelle Faust Templin Memorial Contest: First—Morton D. Prouty, Jr., for "Evening"; Second—Elaine McDermott, for "Van Gogh's Starry Night"; Third—June Owens, for "Among The Breakers."
   Marjorie Lees Linn Memorial Contest: First—Lucille Morgan Wilson, for "The Grand Marche"; Second—Dr. John T. Morris, for "Sonnet Sequence"; Third—Sue Scalf, for "From the Ruins."
   Nixon R. Daniel Memorial Poetry Contest: First—Vivian Smallwood, for "September Harvest"; Second—Vesle Fenstermaker, for "In Venetian Light"; Third—Stella Worley, for "Hollyhock And Blue Plaid Shirt."
   Riley Nicholas Kelly Award: First—Ann Gasser, for "Echoes In Silence"; Second—June Owens, for "Mood Piece For A Metalurgist"; Third—Elaine McDermott, for "Traveling Highway 13."
   Fall Contest—
   Contest 1: First—Sue Scalf; Second—Agnes Homan; Third—Charles B. Dickson.
   Contest 2: Agnes Homan; Dorothy Winslow Wright; Ruth T. Halbrooks; Sue Scalf; Laquita Thomson; Elaine McDermott; Gertrude B. Byram; Sue Walker; Ida Will Smith; Charles B. Dickson.
   Contest 3: First—Sue Scalf; Second—Dorothy Winslow Wright; Third—Elaine McDermott; Fourth—Charles B. Dickson.

Amelia
P. O. Box 2385
Bakersfield, CA 93303
> *Amelia Awards:* First—David Ray, for "Ajanta,"
> Second—Esther M. Leiper, for "Approach To
> The Second Coming"; Third—Rhina P. Espail-
> lat, for "Theme and Variations."
> *Montegue Wade Award:* Joyce Kahn, for "Sailing
> For The Cup."
> *A & C Limerick Contest:* First—Patty Duffy, for
> "T'was Once A Gay Whale We Dubbed Cisco";
> Second—Gordon Kidd, for "There Once Was A
> Legal Named Blaising"; Third—Dennis C. Cook,
> for "The Wheel Was A Marvelous Fad."
> *Hildegarde Janzen Prizes for Oriental Forms of
> Poetry:* First—Patricia Duffy, for "Bald"; Sec-
> ond—Naomi Sling, for "Fire In Bat Guano";
> Third—Lee Yay Seok, for "Moving In Water."
> *Anna B. Janzen Romantic Poetry Award:* Earl C.
> Pike, for "Untitled."
> *Bernice Jennings Traditional Poetry Award:*
> David Ray, for "Syllabics."
> *Georgie Starbuck Galbraith Light/Humorous
> Verse Awards:* First—Ned Pastor, for "Paradise
> Lost—On Wall Street"; Second—Margaret Bla-
> ker, for "Minerva Cheevy"; Third—Eileen Ma-
> lone, for "Overworked Poetic Expressions."
> *Charles William Duke Longpoem Award:* John
> Gery, for "From 'Davenport's Version' Book IV:
> The Burning Of New Orleans."
> *Lucille Sandberg Haiku Awards:* First—Craig W.
> Steele; Second—H. F. Noyes; Third—Ann Newell.
> *Amelia Student Awards:* First—Kelly Henson, for
> "Sweets & Fruits"; Second—Sandra Sotelo, for
> "Hope."
> *Grace Hines Narrative Poetry Prize:* Don Scho-
> field, for "Summer Rain."
> *Amelia Chapbook Award* (poetry): David Price-
> Gresty, for "Hymnal."
> *Johanna B. Bourgoyne Poetry Prizes:* First—R.
> Nikolas Macioci, for "Kamikaze"; Second—
> Alinda Dickinson Wasner, for "Untitled"; Third—
> Catherine L. Marconi, for "Peace Offering."
> *Amelia Short Poem Prizes:* First—Phebe E. Dav-
> idson, for "Water Bearer"; Second—Elisavietta
> Ritchie, for "Bumper Crop"; Third—Marion
> Ford Park, for "I Want To Go Where Poets Go."
> *Douglas Manning Smith Epic/Heroic Poetry Prize:*
> Alice Morrey Bailey, for "Death of James."
> *Eugene Smith Prizes for Sonnets:* First—Nancy
> Breen, for "One Mother's Story"; Second—
> Marilyn Shea, for "The Abbey At Bath";
> Third—Esther M. Leiper for "An Old Man's
> Early Sleep."

American Academy and Institute of Arts and Letters
633 W. 155th St.

New York, NY 10032-7599
> *Awards in Literature* (poets): Sandra McPherson;
> Robert Phillips.
> *Witter Bynner Poetry Prize:* Antler.
> *Rome Fellowships in Literature:* (this year not
> awarded to a poet).
> *Jean Stein Award:* (this year not awarded for
> poetry).
> Rosenthal Award: Norman Rush, for "Whites."

The American Scholar
United Chapters of Phi Beta Kappa
1811 Q St., N.W.
Washington, DC 20009
> *Mary Ellinore Smith Poetry Prize:* Michael
> Spence, for "The Right Way To Escape From A
> Sinking Ship."

Andrew Mountain Press
P. O. Box 14353
Hartford, CT 06114
> *Memorial Chapbook Series:* Anne Ohman-Youngs,
> for "Markers."

Appalachian Literary League
Griffithsville, WV 25521
> *Davis Grubb Memorial Poetry Award:* Michael
> Joseph Pauley, for "Parade's End."
> *Poetry Competition:* First—Joseph Barrett, for
> "Blue Planet Memoir"; Second—Terrance Hill,
> for "To A Gemini."

Arizona Commission on the Arts
417 W. Roosevelt St.
Phoenix, AZ 85003
> *Fellowships in Poetry:* Rolly Kent; Jim Simmerman.

Artemis
P. O. Box 945
Roanoke, VA 24005
> *Artemis Poetry Contest:* First—Susan Grimes, for
> "Shady Grove Singing"; Second—Barbara Wil-
> son, for "Sitting With Bass Masters, Thinking
> About Love"; Third—Vesle Fernstermaker, for
> "Next Door."

The Artists Foundation, Inc.
110 Broad St.
Boston, MA 02110
> *Massachusetts Artists Fellowship* (poetry): Maria
> Howe; Mary Karr; Thylias Moss; William Pa-
> trick; Candice Reffe; Paula Tatarunis.

Associated Writing Programs
Old Dominion University
Norfolk, VA 23529-0079
> *AWP Award Series in Poetry:* Robin Behn, for
> "Paper Bird."

Atlanta Writing Resource Center
Room 206, The Arts Exchange

750 Kalb St., S.E.
Atlanta, GA 30312

> *Poetry Competition:* First—Kathy May, for "My Grandmother's Hands"; Second—Michael Chitwood, for "Martyrdom Of The Onions"; Ron Hendricks, for "Upon G. C. Murphy's Closing, 1986."

Barnard College
Columbia University
Women Poets at Barnard
3009 Broadway
New York, NY 10027-6598

> *Barnard New Women Poets Prize:* Elizabeth Socolow, for "Laughing At Gravity: Conversations with Isaac Newton."

Bitterroot
P. O. Box 489
Spring Glen, NY 12483

> *William Kushner Award:* First—Antonio Machado, for "Los Ojos (The Eyes)"; Second—Eva Rothberg, for "The Wine Shop"; Third—Vivian Baumgartner, for "Recent Gravestone."
> *Heersche Dovid Badonneh Award:* First—None; Second—Lynn Kozma, for "Sequence"; Third—Elizabeth Bowman Kurz, for "Old Woman."

Blue Unicorn
22 Avon Rd.
Kensington, CA 94707

> *Annual Poetry Contest:* First—Don Welch, for "Sapphire"; Second—Annette Allen, for "The Dark Continent"; Third—June Owens, for "The Carvings of Chauthandi."
> *Carole Elzer Memorial Prize:* Charles Atkinson, for "Elkhorn Slough On A Wedding Anniversary."

The Boston Globe
Public Affairs Dept.
Boston, MA 02107

> *Literary Press Competition* (poetry): Ecco Press, for "The Triumph Of Achilles," by Louise Gluck, and "Poems Of Fernando Pessoa," (edited and translated by Edwin Honig and Susan M. Brown).

Brandeis University
Creative Arts Commission
Waltham, MA 02254

> *Special Recognition in Poetry:* Willilam Meredith.

Bush Artist Fellowships
E-900 First National Bank Building
St. Paul, MN 55101

> *Bush Artist Fellowships* (poets): John Engman; Patricia Hampl.

Byliners of Corpus Christi
P. O. Box 6218
Corpus Christi, TX 78412

> *Byliners Writers Contest* (rhymed poem): First—Shirley J. McKee, for "Aunt Essie's Trunk"; Second—Joy Murphy, for "The Poem"; Third—Martha Fuller, for "A Time To Stay—A Time To Go." (unrhymed poem): First—Kirk Wilson, for "Copperhead"; Second—Dorothy J. Gottschall, for "A Thousand Pardons"; Third—Sarah Patton, for "One of Dot's Freckled Pears."

California State Poetry Society
Helen Shanley, President
6601 Eucalyptus Dr., #97
Bakersfield, CA 93306

> *CQ Poems Competition:* First—Donna Prinzmetal, for "New Mexico"; Second—Denise Dumars, for "A Woman At A Sherlock Holmes Convention"; Third—Sibyl James, for "The Road From Mandalay."
> *Third Dial-A-Poem Contest:* First—Regina de Cormier, for "January 1" and Glenna Holloway, for "Old Wives The Tales Come From"; Second—Mark Defoe, for "In The Tourist Cave" and Claire Peterson, for "Ex Husband"; Third—Israel Halpern, for "Sound Catcher" and Grace Morton for "The Leopard Mansion."
> *Fourth Dial-A-Poem Contest:* First—Diane Wald, for "What She Said When She Sat Up" and Don Schofield, for "Mud And Marble"; Second—Morgan Finn, for "Insubstantial Women" and Timothy Russell, for "In Exitu"; Third—James E. MacWhinney, for "Eating In Forbidden Places" and Nancy Edwards, for "The Road To Nowhere."

Columbia University
Advisory Board on Pulitzer Prizes
New York, NY 10027

> Pulitzer Prize in Poetry: Rita Dove, for "Thomas And Beulah."

Commonwealth Club of California
595 Market St.
San Francisco, CA 94105

> *Silver Medal* (poetry): Gary Snyder, for "Left Out In The Rain: New Poems 1947-1985"; Timothy Steele, for "Sapphics Against Anger And Other Poems."

Crazy Quilt Literary Quarterly
3341 Adams Ave.
San Diego, CA 92116

> *Annual Poetry Contest:* First—Glenna Preston Holloway, for "Weather Message."
> *Southern California Poets' Pen Contest:* First—Elizabeth R. Curry, for "My Father's Death Day"; Second—Barbara Brent Brower, for "Symphonic Variations"; Third—Madeline Tiger, for "The Kinneret."

Cross-Canada Writers' Quarterly
Box 277, Sta. F

Toronto, Ont. M4Y 2L7, Canada
Editors' Prize Writing Competition (poetry):
First—Roberta Olenick, for "Lyell Island";
Second—Carol Malyon, for "Iris"; Third—Bert
Almon, for "Avenida De Juarez"; Fourth—
Allison Beaumont, for "Solstice."
International Prize (this year awarded to a poet):
Denise Duhamel, for "A Pretty Face Considers."

Crowder College
Neosho, MO 64850
Ozark Writers and Artists Guild (poetry): First—
Betty Henderson, for "Inspiration Point"; Sec-
ond—Dick Zahm, for "Untitled"; Third—
Bonnie Schmidt, for "Ode To A Sister-In-Law."

Denver Quarterly
Dept. of English
University of Denver
Denver, CO 80208
Annual Poetry Competition: Mark Rudman, for
"The Bus To The Ruins."

Earthwise Publications
P. O. Box 680-536
Miami, FL 33168
T. S. Eliot Award: Tom Smith, for "Mummer's
Echo."

The Edmonton Journal
Box 2421
Edmonton, Alta. T5J 2S6, Canada
Annual Literary Contest (poetry): First—Derek
Hanebury; Second—Dianne Linden; Mark
McCawley.

Electrum Foundation
2222 Silk Tree Drive
Tustin, CA 92680-7129
Alice Jackson Poetry Prize: First—Billy Collins,
for "Strange Lands"; Second—Joanna Warwick,
for "Frau Lou"; Third—Charles Webb, for
"First Elegy."

George Elliston Poetry Foundation
Elliston Poetry Collection
646 Central Library
University of Cincinnati
Cincinnati, OH 45221
George Elliston Poetry Prize: Walter McDonald,
for "The Flying Dutchman."

Maurice English Foundation for Poetry
2222 Rittenhouse Square
Philadelphia, PA 19103
Maurice English Poetry Award: Philip Booth, for
"Relations: Selected Poems 1950-1985."

Friends of the Chicago Public Library
78 E. Washington St.
Chicago, IL 60602

Carl Sandburg Literary Arts Award: Paul Hoover,
for "Idea."

Georgia State Poetry Society
c/o Edward Davin Vickers
P. O. Box 7695
Atlanta, GA 30357
Laurraine Goreau Memorial Poetry Award:
First—Jeanne Osborne Shaw, for "You Can't
Draw Circles Freehand"; Second—John T. Hen-
dricks, for "May, AM, 1987: Old Man And His
Red Radio Special Wagon"; Third—June Owens,
for "Pale Fire."
Summer Splendor Award: First—Ruth Tiller, for
"Without Knowing"; Second—June Owens, for
"Walking Through Seagull Summer"; Third—
Melanie A. Rawls, for "Summer Storm."
Edward Davin Vickers Award: Dorothy William-
son Worth for "Overture."
Eighth Anniversary Awards (traditional): First—
June Owens, for "Upward, Through Snow";
Second—Ruth Tiller, For "Clocks And Time";
Third—John Hendricks, for "Hoover Rock
Reflections."
Eighth Anniversary Awards (contemporary):
First—Edward Davin Vickers, for "Celebration
By Death"; Second—Beverly V. Head, for
"Through A Neighborhood Silently"; Third—
Betty Maine, for "Endless Marching Names
from Vietnam."
Byron Herbert Reece National Awards—
Literary Ballad: First—John Crawford, for "The
Vengeance of Jehu."
Rhymed Lyric: First—Dorothy Williamson Worth,
for "Villanelle For Spring."
Sonnet: First—Lethe Hunter Bishop, for "In A
Garden Of Blue Ferns."

John Simon Guggenheim Memorial Foundation
90 Park Ave.
New York, NY 10016
Guggenheim Fellowships (poetry): Robert Bring-
hurst; Louise Gluck; Debora Greger; John
Koethe; Sydney Lea; J. D. McClatchy; Katha
Pollitt; Dabney Stuart; C. D. Wright. (poetry
and translation): T. Carmi; Richard Zenith.

Hawaii State Foundation on Culture and the Arts/
Hawaii Literary Arts Council
Governor's Office
Honolulu, HI 96813
Hawaii Award for Literature (this year awarded
to a poet): M. S. Merwin.

Chester H. Jones Foundation
P. O. Box 498
Chardon, OH 44024
National Poetry Competition: First—Victoria Re-
del, for "Soke Crazy Dancing"; Second—Naomi

Clark, for "The Congregation"; Third—Roger Mitchell, for "Why We're Here"; Fourth—Leonard Kress, for "Poppy Seeds."

Kansas Quarterly
Denison Hall
Kansas State University
Manhattan, KS 66506

KQ/Kansas Arts Commission Awards (poetry): First— Bruce Cutler, for "From The Book Of Naples: Angelita"; Second—Tom Hansen, for "Reflections On Wittgenstein" and B. D. Love, for "Grace."

Seaton Awards: First—Carol Hebald, for "Fantasy In A Floating Cafe Aboard A Cruise Ship Somewhere Near Southampton," Elmer Suderman, for "Saturday Night In The Depression," and Michael L. Johnson, for "Delirium Tremens"; Second—Daniel Glynn, for "First Geese," Jim Thomas, for "On Grace," Adej Ross, for "Your Bavarian Cremes," Victor Contoski, for "The Things Of The Dead," Till McPherron, for "Front Porch," and Ken Shedd, for "The Inheritance". Third—Mahlon Coop, for "Birdcall," Bruce Cutler, for "From The Book Of Naples: Angelita," Ken Shedd, for "We Were Drinking Margaritas," and Carol Hebald, for "Letter To A Gay Artist Aboard A Cruise Ship Somewhere Near Stockholm"; Fourth—Steve Hind, for "A Kind Of Divorce," Thomas Hawkins, for "The Tractor Driver," and Vic Contoski, for "Conversation Over Hot Coffee."

Kentucky State Poetry Society
c/o James W. Proctor, Contest Chairman
505 Southland Blvd.
Louisville, KY 40214

Grand Prize: First—Jennifer B. McPherson, for "The Explorer"; Second—Myrtle Marmaduke, for "And Having Writ, Moves On"; Third—Henry Jacquez, for "Mary's Request."

Stuart Speckter Memorial Award: First—L. Bradley Law, for "White Irises In The Vase"; Second—Sylvia Turk Weinberg, for "Album"; Third—Elizabeth W. Schmitt, for "Love Poem—1943"; Fourth—Verna Lee Hinegardner, For "To The Bride."

Through A Child's Eyes (elementary students): First—Kate Coltharp, for "What Camping Is All About"; Second—Erik Scott, for "My Bus Driver"; Third—Amanda Jo Hardman, for "Fireflies."

On Golden Trails (elementary students): First—Chris Jones, for "Best Friends"; Second—Matthew Anderson, for "The Skier"; Third—Christopher Rees, for "The Icy Sabers"; Fourth—Jason Coltharp, for "Snow."

High School Poets: Second—David Wesley Poe,

for "Gone Again"; Third—Lenora Roberts, for "Friends And What We Have To Do."

College Poets: First—Lisa Calderon, for "Miracles Of Life"; Second—Darlene Miller, for "Alone"; Third—Charlene Davison, for "You Linger Still."

Let's Get Acquainted: First—Darling Harris Pate, for "Circles"; Second—Elsie Klute, for "In Staring"; Third—Daniel L. Nelson, for "Midway."

Kentucky Women: First—Charles M. Whitt, for "Logan Woman"; Second—L. Bradley Law, for "Eulogy For A Common-Law Wife"; Third—Grace Haynes Smith, for "Someone Walks In The Twilight."

Wind/Literary Journal Award: First—L. Bradley Law, for "The Sweet Suffering Of Misplaced Hours"; Second—Vonnie Thomas, for "The House Of Elizabeth Bishop"; Third—Thelma Scott Kiser, for "Preference, Saltbox"; Fourth—Donald R. Maley, for "Cygnet Song."

Traditional Award: First—Judy Gill Milford, for "I. C. U."; Second—Deborah Adams, for "Joan D'Arc—Trial By Fire"; Third—Cecilia Parsons Miller, for "The Question We Pursue."

Swamps: First—Deborah Adams, for "Why Lucas Finley Gave Up Gin For Good"; Second—Grace Haynes Smith, for "On Canoeing Through Okefenokee"; Third—Roger Selvidge, for "Everglades."

Haiku (single): First—Miriam Bralley Campbell, for "Poplars Are Fingers"; Second—Miriam Woolfolk, for "Hot Month To Have A Child"; Third—Fran Cornett, for "The Old Rooster's Crow."

Haiku Sequence: First—Ann Gasser, for "Yasaka In Snow"; Second—Dorothy Swaner Daniels, for "The Long Night"; Third—Grace Haynes Smith, for "Phantom: Summer Night."

Let Freedom Ring: First—Lila Borg Rohrer, for "On December 7, 1941"; Second—Donald R. Maley, for "The Circle"; Third—Mary Ernestine O'Dell, for "Freedom's Cost."

Bread: First—LaNita Lane Moses, for "Midnight Shadow"; Second—Grace Haynes Smith, for "Bread is The Need Of The World"; Third—Louise Lamar, for "La Pandaderia."

Holding on to Life: First—Mary Ernestine O'Dell, for "If At First . . ."; Second—Grace Haynes Smith, for "The Parable Of The Elm"; Third—Donald R. Maley, for "Garden Burial."

Ben Ray Memorial Award: First—Grace Haynes Smith, for "My Polonius"; Second—Beatrice G. Holt, for "Latin IV"; Third—James R. O'Dell, for "A Sum Of Fingers."

Mountain Ballad: First—Nida E. Jones, for "Ballad of The Phantom Bell"; Second—Deborah Adams, for "The Wife Of Sarlis

Shadd"; Third—Rachel Branch Shelton, for "Legend Of Three Friends."

A Grin to Help You Bear It: First—Jewell Newburn, for "Sailor's Wife"; Second—Barbara Shirk Parish, for "Family History: Surprise Ending"; Third—Ann Gasser, for "At G. N. C. (General Nutrition Center)."

Sunrise, Sunset: First—L. Bradley Law, for "The Child King's Blessing"; Second—Thelma Scott Kiser, for "Growing Pains"; Third—Jeani Picklesimer, for "Serenade."

The Land and Its People: First—L. Bradley Law, for "Steps of Mystic Understanding"; Second—Ernestine Gravley, for "Kentucky, My Kentucky"; Third—Faye Kaestner, for "Old Brown Woman."

James T. Ellington Memorial Award: First—Thelma Scott Kiser, for "A Day With Grandad"; Second—Grace Haynes Smith, for "Grandfather's Victory"; Third—Alice Mackenzie Swaim, for "Evening at Grandfather's."

World Peace Award: First—Hazel T. Ray, for "At The Edge Of Boston Commons"; Second—Lucy Ann Marsh, for "All Men"; Third—L. Bradley Law, for "We Seldom Choose To Speak Of Common Things."

Black And All Colors Are Beautiful: First—Harry B. Sheftel, for "Soliloquy"; Second—Barbara Shirk Parish, for "Last Battle"; Third—Verna Lee Hinegardner, for "1985 Reunion On Iwo Jima."

Philip A. Moore Memorial Award: First—L. Bradley Law, for "Yellow Ledgers and Empty Envelopes"; Second—Ernestine Gravley, for "Leaving The Old Home"; Third—Barbara Shirk Parish, for "Mother Of Twelve."

Jesse Stuart: First—Ernestine Gravley, for "Hope Incessant"; Second—Charles M. Whitt, for "Healing"; Third—Jeani Picklesimer, for "Cradles For Jesse."

Bertha Law Memorial Award: First—Mary Alice Countess, for "Tease"; Second—Betty Jane Simpson, for "Quiet Mist"; Third—Barbara Barnard Greer, for "Lady Saviour."

Blank Verse Award: First—Grace Haynes Smith, for "Inherit The Earth"; Second—Thelma Scott Kiser, for "Still Life In July"; Third—Betty Jane Simpson, for "The Old Soddie."

Dr. Vernon O. Kash Memorial: First—Donald R. Maley, for "Back Talk"; Second—Mary Ernestine O'Dell, for "Like Mary"; Third—Jeani Picklesimer, for "Female Touch."

Evelyn & William Pate Memorial: First—L. Bradley Law, for "The Theory Of The Leash And Collar"; Second—Burdell Swain, for "Patience"; Third—Barbara Shirk Parish, for "Hereford."

Engle's Angle Award: First—Beatrice G. Holt, for "Today Not Yesterday"; Second—Sylvia Turk Weinberg, for "Safe Talk"; Third—Alice Mackenzie Swaim, for "This Deathless Stallion."

Villanelle: First—Donald R. Maley, for "Sweet Singer, Bid The Music Cease To Be"; Second—Deborah Adams, for "Walking To The Light"; Third—Marguerite A. Brewster, for "Full Spinnakers' Red Gleam."

Apprentice Award: First—Sandi Girdley, for "Ballad Of The Unicorns."

Journeyman Award: First—L. Bradley Law, for "Among The Things Of This Room"; Second—Barbara Barnard Greer, for "Terra Femina"; Third—Timothy Russell, for "Vigilance."

Bond Between Youth and Age: First—Grace Haynes Smith, for "Another Socrates"; Second—Hazel Firth Goddard, for "Verse Maker?"; Third—Esther Priest Brewer, for "Let's Save A Place For Jim."

President's Award: (No Nukes is Good Nukes): First—Donald R. Maley, for "The Answer"; Second—Charles M. Whitt, for "Old Tires"; Third—Jeani Picklesimer, for "Dichotomy."

Doris Publications Literary Award: First—Linda Frisa, for "Paper Dolls"; Second—Deborah Adams, for "Missing Ingredients"; Third—Timothy Russell, for "At The Window."

Bless the Beasts (dogs and cats): First—Ann Gasser, for "Sparks In The Snow"; Second—Grace Haynes Smith, for "Terrier Passing"; Third—Judy Gill Milford, for "J. J. And The Intruder."

Bob Ward Memorial: First—Ann Gillgam, for "Kayak"; Second—Harry B. Sheftel, for "Rites"; Third—Sister Mary Martina, for "Sufficiency."

The Kindred Spirit
Rt. 2, Box 111
St. John, KS 67576

Groovy Gray Cat Poetry Contest: First—Mary Lou Pilkinton, for "Straw"; Second—Jennifer Jesseph, for "Poem On A Compact"; Third—John Eberly, for "Interpersonal Communications," R. Franklin Pate, for "Long Distance," Sandra A. Fender, for "Humanity," Jallelah Karriem, for "In A Deep Breath," and Janet McCann, for "Explanation."

Ellen La Forge Memorial Poetry Foundation
6 Plympton St.
Cambridge, MA 02138

Grolier Poetry Prize: Iain Higgins; Susan Wheeler.

Grolier Poetry Peace Prize: Lowell Jaeger, for "Ernesto De Fiori's Soldier."

League of Canadian Poets
24 Ryerson Ave.
Toronto, Ont. M5T 2P3, Canada

Lowther Memorial Award: Heather Spears, for "How To Read Faces."
Lampert Memorial Award: Rosemary Sullivan, for "The Space A Name Makes."
F. R. Scott Translation Award: Gertrude Sanderson, for "Within A Mystery."

Lincoln College
Lincoln, IL 62656
Billee Murray Denny Poetry Award: First—Marjorie Stelmach, for "Playing The Long Joke"; Second—Arlene Jones, for "Madonna Del Parto"; Third—Chris Donodeo, for "Snow White At Sunrise."

The Literary Review
Fairleigh Dickinson University
285 Madison Ave.
Madison, NJ 07940
Charles Angoff Awards (poetry): Eamon Grennan, for "Jewell Box"; David Hopes, for "The Saint Francis Poems."

Loft-McKnight Writers Awards
2301 E. Franklin Ave.
Minneapolis, MN 55406
Loft-McKnight Awards (poetry): John Caddy; Louis Jenkins; Barton Sutter; Cary Waterman.
Loft-Mentor Series (poetry): Barrie Jean Borich; Jennifer Jesseph; Jerry Neren; Patricia Zontelli.

Long Island University
C. W. Post Poetry Center
Brookville, NY 11548
Young Poets of Long Island/Floyd Lyon Award: Ian Brand, for "John Coltrane (A Lament)."
Poetry Center Awards: Undergraduate/Winthrop Palmer Award—Bill Dunne, for "A Sonnet To James T. Farrell"; Graduate—Edward Dumas, for "A Moment Of Disturbance On The Expressway"; Alumni—Olga Abella, for "First Love"; Staff—Barbara Thomson, for "Even On Christmas"; Faculty—R. B. Weber, for "Cello Lovers."
Post Library Association Community Award: Susan Astor, for "Spider Lies."

Los Angeles Times
Times Mirror Square
Los Angeles, CA 90053
Book Prize (poetry): William Meredith, for "Partial Accounts: New And Selected Poems."

Louisiana State Poetry Society
c/o Jessica Gonsoulin, Contest Chairperson
2300 Severn Ave., #L-201
Metairie, LA 70001
Annual Poetry Day Contest—
Myths and Legends: First—Arlyle Mansfield Losse, for "Pygmalion And Galatea" and Ruth Shaver Means, for "The Magic Chain Of

Asgard"; Third—Grace Haynes Smith, for "Sestina On The Abduction Of Helen."
Nostalgia: First—Darla Burris, for "When Grandpa Used To Mow"; Second—Grace Haynes Smith, for "September Fields"; Third—Betty Jane Simpson, for "Deja Vu."
Peace: Lila Borg Rohrer, for "If I Were Starman"; Second—Lila Borg Rohrer, for "Peace Raggedy Man"; Third—William Schroll, for "The Quest."
Inspirational Poem: First—Miriam J. Smithers, for "Prayer"; Second—Todd Michael Phillips, for "Harriette, The Bag Lady"; Third—Trebor H. Taylor, for "Beginner At 81."
Humorous Poem: First—Elizabeth House, for "Sexpanation"; Second—Betty Jane Simpson, for "Psychedelic Speller"; Third—Alice Mackenzie Swaim, for "Did You Notice?"
Traditional Haiku: First—Linda Swift Reeder, for "Seven Cawing Crows"; Second—Todd Michael Phillips, for "Four Little Ducklings."

The Lyric
307 Dunton Dr., S.W.
Blacksburg, VA 24060
Lyric Memorial Prize: Marthe E. Bosworth, for "November Violets."
Nathan Haskell Dole Prize: Marion Shore, for "Oje Doesn't Die."
Roberts Memorial Prize: Elsie B. Kurz, for "Theater."
Leitch Memorial Prize: Kay Harvey, for "Contemporary Love Song."
Virginia Prize: Vonnie Thomas, for "The Final Bill Is Here—Is Fair."
New England Prize: Jason Sommer, for "Lachrymal."
Muriel Craft Bailey Prize: Cecil J. Mullins, for "New Rules."
Margaret Haley Carpenter Prize: Mildred Dunetz, for "World Narrowed Down."
Louise Hajek Prize: Rhina P. Espaillat, for "Reading" and Caroline Rowe Martens, for "A Psychologist Evaluates Santa."
College Poetry Contest: First—Bradin Cormack, for "Horus Watches Over The Child Ramses"; Second—Katherine Riegal, for "Sonnet: Dreaming"; Third—Marilyn Carder, for "Locked Courtyard And Sculpture."

Midwest Poetry Review
Box 776
Rock Island, IL 61201
Autumn Gold Contest: First—Helen J. Alsop, for "Autumn's Last Sunset"; Second—Christine Christian, for "October Walk"; Third—Verna Lee Hinehardner, for "Autumn Stars."
Gala Contest: Grand Award—Lolete Falck Bar-

low, for "Shenandoah Sunday"; Second—Pat Anthony, for "Sincerely"; Third—Marcia Wilkins Grant, for "Symphony"; Fourth—Nancy Niemeyer Graham, for "A Shadow Stirs"; Fifth—Jo Hoover, for "A Queen Incarnate"; Junior Award—Dawn, for "Center Stage, Left."

The Nation/New Hope Foundation
72 Fifth Ave.
New York, NY 10011
Lenore Marshall/Nation Prize for Poetry: Donald Hall, for "The Happy Man."

Natinal Book Critics Circle
c/o Robert Harris
4000 Tunlaw Rd., N.W., #1019
Washington, D.C. 20007
Poetry Award: Edward Hirsch, for "Wild Gratitude."

National Endowment for the Arts
The Literature Program
1100 Pennsylvania Ave., N.W.
Washington, DC 20506
Fellowships (poetry): P. Chase Twichell; Naomi H. Clark; Corrinne Hales; Philip Levine; Duncan W. McNaughton; Benjamin Saltman; Anne Winters; Jeffrey T. Skinner; Gerald R. Stern; Mary L. Swander; Julia A. Alvarez; Li-Young Lee; Michael J. Van Walleghen; Michael J. Heffernan; Tony D. Hoagland; Robert B. Shaw; Jane Shore; Geraldine R. Connolly; Deborah L. Digges; Baron C. Wormser; Stephen H. Tudor; Deborah A. Keenan; Sherod A. Santos; Tom R. Sleigh; Jimmy S. Baca; Ruth E. Borson; Phillip O. Foss; Laurel Blossom; Nancy Lee Couto; David J. Dwyer; Irving M. Feldman; Allen Ginsberg; Daniel Halpern; Brooks Haxton; Richard J. Howard; Joan Larkin; David C. Lehman; Joseph D. McClatchy; Robert R. Morgan; Ed Sanders; Armand Schwerner; Michael A. McFee; John Skoyles; Terry R. Hummer; Christopher I. Bursk; John Repp; Sharon Bryan; Robert J. McNamara; Mark A. Doty; David W. Romtvedt.
Senior Fellowship (one awarded to a poet this year): Thomas McGrath.

National Federation of State Poetry Societies
c/o Amy Jo Zook, Contest Chairman
3520 State Rd. 56
Mechanicsburg, OH 43044
NFSPS Award: First—Susan D. Tucker, for "Felinity"; Second—Frank M. Decaria, for "Bird On The Ice"; Third—Alfred Dorn, for "Walking Home."
Ward Fulcher Memorial Award: First—Ann Sandifur, for "Underwater With Lilies"; Second—Grace Haynes Smith, for "Sestina Written Under Stars"; Third—Grace Simpson, for "Elephants At The Salt Cave."

Poetry Society of Texas Award: First—Ernestine Hoff Emrick, for "White On White"; Second—Cathryn Essinger, for "Patching The Sky"; Third—Rod Best, for "Interstate."
Jack Murphy Appreciation Award: First—Marianne McFarland McNeil, for "The Winds Of Change"; Second—Lucille Morgan Wilson, for "Voice Of The Quarter Past Ten"; Third—Grace Haynes Smith, for "Andromache's Goodbye."
NFSPS Past President's Award: First—Patricia S. Grimm, for "The Prince"; Second—Violette Newton, for "Critics At The Retrospective"; Third—Sy Swann, for "Letter To My Piano Pedagogue."
Florida State Poets Award: First—Lou Layman, for "Innocence"; Second—Ruth Shaver Means, for "Created On The Eighth Day—A Poet"; Third—Max Golightly, for "Love Letter To An Unrealized Idea."
John A. Lubbe Memorial Award: First—J. A. Totts, for "Seven Springs"; Second—John Bart Gerald, for "Double You"; Third—Clara Laster, for "Mother In Waiting."
Music Award: First—Joy Gresham Hagstrom, for "Lyrics Born Of Prayer"; Second—J. William Griffin, for "Living In The Music"; Third—Robert Vessey, for "Sound Track Of Heaven."
Beymorlin Sonnet Award: First—Meredith R. Cook, for "Nightmare"; Second—Jack E. Murphy, for "Bonus Hours"; Third—Patty McCoy Horton for "Metamorphosis."
Leona Jones Smith Award: First—Patricia S. Grimm, for "The Fungus"; Second—David L. Byrn, for "Principal's Lament"; Third—Marion Brimm Rewey, for "My Brother In Sunlight And Shadow."
Mary Ellen Riddell No. 88 Award: First—Marie Davis McCobbin, for "The Benchwarmers"; Second—Marcella Siegel, for "Joint Venture"; Third—Helen Mar Cook, for "An Old Woman Looks At Old Barns."
Arlena Robbins Honorary Award: First—Deborah Adams, for "The Valiant"; Second—Vonnie Thomas, for "The Mason-Dixon Line Has Been Erased"; Third—Robert M. Howell, for "Steamboat Whistle."
Alabama State Poetry Society Award: First—Barbara Brent Brower, for "Remembering Bread In The Morning"; Second—Kittie Yeager, for "A Rag Doll Named Katie"; Third—Donna Thomas, for "Campsite With Ghosts."
Indiana Federation Award: First—Lois Beebe Hayna, for "Second Sight"; Second—Rose Ann Spaith, for "Mid-Life Career Change"; Third—Harriett G. Hunt, for "Broken Dreams."
Amelia Reynolds Long Award: First—Carlee

Swann, for "Advice To Sister, Or Better Than A Top, Sis"; Second—Anita Tanner, for "Oh To Be Tan"; Third—Meredith R. Cook, for "Dead Reckoning."

Arkansas Award: First—Violette Newton, for "The Cameras Rolled"; Second—Esther M. Leiper, for "Tale Of A Whittling Woman"; Third—Kitty Yeager, for "Arkansas Sesquicentennial."

Poetry Society Of Oklahoma Award: First—Ida Fasel, for "Staying"; Second—Sy Swann, for "Migrants"; Third—Kathi Hill, for "Wilderness Cocoon."

American Indian Heritage Award: First—Glenna Holloway, for "No Man Can Sell What He Does Not Own"; Second—Linda Hutton, for "(Haiku) Abandoned Teepee"; Third—Pat DeWitt, for "Spirit Wind."

South Dakota Award: First—Dorothy W. North, for "Off The Trail"; Second—Doris K. Ferguson, for "Snapshot In Sepia"; Third—Agnes Homan, for "Under A White Moon."

Manningham Award: First—Dian S. Barnett, for "Won By A Nose!"; Second—Pearl Bloch Segall, for "Alison"; Third—Shirley S. Stevens, for "Visa Vise."

Humorous Award: First—Richard Bodner, for "Ballott Dancing"; Second—Robert M. Howell, for "Salute"; Third—Mary Lou Gipson, for "Pill Age"

Modern Award: First—Mary Logan Sweet, for "Apartment House Windows"; Second—Alfred Dorn, for "Walking On Wall Street"; Third—Grace Simpson, for "Dog Day."

Traditional Award: First—Victoria Gibson, for "Franz Hals: A Jester With A Lute"; Second—Stella Worley, for "Conversation With A Fire Tender"; Third—Marion Brimm Rewey, for "Line Drawing At Swan Cove."

Mabel Meadows Staats Award: First—Alfred Dorn, for "Books"; Second—Jules M. Klagge, for "Envy"; Third—June Owens, for "Making The Pieces Sing."

Evans Spencer Wall Award: First—Lois Beebe Hayna, for "Ink Gardens"; Second—Helen Kenney, for "Letter To The World"; Third—June Owens, for "Wind From The Wings."

Arizona State Poetry Society Award: First—Agnes J. Homan, for "Early Harvest"; Second—Marion Brimm Rewey, for "Misreading The Tea Leaves In A Local Tea Room"; Third—Arthur Madson, for "Of Lines."

Louisiana Award: First—Benny McAdams, for "The Bone Pipe"; Second—Helen S. Riik, for "Song Of The Bridges"; Third—Jack E. Murphy, for "Quick Learning."

Wisconsin Poetry Award: First—Diane Glancy, for "Old Eskimo Woman"; Second—Grace

Simpson, for "Snake Time"; Third—Betty Strickland Kersh, for "Duck Hunter."

Verse Writers' Guild of Ohio Award: First—Paula G. Fehn, for "The Jade Flute"; Second—Max Golightly, for "Prairie Song"; Third—Grace Simpson, for "Closing In."

Poet Laureate of Texas Award: First—Clara Laster, for "Into A Gopher-Wood Womb Of Weeping"; Second—Ida Fasel, for "Journey Less Longer Than It Seems"; Third—Marion Brimm Rewey, for "Touchstone."

Leona Lloyd Memorial Award: First—Harriet G. Hunt, for "Wing Dust"; Second—Billie Menifee, for "Bittersweet Realization"; Third—Cynthia C. Bergen, for "The Looking Glass."

Poetry Society of Tennessee Award: First—Nancy Esther James, for "Sarah, Aunt Martha, And The Bottles"; Second—Ernestine Gravley, for "Song Of The Poet"; Third—Ruth Stewart Schenley, for "Dumb Innocence."

West Virginia Award: First—Harriet Stovall Kelley, for "Yonahlossee"; Second—R. Franklin Pate, for "A Tour Of The Mine"; Third—Marcella Siegel, for "Mountain Music Man."

Perryman-Visser Award: First—Patty McCoy Horton, for "Mr. Browning, How You Prevaricate!"; Second—Kitty Yeager, for "Timothy's Terror"; Third—Nelle Fertig, for "Having Weathered The Storms Until Retirement."

Massachusetts Award: First—Patricia A. Lawrence, for "The Devil's Purse"; Second—LaVon B. Carroll, for "Echoes of Fern Hill"; Third—Maureen Cannon, for "Monk, Running."

New York Poetry Forum Award: First—Violette Newton, for "To See, To See"; Second—Marion Brimm Rewey, for "Agatha"; Third—Harriett Messer, for "The Duccio Block."

Rhode Island Award: First—Gene Fehler, for "War Wound"; Second—Vivian Ricker, for "Unclaimed Heritage"; Third—Joy Gresham Hagstrom, for "Nurse In Appalachia."

Ethel B. Allen Memorial Award: First—Richard Bodner, for "After A Short Sleep In The Bitteroots"; Second—William Schroll, for "Ghost-Birds"; Third—Lois Beebe Hayna, for "Still Life But Still My Life."

Tri-City Poetry Society Award: First—Phyllis Mahn Potter, for "Flying Past The Moon"; Second—Mildred Williams Boggs, for "In The Old Graveyard"; Third—Florence A. Kotraba, for "Cleaning The Fish Catch."

Earthwise "Save Our World" Award: First—Mareye Yeates, for "Chernobyl"; Second—Vera L. Eckert, for "The Question"; Third—Dian S. Barnett, for "This Tiny Planet."

Kentucky State Poetry Society Award: First—LaVonn B. Carroll, for "Country Autumns

Past"; Second—Kay Ellison, for "Fortress"; Third—Helen Bradford, for "On The Turntable."
Poetry Society of Michigan Award: First—Maxine Jennings, for "For Jane Ambrosia Hemmings"; Second—Dian S. Bennett, for "The Gift"; Third—David L. Byrn, for "The Seeds Of Silence."
Foster Sonnet Award: First—Clarence P. Socwell, for "Young Runaway Returns"; Second—Vivian Ricker, for "The Portrait"; Third—Vonnie Thomas, for "Misplaced Jewels At My Love's Feet."
Bessie Archer Smith Memorial Award: First—Marion Brimm Rewey, for "Sing A Song Of Sarah"; Second—Jeani Picklesimer, for "Twisted Oak"; Third—Maxine Jennings, for "Christa's Story."
New Madrid Writers Award: First—Diane Glancy, for "Daughter Of Delight"; Second—Margaret E. Slack, for "Madness"; Third—James W. Proctor, for "Telling Liz Goodbye."
Nevada Poetry Society Award: First—June Owens, for "Why The Sea Sings Lovesongs"; Second—Jessie Ruhl Miller, for "Time Has Laid His Hand Gently"; Third—Lily D. Angle, for "Sonnet To A Sonnet."
Inspirational Lyric Award: First—Jeanette Maes, for "A Word To The Wise Is Sufficient"; Second—Eve Braden-Hatchett, for "The Greatest Port"; Third—Patricia A. Lawrence, for "Brush Fire Along The Marsh."
Lighten Your Life Award: Alfhild Wallen, for "Once In Portugal"; Second—Mary L. R. Johnson, for "My Sister's Cat"; Third—Yvonne Hardenbrook, for "On Getting Word That."
Phillipp and Christine Cook Hammann Award: First—Clara Laster, for "A Leaf Of Laurel Love (Ruth Speaking)"; Second—Grace Simpson, for "My Lord Lay Low"; Third—Ernestine Gravley, for "Stable Boy."
Student Award: First—Michelle Stoll, for "Momentarily Captured"; Second—Joy Kennedy, for "California/Byzantium"; Third—Doug Hambel, for "Stephen Crane."

National Poetry Series
26 W. 17th St.
New York, NY 10011
Open Competition: Jeffrey Harrison, for "The Singing Underneath"; Marie Howe, "The Good Thief"; William Olsen, for "The Hand Of God And A Few Bright Flowers"; Jeffrey Skinner, for "A Guide To Forgetting"; Leigh Cole Swensen, for "New Math."

New England Review and Bread Loaf Quarterly
Middlebury College
Middlebury, VT 05753

Narrative Poetry Prize: Lucie Brock-Broido, for "Elective Mutes."

New Jersey State Council on the Arts
109 W. State St., CN 306
Trenton, NJ 08625
Fellowship Awards in Poetry: Sheila Cowling; Michael D. Madonick; Carol Becker; Dina Cole; Joe-Anne M. McLaughlin; Lynn C. Powell; Rod Tulloss; Richard E. Grazide; Victoria A. Reiners; J. Allyn Rosser; Penelope S. Schott; Madeline J. Tiger.

New Mexico, State of
Office of the Governor
Santa Fe, NM 87503
Award for Literature (poetry): Sabine Ulibarri.

New York Community Trust and Community Funds
415 Madison Ave.
New York, NY 10017
Oscar Williams and Gene Derwood Fund Award: W. S. Merwin.

Nimrod
Arts & Humanities Council of Tulsa
2210 S. Main
Tulsa, OK 74114-1190
Pablo Neruda Prize for Poetry: First—Lisa Steinman, for "A Book Of Other Days"; Second—Lucia Cordell Getsi, for "Intensive Care."

92nd Street Y
The Poetry Center
1395 Lexington Ave.
New York, NY 10128
"Discovery"/The Nation Contest: Fred O. Baysa, for "Ka Anahulu"; Nancy Eimers, for "Rose-Fever"; Florence Grossman, for "Gale Meadow"; David Mura, for "Revery In Hawaii."

Alfred B. Nobel Foundation
Nobel House
Sturegatan 14
11436 Stockholm, Sweden
Nobel Prize in Literature (this year awarded to a poet): Joseph Brodsky.

North American Mentor Magazine
Fennimore, WI 53809
Annual Poetry Contest: First—Robert Hays, for "Shape On The Coronardo Ferry"; Second—Emil Schmit, for "Big River"; Third—Linda and Stephen Colley, for "Daisies Are Pinwheeling."

North Carolina Literary and Historical Association
109 E. Jones St.
Raleigh, NC 27611
Roanoke-Chowan Award for Poetry: Charles Edward Eaton, for "New And Selected Poems, 1942-1987."

North Carolina Poetry Society
c/o Sam L. McKay
12 Knollwood Dr.
P. O. Box 160
Broadway, NC 27505

Thomas H. McDill Award: First—Richard DeLos Mar, for "Harbor"; Second—D. L. McCollum, for "Winter Winds"; Third—Rebecca Rust, for "Today My Right Heel Hurts Again."

Sidney Lanier Award: First—Anne F. Stuck, for "The Jung Man"; Second—Alice Carver Cramer, for "Old Snapshot"; Third—Emily Exner Chi, for "You've Come A Long Way."

Caldwell W. Nixon, Jr. Award: First—Mollie W. Christie, for "The Party"; Second—D. L. McCollum, for "Saturday Night"; Third—Janet Adkins, for "Clyde Of Port Clyde."

Brotherhood Award: First—Amy Hernandez, for "For Charles"; Second—Ree Young, for "George Turns 60"; Third—Billie Marsh, for "The Brotherhood Of Grey Men."

Carl Sandburg Award: First—Ree Young, for "For The Sake Of Brevity"; Second—Lucille Morgan Wilson, for "Albuquerque"; Third—Kinloch Rivers, for "That Trip By Train In January."

Ogden Nash Award: First—Mollie Christie, for "Yuppie Nouvelle"; Second—Janet Adkins, for "Poetic License"; Third—Nina A. Wicker, for "This Line Forms To The Left."

Sallie Paschall Award: First—Elizabeth Roberts, for "Leak In Stable Roof"; Second—Nancy Frost Rouse, for "Eggs On The Table"; Third—Hazel Foster Thomas, for "White Morning Glories."

Hayman "America" Award: First—Raymond Dotson, for "Divinin' Joe Murtie"; Second—Marie Kennedy Robins, for "Port Of Carolina"; Third—Elizabeth Roberts, for "Memorial Day Parade."

Travis Tuck Jordan Award: First—Wendy Gatewood, for "Great Grandmother"; Second—Jacqueline Kellum, for "The Unicorn"; Third—Elizabeth Gardner, for "Friendship."

Marie Barringer Rogers Award: First—Lilla Somerville, for "No Exit"; Second—Martha McLean, for "To Catch A Sky"; Third—Sara Layton, for "The Rose."

Poet Laureate Award: Nancy Frost Rouse, for "Wildflowers."

Zoe Kincaid Brockman Book Award: Charles Edward Eaton, for "The Work Of The Wrench."

Northeastern University Press
English Dept.
Boston, MA 02115

Samuel French Morse Poetry Prize: Yvonne Sapia, for "The Rooms Of Ruined Light."

Owl Creek Press
1620 N. 45th, #205
Seattle, WA 98113

Owl Creek Press Poetry Book Award: Dennis Nurkse, for "Staggered Lights."

Owl Creek Press Chapbook Contest: Jan Minich, for "Occasional Starlight."

Pacific Northwest Writers Conference
1811 NE 199th
Seattle, WA 98155

High School Contest (poetry): First—Ben Hanson, for "The Moon"; Second—Cynthia Schuh, for "Hard Days"; Third—Natalie McNair, for "On The Lady Walking."

Adult Creative Writing Contest (poetry): First—Arlene E. Paul, for "There's A Mark On Our House"; Second—Lynn Rigby Schott, for "Five Poems: Seasons Of The River"; Third—Amelia Haller, for "From The Potter's Wheel."

The Paris Review
45-39 171st Place
Flushing, NY 11358

Bernard F. Conners Poetry Prize: John Koethe, for "Mistral."

Passages North
William Bonifas Fine Arts Center
7th St. and 1st Ave., S.
Escanaba, MI 49829

Michigan Sesquicentennial Poetry Competition: First—Laura Kasischke, for "Parade"; Second—John Palen, for "For Ann On Her 21st Birthday"; Third—Tom Murdock, for "Horses."

Phillips Exeter Academy
Exeter, NH 03833

George Bennett Fellowship: This year awarded to a prose writer.

Poet Lore
The Writer's Center
7815 Old Georgetown Rd.
Bethesda, MD 20814-2415

John Williams Andrews Narrative Poetry Contest: Paul Allen, for "Youngblood Tells Beekman And Jimmy, Jr. About Crow."

Ratner-Ferber Prize: Michael Pfeifer, for "Red Cadillac" and Maureen Seaton, for "The Bell Tower."

Poetry
60 W. Walton St.
Chicago, IL 60610

Levinson Prize: Stephen Dunn.

Oscar Blumenthal Prize: Tess Gallagher.

Eunice Tietjens Memorial Prize: Gregory Djanikian.

Bess Hokin Prize: Ralph Angel.
Frederick Bock Prize: Kevin Stein.

Poetry Society of America
15 Gramercy Park
New York, NY 10003
Alice Fay Di Castagnola Award: Harriet Levin.
Shelley Memorial Award: Mona Van Duyn.
William Carlos Williams Award: Alicia Ostriker, for "The Imaginary Lover."
Norma Farber First Book Award: Aleda Shirley, for "Chinese Architecture."
Robert H. Winner Memorial Award: Marilyn Hacker.
Gustav Davidson Memorial Award: Rhina P. Espaillat.
John Masefield Memorial Award: Nancy Nahra.
Lucille Medwick Memorial Award: Terese Svoboda.
Melville Cane Award: Lewis Tirco, for "Visions And Revisions Of American Poetry."
Cecil Hemley Memorial Award: Carolyne Wright.
Celia B. Wagner Award: Craig Taylor.
Consuelo Ford Award: Arthur Smith.
Gertrude B. Claytor Memorial Award: Charles Fishman.
Mary Carolyn Davies Memorial Award: Gardiner Quartermaine.
Gordon Barber Memorial Award: Nancy Esposito.
Elias Lieberman Student Poetry Award: Sharon Solomon.
Emily Dickinson Award: Flavia R. Prishtina.
Ruth Lake Memorial Award: Justine Buisson.

Poetry Society of Texas
c/o Don Stodghill, Awards Chairman
1424 Highland Rd.
Dallas, TX 75218
Voertman Award: Gene Fehler, for "Piano Tuner."
Poetry Society of Texas Award: Louise Branson Pollard, for "Line For A Bereaved Dove."
Mahan Award: Julia Hurd Strong, for "To Robert."
Mrs. Clark Gresham Memorial Award: Marianne McFarland McNeil, for "Blue Memories."
Great Plains Canal Award: Marcella Siegel, for "Prayer In Time Of Thirst."
Old South Prize: Jack E. Murphy, for "Pastoral Poet."
John A. Lubbe Memorial Award: Julia Hurd Strong, for "The Cry."
President's Award: Ruby Hughes Bussey, for "Manhunt."
Abbie Frank Smith Memorial Award: Shirley Handley, for "Listen! Do You Hear Them?"
Catherine Brooks Shuford Memorial Award: Har-

riet Stovall Kelley, for "Ironing."
Appreciation Prize: Janelle Burk, for "Celebration."
Eloise Kelley Adamson Memorial Award: Nelle Fertig, for "A Grievance For You."
Eloise Roach—Frances Massie Lyric Prize: Violette Newton, for "The Wildness; Driving Route One."
Montgomery Award: Wendy Dimmette, for "Dividing The Indivisible."
William E. Nichols Memorial Award: Maurene McDonald, for "The Builder's Legacy."
Lubbe Award: Doris K. Ferguson, for "Dance, Dragon, Dance."
Texas Sesquicentennial Epic Award: Pauline Crittenden, for "Hill Country Heritage."
Helen S. Chambers Memorial Award: Ida Fasel, for "Desert Flowers."
David Atamian Memorial Award: Hugh Pendexter III, for "Twentieth Olympiad."
Odessa Prize: Carlyse Bliss, for "Crystal Tears."
Joy Award: Kay Ellison, for "Echoes."
Arthur and Hannah Bluhm Memorial Award: Ovon Ross, for "Blase' Clown."
Experimental Poetry Award: Kay Merkel Boruff, for "Coupling."
Lyndon Baines Johnson Award: Julia Hurd Strong, for "The Drought."
Austin Poetry Society Memorial Award: Libby Stopple, for "If They Could Speak."
Inez Puckett McEwen Award: June Owens, for "Like An Enormous, Muffled Voice."
Vivian Page Wheeler Memorial Award: Christine Rosamond Stedman, for "When Winter Lays My Final Bed."
Dedication Award: Harriet Stovall Kelley, for "Braillebarde."
San Antonio Poetry Forum Award: Maurene McDonald, for "Fireside Meditations."
Sesquicentennial Award: Violette Newton, for "This Was Their Death."
Carl and Evie Stripling Memorial Award: Sue Blythe, for "Silhouettes."
F. G. Jeffers Memorial Award: Alice Glenn, for "Fort Davis Festival."
Light Verse Award: Julia Hurd Strong, for "'Roots' And Stuff."
William Arthur Bair Memorial Award: Jack E. Murphy, for "Land Lover."
David and Hallie Harner Preece Award: Andrew T. Roy, for "Bristlecone Pine."
Abstract In Action-Beauty Award: Merle M. Hudson, for "My Aunt Orlie."
Anne Pence Davis Award: Ida Fasel, for "Staying Powers."
San Jacinto Chapter Award: Arlene Maass, for "A Long Time Ago From Fez."

Land Award: Marianne McFarland McNeil, for "A 50 Year Old Street."

Mockingbird Chapter Award: Jack E. Murphy, for "San Jacinto."

Newton Award: Wendy Dimmette, for "Directions."

Reverence Award: Geneva Fulgham, for "The Message."

Pen Woman Award: Ida Fasel, for "To A Violet."

Free Verse Award: Buz Craft, for "The Dinner Bell."

Poet's Ink Award: Harriett Stovall Kelley, for "China Shapes."

Children's Award: Gayle Briscoe, for "How I Became A Poet At Age Ten."

Thanks Award: Opie R. Houston, for "Reality."

Hughs Metaphysical Poetry Award: Helen Rilenge, for "Goldbeater's Skin."

Bowman Award: Alice Glenn, for "Texas 1835."

Wichita Falls Poetry Society Award: Margarete Schuette, for "My Welcome Home."

High Plains Chapter Award: Gene Fehler, for "Problem Child In Third Grade Classroom."

Palestine Poetry Society Award: Maurene McDonald, for "Deep Wells."

Major Donald J. Crocker Purple Heart Award: Ruth E. Reuther, for "Arlington Remembered."

Harry Kovner Memorial Award: Harriet Stovall Kelley, for "Winterlude."

Ernest Bobys Memorial Award: Jack E. Murphy, for "Dear Son."

Bruce Bobys Lyric Award: Virginia Long, for "I Can Remember Maples."

Helen Claire Mueller Memorial Award: Vera L. Eckert, for "Two Friends."

Alamo Prize: Gene Fehler, for "Mender of Roads."

Globe Peace Award: Nelle Fertig, for "A Standard For Peace."

Horse In Poetry Prize: Harriet Stovall Kelley, for "Sleepthief."

Julia H. Ricker Memorial Award: Jack E. Murphy, for "Titanic."

Bible Award: Shirley Handley, for "Train Up A Child."

Grace and Jerry Huffaker Memorial Award: Margarete Schuette, for "The Whistle Still Blows."

A Galaxy of Verse Award: Shirley Handley, for "Mary McLeod Bethune—Victorious."

Odessa Chapter Award: Helene Rilenge, for "Generations."

Saturday "Poetry In The Arts" Endowment Award: Kathleen Henry Harris Curry, for "One Day At A Time."

Garland Chapter Award: Bernice Chenault Howard, for "Masterpiece In White."

Lone Star Sesquicentennial Celebration Award: Carlyse Bliss, for "Cowboy Recruit."

Katherine Schutze Haiku Memorial Award: Martha Freeman France, for "Haiku."

San Antonio Poets Association Award: Marcella Siegel for "Aging Collie."

Sons and Daughters Award: Wendy Dimmette, for "This is Not A Reasonable Place."

Vera and Arthur Sampley Memorial Award: Virginia Hampton Justice, for "The Challenge."

Beth Dolan Memorial Award: Budd Powell Mahan, for "A Jumping Fish."

Wisdom Award: Mildred Vorpahl Baass, for "Guidelines."

Springforth Award: Jack E. Murphy, for "Jamie Wyeth's Pig."

Poetry Forum of San Antonio Award: Julie Hurd String, for "Sunday."

Houston Chapter Award: Bea M. Land, for "Death Of A Famous Poet."

Earl Bonnie Memorial Award: Vivian Ricker, for "Remembered Town."

Shakespearean Sonnet Award: Nelle Fertig, for "The Hatching Of Strange Eggs."

PZL Award: Evelyn McDaniel Morris, for "Efficiency Apprentice."

Daisy Elmore Tennant Memorial Award: Alice Glenn, for "Derelict."

Rachel Award: Katharine Dee, for "The Cross And The Lily."

Sallie Jenkins Thomas Award: Marcella Siegel, for "For Rachel, Who Was Four."

Harriet Cameron Havens Award: Harriet Stovall Kelley, for "Generation Bridge."

Gillie T. and Neta Hall Pounds Memorial Award: Jack E. Murphy, for "I Take This Man."

Emma Jean Pounds Terry Award: Carlyse Bliss, for "To A Dear Daughter."

Dr. Glenn Mitchell Award: Vivian Ricker, for "Dr. Bill."

Seth Award: Claudia Nabors, for "Beyond Three Dimensions."

Dancearth Award: Carlyse Bliss, for "We Visit A Disco."

Annual Awards Banquet Award: Nelle Fertig, for "Catching The Highwire Performance."

Annual Critic's Award: Janelle Burk, for "Blue Norther."

Poets Club of Chicago
c/o Carol Spelius, Contest Chairman
373 Ramsay Rd.
Deerfield, IL 60015

International Shakespearean Contest: First—Charles Dickson, for "When Chieftains Speak" and Dorothy Van H. Harrison, for "Extrovert"; Second—C. Webster Wheelock, for "The Room A Child Inhabits"; Third—Rose B. Akerman, for "Time."

Poets of the Foothills Art Center
809 Fifteenth St.
Golden, CO 80401
   Riverstone International Poetry Chapbook Competition: John Spaulding, for "The Roses Of Starvation."

Poets of the Vineyard
P. O. Box 77
Kenwood, CA 95452
   Grand Prize: Ernestine Gravley, for "Because She Loved That Land."
   Traditional Form: First—Marguerite A. Brewster, for "The Passing Amber Of These Autumn Days"; Second—Margaret Stavely, for "The Voice Of The House"; Third—Ruth Holter, for "Autumn Counterpoint, A Villanelle."
   Free Verse: First—Delores G. Beggs, for "Morning"; Second—Peter Ulisse, for "Private Solomon"; Third—Nicole Dobson, for "Growing."
   Free Verse: First—Nan Rigotti, for "Dragon"; Second—Judy Hardin, for "Monica John"; Third—Patricia M. Johnson, for "From The Bookshelf."
   Light/Humorous: First—Ernestine Gravley, for "Lines To A Male Shopper"; Second—Clara G. Willis, for "No Pad For Dad"; Third—Clara G. Willis, for "Pest Question."
   Short Verse: First—Marguerite A. Brewster, for "Return To Copper-Burnished Sea"; Second—Alice M. Swaim, for "Soon The Lake Forgets"; Third—Delphine LeDoux, for "Courtesy."
   Haiku, Senryu, Tanka: First—Ruth Holter, for "My Little Daughter"; Second—Nida E. Jones Ingram, for "Crossing Autumn Hills"; Third—Sheila Jetter, for "Daisies In A Vase."
   Wines, Grapes, Vineyards: First—Marguerite A. Brewster, for "In Autumn's Ambered Valley"; Second—Eileen Malone, for "Becoming Wine"; Third—Winnie E. Fitzpatrick, for "Harvest Of Years."

Pudding House
60 N. Main St.
Johnstown, OH 43031
   National Looking Glass Poetry Competition: First—M. Truman Cooper, for "Substantial Holdings"; Second—Carol Hamilton; Third—Gilbert Allen.
   Columbus Zoo Poetry Competition: First—Margaret Honton, for "Zebra's Sanctuary"; Second—Martha Collins; Third—Victoria Wyttenberg.
   Pudding House Chapbook Competition: First—Walter Pavlich, for "Theories Of Birds And Water"; Second—Wilson Wise; Third—Larry D. Griffin.

Pulitzer Prize (see Columbia University)

Quarterly Review of Literature
26 Haslet Ave.
Princeton, NJ 08540
   QRL Prize: Dannie Abse, for "Sky In Narrow Streets"; Joan Aleshire, for "This Far"; David Keller, for "A New Room"; Peter Stambler, for "Unsettled Accounts"; Eugenio de Andrade, for "White On White."

Rhino
Enid Baron and Carole Hayes, Editors
1040 Judson Ave.
Evanston, IL 60202
   Rhino Annual Poetry Contest: Carole Wade Lundberg, for "Mapping."

Rhyme Time Poetry Newsletter
Hutton Publications
P. O. Box 2377
Coeur d'Alene, ID 83814
   Poet of the Year: Thomas Lynn.
   Open Title Contest: First—Thomas Lynn, for "A Good Ship"; Second—Rosa Nelle Anderson, for "Water Lillies"; Third—James F. Webb, for "Cherry Tree."
   Assigned Title ("Keepsake"): First—James F. Webb; Second—Helen V. Johnson; Third—Ivan Bernard Robson.
   Assigned Title ("Charades"): First—Sandra Smith; Second—Bill Withers; Third—May Wareberg.
   Four-Line Contest: First—Betty Lou Hebert, for "Autumn's Gift"; Second—Elisabeth Winstead, for "Springtime"; Third—Alice Cowan, for "True Friendship."
   Assigned Title ("Rainbows"): First—Erick Wruck.
   Assigned Title ("Encore"): First—Laura Dennison Vargas.
   Assigned Title ("Debut"): First—Jonathan P. Rose.
   Quatrain Contest: First—James F. Webb, for "Summer."

St. Mary's College of Maryland
Festival of Poets and Poetry
St. Mary's City, MD 20686
   Chaucer Award: Mary M. Pronovost, for "Ladder In The Marketplace."

San Francisco State University
The Poetry Center
1600 Holloway Ave.
San Francisco, CA 94132
   Poetry Center Book Award: Yusef Komunyakaa, for "I Apologize For The Eyes In My Head."

Southern Poetry Review
Dept. of English
University of North Carolina
Charlotte, NC 28223

Guy Owen Poetry Prize: Joe Bolton, for "American Variations."

Southwest Review
Southern Methodist University
Box 4374, 6410 Airline Rd.
Dallas, TX 75275
Elizabeth Matchett Stover Award: Edward Hirsch, for "Proustian."

Stone Country
P. O. Box 132
Menemsha, MA 02552
Phillips Award: Martha McFerren, for "We Know Where"; Jonas Zdanys, for "Freight Trains."

Syracuse University
Dept. of English
Syracuse, NY 13210
Creative Writing Contest (poetry)—
Raymond Carver Prize: Karen Parrish, for "The Price You Pay For Comparisons."
Alan Birk Prize: Josef M. Sparacio.
Loring Williams Prize: Catherine Rankovic.
Edwin T. Whiffen Prize: John K. Riggin, for "When It Rains, She Soars."
Delmore Schwartz Prize: Kathryn M. Anderson, for "Summer Count."

Texas Institute of Letters
Box 8594
Waco, TX 76714
Poetry Award: Edward Hirsch, for "Wild Gratitude."

Thorntree Press
547 Hawthorn Lane
Winnetka, IL 60093
Goodman Competition: Mary Makofske; Katherine Androski; Judith Neeld; Hilda Ray.

University of Massachusetts Press
Box 429
Amherst, MA 01004
Juniper Prize: Walter McDonald, for "After The Noise Of Saigon."

University of Michigan
Hopwood Room
1006 Angell Hall
Ann Arbor, MI 48109-1003
Hopwood Awards Program—
Summer Hopwood Poetry: First—Anna Maria McEwen, for "Crossing The Sands"; Second—Howard Schott, for "Stephen's Adventures."
Hopwood Underclassmen Poetry: First—Audrey Joan Gebber, for "Tradition And Admiration"; Second—Stephanie Fody, for "Graffiti"; Third—Emily Severance, for "Sunday Afternoon."
Major Hopwood Poetry: First—T. J. Anderson III, for "The Message Of Fire," and Su Nor-

molle, for "At Home"; Second—Dawne Adam, for "Home And The World," and Blake Walmsley, for "Expecting."
Minor Hopwood Poetry: First—Barbara Bizek, for "Resurrection"; Second—Stacey M. Kaufman, for "Retrospection," and Suzanne Misencik, for "Three Things"; Third—Laura Janis Bernstein, for "Like A Family"; Fourth—Stephanie Ivanoff, for "Suffrage."
Academy of American Poets Prize: Paula K. Gover, for "On The Migration Corridor."
Bain-Swiggett Poetry Prize: Renee A. Bowles, for "Don't Leave Home Without It" and "Over The Turnpike And Through The Tollbooths."
Michael R. Gutterman Award in Poetry: First—Renee A. Bowles, for "Floral Arrangement"; Second—Paula K. Gover, for "The Fat Girl."
Marjorie Rapaport Award in Poetry: First—Kristen C. Hendricks, for "Brigadoon, For My Father"; Second—Margaret Reutter, for "Karen's House."
Jeffrey L. Weisberg Memorial Prize in Freshman Poetry: First—Jody Blanco, for "On Long Lost Friends" and "Bookstore"; Second—Emily Severance, for "Song Of Janus" and "The Crooked Growth Of Tree."

University of Pittsburgh Press
127 N. Bellefield Ave.
Pittsburgh, PA 15260
Agnes Lynch Starrett Poetry Prize: David Rivard, for "Speedway."

University of Puget Sound
Dept. of English
1500 N. Warner
Tacoma, WA 98416
Nixeon Civille Handy Prizes for Poetry: First—Maria Pao, for "The Piano Tuner"; Second—Jeff Gollnick, for "Sister's Freedom"; Third—Thea Reed, for "Foto Booth."

University of Toronto
University College/The Registrar
Toronto, Ont. M5S 1A1
This year not awarded to a poet.

West Virginia Poetry Society
c/o Regina Skeen, Contest Chairman
Rt. 2, Box 13, White Pine Rd.
Kentuck, WV 25249
West Virginia Poetry Society Award: First—LeAnne Snyder Setlak, for "In learning You Too Late"; Second—Lucille Morgan Wilson, for "Kaleidoscope."
WVPS Award Modern: First—Geraldine Jackson, for "February's Chill"; Second—Lucille Morgan Wilson, for "Mending The Harness."
Limerick: First—Thelma Scott Kiser, for "Dish

Of Tye Day"; Second—Mary Holmes Jones, for "Mis-Matched."

Haiku: First—Anne Gasser, for "Beneath Loblolly"; Second—Timothy Russell, for "So Many Bull Frogs."

WVPS Student Award: First—Stephanie Wotring, for "Sunset"; Second—Christopher Poe, for "Mr. Spock."

Parkersburg Chapter, Light Verse: First—Louise Marsh Gabriel, for "Ain't English Funny?"; Second—Wilma Miller, for "Old Age"; Third—Anne Gasser, for "Who's Minding The Store?"

Lee Mays Chapter Award: First—Grace Haynes Smith, for "The Riddle Of The Hills"; Second—Thelma Scott Kiser, for "A Cold Wind Sweeps My Valley"; Third—Anne Barlow, for "The Little Hills."

Charleston Chapter: First—Rea Reaney, for "Night Sounds"; Second—Anne Clendening, for "Mojave Scenes."

Harold C. Jacobs Memorial Award: First—Anne Barlow, for "Forest Therapy"; Second—Harold Slate, for "Respite."

Morgantown Chapter: First—Thelema Scott Kiser, for "Portrait Of A West Virginian"; Second—Earl Bee, for "Prayer Of A Mountaineer."

Mary Holmes Jones Award: First—Margarette Parker, for "The Covered Bridge"; Second—Timothy Russell, for "In Conseptu Ejas For ERK."

Skip McGinley Memorial Award: First—Grace Haynes Smith, for "The Candy Striper."

Elaine Rowley Memorial Award: First—Grace Haynes Smith, for "Going Home For The Holidays"; Second—Anne Gasser, for "Coming Home"; Third—Mary Holmes Jones, for "The Day After."

Beulah Tubbs Dungey Memorial Award: First—Mary Holmes Jones, for "Miss Em's Flowers"; Second—Anne Gasser, for "Twilight Reprieve"; Third—Rea Reaney, for "Garden Talk."

Children's Award: First—Bevin Hassig, for "I Am Like The Wind"; Second—Emily Goodwin, for "Winter To Spring"; Third—Tricia Bush, for "Sue's Trash Problem."

Parker-O'Connor Award: First—Grace Haynes Smith, for "What Sylvan Giants"; Second—Lucille Morgan Wilson, for "Home From The Seas"; Third—Amy Jo Zook, for "A Renascence."

Vance McKee Iker Award: First—Lucille Morgan Wilson; Second—Grace Haynes Smith.

Walter E. Pratt Memorial Award: Anne Barlow, for "Back Yard Odyssey."

Osa Mays Memorial Award: First—Anne Gasser, for "After The Final Curtain"; Second—B. R. Culbertson, for "Legacy"; Third—Harold Slate, for "The Example."

Betty D. Grugin Award (Ballad): First—Grace Holliday Scott, for "The Bells of Kingston Bay"; Second—Margarette Parker, for "Ballad Of The Blowing Rock"; Third—James Proctor, for "Weeping Willow Ballad."

Strictly Humorous Award, Miller & Miller: First—LeAnne Snyder Setlak, for "Werewolves Are Lovable"; Second—Anne Gasser, for "Fidgital Digital"; Third—Linda Banks, for "Two-Step."

West Virginia Writers, Inc.
4651 Victoria Rd.
Charleston, WV 25313

Jug Award for Lifetime Achievement: Shirley Young-Campbell.

Lyric Poetry: First—Barbara A. Smith, for "The Omen"; Second—Keith Sarver, for "A Horse And His Boy"; Third—Rosanna Swearington, for "Whole."

Narrative Poetry: First—Randal O'Field, for "I Sink In Deep Mire"; Second—Earl R. Kenner, for "A Long Distance Call"; Third—LeAnne Setlak, for "The Last Great Comedy."

Light Verse: First—Betty Gill, for "Magic World"; Second—LeAnne Setlak, for "Do Not Go Gently Into Bankruptcy"; Third—Timothy Russell, for "The Bills."

Mrs. Giles Whiting Foundation
Pierpont Morgan Library
29 E. 36th St.
New York, NY 10016

Whiting Writers Award (poets): Mark Cox, for "Smoulder"; Michael Ryan, for "In Winter."

Witter Bynner Foundation for Poetry, Inc.
Box 2188
Santa Fe, NM 87504

Grant Awards—

Support of Individual Poets Through Non-Profit Institutions: Susan Eisenberg, "Work Poems In Performance," Word of Mouth Productions, Jamaica Plain, MA; Susan B. Slocum, "Poets In Residence," Fine Arts Work Center in Provincetown, Provincetown, MA.

Developing the Poetry Audience: Grace Cavalieri, "The Poet And The Poem," WPFW-FM, Washington, DC; Roland Legiardi-Laura, "Azul" (Nicaragua—Land of Poets), New York Center for Visual History, New York, NY; Leita Hagemann, "Poetry Breaks," WGBH-TV, New Television Workshop, Boston, MA; Rhea Lehman, "Staging Romantic Poetry," Actors Theatre of Louisville, Louisville, KY; Francine Ringold, "NIMROD: On The Air," Arts & Humanities Council of Tulsa, Tulsa, OK.

Uses of Poetry: Mary Jane Hurst, "The Effect Of Poetry On The Brain," Texas Tech University, Lubbock, TX; Virginia Schatz, "Poet And Teacher: Collaboration For Deaf Students," Western Pennsylvania School for the Deaf, Pittsburgh, PA; Karen Chase, "The Poetry Project," New York Hospital/Cornell Medical Center, White Plains, NY.

Translation and the Process of Translation: Molly Seale Edwards, "Translations Of The Complete Poems (Stikhi And Shaski) By Kornei Chukovski For Children," American Institute for Learning, Austin, TX; Rachael Newton Bellow, "Poets House Translation Fund," Poets House, New York, NY.

The Word Works
P. O. Box 42164
Washington, DC 20015
    Washington Prize: Lisa Ress, for "Setting The Table: Eating What Is Served."

World Literature Today
University of Oklahoma
630 Parrington Oval, Room 110
Norman, OK 73019
    Neustadt International Prize for Literature: Not awarded this year.

Writer's Digest
9933 Alliance Rd.
Cincinnati, OH 45242

Writing Competition (poetry): First—Frances Balfour, for "Moonsail"; Second—Deborah Adams, for "Need Hope For Nothing."

Writer's Journal
P. O. Box 65798
St. Paul, MN 55165
    Spring Poetry Contest: First—Lila Borg Rohrer, for "Lessons Mama Never Taught"; Second—Michael Bourgo, for "My Bag Lady"; Third—Yvonne Pearson, for "One For Each Hand."

Yale University
Beinecke Rare Book and Manuscript Library
1603A Yale Sta.
New Haven, CT 06520
    Bollingen Prize: Stanley Kunitz, for "Next To Last Things."

Yale University Press
92A Yale Sta.
New Haven, CT 06520
    Yale Series of Younger Poets: Brigit Pegeen Kelly, for "To The Place Of Trumpets."

Yankee Magazine
Dublin, NH 03444
    Yankee Poetry Awards: First—Jean Nordhaus, for "Roofer"; Second—Peter Meinke, for "Chipmunk Center"; Third—Charles Darling, for "At The Airport Baggage Claim."

Acknowledgments

The publisher expresses appreciation to the authors represented in the Anthology for graciously permitting the inclusion of their poetry.

In addition, credit has been given to all magazines where material in this volume first appeared, with their names listed under each respective poem.

In individual instances where certain authors, magazines or book publishers require special mention or credit lines for copyrights they control or administer, such recognition is hereby indicated as follows:

"Walker Evans: House and Graveyard, Rowlesburg, West Virginia, 1935," by Maggie Anderson, is from her book, *Cold Comfort*. Reprinted by permission of the University of Pittsburgh Press. Copyright © 1986 by Maggie Anderson.

"Abyss," by Charles Baudelaire, translated from the French by David Ferry, copyright © by David Ferry, is reprinted by permission of David Ferry and by *Raritan: A Quarterly Review,* Vol. VII, No.1 (Summer, 1987).

"Everlasting Peace" is translated from the German of Wolf Biermann by Maurice Taylor, and appeared originally in *Die Zeit* #34 (August 26, 1983, Feuilleton, P. 17) and, later, in *The Malahat Review.*

"A Trenta-Sei of The Pleasure We Take in The Early Death of Keats," by John Ciardi (dec.) is reprinted by permission of Miller Williams, Literary Executor.

"Everything Else You Can Get You Take," by Robert Dana, is from his book, *Starting Out for the Difficult World.* Copyright © 1987 by Robert Dana. Reprinted by permission of Harper & Row, Publishers, Inc.

"Flash Cards," by Rita Dove, is copyright © 1987 by Rita Dove. Reprinted by permission of the author.

"Supplication," by Joseph Duemer, is from his book, *Customs,* copyright © 1987 The University of Georgia Press. Reprinted by permission of the University of Georgia Press.

"On the Deepest Sounds," by Lars Gustafson, is from his book, *New Selected Poems.* Copyright © 1986 by Lars Gustafson. Reprinted by permission of New Directions Publishing Corporation.

"The Owl," by Craig Hancock, appeared originally in *Blueline,* and also in *North Country*, published by Greenfield Review Press.

"Los Ojos," by Antonio Machado, translated from the Spanish by Lilly McCue, first appeared in *Bitterroot International Poetry Journal.*

"Spring Planting," by Gail Mazur, is from her book, *Pose of Happiness.* Copyright © 1986 by Gail Mazur. Reprinted by permission of David R. Godine, Publisher.

"Wind and Hardscrabble," by Walter McDonald, is from his book, *The Flying Dutchman*, copyright © 1987 by The University of Ohio Press. Reprinted by permission.

"Old, Old Lady," by Lillian Morrison, first appeared in *The Creative Woman.* Copyright © by Lillian Morrison. Reprinted by permission of the author.

"Concerning Stars, Flowers, Love, Etc.," by John Newlove, is from his book, *The Night The Dog Smiled,* published by ECW Press, Toronto. Copyright © by John Newlove.

"Autumn Day," by Rainer Maria Rilke, translated from the German by David Ferry, copyright © by David Ferry, is reprinted by permission of David Ferry and by *Raritan: A Quarterly Review*, Vol. VII, No.1 (Summer, 1987).

"Dodge Elegy," by Susan Snively, is from her book, *Voices in the House,* published by The University of Alabama Press. Reprinted by permission of Susan Snively.

"Ode to Entropy," by John Updike, is from his book, *Facing Nature,* copyright © 1985. Reprinted by permission, Alfred A. Knopf, Inc.

"The Aging Actress Sees Herself A Starlet on The Late Show" and "For Lucinda, Robert and

A Woman," by Ralph Burns; "Camouflage," by Henry Carlile; "What People Make," by Thomas Carper; "The Autoscopic Experience," by Turner Cassity; "A Trenta-Sei Of The Pleasure We Take In The Early Death of Keats," by John Ciardi; "Faculty Offices, Circa 1985," by James Cole; "Autistic Boy," by Kevin Cole; "Elegy For John, My Student Dead Of Aids," by Robert Cording; "The Blooming Of Sentimentality," by Stephen Corey; "The Spaniel (formerly entitled 'The Task')," by Carl Dennis; "Angelus," by Stuart Dybek; "Child Burial," by Maria Flook; "Our Father Who Art On Third," by William Greenway; "The Coming Day," by Eamon Grennan; "Because You Asked For A Bedtime Story," by Ben Howard; "Spring Planting," by Gail Mazur; "So many Americans, Driving Late On Country Roads," by Bill Meissner; "Northern Exposure," by G. E. Murray; "The Mariner," by Jay Parini; "Car Radio," by Donald Revell; "Illinois At Night, Black Hawk's Statue Broods," by J. W. Rivers; "Waiting Room In Missouri," by Judith Root; "Postscript To An Elegy," by Gibbons Ruark; "The Wandering Year," by Aleda Shirley; "The Librarian Decides on Cryonics," by Judith Skillman; "Brief Sparrow," by Barry Spacks; "Walking Back," by William Trowbridge; "My Mother Is Not Watching," by Leslie Ullman; "Views," by Mona Van Duyn; "Martha," by Jon Veinberg; "Barn Cat Summer," by Roger Weingarten; "On The Return Of Halley's Comet," by J. P. White; "The Aging Actress Sees Herself A Starlet On The Late Show," by Miller Williams; "A Reply To The Journalist Who Informed the Russian People in *Izvestia* That There Was No Santa Claus," by Baron Wormser; "Winter Rain," by Sevag Yaralian; "Champagne On The M," by Paul Zarzyski.

The following poems first appeared in *Poetry*. Copyright © 1987 by The Modern Poetry Association, and are reprinted with permission of the Editor of *Poetry*: "St. Louis Botanical Gardens," by Diana Ackerman; "Barge Lights On The Hudson," by Dick Allen; "Self-Portrait," by Barri Armitage; "The Diver," by Michael Collier; "Isaac," by George Evans; "Station Music," by Elliot Figman; "Penelope Gardening," by Susan Fox; "After Thanksgiving," by Sandra M. Gilbert; "Dancing Lessons," by Elton Glaser; "Red Tide, A Beach of Salvage" by Greg Glazner; "Commuter's Log," by Art Homer; "Letter To Monet," by Mark Madigan; "Exchange Of Gifts," by Stanley Moss; "Spring's Awakening," by Robert B. Shaw; "The Sadness Of Rivers," by Maurya Simon; "Foggy Notion," by Alison Stone.

The following poems first appeared in *Shenandoah*: The Washington & Lee University Review, with the permission of the Editor. Copyright 1986 by Washington & Lee University: "Filling Canvas," by Elizabeth Arthur; "Waiting," by David Neelin; "Frozen Lasagne," by Alan Michael Parker.

The following poems first appeared in *TriQuarterly*, a publication of Northwestern University: "The Morning After," by Stanislaw Baranczak; "The Scale," by Paul Breslin; "The Condolence," by Timothy Dekin; "The Apricot Trees," by W. S. DiPiero; "West Texas Interlude," by Robert A. Fink; "Meyer Levine," by David Galler; "Dinner At Grandpa's," by Morton Marcus; "The Descent," by Linda Pastan.

The following poems appeared originally in *Yankee* and are reprinted with permission from Yankee Publishing: "The Nature of Literature," by Richard Behm; "Learning the Language," by Martha Christina; "Boonies," by Robert DeYoung; "Marc Chagall," by Margaret Toarello Diorio; "There's Something Left Out in the Rain," by Alice B. Fogel; "Rain," by Thomas Johnson; "Sorrow Trees," by Jeanne Lohman; "Vineyard Conjuring," by Mildred J. Nash; "Balance of Power," by Barry Sternlieb; "A Prayer to Feet," by Mary Ann Waters.